H. Lee Jones

BIRDS

Illustrated by Dana Gardner

BELIZE

University of Texas Press, Austin

Copyright © 2003 by H. Lee Jones
Illustrations © 2003 by Dana Gardner
All rights reserved
Printed in China
Sixth paperback printing, 2016

Requests for permission to reproduce material from this work should be
sent to:

Permissions
University of Texas Press
P.O. Box 7819
Austin, TX 78713-7819
http://utpress.utexas.edu/index.php/rp-form

♾ The paper used in this book meets the minimum requirements of
ANSI/NISO Z39.48-1992 (R1997) (Permanence of Paper).

Library of Congress Cataloging-in-Publication Data

Jones, H. Lee.
    Birds of Belize / by H. Lee Jones ; illustrated by Dana Gardner.
        p.   cm. — (The Corrie Herring Hooks series ; no. 57)
Includes bibliographical references and index.
    ISBN 978-0-292-70164-9 (pbk. : alk. paper)
    1. Birds—Belize—Identification. 2. Birds—Belize—
Pictorial works.
    I. Gardner, Dana. II. Title. III. Series.
QL687 .B45 J66   2004
598'.097282—dc21   2003010956

doi:10.7560/740662

CONTENTS

Without the pioneering work of Steve Howell and Sophie Webb, this book would not have been possible. The publication in 1995 of their book *A Guide to the Birds of Mexico and Northern Central America* immediately elevated birding in Belize to a higher plane. Previously, the only publications on Belize birds were Steve Russell's *Distributional Study of the Birds of British Honduras* (1964), which was long out of date and nearly impossible to find, and several equally out-of-date checklists. John Moore's excellent *A Bird Walk at Chan Chich* audiotape was produced around the same time I arrived in Belize in 1992 and became my constant field companion. Ultimately, I was able to resolve the myriad jungle sounds by listening to Moore's tape over and over and over again.

I obtained much additional valuable information from the published literature and numerous unpublished documents and newsletters. These are cited in the references section at the end of the book. But, without doubt, the bulk of information on the status and seasonality of birds in Belize has come from the unpublished field notes and verbal and e-mail communications received from a growing network of birders in Belize. I am especially indebted to Philip Balderamos, Jim and Dorothy Beveridge, Steve Howell, Susan Lala, Ellen McRae, Martin Meadows, and Nick Smith for generously providing me with their excellent field notes. Many others have provided their trip reports and noteworthy sightings. These included Tim Brush, Rudi Burgos, John and Agnes Caulfield, Micky Craig, Glenn Crawford, Thomas Donegan, Marcus England, Omar Figueroa, John Gilardi, Alvaro Jaramillo, Andy Johnson, Jacques Laesser, Mark and Karen MacReynolds, Jan Meerman, Mario Muschamp, Wilfred Requena, Paul Rodewald, John Rowlett, Chris Sharpe, Mary Beth Stowe, Sam Tillett, Jonathan Urbina, Andrew Vallely, and Barry Zimmer.

Van Remsen, Steve Cardiff, and Donna Dittmann (Louisiana State University Museum of Natural Science), Kimball Garrett (Los Angeles County Museum of Natural History), Manuel Marin (Western Foundation for Vertebrate Zoology), Peter Capainolo (American Museum of Natural History), Steve Howell (Point Reyes Bird Observatory), Bruce and Carolyn Miller (Wildlife Conservation Society), Jon Dunn, and numerous members of the NEOORN listserv have helped in many other ways by providing access to specimens, tracking down obscure documents, providing vital information on unpublished records, or lending their expertise in helping to resolve any of a number of sticky identification issues. I would especially like to thank Kimball Garrett for his meticulous scrutiny of and thoughtful comments on the draft manuscript.

The knowledge and assistance of Amos Capps and Betsy Mallory in developing the range maps, and Capps in creating a database of bird observations, were invaluable. Early on, Bob Ridgely generously donated his personal copy of the hard-to-find *Distributional Study of the Birds of British Honduras*. Sharon Matola and Conservation International were instrumental in arranging for both Dana Gardner and myself to participate in a two-week expedition into the Maya Mountains to explore the little-known flora and fauna of that region. William (Chet) Schmidt provided assistance early in the project in introducing me to a number of unexplored areas of southern Belize. The Belize Audubon Society provided transportation to Half Moon Caye and unlimited access to its library. The inclusion of local Creole, K'ekchi, and Mopan Maya names in the "Other Names" section of the species accounts was made possible largely through the efforts of Sam Tillett (Creole names), Marcus Ack and Carol Smith (K'ekchi names), and Juan Chun, Juan Sho, Sylvano Sho, and Victor Sho (Mopan Maya names).

During the 10 years I have been living part-time in Belize, I have received generous support and encouragement from many sources. Jim and Dorothy Beveridge, Mark and Monique Howells, Susan and Wil Lala, Matthew and Marga Miller, Tina and Kirby Salisbury, and Sam and Rita Tillett have at one time or another provided excellent accommodations and an endless supply of hospitality and friendship during my frequent travels around the country. Several nongovernmental organizations such as TIDE, PLENTY Belize, and the Toledo Ecotourism Association have generously provided logistical support and field assistance whenever called upon.

Special thanks are due to Philip Balderamos, Brian Holland and Anne Brorsen, Martin Meadows, and Larry Munsey for their support and encouragement throughout the project and to Len Zeoli and Wilfred Requena for their near constant companionship and support in the field during the last year of the project. Jacquie Strickland managed my stateside affairs during my lengthy absences. Without her support, I could not have devoted anywhere near the time I did to fieldwork in Belize.

Finally, the still small but ever growing army of Belizean birders is adding exponentially to our knowledge of Belize's remarkable avifauna. More than anyone else, this book is dedicated to them. It is hoped that they will find this book a source of information and encouragement in their pursuits and will use it to extend and improve our knowledge still further.

DISTRICTS
BE = Belize District
CA = Cayo District
CO = Corozal District
OW = Orange Walk District
SC = Stann Creek District
TO = Toledo District

REGIONS OF THE WORLD
Afr. = Africa
Aust. = Australia
Can. = Canada
C.A. = Central America
C.R. = Costa Rica
E.S. = El Salvador
Eur. = Europe
Guat. = Guatemala
Hon. – Honduras
Mex. = Mexico
N.Z. = New Zealand
Nic. = Nicaragua
N.A. = North America
Pan. = Panama
S.A. = South America
U.S. = United States
W.I. = West Indies

The modifiers *n* (northern), *s* (southern),
e (eastern), *w* (western), *c* (central),
ne (northeastern), and so on are used with the
above geographical entities to indicate the
specific portion of the region referred to (for
example: c TO = central Toledo District; nw
S.A. = northwestern S.A.).

These same symbols are used with a period
to denote compass direction: n., s., e., w., n.e.,
and so on.

ABUNDANCE
VC = very common
C = common
FC = fairly common
UC = uncommon
VU = very uncommon
R = rare

PLUMAGE, AGE, AND SEX
alt. = alternate plumage
basic = basic plumage
ad(s). = adult(s)
imm(s). = immature(s)
juv(s). = juvenile(s)
subad(s). = subadult(s)
♂ = male
♀ = female

OTHER NAMES
alt. = alternative English names
arch. = "archaic" names, no longer in general
usage
C = Creole (Kriol)
coll. = colloquial
I. Davis = names coined by Irby Davis
K = K'ekchi names
M = Mopan Maya names
S = local Spanish names
U.K. = English names that may be more
familiar to birders from the United Kingdom

OTHER ABBREVIATIONS
Hwy. = Highway
ID = identify, identification
Isl. = Island(s)
Mtn(s). = Mountain(s)
occas. = occasional(ly)
Pen. = Peninsula
R. = River
sp. = species
ssp. = subspecies

BIRDS OF BELIZE

GEOGRAPHY AND CLIMATE

Located at the southeastern tip of the Yucatán Peninsula, Belize is the only English-speaking country in Central America and one of the few in all of Latin America. At 16° to 18°30′ north latitude and 87°30′ to 89°5′ west longitude, it is well within the New World Tropics. The Caribbean Sea lies to the east, Guatemala to the west and south, and Mexico to the north. Belize is about 180 miles (290 km) north to south and 65 miles (105 km) east to west at its widest point, with a land area of 8,867 square miles (22,965 km²). It is only slightly larger than El Salvador, Central America's smallest country; yet with only 250,000 people, it has one-twenty-fifth of El Salvador's population.

Belize has a broad, flat coastal plain, broken only by the relatively low-lying Maya Mountains in the south and some low hills in the northwest. Belize's highest peak, located in the southern Maya Mountains, is only 3,688 feet (1,124 m). Composed of granitic, metasedimentary, and volcanic rocks, overlain in some areas by limestone, the Maya Mountains rise abruptly from the coastal plain, then slope gradually to the west. The Vaca Plateau, for example, which lies west of the Maya Mountains, has an average elevation of about 1,600 feet (490 m). A number of rivers drain the Maya Mountains watershed, most prominent among them being the Raspaculo-Macal-Belize river system, the Sibun River, North and South Stann Creek, and the Sittee River in the north, and Monkey River, the Deep River, and the Rio Grande in the south. North of the Maya Mountains are the New River, with its network of bird-rich lagoons, and the Rio Hondo, which defines much of the Mexico-Belize border. South of the Maya Mountains watershed are the Temash and Sarstoon rivers, the latter defining Belize's southern border with Guatemala.

East of the coastal plain lies the world's second-longest barrier reef, which begins just north of the Belize-Mexico border and extends south nearly the length of the country, a distance of approximately 175 miles (280 km). Along and within the reef are hundreds of small- to moderate-sized cayes (pronounced "keys") plus the much larger Ambergris Caye, which is actually a long, thin peninsula extending south from Mexico for 17 miles (27 km) just inside the reef. Beyond the barrier reef are three coral atolls: Lighthouse Reef, Turneffe Islands, and Glovers Reef.

Belize has a tropical climate. Monthly mean maximum temperatures range from 82.5°F (28°C) in winter to 91.5°F (33°C) in summer. Although winter lows may occasionally dip into the high 50s (midteens), and even lower at high elevations, frost is unknown. Belize has a distinct rainy season, with most of the rain falling in July and August, then gradually tapering off through December. The rainy season begins abruptly with several days of heavy rain, typically commencing in late May or early June, whereas the onset of the dry season is gradual and virtually imperceptible. The rainy season is characterized by moderate to strong trade winds that blow from the east. By early winter, the trade winds and their associated thunderstorms give way to mild westerlies and occasional "northers," cold fronts that sweep through North America with their southern tip often extending into the Tropics. With the northers come cooler temperatures and modest rains of longer duration.

Mean annual rainfall varies dramatically from north to south, with less than 45 inches (110 cm) in the far north and more than 160 inches (400 cm) in southernmost Belize. Although no official record exists, it is likely that higher elevations in the Maya Mountains receive in excess of 180 inches (460 cm) of rainfall annually.

VEGETATION

For its size, Belize possesses an impressive diversity of plant and animal life. Nearly 75% of the country's land area is still dominated by natural vegetation, owing largely to Belize's small human population and relatively strong conservation ethic. In addition, Belize possesses a complex underlying geology, a wide variety of soil types, and a strong north-south cline in precipitation. These factors, coupled with its relatively varied topography, all contribute to a greater variety of vegetation types than would otherwise be expected in a country this size. Approximately two-thirds of the country is covered with forests in various states of maturity. Dominant among these is subtropical, moist, semideciduous broadleaf forest, with pine woodland and savanna composing a much smaller proportion. Nearly half of the country's land and adjacent waters has achieved Protected Area status as forest reserves, wildlife sanctuaries, national parks, or other similarly designated areas.

Natural vegetation along much of the coastal plain, except Corozal District and all but northeastern Toledo District, comprises open pine woodland and savannas and seasonally wet meadows. Mangrove forests line much of the coastline and the majority of cayes. The northern half of the country is dotted with freshwater marshes and lagoons. These are virtually lacking in the south. On its two highest peaks, Belize has a very limited amount of cloud forest.

HABITAT TYPES

The habitat types presented below are necessarily broad and relatively few. They are not intended to reflect in any significant way a botanist's view of the world, but more a bird's view of its world. To specify more narrowly defined habitats would be unnecessarily complex and would likely exceed our current knowledge of what actually limits most species' distribution across or within the various vegetation zones (see discussion in the section "Habitat," p. 14).

CLOUD FOREST

At the top of 3,675 feet (1,120 m) Victoria Peak and 34 miles (55 km) to the southwest atop Belize's 3,688 feet (1,124 m) unnamed highest peak (unofficially dubbed Doyle's Delight after Arthur Conan Doyle's *The Lost World*), are small stands of dwarf forest, perhaps closest in type to elfin woodland and palm brake cloud forest. Because these peaks are enveloped in clouds much of the year, the vegetation is almost completely covered with mosses and ferns, and the under-

lying soil and rocks are covered additionally with sphagnum, club mosses, and lichens. The tallest trees are typically no more than 20 feet (6 m) tall on Victoria Peak and 30 feet (9 m) tall on Doyle's Delight.

SUBMONTANE BROADLEAF FOREST

The forest cover in most of the Maya Mountain range roughly above 1,300 feet (400 m) is dominated by evergreen trees 80 to 120 feet (25 to 35 m) tall with buttressed trunks. The forest is structurally complex, with a high incidence of epiphytes and lianas, and a substory dominated by tree ferns, a variety of palms, and other shrubs and trees of low to moderate stature. Because the canopy is closed, little light penetrates to the forest floor. Understory vegetation is sparse.

LOWLAND BROADLEAF FOREST

This forest type, the dominant forest cover in Belize, is similar to, but less luxuriant than, forests at higher elevations. It typically contains more dry-season deciduous tree species, fewer epiphytes and palm species, and few if any tree ferns in the substory. As in the submontane forest, the understory is sparse; however, toward the end of the dry season, the leaf litter on the forest floor can become quite dense. In the south, the lowland forest, like that at higher elevations, has a closed canopy with tree height averaging in excess of 100 feet (30 m). North of the Maya Mountains, the forest is both drier and of smaller stature, with many more deciduous species and an average canopy height seldom exceeding 80 feet (25 m) away from the major rivers. The canopy is more open, allowing for a denser understory.

Bajo forest, a specific type of seasonally flooded lowland broadleaf forest, is relatively widespread in the north but becomes increasingly scarce southward. Because bajo forests are structurally similar to other types of lowland broadleaf forest and their avifauna, for the most part, is similar, they are not classified as a separate habitat type here.

SUBMONTANE PINE WOODLAND

The Mountain Pine Ridge, a 125-square-mile (325 km²) westward extension of the northern portion of the Maya Mountains, has underlying soils that are predominantly sandy, resulting from decomposed granite. Here, the broadleaf forest is replaced by an open pine woodland (primarily *Pinus caribaea*) with a smaller component of oaks. In many areas the understory is relatively sparse, with grasses predominating, but in recently burned areas a low-growing, nearly impenetrable tangle of ferns (*Dicranopteris* sp.) predominates.

LOWLAND PINE WOODLAND AND SAVANNA

In the coastal lowlands from the Mexican border in northern Orange Walk District, somewhat discontinuously south to northeastern Toledo District, the terrain is dominated by a pine woodland similar in many respects to that in the Mountain Pine Ridge. As in the pine ridge, pines dominate the landscape and are typically found in close association with oaks. However, the understory is much more varied and complex. In many areas, a variety of shrubs and grasses compose the understory. In other areas, palmettos, calabash, and sedges are the dominant understory species. The woodland ranges from relatively dense to open and savanna-like.

SEASONALLY WET MEADOWS

Pine woodland transitions to savanna, and savanna to wet meadow, in many areas almost imperceptibly, in others quite abruptly. Together, the meadows, savannas, and woodlands form a complex mosaic that, although quite different at the two extremes, are often almost impossible to delineate as separate vegetation types because of the many broad transition zones. Extensive seasonally flooded areas with few or no trees are considered separately here because of their distinctive avifauna.

MARSHES AND LAGOONS

Freshwater marshes and lagoons dot the lowland landscape north of Stann Creek but are much less frequent in the south. They range from small ponds with emergent grasses, sedges, rushes, and cattails to expansive shallow lagoons. Unlike seasonally wet meadows, marshes are flooded year-round, have taller emergent vegetation, and are usually found in association with ponds or lagoons. Lagoons may be essentially isolated bodies of water, especially those just back of the coast, or they may be wide areas in sluggish rivers (e.g., New River Lagoon). They are usually shallow, often with seasonally fluctuating water levels. Poorly drained lagoons, such as those at Crooked Tree, have a remarkably rich avifauna that changes compositionally along with the water level through the year. It is these lagoons that attract impressive numbers of waterfowl, waders, and shorebirds in the dry season.

MANGROVE AND LITTORAL FORESTS

Mangroves, especially the red mangrove *(Rhizophora mangle),* line the coast in many areas and may extend some distance inland along major rivers. They are also a significant component of many cayes. The "drowned" cayes are mangrove cayes with no dry land. Mangroves are essential in stabilizing coastlines and serve as important nurseries for many fish species. Behind the red mangroves, on higher land but still within the highest reaches of the tidal zone, are several larger unrelated species that are collectively referred to as black mangroves and white mangroves, depending on their growth form. Above the tide line, mangroves are replaced by littoral forest, which reaches its greatest expression on the cayes. Dominant tree species in the littoral forest vary from 20 to 40 feet (6 to 12 m) tall and typically have broad, tough, leathery leaves.

HUMAN-ALTERED HABITATS

Humans have altered the native landscape of Belize in many and various ways. Such human-altered habitats range from towns and villages, with their trees, lawns, and parks, to agricultural fields, orchards, rice fields, and aquaculture ponds. Recovering forests are often the result of human activities, but at some point in their recovery, they become "natural" habitats again. Human-altered habitats vary from virtually unvegetated, recently disked fields to vegetationally complex and dense second-growth scrub. Each has its own complement of birds, and some, such as rice fields, and aquaculture ponds at harvest time, can attract a remarkably diverse avifauna.

AVIFAUNA

With its extensive tropical forests, pinelands, species-rich lagoons, and countless cayes along its barrier reef, Belize has an avifauna approaching 600 species. As such, it serves as an ideal introduction to tropical birding, especially for English-speaking tourists.

As expected for a country located at 16° to 18° north latitude, its avifauna includes both North Temperate and tropical elements in roughly equal proportions. Of the approximately 574 species reliably recorded in Belize through early 2003, a little more than half do not reach the Temperate Zone and are thus truly tropical. Of those that do, 80% are migratory, reaching or passing through Belize only in winter or during migration.

The terms "resident" and "migrant" are somewhat relative. A number of non-migratory species turn up, at least occasionally and sometimes regularly, on the cayes where they are clearly not resident. Others may be resident in one part of Belize and seasonal in another. For presumed residents, we know little about seasonally fluctuating numbers. For example, many species follow seasonal food supplies. Some hummingbirds move considerable distances at certain seasons timed to correspond with the blooming period of favored plants. Scarlet Macaws are considered to be resident west of the Maya Mountains but seasonal (January to April) east of the Maya Mountains. Hook-billed Kites are thought to be essentially resident throughout their range from northern Mexico to central South America, yet thousands can be observed migrating south in coastal southern Belize every autumn. Where are they coming from? Where are they going? No one knows. Green Shrike-Vireos are common in the dry season yet inexplicably scarce in the rainy season. Is this because they largely vacate much of Belize during the rainy season?

Or is it because they are much less in evidence when they are not singing? Perhaps it is a little of both. A few species—such as Slate-colored Seedeater, Blue Seedeater, and Grassland Yellow-Finch—are nomadic, appearing in an area and breeding for one to several seasons, then disappearing.

Truly migratory species have precisely set biological clocks. With few exceptions, Black-and-white Warblers appear every year in the third week of July, Golden-winged Warblers in the third week of August, and Palm Warblers in the third week of September. An individual seen a mere two weeks earlier would be noteworthy, and one seen even a week ahead of schedule would be considered early. Most species migrate at night, presumably to minimize predation, but a few, like migratory hawks, swallows, Chimney Swifts, and Eastern Kingbirds, migrate during the day, and at least one, the Dickcissel, may migrate both at night and during the day.

Whereas migrants could turn up in almost any habitat, most of the resident avifauna is much more habitat specific. Of three broadleaf-forest species in southern Belize, the Nightingale Wren is found exclusively in hill country (karst limestone hills, Maya Mountains), the Western Slaty-Antshrike only in coastal lowlands, and the Orange-billed Sparrow in both. A number of species are confined to the pinelands. In fact, one species, the Grace's Warbler, is seldom seen outside a pine tree! Although most pineland species are found in both the lowland pine savannas and the Mountain Pine Ridge, a few such as the Ladder-backed Woodpecker are confined to the lowlands, whereas others such as Greater Pewee are confined to the uplands, even though the dominant plant species in both areas is the Caribbean pine.

A few bird species seem to be confined not by gross habitat or topographical parameters but by some other, as yet unknown factor. The Azure-crowned Hummingbird is found in a wide swath across central Belize that includes both lowland and upland pine woodlands as well as upland broadleaf forest. But it is not found in lowland pines and upland broadleaf forest (or any other habitat) north or south of this seemingly arbitrary line. The Plumbeous Vireo is found in the Mountain Pine Ridge (pine forest) and at higher elevations in the Maya Mountains (broadleaf forest). Yet it does not appear to be confined elevationally, because a small population also persists in the lowland pine savannas of Stann Creek District.

Many bird species have dramatically increased in number in the 39 years since the publication of Steve Russell's *Distributional Study of the Birds of British Honduras*. Nearly all of these are birds associated with cleared land, urban areas, second-growth scrub, and manufactured wetlands such as rice fields and shrimp farms. At the same time, although not as apparent, *all* birds of mature broadleaf forest, littoral forest, and mangrove forest have surely decreased in number as man-made habitats have gradually replaced Belize's original forested habitats. While grackles, cowbirds, seedeaters, and some species of pigeons and doves have proliferated as the result of human activities, many forest birds—especially those requiring large territories, like birds of prey—and colonial seabirds, especially terns, have become perilously scarce. On the other hand, migratory waterfowl, shorebirds, and waders, including the Jabiru, have benefited at the expense of grassland and savanna species such as the Black-throated Bobwhite, Botteri's Sparrow, and Grasshopper Sparrow. Several terns (Roseate, Bridled, Sooty, and Brown Noddy) have been nearly extirpated as breeding species in Belize since the mid-1960s, and one, the Black Noddy, was extirpated long before the 1960s. Some birds of prey such as Ornate Hawk-Eagle and Harpy Eagle are almost certainly scarcer now than 40 years ago, although the early data (before the influx of birders) on these species are too sparse for any meaningful comparison.

On the other hand, several now-common species (Double-crested Cormorant, Black-bellied Whistling-Duck, Red-billed Pigeon, and Bronzed Cowbird) were rare in the early 1960s, and the White-winged Dove and Yellow-faced Grassquit were yet to be recorded. Other species, not yet common but clearly on the increase, include American White Pelican, Glossy Ibis, Fulvous Whistling-Duck, and White-winged Becard. All of these species are likely responding to a changing landscape that favors them at the expense of other species. As of early 2003, the Shiny Cowbird has not yet been recorded, and the Eurasian Collared-Dove has been recorded only twice. These two species are rapidly expanding their ranges into Central and North America and may well be common, at least locally, in Belize within the next couple of decades.

Successful bird identification is directly related to the time spent observing an unknown bird, not time spent perusing the book for vital information. The layout of this book is designed to facilitate the identification process by minimizing the time spent consulting the book while the bird is under study. Ideally, the book should not be consulted until *after* the bird has been thoroughly studied, notes taken, and sketches made. The more time spent studying the bird, not the book, while the bird is in view means more time absorbing important information about the bird.

When consulting the book, knowing what family or group the bird belongs to will save a lot of time in narrowing down the choices. For the beginner, the first step then is to become familiar with the arrangement of the families and species (see the sections "Taxonomy" and "Nomenclature," below), then the family and group characteristics (see "Family and Group Headings," p. 10). Bird terminology can be confusing, if not overwhelming, to the person just starting out. Understanding plumage sequences and molt is vital to the identification process (see "Plumage and Molt," p. 8), as is an understanding of the terminology used to describe the various parts of a bird (see "Bird Topography," p. 16).

The advanced birder can skip these sections. For the more skilled birder who is more likely to know at the outset the family or group to which a puzzling species belongs, this book has a feature called "Things to note" that is designed to assist the observer, not in determining immediately which species the bird is, but in noting key field marks to look for while the bird is still under observation. After the bird is gone, and with this key information in hand, successfully identifying the species should be relatively straightforward.

TAXONOMY

The class Aves is divided into orders, and the orders into families. Within each family are genera, and within each genus are the species. For a person just beginning to learn the birds, this grouping may seem somewhat capricious. For example, why are New World vultures grouped with storks instead of hawks? American Coot with rails instead of grebes? Eastern Meadowlark with the blackbirds? And Dickcissel with the buntings? Although taxonomists may disagree on some aspects of how birds should be classified, there really is a considerable amount of scientific evidence to support the manner in which birds are grouped. Birds thought to be the most primitive are listed first, and the most recently derived last. Species are grouped into families, and families into orders, based on shared morphological, biochemical, behavioral, and genetic characters. Although a beginner may lament that birds are not listed alphabetically or arranged according to some color scheme, any veteran can tell you that once you have a fundamental understanding of avian classification, the grouping of species according to their "phylogenetic" relationships is useful in developing a basic framework for bird identification. Having the tyrant flycatchers all placed together makes a lot more sense than having the closely related Great Kiskadee and Boat-billed Flycatcher grouped with the *K*'s and *F*'s, respectively, or the quite unrelated Blue-gray Tanager and Blue-gray Gnatcatcher placed together because of their similar color.

To help the user of this book better understand the higher-level groupings of birds, brief paragraphs highlighting the shared traits of each family are included in the text. Ibises and spoonbills are grouped together in the family Threskiornithidae because of certain shared characters that are believed to be genetically linked. Note that in the world of animals family names always end in "-idae."

Not surprisingly, in a field in which we still have so much to learn, there are several widely accepted classification schemes for birds, some quite disparate at the higher taxonomic levels. In this guide, the convention adopted by the American Ornithologists' Union (AOU) is used because that is the convention most familiar to New World ornithologists and birdwatchers, not because it is any more "correct" than other schemes.

NOMENCLATURE

Like all living things, birds have a scientific name comprising a genus name and a species name. The first letter of the genus is *always* capitalized, and the species name is *never* capitalized (e.g., *Ara macao,* the Scarlet Macaw). Some species are further divided into subspecies. These have a third name, also never capitalized. The scientific name is always written in italics. Thus the subspecies of Yellow Warbler that breeds in Belize, known as the Mangrove Warbler in English, is *Dendroica petechia bryanti.*

Because birding enjoys a popularity among amateurs that is without parallel in any other scientific endeavor, and most amateur birdwatchers do not know the scientific names of birds, their English names have become increasingly standardized to eliminate confusion. The AOU has adopted a rigorous standard for English name usage to thwart the proliferation of names in field guides, handbooks, and other publications. Exceptions remain, however, for many species that range well beyond the geographical area covered by the AOU. The cosmopolitan species *Ardea alba,* which is variously known as Great Egret, Great White Egret, American Egret, and Common Egret, has been dubbed "Great Egret" by the AOU. Other conventions, especially in the Old World, use the name "Great White Egret." Again, the latter is no less "correct" than the name "Great Egret."

PLUMAGE AND MOLT

Many species of birds change their appearance with age or the seasons. They do this through a combination of changing their feathers (molt) and feather wear. When molt results in a plumage that is recognizably different from the preceding plumage, the different plumages are given specific names that refer to their age-related or seasonal set of feathers. Recognizing the plumage that a bird is in can be a convenient means of determining the bird's age or sex and in some cases aids greatly in determining the identity of the species.

Various terminologies for plumage and molt have been proposed over the years, but the one proposed by Humphrey and Parkes (1959, 1963) has become the one most widely used by authors of field guides and handbooks in the Western Hemisphere (e.g., Howell and Webb 1995; National Geographic Society 1999; Sibley 2000). Very recently, a modified version of the Humphrey-Parkes system has been proposed by Steve Howell and others. Although not yet published in late 2002, this modified, simplified approach is eloquently summarized by David Sibley in his excellent new book *Sibley's Birding Basics* (2002). The first true plumage of contour and flight feathers is the **juvenal plumage.** It grows in over the feathers of the downy young. The bird in this plumage is referred to as a **juvenile** (note the different spelling). Some molt out of juvenal plumage almost immediately; others retain juvenal plumage until after they have migrated to their wintering grounds. Through either a partial or a complete replacement of its feathers, the juvenile molts into its **first basic plumage.** In some species, the first basic plumage is indistinguishable from that of the adult; thus, the only recognizable postnatal plumages are the juvenal plumage and *formative,* or adult-like plumage (e.g., Orange-billed Sparrow).

Many species replace at least some of their feathers twice a year, with each corresponding plumage being recognizably different. These plumages are referred to as the **basic plumage** and the **alternate plumage.** For most species, the alternate plumage is worn during the breeding season, and the basic plumage is worn the remainder of the year (Sanderling, Chestnut-sided Warbler). Some species have a very protracted basic plumage (Royal Tern); others a very brief basic plumage (Blue-winged Teal).

Alternate plumage may be attained in a variety of ways. Very few species molt all of their body and flight feathers during the pre-alternate molt. One exception is the male Bobolink, which undergoes a complete transformation from the rather dull-colored basic plumage to the gaudy black, white, and buff alternate plumage. Most Temperate Zone species, however, go through a partial molt, often involving only the body, or contour, feathers. An example is the male Scarlet Tanager, which replaces its green body feathers with bright scarlet feathers while retaining its black wing and tail feathers. Many tropical species, on the other hand, retain much or all of their basic plumage through the breeding season, molting only once a year, usually in late summer or autumn.

Still others attain their "alternate plumage" not through molt but through feather wear. The male Blue-black Grassquit, for example, molts into what appears to be a femalelike dull brown plumage after the breeding season. However, only the fragile tips of its overlapping body feathers are brown. These soon wear off, revealing the glossy blue-black feathers of breeding plumage that were there all along, just not visible. This is an interesting strategy that enables many species to transform themselves from a protective plumage of browns and olives into a showy breeding plumage without the significant expenditure of energy required for shedding and regrowing feathers.

In many species the male and female wear different plumages for part or all of the year. Species with distinctive male and female plumages are more prevalent in the Temperate Zone than in the Tropics, and in a few species, such as Black-cowled Oriole, males and females differ significantly in the northern part of their range but are indistinguishable in the southern part of their range. In some species the male and female wear different plumages year-round (Great-tailed Grackle), in others the male resembles the female only in basic plumage (Bobolink), and in still others the male and female are indistinguishable year-round (Melodious Blackbird).

Aging in birds is defined by the progressive sequence of molts leading to the adult-type plumage. Most tropical species and many temperate species molt directly from their juvenal plumage into adult plumage within one to a few months after fledging. The vast majority of these species breed in their first spring. Other species, notably

hawks and gulls, require more than one year to attain adult plumage. Some examples of the aging process are as follows:

Green Jay: Molts directly from downy plumage into a plumage that is indistinguishable in the field from adult plumage. It has no discernible juvenal plumage.

Orange-billed Sparrow: Has a distinctive juvenal plumage but attains adultlike plumage with its first molt.

Short-billed Dowitcher: Retains a distinct juvenal plumage through November, then acquires the adult-type alternate plumage by spring, well before the end of its first year.

American Redstart: Retains juvenal plumage only briefly, followed by a molt into first basic plumage shortly after leaving the nest. Its first alternate plumage, acquired in spring, is recognizably different from that of the adult (this is especially noticeable in the male). It is not until late in its second summer that the young bird attains adult-type plumage.

Great Black-Hawk: Retains juvenal plumage through its first year, molts into its first basic plumage in its second year, and molts into its second basic plumage shortly after the beginning of its third year. It does not molt into adult-type plumage until it is nearly four years old.

Herring Gull: Retains juvenal plumage only for a short period after fledging and, through a process of protracted molts, proceeds through three basic plumages (three years) before molting into adult basic plumage in its fourth year.

In birds that take more than one year to mature, it is often simpler to refer to nonadult birds collectively as "immatures" or "subadults," as opposed to "juveniles," "first basic," "second basic," and so on. This policy has been adopted, where appropriate, in the species accounts.

In a few more challenging species, the plumage that the bird is in, and even the state of feather wear, may be critical to its correct identification (e.g., some shorebirds, gulls, and flycatchers). Many birds, especially small flycatchers in the genus *Empidonax,* are very similar, and the juvenile of one species may look more like the adult of another species, and an adult with worn feathers may look similar to yet another species with a fresh set of feathers.

ORGANIZATION OF THE SPECIES ACCOUNTS

Bird identification is often a multistep process and requires practice. Birds do not always sit still. Success often depends on how much the observer can absorb in a short period of time or from a bird mostly hidden in foliage. Knowing which aspects of the bird's plumage, shape, and behavior are important for identification and which are not can be critical for a bird that is only in sight momentarily. Size, posture, and shape, especially bill shape, are often important in determining the bird's family or genus. Plumage patterns are often important in identifying the species, but a bright red breast may be far less important than the presence or absence of a small white mark behind its eye. Subtle differences in bill size or shape can be more important to note than wing pattern. The underwing pattern of an overhead buteo or buzzard may be critical to its identification; the underwing pattern of a falcon may not. Noting the vocalizations of a small flycatcher may be more critical to its identification than the calls of a confusing fall warbler. The species accounts are organized to facilitate this multistep identification process and to aid the user in recognizing key field marks.

FAMILY AND GROUP HEADINGS

Under each family heading is a general description of the characteristics unique to that family. This is the place to go to learn the difference between a warbler and a vireo or between a woodcreeper and a woodpecker. For closely related species within a family, an additional paragraph describes the characters shared by species in the group, as well as their key differences.

The species group may be a subfamily (e.g., the Anserinae, or geese), a tribe (e.g., the Anatini, or surface-feeding ducks), a collection of related genera (e.g., the kites), a specific genus (e.g., the hawk genus *Accipiter*), or a group of

closely related birds within a genus (e.g., the *virens* group of *Dendroica* warblers).

THINGS TO NOTE

At the end of most family or group descriptions is a brief section entitled "Things to note." The purpose of this tool is to allow the observer to spend as much time studying the bird and as little time as possible flipping through the book and memorizing complex details. This is *not* the place to go to learn how to tell the two dowitchers apart. It *is* the place to go when studying a puzzling dowitcher to learn which field marks to look for and which to ignore, so that the bird can be identified later—after it has flown. It would take at least several minutes to wade through the intricacies of how to tell a Short-billed Dowitcher from a Long-billed, during which time the bird may flush unidentified. But it only takes a few seconds to note which characters are critical to the bird's identification and which are not. For example, it is not as important to determine the length of the bird's bill as it is to note what plumage it is in, whether the folded wings project beyond the tail, and what habitat it is in. If these items are carefully noted while the bird is under observation, chances are good that the bird can be successfully identified long after it has flown, by referring to the detailed information presented in the species accounts.

THE SPECIES

Introducing each species account is the species' currently accepted English name and scientific name. These are the names designated by the AOU in the seventh edition of its *A.O.U. Checklist of North American Birds* (1998), along with the few name changes specified in the 42nd and 43rd supplements to the check-list published in 2000 and 2002, respectively. With few exceptions, subspecies are not given full accounts in the text. A few strikingly different subspecies, such as the "Mangrove" subspecies of Yellow Warbler, and the Myrtle and Audubon's subspecies of Yellow-rumped Warbler, are, however, accorded separate accounts.

In addition to the 574 species reliably reported from Belize, 6 additional species reported but not confirmed, and 1 species not yet reported, are included in the species accounts. They are distinguished from the species generally accepted as having occurred at least once by having their English name placed in brackets. Although the Baird's Sandpiper, Great Black-backed Gull, Great Potoo, Sparkling-tailed Hummingbird, Eastern Phoebe, and Connecticut Warbler may well have been correctly identified within the boundaries of Belize, the evidence thus far is less than convincing (Jones 2002). All have a reasonable chance of turning up in Belize in the future and are included to bring attention to their as yet unconfirmed status. The seventh species, Shiny Cowbird, has not been reported but is rapidly expanding its range and may soon "invade" the country, as it has the northern West Indies and southern United States.

OTHER NAMES

Following the English and scientific name heading for most species is a list of other names. Many Belizeans are not familiar with the standard English names but know the birds by their local Creole, Maya, or Spanish names. Still others have learned the birds from older books that use English names different from those adopted by the AOU. Of the older bird guides, *A Field Guide to the Birds of Mexico and Central America* (1972), by Irby Davis, easily has the most English names that never found their way into standard usage. Davis's unique names are also provided here for those who are most familiar with his book. Thus, the section on other names includes, where applicable, alternative English names (alt.), names no longer in general usage (arch., for "archaic"), colloquial names (coll.), English names that may be more familiar to birders from the United Kingdom (U.K.), names coined by Irby Davis (I. Davis), K'ekchi names (K), Mopan Maya names (M), and local Spanish names (S). Add to this the many "lumps" and "splits" of species over the past several decades. In many cases, such regroupings have resulted in a new English name for one or both of the split species or for the combined form in cases where two species were lumped. For example, the Gray-fronted Dove

is considered by some authorities, but currently not the AOU, to comprise two different species, the Gray-fronted Dove and the Gray-headed Dove. Under this scheme, the bird found in Belize and the rest of Central America would be the Gray-headed Dove, with the Gray-fronted Dove found only in South America. Under "Other Names" for this bird is the entry "Gray-headed Dove (is part of)," meaning that if the two forms are split, the species in Belize would be called the Gray-headed Dove. Conversely, the Black-headed Trogon was once thought to include populations on both the Caribbean and Pacific slopes of Mexico and Central America and was called collectively the Citreoline Trogon. Now birds on the Caribbean slope are considered a separate species known as the Black-headed Trogon, and those on the Pacific slope are still referred to as the Citreoline Trogon. Under "Other Names" for this bird the reader will find "Citreoline Trogon (combined form)," meaning that if the classification scheme in which all populations are considered to be one species is used, the birds in Belize would be known as the Citreoline Trogon.

IDENTIFICATION

In addition to descriptions of the bird's plumage and soft parts (bill, eyes, legs, and feet), the identification section includes an indicator of the species' size and frequently includes important behavioral notes when a species' distinctive behavior may facilitate its identification. Before wading too deeply into this section, it is imperative that the reader become familiar with the terminology used to describe the different parts of a bird (see "Bird Topography," p. 16).

Size

The approximate overall length of each species is given in both inches and centimeters. For simplicity, only one, average measurement is given, rather than a range, and this should be taken into account when considering the stated size of the bird. Most birds have a range in size of about 5% to rarely 10% or more. In many of the larger species (e.g., hawks) and a few smaller ones (e.g., some of the cowbirds), males and females differ significantly in size. In such instances, male and female measurements are given separately. In some birds that spend much of their time on the wing, wingspread is given as well.

Determining the overall length of a bird is problematical. Unlike the measurement of the folded wing, for example, the measured bill-tip to tail-tip of a bird may vary widely, depending on whether one is measuring a specimen in a museum tray or a live or freshly dead bird in the hand. Even the manner of repose of the living bird can greatly affect its overall length. All birds have extendable necks to some degree. Museum specimens may vary greatly in length, depending on the method of preparing the specimen. For this reason, most recent bird guides have used measurements of living birds. Thus, overall length is given only as a rough indicator of a bird's size relative to similar species. For example, the Lesser Yellowlegs is about 9¾ inches long; the Greater Yellowlegs approximately 12 inches. Although not precise, and representing roughly the median size for each, these size measurements are a pretty good indicator that the Greater Yellowlegs is a substantially larger bird than the Lesser Yellowlegs, an important field character. Nevertheless, the size of a yellowlegs feeding alone in a shallow pond can be very difficult to determine, even within a range of 2–3 inches. In cases of lone birds like this, other field characters may be necessary to determine the bird's identity.

Plumage Characteristics

In the species accounts, special attention is paid to plumage characteristics, which are usually the primary features but by no means the only ones used in bird identification. In species with recognizably different plumages (male vs. female, basic vs. alternate, juvenile vs. adult, etc.), the differing plumage characters of each are given. Also, on the pages facing the color plates are identification notes for each species and plumage that is illustrated. These notes are condensed versions of what appears in the text.

Behavior

The behavior of a bird can be critical to its identification, especially in species with similar plumages or a confusing variety of plumages. Behavior includes everything from a bird's manner of foraging to its flight characteristics and its posture. In some species such as birds of prey and shorebirds, the identification of birds in flight is called out separately in the species accounts.

VOICE

The sounds that birds make are often more important than what the birds look like. After all, if the bird is not seen, its voice may be the only clue to its identification. And it is said that for every bird seen, four others are heard only. Learning bird vocalizations is not as daunting as many people believe. Nearly everyone can instantly identify the voices of their friends and relatives on the telephone, even some friends they may not have spoken with for years. Bird vocalizations should be no more difficult to learn than "people vocalizations."

One of the greatest challenges facing anyone writing a bird guide is how to depict bird vocalizations as text. No one has yet devised a method of accurately describing complex sounds in nature through use of the written word. Many techniques have been used, some more successfully than others. Although written descriptions of bird sounds can never match the actual or recorded sounds, they can serve as a learning tool. Even with a recording in hand, most people need to catalog a sound in their memory through verbal associations in order to facilitate the learning process.

No one can be expected to read a vocal description and then go out and recognize the bird the first time he or she hears it. The verbal descriptions, though, should serve as an aid in *remembering* the sounds heard in the field through association. The use of CDs or tapes as a supplement to this book is strongly encouraged. But they should be used in conjunction with, not to the exclusion of, verbal descriptions.

This guide employs a combination of phonetic sounds and modifiers such as flat, sharp, metallic, hollow, dry, liquid, squeaky, harsh, buzzy, and nasal to describe the tone, clarity, pitch, modulation, and other qualities. In some cases, soundalike phrases are used, such as *Chick, see the vireo, chick!* for the song of the White-eyed Vireo and *hope, nope,* and *no hope* for the sounds the various ground-doves make. If the descriptions given in the text are read immediately *after* hearing a bird's song in the field or on tape, they should help commit the sound to memory through association.

A word of caution in learning bird sounds from a commercial tape or CD: many species in the Tropics have rather pronounced regional dialects. This is especially true of some groups like the woodcreepers. With few exceptions, tapes of woodcreeper vocalizations made in southern Central America or in South America are of little use in learning what woodcreepers in Belize sound like.

To successfully make the leap from the written word to the actual sounds heard in nature, you will need to know how to interpret these textual representations. I have made liberal use of the standard diacritical marks for vowel sounds found at the bottom of every page in a standard dictionary. If you are not already familiar with these, learn them first. Spacing of notes in a vocal sequence is represented in the following manner: a pause between notes that is noticeably longer than the spacing between other notes is indicated by one or more extra spaces between notes. A "normal" spacing of notes is indicated with a single space between notes. A rapid sequence of notes (for example, a rattle or slow trill) is indicated with a hyphen between notes, and a very rapid sequence in which the individual notes are virtually impossible to distinguish is represented with no spaces or hyphens between notes. Thus, the widely spaced individual notes of the Spotted Woodcreeper are represented as *keeoo   keeo   keeo   keeo;* the more rapidly paced song of the Green Shrike-Vireo as *dear dear dear dear;* the short rattle or slow trill of the Common Tody-Flycatcher as *d-d-d-dt;* and the rapid trill or buzz of the Grasshopper Sparrow as *tp tipit zzzzzzzzzzzzzzzzz.*

But bird vocalizations are a lot more than the relative spacing of notes in a song or call. Songs have rhythm and cadence, pitch and tone, flatness, sharpness, musicality, richness, amplitude, and many other traits. Wherever possible, I have used words and parts of words to describe these sounds. For example, *dee* represents a higher note than *doe; t* is a sharper sound than *d,* and *d* is sharper than *ch* or *sh.* Other words such as "clear," "hollow," "liquid," "dry," "nasal," and "guttural" are standard written descriptions used to portray familiar sounds. Even with all these aids, will you really know what a Black-faced Grosbeak sounds like from the description given in this book? Probably not. But *after* you have heard the bird and compared what you heard with the description in the book, you should be able to recall at least some of its vocalizations the next time you hear it or read its vocal description a few weeks, or even months, later.

The best way to expand your knowledge of bird vocalizations is to compare an unfamiliar sound with a similar one you already know. At first, this may be difficult, but as you learn more and more, your accumulated knowledge helps considerably in building upon what you have learned. Thus, the rate of learning can be nearly exponential, at least for awhile. If you have the patience and perseverance to get past the early learning stages, it actually gets easier as you go. Having spent the majority of my adult life in California, I noticed when I first came to Belize that one of the vocalizations of the Rufous-browed Peppershrike reminded me of the rich cascading song of the familiar Canyon Wren, and that the simple call of the Green-backed Sparrow reminded me of an Orange-crowned Warbler's. Whether you are a tourist or a native, a professional or an amateur, you are probably already familiar with many bird sounds. Just as with learning a foreign language, you can build upon this knowledge; use it as a nucleus for expanding your vocabulary of bird sounds.

Vocalizations are traditionally divided into calls and songs; however, this distinction is not as straightforward as you might think, even for the "songbirds," or passerines. Most birds have a more complex vocabulary than that. For example, one vocalization may be a simple "contact" or "location" call. Another may be given when a bird is slightly agitated, yet another when pursuing an intruder, announcing a nearby predator, or defending a nest. Songs may include a dawn song, as well as the "typical" song. Other vocalizations defy classification. For example, the Rufous-browed Peppershrike gives, in addition to its various calls, a complex whistled jumble of notes at various pitches—clearly its song. However, it also gives a very different series of clear, whistled notes that descend the musical scale, as mentioned above. Is this an alternate song? Or does it serve some other function?

The full vocal repertoire of many neotropical species is extensive, but nearly all have one to several characteristic vocalizations that they give frequently. This book does not attempt to present a comprehensive repertoire; instead, the focus is on the more typical utterances. Wherever possible, I have attempted to separate vocalizations normally referred to as calls from those that are considered to be songs. For most passerines, or "songbirds," the distinction is fairly straightforward. But for many other species, this distinction is blurred, and the use of the word "song" for some nonpasserines is not entirely accurate.

HABITAT

Habitats are complex and can be defined in many different ways. They are not discrete units; there is often broad overlap between different habitat types. No single accepted classification system exists. Botanists classify vegetation types according to dominant plant types, vegetation structure, soil type, and underlying topography. Birds, on the other hand, are often limited by a combination of vegetation structure, presence of preferred food plants, absence of certain potential predators, temperature regimes, and other, more subtle parameters. Rarely are bird species confined specifically to one vegetation type. Some are limited exclusively by food type, others by cover type, and still others by competition with similar species or dissimilar

species with similar life requirements. Often, these species segregate themselves on the basis of elevation, type of cover, rainfall patterns, or other factors in combination that may not be readily discernible to humans. And these requirements may change with the seasons, according to a north-south, east-west (coastal-inland), or altitudinal gradient. Thus, "habitat" necessarily becomes a loose criterion in framing the physical, geographical, and environmental limitations on a species' distribution. It may or may not correspond with the vegetation types defined by botanists. For the broadly defined habitat types used in this book, see the section "Habitat Types" (pp. 2–4).

DISTRIBUTION

The section on distribution frames in very general terms the species' worldwide distribution. It provides a broader context for the species' distribution, status, and seasonality in Belize. For example, when pondering a pewee in January, it helps to know that the Eastern Wood-Pewee and the Western Wood-Pewee both winter in South America, thus leaving the Tropical Pewee as the only reasonable choice.

STATUS IN BELIZE

A bird's status in an area includes (1) its geographic range within the area covered (in this case within the political boundaries of Belize); (2) whether it is present year-round or only during a portion of the year; (3) if the latter, in which season of the year it is expected to be present; and (4) its relative abundance. Its geographic range includes only those habitats in which it is expected to occur; thus, a bird "found on the mainland throughout" can be found wherever its preferred habitat is present on the mainland, but it would not be found anywhere on the cayes, even in its preferred habitat.

Seasonality

Thirty percent of the birds in Belize (about 170 species) are present during only a portion of the year. Knowing which species to expect during any given season can be very helpful in the identification process. A waterthrush in July seen too briefly to identify with certainty would be Louisiana; one seen in May would be Northern. The arrival and departure times given in the text reflect the earliest and latest dates the species can reasonably be expected in Belize. There are, of course, exceptions to this generally predictable pattern of occurrence, but any bird seen outside the expected period should be studied carefully to make sure it is not a similar species more likely at that season. In some years, certain species may arrive or depart significantly earlier or later than the norm, but such instances are rare.

Because migrants appear in "waves" according to changing regional weather patterns, a species that may, on average, be a "fairly common migrant" could be absent or, alternatively, very common for several days at a time. Typically, birds do not become common until several weeks after the arrival of the first individuals. Likewise, numbers become greatly reduced before the last individuals depart. At the same time, stragglers occasionally may be seen as much as a week or more after the normal departure date or a week or so before the typical arrival date.

In the Tropics, terms such as "winter" and "summer" are not as meaningful as in temperate areas. Some species breed in the Arctic and spend the "winter" in Belize, although they may arrive as early as July and not leave until late May. Likewise, several "summer" species that leave Belize in the winter for South America may arrive as early as February. One "summer" resident, the Gray-breasted Martin, sometimes appears as early as the last week of December! Some observers refer to these species as dry-season residents rather than summer residents, but even that term is less than accurate, because, without exception, species in Belize that appear near the beginning of the dry season do not depart until two to four months after the heavy rains begin in June.

Relative Abundance

The words "common," "fairly common," and "uncommon" reflect a matter of degree. They are subjective terms. Where does one draw the line between something that is fairly common and something that is uncommon? Where in this continuum, for example, would you place a bird that you might see on average once in every five trips afield? Although these terms are very general, they do serve a useful purpose if properly defined and used only according to each one's definition. As used in this book, these terms are defined below.

For a resident species in appropriate habitat within its normal range:

- *Very common (VC):* Present in large numbers; seen on every trip afield (Great-tailed Grackle in any urban area)
- *Common (C):* Seen in small to moderate numbers on nearly every trip afield (Red-throated Ant-Tanager in most woodland habitats; Common Tody-Flycatcher in open areas with trees)
- *Uncommon (UC):* Seen periodically; not expected on every trip afield (White Hawk in rainforest and forest edge)
- *Very uncommon (VU):* Seen only once or twice a year (Uniform Crake)
- *Rare (R):* Seldom seen; distribution spotty, even within seemingly appropriate habitat (Harpy Eagle in mature rainforest)

For transients, these terms are applied somewhat differently, and one additional term is used:

- *Very common (VC):* Seen frequently in moderate to large numbers but may be scarce or absent on any given day, even during normal periods of migration (Eastern Kingbird in September along the coast)
- *Common (C):* Seen frequently in small to moderate numbers but occasionally scarce or absent (Red-eyed Vireo in April and October)
- *Uncommon (UC):* Not seen on most days; rarely present in large numbers (Golden-winged Warbler in April and September)
- *Occasional (occas.):* Occurs on an infrequent basis; may be missed during an entire period of migration (Canada Warbler)

For species with three or fewer records, each occurrence is given in the text. These species are often referred to as "vagrants" or "accidentals."

REFERENCES

The reference section lists articles, books, and audiocassettes and CDs that may be of interest to the reader. Material consulted in developing the species accounts is also listed here. Major works such as Russell (1964), Howell and Webb (1995), and other books with broad coverage of birds in Belize generally are not cited in the species accounts.

BIRD TOPOGRAPHY

One cannot approach the subject of bird identification without referring to specific external parts of a bird. The parts usually refer to feather groups, feather tracts, or soft parts (bill, eyes, legs, and feet). The parts of a bird that are mentioned in the text are shown in the illustrations below. Learning these terms will help considerably in the identification process.

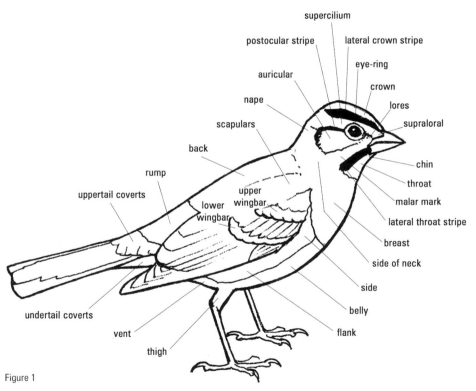

Figure 1

Parts of a bird.

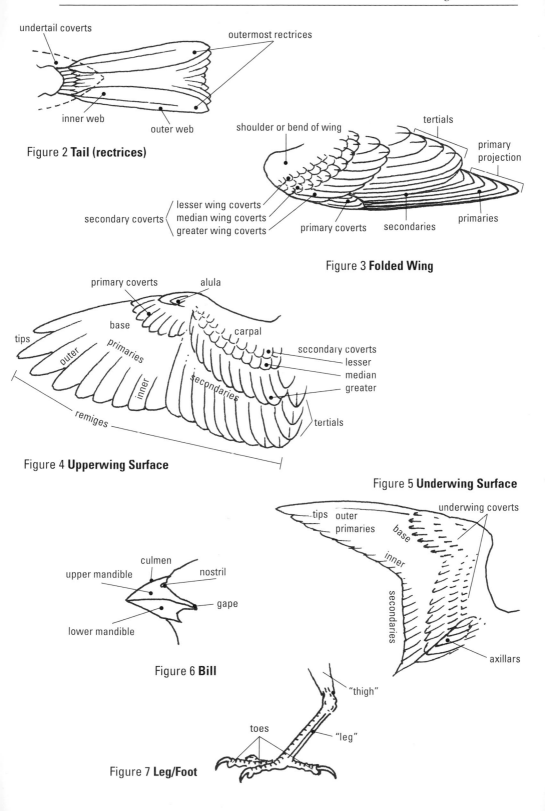

undertail coverts

outermost rectrices

inner web

outer web

Figure 2 **Tail (rectrices)**

shoulder or bend of wing

tertials

primary projection

lesser wing coverts
secondary coverts { median wing coverts
greater wing coverts

primary coverts

secondaries

primaries

Figure 3 **Folded Wing**

primary coverts

alula

base

carpal

tips

outer

primaries

secondary coverts

lesser

median

greater

inner

secondaries

remiges

tertials

Figure 4 **Upperwing Surface**

Figure 5 **Underwing Surface**

tips   outer
primaries

base

underwing coverts

inner

culmen

upper mandible

nostril

secondaries

gape

lower mandible

axillars

Figure 6 **Bill**

"thigh"

toes

"leg"

Figure 7 **Leg/Foot**

RANGE MAPS

At the back of the book are range maps for 234 species. For species found throughout the country, and for most widespread migrants, range maps are not given. Nor are range maps given for those species with very few records. Locality information for these vagrant species is presented in the text.

In the maps, the distribution of resident species is shown in gray (see Hypothetical Range Map). The distribution of species found in Belize only in summer is shown with diagonal lines that run from upper right to lower left (e.g., Swallow-tailed Kite, Map 27). Winter distributions are indicated with diagonal lines that run from upper left to lower right. A dot (•) is used to mark a specific locality of occurrence of a resident species, such as a breeding colony (for colonially nesting species) or a very small, isolated population. An asterisk (*) is used to show a single occurrence of a species, and a question mark is used to show uncertain occurrence or uncertain status. A dashed line is used to indicate expanded seasonal distribution beyond the limits of the species' breeding range.

Major place names and topographic features are shown on the Localities and Features Map on p. 19.

Hypothetical Range Map

Localities and Features Map

by Dana Gardner

PLATE **1** PELECANIFORMES

BOOBIES: Fairly large seabirds with long, pointed wings, tail, and bill; webbed feet, no pouch.

1 BROWN BOOBY *Sula leucogaster* · p. 26
FC offshore. Pale underwing coverts; straight culmen; sharp breast/belly contrast (except juv.), yellow feet. *Ad. ♂:* yellow bill, blue face. *Ad. ♀:* yellow face. *Juv.:* similar to juv. **3** but slightly larger; underwing coverts contrast lighter; may show slight breast-belly contrast; bill gray; culmen straight.

2 MASKED BOOBY *Sula dactylatra* · p. 25
Vagrant. *Ad.:* white, with black flight feathers (including tail), pale bill, straight culmen. *Imm.:* dark above, white below, with black hood, white collar.

3 RED-FOOTED BOOBY *Sula sula* · p. 26
Half Moon Caye only. Narrow bill with concave bill/forehead angle. *White morph:* red feet, pale blue bill, pink face, white tail; in flight (not shown), inner secondaries white (black in **2**). *Brown morph:* brown, with white posterior; 1 in 30 ads. is brown morph. *Juv.:* uniformly brown; nearly black bill; yellowish feet (see juv. **1**).

4 MAGNIFICENT FRIGATEBIRD
Fregata magnificens · p. 30
C on coast, R inland. Large size, distinctive flight silhouette with very long, narrow wings; strong angle at wrist; deeply forked tail; and long, hooked bill. *Ad. ♂:* all black, with red pouch (usually not visible except when inflated on breeding grounds). *Ad. ♀:* white breast, black hood. *Juv.:* white breast and head.

PELICANS: Very large, with immense bill, webbed feet, large pouch.

5 AMERICAN WHITE PELICAN
Pelecanus erythrorhynchos · p. 27
Local on coast, R inland. Largest bird in W. Hemisphere (Jabiru smaller but weighs more). White with extensive black in wings. From **2** by immense orange bill, long neck, white tail, large size. From Wood Stork (Plate 3) by immense bill that rests on curved neck in flight (storks fly with neck outstretched), by

short legs, and by feathered white head and neck.

6 BROWN PELICAN *Pelecanus occidentalis*
p. 27
C on coast, R inland. Immense bill, short tail, rounded wings. *Ad.:* silvery gray upperparts, blackish underparts, white neck, yellow head. *Prebreeding ad.:* rich brown stripe up back of neck. *Juv. and 1st basic:* mostly brown, with white belly and white stripe in underwing. *2nd year* (not shown): like ad. but head and neck mottled white; lacks silvery gray highlights in upperparts.

7 ANHINGA *Anhinga anhinga* · p. 29
UC to FC in lowlands. Mostly black, with silvery white back plumes and wing patch. Long, thin neck and bill; long tail. Frequently swims with just head and neck above water. Like cormorant, often rests with wings outstretched. Unlike cormorant, will soar high overhead with outstretched neck and fanned tail. ♂: black foreparts. ♀: light brown foreparts.

CORMORANTS: Medium-sized body, gular pouch, long neck, webbed feet. Often rest with outstretched wings. Fly with outstretched, slightly crinkled neck; frequently glide for short periods in steady flight but do not soar.

8 DOUBLE-CRESTED CORMORANT
Phalacrocorax auritus · p. 28
C on n. coast and cayes. Yellow-orange bill and pouch; pouch with curved to straight posterior edge; orange supraloral stripe. *Ad.:* blackish plumage; black ear tufts when breeding. *Juv.:* pale brown head, neck, and breast.

9 NEOTROPIC CORMORANT
Phalacrocorax brasilianus · p. 28
C, except cayes. Smaller than **8**; sharp angle at rear edge of pouch, longer tail, black supraloral. *Ad.:* white line at rear edge of pouch (sharper in breeding birds); thin white ear plumes when breeding. *Juv.:* lacks white at base of pouch; from juv. **8** by smaller size, longer tail, shorter bill, sharp angle at base of bill.

1 ♀ ♂

1 Juvenile

Juvenile

2 Immature

4

2 Adult

Adult
Brown
Morph
3

♂

3

Juvenile

5

♀

Adult White Morph

Prebreeding
Adult

First
Basic

6

6

♀

♂

7

Breeding

8

Adult

Juvenile

Adult

9

Breeding

Adult

Juvenile

PLATE **2** WADERS

SMALL HERONS: Decidedly smaller than other herons (especially **1**).

1 LEAST BITTERN *Ixobrychus exilis* · p. 31
R and local; marshes. Tiny, secretive. ♂: black back and crown; faintly streaked breast. ♀: duller, with dark brown back and crown.

2 GREEN HERON *Butorides virescens* · p. 34
C throughout. Small, squat. When alarmed raises neck, head, and shaggy crest, flicks tail nervously. *Ad.:* chestnut, blue gray, and green. *Imm.:* brown above, streaked below.

NIGHT-HERONS: Colonial; active at night; roost in trees during day.

3 BOAT-BILLED HERON *Cochlearius cochlearius* p. 36
Local, rivers and lagoons. Large, bulbous bill and pinkish buff breast distinguish it from **4**. *Ad.:* chestnut belly, gray back, and black crown with long, bushy plumes. *Imm.:* brown back and crown; short plumes; lacks chestnut belly of ad.

4 BLACK-CROWNED NIGHT-HERON
Nycticorax nycticorax · p. 35
Local, wetlands. Usually keeps head retracted. In flight, only distal portion of feet project beyond tail. *Juv.:* pale "teardrop" edges to feathers; underparts streaked; greenish yellow base to bill. *Ad.:* black crown with 2 white plumes; black back, gray wings, white underparts.

5 YELLOW-CROWNED NIGHT-HERON
Nyctanassa violacea · p. 35
C and widespread. More often seen with head and neck extended than **4**. In flight, entire length of feet project beyond tail. *Juv.:* similar to **4** but thicker bill without pale base; spots in wing reduced to small triangles; darker overall; larger eyes in smaller head. *Ad.:* blue gray, with black and pale yellow head.

6 LIMPKIN *Aramus guarauna* · p. 77
Locally C, wetlands. Most like Glossy Ibis (Plate 3) but larger, with short white streaks in plumage; thicker, less downcurved bill (herons

have straight bill). Distinctive flight, with rapid upstroke and slow downstroke; neck and head outstretched and slightly drooped.

7 AGAMI HERON *Agamia agami* · p. 35
UC and local. Very long, thin neck and bill. Skulker. *Ad.:* striking silvery gray-blue plumes on head, lower neck, and lower back; yellow face; underparts chestnut. *Imm.:* gray brown above; creamy white below; lacks plumes.

BITTERNS: Large brown marsh herons. Secretive, often remaining motionless with bill pointed skyward as means of camouflage.

8 PINNATED BITTERN *Botaurus pinnatus* p. 30
UC, marshes. Larger than **9** and lacks black malar streak; has finely barred neck, black streaks on pale back, and darker tail. Smaller than imm. **10**, lacks bold barring across back. In flight, dark flight feathers contrast with warm brown wing coverts.

9 AMERICAN BITTERN *Botaurus lentiginosus* p. 31
Occas. in winter, marshes. Differs from **10** in same ways as **8**. From **8** by smaller size; conspicuous black malar stripe; streaked, not barred, neck; unstreaked back. In flight, tail does not contrast darker.

10 BARE-THROATED TIGER-HERON
Tigrisoma mexicanum · p. 31
FC throughout. Larger than bitterns. Unfeathered yellow throat. Labored flight, especially on takeoff. *Ad.:* gray face; finely barred light brown neck; dark cinnamon belly. *Imm.:* strongly barred throughout.

11 GREAT BLUE HERON *Ardea herodias* · p. 32
FC throughout. Large; flies with very slow wingbeats. *Ad.:* white head with black stripe continuing behind as plume; yellow bill. *Imm.* (not shown): dark gray crown; light gray head, with lighter chin and throat; dark bill. (See Plate 3 for rare white morph.)

♂

♀

1

Immature

Adult

2

Immature

Adult

3

Adult

Immature

5

Immature

4

6

Adult

7

Immature

Adult

Immature

10

Adult

11

8

9

Adult

PLATE **3** WADERS

STORKS: Large; unfeathered head and neck; heavyset bill; soaring flight with outstretched neck.

1 JABIRU *Jabiru mycteria* · p. 38
Local, wetlands. Massive bill; red sac at base of neck; lacks black flight feathers of **2**. *Imm.* (not shown): plumage washed dirty brown.

2 WOOD STORK *Mycteria americana* · p. 38
FC throughout. Half the size of **1**; slimmer bill droops at tip; lacks red skin at base of neck; black remiges conspicuous in flight. *Ad.:* unfeathered head and neck, dusky bill. *Imm.:* feathered neck, bill yellowish.

3 GREAT BLUE HERON *Ardea herodias* · p. 32
Rare white morph: from **6** by yellow legs, heavier-set bill, larger size, white plume on hindcrown, slower wingbeats.

4 GREATER FLAMINGO *Phoenicopterus ruber*
p. 41
Vagrant. Long, thin neck and legs; sickle-shaped, black-tipped bill. *Ad.:* bright pink. *Juv.* (not shown): grayish buff, with pink only on underparts.

5 ROSEATE SPOONBILL *Platalea ajaja* · p. 37
Locally FC, wetlands. Spatulate bill; flies with shallow wingbeats. *Ad.:* rose pink, with red patch in wing, unfeathered greenish head, orange tail. *Juv.:* mostly white.

EGRETS: All but **8** are white or have white morph (**7**) or imm. (**9**). Hold neck retracted in flight.

6 GREAT EGRET *Ardea alba* · p. 32
C throughout. Large; long, yellow bill; black legs; has white plumes on lower neck and back when breeding.

7 REDDISH EGRET *Egretta rufescens* · p. 34
UC on cayes, coast. White eyes and gray legs in all plumages. Forages by actively stirring up water with its feet while spreading and closing wings. In flight, slow, deep wingbeats. When breeding, plumes on crown, neck, and back. *Dark morph:* reddish head and neck, grayish

body; pale stripe on underwing conspicuous in flight. *Ad.:* blue-gray body, brighter reddish head and neck, pink-and-black bill. *Imm.:* duller. *Juv.* (not shown): chalky grayish plumage with pale pinkish cinnamon head and neck. *White morph:* from other white herons by gray legs, dark bill (pink with black tip in ad.); much less frequent than dark morph.

8 TRICOLORED HERON *Egretta tricolor* · p. 33
C throughout. Longer, thinner neck and bill than all but Agami. *Ad.:* slaty blue upperparts, white belly and foreneck; 2 white crown plumes in breeding season. *Imm.:* brownish and gray.

9 LITTLE BLUE HERON *Egretta caerulea* · p. 33
C in winter, UC in summer. *Ad.:* slaty blue gray throughout; blue bill with black tip; greenish legs. *Imm.:* white, with black-tipped blue bill, greenish legs. *1st summer* (not shown): pied slate-and-white plumage.

10 SNOWY EGRET *Egretta thula* · p. 33
C throughout. White in all plumages. White plumes on crown, neck, and back in breeding season. Black bill and legs; yellow face and feet. *Juv.* (not shown): greenish yellow legs, usually with black on fore-edge.

11 CATTLE EGRET *Bubulcus ibis* · p. 34
C throughout. *Ad. alt.:* orange-buff plumes on crown, breast, and lower back; yellow bill, dark olive-gray legs. *Basic ad. (and imm.):* all-white body.

IBISES: Long, decurved bill; shallow, fast wingbeats; outstretched neck in flight.

12 GLOSSY IBIS *Plegadis falcinellus* · p. 37
Local in winter, wetlands. *Ad. alt.* (not shown): dark chestnut plumage with iridescent purplish green feathers in back and wings. *Ad. and imm. basic:* dusky brown; fine white streaks on head and neck; thin, pale blue supraloral stripe.

13 WHITE IBIS *Eudocimus albus* · p. 36
Locally C, wetlands. *Ad.:* white, with black outer primary tips; face and bill red. *Imm.:* brown above and white below; pale bill.

1

2 Immature / Adult

3

4

5 Juvenile / Adult

6

7 White Morph / Adult / Immature

8 Adult / Immature

9 Adult / Immature

10

11 Adult Alternate / Adult Basic

12

13 Immature / Adult

PLATE **4** WATERFOWL

1 **MUSCOVY DUCK** *Cairina moschata* · p. 44
Locally FC, often domesticated. Large black duck with conspicuous white wing patch. *Ad. ♂:* warty protuberances on face. *Ad. ♀:* lacks warty protuberances. *Imm.:* white in wing much reduced.

WHISTLING-DUCKS: Large, long-legged waterfowl with rounded bill.

2 **FULVOUS WHISTLING-DUCK**
Dendrocygna bicolor · p. 42
Crooked Tree in winter. Rich tawny below, with white stripes on sides, white uppertail coverts, and gray bill and legs. In flight, black underwings contrast with pale tawny body.

3 **BLACK-BELLIED WHISTLING-DUCK**
Dendrocygna autumnalis · p. 41
Locally C. *Ad.:* gray face, dark tawny brown body, black belly, red bill and pinkish legs, large white wing patch. *Juv.:* paler with whitish belly, dark gray bill and legs.

4 **MASKED DUCK** *Nomonyx dominicus* · p. 49
Vagrant. Small; long, pointed tail; thick-based blue bill; white wing patch conspicuous in flight. *♂ alt.:* chestnut body, black face, blue bill. *♂ basic, ♀, and juv.:* 2 dark stripes across face; duller bill and body.

DABBLING DUCKS: ♂s in alt. plumage showy, ♀s brown; most have diagnostic wing patch.

5 **AMERICAN WIGEON** *Anas americana* · p. 44
UC and local in winter. Conspicuous white wing patch, reduced in ♀ and imm. *♂ alt.:* white crown, green head, salt-and-pepper neck and face, blue bill. *♀:* pale forehead, face, and neck; blue bill; white bar in upperwing coverts evident in flight.

6 **GREEN-WINGED TEAL** *Anas crecca* · p. 46
R in winter. Small, with green inner secondaries (speculum). *♂ alt.:* green-and-chestnut head; vertical white stripe on side; black-bordered buff undertail coverts. *♀:* small; from other ♀ *Anas* by green speculum, pale area on undertail coverts. In flight, contrasting whitish belly.

7 **BLUE-WINGED TEAL** *Anas discors* · p. 44
C in winter. Blue upperwing coverts; larger than **6**, with longer bill, flatter head, longer neck. *♂ alt.:* white crescent in blue-gray face; white patch at rear of flanks. *♀:* facial area at base of bill (variable); blue upperwing coverts visible in flying bird.

8 **CINNAMON TEAL** *Anas cyanoptera* · p. 45
R in winter. Except for ♂ alt., very similar to **7**; bill slightly longer, broader, spatulate. *♂ alt.:* bright chestnut body, red eyes, yellow legs. *♀:* very similar to ♀ **7** but usually with plainer face and longer, more spatulate bill. *♂ basic* (not shown): richer brown than ♀, with red eyes.

9 **NORTHERN SHOVELER** *Anas clypeata*
p. 45
UC in winter. Very large spatulate bill forms nearly straight line with forehead; blue upperwing coverts. *♂ alt.:* green head, white breast, chestnut sides. *♀:* from **7** and **8** by larger size, unique bill-head profile.

10 **NORTHERN PINTAIL** *Anas acuta* · p. 45
Occas. in winter. Long, pointed central tail feathers; long neck; no conspicuous wing pattern. *♂ alt.:* brown head with white stripe up neck; gray body. *♀:* lead gray bill; plain head; central tail feathers less elongated than in ♂.

9

♀

7

♀

6

♀

5

♀

Adult

3

Juvenile

Immature

2

Adult

♂

1

♂ Alternate   4   ♂ Basic

♀

♂

♂ Alternate   6   ♀

5

♀

♂ Alternate   7   ♀

♀   8

♂ Alternate

♀ ♂ Alternate

9

♂ Alternate   ♂ Alternate

PLATE 5

VULTURES, ZONE-TAILED HAWK, BLACK-HAWKS,
EAGLES, AND OSPREY

NEW WORLD VULTURES: Unfeathered head; distinctive wing pattern and flight characteristics; broad wings with primary feathers held apart, creating rounded wingtip.

1 TURKEY VULTURE *Cathartes aura* · p. 39
C throughout. Flies with wings held above horizontal plane, rocks side to side; relatively long, unbarred tail; gray remiges contrast with rest of plumage. *Ad.:* unfeathered red head, white bill. *Juv.:* blackish head and bill.

2 LESSER YELLOW-HEADED VULTURE
Cathartes burrovianus · p. 40
FC, lowlands. Like **1**, but white primary quills visible on upper surface in flight. Flies lower, typically foraging only a few meters aboveground. *Ad.:* unfeathered yellow-and-orange head, white bill. *Juv.:* brown feather edges, dusky head with small swath of yellow.

3 BLACK VULTURE *Coragyps atratus* · p. 39
C throughout. Shorter, broader wings and shorter tail than **1** and **2**, with conspicuous pale silvery gray patch at base of primaries. Wings often held above horizontal plane in soaring flight, but does not rock side to side like **1** and **2**. *Ad.:* unfeathered dark gray head, dark bill with whitish tip, whitish legs. *Juv.* (not shown): all-dark bill, darker legs.

4 KING VULTURE *Sarcoramphus papa* · p. 40
UC to FC throughout. Very large. *Ad.:* multicolored head. In flight: white with black flight feathers, dark head; much shorter neck and bill than Wood Stork. *Juv.:* much larger than **3**; wings held flat; pale mottling on underparts.

5 ZONE-TAILED HAWK *Buteo albonotatus*
Plates 6, 10; p. 62
Occas. in winter. Turkey Vulture mimic; soars and rocks side to side on wings held above horizontal. Banded tail, finely barred remiges, feathered head, yellow cere (ad. shown).

BLACK-HAWKS: Nearly black plumage; broad white band in tail; broad, rounded wings.

6 COMMON BLACK-HAWK
Buteogallus anthracinus · Plate 10; p. 57
FC, primarily coastal. Slightly smaller than **7**, with noticeably shorter tail. *Ad.:* all-black thighs; yellow cere and lores; folded wings reach tip of tail. *Juv.:* blackish malar stripe; dusky flanks (mostly covered by wing); longer tail than ad. (folded wings do not reach tip).

7 GREAT BLACK-HAWK *Buteogallus urubitinga*
Plate 10; p. 58
Widespread; more C than **6** inland. Tail extends well beyond folded wings. *Ad.:* thigh feathers finely barred with white; gray lores. *Juv.:* lacks malar mark and dusky flanks; tail more finely barred; shorter primary extension than in juv. **6**. See text for IDing older imms.

8 SOLITARY EAGLE *Harpyhaliaetus solitarius*
Plate 10; p. 58
R in mountains. Much larger than preceding two species, with larger bill, slight crest; wing and tail proportions like **6**. *Ad.:* plumage dark gray (lighter than black-hawks). *Juv.:* dark breast and thighs contrast with pale belly and head; barring in tail indistinct. See text for older imms.

9 OSPREY *Pandion haliaetus* · p. 49
FC in coastal areas, less C inland. Large hawk, dark above, white below; flies with downcurved wings and strong bend at wrist; conspicuous black patch at bend of wing on undersurface. Resident *ridgwayi:* unbarred breast; pale postocular stripe. Migrant *carolinensis:* barring in breast, bold black postocular stripe.

EAGLES: Very large; live inside forest canopy; do not soar high above forest.

10 CRESTED EAGLE *Morphnus guianensis*
p. 63
R, undisturbed forest. *Imm.:* gray and white, with 5–7 bands in tail; forewing contrasts lighter than hindwing; single crest. *Ad. light morph:* gray head and breast, single crest, smaller bill than **11**. See text for juv.

11 HARPY EAGLE *Harpia harpyja* · p. 63
R, undisturbed forest. World's largest bird of prey; massive bill and talons; double crest. *Imm.:* partial breast band; fewer tail bands than imm. **10**; little contrast in wings. *Ad.:* black breast band; split crest; neck ruff. See text for juv.

Juvenile

Adult

1

Adult

2

Adult

Adult

5

Adult

3

Adult

4

Adult

Juvenile

2

Juvenile

Adult

3

1

Adult

Juvenile

Adult

6

Adult

4

Juvenile

7

Juvenile

8

Adult

9

Adult

9

Resident
ssp.

Migrant
ssp.

Immature

11

10

Adult

Adult

Immature

PLATE **6** BUZZARDS (PERCHED)

BUZZARDS: Small to medium-sized hawks, mostly in the genus *Buteo,* with broad, usually rounded wings and short to medium-length tail; frequently soar.

1 ROADSIDE HAWK *Buteo magnirostris*
Plate 11; p. 59
C throughout. Small. Relatively long tail; soars less frequently than other buzzards. *Ad.:* gray brown above, diffusely streaked breast, barred belly. *Juv.:* from **2** and **3** by streaked breast and barred belly; dark auriculars; indistinct supercilium.

2 BROAD-WINGED HAWK *Buteo platypterus*
Plate 11; p. 60
R in winter. Small. Relatively short tail, with longer primary projection than **3** or **1**; frequently soars. *Ad.:* barred breast (sometimes coalescing into a band) with contrasting white throat; black-and-white-banded tail. *Juv.:* streaked breast and belly; dark auriculars.

3 GRAY HAWK *Asturina nitida* · Plate 11; p. 59
FC throughout. Small. Medium-length tail, with shorter primary projection than **2**; occasionally soars. *Ad.:* gray above, with finely barred gray breast and belly; black-and-white-banded tail. *Juv.:* streaked breast and belly; white auriculars.

4 RED-TAILED HAWK *Buteo jamaicensis*
Plate 11; p. 62
Mtn. Pine Ridge. Medium size, with white mottling in scapulars. Folded wings do not reach tail tip; white flecks in upperparts. *Ad.:* red tail; streaks concentrated on belly and flanks. *Juv.:* tail barred dark and light brown.

5 ZONE-TAILED HAWK *Buteo albonotatus*
Plates 5, 10; p. 62
Occas. in winter. *Ad.:* all dark, with black and pale gray tail bands; wings extend to tail tip.

6 SHORT-TAILED HAWK *Buteo brachyurus*
Plates 10, 11; p. 60
FC throughout. Small. Wings reach tail tip. *Ad. dark morph:* like **5** but smaller; shorter tail with more bands. *Ad. light morph:* all-white underparts.

7 SWAINSON'S HAWK *Buteo swainsoni*
Plate 11; p. 61
R transient. Medium-sized, long-winged buzzard; folded wings reach tail tip. *Juv. light morph:* brown-and-white-patterned head like **3**. *Ad. light morph:* chestnut band across upper breast; unstreaked flanks; banded tail.

8 WHITE-TAILED HAWK *Buteo albicaudatus*
Plates 10, 11; p. 61
UC, open areas. Medium-sized, long-winged buzzard; wingtips exceed tail. *Ad.:* gray above, with rufous scapular patch; mostly white below; white tail with black subterminal band. *2nd year:* partial band across breast, all-dark head. *Juv.* (not shown): white markings on head.

9 WHITE HAWK *Leucopternis albicollis*
Plate 11; p. 57
UC in south, forests. Mostly white buzzard with black band in tail and black primary tips. *Juv.:* black bars in remiges and wing coverts.

10 BLACK-COLLARED HAWK *Busarellus nigricollis*
Plate 10; p. 54
UC in north, rivers and lagoons. Medium size; short tail with broad black band. *Ad.:* orange-rufous underparts, with black breast band and white head. *Juv.:* similar, but reduced rufous; barred underparts.

Adult

Juvenile

1

Adult

Juvenile

2

Adult

3

Juvenile

Juvenile

4

Adult

5

Dark
Morph

6

Light
Morph

Juvenile
Light
Morph

7

Adult
Light
Morph

Adult

8

Second
Year

Juvenile

9

Adult

Adult

10

Juvenile

PLATE 7

FOREST KITES, FOREST-FALCONS, AND
HAWK-EAGLES (PERCHED)

FOREST KITES: Relatively short, broad, rounded wings for maneuvering through forest foliage.

1 HOOK-BILLED KITE *Chondrohierax uncinatus*
Plates 10, 11; p. 50
UC and local, forests. Very variable: several plumage morphs, plus age and sex differences. *Ad. dark morph:* all dark; from Zone-tailed Hawk (Plate 6) by habitat, smaller size, larger bill and head, pale eyes, one visible tail band. *Ad. ♂ light morph:* from Gray Hawk (Plate 6) by larger bill and head, pale eyes, darker gray underparts. *Ad. ♀ light morph:* from Roadside Hawk (Plate 6) by larger head and bill, pale eyes, rufous nape, barred throat and breast. *Juv. variants:* from **4** and **5** by different proportions.

2 GRAY-HEADED KITE *Leptodon cayanensis*
Plates 10, 11; p. 50
UC and local, forests. Long-tailed kite with short wings, boldly banded tail (3 visible bands in tail). *Juv. dark morph:* thinly to heavily streaked breast. *Juv. light morph:* white head and underparts with black cap; from **8** by smaller size, dark eyes, pale lores, paler tail bands. *Ad.:* pale gray head contrasts with dark brown back; white underparts.

3 DOUBLE-TOOTHED KITE *Harpagus bidentatus*
Plate 11; p. 53
UC, forests. Small, accipiter-like. Black stripe in center of white throat; thin white bands in tail. *Ad.:* gray head; brown back; chestnut bars underneath often coalesce into broad band across breast. *Juv.:* variably streaked underparts.

FOREST-FALCONS: Long-legged falcons with short, rounded wings and unfeathered facial skin.

4 BARRED FOREST-FALCON *Micrastur ruficollis*
p. 65
UC, undisturbed forest. Small, slim. Does not soar above canopy. Thin white bands in tail; long legs; throat lacks central stripe. *Ad.:* upperparts all gray; fine dark gray bars on underparts.

Juv. variants: brown; barred to unbarred underparts; unbarred juv. (not shown) from juv. Bicolored Hawk by thin bands in tail and more compact, rounded head.

5 COLLARED FOREST-FALCON
Micrastur semitorquatus · p. 65
FC throughout. Large, slim. Long, rounded tail with thin bands, small head. Frequently perches hunched over (not shown). Does not soar above canopy. Often heard, seldom seen. Highly variable plumage. *Ad. dark morph:* all black except for finely barred thighs sometimes extending to belly and breast; thin tail bands. *Ad. light morph:* white to creamy buff below, with pale collar and black "hook" posterior of auriculars. From similar-plumaged Bicolored Hawk (Plate 8) by thinner bands in longer tail, better-defined collar and hook, and dark eyes. *Juv. light morph:* barred beneath; collar and auricular hook less distinct.

HAWK-EAGLES: Fully feathered tarsi, large size.

6 BLACK HAWK-EAGLE *Spizaetus tyrannus*
Plates 10, 11; p. 64
UC throughout. Bushy crest, white at base; boldly barred thighs and tarsi. *Juv.:* dark brown upperparts; streaked black-and-white head, neck, and breast, with dark auricular patch. *Ad.:* mostly black.

7 ORNATE HAWK-EAGLE *Spizaetus ornatus*
Plates 10, 11; p. 64
R, primary forests. Long crest plumes; boldly barred thighs and tarsi. *Juv.:* white head and breast. *Ad.:* striking black crown and erect crest plume; rufous auriculars, nape, neck, and breast band; black malar stripe; white throat; boldly barred underparts.

8 BLACK-AND-WHITE HAWK-EAGLE
Spizastur melanoleucus · Plate 11; p. 63
VU, forests. White head and underparts, black cap. Black lores, yellow eyes, shorter tail, and feathered tarsi distinguish it from juv. **2**.

1
Adult Dark Morph
Light Morph ♂
Light Morph ♀
Juveniles
Intermediate Morph
Light Morph

2
Juveniles
Adult

3
Adult
Juvenile

4
Adult
Juveniles

5
Dark Morph
Adults
Light Morph
Juvenile Light Morph

6
Juvenile
Adult

7
Juvenile
Adult

8
Adult

PLATE **8**

ACCIPITERS AND FALCONS (PERCHED AND IN FLIGHT)

ACCIPITERS: Small, long-tailed, round-winged hawks; ♀s noticeably larger than ♂s.

1 **COOPER'S HAWK** *Accipiter cooperii* · p. 55
R in winter. Similar to **2** but larger and has more head projection in flight. *Ad.:* gray above; barred rufous below; black crown; white upper nape (strong crown-nape contrast); slightly peaked hindcrown. *Juv.:* brown above; streaked below; less distinct supercilium; thinner, sparser streaking underneath than **2**.

2 **SHARP-SHINNED HAWK** *Accipiter striatus* p. 55
VU in winter. Similar to **1** but smaller, has square-tipped tail, less head projection in flight, wings held slightly forward in flight. *Ad.:* rounded head, little contrast between gray crown and nape. *Juv.:* like **1** but with distinct supercilium; heavier streaking underneath.

3 **BICOLORED HAWK** *Accipiter bicolor* · p. 56
UC, forests. ♀ much larger than ♂. *Juv.:* brown above; varies from deep cinnamon to nearly white below, never barred; light morph, especially the larger ♀, can be similar to Collared Forest-Falcon (Plate 7), but profile different, shorter tail, longer wings. *Ad.:* gray above; pale gray underparts; rufous thighs (often obscured by flank feathers).

FALCO FALCONS: Strong fliers with pointed wings and long, compact tail; usually seen in open country or flying above forest canopy; occasionally soar.

4 **AMERICAN KESTREL** *Falco sparverius* p. 67
UC in winter. Smaller, less compact than others; tail usually held straight or slightly spread in flight. Flight less direct, slower; occas. pumps tail when perched; hovers when foraging. ♂: unmistakable. ♀: streaked breast; barred brown back, wings, and tail.

5 **MERLIN** *Falco columbarius* · p. 67
UC in winter. Small and compact; strong, fast, direct flier. In flight, has broad-based, strongly tapered wings; tail compressed distally, with fewer pale bands than larger **9**. Seldom soars. ♂: blue gray above, brown streaks and chevrons below; thin supercilium; faint to prominent "teardrop." ♀ *and juv.:* brown above, more heavily streaked below.

6 **BAT FALCON** *Falco rufigularis* · p. 68
FC throughout. Small and compact; fast, direct flier with narrow-based wings. Throat, upper breast, and sides of neck clean white, sometimes with pale cinnamon wash (some juvs.); narrower barring on lower breast and upper belly than **7**, smaller feet and bill.

7 **ORANGE-BREASTED FALCON** *Falco deiroleucus* · p. 68
R and local. Medium-sized and compact; powerful flier; often soars. Breast and sides of neck usually orangish buff; broader barring on breast and belly than **8**; large feet and bill. *Juv.* (not shown): barred thighs.

8 **APLOMADO FALCON** *Falco femoralis* · p. 68
FC, savannas. Slimmer and longer-tailed than **9**. *Ad.:* from **9** by paler upperparts, narrower "teardrop," light supercilium, dense black-and-white barring on sides and flanks, and pale cinnamon thighs, belly, and undertail coverts. *Juv.* (not shown): dark brown above, with heavily streaked breast and unbarred black sides.

9 **PEREGRINE FALCON** *Falco peregrinus* p. 69
UC in winter. Large and compact; strong, fast, direct flier. Occasionally soars. ♀ slightly larger than ♂, otherwise similar. *Ad.:* dark blue gray, with black crown, nape, and broad "teardrop"; partial white collar; barred underparts. *Juv.:* brown above, with streaked, not barred, underparts; "teardrop" narrower; partial supercilium. Subspecies *F.p. anatum* is illustrated.

1 Adult

2 Adult

5 ♀

8 Adult

9 Juvenile

4 ♀

Juvenile ♂

1 Adult ♀

6

7

Juvenile ♂

2 Adult ♀

Juvenile Light Morph ♀

Juvenile Dark Morph ♂

3 Adult ♂

4 ♂

9 Adult

8 Adult

7 Adult

6 Adult

5 ♂

PLATE **9**

OPEN-COUNTRY KITES, LAUGHING FALCON,
CRANE HAWK, AND HARRIER

OPEN-COUNTRY KITES: Typically seen in open areas or soaring over canopy of open forest.

1 PLUMBEOUS KITE *Ictinia plumbea* · p. 54
FC dry-season resident. Long, rather pointed wings; rufous patch in primaries visible in flight; outer primary much shorter than others; folded wings extend well past tail tip; medium-length tail. *Ad.:* all gray, with red eyes; tail banded below, unbarred above; primaries do not contrast darker than rest of upperparts. *Juv.:* brown above; heavily mottled underwing coverts; gray-streaked underparts; reduced rufous in primaries.

2 MISSISSIPPI KITE *Ictinia mississippiensis*
p. 54
R transient. Lacks rufous in wing; folded wings extend only slightly past tail; black primaries contrast darker than rest of upperparts; longer tail than **1**. *Ad.:* pale head; unbarred tail; conspicuous pale gray secondaries on upper surface. *Juv.:* reddish streaks underneath. *Subad.* (not shown): mostly gray like ad. but lacks pale secondary patch and has partially banded tail.

3 WHITE-TAILED KITE *Elanus leucurus* · p. 52
Local, fields and marshes. Hovers when foraging. *Ad.:* gray above with large black "shoulder" patch; white head, tail, and underparts; black around eyes; black spot in underprimary coverts conspicuous in flight. *Juv.* (not shown): like ad. but light rufous wash across breast; streaks in crown and back.

4 SWALLOW-TAILED KITE *Elanoides forficatus*
p. 52
FC dry-season resident. Unmistakable white hawk with black flight feathers and long, forked tail; slow, graceful flight.

5 SNAIL KITE *Rostrhamus sociabilis* · p. 53
Locally C, marshes. Long, rounded wings; white tail coverts and base of tail form broad white band; thin, deeply hooked bill. Gracefully glides and circles low over marshes. ♀: heavily streaked head and underparts; pale patch at base of primaries; orange cere and legs. ♂: dark gray back, with red cere and feet. *Juv.* (not shown): similar to ad. ♀ but less densely streaked; cere gray; yellow legs.

6 LAUGHING FALCON *Herpetotheres cachinnans*
p. 67
FC throughout. Pale buff head and underparts, with bold black mask; banded tail; rounded wings with conspicuous pale cinnamon patch at base of primaries noticeable in flight. Flies with rapid, shallow wingbeats; does not soar.

7 CRANE HAWK *Geranospiza caerulescens*
p. 56
UC and local. Slender, long-tailed, small-headed black hawk with long, thin "double-jointed" orangish red legs and 2 white tail bands. In flight, white bar on underwing in outer primaries; short, rounded wings. Often forages in bromeliads of large trees near water. Rarely soars.

8 NORTHERN HARRIER *Circus cyaneus* · p. 54
UC in winter. Flies low over marshes and grasslands with long wings held above horizontal; long, banded tail with conspicuous white uppertail coverts; owl-like facial disks. Birds in Belize most likely to be juvs. *Ad.* ♂: all gray except for dark wingtips and tail tip and white uppertail coverts. *Juv.:* brown and streaked above, with bright cinnamon underparts (fading to whitish through winter). *Ad.* ♀: like juv. but lacks cinnamon; streaks extend through belly.

PLATE **10** HAWKS IN OVERHEAD FLIGHT (DARK)

HAWK-EAGLES: Large, with long wings pinched in at base.

1 ORNATE HAWK-EAGLE *Spizaetus ornatus*
Plates 7, 11; p. 64
Rufous head; white throat; boldly barred underparts; broad wings; underwing coverts mostly white; remiges less conspicuously barred than in **2**.

2 BLACK HAWK-EAGLE *Spizaetus tyrannus*
Plates 7, 11; p. 64
Long, broad wings pinched in at base; long tail; wings and tail boldly banded; dark underwing coverts.

BLACK-HAWKS: Broad, rounded wings and short tail, often spread wide; adults mostly black with broad white tail band; juveniles pale beneath with multiple thin tail bands.

3 SOLITARY EAGLE *Harpyhaliaetus solitarius*
Plate 5; p. 58
Very large; head projects more than in similar but much smaller **4** and **5**. *Ad.:* dark gray body, including underwing coverts, accentuates black tips to remiges. *Juv.:* dark sides and thighs; creamy white unbarred panel in outer wing.

4 GREAT BLACK-HAWK *Buteogallus urubitinga*
Plate 5; p. 58
Medium size, with longer, narrower wings, longer tail. *Ad.:* white-tipped uppertail coverts (not shown) diagnostic when bird viewed from above or behind; 2nd white tail band usually visible. *Juv.:* malar streak inconspicuous or absent; less heavily streaked underparts than **5**.

5 COMMON BLACK-HAWK
Buteogallus anthracinus · Plate 5; p. 57
Shorter tail and shorter, broader wings than **4**. *Ad.:* one broad white tail band; lacks white-tipped uppertail coverts. *Juv.:* dark malar stripe, sides, and flanks; darker tail tip.

6 ZONE-TAILED HAWK *Buteo albonotatus*
Plates 5, 6; p. 62
Juv.: Like juv. dark-morph **7** but larger; lacks pale panel in primaries; has longer tail that is usually not spread and has longer, less pointed wings; rocking flight on wings held above horizontal.

7 SHORT-TAILED HAWK *Buteo brachyurus*
Plates 6, 11; p. 60
Broad, relatively pointed wings with pale panel in primaries; short, broad tail. Soars with wings held flat and primary tips curled upward. *Ad. dark morph:* black wing coverts contrast with paler flight feathers. *Juv. dark morph:* finely spotted belly and underwing coverts.

8 WHITE-TAILED HAWK *Buteo albicaudatus*
Plates 6, 11; p. 61 ,
Juv.: small white auricular patch; white central throat/breast, and undertail coverts; mostly dark underwing coverts; short tail, usually spread.

9 GRAY-HEADED KITE *Leptodon cayanensis*
Plates 7, 11; p. 50
Juv. dark morph: dark head and throat, lightly to boldly streaked breast; white belly and underwing coverts; barred flight feathers; relatively long tail.

10 HOOK-BILLED KITE *Chondrohierax uncinatus*
Plates 7, 11; p. 50
Rounded wings are pinched in at base; relatively long tail frequently fanned when soaring; large bill. *Ad. intermediate morph:* barred underparts, white undertail coverts, 2 or 3 white tail bands, strongly barred primaries. *Ad. dark morph:* all black, with one broad white tail band.

11 BLACK-COLLARED HAWK *Busarellus nigricollis*
Plate 6; p. 54
Ad.: distinctive orange-rufous color, black breast band, white head, broad wings. *Juv.* (not shown): brown replaces orange rufous; lightly streaked.

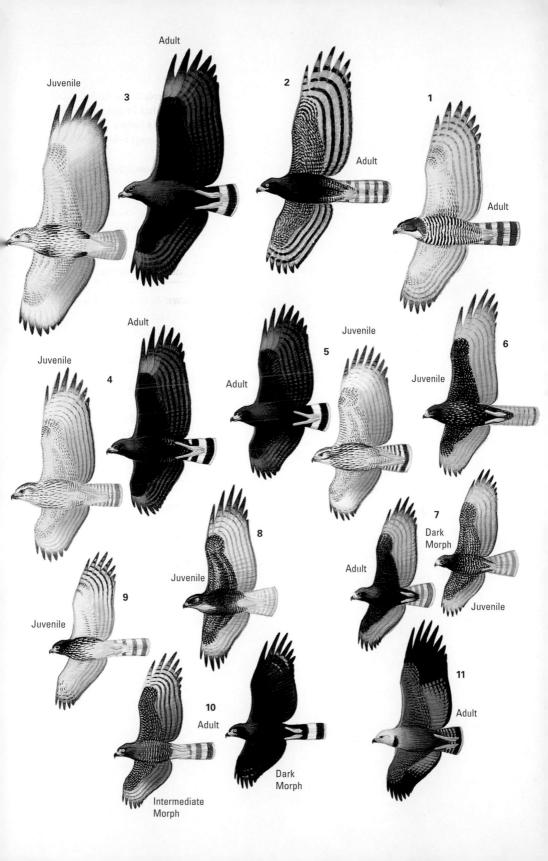

Juvenile

Adult

3

2

1

Adult

Adult

Adult

4

Juvenile

Adult

5

Juvenile

6

Adult

Juvenile

7

Dark
Morph

Adult

9

8

Juvenile

Juvenile

Juvenile

10

Adult

11

Adult

Dark
Morph

Intermediate
Morph

PLATE **11** HAWKS IN OVERHEAD FLIGHT (LIGHT)

SMALL BUZZARDS: Short, broad wings; short to medium-length banded tail.

1 ROADSIDE HAWK *Buteo magnirostris*
Plate 6; p. 59
Juv.: streaked breast and barred belly; dark auriculars; relatively long, compressed tail.

2 GRAY HAWK *Asturina nitida* · Plate 6; p. 59
Juv.: streaked breast and belly; barring only on thighs; pale auriculars; tail often slightly fanned; white-tipped uppertail coverts (not shown).

3 SHORT-TAILED HAWK *Buteo brachyurus*
Plates 6, 10; p. 60
Ad. light morph: dark head contrasts with white underparts; white underwing coverts contrast with gray remiges; pale panel in outer primaries.

4 BROAD-WINGED HAWK *Buteo platypterus*
Plate 6; p. 60
Juv.: like **2** but with dark auriculars; wings have dark trailing edge; bolder subterminal tail band. *Ad.:* underparts barred rufous; boldly black-and-white-banded tail.

FOREST KITES: Rounded wings; live within forest canopy but also soar above canopy.

5 GRAY-HEADED KITE *Leptodon cayanensis*
Plates 7, 10; p. 50
Juv. light morph: similar to **12** but longer tail with bolder bands, more extensively barred remiges. *Ad.:* blackish underwing coverts.

6 DOUBLE-TOOTHED KITE *Harpagus bidentatus*
Plate 7; p. 53
Small, accipiter-like; white throat with dark central stripe. Glides on downwardly curved wings. *Ad.:* white underwing with barred remiges, gray-and-white-banded tail. *Juv.:* dark head, streaked breast, pale underwings.

7 HOOK-BILLED KITE *Chondrohierax uncinatus*
Plates 7, 10; p. 50
Rounded wings pinched in at base, fairly long tail, large bill. *Juv. light morph:* dark brown crown, mostly white beneath with barred flight feathers. *Ad. light morph:* gray above, finely to heavily barred underparts, white undertail coverts, and barred flight feathers.

LARGE BUZZARDS: Medium-sized; most soar with wings held slightly to distinctly above horizontal.

8 SWAINSON'S HAWK *Buteo swainsoni*
Plate 6; p. 61
Juv. light morph: relatively pointed wings (more so than shown); pale underwing coverts with no carpal bar; darker remiges; streaked upper breast and sides; fairly long tail; soars with wings held well above horizontal.

9 RED-TAILED HAWK *Buteo jamaicensis*
Plate 6; p. 62
Only hawk with dark carpal bar; more rounded wingtips than **8** or **11**, and flies with wings held closer to horizontal. *Ad.:* red tail, barred flanks and belly, unbarred breast. *Juv.:* similar to ad. but with banded brownish tail and more extensively barred underparts; sometimes with white mottling in upperparts.

10 WHITE HAWK *Leucopternis albicollis*
Plate 6; p. 57
All white, with short, broad, black-tipped tail; limited black barring in remiges (more so in juv.).

11 WHITE-TAILED HAWK *Buteo albicaudatus*
Plates 6, 10; p. 61
Ad.: black-tipped white tail; white underparts and underwing coverts; gray remiges with pale panel in primaries (wings longer and more pointed than shown). *Subad.* (not shown): similar to juv. **9** but with longer, more pointed wings and no carpal bar.

HAWK-EAGLES: Large birds of prey with long wings pinched in at base.

12 BLACK-AND-WHITE HAWK-EAGLE
Spizastur melanoleucus · Plate 7; p. 63
Like juv. **5** and **10** but larger. From **10** by longer, narrower, multibanded tail; longer wings; and black cap. From **5** by shorter tail with thinner bands and virtually unbarred remiges.

13 ORNATE HAWK-EAGLE *Spizaetus ornatus*
Plates 7, 10; p. 64
Juv.: similar to **12** but with barred flanks and thighs, dark mottling in underwing coverts. From juv. **14** by less strongly barred remiges, white breast.

14 BLACK HAWK-EAGLE *Spizaetus tyrannus*
Plates 7, 10; p. 64
Juv.: like **13** but heavily barred breast and more heavily barred remiges; dark head with contrasting white throat and supercilium.

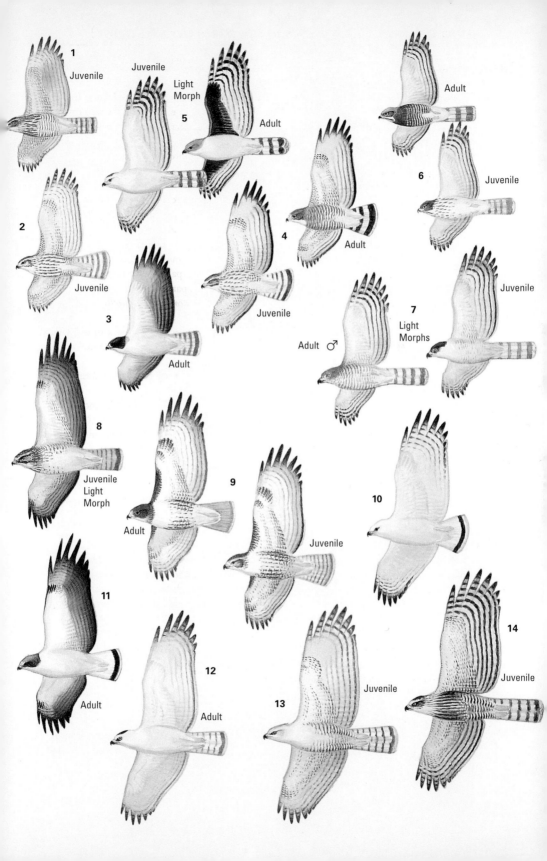

1 Juvenile

Juvenile

5 Light Morph

Adult

6 Adult

Juvenile

2 Juvenile

4 Adult

Juvenile

3 Adult

7 Light Morphs

Adult ♂

Juvenile

8 Juvenile Light Morph

9 Adult

Juvenile

10

11 Adult

12 Adult

13 Juvenile

14 Juvenile

PLATE **12** TINAMOUS AND GALLINACEOUS BIRDS

NEW WORLD QUAILS: Small, plump, nearly tailless birds with short, rounded bill.

1 SINGING QUAIL *Dactylortyx thoracicus* p. 72

R and local, woodland. ♀: whitish supercilium and throat; cinnamon breast lightly streaked white. ♂: mostly cinnamon head; grayish breast streaked white.

2 BLACK-THROATED BOBWHITE

Colinus nigrogularis · p. 71

FC, savannas and fields. ♂: black-and-white-striped head; black throat; prominent scaly-looking black-and-white underparts. ♀: buffy supercilium and throat; underparts brown and white, less "scaly" than ♂.

3 SPOTTED WOOD-QUAIL

Odontophorus guttatus · p. 72

Locally FC, forests; often heard, rarely seen. Brown to cinnamon rufous, with white spots on breast; black-and-white-spotted throat. ♂: crest, when raised, reveals bright orange feathers.

TINAMOUS: Primitive plump chickenlike birds of the forest with small head, thin neck and bill, haunting vocalizations.

4 LITTLE TINAMOU *Crypturellus soui* · p. 21

FC, second growth. Small, unmarked. Dull cinnamon belly, yellowish olive legs.

5 THICKET TINAMOU *Crypturellus cinnamomeus* p. 21

FC in north and west, woodland. Boldly barred wings, back, and rump; cinnamon breast; red legs. ♀: fine barring on breast and neck.

6 SLATY-BREASTED TINAMOU

Crypturellus boucardi · p. 22

FC, forests. Gray breast; rich buff belly with fine bars on flanks; red legs. ♂: grayer foreparts. ♀: barred wings and rump, but not as bold as in **5**.

7 GREAT TINAMOU *Tinamus major* · p. 21

FC, woodland. Largest tinamou; relatively plain, but with inconspicuous barring on upperparts and flanks; gray legs.

GUANS AND CURASSOWS: Medium-sized to large, long-tailed birds with bushy crests.

8 PLAIN CHACHALACA *Ortalis vetula* · p. 69

C throughout. Medium-sized brown bird with long, pale-tipped tail; fairly long, thin neck; small head; red gular stripe visible when displaying.

9 CRESTED GUAN *Penelope purpurascens* p. 70

Local and UC, forests. Widely extirpated. Similar in body proportions to **8** but much larger and darker; white spots on neck and breast; short, bushy crest; unfeathered blue face; red throat wattle; tail not pale tipped; spends most of its time in trees in forest interior.

10 GREAT CURASSOW *Crax rubra* · p. 70

Local and UC, forests. Very large, secretive; spends most of its time foraging on forest floor. Extirpated from most populated areas. Unmistakable curly crest. ♀: salt-and-pepper pattern on head; neck, back, and breast uniformly dark brown (dark morph) or boldly barred (barred morph, not shown). ♂: jet black, with white undertail coverts; banded bill with large butter-yellow knob at base.

11 OCELLATED TURKEY *Meleagris ocellata* p. 71

Local in west, forest clearings. Unmistakable large ground bird with unfeathered blue head covered with orange warts. Showy tail, spur on legs. Rarely seen away from areas where it is protected. Unlike **9** and **10**, becomes tame within a few generations when not hunted.

PLATE **13** RAILS AND CRAKES

SMALL RAILS: Tiny birds, no larger than a Least Sandpiper; seldom seen, even where common, because of their habit of staying hidden in dense grasses and matted vegetation. Best detected by their vocalizations.

1 GRAY-BREASTED CRAKE *Laterallus exilis* p. 73
Local in south; marshes, wet meadows. Like **2** but differs in having paler gray head and breast, unspotted brown back, and lime green at base of bill.

2 BLACK RAIL *Laterallus jamaicensis* · p. 73
Few records, possibly R resident; savannas. Like **1** but with nearly black head and breast, fine white barring on back, and black bill.

3 YELLOW-BREASTED CRAKE
Porzana flaviventer · p. 75
Vagrant or R resident, marshes. Breast and side of neck rich yellow buff; conspicuous white supercilium sometimes split by diagonal black line; upperparts a complex pattern of black and dark brown, streaked with yellow buff and white; lower sides, flanks, and undertail coverts barred black and white.

4 RUDDY CRAKE *Laterallus ruber* · p. 73
FC, frequently heard but rarely seen; grassy ditches, marshes, weedy fields. Like a small version of **5** but with short black bill, gray head, and olive-gray legs.

MEDIUM-SIZED RAILS: These rails, though secretive, are not as difficult to see as the preceding. Like all the rails, best IDed by their distinctive vocalizations.

5 UNIFORM CRAKE *Amaurolimnas concolor* p. 74
R and local, swampland and seasonally wet forests. Like large version of **4** (size of a Sora) but with head same color as body, longer greenish yellow bill, and pinkish red legs. Smaller than **10** and lacks its gray saddle and black posterior.

6 SORA *Porzana carolina* · p. 75
Local in winter, marshes. *Juv.:* similar to **3** but much larger, with thicker yellow bill; lacks white supercilium. *Ad.:* black face; gray neck and breast.

7 SPOTTED RAIL *Pardirallus maculatus* · p. 75
VU to R, marshes. Unmistakable—black with white-spotted head, breast, and upperparts, becoming barred on belly and flanks; moderately long, lime green bill with red spot at base. *Juv.* (not shown): similar but dark brown, with less spotting and duller bill.

LARGE RAILS: Decidedly larger and more easily seen than the preceding.

8 CLAPPER RAIL *Rallus longirostris* · p. 74
FC, mangrove forests. Dull gray brown; belly and flanks barred with white; long bill.

9 GRAY-NECKED WOOD-RAIL *Aramides cajanea* p. 74
FC, wide variety of habitats. The most conspicuous and widespread rail. Very distinctive, with gray head, neck, and upper breast; rufous hindcrown, cinnamon-rufous lower breast and belly, black hindquarters, yellow bill, and pinkish red legs.

10 RUFOUS-NECKED WOOD-RAIL
Aramides axillaris · p. 74
UC and local, mangrove forests. Somewhat like **5** but larger, with longer bill, black hindquarters, and gray saddle on upper back.

1

2

3

6

Adult

4

Juvenile

5

8

7

9

10

PLATE **14** GREBES, SUNGREBE, JACANA, AND GALLINULES

GREBES: Small waterbirds, superficially ducklike but without ducklike bill; toes are lobed, not webbed.

1 PIED-BILLED GREBE *Podilymbus podiceps* p. 22
Locally FC in winter, breeds locally. Small bird with chickenlike bill; fine, fluffy feathers at rear. *Basic:* cream-colored bill with no bar. *Alt.:* white bill with conspicuous black bar; black throat.

2 LEAST GREBE *Tachybaptus dominicus* · p. 22
Local, lagoons and rivers. Tiny; thin, pointed bill; yellow eyes; often swims with feathers at rear fluffed up. In flight, shows broad white wing stripe. *Basic:* whitish throat. *Alt.:* black throat. *Chick:* streaked head and neck.

---

3 SUNGREBE *Heliornis fulica* · p. 77
Local, rivers and swamps. Larger than grebe, with much longer tail, black-and-white-striped neck, white supercilium, black bands on lobed pale yellow feet (not shown). Thinner, longer bill than **1**. ♂: white auriculars. ♀: tawny auriculars; bill becomes scarlet prior to breeding.

4 NORTHERN JACANA *Jacana spinosa* · p. 81
C, marshes. Highly distinctive bird with long legs and extremely long toes and claws; bright yellow primaries and secondaries revealed in spread wings (note spur at bend of wing). *Ad.:* deep chestnut body with black head; 3-lobed orange-yellow frontal shield; yellow bill with light blue base. *Juv.:* white face and underparts; black postocular line.

GALLINULES: Plump marsh birds with long legs and toes (except coot) and chickenlike bill.

5 PURPLE GALLINULE *Porphyrio martinica* p. 76
Local, marshes. All-white undertail coverts. *Ad.:* blue-violet body, pale blue frontal shield, red bill with yellow tip, and orange-yellow legs. *Juv.:* brownish.

6 COMMON MOORHEN *Gallinula chloropus* p. 76
UC to FC in winter, breeds locally; marshes, occas. open water. Dark gray stripe splits white undertail coverts. *Ad.:* mostly gray body with brownish back and white bars on flanks; red frontal shield; red bill with yellow tip. *Juv.:* dull version of ad., with white in face; grayer than juv. **5**, with white bars on sides.

7 AMERICAN COOT *Fulica americana* · p. 76
Locally abundant in winter, open water and edge of marshes. Like gallinules but without long legs and toes. Black head and neck, gray body, small red frontal shield, stark white bill with reddish bar near tip.

1 Basic Alternate

2 Alternate Chick Basic

3 ♂ ♀

4 Juvenile Adult

5 Juvenile Adult

6 Juvenile Adult

7 Adult

PLATE **15** PLOVERS

TUNDRA PLOVERS: Unmistakable in alternate plumage. In basic plumage, best field marks are flight pattern and length of folded wings relative to tail.

1 BLACK-BELLIED PLOVER *Pluvialis squatarola* p. 78
Locally C, coast and cayes. Folded wings do not extend significantly beyond tail tip. Distinctive call. *Basic:* brownish gray, with paler feather edges; unbarred flanks; in flight, white underwing with black axillars, white wing stripe on upper surface, white uppertail coverts. *Juv.* (not shown): similar but feather centers darker, edges paler, sometimes tinged golden on back. *Alt.:* unmistakable; note white undertail coverts.

2 AMERICAN GOLDEN-PLOVER
Pluvialis dominica · p. 78
UC and local spring transient. Smaller and slimmer than **1**, with proportionately smaller bill. Folded wings easily exceed tip of tail. Distinctive call. *Basic:* very similar to **1** but browner on average and has faintly barred flanks and darker crown than **1**, with more prominent supercilium. In flight, grayish underwing without black axillars; lacks wing stripe; tail and uppertail coverts same color as rump and back. ♂ *alt:* black extends to undertail coverts; feathers on upperparts edged golden. ♀ *alt.* (not shown): similar, but black underparts less extensive, often mottled.

BANDED PLOVERS: All have partial or complete breast band (2 bands in Killdeer), and all but collared (!) have white collar.

3 KILLDEER *Charadrius vociferus* · p. 80
FC in winter, pastures and lawns. Diagnostic double band across breast, red-orange uppertail coverts and base of tail; long tail easily exceeds folded wings. Diagnostic calls.

4 SNOWY PLOVER *Charadrius alexandrinus* p. 79
R winter visitor, beaches and sandflats. Small bill, gray legs; pale upperparts the color of sand, white lores. *Alt.:* partial black breast band, black auricular stripe, and black forecrown. *Basic and some* ♀ *alt.* (not shown): black highlights reduced or absent. *Juv.* (not shown): pale feather tips on upperparts give scaly appearance.

5 COLLARED PLOVER *Charadrius collaris* p. 79
VU and local along coast. *Ad.:* tiny (smaller than shown), slim, with small head; long, thin black bill; flesh-colored legs; thin black breast band; pale chestnut hindcrown and auriculars; lacks white collar. *Juv.* (not shown): lacks black highlights and reddish tones on head and neck; dark patch on side of breast only; thin pale feather edges.

6 WILSON'S PLOVER *Charadrius wilsonia* p. 79
UC, coast and cayes. Larger than all but Killdeer; long, thick, all-dark bill; flesh-colored legs. *Alt.:* broad black breast band, forecrown, and lores (dark brown in ♀). *Basic:* brown breast band and forecrown. *Juv.* (not shown): pale edges to feathers of upperparts.

7 SEMIPALMATED PLOVER
Charadrius semipalmatus · p. 79
Locally C in winter. Smaller than **6** but larger and much darker brown than **4**, with yellow-orange legs, complete breast band, and dark lores that separate white forehead and throat. Much larger and plumper than **5** and has full white collar; yellow-orange legs. *Alt.:* black breast band, auriculars, lores, and forecrown; white forehead and postocular stripe; orange bill with black tip. *Basic:* brown instead of black collar and facial features. *Juv.* (not shown): fine pale edges to feathers of upperparts, duller legs.

Basic

Basic

1

Basic

2

♂ Alternate

Basic

1

Alternate

Basic

3

3

4

♂ Alternate

5

Adult

6

6

7

♂ Alternate

6

Basic

Alternate

Basic

PLATE **16**

STILT, AVOCET, OYSTERCATCHER, AND SANDPIPERS

1 BLACK-NECKED STILT *Himantopus mexicanus*
p. 81
Locally C in winter, breeds locally; wetlands.
Unmistakable—very long, bright pink legs;
thin, straight bill; black-and-white plumage. ♂:
upperparts black. ♀: dark brown back. *Juv.* (not
shown): pale feather edges on dark gray upperparts; white hindneck.

2 AMERICAN AVOCET *Recurvirostra americana*
p. 81
R in winter, wetlands. Unmistakable—black
and white, with long, blue-gray legs and long,
thin upturned bill, less sharply upturned in ♂
than in ♀. *Basic:* head and neck with pale gray
wash. *Alt.:* rusty cinnamon head and neck.

3 AMERICAN OYSTERCATCHER
Haematopus palliatus · p. 80
R in winter, sandy beaches. Unmistakable—
dark blackish brown and black, with white
belly, wing stripe, and uppertail coverts; bright
orange-red, oddly shaped bill; flesh-colored
legs; yellow eyes.

4 BUFF-BREASTED SANDPIPER
Tryngites subruficollis · p. 89
VU transient; short-grass meadows, flats. Small
warm-brown-and-buff shorebird with short,
straight, thin bill and small head; dark eyes
highlighted in plain buff face; bright buff
below; yellow legs. In flight, stark white underwings.

5 UPLAND SANDPIPER *Bartramia longicauda*
p. 84
R transient, open areas usually away from water.
Long, thin neck and small head, with disproportionately large eyes; long, rounded tail;
short, straight orange-yellow and black bill;
orange-yellow legs; upright posture (often more
so than shown). In flight, nearly black unmarked outer wing contrasts with lighter inner
wing.

6 WILSON'S PHALAROPE *Phalaropus tricolor*
p. 92
R transient, lagoons and ponds. Long, thin,
straight bill; swims less than other phalaropes.
Basic: uniform gray above, with white face
and underparts; lacks dark auricular stripe and
white wing stripe of Red-necked (Fig. 15); white
uppertail coverts much like those of Stilt Sandpiper. ♀ *alt.:* unmistakable. ♂ *alt.* (not shown):
similar but duller.

CURLEWS: Medium to large sandpipers
with downcurved bill.

7 LONG-BILLED CURLEW *Numenius americanus*
p. 84
R in winter. Extremely long bill, longest in ♀
(shown). *Ad.* ♂, and especially juv., have shorter
bill. Lacks boldly striped head of **8**. In flight,
shows bright cinnamon unbarred underwings.

8 WHIMBREL *Numenius phaeopus* · p. 84
Locally FC in winter. Smaller than **7,** with
shorter bill, dark- and light-brown-striped head.
Barred underwings lack cinnamon color of **7**.

GODWITS: Large, long-legged sandpipers
with long, upturned bill.

9 MARBLED GODWIT *Limosa fedoa* · p. 85
R in winter. Long, upturned bill, pink at base.
Plumage otherwise similar to that of **7**, including cinnamon underwings. *Juv.* (shown) *and
basic:* unstreaked underparts. *Alt.:* finely barred
underparts.

10 HUDSONIAN GODWIT *Limosa haemastica*
p. 85
Spring vagrant. Slightly upturned bill, shorter
than in **9**. Unmistakable in alt. plumage (birds
in juvenal and basic plumages unrecorded in
Belize). Underwing linings black, contrasting
sharply with white wing stripe; black tail; white
uppertail coverts. ♂ *alt.:* rich chestnut underparts. ♀ *alt.:* much less chestnut and more
heavily barred underparts than ♂.

1

♂

♀

3

2

♀ Alternate

5

7

♂ Basic

3

4

9

♀ Alternate

4
Alternate

6

♂
Alternate

5

Basic

8

10

♀ Alternate

7

8

9
Juvenile

PLATE **17** SANDPIPERS

1 SPOTTED SANDPIPER *Actitis macularia*
p. 83
C visitor nearly year-round. Constantly bobs posterior; unique flight, with alternating rapid shallow flapping and gliding. Pale supercilium, fairly distinct wing band, mostly dark tail. *Basic:* dusky patch on side of lower neck; white underparts. *Alt.:* spots on undersides. *Juv.* (not shown): pale edges to back and wing feathers.

2 RUDDY TURNSTONE *Arenaria interpres*
p. 85
Local visitor nearly year-round. Distinctive head pattern in all plumages; red-orange legs; short upturned bill. *Basic:* complex dusky-and-white pattern on head and breast. *Alt.:* striking black-and-white head and breast pattern; black, rufous, and white upperparts, including wings and tail. *Juv.* (not shown): similar to basic but with scaly-looking upperparts, duller legs.

3 WILSON'S SNIPE *Gallinago delicata* · p. 91
UC in winter, marshes. Very long bill and disproportionately short legs; eyes set high and back on striped head; heavily mottled upperparts, with conspicuous pale stripe on each side of back. Fast, erratic flight; distinctive flight call.

DOWITCHERS: Long bill for probing in mud; legs dull green. In flight, distinctive white wedge up back, finely banded black-and-white tail. Distinguishing the two dowitchers by plumage characters is difficult (see text). Distinctive calls; silent birds, especially in basic plumage, may go unidentified. Bill length not reliable.

4 LONG-BILLED DOWITCHER
Limnodromus scolopaceus · p. 91
UC in winter; marshes, vegetated mudflats; coast and interior. Distinctive *pik* or *peek* call. *Juv.:* unmarked gray tertials; brown back; grayer underparts than **5**. *Alt.:* reddish underparts, including undertail coverts, heavily barred throughout. *Basic:* see Short-billed account (next) and text.

5 SHORT-BILLED DOWITCHER
Limnodromus griseus · p. 90
Locally C in winter along coast; mudflats, shallows. Distinctive *tu-tu* flight call. *Juv.:* brown tertials are barred; rich buffy underparts. *Basic:* grayish above and across breast; nearly identical to **4** (see text). *Alt.:* some subspecies (*griseus*

shown) have white belly and heavily spotted breast; *hendersoni* very similar to **4** (see text).

6 WILLET *Catoptrophorus semipalmatus* · p. 83
Local in winter, coast only. Large and grayish, with blue-gray legs and fairly thickset, straight, medium-length bill; bold black-and-white wing pattern in flight. *Alt.:* fine black feather edges create barred and speckled appearance. *Basic:* rather uniformly gray above, paler below. *Juv.* (not shown): warm brownish gray, with pale feather edges on upperparts. Eastern subspecies illustrated. Western subspecies differs (see text).

YELLOWLEGS: Long-necked shorebirds with medium-length bill and long, yellow legs. In flight, white lower rump and uppertail coverts; finely banded black-and-white tail; pale underwings; no wing stripes. The two species are essentially alike except for size and voice.

7 GREATER YELLOWLEGS *Tringa melanoleuca*
p. 82
Local visitor nearly year-round, wetlands. Larger than dowitcher; thick-based, slightly upturned bill 1½ times diameter of head. *Alt.:* heavily barred and speckled black and white; short black bars on flanks. *Basic:* barring and speckling less apparent. *Juv.* (not shown): heavily spotted above, streaked on breast.

8 LESSER YELLOWLEGS *Tringa flavipes*
p. 82
Local visitor nearly year-round, wetlands. Slightly smaller than dowitcher; thin, straight bill 1¼ times diameter of head. *Alt.:* similar to **7** but finer barring on neck; barring sparse or absent on flanks. *Basic:* similar to **7** (see text). *Juv.* (not shown): like **7** but with streaking on breast less distinct.

9 SOLITARY SANDPIPER *Tringa solitaria*
p. 83
FC in winter. Halfway between Spotted Sandpiper and Lesser Yellowlegs in size; general aspect like small, dark yellowlegs; bobs head like yellowlegs, not posterior like Spotted Sandpiper. Bill like **8** but shorter. Fine spots in back and wings; distinct white eye-ring; legs shorter than yellowlegs and dull greenish. In flight, tail dark in center, strongly barred laterally; very dark underwing.

PLATE **18** *Calidris* SANDPIPERS

CALIDRIS SANDPIPERS: Small sandpipers, most with short neck and legs, moderately short bill. The smaller *Calidris,* often called peeps, can be notoriously difficult to ID.

1 LEAST SANDPIPER *Calidris minutilla* · p. 87
C in winter, flats and marshes. Smallest peep; greenish yellow legs; brown plumage; short, thin bill. Darker than **2** or **3**. *Basic:* brownish upperparts and breast band. *Juv.:* rufous upperparts; buffy wash across breast. *Alt.:* darker and browner than **2** or **3**; densely streaked breast band.

2 SEMIPALMATED SANDPIPER *Calidris pusilla*
p. 86
Locally FC transient, flats. Black legs; grayer, paler, plumper than **1**, with thicker bill than **1**, straighter and usually shorter bill than **3**. *Juv.:* more uniformly brown above, with darker crown and auriculars than juv. **3**. *Alt.:* more uniformly brown above than **3**, without strong rufous highlights on scapulars and head; lacks spotting on flanks. *Basic* (not shown): very similar to basic **3** (see next account and text).

3 WESTERN SANDPIPER *Calidris mauri*
p. 87
Locally VC migrant, less C in winter; coastal flats. Black legs; moderately long bill (length varies), with slight droop. *Basic:* brownish gray above; feathers without dark centers and white edges; slightly paler face than **2**. *Juv.:* rufous in scapulars and auriculars; less prominent supercilium than **2**. *Alt.:* like juvenile, but rufous also in crown; heavily streaked breast, sides, and flanks.

4 SANDERLING *Calidris alba* · p. 86
Local in winter along coast; prefers beaches. Larger and paler than preceding three. *Basic:* pale gray above; white below; mostly white head accentuates black eyes, bill, and dark shoulder patch. *Juv.:* back and scapular feathers nearly black with broad white edges. *Alt.:* pale (♀) to bright (♂) chestnut head and breast.

5 PECTORAL SANDPIPER *Calidris melanotos*
p. 89
FC transient. Medium-sized peep with breast streaks abruptly cut off from white belly; yellow legs. ♂ distinctly larger, darker than ♀. *Juv.:* buffy wash on streaked breast. *Alt.* (not shown): fine black streaks on white breast.

6 WHITE-RUMPED SANDPIPER
Calidris fuscicollis · p. 88
C spring transient, wet areas. Medium-sized peep with white uppertail coverts. Primaries project well past tertials. *Alt.:* streaked breast, sides, and flanks; rufous highlights on crown, auriculars, and back; gray wing coverts; lower mandible has pale base.

7 BAIRD'S SANDPIPER *Calidris bairdii* · p. 88
Possible vagrant, drier upper edges of wetlands. Similar to **6** but without all-white uppertail coverts and streaks on flanks; has all-black bill. *Juv.:* brownish buff plumage with scaly back pattern. *Ad.* (not shown): see text.

8 STILT SANDPIPER *Calidris himantopus*
p. 89
UC transient, local in winter; wetlands. Relatively long neck and small head; moderately long bill has a distinct droop. Long yellow-green legs; white uppertail coverts and lower rump. Probes in shallow water much like dowitcher, but with posterior raised above head. *Alt.:* chestnut auriculars; streaked throat; mottled neck and breast; barred belly through undertail coverts. *Basic:* grayish above, without contrasting pale rufous feather edges. *Juv.:* finely streaked breast; dark brown back with pale rufous feather edges.

9 DUNLIN *Calidris alpina* · p. 89
Vagrant, coastal wetlands. Longer bill than **3**, with more distinct droop; shorter neck and legs than **8** and lacks fully white uppertail coverts. Legs dark gray. *Basic:* brownish gray; in flight, indistinct wing stripe, center of uppertail coverts dark. *Alt.:* distinctive pattern but unlikely to turn up in Belize.

10 RED KNOT *Calidris canutus* · p. 86
UC transient, local in winter; mudflats, beaches. Distinctly larger and plumper than the peeps. Short legs, medium-length bill, and lack of white wedge in rump distinguish it from dowitchers. *Basic:* grayish above; whitish below; in flight (not shown), rump and uppertail coverts only slightly paler than back. *Juv.:* feathers of upperparts finely edged dark gray and white; warm, light brown wash on body in fresh plumage. *Alt.:* chestnut above and below; mottled black above; finely barred black-and-white rump and tail.

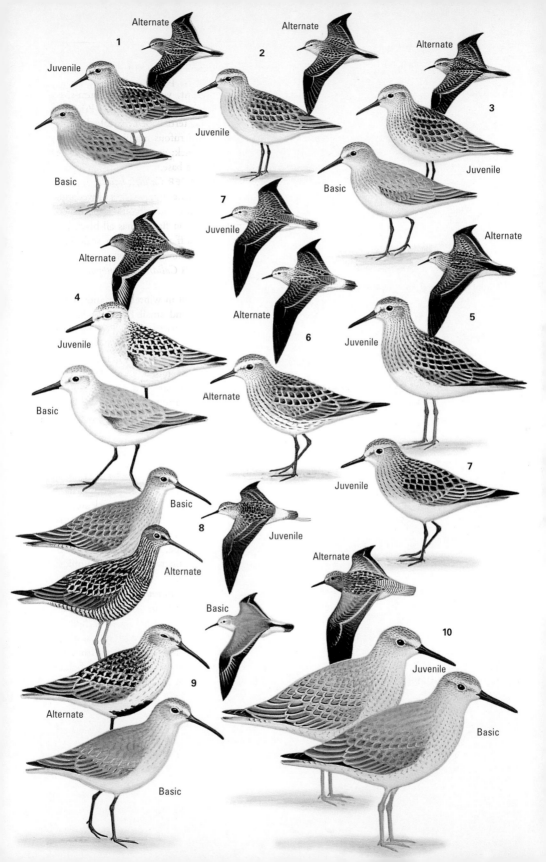

PLATE **19** GULLS

BLACK-HOODED GULLS: Adults in alt. plumage have black hood. In basic and imm. plumages, hood reduced or absent. Only Laughing is common in Belize.

1 BONAPARTE'S GULL *Larus philadelphia*
p. 97
R in winter; coast, cayes, lagoons. Tiny gull with delicate bill, buoyant flight. *Alt.:* black hood; gray mantle with white bar on anterior outer wing outlined in black. *Ad. basic* (not shown): black hood replaced by small black auricular spot. *1st basic:* black subterminal tail band; dusky brown median wing coverts; remiges mixed gray, white, and black; mostly white head with black auricular spot.

2 FRANKLIN'S GULL *Larus pipixcan* · p. 97
Occas. transient; coast, cayes, lagoons. Like **3** but smaller, with thinner bill. *Ad. alt.:* white wingtip split by black bar. *1st alt.:* reduced white in wingtip; easily confused with ad. basic **3**, but black partial hood more extensive, accenting partial white eye-ring. *1st basic:* similar to 1st basic **3**, but tail band does not extend to lateral edge of tail; partial hood usually better defined; clean white underparts.

3 LAUGHING GULL *Larus atricilla* · p. 96
C, coast and cayes. Larger than others in group, with larger bill and darker mantle. *Ad. alt.:* uniformly dark gray mantle contrasts less with black wingtips. Basic ad. (not shown): mostly white head. *2nd basic:* like ad. basic but with partial tail band. *1st basic:* gray back and scapulars; inner wing dusky brown, with extensive black outer wing and trailing edge; full black subterminal tail band; partial hood; dusky wash on nape and breast. *Juv.:* dark brown mantle and head; dark smudge across breast; thick black tail band.

PALE-HEADED GULLS: Lack dark hood in all plumages. Most recorded in Belize are imms.

4 RING-BILLED GULL *Larus delawarensis*
p. 98
Occas. in winter, coastal. Size of **3** but mantle paler. *1st basic:* pale gray back; patchy gray, brown, and dusky wings; mottled, mostly white head and rump; white tail with black subterminal band; white underparts; pale bill with dark tip. *Ad. basic:* mostly white head (all white in alt.), yellow eyes, yellow bill with black ring near tip. Mantle (not shown) pale gray with white spots in black wingtip; tail all white. *2nd basic* (not shown): similar to ad. but bill not yet bright yellow; white spots in wingtip absent. *Juv.* (not shown): see text.

5 HERRING GULL *Larus argentatus* · p. 98
UC in winter, coastal. Largest expected gull in Belize. *1st basic:* brownish, with dark mottling throughout; mottled rump does not contrast much lighter than back; tail mostly black; inner primaries paler, grayer than rest of wing; face paler than rest of body; dark bill often pale at base and may be distinctly bicolored. *2nd basic:* similar to 1st basic **6** but smaller, with more black in tail and light gray in back and remiges; larger than 1st basic **4**, with heavier bill, broader black tail band, pale eyes, and clean white uppertail coverts. *Ad.:* yellow eyes; yellow bill with red spot near tip; mantle (not shown) pale gray, with white spots in black wingtips; all-white tail.

6 GREAT BLACK-BACKED GULL *Larus marinus*
p. 99
Possible vagrant, coast and cayes. Very large and chunky, with thick, all-black bill. *1st basic:* dark mottling on light brown background above; mostly white with fine speckling below; tail white basally and dark distally, forming indistinct tail band. *2nd basic:* more white in head; bicolored bill; dark slate gray back and patchy wing pattern (not shown).

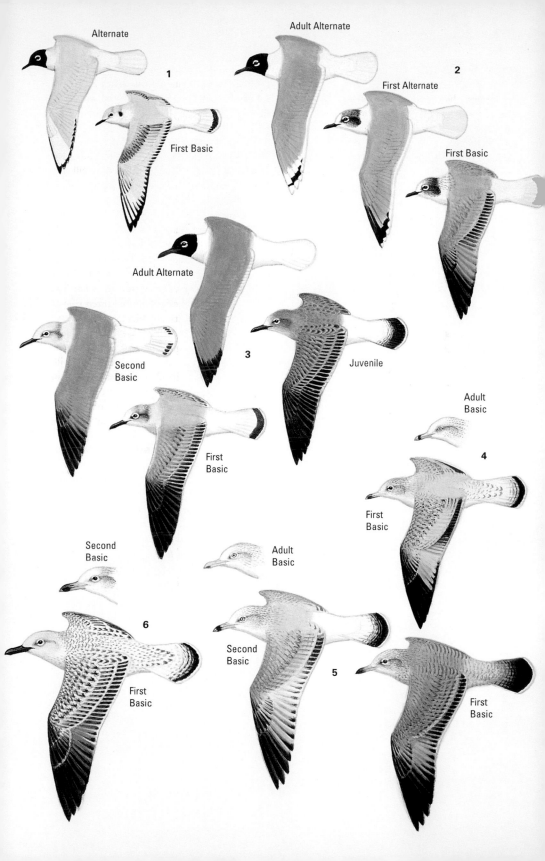

Alternate

1

First Basic

Adult Alternate

2

First Alternate

First Basic

Adult Alternate

Second
Basic

3

Juvenile

First
Basic

Adult
Basic

4

First
Basic

Second
Basic

Second
Basic

Adult
Basic

6

5

First
Basic

First
Basic

First
Basic

PLATE **20** TERNS

1 GULL-BILLED TERN *Sterna nilotica* · p. 100
Local in winter, lagoons and coast. Medium-sized, with short, thick, black bill and shallowly forked tail. Mantle and tail very pale gray. *Alt.:* black crown, no crest. *Basic:* white head, short streak behind eyes.

CRESTED TERNS: Diagnostic bill color, shaggy hindcrown.

2 CASPIAN TERN *Sterna caspia* · p. 101
Locally FC in winter, lagoons and coast. Largest tern, with heavy red bill, shallowly forked tail, gull-like flight; shaggy hindcrown often not noticeable. *Basic:* black crown finely streaked white, especially on forecrown; contrasting dark gray primaries in underwing. *Alt.:* all-black crown.

3 SANDWICH TERN *Sterna sandvicensis* · p. 101
C, coast and cayes. Moderately small, with long, thin, yellow-tipped black bill, forked tail, and pale gray mantle. Reduced dark areas in primaries. *Basic:* black restricted to posterior half of shaggy crown. *Alt.:* full black crown. *Juv.* (not shown): reduced yellow in bill tip, may be difficult to see; mantle has dusky feather tips.

4 ROYAL TERN *Sterna maxima* · p. 101
C year-round visitor, coast and cayes. Medium-large tern with fairly long, orange bill and forked tail. Less extensive dark underprimaries than **2**. *Basic:* black restricted to postocular bar and hindcrown. *Alt.:* full black shaggy crown. *Juv.* (not shown): dark carpal bar, yellow bill.

SMALL GRAY-AND-WHITE TERNS: Small size, deeply forked tail, and thin, dark bill. Wingtip pattern and length of folded wing vs. tail are key ID features.

5 FORSTER'S TERN *Sterna forsteri* · p. 103
Occas. in winter. Folded wings extend to tail tip; legs moderately long; outer wing pale. *Basic:* black postocular bar; all-dark bill. *Alt.:* black crown; orange bill with black tip.

6 COMMON TERN *Sterna hirundo* · p. 102
Irregular transient and winter visitor, coastal. Wingtips darker than rest of wing; slightly darker mantle than **5** or **7**; folded wings usually exceed tail tip. *Basic:* anterior half of crown white; all-dark bill; dark carpal bar. *Alt.:* black crown; red-orange bill with black tip.

7 ROSEATE TERN *Sterna dougallii* · p. 102
Local in summer, cayes. Folded wings do not reach tail tip; in flight, only leading edge of outer primaries dark; shorter legs and longer, thinner bill than **5** or **6**. Flies with rapid, shallow wingbeats. *Basic:* lacks carpal bar of **6**; white forecrown; bill all black. *Alt.:* black crown; at height of breeding season has pinkish cast below, and basal half of bill turns red to orange.

8 LEAST TERN *Sterna antillarum* · p. 103
Local summer resident, coastal. Very small pale gray-and-white tern with bounding flight. *Juv.:* warm gray back with dark feather edges; bill mostly black. *Alt.:* black crown with white forehead; yellow bill with small black tip.

9 BLACK TERN *Chlidonias niger* · p. 104
FC autumn transient, scarce in spring; ocean, lagoons. *Basic:* smoke gray above, white below, dusky patch on side of breast, dark crescent behind eyes, notched gray tail. *Alt.:* black head and underparts, gray upperparts, light gray underwings.

BLACK-BACKED TERNS: Pelagic; dark gray or black upperparts, white underparts, white forehead, and deeply forked tail.

10 SOOTY TERN *Sterna fuscata* · p. 104
Local seasonally offshore. *Juv.:* all dark except for white lower belly and undertail coverts and small white spots in back and wings. *Ad.:* similar to **11** but underside of remiges dark, contrasting with white underwing coverts; white on head restricted to forehead; upperparts black.

11 BRIDLED TERN *Sterna anaethetus* · p. 104
Local seasonally offshore. *Juv.:* white below; brownish gray above, with white feather edges. *Ad.:* similar to **10**, but underwing mostly white; white in forehead extends past eyes; upperparts dark gray.

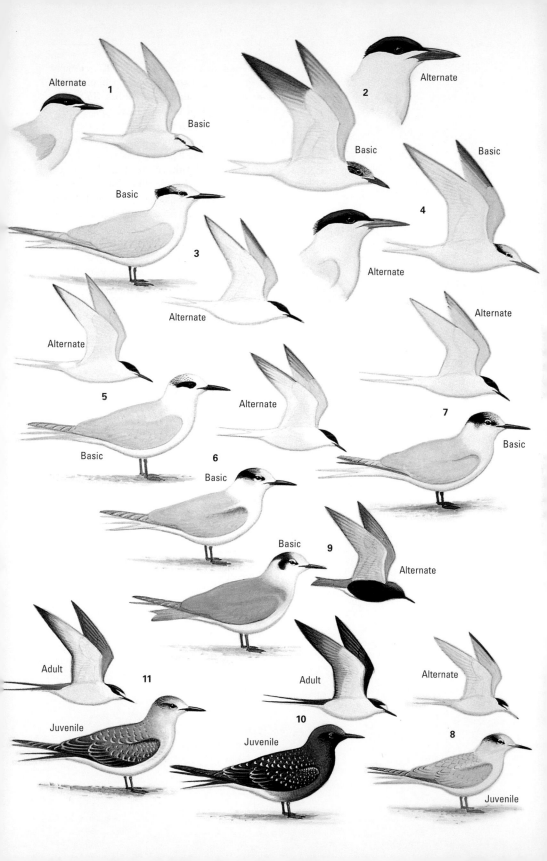

Alternate

1

Basic

Basic

2

Alternate

Basic

Basic

Alternate

4

3

Alternate

Alternate

Alternate

Alternate

Basic

5

Alternate

7

Basic

Alternate

6

Basic

Basic

9

Alternate

Adult

11

Adult

Alternate

Juvenile

10

8

Juvenile

Juvenile

PLATE **21** PIGEONS AND DOVES

PIGEONS: Stocky birds with rather short tail; fast fliers, often traveling in flocks. Often perch inconspicuously in foliage. Heard more often than seen.

1 WHITE-CROWNED PIGEON
Columba leucocephala · p. 109
FC summer resident, cayes. Dark slaty plumage with white crown; iridescent green hind neck. *Juv.* (not shown): white restricted to forehead.

2 RED-BILLED PIGEON *Columba flavirostris*
p. 109
C in north and west. Whitish bill with red base usually visible only at close range. Three-toned body: dull vinaceous foreparts, blue-gray hindparts, nearly black tail.

3 SCALED PIGEON *Columba speciosa* · p. 108
Local, forests; less common in south. Conspicuously scaled neck and underparts; pale belly and undertail coverts contrast with dark tail in flight. Red bill with pale yellow tip. ♂: purplish chestnut upperparts. ♀: olive-brown upperparts.

4 SHORT-BILLED PIGEON *Columba nigrirostris*
p. 109
C nearly throughout, forests. Small, dark pigeon with dark brown back and wings and vinaceous gray head, neck, and underparts. Tail does not contrast strongly with undertail coverts; black bill. Vocalizations distinctive.

5 PALE-VENTED PIGEON *Columba cayennensis*
p. 107
C, widespread. Larger and paler than **4**. Body a subtle mix of blue grays, browns, and vinaceous purples. Bill all dark. Two-toned gray-brown tail, lighter in distal half, clearly visible when birds spread tail for landing. Paler undertail coverts contrast with darker tail in flight.

ZENAIDA DOVES: Smaller, paler, and browner than pigeons; distinctive wing markings. Found in open country.

6 WHITE-WINGED DOVE *Zenaida asiatica*
p. 110
C in n.e., autumn migrant in south and west. Pale gray brown, with conspicuous white band in wing; square-tipped tail with black-and-white corners. Larger and plumper than **7**.

7 MOURNING DOVE *Zenaida macroura* · p. 110
UC in winter. Slender pale pinkish brown dove with parakeet-like pointed tail and flight silhouette; spots in wing.

PLATE **22** TERRESTRIAL DOVES

GROUND-DOVES: Except for Blue Ground-Dove, found exclusively in open country, usually on or near the ground. Blue Ground-Dove usually in forest interior. All have rufous wing panel, conspicuous in flight.

1 PLAIN-BREASTED GROUND-DOVE
Columbina minuta · p. 111
FC in e. half, open areas. Noticeably smaller than other ground-doves. Rufous wing patch not as conspicuous as in **2** and **4**; both sexes have dark violet spots in wing. ♂: bluish gray head, gray-brown body. ♀: duller than ♂, with little head-body contrast.

2 COMMON GROUND-DOVE
Columbina passerina · p. 111
FC, savannas and n. cayes. Scaly breast and head. ♂: face, neck, and underparts pinkish; crown blue gray; dark violet spots in wing; bill pinkish red with dark tip. ♀: face, neck, and underparts buffy gray; scaling less prominent; purplish chestnut spots in wing.

3 INCA DOVE *Columbina inca* · p. 111
Vagrant. Somewhat similar to **2**, but rounded dark feather edges give entire body a scaly appearance. Longer-tailed than other ground-doves, with conspicuous white in outer rectrices.

4 RUDDY GROUND-DOVE *Columbina talpacoti*
p. 112
C and widespread, open areas. Longer-tailed than **1** or **2**; both sexes have all-dark bill. ♂: blue-gray crown; ruddy vinaceous below; pinkish ruddy above; black spots and bars in wing. ♀: lacks ruddy color of ♂; lacks scaly appearance of **2**; larger and browner than **1**, with black spots in wing.

5 BLUE GROUND-DOVE *Claravis pretiosa*
p. 112
C in south, UC in north; forests and clearings. Sexes strongly dimorphic; bill dull yellowish. ♂: distinctive; soft grayish blue throughout, with black bars and spots in wing. ♀: blue replaced with brown; dark rufous spots and bars in wing; rump and central tail also rufous.

FOREST DOVES: Often heard but seldom seen dwellers of the forest floor. Some sound confusingly similar, and all but quail-dove look similar.

6 RUDDY QUAIL-DOVE *Geotrygon montana*
p. 114
Relatively UC, woodlands. Bill, eye-ring, and legs reddish. Peculiar profile, with bill projecting sharply downward from flat forehead; eyes set high in head. Typically louder wing whir than *Leptotila* doves when flushed; lacks white tail corners. ♂: brownish rufous, with pale cheeks and throat broken by dark slash; white bar at bend of wing. ♀: duller; retains ghost of ♂'s head pattern.

7 GRAY-CHESTED DOVE *Leptotila cassini*
p. 113
FC in s. half, forests. Crown and nape warm brown; breast vinaceous gray. Lacks iridescence on neck. Darkest of the group, especially on underparts, with white only on undertail coverts. Least amount of white in tail corners.

8 CARIBBEAN DOVE *Leptotila jamaicensis*
p. 113
FC, Ambergris Caye and ne CO. Blue-gray hindcrown and nape like **10**; sides of neck iridescent rose. Whitest underparts and face and brightest red legs of the group. Most extensive white in tail corners.

9 WHITE-TIPPED DOVE *Leptotila verreauxi*
p. 112
C in n. two-thirds, woodland and second growth. Head and breast grayish vinaceous, paler on face, darker on crown; nape has iridescent violet sheen. Pinkish red legs.

10 GRAY-FRONTED DOVE *Leptotila rufaxilla*
p. 113
FC nearly throughout, woodland. Crown and nape blue gray like **8**, becoming whitish on forehead, throat, and belly, but less extensive than in **8**; breast pale vinaceous, pinker than rest. Lacks iridescence on neck.

PLATE **23** PARROTS

LONG-TAILED PARROTS: Long, pointed tail; largest and smallest species in Belize.

1 SCARLET MACAW *Ara macao* · p. 114
UC; restricted to Vaca Plateau, c Maya Mtns. Unmistakable large red, yellow, and blue parrot with long, pointed tail and massive bill.

2 OLIVE-THROATED PARAKEET *Aratinga nana* p. 114
C throughout, forest edge and second growth. Small, mostly green parakeet with bluish remiges. Usually travels in small to moderate-sized groups. Rapid, twisting flight.

SMALL SHORT-TAILED PARROTS: Rapid flight with relatively deep wingbeats quite unlike those of amazons.

3 BROWN-HOODED PARROT
Pionopsitta haematotis · p. 115
C in south and west, UC in n.e.; woodland. Small green parrot with short, square-tipped tail. In flight, note all-green body, dark brown head, and bright red axillars. Usually travels in pairs or small groups. *Ad.:* conspicuous dark brown hood, white eye-ring, and pale bill; remiges blue on upper surface. *Juv.:* much paler hood than adult.

4 WHITE-CROWNED PARROT *Pionus senilis* p. 115
C nearly throughout, woodland. Small, dull bluish green parrot with blue-and-white head and short, square-tipped tail. In flight, appears darker and more uniform than **3**, showing little contrast between body and head. Lacks red axillars. *Ad.:* dark bluish head, white forecrown and throat, bronzy forewing, red tail coverts. *Juv.:* greener than adult, with white on forehead only; lacks blue head. Could be confused with **6** at a distance, but note red undertail coverts and lack of red in wings and face.

AMAZONS: Distinctive slow flight on rapid, shallow wingbeats, with wings bowed downward below horizontal plane.

5 YELLOW-LORED PARROT *Amazona xantholora* p. 116
VC in n.e., local in n.w.; open woodland. Larger than **3** and **4**, smaller than **7–10**. Often travels in large flocks. ♂: yellow lores, white forecrown, and dusky auriculars; white eye-ring with red border; red patches in upper wing. ♀: similar but lacks white forecrown and red wing patches.

6 WHITE-FRONTED PARROT *Amazona albifrons* p. 116
C in n. half, open woodland. Like **5** but lacks yellow lores and dusky auriculars. ♂: white forehead, red face and upper primary coverts. ♀: similar but with reduced amount of white in forehead; lacks red upper primary coverts.

7 YELLOW-HEADED PARROT *Amazona oratrix* p. 117
FC, pine savannas; threatened by pet trade. Larger than **5** and **6**; distinctive yellow face and crown, pale brown bill, and white eye-ring; yellow reduced in juvenile. Travels in pairs.

8 YELLOW-NAPED PARROT
Amazona auropalliata · p. 117
Vagrant, Turneffe Isl. Yellow restricted to nape and forehead; cere dark gray, bill grayish; eye-ring gray.

9 RED-LORED PARROT *Amazona autumnalis* p. 116
C throughout. Same size as **7** and **8** but with very different head pattern: blue crown, red forehead, yellow cheeks, and darker bill.

10 MEALY PARROT *Amazona farinosa* · p. 116
C, forests. Largest of amazons; broad, pale eye-ring; blue crown; dark bill. Tail more broadly tipped yellow than in others.

1

9

5 ♂

10

6 ♂

7

2

2

3

4

2

Adult

3

♀ 5

♂

Juvenile

Adult

4

6

♂

Juvenile

♀

8

7

9

10

PLATE **24** CUCKOOS AND ANIS

COCCYZUS CUCKOOS: Gray brown above; creamy buff or white below; graduated tail with white spots on underside.

1 YELLOW-BILLED CUCKOO

Coccyzus americanus · p. 118

FC transient, especially on cayes. Rufous patch visible in spread wing; yellow-and-black bill; yellow eye-ring. *Ad.:* tail black, with broad white feather tips on undersurface; most of lower mandible and base of upper mandible yellow. *Juv.:* tail grayish, with white feather tips less extensive (not shown); yellow restricted to base of lower mandible.

2 BLACK-BILLED CUCKOO

Coccyzus erythropthalmus · p. 118

Occas. transient. Lacks rufous in spread wing; undertail gray, with thin white feather tips. *Ad.:* all-black bill, red eye-ring. *Juv.:* creamy white to grayish buff throat and upper breast; buffy eye-ring; white tail feather tips indistinct.

3 MANGROVE CUCKOO *Coccyzus minor*

p. 118

VU and local, cayes and riparian woodland. Buff underparts, blackish mask, grayish crown, and black tail with broad white rectrix tips as in **1**, but lacks rufous in primaries. *Juv.* (not shown): less well defined mask; gray-and-white tail.

4 SQUIRREL CUCKOO *Piaya cayana* · p. 119

C throughout. Large cuckoo with very long, graduated black tail with broad white rectrix tips; rufous upperparts; cinnamon-and-gray underparts; yellow-green bill and eye-ring.

GROUND-CUCKOOS: Streaked or spotted cuckoos with erectile crests.

5 PHEASANT CUCKOO *Dromococcyx phasianellus*

p. 119

R, seldom seen; forested areas. Larger than **6**; long, broad graduated tail, with white-tipped gray rectrices. Small black-and-white-striped head; uniform chestnut crest; thinner, darker bill; spotted breast (unmarked in juvenile).

6 STRIPED CUCKOO *Tapera naevia* · p. 119

UC to FC; second growth, edge. White supercilium, shaggy crest, yellow bill. Larger **5** has thinner bill, different tail pattern. *Ad.:* streaked cinnamon-brown upperparts, unstreaked underparts. *Juv.:* pale cinnamon spots on upperparts, including crest; fine dark spots or bars on breast.

ANIS: Black, grackle-like birds with disjointed flight; grotesquely large bill.

7 SMOOTH-BILLED ANI *Crotophaga ani*

p. 120

Occas. in winter, cayes; may occas. breed. Larger than **6**. *Ad.:* bill lacks grooves, has hump at base of upper mandible; feathers on head and nape reflect brownish bronze gloss in good light, contrasting with glossy green-edged back feathers. *Juv.* (not shown): very similar to **8**; best told by vocalizations.

8 GROOVE-BILLED ANI *Crotophaga sulcirostris*

p. 120

C throughout. *Ad.:* grooves on upper mandible (not always apparent); feathers on head, nape, and back edged glossy blue green (apparent only in good light).

1

2

1

Juvenile

2

Juvenile

3

5

4

8

7

Adult

6

Juvenile

PLATE **25** OWLS

1 VERMICULATED SCREECH-OWL

Otus guatemalae · p. 121

FC, woodland. Small dark owl with short ear tufts, finely barred and streaked underparts, yellow eyes, and greenish bill. The only *Otus* in Belize.

PYGMY-OWLS: Tiny owls, no larger than pewees, with earless head; 2 white-bordered black "eye" spots on nape (not shown); brown sides with pale spots; streaked flanks. Often active during day.

2 FERRUGINOUS PYGMY-OWL

Glaucidium brasilianum · p. 123

Locally FC, open forest and towns. Highly variable: rufous to dull brown upperparts; streaked crown and nape; white spots in wings, as well as conspicuous row of white spots in scapulars; tail longer than in **3**, varies from rufous to brown, with 5–7 narrow dark bands, whitish bands, or no bands at all.

3 CENTRAL AMERICAN PYGMY-OWL

Glaucidium griseiceps · p. 122

UC, forests. Smaller than **2**; shorter, black tail with only 3 or 4 whitish bands. Spotted crown and unspotted nape; wing and scapular spots faint or absent.

4 BURROWING OWL *Athene cunicularia*
p. 123

Vagrant. Small ground owl; conspicuously spotted back and wings; spotted and barred underparts; distinctive black-and-white band across lower throat and upper breast. Yellow eyes. Stands erect on long legs and frequently bobs.

5 STRIPED OWL *Pseudoscops clamator* · p. 125

FC in south, e. of Maya Mtns.; open woodland, edge. Medium-sized, pale, striped owl with conspicuous ear tufts. White facial disks outlined in black. The only owl in Belize with combination of ear tufts and dark eyes.

6 BARN OWL *Tyto alba* · p. 121

Locally FC, urban and agricultural areas. Medium size; heart-shaped white facial disk, finely spotted nearly white breast. Buff and silvery upperparts with intricate pattern of fine spots. Dark eyes.

7 CRESTED OWL *Lophostrix cristata* · p. 122

UC in s. interior, forests. Unmistakable dark chestnut face accentuated with snow-white whiskers continuing as long, white, erect ear tufts. Only eared owl in Belize without prominent streaks or bars underneath.

8 STYGIAN OWL *Asio stygius* · p. 124

R, pine forests. Medium-sized dark owl; boldly streaked underparts with fine crossbars. Diagnostic whitish diamond on forehead stands out against dark blackish facial disks. Close-set ear tufts; yellow eyes.

9 GREAT HORNED OWL *Bubo virginianus*
p. 122

FC, Ambergris Caye and locally along n. coast. Large owl with orangish facial disks separated by white X (eyebrows and whiskers); white throat band; bold streaks on upper breast; fine barring on rest of underparts. Yellow eyes.

10 SPECTACLED OWL *Pulsatrix perspicillata*
p. 122

UC in south and west, forests. Large and unmistakable, with its strongly patterned dark-brown-and-white face and throat, clean buff underparts, and yellow eyes.

11 BLACK-AND-WHITE OWL *Ciccaba nigrolineata*
p. 124

UC and local, forests. Nearly black upperparts, black-and-white-barred underparts, sides of neck, and eyebrows. Dark eyes set in dark facial disks. Bill orangish yellow.

12 MOTTLED OWL *Ciccaba virgata* · p. 123

C and widespread, woodland. Smaller than **11**. Dull brown, dark-eyed owl. *Light morph:* conspicuous whitish eyebrows and "moustache"; sparse, narrower streaking on pale underparts. *Dark morph* (not shown): less conspicuous facial markings, more heavily streaked brownish buff underparts.

PLATE **26** CAPRIMULGIDS AND POTOO

1 NORTHERN POTOO *Nyctibius jamaicensis*
p. 129
UC to FC; open woodland, clearings. Remarkably well camouflaged and rarely seen during the day, even when perched in the open. At night, large eyes and long tail readily distinguish it from owls, and upright posture distinguishes it from nightjars and nighthawks. Large, with large yellow eyes. *Left:* alert, at night. *Right:* sleeping, daytime. See similar **Great Potoo** (Fig. 21a), which may occur in south.

NIGHTHAWKS: Usually seen in flight at dawn and dusk; perch parallel on branch during the day. Bounding flight, with frequent changes in direction; wings pointed.

2 COMMON NIGHTHAWK *Chordeiles minor*
p. 126
C transient and local summer resident, pine savannas. White bar in outer wing halfway between bend and tip, usually not visible in folded wings. Wingtip more pointed than in **3**. Folded wings exceed tail tip. Back and scapulars contrast darker than wing. Generally flies slower and higher than **3**, with more gliding and abrupt turns. ♂: white throat and tail band. ♀ (not shown): buffy throat and tail bars.

3 LESSER NIGHTHAWK *Chordeiles acutipennis*
p. 126
C transient, UC in winter; most open areas. Wingtip more rounded than in **2**. Folded wings do not exceed tail tip. Little contrast in back, scapulars, and wings. ♂: prominent white primary bar is ⅔ of the way from bend to tip. ♀: buffy throat and tail bars; bar in wing buffy and not always apparent; additional buffy barring in inner primaries.

4 SHORT-TAILED NIGHTHAWK
Lurocalis semitorquatus · p. 125
Possibly a R resident in south; forages over wooded streams. Very dark, with straighter wings, shorter tail, and more batlike flight than **2** or **3**. Lacks white bar in primaries.

ROUND-WINGED NIGHTJARS: With the exception of Common Pauraque, rarely seen. Inhabit forested areas, where they remain well camouflaged during the day. Best detected by their distinctive vocalizations.

5 YUCATAN POORWILL
Nyctiphrynus yucatanicus · p. 127
UC to FC in n. half, woodland. Small, short-tailed bird. Warm brown, relatively unpatterned body; holds breast feathers out from body in fashion of a bib. *Voice:* burry *will.*

6 YUCATAN NIGHTJAR *Caprimulgus badius*
p. 128
UC to FC in north, may breed locally; woodland and edge. Like **7** but with prominent tawny cinnamon collar. Breast mottled with white spots. Green reflected eyeshine. ♂: conspicuous white tail corners; tail appears nearly all white from below. ♀: lacks white in tail. *Voice: toe reo-a-reo.*

7 WHIP-POOR-WILL *Caprimulgus vociferus*
p. 128
Probably R or VU transient, few records. Like **6** but tawny cinnamon collar much reduced or lacking; tail pattern somewhat different. ♂: white tail corners nearly rectangular. ♀: outer tail feathers narrowly tipped buff. *Voice:* loud *whip-poor-will.*

8 CHUCK-WILL'S-WIDOW
Caprimulgus carolinensis · p. 127
UC transient, R in winter; open wooded areas. Large; dark warm brown throughout, with heavy mottling; banded tail. ♂: thin white throat stripe (often obscured); ad. ♂ also has white inner webs of rectrices, sometimes visible in flight. ♀ *and imm.* ♂ (not shown): pale buff throat stripe; tail feathers lack white inner webs. *Voice:* burry *chuck whido whido.*

9 COMMON PAURAQUE *Nyctidromus albicollis*
p. 127
C throughout; often seen on road at night. Large, with long tail and relatively short wings. Gray morph illustrated; rufous morph has body of cinnamon brown, most noticeable on crown. ♂: 2 full-length white stripes in tail, bold white bar in primaries like that of nighthawks (visible when flushed). ♀: small white patch in tail corners; bar in primaries narrower and buff, not apparent in poor light. *Voice:* typically a faint *wh-what wh-what wh-what* followed by a loud *P'WEEOO!* or a simpler, often repeated *wiull.*

PLATE **27** HUMMINGBIRDS

SABREWINGS: Large hummingbirds with all-black, decurved bill; long, broad tail.

1 VIOLET SABREWING
Campylopterus hemileucurus · p. 135
FC in Maya Mtns., foothills. Large, with downcurved bill; broad white tail corners. ♂: unmistakable dark violet body; small white postocular spot. ♀: blue to blue-violet throat.

2 WEDGE-TAILED SABREWING
Campylopterus curvipennis · p. 135
FC in interior; open woodland, edge. Fairly large. Wedge-shaped tail; bill only slightly downcurved; violet crown; uniformly pale gray underparts. ♂: tail distinctly wedge-shaped, does not have white corners. ♀: tail less wedge-shaped, with outer feathers tipped white.

HERMITS: Small to large, with decurved bill and striped head.

3 STRIPE-THROATED HERMIT
Phaethornis striigularis · p. 134
C nearly throughout, woodland. Tiny, with short bill and moderate central tail extension. Blackish auriculars; cinnamon underparts; rufous uppertail coverts; pale cinnamon tips to tail feathers.

4 LONG-BILLED HERMIT *Phaethornis longirostris*
p. 134
C in s. two-thirds, woodland. Much larger than **3** and lacks cinnamon underparts. Tail tipped white; long central tail feather extension.

5 BAND-TAILED BARBTHROAT *Threnetes ruckeri*
p. 134
UC in s. interior, woodland. Black wedge-shaped tail with white base and tip; lacks extended central tail feathers. Black auriculars and throat outlined in white; breast cinnamon rufous; bill less decurved than in other hermits.

6 WHITE-NECKED JACOBIN *Florisuga mellivora*
p. 136
FC in s. two-thirds, mostly wooded streams. Medium size, with square-tipped tail and fairly

short, straight bill. ♂: striking violet blue head and breast; white nape, belly, and tail. ♀: variable; at one extreme, similar to ♂; others (shown) are distinctly different, with strongly speckled throat and white-tipped tail.

7 PURPLE-CROWNED FAIRY *Heliothryx barroti*
p. 139
FC in south and west, forests. No similar species in Belize. Long, slim hummingbird with short, needlelike bill, long tail, gleaming white underparts, and black mask. ♂: violet forecrown and rear of mask. ♀: lacks violet; longer tail.

8 BROWN VIOLET-EAR *Colibri delphinae*
p. 136
UC, Maya Mtns. Brown plumage with black-and-cinnamon scalloping on rump and uppertail coverts; broad, dark subterminal tail band; iridescent green throat; conspicuous pale grayish malar mark; dark auriculars reflect violet in sunlight.

9 GREEN-BREASTED MANGO
Anthracothorax prevostii · p. 136
C on cayes, UC to FC on mainland. Medium-sized, mostly green hummingbird with moderately decurved, all-black bill. ♂: black median throat and upper breast bordered laterally by reflective blue; tail mostly blackish violet. ♀: white below, with distinctive dark median line from throat to belly; blue-black tail broadly tipped white.

10 VIOLET-CROWNED WOODNYMPH
Thalurania colombica · p. 137
Local and UC, foothills of s Maya Mtns. Medium size, with short, moderately decurved, all-black bill. ♂: glittering green throat, violet forecrown and upper back, forked violet-black tail. ♀: underparts pale gray with green flanks; dark, slightly notched tail tipped white; lacks white postocular mark.

PLATE **28** HUMMINGBIRDS

1 BLACK-CRESTED COQUETTE
Lophornis helenae · p. 136
R in s. half, forests. The smallest bird in Belize. Very short red bill with black tip; white rump band; greenish bronze spotted underparts. ♂: spectacular long, black-and-green filamentous crest; throat sparkling green with showy black-and-buff gorget feathers extending from lower throat. ♀: lacks showy crest and gorget; has blackish auriculars.

2 BLUE-THROATED GOLDENTAIL
Hylocharis eliciae · p. 137
Vagrant or R resident. Green above; golden tail and uppertail coverts highly conspicuous in good light, but otherwise appear grayish. Short black-tipped red bill. ♂: blue-violet throat. ♀: blue-violet specks on throat.

3 AZURE-CROWNED HUMMINGBIRD
Amazilia cyanocephala · p. 138
FC, pine woodland and savannas; also locally in broadleaf forest. Medium-sized, with green-and-brownish upperparts, white underparts, unmarked tail, and black-tipped red bill. Crown turquoise to violet blue, but mostly green in imm.

4 CANIVET'S EMERALD *Chlorostilbon canivetii*
p. 137
FC in n. two-thirds; savannas, other open areas. Small hummingbird with short, black-tipped red bill. ♂: emerald green; face and throat fluorescent green in reflected sunlight; tail deeply forked, blue black. ♀: white below, with white postocular stripe and pale grayish lower underparts. Slightly forked tail has black subterminal band; outer rectrices white at tip and base.

5 RUBY-THROATED HUMMINGBIRD
Archilochus colubris · p. 140
FC spring transient, UC in autumn and winter. Small hummingbird with short, black bill. ♂: ruby red throat outlined below in white; underparts whitish with greenish sides; moderately forked black tail. ♀: like **4** but with only

a tiny white postocular spot, whiter underparts; unnotched green-and-black tail, with white restricted to feather tips.

6 STRIPE-TAILED HUMMINGBIRD
Eupherusa eximia · p. 139
C in Maya Mtns. Rufous panel in wings. Inner webs of outer rectrices white—very conspicuous from below. ♂: emerald green nearly throughout. ♀: grayish white below.

7 WHITE-BELLIED EMERALD *Amazilia candida*
p. 138
FC nearly throughout, woodland. Green above, white below, with green flecking on sides. Auriculars green, not dusky. Straight bill with red on lower mandible. Tail has dark grayish subterminal band and lighter gray tip.

8 BUFF-BELLIED HUMMINGBIRD
Amazilia yucatanensis · p. 139
UC to locally C in north, primarily in savannas. Very similar to **9** but with cinnamon belly and undertail coverts and green-and-rufous tail.

9 RUFOUS-TAILED HUMMINGBIRD
Amazilia tzacatl · p. 138
C nearly throughout. Green above, with glimmering green throat and breast; grayish belly contrasts with cinnamon-rufous undertail coverts and white leg tufts. Tail rufous; bill red, tipped black. ♂: entire throat and breast glimmering green, belly grayish cinnamon. ♀: reduced amount of green in throat and breast; belly paler, grayer.

10 CINNAMON HUMMINGBIRD *Amazilia rutila*
p. 139
C on cayes, locally along coast. Like **8** and **9** but entire underparts cinnamon; mostly rufous tail.

11 SCALY-BREASTED HUMMINGBIRD
Phaeochroa cuvierii · p. 135
UC to FC in interior. Green above, with green mottling on throat and breast; belly dusky cinnamon. Small white postocular spot. Outer rectrices broadly tipped white. Bill all black.

PLATE **29**

TROGONS, JACAMAR, MOTMOTS, AND PUFFBIRDS

TROGONS: Red or yellow belly, prominent eye-ring; most have diagnostic white pattern on underside of tail.

1 VIOLACEOUS TROGON *Trogon violaceus* p. 141

FC to C throughout, woodland. Yellow belly, latticelike bars on undersurface of tail. Shorter-tailed than **3** (shorter than shown). ♂: yellow eye-ring, black hood with violet gloss, green back and rump, salt-and-pepper pattern in wing coverts (looks gray at a distance). ♀: incomplete white eye-ring, dull blackish hood, back and rump without iridescence, thin tail bars restricted to lateral edge of tail, wing coverts thinly barred black and white.

2 COLLARED TROGON *Trogon collaris* · p. 142

UC to FC, interior forests. Red belly, separated from breast by conspicuous white bar; yellow bill. ♂: iridescent green hood and upperparts; black face; red eye-ring; tail and wing covert pattern similar to that of **1**. ♀: hood and upperparts (including wing panel) noniridescent brown; incomplete white eye-ring; tail mostly gray.

3 BLACK-HEADED TROGON

Trogon melanocephalus · p. 141

C throughout. Yellow belly, pale blue eye-ring. Longer-tailed than **1** (tail on Violaceous shown is too long). ♂: hood black without iridescence; back blue green, becoming violet on rump; undertail mostly white, lacks latticelike tail bars. ♀: hood and upperparts dark gray; less white in tail; white more extensive than in **1**, but lacks thin latticelike bars. *Imm.* (not shown): white latticelike bars at base of outer rectrices.

4 SLATY-TAILED TROGON *Trogon massena* p. 142

FC, forests. Largest of the four trogons. Red belly without white breast bar. Bill and eye-ring orangish red. Tail dark gray. ♂: mostly iridescent green above; salt-and-pepper wing coverts. ♀: all gray except for red belly; gray extends farther down breast than in ♂; bill and eye-ring duller.

5 RUFOUS-TAILED JACAMAR

Galbula ruficauda · p. 146

UC to FC, except CO, woodland. Long, thin, daggerlike bill; metallic green, with rich cinnamon-rufous belly and undertail. ♂: white throat. ♀: cinnamon-buff throat.

MOTMOTS: Distinctive green-and-turquoise-blue birds with black mask. Head and bill rather large. Motmots have distinctive vocalizations given most frequently around dawn.

6 KEEL-BILLED MOTMOT *Electron carinatum* p. 143

UC to FC in Maya Mtns. and interior foothills, but restricted to undisturbed forest. Double black central breast spot; racketlike tail. Bare part of elongated central tail feathers generally less extensive than in **7**; bill distinctly broader when seen from below. Rufous forehead, turquoise blue above eyes and on chin. ♂: green breast. ♀: mustard yellow breast.

7 BLUE-CROWNED MOTMOT *Momotus momota* p. 143

FC to C throughout, forests. Like **6** but larger and with narrower bill (viewed from below); black crown, broadly bordered with turquoise blue.

8 TODY MOTMOT *Hylomanes momotula* p. 142

FC in s. two-thirds, forests. Much smaller than **6** and **7**, with shorter tail lacking racketlike extension. Rufous crown and nape, turquoise blue eyebrow, black mask bordered below by 2 white stripes.

PUFFBIRDS: Large-headed, large-billed birds with prominent whiskers and lax plumage. Sit motionless for long periods and often overlooked.

9 WHITE-NECKED PUFFBIRD

Notharchus macrorhynchos · p. 145

UC; open woodland, forest edge. Boldly marked, with black upperparts and breast band and broad white forecrown, collar, and belly.

10 WHITE-WHISKERED PUFFBIRD

Malacoptila panamensis · p. 145

UC to FC in south and west, forests. Brown above, with fine pale spots, streaked below; bushy white face and whiskers. ♂: cinnamon brown. ♀: gray brown, with more distinct pale spotting above.

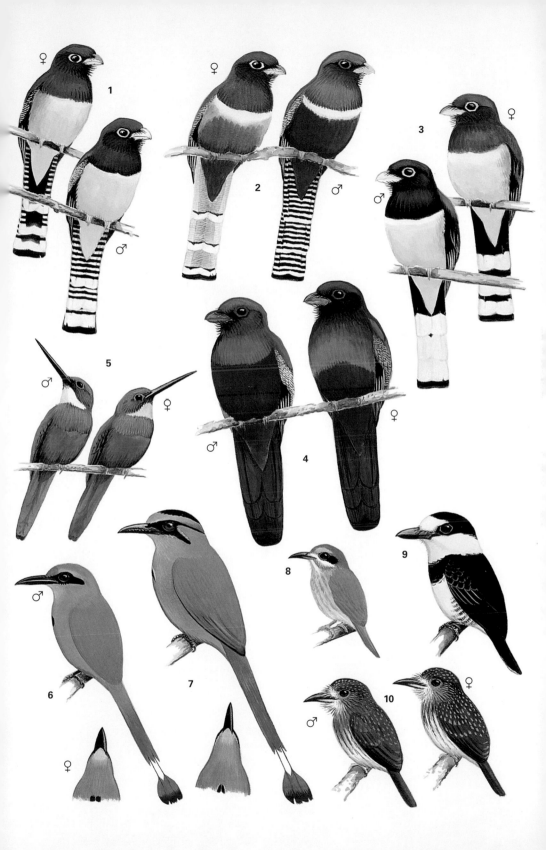

PLATE **30** TOUCANS AND KINGFISHERS

TOUCANS: All have grotesquely large, colorful bill.

1 COLLARED ARACARI *Pteroglossus torquatus*
p. 147
FC to C throughout, woodland. Striking black bird with large black-and-grayish-brown bill; yellow eyes; unfeathered reddish face, rump, and thighs; and yellow lower breast and belly, with black and red highlights.

2 KEEL-BILLED TOUCAN *Ramphastos sulfuratus*
p. 147
FC to C throughout, woodland. Unmistakable. Enormous green, orange, and blue bill with maroon tip. Black plumage with yellow foreparts, white uppertail coverts, and red undertail coverts.

3 EMERALD TOUCANET *Aulacorhynchus prasinus*
p. 146
C in mtns., UC and seasonal in foothills. Smaller than **1** and **2**, with large yellow-and-black bill, emerald green plumage, and chestnut undertail coverts.

KINGFISHERS: Blue or green birds with daggerlike bill, bushy crest, pale collar, and banded breast.

4 BELTED KINGFISHER *Ceryle alcyon* · p. 144
C in winter. Blue gray above, with broad white collar and gray breast band; crest often appears double-peaked. ♀: rufous band on upper belly and flanks. ♂: lacks chestnut belly band.

5 RINGED KINGFISHER *Ceryle torquata*
p. 143
FC to C throughout, most freshwater aquatic areas. Largest kingfisher in Belize. Like **4** but with entire belly rufous and much larger bill. ♀: blue-gray breast band bordered below with white; undertail coverts rufous. ♂: lacks blue breast band; undertail coverts white.

6 AMAZON KINGFISHER *Chloroceryle amazona*
p. 144
UC to FC, wooded streams. Slightly smaller version of **4**, with dark glossy green to blue-green head and upperparts and single-peaked crest. ♂: broad rufous breast band. ♀: green, often incomplete, breast band.

7 GREEN KINGFISHER *Chloroceryle americana*
p. 144
Locally C, wooded streams. Much smaller than **6**, with thinner bill and less of a crest. Wings spotted with white; outer tail mostly white. ♀: mottled green bands on breast and upper belly. ♂: broad rufous breast band.

8 AMERICAN PYGMY KINGFISHER
Chloroceryle aenea · p. 145
UC to locally C; wooded streams, ponds, lagoons. Tiny. Dark glossy green above; cinnamon below; hind collar pale cinnamon to nearly white; wings spotted with pale cinnamon. ♀: mottled dark green breast band. ♂: lacks green breast band.

PLATE **31** WOODPECKERS

1 GOLDEN-OLIVE WOODPECKER
Piculus rubiginosus · p. 150
FC throughout, woodland. Olive green, with bronzy wings; underparts barred olive and cream; gray crown, red nape, and pale face. ♂: red border of crown from nape to eyes, red malar stripe. ♀: no malar stripe, red restricted to nape.

2 GOLDEN-FRONTED WOODPECKER
Melanerpes aurifrons · p. 148
C throughout, open areas with trees. Black back and wings, with narrow white bars; head and underparts pale grayish buff; white rump. ♂: red crown and nasal tufts separated by pale forehead (only the subspecies n. of Belize have golden yellow nasal tufts). ♀: red restricted to nape and nasal tufts.

3 RED-VENTED WOODPECKER
Melanerpes pygmaeus · p. 148
FC in n.e., open woodland. Small short-billed, short-tailed version of **2**, with yellow nasal tufts. ♂: crown and nape red. ♀: red restricted to nape.

4 LADDER-BACKED WOODPECKER
Picoides scalaris · p. 149
UC to FC, lowland pine woodland and savannas. Black-and-white-barred upperparts (white bars broader than in **2** and **3**); black-and-white-patterned head; underparts dusky brown, with fine black bars and spots. Lacks white wing patch of **6**. ♂: red hindcrown, black-and-white-flecked forecrown. ♀: crown all black.

5 SMOKY-BROWN WOODPECKER
Veniliornis fumigatus · p. 149
FC throughout; woodland, second growth. Tawny brown back; duller, dark brown wings, tail, and underparts; paler on face. ♂: mottled reddish crown. ♀: dark brown crown.

6 YELLOW-BELLIED SAPSUCKER
Sphyrapicus varius · p. 149
UC in winter. Black-and-white-barred woodpecker with broad white patch in wing and yellowish underparts. *Imm.:* washed-out brownish barred back, head, and underparts; dingy, pale yellow underparts. *Ad.* ♂: red forecrown and throat; ♀ (not shown): white throat.

7 ACORN WOODPECKER
Melanerpes formicivorus · p. 147
FC to C, pine-oak woodland. Highly distinctive black-and-white woodpecker with red crown, yellow and white foreparts, clownlike appearance. ♂: no black in crown. ♀: black bar separates red hindcrown from white forecrown.

8 BLACK-CHEEKED WOODPECKER
Melanerpes pucherani · p. 148
FC in s. two-thirds, woodland. Like **2**, but with black mask and yellow nasal tufts, more heavily barred flanks and sides, and black-and-white-banded central tail feathers. ♂: red nape and crown. ♀: red on nape only.

9 PALE-BILLED WOODPECKER
Campephilus guatemalensis · p. 151
FC throughout, woodland. Large woodpecker with bushy, rounded crest and red head; lateral white line from neck through scapulars to lower back; barred underparts; whitish bill; pale yellow eyes. ♂: entire head red. ♀: forecrown black.

10 LINEATED WOODPECKER *Dryocopus lineatus*
p. 150
FC to C throughout, woodland. Like **9** but white line continues anteriorly through face to base of bill. Crest more pointed. ♂: crown, forehead, and malar region red. ♀: forehead and malar area black.

11 CHESTNUT-COLORED WOODPECKER
Celeus castaneus · p. 150
UC to FC, forests. Black-barred chestnut body with pale ochre head. Prominent crest, greenish yellow bill. ♂: red patch below eyes. ♀: lacks red.

PLATE **32**
WOODCREEPERS, FOLIAGE-GLEANERS,
AND LEAFTOSSERS

SMALL WOODCREEPERS: Small and slim, with short, straight bill; rufous hindparts.

1 WEDGE-BILLED WOODCREEPER
Glyphorynchus spirurus · p. 154
FC in south and west, forests. Pale brown supercilium; spotted and streaked face, throat, and breast; picklike bill, slightly upturned.

2 OLIVACEOUS WOODCREEPER
Sittasomus griseicapillus · p. 153
FC, woodland. Slightly larger than **1**, with slightly longer, slightly downcurved bill. Head and underparts gray.

MEDIUM-SIZED UNMARKED WOOD-CREEPERS: Relatively straight bill, shaggy crown. Ant followers.

3 RUDDY WOODCREEPER
Dendrocincla homochroa · p. 153
UC to FC, woodland. Rufous throughout except for gray eye-ring and lores. Shaggy crown.

4 TAWNY-WINGED WOODCREEPER
Dendrocincla anabatina · p. 153
FC, woodland. Brown body with bright tawny remiges and chestnut tail; pale brown throat and supercilium.

STREAKED, BARRED, AND SPOTTED WOODCREEPERS: Medium-sized to large woodcreepers with rufous rump and flight feathers. Most have relatively long, slightly decurved bill and streaked, barred, or spotted head, back, and underparts.

5 STREAK-HEADED WOODCREEPER
Lepidocolaptes souleyetii · p. 155
UC to locally FC, woodland. Small version of **6**, with thinner, slightly decurved bill, darker on upper mandible. Easily mistaken for **6** when size is difficult to judge. Best told by vocalizations.

6 IVORY-BILLED WOODCREEPER
Xiphorhynchus flavigaster · p. 154
C throughout. Streaked head, back, and underparts; pale supercilium and throat. Like **5**, but larger with proportionately heavier, all-pale bill with a nearly straight lower mandible.

7 STRONG-BILLED WOODCREEPER
Xiphocolaptes promeropirhynchus · p. 154
UC and local in west, forest. Largest of the woodcreepers, with the heaviest bill. Fine streaks on head, back, and breast not as prominent as in **5** and **6**. Contrasting white throat.

8 SPOTTED WOODCREEPER
Xiphorhynchus erythropygius · p. 155
FC in Maya Mtns. Like **6** but with spotted instead of streaked head, back, and underparts. Bill slightly shorter, and with dark upper mandible.

9 NORTHERN BARRED-WOODCREEPER
Dendrocolaptes sanctithomae · p. 154
Locally FC, woodland. Head, back, and underparts uniformly tawny brown, barred black. Long, relatively straight dark gray bill, lighter at base of lower mandible. Bars can be hard to see in deep shade; best seen on slightly paler breast.

FOLIAGE-GLEANERS: Brown, with rufous rump and tail, prominent "spectacles," and pale throat.

10 BUFF-THROATED FOLIAGE-GLEANER
Automolus ochrolaemus · p. 152
FC, forests. Forages close to ground in forest interior. Well-defined, ochraceous buff of throat extends laterally at the corners toward the nape. Sometimes shows diffuse mottling, but not scales, on upper breast.

11 SCALY-THROATED FOLIAGE-GLEANER
Anabacerthia variegaticeps · p. 151
Restricted to highest peak in s Maya Mtns. Forages in trees at epiphytes, vines, and tangles; often hanging upside down. Smaller than **10**, with shorter bill. Gray crown and auriculars; scaly-looking throat and upper breast.

LEAFTOSSERS: Predominantly dark brown ground and understory dwellers with short tail and moderately long bill.

12 TAWNY-THROATED LEAFTOSSER
Sclerurus mexicanus · p. 152
UC, higher elevations in Maya Mtns. Tawny rufous throat and upper breast; chestnut rump. Longer, thinner bill than **13**.

13 SCALY-THROATED LEAFTOSSER
Sclerurus guatemalensis · p. 152
Locally FC (except highest elevations), forests. Whitish speckled throat and upper breast. Shorter, thicker bill than **12**.

PLATE **33**

XENOPS, SPINETAIL, ANTBIRDS, AND ANTTHRUSH

1 PLAIN XENOPS *Xenops minutus* · p. 152
FC, forests. Small brown bird with short, up-turned bill; white malar stripe; thin buff supercilium; and rufous-and-black flight feathers.

2 RUFOUS-BREASTED SPINETAIL
Synallaxis erythrothorax · p. 151
FC, dense scrub. Long, spiny-tipped tail; rufous breast and wings; finely mottled black-and-white throat. Skulks in dense tangles.

ANTBIRDS: Diverse group exhibiting strong sexual dimorphism. Most have moderately thick bill with hooked tip, and many have spots in wing.

3 PLAIN ANTVIREO *Dysithamnus mentalis*
p. 157
UC and local in west, forests. Small and short-tailed, with short, moderately thick bill; much like a vireo. Whitish throat, darker breast, pale yellow belly, faint wingbars. ♂: grayer than ♀, with dark gray auricular patch. ♀: browner, with rufous crown and white eye-ring.

4 DUSKY ANTBIRD *Cercomacra tyrannina*
p. 157
C, except in far north, scrub and second growth. Medium-sized, with relatively thin bill, plain coloration. ♂: dusky gray, with rows of fine white spots in wing coverts. ♀: undistinguished; olive brown above and dull tawny brown below, with plain-looking face; no markings in wing; face and throat darker than in smaller **5**.

5 SLATY ANTWREN *Myrmotherula schisticolor*
p. 157
UC to FC, Maya Mtns. Smaller than **4**, with much shorter tail and thinner bill; not a skulker. ♂: slate gray, with black throat and central breast; rows of white dots in wing coverts. ♀: paler face and underparts than ♀ **4**; little altitudinal overlap.

6 DOT-WINGED ANTWREN
Microrhopias quixensis · p. 157
C in south, local in north; forests. Small, moderately long-tailed bird with thin bill. Conspicuous white dots and bar in wing. Carries graduated tail slightly spread, revealing white feather tips. Travels in small flocks. ♂: mostly black. ♀: slate gray above, rufous below.

7 RUSSET ANTSHRIKE *Thamnistes anabatinus*
p. 156
FC in Maya Mtns., UC in foothills; forest. Medium-sized, with heavyset hooked bill. Rufous wings and tail. Underparts and prominent supercilium pale buff. Head pattern and bill resemble those of a vireo.

8 BARE-CROWNED ANTBIRD
Gymnocichla nudiceps · p. 158
VU in south, second growth and scrub. Unfeathered blue skin on face. ♀: gray brown above, with cinnamon-rufous underparts and wingbars. ♂: black, with thin white wingbars and unfeathered blue face and crown.

9 BARRED ANTSHRIKE *Thamnophilus doliatus*
p. 156
C, second growth and forest edge. Strongly sexually dimorphic, medium-large antbird with crest and pale eyes, fairly thick bill. ♀: rufous above, ochraceous buff below; except for rufous crest, head striped black and white. ♂: barred black and white throughout.

10 WESTERN SLATY-ANTSHRIKE
Thamnophilus atrinucha · p. 156
FC in lowland forests of TO. Medium-sized, with moderately thick bill and barred and spotted wings. ♂: slaty gray, with black crown and center of back; wings black with feathers edged white; tail black, tipped white. ♀: olive brown above, with tawny brown crown; wings and scapulars dark brown, with pale buff feather edges.

11 GREAT ANTSHRIKE *Taraba major* · p. 155
FC in s. two-thirds, dense scrub and forest edge. Large antbird with red eyes and heavyset hooked bill. Both sexes clean white below, dark above. ♂: black above, with white wingbars. ♀: rufous above, without wingbars.

12 BLACK-FACED ANTTHRUSH
Formicarius analis · p. 158
FC to C, forests. Walks on forest floor. Plump, dipperlike ground bird with short tail and long legs; holds tail cocked. Brown above, gray below, with black face and throat, chestnut bar on upper breast, chestnut uppertail coverts, and cinnamon undertail coverts. Blue eye-ring.

PLATE **34**

TYRANNULETS, ELAENIAS, TODY-FLYCATCHERS, ETC.

SMALL TO MEDIUM-SIZED RESIDENT FLYCATCHERS: Mostly greenish to brownish, with a pale yellowish, greenish, or cinnamon wing panel. Bill shape, posture, behavior, and voice help to distinguish them.

1 NORTHERN BENTBILL *Oncostoma cinereigulare* p. 162
FC to C; forest and edge, scrub. Wings with greenish yellow feather edges; oddly decurved bill; lacks "spectacles" and flattened bill of **3**.

2 STUB-TAILED SPADEBILL
Platyrinchus cancrominus · p. 163
FC, forests. Tiny, with squat body, large head, and very short tail. Distinctive face pattern with whitish eye-ring, supercilium, and ear spot. Extremely broad bill evident when viewed from below.

3 SLATE-HEADED TODY-FLYCATCHER
Poecilotriccus sylvia · p. 162
Locally FC, dense scrub. Like **1** but with straight, flattened bill, bolder yellow wingbars, and white "spectacles"; horizontal posture.

4 COMMON TODY-FLYCATCHER
Todirostrum cinereum · p. 162
C except in CO, open woodland. White eyes set in jet black head; yellow underparts and feather edges in wing. Swishes cocked tail from side to side.

5 NORTHERN BEARDLESS-TYRANNULET
Camptostoma imberbe · p. 159
FC in north and east, UC in west and south; open woodland. Small, olive gray, with small bill and pinkish orange on lower half; short bushy crest. Indistinct pale wingbars, short supercilium, and eye-ring. Methodically pumps tail while foraging.

6 RUDDY-TAILED FLYCATCHER
Terenotriccus erythrurus · p. 164
UC, forests. Tiny and inconspicuous, but once seen, its gray-and-cinnamon plumage are highly distinctive.

7 YELLOW-BELLIED TYRANNULET
Ornithion semiflavum · p. 159
FC n. to OW. Tiny canopy dweller. Very short tail and bill; yellow underparts; bold white supercilium.

8 YELLOW-BELLIED ELAENIA
Elaenia flavogaster · p. 160
C, open woodland. Medium-sized brownish olive flycatcher with pale eye-ring; whitish wingbars and tertial edges. Crest nearly always raised, showing white feather bases. Highly vocal and social.

9 SEPIA-CAPPED FLYCATCHER
Leptopogon amaurocephalus · p. 161
UC to FC, forests. Dark sepia-brown crown, pale grayish face with dark postauricular crescent, and ochre wingbars. Perches nearly vertically. Curious habit of flicking one wing.

10 CARIBBEAN ELAENIA *Elaenia martinica* p. 160
Resident on Caye Caulker; Ambergris Caye in winter. Medium-sized grayish olive flycatcher with pale lemon-buff wing panel and indistinct wingbars; no eye-ring. Crest rarely raised.

11 GREENISH ELAENIA *Myiopagis viridicata* p. 160
C, woodland and edge. Most like **12** and **13**, but with narrower bill (as viewed from below); dark eye; flatter, more olive head; typically more vertical posture; different vocalizations. Concealed yellow crown patch.

12 YELLOW-OLIVE FLYCATCHER
Tolmomyias sulphurescens · p. 163
C, woodland and edge. Like **11** and **13** but with larger, rounder head, grayer than **11**; different posture; pale eyes (dark in juv.). When viewed from below, note broad-based bill. Typically perches more horizontally than **11** and seldom cocks its tail like **13**.

13 PALTRY TYRANNULET *Zimmerius vilissimus* p. 161
UC in s TO. Most similar to **11** and **12**, but with stubby bill and more pronounced supercilium extending well behind eyes. Typically perches horizontally, with tail slightly cocked.

14 SULPHUR-RUMPED FLYCATCHER
Myiobius sulphureipygius · p. 164
FC, forests. Ochre breast, black tail, conspicuous sulfur-yellow rump. Plain face sets off beady black eyes.

PLATE **35** TYRANT FLYCATCHERS AND MOURNERS

1 BRIGHT-RUMPED ATTILA *Attila spadiceus*
p. 170
FC, forest and edge. Oddly shaped, fairly large, noisy flycatcher with large head, prominent whiskers, and long, hooked bill. Angled lower mandible gives bill an upturned look. Conspicuous golden tawny rump. Perches upright, with tail drooped.

2 OCHRE-BELLIED FLYCATCHER
Mionectes oleagineus · p. 161
FC to C, forest and edge. Drab olive flycatcher with grayish lores and throat, faintly streaked olive breast, and ochre belly. Dark eyes stand out in plain face. Characteristically hovergleans insects and small berries. Nervously flicks one wing, like Sepia-capped (Plate 34).

3 EASTERN PHOEBE *Sayornis phoebe* · p. 169
Potential vagrant. Dark olive gray above; darker on head; wings have pale feather edges but lack wingbars. Whitish underparts with dusky sides; belly often pale lemon. Flicks tail downward.

4 BLACK PHOEBE *Sayornis nigricans* · p. 169
Local, fast-flowing streams. All black except for sharply contrasting white belly. Flicks tail down.

5 EYE-RINGED FLATBILL
Rhynchocyclus brevirostris · p. 162
UC to locally FC, forests. Large head and large eyes with thin but conspicuous white eye-ring. Diffusely streaked breast and pale yellow belly. Very broad-based bill. Perches upright, with slightly drooped tail.

6 ROYAL FLYCATCHER
Onychorhynchus coronatus · p. 163
UC to FC, forest and edge. Slender and brown, with fairly long bill and tail, prominent whiskers. Bright tawny rump, cinnamon tail. Spectacular crest rarely erected; when folded, projects from back of head.

7 VERMILION FLYCATCHER
Pyrocephalus rubinus · p. 169
FC to C in n. two-thirds, open country and savannas. Sexes very different. ♂ has distinctive hovering courtship flight. *Ad.* ♀: gray brown above; paler below, with streaked breast; rose-pink vent and undertail coverts. *Imm.* ♀: pale yellow lower vent and undertail coverts. *Ad.* ♂: brilliant red crown and underparts; dark brownish black upperparts, including nape and face.

8 THRUSH-LIKE SCHIFFORNIS
Schiffornis turdinus · p. 177
FC to C, forests. Forest interior. Brownish olive throughout; relatively plump with short tail; distinctive vocalization. Uncertain taxonomic relationship.

MOURNERS AND PIHA: These superficially similar plain rufous birds each have highly diagnostic vocalizations. Most taxonomists agree that the Rufous Mourner is a tyrant flycatcher, but the Speckled Mourner and Rufous Piha have uncertain taxonomic affinities.

9 RUFOUS PIHA *Lipaugus unirufus* · p. 178
UC to FC, forests. Largest of the three; rufous brown throughout; distinctly paler on throat and belly. Narrow gray eye-ring, larger bill, small tuft of feathers at base of bill.

10 RUFOUS MOURNER *Rhytipterna holerythra*
p. 170
UC to FC, forests. Smaller than **9**; rufous brown, with paler belly, but throat not contrasting lighter than rest of foreparts. Lacks gray eye-ring. Bill proportionately smaller.

11 SPECKLED MOURNER *Laniocera rufescens*
p. 178
R, forests. Similar in size and color to **10** but with mottled dark brown-and-rufous wing coverts, scaly-looking breast, distinctive yellow patch on sides (often covered by folded wings), stouter bill.

Adult
♂

Immature
♀

Adult
♀

PLATE **36**

EMPIDONAX, PEWEES, AND MYIARCHUS FLYCATCHERS

EMPIDONAX FLYCATCHERS: Small, similar-appearing flycatchers with eye-ring and wingbars. Best told by their vocalizations. Birds illustrated are in fresh plumage (autumn). Birds in worn, faded plumage may differ significantly from those illustrated, complicating ID.

1 LEAST FLYCATCHER *Empidonax minimus*
p. 168
C in winter, forest edge and scrub. Brownest empid, with less wing-back contrast than **2**; conspicuous white eye-ring and throat; short primary extension; relatively short tail and bill. *Call:* soft *pit* or *wit*.

2 YELLOW-BELLIED FLYCATCHER
Empidonax flaviventris · p. 166
C in winter, forests. Greener above than **1**; yellowish underparts, including throat; black wings contrast with green back; yellow eye-ring, usually with slight posterior projection. Moderate primary projection, tail length. *Call: peeup.*

3 ACADIAN FLYCATCHER *Empidonax virescens*
p. 167
UC to FC transient. Greenish like **2** but larger; whitish throat contrasts less with face than in others; even-width white eye-ring. Long primary projection; relatively long tail. Largest, broadest-based bill. *Call: peeip!*

4 ALDER and **WILLOW FLYCATCHERS**
Empidonax alnorum and *Empidonax traillii*
pp. 167, 168
FC transient. Essentially indistinguishable except by voice. Browner than **3**, with eye-ring thin to nearly absent; stronger head-throat contrast. Fairly long primary extension. *Willow's call: whit.* Alder's call: *pip.*

5 WHITE-THROATED FLYCATCHER
Empidonax albigularis · p. 168
R and local in winter, edge of marshes. Like **4** but warmer brown above, with buffy cinnamon wingbars and pale ochre flanks. Whiter throat flares onto side of neck. *Call:* rough, nasal *r-reeah.*

PEWEES: Darker and browner than *Empidonax,* with less wing-back contrast, no eyering, longer primary projection, and wingbars less well defined. Do not flick tail.

6 TROPICAL PEWEE *Contopus cinereus* · p. 165
FC, forest edge and open woodland. Flanks average duskier, and belly yellower, than in **7**.

Lower mandible orangish throughout. Shorter primary projection; slightly darker, more crested crown than in **7**. *Call:* typically a brief *pee-it.*

7 EASTERN WOOD-PEWEE *Contopus virens*
p. 165
VC transient. Paler underparts on average than **6**. Distal ⅓ to ½ of lower mandible dark. Longer primary projection. *Song:* sweet, mournful *peeaahh* to *peeeah weee.*

8 GREATER PEWEE *Contopus pertinax* · p. 165
FC in Mtn. Pine Ridge. Lacks bold white markings on undersides. Distinctly crested head; bright yellow-orange lower mandible.

9 OLIVE-SIDED FLYCATCHER *Contopus cooperi*
p. 164
UC transient, local in winter. Shorter, rounder crest than **8**. White underparts sharply delineate dark dusky sides and flanks. White tuft on side of rump may be visible above folded wings.

MYIARCHUS FLYCATCHERS: Olive brown above, pale yellow below, with gray throat and varying amount of rufous in flight feathers. All have peaked head, slender body, moderately large bill, distinctive vocals (see text).

10 DUSKY-CAPPED FLYCATCHER
Myiarchus tuberculifer · p. 171
C throughout. Smallest, darkest of group; like **13**, but with more peaked, brownish head; brown extends to lores and cheeks; brownish wingbars; pale cinnamon tertial edges.

11 GREAT CRESTED FLYCATCHER
Myiarchus crinitus · p. 171
C transient, less C in winter; forests. Medium-gray throat and upper breast, lemon yellow belly, extensive rufous in tail, flesh-colored base of bill.

12 BROWN-CRESTED FLYCATCHER
Myiarchus tyrannulus · p. 171
C summer resident, VU in winter. Like **11**, but paler gray throat contrasts more strongly with brown crown and less with pale lemon yellow belly. Upperparts paler, grayer; bill all dark.

13 YUCATAN FLYCATCHER
Myiarchus yucatanensis · p. 170
UC to C in north, woodland and edge. Paler, grayer lores than similar **10**, with gray in cheeks often extending over eyes; grayish wingbars; white-edged tertials. Head less peaked.

PLATE **37** KINGBIRDS, STREAKED FLYCATCHERS, AND DERBY FLYCATCHERS

FORK-TAILED FLYCATCHERS: Striking plumage; long, forked tail.

1 SCISSOR-TAILED FLYCATCHER

Tyrannus forficatus • p. 176

Locally FC in winter. Pale gray foreparts and black-and-white tail. *Ad.:* pink sides, brightest at bend of wing. *Juv.:* sides and flanks orange pink to pinkish yellow; much shorter tail.

2 FORK-TAILED FLYCATCHER *Tyrannus savana*

p. 177

C, savannas and pastureland. Highly gregarious. *Ad.:* lacks pink of **1**, has black head and longer, mostly black tail. *Juv.* (not shown): black mask and much shorter tail.

KINGBIRDS: Medium-large, moderately short-tailed flycatchers of open country; gray to olive above; white to yellow below.

3 GRAY KINGBIRD *Tyrannus dominicensis*

p. 176

Occas. on cayes and along coast. Gray head with dark mask, notched tail. Larger bill than in other kingbirds. In flight, underwing coverts nearly white.

4 TROPICAL and **COUCH'S KINGBIRDS**

Tyrannus melancholicus and *Tyrannus couchii*

p. 174

C (Couch's) to VC (Tropical) throughout, open areas. Virtually indistinguishable in the field except by voice. Even their habitats overlap broadly. Note dark mask, dull olive back, pale feather edges in wings, yellow underparts with dusky smudge across upper breast, white throat, and notched tail. To distinguish these from Western and Cassin's kingbirds (Fig. 24a,b), both of which occur as vagrants, see text.

5 EASTERN KINGBIRD *Tyrannus tyrannus*

p. 176

VC autumn and C spring transient, especially along coast. Mostly black above, with dark gray back; unnotched tail, tipped white. White below, with dusky smudge on breast. In flight, underwing mostly dark.

STREAKED FLYCATCHERS: Lightly to heavily streaked plumage.

6 SULPHUR-BELLIED FLYCATCHER

Myiodynastes luteiventris • p. 173

C summer resident, woodland. Heavily streaked on back, head, and underparts. Dark lateral throat stripe and chin. Lower underparts pale lemon yellow. Bill all dark.

7 STREAKED FLYCATCHER

Myiodynastes maculatus • p. 173

Local and UC summer resident, woodland. Thinner lateral throat stripes that do not connect across chin, and paler yellow underparts than **6**, with less streaking on belly. Bill heavier; lower mandible has pale base.

8 PIRATIC FLYCATCHER *Legatus leucophaius*

p. 173

FC summer resident, forest clearings and woodland. Intermediate between *Myiodynastes* (**6** and **7**) and *Myiozetetes* (**9**). Much smaller than the former and slightly smaller than the latter; diffuse streaking confined to breast; upperparts unstreaked; wing feathers edged white to pale lemon. Faint lateral throat stripe.

DERBY FLYCATCHERS: Moderately small to large, unstreaked flycatchers with black-and-white head pattern, and yellow underparts. All are very vocal.

9 SOCIAL FLYCATCHER *Myiozetetes similis*

p. 172

VC, open areas and forest edge. Much smaller than other two, with proportionately smaller bill. Head is dark gray and white. Lacks streaks and lateral throat mark of **8**.

10 GREAT KISKADEE *Pitangus sulphuratus*

p. 172

VC, open areas. Like **11**, but with smaller bill and rufous panel in secondaries. Vocalizations very different.

11 BOAT-BILLED FLYCATCHER

Megarynchus pitangua • p. 172

FC to C, forests and edge. Size of **10** but has larger (thicker and broader) bill and lacks rufous panel in wing.

Juvenile

1

Adult

2

Adult

3

4

8

5

7

9

6

11

10

PLATE **38** MANAKINS, BECARDS, COTINGA, AND TITYRAS

MANAKINS: Small, plump, short-tailed birds with large head; strong sexual dimorphism. Famous for forming courtship leks.

1 WHITE-COLLARED MANAKIN *Manacus candei* p. 181
C except in north; woodland. Yellow-orange legs; larger than **2**. ♂: very showy; black and white, with yellow belly and olive rump; throat feathers often fluffed to give throat an inflated appearance. ♀: olive with yellowish belly.

2 RED-CAPPED MANAKIN *Pipra mentalis* p. 181
FC to C, forests and edge. Smaller than **1**, with grayish legs. ♂: unmistakable, with its red head, white eyes, yellow thighs. ♀: dull olive throughout.

BECARDS: Relatively small birds, with short bushy crest.

3 CINNAMON BECARD
Pachyramphus cinnamomeus · p. 178
UC to FC, absent in north; forest interior and edge. Pale supraloral stripe, dusky lores and tawny underparts readily distinguish it from larger, bigger-eyed mourners (Plate 35). Lacks dark crown of Rose-throated and has graduated tail.

4 WHITE-WINGED BECARD
Pachyramphus polychopterus · p. 179
UC to FC in s. two-thirds; forest edge, open woodland. Strongly patterned bird, closely related to **5**. ♀: white spectacles; wing feathers and tail tip edged pale cinnamon. *Imm.* ♂: like ♀ but grayer head and throat, pale yellow edges to wing feathers, and more black in tail. *Ad.* ♂: black above, gray below, with white scapular bar, wingbars, and tertial edges. Hindneck black. Lacks pale supraloral stripe.

5 GRAY-COLLARED BECARD
Pachyramphus major · p. 179
R, forest and edge. ♂ much like **4**, ♀ more like **6**; both sexes have pale supraloral stripe. ♀: pale supraloral and black-and-cinnamon tail and wings readily distinguish it from ♀ **6**. *Imm.*

♂: variable; generally similar to adult ♂ but with cinnamon-brown back and rump, pale lemon-buff wing feather edges, pale grayish to creamy-white underparts. *Ad.* ♂: from **4** by paler gray underparts, with gray extending as collar around back of neck; pale supraloral.

6 ROSE-THROATED BECARD
Pachyramphus aglaiae · p. 179
C in north, UC in south; woodland and edge. Both ♂ and ♀ lack prominent pale edges to wing feathers and pale supraloral stripe. ♂: dark gray above, paler below, darker on crown; birds in north have rose coloring in throat; birds in south have rose reduced or absent. ♀: dark rufous above; ochraceous brown below; blackish crown; no prominent wing or tail markings.

7 LOVELY COTINGA *Cotinga amabilis* · p. 180
VU to R, forests. One of Belize's most beautiful—and rarest—birds. Plump body, with small round head and short tail. ♂: brilliant turquoise blue, with dark purple throat and belly; flight feathers black, broadly edged with turquoise blue. ♀: brownish gray, with scaly-looking white feather edges on back and speckling on head and breast; wings dark brown, edged with light brown.

TITYRAS: Two similar species in Belize: ♂s are mostly white, with black on head and flight feathers; ♀s have grayish brown back. The taxonomic relationship of tityras is uncertain.

8 BLACK-CROWNED TITYRA *Tityra inquisitor* p. 180
UC, woodland and edge. Relatively slender all-black bill. ♀: black crown with chestnut brown face and whitish forehead. ♂: black crown.

9 MASKED TITYRA *Tityra semifasciata* · p. 180
C, woodland and edge. Like **8**, but with unfeathered red face and heavyset black-tipped red bill. ♂: broad black border around red face. ♀: like ♂ but with black in head replaced by dark brownish gray.

PLATE **39** VIREOS

1 GREEN SHRIKE-VIREO *Vireolanius pulchellus*
p. 187
C, forests. All green, with yellow throat and
blue crown; heavyset bill. Sexes similar.

2 RUFOUS-BROWED PEPPERSHRIKE
Cyclarhis gujanensis · p. 187
FC in n.e. half, woodland and edge. Distinctive
medium-sized green-and-yellow bird with gray
head and rufous supercilium and forecrown.

3 RED-EYED VIREO *Vireo olivaceus* · p. 184
C to VC transient. Distinguished by gray crown
bordered laterally with thin black line; lacks
yellow on underparts. *Imm.* (not shown): dark
brown eyes.

4 BLACK-WHISKERED VIREO *Vireo altiloquus*
p. 185
Vagrant. Like **3**, but with less distinct facial
markings and dark brown eyes; thin lateral
throat stripe can be hard to see. Bill longer than
in **3**.

5 YELLOW-GREEN VIREO *Vireo flavoviridis*
p. 185
C summer resident, woodland. Like **3**, but with
dark brown eyes and mostly yellow underparts;
lacks sharp black border to gray crown.

6 YUCATAN VIREO *Vireo magister* · p. 185
C on cayes, local on mainland coast; mangroves
and littoral forest. Larger and browner than **3**,
4, and **5**, with supercilia that nearly meet across
forehead. Proportionately larger bill. Legs/feet
blue gray.

7 PHILADELPHIA VIREO *Vireo philadelphicus*
p. 184
FC transient, UC in winter; forest edge and
open woodland. Smaller and duller than **3**, with
shorter, stubbier bill. From **8** by dark lores,
yellow breast and throat. Birds in spring (not
shown) have much duller area of yellow. Thicker
bill, darker eyeline, and more sluggish actions
than in Tennessee Warbler.

8 WARBLING VIREO *Vireo gilvus* · p. 184
Vagrant. Like **7** but duller, grayish olive; never
has yellow on throat and breast but may have
pale yellow-buff sides and flanks. Pale lores.

9 YELLOW-THROATED VIREO *Vireo flavifrons*
p. 183
FC in winter, forests and edge. Yellow throat
and breast sharply separated from white belly;
blue-gray scapulars and rump; bold white wingbars; yellow spectacles.

10 PLUMBEOUS VIREO *Vireo plumbeus* · p. 183
FC in Mtn. Pine Ridge, Maya Mtns. Gray
above and white below, with white spectacles
and 2 bold white wingbars; often has olive tinge
to wings and rump, hint of pale yellow buff on
sides. Subspecies in Belize is smaller than bird
shown.

11 BLUE-HEADED VIREO *Vireo solitarius*
p. 183
Vagrant. Distinctive blue-gray head sharply set
off from green back and white throat; bright
yellow-buff sides and flanks; bold white spectacles and wingbars.

12 MANGROVE VIREO *Vireo pallens* · p. 182
C in lowlands nearly throughout, scrub and forest edge. Like **13,** but broad yellow lores and
thin, incomplete eye-ring do not give spectacled
appearance. Underparts, including throat, yellowish.

13 WHITE-EYED VIREO *Vireo griseus* · p. 182
FC to C in winter, scrub and forest edge. Like
12 but distinct yellow spectacles, white throat.
1st winter (not shown): dark eyes.

14 TAWNY-CROWNED GREENLET
Hylophilus ochraceiceps · p. 186
C, forests. Green above, with tawny crown and
white iris; ochre breast; no wingbars.

15 LESSER GREENLET *Hylophilus decurtatus*
p. 186
C, forests and edge. Tiny green vireo with gray
head, white throat, yellowish flanks, and thin
white eye-ring. Distinguished from rare Nashville Warbler by white throat and breast and different habits and habitat.

PLATE **40** GNATCATCHERS, JAYS, AND MIMIDS

GNATCATCHERS: Small blue-gray birds with white underparts and long, frequently cocked black-and-white tail.

1 BLUE-GRAY GNATCATCHER
Polioptila caerulea · p. 197
C in pine woodland; UC to FC in winter elsewhere. Blue-gray crown and plain face. ♂ *alt.:* thin black lateral crown stripe.

2 TROPICAL GNATCATCHER *Polioptila plumbea*
p. 198
UC to FC nearly throughout, broadleaf forest. Like **1** but with distinct white supercilium. ♂: black crown and thin postocular stripe accentuate white supercilium. ♀: like **1**, but thin gray postocular stripe and gray crown (slightly darker than back) accentuate white supercilium.

JAYS: Medium-large, inquisitive, raucous birds, usually found in small flocks. Sexes similar.

3 BROWN JAY *Cyanocorax morio* · p. 188
C to VC in most wooded areas. Large, raucous brown jay with white belly and white-tipped tail. *Ad.:* black bill. *1st year:* yellow bill and eyering.

4 GREEN JAY *Cyanocorax yncas* · p. 188
UC to FC, forest. Striking green-and-yellow jay with black-and-blue head and yellow eyes (dark in juv.).

5 YUCATAN JAY *Cyanocorax yucatanicus*
p. 188
C to VC in n.e., woodland. Striking blue-and-black jay and, like all jays, highly vocal. *Juv.:* white head and underparts, yellow bill and eyering. *Imm.:* white parts replaced with black. *Ad.:* like imm. but with black bill and no eyering.

MIMIDS: Medium-sized gray or black birds with medium-length tail and relatively small bill. Catbirds are somewhat inconspicuous inhabitants of scrub and second-growth woodland; mockingbird is conspicuous bird of open country.

6 TROPICAL MOCKINGBIRD *Mimus gilvus*
p. 203
C in open country, especially near settlements, mostly in north and east. Conspicuous gray-and-white bird with long, dark gray-and-white tail, white wingbars, and yellowish eyes.

7 BLACK CATBIRD *Melanoptila glabrirostris*
p. 202
C on Ambergris Caye and Caye Caulker; scattered populations on mainland in n.e. Jet black, with bluish gloss or sheen.

8 GRAY CATBIRD *Dumetella carolinensis*
p. 202
C in winter. Medium-dark gray, with black crown and chestnut undertail coverts.

1

♀

♂ Alternate

2

♀

♂

First Year

3

Adult

Adult

4

Juvenile

5

Immature

6

7

8

PLATE **41** SWALLOWS

ROUGH-WINGED SWALLOW COM-PLEX: Two resident populations in Belize and migratory birds from North America, all differing slightly.

1 RIDGWAY'S ROUGH-WINGED SWALLOW
Stelgidopteryx [serripennis] ridgwayi · p. 192
Locally C near limestone caves in interior. Noticeably darker than **2**. Blackish undertail coverts give base of tail a squared-off look. Tiny white spot on forehead noticeable at close range.

2 NORTHERN ROUGH-WINGED SWALLOW
Stelgidopteryx serripennis · p. 191
C in winter and local resident; open areas, especially in coastal plain. Brownish above; dusky throat and breast, fading to white on belly; light panel in underwing visible in flight. Paler than **1**, but relative darkness not always easy to discern. All-white undertail coverts form wedge on undertail. Resident birds have dark tips to some undertail covert feathers, thus somewhat convergent with **1**.

---

3 BANK SWALLOW *Riparia riparia* · p. 192
UC to C transient, especially in autumn along coast. Like **2** but slightly smaller, with distinct brown breast band. In flight, appears slimmer, with narrower wings. More direct flight with quick wingbeats and short glides, without lazy turns and sweeps of Rough-winged.

4 TREE SWALLOW *Tachycineta bicolor* · p. 190
C to locally VC in winter in north, much less C in south. Stark contrast between all-dark upperparts and clean white underparts. Larger, more heavyset, and broader-winged than **5**, with all-dark underwings. *Ad.:* dark metallic greenish blue above, contrasting sharply with white underparts. *Imm.:* dark brown above, white below.

5 MANGROVE SWALLOW *Tachycineta albilinea*
p. 191
FC (inland) to C (coast); rivers, lagoons. Smallest of the swallows; like **4** but with white rump and white underwing coverts. *Ad.:* metallic blue green above. *Juv.:* gray brown above.

6 BARN SWALLOW *Hirundo rustica* · p. 193
C to VC transient and local in winter. Deeply forked tail (except in molting birds and juveniles). Deep blue black above, with chestnut

forehead and throat and buffy cinnamon to pale buff lower breast and belly. White inner webs of undertail feathers visible when tail is fanned.

PETROCHELIDON SWALLOWS: Glossy blue black above and pale buff below, with buff to chestnut forehead, cinnamon to chestnut throat, and buff to chestnut rump; square-tipped tail.

7 CLIFF SWALLOW *Petrochelidon pyrrhonota*
p. 193
UC spring and C autumn transient, especially along coast. Pale buff forehead, pale rump, and square-tipped tail distinguish it from **6**. Chestnut throat and pale forehead distinguish it from **8**.

8 CAVE SWALLOW *Petrochelidon fulva* · p. 193
VU transient. Chestnut forehead, little contrast between cinnamon-buff throat and pale buff underparts. Square-tipped to slightly notched tail. *Pallida group:* pale cinnamon-buff rump. *Fulva group:* dark chestnut rump.

MARTINS: Larger and with bigger head than other swallows. [Throat not paler than breast, as mistakenly shown on plate.]

9 GRAY-BREASTED MARTIN *Progne chalybea*
p. 190
C breeding visitor, Jan.–Sept. Small for a martin and easily mistaken for a swallow in flight. Uniformly dark head and neck usually distinguish it from ♀ **10**, except when viewed directly from below. Tail averages less notched than in **10**.

10 PURPLE MARTIN *Progne subis* · p. 189
Relatively UC spring and C autumn migrant. Largest of the swallows in Belize. ♂: dark glossy blue black throughout. ♀: from **9** by pale forehead and collar, larger size, and more deeply notched tail, on average.

11 SNOWY-BELLIED MARTIN *Progne dominicensis*
p. 189
Vagrant. Strong contrast between white belly and uniformly dark breast and throat. ♂: dark, glossy blue black throughout except for sharply contrasting white belly and undertail coverts. ♀: similar to **9**, but with darker throat and breast contrasting more sharply with white belly (see text).

fulva

pallida

PLATE **42** WRENS AND GNATWREN

1 BAND-BACKED WREN
Campylorhynchus zonatus · p. 194
Local in s. half, woodland. Large, distinctive wren of the forest canopy. Much larger and longer-tailed than **3**, with boldly barred or streaked upperparts and prominent supercilium. Very harsh, raucous vocalizations. *Ad.:* spotted breast, black-and-white-barred back. *Juv.:* lacks spots; back streaked, not barred; buffy coloration.

THRYOTHORUS WRENS: Brown above, paler below, with conspicuous white supercilia and moderately long tail.

2 PLAIN WREN *Thryothorus modestus* · p. 195
Local in and near Mtn. Pine Ridge. Plain face with weak eyeline; unstreaked auriculars; unbarred cinnamon undertail coverts.

3 SPOT-BREASTED WREN
Thryothorus maculipectus · p. 194
C, woodland and scrub. *Ad.:* heavily spotted face, throat, and breast, cinnamon-brown flanks and belly. *Juv.* (not shown): lacks spots; similar to **2** and **4** but has dull plumage and indistinct marks on breast.

4 CAROLINA (WHITE-BROWED) WREN
Thryothorus [ludovicianus] albinucha · p. 195
Very local in OW and w CA, woodland. Like juv. **3** but has barred remiges and clean white underparts. Unlike **2**, has barred undertail coverts and bold eyeline that accentuates supercilium. Auriculars lightly streaked.

5 HOUSE WREN *Troglodytes aedon* · p. 195
C in towns and open scrub habitats on mainland. Plain brown wren with finely barred wings, tail, and undertail coverts; faint supercilium.

6 WHITE-BELLIED WREN *Uropsila leucogastra*
p. 196
C in north and west, woodland. Small, short-tailed wren with white supercilium. Smaller and shorter-tailed than **2** and **4** and has plain face with white lores. Lacks cinnamon flanks and undertail coverts of **2** and streaked auriculars of **4**.

7 SEDGE WREN *Cistothorus platensis* · p. 196
C in sedge savannas of ne TO and se SC; local in Mtn. Pine Ridge. Small wren with relatively long tail, which is typically strongly cocked. Streaked crown and back, barred wings and tail. Uniformly pale underparts.

8 WHITE-BREASTED WOOD-WREN
Henicorhina leucosticta · p. 196
C in south and west, less C in n.e.; forest interior and edge. Small, secretive, but highly vocal stub-tailed forest wren. White supercilium, black-and-white-barred auriculars; white throat and breast contrast with gray sides and cinnamon lower underparts. *Juv.* (not shown): pale gray throat and breast.

9 NIGHTINGALE WREN *Microcerculus philomela*
p. 197
FC in Maya Mtns. and foothills, including limestone hills in south; forest interior. Dark brown, virtually tailless wren with disproportionately long bill and legs. Rarely seen, but its unique song is frequently heard.

10 LONG-BILLED GNATWREN
Ramphocaenus melanurus · p. 197
C resident. Tangles, forest edge. Superficially wrenlike but more closely related to the gnatcatchers. Characterized by exceptionally long, thin bill and moderately long, graduated tail; cinnamon-colored face, breast, and flanks.

Juvenile

1

2

3

4

5

6

7

8

9

10

PLATE **43** WAXWING AND THRUSHES

1 CEDAR WAXWING *Bombycilla cedrorum*
p. 204
Sporadic late winter and spring visitor in small numbers. Grayish cinnamon brown anteriorly and blue gray posteriorly, with yellow-tipped tail, yellow belly, prominent crest, black face outlined in white, and waxy red extensions to inner secondaries. Typically seen in groups.

2 SLATE-COLORED SOLITAIRE
Myadestes unicolor · p. 199
C in Maya Mtns., occas. seen at lower elevations; forest interior. Slim, uniformly gray thrush with conspicuous white partial eye-ring and white lateral tail edges. One of the most accomplished songsters in the world.

3 EASTERN BLUEBIRD *Sialia sialis* · p. 198
UC and local in Mtn. Pine Ridge. Unmistakable blue-and-rufous plumage. ♂: brilliant blue upperparts; rufous throat, breast, and flanks; white belly. ♀: head and upper back gray, throat whitish, breast and flanks duller rufous than in ♂.

SPOT-BREASTED THRUSHES: Brown to rufous above, faintly to boldly speckled below. Three of the four species in Belize present an ID challenge.

4 VEERY *Catharus fuscescens* · p. 199
UC to FC transient, most often seen on cayes. Brown to reddish brown above and whitish below, with faint to fairly conspicuous spotting on breast. Gray flanks contrast with buff wash across breast. *C. f. salicicola* (shown) averages more distinct spots on upper breast; upperparts less rufous than in *C. f. fuscescens*. Not all individuals can be safely IDed to subspecies.

5 GRAY-CHEEKED THRUSH *Catharus minimus*
p. 199
UC transient, most often seen on cayes. Less frequent than **4**. Like **4** but lacks any hint of rufous in upperparts; face pale grayish, finely streaked darker; indistinct eye-ring; lacks buffy background color on face and breast of **6**.

6 SWAINSON'S THRUSH *Catharus ustulatus*
p. 200
FC to C transient and occas. in winter, woodland. Distinctive buff eye-ring and buffy wash across breast distinguish it from **5**. From **4** by buff eye-ring, distinct spots on breast, and olive flanks. Upperparts also lack rufous tones of **4**.

7 WOOD THRUSH *Hylocichla mustelina* · p. 200
C in winter, most woodland. Larger than preceding three, with rich rufous upperparts except for brownish olive rump and tail. Boldly spotted black on breast and flanks; brown-and-white-streaked auriculars; white eye-ring.

***TURDUS* THRUSHES:** Larger thrushes with yellow bills. Adults have unspotted breasts.

8 WHITE-THROATED ROBIN *Turdus assimilis*
p. 201
C in Maya Mtns., generally UC and local in foothills, occas. in coastal plain; broadleaf forest. Upperparts, breast, and flanks dark gray, becoming nearly black on head; black-and-white-streaked throat, with white band on lower throat. Bill, eye-ring, and legs bright yellow to orange yellow.

9 CLAY-COLORED ROBIN *Turdus grayi* · p. 200
C away from densely forested areas. Clay brown above, paler tawny buff below, streaked throat, yellow bill, flesh-colored legs.

PLATE **44** WOOD-WARBLERS

1 PROTHONOTARY WARBLER

Protonotaria citrea · p. 217

C autumn and UC spring transient. Striking golden yellow, green, and blue-gray bird with prominent white flashes in spread tail. *Ad. ♂:* golden yellow head and underparts to legs; prominent black eyes and bill. *Imm. ♀:* green extends to crown and face.

2 NORTHERN PARULA *Parula americana*

p. 207

UC (mainland) to C (cayes) in winter. Tiny; blue gray, with yellow throat and breast, olive back patch, and conspicuous white wingbars. *Imm. ♀:* unmarked yellow throat and breast; greenish wash on head and rump. *♂ alt.:* black face with prominent white eye crescents; black-and-rufous breast band; duller in basic plumage.

3 TROPICAL PARULA *Parula pitiayumi* · p. 208
FC in s Maya Mtns., UC in s CA; forest canopy. Sexes similar. Lacks white eye crescents and black-and-rufous breast band; wingbars thinner; yellow underparts extend nearly to undertail coverts.

4 GOLDEN-WINGED WARBLER

Vermivora chrysoptera · p. 205

UC to FC transient and VU in winter. Gray and white, with broad yellow wingbars and prominently marked head with yellow forecrown. ♂: black auriculars and throat, yellow forecrown and wing patch. ♀: black areas replaced with gray.

5 BLUE-WINGED WARBLER *Vermivora pinus*

p. 205

UC to FC transient and UC in winter. Yellow-and-green warbler with blue-gray wings and tail and white wingbars; thin dark line through eyes. ♂: mostly yellow head; black stripe through eyes. ♀: green extends into hindcrown and auriculars; line through eyes dusky.

6 LAWRENCE'S WARBLER

Vermivora chrysoptera × *Vermivora pinus*

p. 205

Vagrant. *Typical ♂:* green and yellow, with black face markings of **4**; wingbars white. ♀: duller, with indistinct face pattern, yellowish wingbars.

7 BREWSTER'S WARBLER

Vermivora chrysoptera × *Vermivora pinus*

p. 205

R in winter. *Typical ♂:* gray and white, with black eyeline, yellow forecrown, varying amounts of yellow on breast; yellow wingbars. ♀: duller.

8 GOLDEN-CROWNED WARBLER

Basileuterus culicivorus · p. 222

C in broadleaf forest interior. Grayish olive above and yellow below, with yellow central crown stripe bordered by black; yellow partial supercilium and eye crescents.

9 BLACK-THROATED BLUE WARBLER

Dendroica caerulescens · p. 210

UC to FC transient and winter visitor, primarily on n. cayes; scarce on mainland. Sexes radically different. ♀: dull olive brown above, dusky yellowish below, thin white supercilium, small white patch at base of primaries (sometimes absent). ♂: blue above, white below, with black face, throat, and sides.

10 RUFOUS-CAPPED WARBLER

Basileuterus rufifrons · p. 222

C in Mtn. Pine Ridge, less C on Vaca Plateau; small disjunct populations on e. side of Maya Mtns.; understory. Olive above and yellow below, with rufous crown and auriculars, white supercilium, and black eyeline. Frequently cocks its long tail.

11 GRAY-THROATED CHAT *Granatellus sallaei*

p. 222

Locally FC in north, R in south; understory. Short, thick bill. Cocks, fans, and flicks tail. ♂ and ♀ differ significantly. ♂: gray above and on throat and upper breast; rest of breast, central belly, and undertail coverts red; sides and flanks white; white supercilium behind eyes. ♀: brownish gray above, with rich buff supercilium and breast.

1

Immature ♀

Adult ♂

2

Immature ♀

Adult ♂

3

4

♂

♀

5

♀

♂

6

♂

7

♂

9

♂

♀

8

10

11

♀

♂

PLATE **45** WOOD-WARBLERS

1 BAY-BREASTED WARBLER *Dendroica castanea*
p. 215
FC spring and UC autumn transient. *Imm.*
♀: much like **2** but with dark gray legs, pale
buff undertail coverts, and unstreaked back. ♀
alt.: distinct pale neck patch, chestnut sides
and flanks. *Basic ad.* (not shown): similar to
♀ alt. but with bright green upperparts, grayish scapulars. ♂ *alt.:* black face; chestnut crown,
throat, sides, and flanks; pale buff neck patch.

2 BLACKPOLL WARBLER *Dendroica striata*
p. 215
R spring transient on cayes; autumn vagrant.
Autumn birds closely resemble **1**; ID with caution. ♂ *alt.:* distinctive black-and-white head
pattern. ♀ *alt.:* similar to ♂ but duller; crown,
face, and lateral throat stripe brownish and diffusely streaked. *Imm.* ♀: duller than **1** in similar
plumage, with streaks on back and sides, thinner wingbars, pale legs, and white undertail coverts; never has pinkish buff wash in flanks and
vent.

3 CHESTNUT-SIDED WARBLER
Dendroica pensylvanica · p. 209
C transient and FC (s.) to UC (n.) in winter.
Imm. ♀: lime green crown, back, and rump; pale
yellow wingbars; pale gray face and underparts.
♂ *alt.:* yellow crown, black facial stripe, chestnut sides. ♀ *alt.* (not shown): similar to ♂, but
features are less prominent.

4 BLACKBURNIAN WARBLER *Dendroica fusca*
p. 213
FC spring and UC autumn transient. Distinct pale streak on each side of back; bold
white wingbars; dark auricular patch; streaked
breast. *Imm.* ♀: olive green, with pale yellowish to orange-yellow face and throat. *Ad.* ♀ (not
shown): similar but with bright orange throat.
♂ *alt.:* mostly black above, with fiery orange face
and throat and bold white wing patch.

5 YELLOW-RUMPED (MYRTLE) WARBLER
Dendroica coronata · p. 211
FC (n.) to relatively R (s.) in winter. Yellow
rump and sides. *Basic* ♂: dull olive above, with
streaked back. *Basic* ♀ (not shown): similar, but
more diffusely marked throughout; throat may
be creamy white. ♂ *alt.:* blue gray above, with
black auriculars, black breast band, and bold
yellow patch on sides. Myrtle (the expected sub-

species in Belize) has triangular white throat
and pale supercilium. Vagrant Audubon's (not
shown) has rounded yellow (ad.) to off-white
(imm. ♀) throat; lacks supercilium.

6 GRACE'S WARBLER *Dendroica graciae* · p. 214
C in pine woodland. Blue gray above, yellow
throat and breast, mostly yellow supercilium,
white wingbars; lacks black-and-white face pattern of **7**. ♂ has black in forecrown.

7 YELLOW-THROATED WARBLER
Dendroica dominica · p. 213
FC to C in winter. Like **6**, but with black face,
white neck patch, and more boldly streaked
sides. ♂ has black in crown. *D. d. albilora:* white
supercilium throughout. *D. d. dominica* (occas.
on cayes): supercilium yellow in front of eyes.

8 BLACK-THROATED GREEN WARBLER
Dendroica virens · p. 212
FC to C in winter. Unstreaked green upperparts, white wingbars, yellow face with green
auricular patch, streaked sides, pale yellow vent
area (between legs). *Imm.* ♀: yellowish throat,
finely streaked sides. *Ad.* ♂: black throat and
upper breast (♀ alt. often lacks black in throat).

9 CERULEAN WARBLER *Dendroica cerulea*
p. 216
UC spring (and VU autumn) transient. Blue
to aqua green above; white to pale yellowish
below; bold white wingbars. *Ad.* ♂: blue above;
white throat set off with dark breast band. *Ad.*
♀: blue green above; broad pale supercilium.
Imm. ♀: aqua green above; broad supercilium;
throat and breast pale yellowish; white undertail
coverts.

10 MAGNOLIA WARBLER *Dendroica magnolia*
p. 209
C in winter. Yellow rump and throat and rectangular pattern of white in tail distinguish it.
Imm. ♀: grayish head, green back, yellow underparts, faint flank streaks. ♂ *alt.:* unmistakable.

11 CAPE MAY WARBLER *Dendroica tigrina*
p. 210
UC in winter, principally on n cayes. Yellow
to yellow-green rump; yellowish neck. *Imm.* ♀:
streaked breast; smaller than **5**, with unstreaked
back and indistinct yellowish neck patch (sometimes absent). ♀ *alt.:* yellow neck patch. ♂ *alt.:*
chestnut auriculars, yellow neck, bold white
wing patch.

Immature
♀

1

Alternate

♂
Alternate

♀ Alternate

♂ Alternate

♀ Alternate

2

Immature ♀

Immature ♀

4

♂
Alternate

♂
Alternate

3

Immature ♀

6

♂

♂ albilora

7

♂ dominica

♂ Basic

5

♂ Alternate

Adult ♂

Adult ♀

9

Immature
♀

Adult
♂

8

Immature
♀

♂
Alternate

11

Immature
♀

10

Immature
♀

♂ Alternate

♀ Alternate

PLATE **46** WOOD-WARBLERS

1 MANGROVE WARBLER *Dendroica petechia* (*erithachorides* group) · p. 209
VC in mangroves. Yellow edges to all wing feathers diagnostic. *Ad. ♂:* prominent chestnut hood; thin chestnut streaks on breast. *Imm. ♀:* dullest birds are mostly gray above, with green confined primarily to rump; yellow confined to undertail coverts and suffusion across breast; yellow to white eye-ring. Virginia's (Plate 47) lacks pale-edged flight feathers, pumps tail.

2 YELLOW WARBLER *Dendroica petechia* (*aestiva* group) · p. 208
C in winter. Black eyes stand out in plain yellow face. *Ad. ♂:* red breast streaks (less prominent in imm.); lacks chestnut hood. ♀: lacks red streaks. *Imm. ♀* (not shown): duller and paler than adult ♀, but never with strong gray tones like imm. ♀ **1**.

3 WILSON'S WARBLER
Wilsonia pusilla · p. 221
UC (cayes and coast) to FC (mtns.) in winter. Like ♀ **2** but darker green above; lacks yellow edges to flight feathers (undertail grayish; yellow in **1** and **2**). *Ad. ♂:* black cap (reduced in ♀). *Imm. ♀:* lacks black in cap.

4 PRAIRIE WARBLER *Dendroica discolor* · p. 214
FC transient, UC in winter, on cayes; R on mainland. Pale supercilium and lower eye crescents; yellowish wingbars; pumps tail. *Imm. ♀:* grayish wash on head; faint streaks and dusky smudge on sides. *Ad. ♂:* yellow face with prominent black markings; black streaks on sides; rufous streaks in back. *Ad. ♀ and imm. ♂* (not shown): reduced areas of black.

5 HOODED WARBLER *Wilsonia citrina* · p. 221
C in winter. Constantly fans tail, flashing white inner webs. ♂: yellow face bordered by black hood. ♀: variable; hood complete (like ♂) to nearly lacking. *Imm. ♀:* from **3** by sharp outline of yellow mask behind eyes, larger size, longer tail, and white tail flashes.

6 CANADA WARBLER *Wilsonia canadensis*
p. 221
UC autumn transient, principally on cayes; vagrant in spring. Blue gray to greenish gray above; yellow below except for white undertail coverts; white eye-ring; yellow supraloral spot; faint to strong breast streaks. ♂ *alt.:* bold band of black streaks across breast. *Imm. ♀:* greenish cast to plumage; faint breast streaks.

7 PALM WARBLER *Dendroica palmarum* · p. 214
C transient and FC in winter, on cayes; UC on mainland. Yellow undertail coverts, streaked underparts, and habit of pumping tail. *Basic:* yellow confined to undertail coverts; rump yellow green; conspicuous supercilium. *Alt.:* yellow throat and supercilium, chestnut crown.

8 MOURNING WARBLER *Oporornis philadelphia*
p. 220
FC transient, mostly in spring on cayes; UC on mainland. Skulker. Green above, yellow below, including undertail coverts. Hops; does not walk. *Imm.:* olive-gray wash in head; thin broken eye-ring, pale supraloral; partial dusky olive breast band. *Ad. ♀:* gray hood with paler throat; eye-ring, when present, is nearly complete. *Ad. ♂:* darker gray hood with black lower throat and upper breast; no eye-ring.

9 CONNECTICUT WARBLER *Oporornis agilis*
p. 219
Possible vagrant. Bold white eye-ring of even thickness; complete gray (ad.) or brown (imm.) hood contrasts sharply with rest of underparts. Lores do not contrast darker or lighter. Undertail coverts extend nearly to tail tip. Walks rather than hops. *Imm.:* brownish hood, paler throat. *Ad. ♂:* full gray hood.

10 COMMON YELLOWTHROAT *Geothlypis trichas*
p. 220
C in winter. Yellow throat and undertail coverts, whitish on breast and belly. Skulker. ♀: like imm. **8** but lacks any semblance of hood. *Ad. ♂:* black mask (less prominent in imm.) bordered above with white.

11 GRAY-CROWNED YELLOWTHROAT
Geothlypis poliocephala · p. 220
C, primarily in pine savannas, s. locally to s TO. Thick-billed, long-tailed warbler; green above; yellow below. ♀: black in face restricted to lores. ♂: gray crown; black extends to forehead.

12 KENTUCKY WARBLER *Oporornis formosus*
p. 219
C in winter in south, less C in north. Distinctive black-and-yellow face pattern. *Ad. ♀* shown. ♂: more extensive black on sides of throat. *Imm. ♀:* black much reduced to nearly absent.

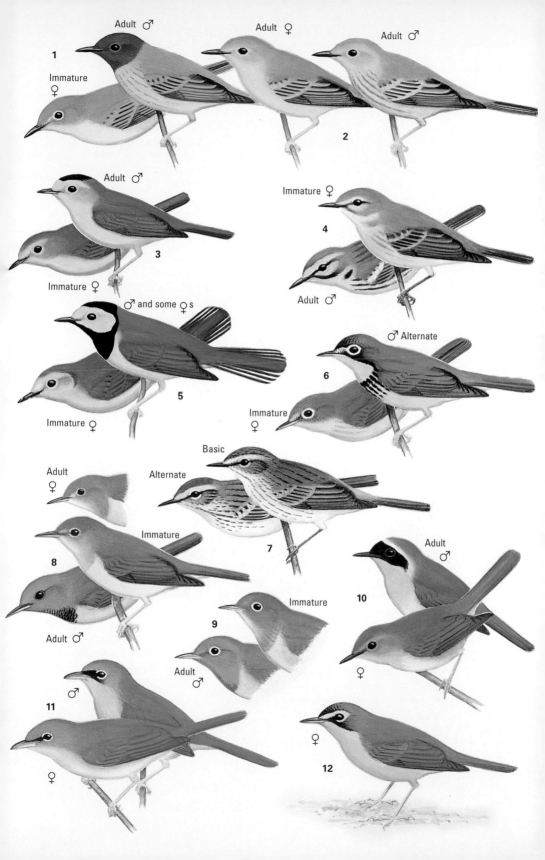

Adult ♂

Adult ♀

Adult ♂

1

Immature ♀

2

Adult ♂

3

Immature ♀

Immature ♀

4

Adult ♂

♂ and some ♀s

♂ Alternate

5

6

Immature ♀

Immature ♀

Basic

Alternate

Adult ♀

Immature

8

7

Adult ♂

Immature

9

Adult ♂

Adult ♂

10

♂

♀

11

♀

12

PLATE **47** WOOD-WARBLERS

1 BLACK-AND-WHITE WARBLER
Mniotilta varia · p. 216
C in winter. Heavily striped black and white above, variable amounts of streaking below. ♂ *alt.:* black throat and auriculars, heavy black streaks below. *Imm.* ♀: white throat, thin or diffuse streaking below, buffy flanks and face. *Ad.* ♀ *and imm.* ♂ (not shown): lack buff tones.

2 AMERICAN REDSTART *Setophaga ruticilla*
p. 216
C in winter. Typically holds tail cocked and spread. ♀: olive above; grayish head; yellow flashes in wings, tail, and sides. *Ad.* ♂: black throughout except for white belly and orange-red flashes. 1st alt. ♂ (not shown): similar to ♀ but with yellow-orange sides and black lores, sometimes with black flecking elsewhere.

3 TENNESSEE WARBLER *Vermivora peregrina*
p. 206
C transient and UC in winter. Tiny greenish warbler with short, thin bill; thin but distinct supercilium; thin pale wingbar; and white undertail coverts. *Imm.:* greenish head; yellow-buff throat and breast. *Ad.* ♀: less buff below, grayish crown. ♂ *alt.:* gray head, all white below.

4 ORANGE-CROWNED WARBLER
Vermivora celata · p. 206
Vagrant. Like imm. **3** but duller, olive gray above, and faintly and diffusely streaked below, with yellowish undertail coverts and less prominent supercilium; lacks thin wingbar of **3**.

5 NASHVILLE WARBLER *Vermivora ruficapilla*
p. 207
Occas. in winter. Gray head, green back, mostly or all-yellow underparts, white eye-ring. *Imm.* (not shown): duller throughout, but same basic pattern. Western subspecies pumps tail.

6 VIRGINIA'S WARBLER *Vermivora virginiae*
p. 207
Vagrant. Mostly gray above, with yellow-green rump, yellow undertail coverts and breast patch, and white eye-ring; pumps tail. *Ad.* ♂ (shown): more extensive yellow in breast than ♀ and has concealed red crown patch. *Imm.:* duller; similar to some imm. ♀ Mangrove Warblers (Plate 46) but lacks yellow edges to wing and tail feathers.

7 WORM-EATING WARBLER
Helmitheros vermivorus · p. 217
UC to FC in winter. Brownish olive above; rich buff head and underparts, with black stripes in head.

8 SWAINSON'S WARBLER
Limnothlypis swainsonii · p. 217
UC and secretive winter visitor, with most records from cayes. Olive brown above, with warm brown crown; broad whitish supercilium; unstreaked below. Flat-headed; bill long and spikelike.

9 OVENBIRD *Seiurus aurocapilla* · p. 218
C transient, FC in winter. Olive above; boldly streaked below; orange crown bordered by black; white eye-ring. Characteristically walks on ground with erect posture and cocked tail.

10 NORTHERN WATERTHRUSH
Seiurus noveboracensis · p. 218
C in winter. Brown above and pale yellowish white to white below, with bold black streaking. Fine streaks in throat. Off-white supercilium tapers to a point posteriorly. Horizontal posture; pumps posterior like Spotted Sandpiper.

11 LOUISIANA WATERTHRUSH *Seiurus motacilla*
p. 218
FC transient; UC to FC in winter principally in interior. Like **10**, but heavier-bodied; white below, with pinkish buff flanks; immaculate white supercilium does not taper posteriorly; central throat usually unstreaked, and streaks on upper breast are less dense. Tail pumping slower and more exaggerated.

12 YELLOW-BREASTED CHAT *Icteria virens*
p. 222
C transient, UC to FC in winter. Skulker. Large and un-warblerlike with thick, tanager-like bill. Olive above, yellow throat and breast, white spectacles. ♂: lores black. ♀ (not shown): dark gray lores.

♂ Alternate

1

Immature ♀

Adult ♂

2

♀

♂ Alternate

3

Adult

5

♀

Immature

♂ Alternate

6

4

7

8

9

10

11

♂

12

PLATE **48** TANAGERS

1 COMMON BUSH-TANAGER

Chlorospingus ophthalmicus · p. 224

VC at high elevations in Maya Mtns.; broadleaf forest. Small; thickset bill; white patch behind eyes; dark gray head; white throat; pale yellow breast, flanks, and undertail coverts.

2 BLUE-GRAY TANAGER *Thraupis episcopus*

p. 228

C nearly throughout, but scarce in n.e.; open woodland. Pale grayish blue body, with bright turquoise blue wings and tail.

3 YELLOW-WINGED TANAGER *Thraupis abbas*

p. 229

C in south and west, local in n.e.; open woodland. Lilac blue, becoming dusky blue on back, olive on underparts; black wings and tail with distinctive yellow patch at base of remiges.

4 ROSE-THROATED TANAGER

Piranga roseogularis · p. 226

UC to FC in n. third of country; forest interior. Grayish, with red or yellow highlights; conspicuous white eye-ring. ♂: red crown and uppertail coverts; rose-red throat and undertail coverts. ♀: yellow-olive crown and wing feather edges, yellow throat and undertail coverts.

5 GRAY-HEADED TANAGER

Eucometis penicillata · p. 224

FC; forest understory. Olive green above and yellow below, with gray hood and short crest. Follows ant swarms. ♀ **8** is larger, with less distinct hood, tawny brown upperparts, and larger, hooked bill; found in higher forest strata.

ANT-TANAGERS: Conspicuously noisy, all-dark forest tanagers best distinguished by their distinctive vocalizations. Typically found in lower forest strata, where they often follow ant swarms.

6 RED-CROWNED ANT-TANAGER *Habia rubica*

p. 225

C at higher elevations, less C to locally absent at lower elevations; forests. Slightly smaller than **7**, with slightly shorter bill and moderately pale lores. ♂: central crown stripe thinly bordered with black. ♀: tawny crown patch; throat only slightly lighter; bill pale below, especially at base.

7 RED-THROATED ANT-TANAGER

Habia fuscicauda · p. 225

C to VC in lowlands, less C than **6** at higher elevations; forests. Slightly larger than **6**, with longer bill (best in direct comparison) and darker lores. ♂: usually lacks thin black border on crown. ♀: lacks crown patch and has paler throat than ♀ **6**; bill all black.

8 BLACK-THROATED SHRIKE-TANAGER

Lanio aurantius · p. 224

UC to C in forested south and west. Found in mixed-species flocks in mid- and upper strata. ♂: highly distinctive black-and-yellow bird; superficially like an oriole, but chunkier, with shorter, thicker, hooked bill. ♀: dirty olive-gray hood and tawny brown upperparts.

PLATE **49** TANAGERS

1 CRIMSON-COLLARED TANAGER
Ramphocelus sanguinolentus · p. 228
FC in s. two-thirds; brush and scrub. Black, with crimson crown, collar, breast, and tail coverts; bluish white bill. Sexes similar.

2 HEPATIC TANAGER *Piranga flava* · p. 226
UC (n.) to C (s.) in pine woodland. Dusky auriculars, large dark gray bill. ♂: brick red throughout. ♀: grayish olive above, ochraceous yellow below.

3 SUMMER TANAGER *Piranga rubra* · p. 226
C in winter. Lacks dusky auriculars of **2**; pale bill. ♂: bright red throughout. ♀: mustard olive above, mustard yellow below; some individuals washed pinkish to orangish throughout; wings do not contrast darker than back; underside of tail greenish. *1st-year* ♂ (not shown): like ♀ but with variable amounts of red concentrated on head and breast.

4 FLAME-COLORED TANAGER
Piranga bidentata · p. 227
Found only on Mt. Margaret CA. Dusky crescent on rear edge of auriculars; gray bill. ♂: orange red, with black wings and tail, black-streaked back, and prominent white wingbars and tertial spots. ♀: olive above and yellow below, with same basic pattern as ♂.

5 WESTERN TANAGER *Piranga ludoviciana*
p. 227
Vagrant. Bill horn-colored. *Basic* ♂: yellow, with black wings, back, and tail; feathers of back edged olive; upper wingbar yellow; lower wing-bar white; face may have suffusion of red. ♂ *alt.:* vivid red face and all-black back. ♀: olive above; yellow olive below and on rump; upper wingbar pale yellow; lower whitish; some ♀s (not shown) have gray back, little yellow underneath, and both wingbars white.

6 SCARLET TANAGER *Piranga olivacea* · p. 226
C autumn and less C spring transient. Bill smaller than in other similar tanagers; diagnostic white underwing coverts in all plumages. ♀: olive green above; yellowish below, brightest on undertail coverts (not shown); darker wings and tail; underside of tail gray. *Basic* ♂: yellow olive above and paler below, with jet black wings and tail. ♂ *alt.:* bright scarlet, with jet black wings and tail.

7 WHITE-WINGED TANAGER *Piranga leucoptera*
p. 227
FC at higher elevations, occas. at lower elevations in interior; forests. Small tanager with stubby bill. ♂: bright red, with black face, wings, and tail; bold white wingbars. ♀: smaller than ♀ **5**, with shorter, darker bill; richer olive above sharply contrasting with yellow below; nearly black wings, with 2 prominent white wingbars.

8 PASSERINI'S TANAGER *Ramphocelus passerinii*
p. 228
C in s. half of country; roadside brush. Bill bluish white. Unlike **1**, highly sexually dimorphic. ♂: black, with vivid scarlet rump and tail coverts. ♀: tawny brown above, with grayish head, bright tawny rump, and tawny ochre breast.

PLATE 50
BANANAQUIT, HONEYCREEPERS, EUPHONIAS, ETC.

1 BANANAQUIT *Coereba flaveola* · p. 223
VC at high elevations, less C in lowlands in s. half and on n. cayes; broadleaf forests and edge. Dark above and yellow below, with pale throat, white supercilium, white patch at base of primaries, and thin, downcurved bill. Distinctive white-throated, dark-backed *C. f. caboti* restricted to Ambergris Caye and Caye Caulker. Mainland *C. f. mexicana* has gray throat and paler back.

2 GOLDEN-HOODED TANAGER *Tangara larvata*
p. 231
FC to C in s. two-thirds in both pine and broadleaf forest. One of Belize's most beautiful birds: golden head with violet, blue, and black face; black body with turquoise rump, violet and turquoise shoulder patch and flanks, and white belly.

HONEYCREEPERS: Small nectarivorous tanagers with thin, down-curved bill. ♂s brightly colored.

3 GREEN HONEYCREEPER *Chlorophanes spiza*
p. 231
UC to FC in south and west in broadleaf forest. Larger than **4** or **5**, with yellow lower mandible and gray legs. ♂: glossy blue-green body, partial black hood, red eyes. ♀: flat green throughout, slightly paler below; less yellow in bill.

4 RED-LEGGED HONEYCREEPER
Cyanerpes cyaneus · p. 231
Seasonally C nearly throughout in most wooded habitats. Red legs; underwings bright yellow. ♂ *alt.:* deep blue, with turquoise crown and black wings, back, tail, and mask. *Basic ♂:* green above; streaked with yellow below; wings and tail black. ♀: green above; streaked yellow on underparts; dark lores; dull red legs.

5 SHINING HONEYCREEPER *Cyanerpes lucidus*
p. 231
FC at higher elevations in Maya Mtns., UC to scarce in foothills; broadleaf forest. Smaller than **4**, with shorter bill and tail and bright yellow legs. ♂: similar to ♂ alt. **4**, but with blue

back and black throat; lacks turquoise crown. ♀: like ♀ **4**, but with pale lores, blue lateral throat stripe, and blue-and-green-streaked breast and flanks.

EUPHONIAS: Tiny, plump tanagers with short tail and short, rounded, finchlike bill.

6 ELEGANT EUPHONIA *Euphonia elegantissima*
p. 230
R to VU in Maya Mtns. and Vaca Plateau; broadleaf forest. Turquoise blue crown and nape; chestnut forehead. ♂: blue-black face, throat, and upperparts; ochraceous orange underparts. ♀: olive above and paler below, with cinnamon throat.

7 YELLOW-THROATED EUPHONIA
Euphonia hirundinacea · p. 229
The most common and widespread euphonia in Belize; found throughout in most wooded habitats. ♂: glossy blue black, with yellow forehead and underparts, including throat and undertail coverts. ♀: olive above and whitish to pale gray below, with yellow sides, flanks, and undertail coverts.

8 WHITE-VENTED EUPHONIA *Euphonia minuta*
p. 230
UC and local in south; broadleaf forest. ♂: similar to **9**, but smaller, with white undertail coverts and orange-yellow underparts. ♀: throat pale gray; yellow extends across breast; white belly and undertail coverts.

9 SCRUB EUPHONIA *Euphonia affinis* · p. 229
FC (n.) to UC in most wooded habitats. ♂: full black hood, yellow forehead and underparts. ♀: olive above, with grayish wash on crown and nape; dusky olive below, with yellow belly and undertail coverts.

10 OLIVE-BACKED EUPHONIA *Euphonia gouldi*
p. 230
C in forest and forest edge throughout except CO. ♂: olive green, with bluish sheen above; yellow forehead; chestnut belly and undertail coverts. ♀: chestnut forehead and undertail coverts; yellow-olive underparts.

mexicana

caboti

1

2

4

♀

♂ Basic

♂ Alternate

♂

3

♀

5

♂

♀

7

♀

♂

6

♂

♀

8

♂

♀

10

♀

♂

9

♂

♀

PLATE **51**

SEEDEATERS, BUNTINGS, AND "BLUE" GROSBEAKS

SEEDEATERS: Small buntinglike birds; ♀s brownish; ♂s black, blue black, black-and-white, or gray.

1 THICK-BILLED SEED-FINCH
Oryzoborus funereus · p. 234
FC to C s. of CO; forest edge, savannas. Thick-based, conical black bill with straight culmen. No angle between bill and slope of forehead. ♂: black, with small white patch at base of primaries (not always visible). ♀: rich dark brown throughout.

2 VARIABLE SEEDEATER *Sporophila americana*
p. 233
C to VC in s. two-thirds; fields and forest edge. Like **1** but smaller, with shorter tail and smaller bill with rounded culmen. ♂: glossy black, with small white patch at base of primaries. ♀: brownish olive throughout, paler below.

3 SLATE-COLORED SEEDEATER
Sporophila schistacea · p. 233
UC and local nomadic resident in south and west; forest edge. ♂: lead gray, with white lower underparts, small white flashes in head and wings, and yellow bill. ♀: olive brown above; dirty buff below, becoming pale yellowish on lower underparts; dark gray bill; paler and browner than ♀ **2**.

4 WHITE-COLLARED SEEDEATER
Sporophila torqueola · p. 233
VC, fields and forest edge. *Basic* ♂: mottled black-and-buff breast band, olive-gray back, buff lower breast and belly. ♂ *alt.:* plumage acquired as pale feather tips wear down; back becomes black; breast collar loses buff fringes; lower breast and belly fade to near white. ♀: olive brown; 2 buff to whitish wingbars.

5 BLUE-BLACK GRASSQUIT
Volatinia jacarina · p. 232
C to VC, fields. Small bill with straight culmen. ♂ *alt.:* plumage acquired through feather wear; glossy blue black throughout; conspicuous white axillars in flight. *Basic* ♂: heavily mottled brown and blue black throughout. ♀: brown above; paler below, with dark brown streaks.

6 BLUE SEEDEATER *Amaurospiza concolor*
p. 234
R and local, w BE and e OW only; bamboo thickets. Larger than **2** and **5**. Bill longer, more

pointed than in **2**, more rounded than in **5**. ♂: flat blue black (not glossy); no white at base of primaries or under wing. ♀: rich cinnamon brown above; slightly paler below; very similar to **7** but slimmer, with smaller, more rounded, dark gray (not black) bill.

BUNTINGS AND "BLUE" GROSBEAKS: Generally larger than seedeaters, with more conical bill; ♂s generally blue to blue black.

7 BLUE BUNTING *Cyanocompsa parellina*
p. 242
FC n. and w. of Maya Mtns., forest and edge. ♂: blue black, with bright blue forecrown, supercilium, malar area, shoulder, and rump; base of lower mandible pale. ♀: warm brown above; slightly paler cinnamon brown below; all-black bill.

8 PAINTED BUNTING *Passerina ciris* · p. 243
UC transient and occas. in winter, open areas. ♀: green above, yellow green below, plain face with pale eye-ring. ♂: bright blue head, yellow-green back, red underparts.

9 INDIGO BUNTING *Passerina cyanea* · p. 243
VC transient and FC to C in winter, open areas. ♂ *alt.:* bright blue throughout. ♀: brown above and paler below, with diffusely streaked breast and indistinct pale wingbars. *Basic* ♂ (not shown): like ♀ but with various amounts of blue in plumage.

10 BLUE-BLACK GROSBEAK
Cyanocompsa cyanoides · p. 242
C nearly throughout, absent in n.e.; forest and second growth. Massive conical bill. Chunkier bird with larger bill and head and shorter tail than **1**. ♂: glossy blue black. ♀: deep rich brown throughout.

11 BLUE GROSBEAK *Passerina caerulea* · p. 243
VC transient, UC in winter; open areas. Bill intermediate in size between **9** and **10**. Short crest often held erect. ♂ *alt.:* bright blue, with black face and chestnut wingbars. *Basic* ♂ (not shown): similar but with brown edges to blue feathers. ♀: mostly brown, with gray rump and buffy brown wingbars.

PLATE **52** SALTATORS, GROSBEAKS, AND SPARROWS

SALTATORS: Large green to grayish birds with black in head; longer bills than in grosbeaks.

1 BLACK-HEADED SALTATOR *Saltator atriceps*
p. 240
C in broadleaf forest edge, scrub. Loud, raucous; travels in groups. Golden olive above, gray and cinnamon below. Center of throat and short supercilium white. Black head contrasts sharply with rest of body.

2 BUFF-THROATED SALTATOR
Saltator maximus · p. 240
FC to C in s. two-thirds; broadleaf forest edge. Like **1** but smaller; dark gray head contrasts less with nape and back; central throat pale cinnamon buff broadly bordered with black. Soft, cheery vocalizations very different from raucous chatter of **1**.

3 GRAYISH SALTATOR *Saltator coerulescens*
p. 240
FC to C.; open scrub and forest edge. Olive gray above, with blackish lateral throat stripe, white throat, and white supercilium. Much duller above than **1** or **2**, without strongly contrasting head-and-throat pattern.

GROSBEAKS: Brightly colored, with thick-based triangular bill.

4 BLACK-FACED GROSBEAK
Caryothraustes poliogaster · p. 241
C n. to n OW, primarily in broadleaf forest. Green above, becoming yellow on head and breast; strongly contrasting black face. Scapulars, rump, belly, and tail coverts gray.

5 NORTHERN CARDINAL *Cardinalis cardinalis*
p. 241
UC to FC in n.e.; forest edge and scrub. Prominent crest, large red-orange bill. ♂: bright red, with black face. ♀: brownish gray above, warmer brown below; dusky black face; red crest.

6 ROSE-BREASTED GROSBEAK
Pheucticus ludovicianus · p. 241
C transient, UC in winter. Boldly patterned; large, whitish bill. ♂ *alt.:* boldly marked black-and-white bird with bright rose-red triangle on breast; underwing coverts red. ♀: streaked brown and white above, with prominent white supercilium, wingbars, and tertial tips; heavily streaked breast and flanks; underwing coverts yellow. *Basic* ♂: black-and-white pattern largely obscured by pale brown feather edges; retains rose-red breast.

7 ORANGE-BILLED SPARROW
Arremon aurantiirostris · p. 235
C in s. half; broadleaf forest interior. *Ad.:* striking black-and-white head and breast; orange bill; conspicuous yellow patch at bend of wing. *Juv.:* dark sooty-olive, with paler supercilium and throat; dark gray bill.

ARREMONOPS SPARROWS: Skulking dwellers of ground and underbrush; greenish to brownish, with gray head streaked with dark brown or black.

8 GREEN-BACKED SPARROW
Arremonops chloronotus · p. 236
FC to C throughout, forest edge and scrub. Olive green above, flanks grayish yellow, undertail coverts lemon-buff. Head gray, with black eye-stripe and lateral crown stripe. Song does not accelerate toward the end.

9 OLIVE SPARROW *Arremonops rufivirgatus*
p. 236
FC to C in n. half; forest edge and scrub. Very similar to **8**, but upperparts grayish olive, flanks dull brownish gray, and undertail coverts pale buff. Primaries contrast brighter olive. Head gray, with dark brown eye-stripe and lateral crown stripe. Song an accelerating series of rich chips.

1

2

3

4

5 ♂

♀

6 ♀

♂ Alternate

Adult

7

♂ Basic

Juvenile

8

9

PLATE **53** SPARROWS

1 **LARK SPARROW** *Chondestes grammacus*
p. 238
Occas. autumn transient. Central black breast spot in otherwise plain white underparts. Boldly patterned black-and-white head, with chestnut auricular patch. Tail black, broadly tipped with white.

2 **VESPER SPARROW** *Pooecetes gramineus*
p. 238
Vagrant. Pale sandy brown above and creamy white below, with thin dark streaks on back and breast; thin but conspicuous white eye-ring; white outer tail feathers conspicuous in flight.

SPIZELLA SPARROWS: Small, slim sparrows with notched tail, streaked upperparts, and unstreaked underparts (except juv.).

3 **CLAY-COLORED SPARROW** *Spizella pallida*
p. 238
Vagrant. *Basic:* like **4** but with light brown, not gray, rump; well-defined auricular patch contrasting strongly below with pale malar stripe; thin but conspicuous dark lateral throat stripe; pale lores; whitish central crown stripe (not visible in illustration). Conspicuous gray nape contrasts with buffy breast.

4 **CHIPPING SPARROW** *Spizella passerina*
p. 237
FC to C in pines. Other than distinctive alt. ad., similar to **3**, but with gray rump, dark lores, and thin, indistinct lateral throat stripe. *Ad. alt.:* rufous crown; strong white supercilium; thin black eye-stripe; unstreaked gray face, nape, and underparts. *Basic ad.* (not shown): similar but duller. *Imm.:* most like **3**, but with gray rump, brownish breast, and little nape-breast contrast; streaked crown with pale central crown stripe usually on forecrown only. *Juv.:* streaked underparts and nape.

5 **GRASSHOPPER SPARROW**
Ammodramus savannarum · p. 239
C in sedge savannas; occas. transient elsewhere (nonresident subspecies). Large-headed

sparrow with short unnotched tail. Residents (shown) are darker than migrants, with gray-tinged auriculars, duller head and breast, and streaks on sides and flanks. *Ad.:* yellow-buff face with paler eye-ring; yellow-ochre loral area; dark crown and postocular stripe; pale central crown stripe; blue-gray nape finely streaked with dark rufous; underparts buff. *Juv.:* finely streaked breast, less buff in head and underparts.

6 **LINCOLN'S SPARROW** *Melospiza lincolnii*
p. 239
Occas. transient, R winter visitor. Peaked head; rufous-brown crown set off by broad gray supercilium; thin white eye-ring; buff malar set off from whitish throat by thin black lateral throat stripe. Breast, sides, and flanks ochraceous buff, with fine black streaks.

7 **SAVANNAH SPARROW**
Passerculus sandwichensis · p. 238
Occas. in winter. Heavily streaked. Most like **2** and **6**, but with yellow supraloral fading to whitish on supercilium; breast streaks coalesce into central breast spot. Black lateral throat stripe and dark auriculars further distinguish it from most other small sparrows.

8 **BOTTERI'S SPARROW** *Aimophila botterii*
p. 236
UC to FC in limited range in pine savannas of nc Belize. *Ad.:* grayish face with dark rufous postocular stripe; lacks yellow supraloral and pale central crown stripe of **5**; underparts grayish buff to brownish buff, with blotchy spots on upper sides and flanks. *Juv.:* similar to juv. **5** but larger and longer-tailed, with larger bill.

9 **RUSTY SPARROW** *Aimophila rufescens*
p. 237
C in Mtn. Pine Ridge and lowland pine woodland of SC and TO. Largest of the sparrows. *Ad.:* gray head with rufous crown, dark eye-stripe, black lateral throat stripe, and white throat; upperparts rufous brown, streaked black; unstreaked brownish buff breast. *Juv.:* streaked breast; head pattern less distinct.

2

1

1

2

3

Basic

Juvenile

5

Adult

Juvenile

4

Immature

Adult
Alternate

6

7

Juvenile

9

Juvenile

8

Adult

Adult

PLATE **54** MISCELLANEOUS SPARROWS AND FINCHES

1 DICKCISSEL *Spiza americana* · p. 244
C spring and less C autumn transient; fields. ♀:
yellowish supercilium, malar stripe, and upper
breast; thin black lateral throat stripe; upperparts streaked brown and black, with one pale
stripe down each side; underparts mostly unstreaked. ♂: chestnut shoulder patch; distinctive
black triangle on upper breast; rest of breast,
malar, and supercilium mostly yellow. *Imm.*
(not shown): fine streaks on breast.

2 YELLOW-FACED GRASSQUIT *Tiaris olivacea*
p. 234
Local in c., w., and s. portions of country in
brush, scrub; spreading rapidly. Yellow throat,
supercilium, and lower eye crescent. ♂: forecrown, face, and breast black, accentuating yellow areas. ♀: black areas absent, yellow areas reduced.

3 RED CROSSBILL *Loxia curvirostra* · p. 254
Local and UC in Mtn. Pine Ridge. Upper and
lower mandibles cross at tip. ♂: varies from
mustard yellow to brick red. ♀: mostly grayish
olive, with bright yellow-olive rump and pale
gray throat.

CARDUELIS FINCHES: Small, somewhat
gregarious birds with small, conical bill and
relatively short, notched tail.

4 LESSER GOLDFINCH *Carduelis psaltria*
p. 254
Recent colonist in n OW. ♀: olive to grayish
olive above and bright to dingy yellowish below;
white markings in wings. ♂: black above and
bright yellow below, with white patch at base of
primaries.

5 BLACK-HEADED SISKIN *Carduelis notata*
p. 254
C in Mtn. Pine Ridge. Striking green, black,
and yellow bird. *Ad.:* black hood, yellow-olive
(♂) to olive (♀) back, yellow underparts and
rump, and black wings and tail, with bold yellow patch in wings and at base of outer tail
feathers. *Imm.:* lacks black hood. From goldfinch by yellow wing patches and rump.

6 GRASSLAND YELLOW-FINCH *Sicalis luteola*
p. 235
Locally C in grasslands and savannas. Bill more
rounded than in **4**; has streaked upperparts and
yellow rump; lacks white highlights in wing.
♂: face, underparts, and rump bright yellow. ♀:
yellow areas duller, especially on auriculars.

7 HOUSE SPARROW *Passer domesticus* · p. 255
Non-native urban resident of Punta Gorda,
Dangriga, and Pomona. ♂: gray, chestnut, and
black crown; nearly white cheeks; black throat
and upper breast. ♀: pale supercilium, absence
of lateral throat stripe, and pale stripe on each
side of its otherwise brown-and-black-streaked
back distinguish it from other species.

8 WHITE-CROWNED SPARROW
Zonotrichia leucophrys · p. 239
Vagrant. Fairly large sparrow with boldly
streaked head, unstreaked underparts, and
pinkish to orangish bill. *Imm.:* head pale
buffy brown, with broad chestnut brown lateral
crown stripe and eyeline. *Ad.:* striking black-
and-white head pattern; nape, face, and underparts pale gray.

PLATE **55** BLACKBIRDS

1 BOBOLINK *Dolichonyx oryzivorus* · p. 244
UC transient on cayes; R on mainland. Conical, sparrowlike bill and short spiny-tipped tail feathers. ♂ *alt.:* black, with golden buff nape patch, white scapulars and rump, and streaked back. *Imm. and basic ad.:* head, rump, and underparts bright buff; blackish lateral crown and postocular stripes; streaked upperparts with pale lateral stripe on each side of back; unstreaked nape; streaks underneath confined to flanks. ♀ *Alt.* (not shown): duller, lacks yellow-buff tones.

2 RED-WINGED BLACKBIRD *Agelaius phoeniceus*
p. 245
C in n. half; marshes, fields. ♂ Daggerlike bill. *alt.:* black, with striking red lesser wing coverts and creamy yellow median wing coverts. *Basic* ♂ (not shown): feathers of head and back edged with rusty brown. *Imm.* ♂: most body feathers edged rusty brown; pale brown supercilium; red-and-yellow wing patch flecked with black. ♀: lacks red-and-yellow wing patch; heavily streaked throughout; prominent supercilium.

3 EASTERN MEADOWLARK *Sturnella magna*
p. 245
C in savannas, farmland. Long, daggerlike bill; flat head; short tail with conspicuous white outer tail feathers noticeable in flight. Yellow throat and breast split by broad black **V**.

OROPENDOLAS: Large blackish birds with long, daggerlike bill and yellow tail. Blackish central tail feathers (not visible from below). ♂ distinctly larger than ♀. Colonial; builds large, pendulous nests in isolated large trees.

4 CHESTNUT-HEADED OROPENDOLA
Psarocolius wagleri · p. 253
Local in south, mostly in broadleaf forest interior. Bill pale greenish yellow; eyes pale blue. Undertail coverts chestnut. Smaller than **5** and flies with faster, deeper wingbeats.

5 MONTEZUMA OROPENDOLA
Psarocolius montezuma · p. 253
C nearly throughout, but local and UC in CO; most wooded habitats. Large. Bill black broadly tipped with red orange; face pale blue and pink. Slow, steady crow-like flight.

6 GREAT-TAILED GRACKLE *Quiscalus mexicanus*
p. 246
VC in open and disturbed areas, including urban centers. Slender bird with small head, pale yellow eyes (except juv.), and rather long, black bill. Highly vocal. ♂: glossy blue black throughout; distinctive long tail strongly bowed up laterally in fashion of a keel. ♀: smaller, with shorter tail that lacks keel; plumage brown, with paler supercilium and throat.

7 MELODIOUS BLACKBIRD *Dives dives*
p. 246
C to VC in open and disturbed areas, forest edge. Well-proportioned; all black, including eyes. Flicks tail frequently. Highly vocal.

8 YELLOW-BILLED CACIQUE
Amblycercus holosericeus · p. 252
C in thickets and forest understory. Similar in size to **7**, but with pale greenish yellow bill and pale yellow eyes (young birds have dusky eyes). Skulks in dense vegetation.

COWBIRDS: Small to relatively large dark brown (some ♀s) to black birds that lay their eggs in other birds' nests, leaving the host species to raise their young. Gather in feeding flocks in winter.

9 BRONZED COWBIRD *Molothrus aeneus*
p. 248
C resident in north, local in south but spreading rapidly; open areas. Red eyes, duller in imm. Relatively large bill with curved culmen. ♀: dark brown throughout, including throat. ♂: glossy black, with bronzy green crown, neck ruff, and back.

10 GIANT COWBIRD *Molothrus oryzivorus*
p. 248
UC to locally FC in open woodland and fields. Glossy black, with relatively long, thick-based bill, relatively long tail, and red eyes. Larger than Melodious Blackbird and much larger than other cowbirds. *Ad.* ♂: prominent neck ruff. *Juv.:* lacks ruff; bill nearly white; eye color variable; distinguished from **8** by bill shape, behavior, and habitat.

Basic 1

♂ Alternate

♀ 2 ♂ Alternate

Immature ♂

3

4

5

♂ 6

♀

7

8

Juvenile 10

9 ♂

♀

Adult ♂

PLATE **56** ORIOLES

ORIOLES: Bright yellow- to orange-and-black birds, some with prominent wing marks. Imms. and some ♀s are less boldly marked. **1** and **4** are migrants from North America; the rest are residents.

1 BALTIMORE ORIOLE *Icterus galbula* · p. 252
C in winter. Bill relatively thin and straight. ♂ *alt.:* black hood, back, wings and tail, with bright orange breast, belly, rump, shoulder, and tail corners; white lower wingbar and tertial edges. *Basic* ♂ (not shown): similar but with pale brown edges to back and nape feathers. *Ad.* ♀*:* variable; some more like basic ♂; others similar to ♀ **3** but with yellow-orange underparts (bird shown is intermediate). *Imm.* (not shown): varies from olive gray (some ♀s) to olive above, and from pale orangish yellow on breast and undertail coverts with a dirty gray wash across midsection (some ♀s) to uniformly orange throughout underparts (some ♂s).

2 ORANGE ORIOLE *Icterus auratus* · p. 251
Locally in ne CO; in winter (possibly resident) on Ambergris Caye. Straighter bill than in Hooded. *Ad.* ♂*:* similar to Hooded but with orange back. *Ad.* ♀*:* similar to ♂ but yellow instead of orange; 2 thin wingbars. *Imm.* ♂ (not shown): olive tail; differs from imm. ♂ **3** in having straighter bill, yellower head and back, and black wings.

3 HOODED ORIOLE *Icterus cucullatus* · p. 250
C in n. half, increasingly less C westward. Most like **2**, **4** and **8**, but with decurved bill and other age- and sex-specific differences. *Ad.* ♂*:* black back; black in face more extensive than in **2**; smaller than **8**, with thinner-based bill, bold white upper wingbar, and no white patch at base of primaries. ♀*:* most like ♀ **4** but larger, with longer tail and decurved bill, orange-yellow undertail coverts. *Imm.* ♂*:* black face and central throat; similar to imm. **2** and imm. ♂ **4** (see text).

4 ORCHARD ORIOLE *Icterus spurius* · p. 249
C in winter. Smallest oriole; straight bill; relatively short tail. ♀*:* like **3** but with shorter, straighter bill and slightly shorter tail; undertail coverts lack orange hue. *Imm.* ♂*:* black in face and throat. *Ad.* ♂*:* chestnut underparts, rump, and shoulder.

5 BLACK-COWLED ORIOLE *Icterus prosthemelas* p. 249
C nearly throughout in most wooded habitats. Decurved slender bill. In some plumages, can be confused with several other species (see text). *Ad.* ♂ *and some* ♀*s:* black hood, back, wings, and tail; yellow underparts, rump, and shoulder; thin chestnut border at hood-breast interface; no white in wing. *Other* ♀*s:* back, nape, and most of head olive yellow, much like imm. **7**, but with black extending to auriculars, and shoulder yellow. Still other ♀s and molting imm. ♂s: have nearly complete black hood. *Imm.* (not shown): dark brown, not black, flight feathers.

6 YELLOW-TAILED ORIOLE *Icterus mesomelas* p. 250
FC to C, often near streams and rivers. Bill fairly long, slightly decurved, and thick at base; yellow bar across inner wing and yellow outer tail feathers; black lores and central throat. *Ad.:* yellow with black back, wings, and central tail feathers. *Imm.:* upperparts, except head, yellow olive; back usually with varying amounts of black flecking; yellow in outer tail feathers confined to inner webs. *Juv.* (not shown): lacks black lores and central throat.

7 YELLOW-BACKED ORIOLE *Icterus chrysater* p. 250
FC, primarily in pines, and on Ambergris Caye and Placencia Pen. *Ad.* ♂*:* yellow, with black wings, tail, face, and throat. *Ad.* ♀ (not shown): brownish orange wash on back and head.

8 ALTAMIRA ORIOLE *Icterus gularis* · p. 251
UC to FC in CO s. to e OW and n BE; forest edge and open woodland. Largest oriole; deep-based, straight bill. *Ad.:* like smaller ♂ **3** but with orange shoulder and white patch at base of primaries. *Imm.:* similar to smaller imm. ♂ **3** but with more extensive yellow on head, different bill, and, by 2nd year, a yellow shoulder.

Alternate ♂

1

Adult ♀

Adult ♂

2

Adult ♀

Immature ♂

3

Adult ♂ 3

♀

Some ♀s

5

♂ and Some ♀s

♀

Some ♀s

Adult ♂

4

Immature ♂

Immature

6

Adult

Adult

8

Adult ♂

7

Immature

FAMILY AND SPECIES ACCOUNTS

FAMILY: TINAMIDAE
(Tinamous)

World: 47. **New World:** 47. **Belize:** 4. New World Tropics and S. Temperate Zone. Tinamous superficially resemble Old World partridges—hence their popular Creole name, "Partridge." They are characterized by a robust body; virtually no tail; stout legs; a long, thin neck; a small head; and a short, slightly decurved bill. All in Belize inhabit forest and second growth, where they walk quietly on the forest floor. They usually freeze when alarmed, making them very difficult to detect. Upon close approach, they will flush explosively, only to disappear quickly into the forest. Tinamous fly with rapid, powerful wingbeats, their wings making a whistling sound. Because they are secretive and difficult to see, learning their distinctive vocalizations can be critical to their correct ID. **References:** *Voice:* Hardy et al. (1993); Moore (1992).

Things to note: vocalizations, size, leg color, breast color, presence/absence of barring on upperparts and flanks.

Great Tinamou   PLATE 12
Tinamus major
OTHER NAMES. Blue-foot Partridge (C), colol (K, M).

Identification. 16½″ (42 cm). Easily the largest tinamou—slightly larger than a Gray-necked Wood-Rail. Brown plumage with upperparts marked with short black bars. Blue-gray legs/feet.
Voice. 1. Low-pitched, haunting, wavering *whooooo-ooooooo* (1–1½ sec), sometimes separated into three or more haunting whistles that fade in and out;
2. tremulous *who who who WHOOO-who WHOOO-who WHOOO-who.*
Habitat. Ground dweller within primary and secondary broadleaf forest; less commonly in pine forest.
Distribution. Resident from s Veracruz and s Yucatán Pen. s. primarily on Gulf-Caribbean slope of C.A. to c S.A.
Status in Belize. UC to FC resident on mainland nearly throughout, scarce or absent in much of CO.

Little Tinamou   PLATE 12
Crypturellus soui
OTHER NAMES. Bawley (C), xulul (K), sh'lul (M).

Identification. 9″ (23 cm). Tiny; size of tailless White-tipped Dove. Lacks barring in plumage. Dull yellowish to olive legs/feet. ♀: cinnamon highlights on wings and underparts.
Voice. 1. Long, hollow, wavering *oooweoo* notes that rise, then fall, in pitch;
2. one long, wavering note on same pitch, higher-pitched and clearer than in Great;
3. short series of wavering trills, each in turn higher in pitch and building in intensity.
Habitat. Ground dweller within tall second-growth scrub and secondary forest.
Distribution. Resident from s Veracruz and s Yucatán Pen. s, primarily on Gulf-Caribbean slope through C.A. to c S.A.
Status in Belize. FC resident on mainland nearly throughout, scarce or absent in much of CO and at higher elevations.

Thicket Tinamou   MAP 1; PLATE 12
Crypturellus cinnamomeus
OTHER NAMES. Rufescent Tinamou (arch.), Partridge (C), pom (M), Perdiz (S).

Identification. 10¾″ (27.5 cm). Larger than Little but much smaller than Great; size of tailless Rock Dove. The only strikingly marked tinamou in Belize, with its boldly barred black-and-white upperparts and cinnamon breast. Red legs/feet. ♀: fine barring on breast and neck. ♂: barring nearly absent.
Voice. Short, clear, penetrating, hollow whistle that ends abruptly: *oooooo* (<1 sec), sometimes rising in pitch at end.
Habitat. Ground dweller within semi-deciduous n. broadleaf forest, second-growth scrub.
Distribution. Resident in Caribbean lowlands from s Tamaulipas to Petén and c Belize; Pacific lowlands from c Sinaloa discontinuously to nw C.R.

Status in Belize. UC to FC resident in CO, OW, n BE, and CA w. of Maya Mtns. Reports e. of Maya Mtns. unsubstantiated.

Slaty-breasted Tinamou   MAP 2; PLATE 12
Crypturellus boucardi
OTHER NAMES. Boucard's Tinamou (arch.), Red-footed Partridge (C), pom (K, M), balee (M).

Identification. 10½″ (26.5 cm). Same size as Thicket. Red legs/feet. ♂: slaty gray head, neck, and breast; rich buff lower belly with thin black bars. ♀: dark and light brown barred upperparts, less extensive gray on breast, paler barring on lower belly.
Voice. Penetrating, *oooooo woooooo,* second part slightly lower in pitch. Similar to sound made by blowing across top of a soda bottle. Much longer (2–2½ sec) than in Thicket and two-parted. Somewhat similar to vocalization of White-tipped Dove but longer, hollower, and not mournful.
Habitat. Ground dweller within extensive tracts of broadleaf forest.
Distribution. Resident on Gulf-Caribbean slope from s Veracruz s. of Yucatán Pen. to n C.R.
Status in Belize. UC to FC resident in interior n. to c CA, and in w and c OW.

FAMILY: PODICIPEDIDAE
(Grebes)
World: 21. **New World:** 15 (2 recently extinct). **Belize:** 2. Worldwide. Grebes are virtually tailless diving birds with a moderately long to very long neck, a stocky body, short wings, a small head, flattened claws (toenails), and powerful, laterally compressed tarsi set far back on their body to provide powerful thrust and maneuverability under water. Consequently, they are front-heavy and cannot stand upright on land. Grebes superficially resemble ducks, but their bill is not laterally flattened and their toes are lobed, not webbed. They may swim low in the water with only their head and neck above the surface, or they may ride high on the water with body feathers fluffed to trap air and increase buoyancy.

They can dive headfirst from the surface or submerge equally fast by compressing their body feathers and exhaling quickly, thus literally sinking. Although they seldom fly, they are strong fliers, and some, like Pied-billed Grebe, are long-distance migrants. Because short wings provide little lift, they must run across the water while flapping vigorously to become airborne. Like ducks, grebes have an eclipse plumage shortly after nesting in which they molt all their flight feathers at one time, rendering them temporarily flightless.

Things to note: bill size, shape, and pattern; throat color; eye color.

Least Grebe   PLATE 14
Tachybaptus dominicus
OTHER NAMES. Diving Dopper (C).

Identification. 9″ (23 cm). Tiny; much smaller than any duck and noticeably smaller than Pied-billed, with thinner, pointed, slightly upturned bill; bright yellow eyes. Often swims with posterior body feathers fluffed, giving it a very rounded look with overlarge posterior. *Flight:* broad white wing stripe. *Alt.:* black crown and throat. *Basic:* white throat.
Voice. Purring and chattering, including rolled purring trill. Softer and lower-pitched than in Ruddy Crake, often starting with a stutter. Begging young utter a constant high-pitched, shrill *pee pee pee pee* . . . like an out-of-tune, nasal toy horn.
Habitat. Forest-lined rivers, streams, swamps, and lagoons; freshwater marshes; small ponds.
Distribution. Resident from s Texas, Mex., and W.I. s. to sc S.A.
Status in Belize. Locally UC to FC resident on mainland.
Reference. *Voice:* Howell and Webb (1995).

Pied-billed Grebe   PLATE 14
Podilymbus podiceps
OTHER NAMES. Diving Dopper (C).

Identification. 12″ (30.5 cm). Larger than Least but smaller than any duck. Bill rather fat and white to cream-colored; white eye-ring. White downy undertail coverts frequently fluffed out.

Sometimes swims with only head above water to avoid detection. *Alt.:* broad black vertical bar on bill; black throat. *Basic:* bill lacks bar; throat whitish.

Voice. In breeding season, resonant *coo-coo-coo-coo-coo-coo-coo cow cow cow cow; coo* notes are clear; *cow* notes are guttural.

Habitat. Freshwater and brackish marshes, lagoons, lakes, and ponds; occas. inshore coastal waters (migrants), large rivers.

Distribution. Primarily Temperate Zone from c Can. to s S.A., but only locally resident in C.A. and n S.A.; n. populations migratory.

Status in Belize. UC to locally FC winter visitor in lowlands on mainland, occas. on Ambergris Caye. A few remain through summer locally; breeds regularly at Crooked Tree BE and occas. elsewhere.

Reference. *Status:* Wood and Leberman (1987).

FAMILY: PROCELLARIIDAE
(Shearwaters)

World: 72. **Atlantic Ocean:** ≈30. **Belize**: 2. Oceans worldwide but reach greatest diversity in S. Temperate Zone. Shearwaters are pelagic, rarely seen from land. They are characterized by a long, thin, hooked bill; webbed toes; and weak legs set far back on their body. They are distinguished in flight by long, narrow, stiffly held wings and their manner of alternately flapping and gliding just above the water's surface. On windy days, they rise on stiff wings in a series of high arcs above the water. On the water, they are distinguished from gulls by their low profile, with their posterior held horizontally, not raised, and by their thinner bill. They are often referred to as "tube-noses" because their nostrils are at the end of a raised tube inset in the base of the upper mandible. A large salt gland in the eye orbit concentrates salt, enabling them to drink seawater. Concentrated salt droplets are extruded from the nostrils, down a groove in the bill, and off the tip. Shearwaters nest in colonies on remote offshore islands free of terrestrial predators. **References:** Harrison (1985, 1987).

With only three records for Belize, all of dead or dying beached birds, shearwaters are not a significant component of the Belizean avifauna;

however, few birders ever travel beyond the barrier reef, where a healthy shearwater is most likely to be seen. Audubon's is far more likely than Manx to occur in Belize waters, the Manx record being an anomaly. Shearwaters are most likely to be seen inside the reef during or shortly after the passing of a tropical storm or hurricane.

Things to note: color of lores, folded wing vs. tail length. *In flight,* color of undertail coverts, flap-to-glide ratio.

Manx Shearwater   FIGURE 8
Puffinus puffinus
OTHER NAMES. Common Shearwater (arch.).

Identification. 14½″ (37 cm); wingspan 32½″ (82.5 cm). Black above, white below, including undertail coverts. Larger than Audubon's, with proportionately longer wings and shorter tail. When at rest on water, wingtips project beyond tail. Lores dark, concolorous with rest of face and crown. *Flight:* alternately glides and flaps, but with longer periods of gliding than Audubon's and with slower, more deliberate wingbeats between glides.

Voice. Silent away from nesting colony.

Habitat. Open ocean, usually well away from land.

Distribution. Nests on islands in n Atlantic; disperses well offshore over most of Atlantic Ocean. R migrant and winter visitor in W.I.

Status in Belize. One record: a beached carcass found near Dangriga, 9 Feb. 1990, is the only record for C.A.

Reference. *Status:* Howell et al. (1992).

Audubon's Shearwater   FIGURE 8
Puffinus lherminieri
OTHER NAMES. Dusky-backed Shearwater (arch.).

Identification. 12¼″ (31 cm); wingspan 27½″ (70 cm). Like small Manx, but with black undertail coverts, proportionately longer tail, shorter wings (tail projects beyond folded wings). White patch in lores. *Flight:* more rapid wingbeats and shorter periods of gliding flight than in Manx.

Voice. Silent away from nesting colony.

Manx Shearwater

Audubon's Shearwater

White-tailed Tropicbird

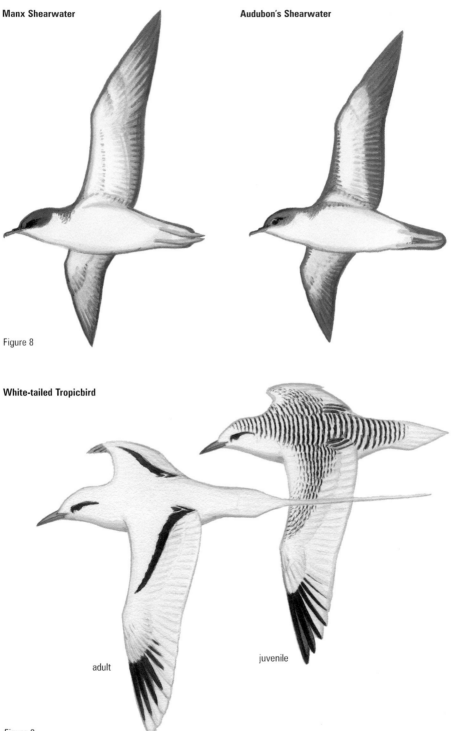

Figure 8

adult

juvenile

Figure 9

Habitat. Open ocean, usually well away from land.

Distribution. Nests on islands in Indian, Pacific, w Atlantic, and e Caribbean oceans. Disperses widely in tropical seas, rarely to w Caribbean off n Quintana Roo.

Status in Belize. Two records: dying bird at Caye Caulker, late July 2000; carcass on beach near Hopkins SC, 2 Aug. 2000.

Reference. *Status:* Jones et al. (2002).

FAMILY: PHAETHONTIDAE
(Tropicbirds)

World: 3. Atlantic Ocean: 2. Belize: 1. Tropical and subtropical oceans worldwide. Tropicbirds are characterized by a long, daggerlike red, orange, or yellow bill; short legs set far back on their body; small totipalmate feet (webbing between all four toes); and direct flight on strong, steady wingbeats. Ads. are unmistakable, with their long, central tail streamers. They nest on islands; otherwise they are pelagic. **References:** Harrison (1985, 1987).

White-tailed Tropicbird   FIGURE 9
Phaethon lepturus
OTHER NAMES. Yellow-billed Tropicbird (arch.).

Identification. 28″ (71 cm), including 10–15″ (25–38 cm) tail streamers of ad. *Ad.:* unlike any tern, has bold black stripe through tertials and wing coverts, black outer primaries, and thin black stripe through eyes; bill orange to yellowish. *Juv.:* lacks black highlights and tail streamers; has fine black barring across back, gray eyeline.

Voice. Silent away from nesting colony.

Habitat. Open ocean; occas. inshore waters.

Distribution. Nests on islands in tropical Indian, Pacific, and Atlantic oceans and locally in W.I.; R in w Caribbean.

Status in Belize. One record: Drowned Cayes BE, 21 Apr. 1976.

Reference. *Status:* Jones et al. (2000).

The possibility of **Red-billed Tropicbird** *(Phaethon aethereus)* turning up in Belize cannot be dismissed and should be reason for caution in IDing any nonadult tropicbird. It is ¼ larger than White-tailed. *Ad.:* red bill; finely barred upperparts. *Juv.:* bill yellow, as in juv. White-tailed, but upperparts more densely barred black, black through eyes extends around nape, and black in outer wing includes primary coverts.

FAMILY: SULIDAE
(Boobies and Gannets)

World: 9. Atlantic Ocean: 6. Belize: 3. Marine waters from Arctic to Antarctic; boobies primarily in the Tropics, gannets primarily at higher latitudes. They are characterized by pale eyes oriented forward just behind the bill; thickset neck; long, straight, pointed, thick-based bill; long, pointed wings; pointed tail; and alternate flapping flight with long glides. In flight, they have a four-point or crosslike profile. When feeding, they plunge into the water from high in the air, then swim underwater in pursuit of prey. **References:** Harrison (1985, 1987); Nelson (1978).

Things to note: bill, face, and leg/foot color; angle of bill at forehead; presence/absence of neck collar. *In flight,* wing and tail pattern (flight feathers, underwing coverts).

Masked Booby   PLATE 1
Sula dactylatra
OTHER NAMES. Blue-faced Booby (arch.).

Identification. 30½″ (77.5 cm); wingspan 64″ (162 cm). *Ad.:* unmistakable white body with black primaries, secondaries, and tail; blackish face; eyes and bill yellow; feet yellowish. *1st year:* mostly dark sooty brown with white breast, belly, undertail coverts, and underwing coverts, and thus superficially similar to ad. Brown Booby; Masked, however, has white collar separating brown head and back; from underneath, brown hood does not extend to wings; gradually attains ad. plumage over 3 years.

Voice. Silent away from nesting colony.

Habitat. Open ocean; healthy birds rarely found near shore.

Distribution. Nests on islands in tropical Indian, Pacific, and Atlantic oceans, including Gulf of Mex. C resident in s Gulf of Mex., R resident in W.I., and UC to R visitor in w Caribbean. Disperses widely at sea.

Status in Belize. R visitor; recorded Feb., May, Aug., and Dec., twice off Ambergris Caye, once off Belize City, and once near Glovers Reef. Although stray boobies are most likely to be imms., all four Belize records are of ads., suggesting that imms., which resemble somewhat the Brown Booby, are being overlooked.

References. *Status:* Jones et al. (2000); Miller and Miller (1992). *Identification:* Dittmann and Cardiff (1999).

Brown Booby   PLATE 1
Sula leucogaster
OTHER NAMES. White-bellied Booby (arch.).

Identification. 28½" (72.5 cm); wingspan 56½" (143.5 cm). Slightly smaller than Masked. *Ad.:* chocolate brown, with sharply contrasting white lower breast through undertail coverts, and white underwing coverts; yellow feet and pale straw-colored bill, becoming bright yellow early in breeding season; lacks white collar of imm. Masked, and hood extends posteriorly to wings. ♂: slaty-blue face. ♀: yellow to greenish yellow face. *Imm.:* whitish underwing coverts like ad., but lower breast, belly, and undertail coverts light brown (finely flecked brown and white) instead of white; like ad., sharp demarcation between breast and belly. *Juv.:* very similar to juv. Red-footed Booby; all-dark underparts except for pale gray in underwing coverts; only some show faint to fairly prominent breast-belly contrast; heavier-billed than Red-footed, with straight culmen (Red-footed has slight concave angle at junction of forehead and bill).

Voice. Generally silent away from nesting colony.
Habitat. Nests on ground on offshore islands; forages at sea both outside and inside the reef; roosts in mangroves on small cayes.
Distribution. Widespread throughout tropical oceans; nests on islands and disperses at sea.
Status in Belize. FC year-round visitor offshore and among smaller cayes; sick or injured birds occas. seen along mainland coast. No credible evidence of nesting.

Reference. *Identification:* Dittmann and Cardiff (1999).

Red-footed Booby   MAP 3; PLATE 1
Sula sula

Identification. 27½" (70 cm); wingspan 56" (142 cm). Smallest of the three boobies, and the only one that nests in Belize. Two color morphs. *White morph* (97% of Belize population): mostly white with yellow suffusion on head; black primaries and outer secondaries; white tail and inner secondaries. *Brown morph* (3% of population): all dark sooty brown except for white posterior (lower rump, lower belly, tail coverts, and tail); some have white patches in tertials and/or dark feathers in tail. *Ad. (both morphs):* bright orange-red legs/feet, blue bill, pink face. *1st year:* all brown, with pale grayish yellow to yellow-orange feet and black bill; darker underwing coverts than in juv. Brown.
Voice. At nest: *chuck* and *check* notes. *In courtship:* guttural screeching and rattling squawks, brays, and chatters. Generally silent away from nesting colony.
Habitat. Nests in trees and shrubs on islands; forages over open ocean, usually beyond sight of land.
Distribution. Widespread throughout tropical oceans.
Status in Belize. Large nesting colony on Half Moon Caye, Lighthouse Reef. Reported occas. on n cayes and once at Belize City, usually following tropical storms.
References. *Status:* Verner (1961). *Identification:* Dittmann and Cardiff (1999). *Voice:* Howell and Webb (1995).

FAMILY: PELECANIDAE
(Pelicans)
World: 8. **New World:** 3. **Belize:** 2. Primarily tropical and subtropical, with both marine and freshwater species distributed nearly worldwide. The Brown Pelican is the only exclusively coastal species. Pelicans are among the world's most familiar birds and among the largest of all birds capable of flight. They are characterized by rounded wings with an unusually long inner

wing; short, thick legs; a short tail; a long, straight bill with a nail at the tip; and totipalmate feet (webbing between all four toes). The lower mandible is modified throughout its length into a highly expandable pouch of skin, which holds its catch prior to swallowing. Unlike cormorants and anhingas, pelicans are very buoyant, with subcutaneous air sacs and very light bones. They typically fly in formation close to the water, with wingtips nearly touching the surface, but some species, like the American Pelican, also soar high in the air on thermals of warm air for extended periods and feed in groups from the surface of the water by herding prey into shallows where they can be reached from the surface. Plunge-diving species like the Brown Pelican will rise suddenly when prey is spotted, then half-fold their wings, turn 90° sideways, and plunge to the surface, extending their wings backward just before spearing the surface. Because of their exceptional buoyancy, only the bill, outstretched neck, and forebody penetrate the surface. **Reference:** Johnsgard (1993).

American White Pelican MAP 4; PLATE 1
Pelecanus erythrorhynchos
OTHER NAMES. White Pilikin (C).

Identification. 61″ (155 cm); wingspan 105″ (266 cm). Largest bird in W. Hemisphere in overall length and wingspan. All-white plumage except for black primaries and outer secondaries. Long, pouched, dull orange bill, with short horn on upper mandible during breeding season. Wood Stork has black tail, and black in wings includes inner secondaries. Storks fly with outstretched necks, pelicans with folded necks.
Voice. Silent away from nesting colony.
Habitat. Estuaries, lagoons, shrimp farms; occas. reservoirs, ocean.
Distribution. Nests in interior Can. and U.S., locally on n coast of Gulf of Mex.; winters from s U.S. to n C.A.
Status in Belize. Other than a sight record in 1901, not recorded until 1981. Numbers have increased steadily in past 20 years; now UC to locally C winter visitor Oct. to May, primarily n. of Belize City (e.g., Crooked Tree and Nova

Shrimp Farm BE), occas. s. along coast to n TO; once inland at Blue Creek OW, and once on Ambergris Caye.
Reference. *Status:* Jones et al. (2000).

Brown Pelican PLATE 1
Pelecanus occidentalis
OTHER NAMES. Pilikin (C).

Identification. 49″ (124 cm); wingspan 88″ (223 cm). Unmistakable. Plumage changes gradually over the first three years, and ads. differ in breeding and nonbreeding seasons. *Ad.:* mostly silvery gray, with nearly black belly; underwings dark, with whitish central stripe; head and neck white, with golden yellow face and forecrown; pouch and facial skin dark gray brown. *Prebreeding:* chestnut stripe along full length of hindneck, yellow patch at base of foreneck; by time of incubation, yellow crown and face become dingy white. *Juv. and 1st basic:* almost entirely dirty gray brown except for white belly. *2nd year:* develops head pattern of ad. but with some dinginess or mottling and no yellow on crown; dark belly, retaining some whitish feathers initially, but lacks silvery gray upperparts of ad.
Voice. Ads. are silent; nestlings give muted groaning and screeching calls.
Habitat. Coastlines, inshore and offshore waters, offshore islands; less common in estuaries and shrimp farms, rarely inshore lagoons and ponds. Nests in colonies in mangroves.
Distribution. Resident along coasts and offshore islands from c U.S. to Venezuela and s Chile. Limited dispersal to coastal (rarely inland) areas outside breeding range.
Status in Belize. Nests on several cayes. C year-round visitor on cayes and along mainland coast; occas. inland, as at Crooked Tree BE.

FAMILY: PHALACROCORACIDAE (Cormorants)
World: 39. **New World:** 11. **Belize:** 2. Nearly worldwide, mostly in N. Temperate Zone. Cormorants are characterized by an elongated body with moderate-length tail; rather short wings; long neck; moderately long, thin bill with hooked tip; relatively small, featherless, expand-

able gular pouch; totipalmate feet (webbing be-tween all four toes); and thick, short legs set far back on their body; but unlike other such birds, they readily stand upright, and some even perch effortlessly on small branches. They never plunge from the air in pursuit of fish but dive from the surface and pursue prey by swimming under-water. To take flight, they must run along the surface of the water with rapidly beating wings. Because of their high body density, take-offs are actually more labored than in the much larger pelicans. When on the water, they characteris-tically swim with their bill held slightly above horizontal. When perched, they frequently hold their wings spread, presumably for thermoregu-lation, although the precise function (or func-tions) is not clear. Both species in Belize fly with their outstretched neck held slightly above hori-zontal, and with a slight kink in the middle. Both frequently glide for brief periods in straight flight but do not soar for extended periods like the Anhinga. Ibises fly with rapid, shallow wing-beats and with neck and head slightly drooped. **Reference:** Johnsgard (1993).

Things to note: size, relative tail and bill lengths, angle of bill/gular pouch at face, pres-ence/absence of white at base of bill.

Neotropic Cormorant   PLATE 1
Phalacrocorax brasilianus
OTHER NAMES. Olivaceous Cormorant (arch.), Shag or Sheg (C), pats i ha (K).

Identification. 26″ (66 cm). Only cormorant found inland; however, both species found to-gether on Ambergris Caye and along much of coast. Noticeably smaller and slimmer than Double-crested, with shorter, thinner bill and proportionately longer tail. Bill-face interface forms a point (straight in Double-crested), but this is not always a reliable character, particularly in imms. When both species seen together, can usually be separated by size. *Flight:* less labored than in Double-crested, with faster wingbeats. *Ad.:* thin white border at base of bill and gular pouch contrasting sharply with orange bill and black head (more conspicuous in breeding sea-son). *Breeding ad.:* white ear plumes. *Juv.:* best

told from Double-crested by size and propor-tions; at close range, pointed base of bill, black lores.
Voice. Usually silent away from nesting colony but occas. utters a deep, short growl. *At nest:* low froglike grunts.
Habitat. Lagoons, estuaries, shrimp farms, rice fields, coastline and inner cayes (especially in south). Nests in colonies in trees.
Distribution. Resident from Mex., s Texas, and W.I. s. to s S.A.
Status in Belize. C resident on mainland and lagoon side of Ambergris Caye; occas. on other inner cayes; unrecorded from outer cayes. Large numbers congregate at Crooked Tree BE.

Double-crested Cormorant
MAP 5; PLATE 1
Phalacrocorax auritus
OTHER NAMES. Shag or Sheg (C).

Identification. 30″ (76 cm). Only cormorant on the cayes s. of Ambergris. Noticeably larger and heavier bodied than Neotropic, with longer, heavier bill and proportionately shorter tail; orange lores (lacking in Neotropic); interface of bill/gular pouch and face usually straight or slightly rounded, not pointed. *Flight:* slightly more labored than Neotropic, with slower wing-beats. *Ad.:* lacks white border at base of bill. *Breeding ad.:* black ear tufts. *Juv.:* differs from Neotropic primarily in size and proportions, straight face–gular pouch interface, orange lores.
Voice. Usually silent away from nesting colony. *At nest:* low, grunting growls.
Habitat. Mangroves, coastline and nearshore waters of cayes, harbors and coastal beaches along n. mainland coast; occas. shrimp farms. Nests in small colonies in mangroves and littoral forest.
Distribution. Nests in interior and coastal Can. and U.S. s. locally to Mex. and n Belize; most inland populations migrate to coastal areas in winter.
Status in Belize. Resident on small cayes w. of Ambergris Caye and off Belize City; FC to C year-round visitor on cayes s. to Sapodillas and along mainland coast s. to n TO. Occas. inland

at Crooked Tree BE and New R. OW. Numbers have increased significantly in past 20 years (noted as unusual as recently as 1982). **Reference.** *Identification:* Patten (1993).

FAMILY: ANHINGIDAE
(Darters)

World: 2. **New World:** 1. **Belize:** 1. Primarily Tropics and subtropics. Anhingas have a much slimmer build than cormorants, with a pencil-thin neck; a small head not much thicker than their neck; a long, thin, pointed bill; and a much longer tail. They inhabit swampy areas with both fresh and brackish water, as well as coastal mangrove forests. They swim low in the water, often with only their head and neck above the surface. Like cormorants, they pursue prey by diving from the surface and swimming underwater. Also, like cormorants, anhingas often perch with their wings held spread, presumably to assist in thermoregulation and perhaps also to facilitate drying their wings when wet. Unlike cormorants, they frequently soar on thermals high above the terrain. In sustained flight, anhingas fly with alternating flaps and glides with their neck outstretched. **Reference:** Johnsgard (1993).

Anhinga   PLATE 1
Anhinga anhinga
OTHER NAMES. Water Turkey (arch.),
Darter (arch.), Snake Bird (C).

Identification. 35″ (89 cm). Although significantly larger in total length than cormorants, it is much slimmer, with a long, thin neck and bill, which is pointed, not hooked, and a long tail. Mostly black, with greenish gloss; bold white greater wing coverts; black-and-white-striped scapulars and wing coverts; pale-tipped tail. Unlike cormorants, typically swims with only neck and head above water; hence its popular name "Snake Bird." *Flight:* alternates gliding with rapid, shallow wingbeats in direct flight, much like an accipiter. Holds neck straight out and slightly below horizontal. Flies higher than cormorants and often soars for long periods, riding the thermals much like a hawk. ♂: black head, neck, and breast. ♀: brown head, neck, and breast, contrasting sharply with black belly and upperparts.

Voice. Deep nasal, guttural *aa-aa-aa-aa-aa-aa-aa;* also, shorter, grunting notes.

Habitat. Forest-lined lagoons, swamps, sluggish tree-lined rivers, coastal estuaries, mangrove forests, innermost mangrove cayes. Nests in trees.

Distribution. Resident from se U.S. to c S.A.; modest s. migration in northernmost populations.

Status in Belize. UC to FC resident on mainland; recorded frequently on mangrove cayes between Punta Ycacos and the Rio Grande TO, and occas. on other inner cayes, including Ambergris.

FAMILY: FREGATIDAE
(Frigatebirds)

World: 5. **Atlantic Ocean:** 2. **Belize:** 1. Tropical and subtropical oceans and coastlines worldwide. Frigatebirds are characterized by extremely long, thin wings held in a strong crook; a long, forked tail; and a long, slim bill with a hooked tip. Unlike cormorants and anhingas, they have a short neck and a rounded head, and small, weak, virtually rudimentary legs and feet that enable them to perch but not to walk or swim. They have a wingspan of up to nearly 8 ft. (2.4 m). The male has a highly distensible, bright red gular pouch. Frigatebirds are exceptionally light, with highly pneumatized bones that account for only 5% of their body weight, allowing them to soar effortlessly for long periods, broken only by occasional slow, deep wingbeats. Frigatebirds are remarkably agile despite their large size and gangly appearance. A frigatebird will relentlessly pursue a gull or tern with a freshly caught fish, harassing it until it drops its prey. Then, with an adroitness that seems to defy the laws of aerodynamics, the frigatebird will whirl around and catch the prey before it hits the water. Frigatebirds also deftly pick fish and offal from the water surface with their bill as they swoop low over the water. **References:** Harrison (1985, 1987).

Magnificent Frigatebird   MAP 6; PLATE 1
Fregata magnificens
OTHER NAMES. Man-o'-War Bird (arch.),
Scissors Tail (C).

Identification. 38½" (98 cm); wingspan 88"
(223 cm). Unmistakable, with its long, thin
wings sharply bent at the wrist; long, hooked
bill; and long, forked tail (usually held shut in
gliding flight). *Ad. ♂:* glossy black throughout
except for paler inner secondaries on dorsal surface; small patch of bare red skin on throat
usually covered by throat feathers; during courtship, inflates red sac to enormous size, many
times size of head when fully inflated. *Ad. ♀:*
black hood, white breast. *Imm.:* white head,
breast, and upper belly; white on head (and
breast in ♂) gradually lost in successive molts
until ad. plumage is attained in about 8 years.
Voice. Away from nesting colony, typically silent; however, occas. emits a guttural *graw*. At
the nest, ♂ emits resonant knocking sounds ac-
companied by bill clacking as part of courtship
display; ♀ responds with short, wheezy calls.
Habitat. Estuaries and other coastal areas, inshore and offshore waters, mangrove cayes. Nests
in large colonies in mangroves.
Distribution. Resident in tropical Atlantic and
e Pacific oceans; widespread dispersal within
breeding range (but rarely inland) and modest
dispersal into temperate areas n. and s. of breeding range.
Status in Belize. Large nesting colony on Man-
o'-War Caye, smaller colony on Half Moon
Caye; elsewhere, C year-round visitor along
mainland coast, all cayes, and at sea. Occas.
inland.

FAMILY: ARDEIDAE
(Herons, Egrets, and Bitterns)
World: 63. **New World:** 25. **Belize:** 16. Worldwide away from polar regions. Herons are wading
birds characterized by a long neck, long legs,
and a very short tail. Nearly all have a spear-
like bill for catching fish and amphibians. Night-
foraging herons have a thicker bill and a generally shorter neck. In the Boat-billed Heron,
the bill is massive and bulbous. Most diurnal
herons show little plumage difference between

imm. and ad.; however, nocturnal species have
marked age-related plumage differences. Some
herons have two morphs, one of which is white.
Egrets and herons are not taxonomically distinct,
but bitterns, tiger-herons, and night-herons are.
Some herons generally keep their neck extended
while standing; others mostly keep their neck
folded (and thus invisible), but all hold their
neck folded in flight. Upon taking flight, some
(notably Little Blue Heron) will keep their neck
extended for a while, but once settled into steady
flight, will fold their neck in. Other long-legged,
long-necked waders such as storks, ibises, and
spoonbills always keep their neck fully extended
both while standing and in flight. **References:**
Hancock (1999); Hancock and Kushlan (1984).

Bitterns

Bitterns are reclusive marsh dwellers characterized by streaked or reticulated brown plumage.
Most often seen in flight when flushed from tall
grass or reeds; seldom visible when perched. In
flight, the two large bitterns are told from tiger-
herons and imm. night-herons by unstreaked,
dark remiges, which contrast sharply with finely
streaked, pale brown wing coverts. Night-herons
are smaller and usually do not flush from tall
grass. Bitterns fly with bill pointed slightly above
horizontal; night-herons have hunchbacked appearance, with bill held at or below horizontal
plane. On the ground, bitterns generally keep
neck folded, except, when alarmed, they extend
neck and point bill skyward to blend in with tall
grass or reeds. Least Bittern is tiny and not likely
to be confused with anything else, except perhaps Green Heron or large rail.
    Things to note (Pinnated vs. American):
pattern and location of streaks and bars, pres-
ence/absence of dark malar stripe. *In flight,* tail
contrast, wing contrast.

Pinnated Bittern   MAP 7; PLATE 2
Botaurus pinnatus
OTHER NAMES. South American Bittern
(arch.), Margarita (C, S).

Identification. 27½" (70 cm). From American
Bittern by finely barred head and neck, contrasting with bold black, reticulated streaks in back

and wings, and absence of black malar stripe. Nearly as large as a tiger-heron. *Flight:* contrasting dark tail, less heavily streaked underparts.

Voice. Simple *gawk,* usually when flushed. In breeding season, ♂ gives deep booming *poonk* or *poonkoo.*

Habitat. Tall grass and reeds in wet areas.

Distribution. Resident from se Mex. locally through C.A. to c S.A.

Status in Belize. UC and rarely seen local resident s. at least to c BE, possibly to TO (presence confirmed; breeding not established). Unrecorded in Belize prior to 1970, but probably overlooked.

References. *Status:* Dickerman (1960); Miller and Miller (1992); Wood and Leberman (1987). *Voice:* Stiles and Skutch (1989).

American Bittern PLATE 2
Botaurus lentiginosus

Identification. 22″ (56 cm). From much larger Pinnated Bittern by conspicuous black malar stripe; tawny brown face; streaked, not barred, neck; and lack of black, reticulated streaks in back and wings. *Flight:* tail not contrasting darker than rump.

Voice. Occas. throaty *ahk* when flushed.

Habitat. Tall-grass marshes, rice fields.

Distribution. Nests from c Can. s. to c U.S.; winters from c U.S. to s Mex. and n W.I., rarely to Pan.

Status in Belize. Occas. winter visitor Oct. to Apr.; recorded from OW, BE, TO, and Ambergris Caye.

Reference. *Status:* Wood and Leberman (1987).

Least Bittern MAP 8; PLATE 2
Ixobrychus exilis

Identification. 11½″ (29 cm). Stays hidden in tall-grass marshes; typically seen only during short flights. Somewhat similar to imm. Green Heron but much smaller. Large ochraceous buff wing panel bordered behind with rufous—very conspicuous in flight. *Ad.* ♂: black, rufous, and buff above; diffusely streaked pale buff and white below; black crown, yellow-buff face, rufous

nape, and black back, rump, and tail, with two narrow white lines down back. *Ad.* ♀: duller; black areas replaced by dark brown. *Juv.:* much like ad. ♀ but back streaked with pale brown; foreneck and breast more prominently streaked.

Voice. Harsh rail-like *chack-chack-chack-chack.* In flight, a short, flat *kuk* or *gik.* On breeding grounds a low, chuckling *ö ö ö ö ö* or *haw haw haw haw haw* with last note softer.

Habitat. Tall-grass marshes, where it stays well hidden.

Distribution. Nests from n U.S. locally to c S.A.; n. populations migratory.

Status in Belize. Resident locally s. at least to s OW and c BE, possibly Ambergris Caye. More widespread in winter, occurring annually as far south as the rice fields near Big Falls, TO. Recorded once on Half Moon Caye, 17 Apr. 1958.

References. *Status:* Dickerman (1973); Wood and Leberman (1987).

Bare-throated Tiger-Heron PLATE 2
Tigrisoma mexicanum
OTHER NAMES. Bare-throated Tiger-Bittern (arch.), Mexican Tiger-Bittern (I. Davis), Barking Gaulin (C), xep jo chai (K), ho'chai (M).

Identification. 30″ (76 cm). From bitterns by very slow, lumbering flight; heavyset neck; different stance; featherless, yellow throat. Does not freeze with bill pointed skyward as a means of camouflage. Heavyset neck makes head seem disproportionately small. *Flight:* less contrast between remiges and wing coverts. Limpkin is superficially similar, but among other features, Limpkin has unique flight with rapid upstroke. *Ad.:* black crown, gray face. *Imm.:* finely barred head and face; prominent black-and-white-barred remiges, especially noticeable in flight.

Voice. *Call:* deep, guttural *woof,* usually repeated, generally given only when flushed. *Courtship call:* far-carrying, low-pitched *grow* or *graw,* repeated frequently.

Habitat. Marshes, lagoons, streamsides, swamp forest, occas. mangroves. Frequently perches in open, either on the ground or in a tree.

Distribution. Resident in lowlands and foothills from n Mex. to Hon.; also C.R. to nw Colombia.

Status in Belize. Locally FC resident at low elevations on mainland and Ambergris Caye.

Egrets and Their Allies

Most "egrets" are white during at least part of their lives or have a white morph. The Great Blue Heron and Reddish Egret both have a dark morph, and the ad. Little Blue Heron is dark. Only the Louisiana Heron lacks a white plumage. More than 95% of Great Blue Herons in Belize are dark-morph birds, as are about 80% of Reddish Egrets. All egrets nest and roost colonially in trees. ID of Louisiana Heron, dark-morph ad. Reddish Egret, and dark-morph Great Blue Heron is usually straightforward. Distinguishing ad. Little Blue Heron from imm. dark-morph Reddish Egret, and imm. Little Blue Heron from Snowy Egret, can be more difficult.

Things to note: body size, bill color, leg and foot color, presence/absence of plumes, feeding behavior. *In flight,* quickness of wingbeats.

Great Blue Heron   MAP 9; PLATES 2, 3
Ardea herodias
OTHER NAMES. Great White Heron (white morph only), Blue Gaulin (C), Toby Full Pot (C), jọ chai (K), ho ho (M).

Identification. 45″ (114 cm). Large grayish heron with yellow legs/feet. *Flight:* dusky remiges contrast darker than rest of plumage; slow, deep wingbeats. *Ad. basic:* blue gray, with dusky vinaceous neck; white head with prominent black supercilium extending as short black plume on back of crown; black crescent at bend of wing; rufous thighs; yellow bill. *Ad. alt.:* attains silvery plumes on lower neck and back. *Imm.:* brownish gray, with blackish crown, white face, and no plumes; streaked underneath; lacks black on sides and belly; bill mostly blackish. *White morph:* all-white plumage; yellow bill and legs/feet; usually has white plume extending from back of crown; from Great Egret by leg color, large size, crown plume.

Voice. Guttural *grock* to *grääwk,* typically upon flushing.

Habitat. Most wet areas that are not densely forested; especially common at shrimp farms and shallow lagoons. White morph confined to mangroves, beaches, littoral forest in coastal areas and cayes. Nests singly or, more typically, in small colonies in mangroves and littoral forest on small cayes.

Distribution. Nests from coastal Alaska and c Can. s. to nw Mex., Yucatán Pen., and Galápagos Isl. N. interior populations migrate southward. White morph resident in Caribbean from s Florida to Venezuela.

Status in Belize. FC winter visitor in lowlands throughout, including cayes, primarily Aug. to May; fewer in summer. Small nesting colonies on Cayo Rosario (off Ambergris Caye) and in Shipstern Lagoon CO. UC white morph found on n cayes and occas. along mainland coast s. to Dangriga.

Great Egret   MAP 10; PLATE 3
Ardea alba
OTHER NAMES. Great White Egret (U.K.), American Egret (arch.), Common Egret (arch.), White Gaulin (C), jo'jo (K), ho ho (M).

Identification. 36″ (91.5 cm). Large white heron with yellow bill and black legs/feet. *Flight:* slow, steady wingbeats; crook of neck when folded in flight dips well below plane of body; legs project considerably past the tail. *Alt.:* plumes on lower neck and back, but not hindcrown; bill and facial skin become brighter, orangish. *Juv. and ad. basic:* greenish yellow facial skin and yellow bill (tipped dusky in juv.).

Voice. 1. Scratchy, guttural *äääawk,* not especially loud;
2. coarse, guttural *gäääää.*

Habitat. Most unforested areas with standing water. Nests in small colonies on small mangrove islands.

Distribution. One of the most widespread birds in the world, nesting in temperate and tropical zones on six continents. N. populations migrate s. in winter.

Status in Belize. C winter visitor, less C in summer, although large numbers congregate at Crooked Tree BE in May and June prior to and at onset of rainy season. Small nesting colonies in Shipstern Lagoon, Northern and Southern Lagoons BE, and Little Monkey Caye TO.

Snowy Egret
MAP 11; PLATE 3

Egretta thula

OTHER NAMES. White Gaulin (C), jo'jo (K), ho ho (M).

Identification. 21″ (53.5 cm). Medium-sized, all-white heron. *Ad. basic:* black bill, yellow face, black legs, and yellow feet. *Alt.:* white plumes on crown, lower neck, and back; red lores and orange feet at height of breeding season. *Juv.:* bill often yellowish at base, and thus, face-bill contrast not as evident as in ad.; back of legs yellow green, sometimes including all but a narrow black strip down the front; when viewed from side or back, legs can appear similar in color to those of imm. Little Blue.

Voice. Similar to that of Little Blue Heron; higher-pitched, more nasal than in Great Egret. Calls less than other herons.

Habitat. Most unforested areas with standing water. Nests in colonies on small mangrove islands.

Distribution. Nests from c U.S. to s S.A.; n. populations migrate s. in winter.

Status in Belize. C winter visitor, less C in summer; however, modest numbers remain at Crooked Tree BE into June. A few may nest on Bird Caye in Northern Lagoon BE.

Reference. *Identification:* Kaufman (1990).

Little Blue Heron
PLATE 3

Egretta caerulea

OTHER NAMES. Carpenter (C), Blue Gaulin (C), pulcha jo̱ chai (K), ta'an ho ho (M).

Identification. 22″ (56 cm). Medium-sized; distinctly different ad. and juv. plumages. In all plumages, has black-tipped blue-gray bill, greenish yellow legs/feet. *Ad. basic:* dark slaty blue gray with dull purplish blue head and neck.

Alt.: elongate plumes on crown, lower neck, and back; reddish purple head and neck. *Imm.:* all white except for dusky tips to outer primaries (usually not visible in folded wings, and often difficult to see even in flight); birds molting into ad. plumage (1st summer) acquire dark feathers gradually through an extended molt beginning in spring and lasting sometimes until early autumn.

Voice. Raspy, nasal *äääääo*, higher-pitched and more drawn out than in Great Egret.

Habitat. Unforested and sparsely forested areas with standing water. Congregates at shallow-water lagoons, shrimp farms, rice fields; less common along forest-lined streams and rivers.

Distribution. Nests from se U.S. to c S.A.; n. populations migrate s. in winter.

Status in Belize. C winter visitor, primarily Aug. to May, with a few imms. remaining through summer. Does not nest in Belize.

Reference. *Identification:* Kaufman (1990).

Tricolored Heron
MAP 12; PLATE 3

Egretta tricolor

OTHER NAMES. Louisiana Heron (arch.), Crabcatcher (C).

Identification. 24″ (61 cm). From most other herons by contrasting white underparts; long, thin bill. *Ad. basic:* slaty blue-gray upperparts; bill yellowish basally. *Alt.:* two short white plumes on hindcrown, creamy buff back plumes; bill blue basally. *Imm.:* gray and dull cinnamon rufous above.

Voice. Raspy *äääää* or *quäää*, similar to that of Little Blue but less drawn out, does not drop in pitch at end.

Habitat. Mudflats, estuaries, lagoons, coastal shorelines, marshes. Nests in mangroves in small colonies, often mixed with other herons.

Distribution. Primarily resident from nw Mex. and se U.S. to n S.A.; some withdrawal from northernmost areas in winter.

Status in Belize. FC to C winter visitor in coastal areas and on cayes; less C inland and in summer. Nests in Shipstern Lagoon CO, and on cayes w. of Ambergris Caye.

Reddish Egret

MAP 13; PLATE 3

Egretta rufescens

OTHER NAMES. Red Gaulin (C).

Identification. 28″ (71 cm). Medium-large heron, distinctly larger than Little Blue with much slower wingbeat. Legs/feet dark blue gray; nearly white eyes contrast with dark face. *Ad. basic dark morph:* reddish head and neck; bluish slate body; bicolored bill, pink with a black tip. *Alt. dark morph:* plumes on crown, lower neck, and back. *Imm. dark morph:* all-dark bill; reddish brown head and neck contrast with slate gray body (Little Blue is uniformly blue gray and has dark eyes). *Juv. dark morph:* distinctive dull, chalky gray plumage with pinkish cinnamon hue on head and neck. *Ad. white morph:* all white with distinctive bicolored bill. *Imm. white morph:* all-dark bill and legs/feet distinguish it from other white egrets. *Flight:* slow, deep wingbeats; pale stripe on underwing (dark morph).

Voice. Mostly silent, but occas. gives a low moaning call or short grunt.

Habitat. Mangrove islands (for nesting), coastal mudflats and estuaries, shrimp farms.

Distribution. Local resident from nw Mex. and se U.S. to s Mex., n Belize, and n W.I. Disperses s. to C.R. and Venezuela.

Status in Belize. UC to FC resident on n cayes and along coast s. to c BE; occas. to n TO. Recorded once inland: New R. OW, 8–14 Apr. 2001. Nests in Shipstern Lagoon CO and cayes w. of Ambergris Caye.

References. *Identification:* Lee and Clark (1988); Kaufman (1990).

Cattle Egret

MAP 14; PLATE 3

Bubulcus ibis

OTHER NAMES. Buff-backed Heron (alt.), White Gaulin (C), jo'jo (K), ho ho (M).

Identification. 19½″ (49.5 cm). Medium-small white egret with relatively short, stocky bill. *Flight:* bouncy compared with steady flight of similar-sized Snowy Egret and imm. Little Blue Heron; bill shape also readily distinguishes it in flight. *Ad. basic and imm.:* all-white plumage with yellow lores and bill, dark olive-gray legs/feet. *Alt.:* orange-buff plumes on crown, lower neck, and back; for brief period at height of breeding season, bill becomes red orange, lores purplish, and legs/feet dusky red.

Voice. Usually silent away from nesting colony, but occas. gives low nasal *onk* to *änk* notes, especially at roost. *At nest:* various squawks and guttural *ick-ack* notes.

Habitat. Pastureland, flooded agricultural fields and grasslands, newly planted rice fields, lawns, mangroves, small, wooded cayes. Nests in mangroves.

Distribution. Prior to late 19th century, confined to tropical Afr. and Asia. With deforestation and spread of irrigated agriculture and domestic livestock grazing, rapidly expanded range in all directions and now found throughout Tropics and much of Temperate Zone worldwide.

Status in Belize. First recorded in Belize in 1956 but undoubtedly arrived earlier. Now C to locally VC winter visitor, with a few remaining throughout the year. May nest on Bird Caye in Northern Lagoon BE.

Reference. *Distribution:* Smithe (1960).

Green Heron

PLATE 2

Butorides virescens

OTHER NAMES. Green-backed Heron (combined form), Little Green Heron (arch.), Poor Joe (C), cak i pulcha jo̱ chai (K), ho ho (M).

Identification. 16″ (40.5 cm). Small, but distinctly larger than Least Bittern. Nervously flicks tail and raises and lowers crown feathers when foraging and when alarmed. *Ad.:* chestnut face, neck, and breast; brown and white streaks down foreneck and central breast; dark green back and rump, with short pale blue-gray back plumes; base of bill, facial skin, and legs/feet yellow; dull brown wing feathers edged with buff. *Imm.:* heavily streaked gray brown, rufous brown, and buff above, brown and white below, with only face and sides of neck unstreaked; more like Least Bittern, but much larger; habits and habitat quite different.

Voice. 1. Loud *keow!* sometimes repeated two to several times;

2. rapid cackling *ak-ak-ak-ak-ak,* often with an emphatic *AK!* at end.

Habitat. Forest-lined lagoons, ponds, rivers, and streams; freshwater and brackish lagoons; mangroves; littoral forest; occas. mudflats. Much more likely to be seen in open than Least Bittern. Nests in littoral forest and mangroves.

Distribution. Nests from s Can. to Pan. N. populations migratory, with some birds reaching n S.A. in winter.

Status in Belize. C winter visitor; less C in summer. Nests on cayes and locally on mainland.

Agami Heron PLATE 2

Agamia agami

OTHER NAMES. Chestnut-bellied Heron (alt.), Blue Jacket (C).

Identification. 28″ (71 cm). Very long, slender bill and relatively short legs give it different body proportions from those of other herons. *Ad.:* dark glossy green above, with chestnut on sides of neck and underparts; short, curled silvery gray plumes on neck, concentrated near base; longer, straight silvery white plumes on hindcrown and lower back in breeding plumage. *Imm.:* gray brown above, streaked dark brown and pale buff below.

Voice. At nesting colony, rough, rolling *d-d-d-d-d* and (nestlings?) froglike *crk crk crk. . . .*

Habitat. Dense foliage along edges of swamps, rivers, lagoons; best seen on exposed shorelines in dry season. Nests in mangroves.

Distribution. Resident from c Veracruz and c Yucatán Pen., mostly on Gulf-Caribbean slope, to c S.A.

Status in Belize. UC and local on mainland in dry season, apparently throughout, but FC at Crooked Tree BE. Nesting colony near mouth of Moho R., possibly also Monkey R. TO.

Night-Herons and Boat-billed Heron

Boat-billed Heron is strictly nocturnal; the two night-herons are also occasionally active during the day. All three nest and roost colonially in trees. Juv. Black-crowned and Yellow-crowned present the greatest ID challenge.

Things to note (juv. night-herons): body proportions, bill color, size of spots in plumage. *In flight,* projection of feet beyond tail.

Black-crowned Night-Heron PLATE 2

Nycticorax nycticorax

OTHER NAMES. Night Heron (arch.).

Identification. 23½″ (59.5 cm). Heavier-set than Yellow-crowned, with shorter neck, proportionately larger head, and smaller eyes. *Flight:* only a portion of feet project beyond tail. *Ad.:* gray above, white below, with black crown and back and two long, white crown plumes. Superficially resembles Boat-billed Heron but lacks its immense swollen bill and pink undersides. *Juv.:* warmer brown plumage than Yellow-crowned; bill greenish yellow with dark tip and culmen; larger, elongate white spots in wing coverts; diffuse streaking on neck. *1st summer:* similar to juv. but paler underneath, darker crown; smaller spots in wings due to feather wear.

Voice. Hoarse *gwok.*

Habitat. Marshes, lagoons, estuaries, mangroves; roosts communally in trees.

Distribution. Widespread; nests on all continents except Aust. and Antarctica. N. populations withdraw s. in winter.

Status in Belize. UC to locally C winter visitor on mainland, mid-Sept. to late May; also recorded on Ambergris Caye and Caye Caulker. Small numbers remain through summer at Crooked Tree, where it may nest.

References. *Identification:* Davis (1999); Kaufman (1988b).

Yellow-crowned Night-Heron PLATE 2

Nyctanassa violacea

OTHER NAMES. King Carpenter (C).

Identification. 21½″ (54.5 cm). More common than Black-crowned in most areas. Slimmer overall, with slightly thicker bill, smaller head, and larger eyes. Proportionately longer neck more frequently held extended than in Black-crowned. *Flight:* feet and lower portion of legs project beyond tail. Darker remiges contrast more with rest of upperparts than in Black-crowned (but not as much as in the bitterns). *Ad.:* distinctive blue-gray plumage with bold black-and-white head pattern. *Juv.:* duller brown plumage than Black-crowned; bill all black; small triangular white spots in wing coverts; more pronounced streaking on neck than Black-crowned. *1st summer:* similar to juv. but with pale auriculars and little, if any, wing spotting.

Voice. 1. Harsh *kaow;*
2. shorter *kow.* Notes louder and higher-pitched than in Black-crowned.

Habitat. Towns, lawns, shores of rivers, estuaries, ponds, swamps, marshes, mudflats, mangroves; often seen foraging beneath streetlights. Roosts communally in large trees and mangrove forests; nests in mangroves and littoral forest.

Distribution. Nests from nw Mex. and e U.S. to c S.A. Northernmost populations withdraw s. in winter.

Status in Belize. FC to C resident in lowlands nearly throughout, including cayes, but confirmed nesting sites relatively few. Generally more C in coastal areas than inland.

References. *Identification:* Davis (1999); Kaufman (1988b).

Boat-billed Heron   PLATE 2
Cochlearius cochlearius
OTHER NAMES. Cooper (C), Spoon-bill Carpenter (C).

Identification. 19½" (49.5 cm). Bloated bill, pinkish buff breast. *Ad.:* chestnut belly and shaggy black plumes on hindcrown. *Imm.:* similar to ad. but with brown, not gray, upperparts, whitish belly, and shorter plumes in crown.

Voice. At colonies and roosts a distinctive, comical *oo oo ah ah oo oo* and similar variations.

Habitat. Forages along shores of estuaries, ponds, and rivers at night; roosts inconspicuously in trees along banks of rivers, lakes, and swamps during the day. Nests in colonies in mangroves and other dense streamside trees.

Distribution. Resident from c Mex. to c S.A.

Status in Belize. UC to locally FC resident primarily in coastal lowlands, including Ambergris Caye and Turneffe Isl., and once on Caye Caulker.

FAMILY: THRESKIORNITHIDAE
(Ibises and Spoonbills)

World: 33. **New World:** 13. **Belize:** 4. Most tropical and subtropical regions worldwide, with several species ranging well into Temperate Zones. Ibises and spoonbills are medium to large wading birds, similar in appearance and behavior to herons but with decurved (ibises) or spatulate bill and usually a small area of bare skin on the face, throat, or nape. Unlike herons, they always fly with their neck fully extended. They have much faster and shallower wingbeats than herons and storks, distinguishing them in flight at any distance.

Things to note (Glossy vs. White-faced): eye color; bill color; presence/absence, extent, and thickness of pale line bordering facial skin.

White Ibis   MAP 15; PLATE 3
Eudocimus albus
OTHER NAMES. American White Ibis (alt.), White Culu (= Curlew) (C), Coco (C), Cocito (S).

Identification. 23" (58.5 cm). *Ad.:* striking white wader with long, decurved red bill, red facial skin, and red legs/feet. *Juv.:* brown above, paler on head and neck; black remiges; white rump, underparts, and underwing; orange soft parts. *1st summer:* plumage mottled brown and white as birds gradually molt into ad. plumage. Orange soft parts gradually become brilliant red. *Flight:* distinctive black tips to outer primaries (ad.); rapid, shallow wingbeats; outstretched neck; White Ibises fly strung out in lines, Glossy Ibises in compact groups with individual birds often changing position within the flock.

Voice. Relatively soft gooselike *hänk,* usually given in flight.

Habitat. Marshes, rice fields, shrimp farms, mangroves, swamp forest, littoral forest. Nests in mangroves and littoral forest.

Distribution. Resident from nw Mex. and se U.S. to nw S.A.; some n. dispersal after the breeding season.

Status in Belize. FC resident in coastal lagoons, larger cayes; absent in most of interior s. and w. of BE and n OW. Congregates in large numbers at shrimp farms when shrimp are being harvested. Nesting colonies in Shipstern Lagoon and at Shipstern Caye CO, cayes w. of Amber-gris, the Turneffe Isl., and Bird Caye in North-ern Lagoon BE. Numbers have increased signifi-cantly in the last 30 years.

Reference. *Status:* Wood and Leberman (1987).

Scarlet Ibis NOT ILLUSTRATED
Eudocimus ruber

Identification. 23″ (58.5 cm). Size and behavior same as White Ibis. *Ad.:* brilliant red plumage throughout, except for black-tipped outer pri-maries. *Juv.:* virtually identical to juv. White Ibis.
Voice. Silent away from nest.
Habitat. Mangrove forests and associated mud-flats, occas. marshes.
Distribution. Trinidad and coastal S.A. Wan-ders occas. to Lesser Antilles, rarely farther n. and w.
Status in Belize. One record: Punta Ycacos TO, 17 Mar. 1999 (with White Ibises).
Reference. *Status:* Jones et al. (2002).

Glossy Ibis MAP 16; PLATE 3
Plegadis falcinellus

Identification. 23″ (58.5 cm). Like juv. White Ibis but all dark. Dark brown eyes in all plum-ages. Limpkin has thicker, less decurved bill and unique flight, with strong upstroke and with neck and head held below horizontal. *Ad. alt.:* dark chestnut throughout, with metallic pur-plish and bronzy green iridescence on rump and wing coverts; head and neck unstreaked. *Ad. basic and imm.:* dusky brown with metal-lic green iridescence, finely streaked brown-and-white head and neck; thin, pale blue line from top of eyes to upper base of bill (supraloral area), and thinner line from bottom of eyes to lower base of bill (visible only at close range); brown bill.
Voice. Usually silent, but when flushed occas. gives a nasal moaning *aak aak aak* or a rapid series of nasal quacks *waa waa waa waa . . . .*
Habitat. Flooded rice fields, marshes, wet mead-ows.
Distribution. Nests locally in s Eur., s Asia,

tropical Afr., se U.S., W.I., n Venezuela, and, re-cently, se Mex. Disperses widely outside breed-ing season. May have colonized New World from Old World in 19th century.
Status in Belize. Local and generally UC win-ter visitor in north-central part, primarily from mid-Sept. to late May; R farther n. and s. Num-bers have increased significantly since first report in Apr. 1969. Thus far, only a nonbreeding visi-tor, but may establish breeding population in the future. While the majority of *Plegadis* ibises in Belize have not been IDed to species (see below), enough have been IDed to suggest that most, if not all, are *P. falcinellus*.
References. *Status:* Howell and de Montes (1989); Jones et al. (2000). *Identification:* Kauf-man (1990). *Voice:* Sibley (2000).

White-faced Ibis *(Plegadis chihi)*, a poten-tial vagrant, is very similar to Glossy. *Ad. alt.:* bright red eyes, feathered white border to bare facial skin, including area behind eyes; gray, not brown, bill, tends toward paler, more golden-rosy iridescence on rump and wings than Glossy. *Ad. basic:* nearly identical to Glossy; legs usually redder; white in face (including powder-blue supraloral line of Glossy) absent. *Imm.:* nearly indistinguishable in the field from Glossy. In short, if the bird clearly has red eyes, it is White-faced. If it does not have red eyes, then the ID may be problematic. Because of the potential for White-faced to turn up in Belize, no all-dark ibis should be assumed to be a Glossy unless field marks specific to that species are seen.

Roseate Spoonbill MAP 17; PLATE 3
Platalea ajaja
OTHER NAMES. Pink Gaulin (C), Cuchara (S).

Identification. 29½″ (75 cm). Long, spatulate bill. Feeds by sweeping head methodically from side to side with tip of bill submerged. *Flight:* rapid, shallow wingbeats and outstretched neck; often glides for short periods. *Ad.:* one of Belize's most striking birds, with rose-pink wings and body, red shoulders, and orange tail. *Juv.:* white, with pale pink underwing and tail. *1st summer:* pale pink nearly throughout.

Voice. Usually silent, but occas. a soft grunting *heh heh heh heh.*

Habitat. Lagoons, flooded rice fields, shrimp farms.

Distribution. Resident from nw Mex., sc and se U.S. to sc S.A.

Status in Belize. Locally FC resident in coastal belt, increasingly less C s. along coast, much less C inland s. of n OW and BE. Nests in Shipstern Lagoon, cayes in Chetumal Bay, and formerly in Doubloon Bank Lagoon OW. Numbers have significantly increased in the last 30 years.

References. *Status:* Miller and Miller (1992); Wood and Leberman (1987).

FAMILY: CICONIIDAE
(Storks)

World: 19. New World: 3. Belize: 2. Worldwide, primarily in Tropics. Storks are large wading birds, among which are some of the largest of all flying birds. They are similar to ibises but heavier-bodied, usually with extensive areas of bare skin on the face (in some, also including neck), a heavier bill usually not markedly decurved, and long, broad wings used to ride thermals to great heights, much in the fashion of hawks. Like ibises and spoonbills, most fly with outstretched neck and long legs trailing behind their short tail. Weighing in at 15½ lb. (7 kg), the ♂ Jabiru is the largest bird in the New World by weight; however, the American White Pelican is larger in both body length and wingspan.

Things to note: wing pattern; bill size, shape, and color.

Jabiru   MAP 18; PLATE 3
Jabiru mycteria
OTHER NAMES. Turk (C), Fillymingo (C).

Identification. 55½″ (141 cm); wingspan 141″ (358 cm). Massive, slightly upturned black bill; unfeathered black head and neck except for conspicuous pinkish red inflatable sac at base of neck. Only stork in the world with all-white plumage. *Ad.:* plumage pure white; sac at base of neck brighter than in imm.; small patch of silvery gray downlike feathers on top of head (lost briefly during breeding season). *Imm.:* plumage

has dirty grayish and brownish cast; dull red skin at base of neck.

Voice. Generally silent; loud bill clapping at nest.

Habitat. Estuaries, rice fields, shrimp farms, wet meadows; for nesting, large trees in savannas, in open farmland, or bordering broad rivers or estuaries. Pairs nest singly, not in colonies.

Distribution. Resident locally from se Mex. to sc S.A.

Status in Belize. Resident in a belt from OW and BE s. in the coastal plain to ne TO and interior s TO. Other than an occas. stray, absent from CO and CA; one record from Ambergris Caye. Nests late Nov.–Apr., after which disperses widely, with majority congregating near coast, especially at shrimp farms. Formerly, present only in nesting season, presumably wintering in s Mex., but has become year-round resident, with protection from persecution and with proliferation of rice fields and shrimp farms, which provide abundant food supply.

Reference. *Conservation:* Jones and Vallely (2001).

Wood Stork   MAP 19; PLATE 3
Mycteria americana
OTHER NAMES. Wood Ibis (arch.), John Crow Culu (= Curlew) (C), Galletan (S).

Identification. 37½″ (95.5 cm). Large; about size of Great Blue Heron, but dwarfed by Jabiru, which is half again larger. Smaller bill than Jabiru; bill turns downward near tip. Only head and upper neck unfeathered; no red at base of neck. *Flight:* conspicuous black flight feathers; outstretched neck and legs; groups frequently soar in circles high overhead, riding the midday thermals much in the fashion of vultures and other birds of prey. *Ad.:* black to light brown bill. *Juv.:* mostly feathered gray-brown head and neck, yellowish bill.

Voice. At nesting colony, hissing and bill clacking; generally silent otherwise.

Habitat. Lagoons, estuaries, marshes, shrimp farms, rice fields. Nests in colonies in swamp forests.

Distribution. Resident from w Mex. and se U.S. to c S.A.

Status in Belize. FC resident; has increased significantly in last 30 years. Nesting colonies in Shipstern Lagoon CO, Doubloon Bank Lagoon OW, cayes in Chetumal Bay, and Aguacaliente Swamp TO. Disperses widely after nesting season, often congregating in large numbers at Crooked Tree BE and shrimp farms. Relatively scarce in CA; unrecorded from c and s cayes.

FAMILY: CATHARTIDAE
(New World Vultures)

World: 7. **New World:** 7. **Belize:** 4. Throughout New World s. of Can. New World vultures are not related to Old World vultures, which are members of the hawk family (Accipitridae). Once thought to be closely related to hawks, New World vultures are actually more closely related to storks, with which they share a featherless head and neck, absence of a syrinx, and perforated nostrils. However, they lack the long neck, bill, and legs of storks and are not aquatic. Like hawks, they have a short hooked bill, an adaptation for tearing away the skin and flesh of carrion. Vultures in the genus *Cathartes* have an acute sense of smell shared by few other birds, notably some shearwaters and the kiwi of N.Z. They use their sense of smell to home in on prey items that may be nearly buried in dense vegetation or within the forest, where they are largely hidden from view. New World vultures spend most of their time in the air and, like many hawks, are exceptionally well adapted for soaring flight. They often soar for hours on thermals, flapping only occasionally to gain altitude or move to a new location. Different wingbeat and soaring patterns among the various species can serve as a useful ID feature for distant birds. The Turkey Vulture is migratory, withdrawing entirely from n. parts of its range in winter. **Reference:** Ferguson-Lees and Christie (2001).

Things to note: color of head and bill, head-body proportions. *In flight,* pattern and location of gray or white in wings, wing shape, presence/absence of white in body, flight silhouette.

Black Vulture   FIGURE 13E,F; PLATE 5
Coragyps atratus
OTHER NAMES. Buzzard (coll.), John Crow (C), so'sol (K), bosh ch'om (M), Sope (S).

Identification. 24″ (61 cm); wingspan 58½″ (149 cm). Larger head on smaller body than in other vultures. *Flight:* from Turkey and Lesser Yellow-headed (genus *Cathartes*) by conspicuous pale silvery gray patch in outer third of each wing, broader wings, much shorter tail, and rapid, shallow wingbeats; like these, often holds wings in dihedral when soaring (compare Fig. 13f,h) but does not rock side to side; often soars higher and congregates in larger flocks than Turkey Vulture; in perched birds, larger head and shorter tail and wings give it squatter appearance than *Cathartes*. *Ad.:* wrinkled gray featherless head, white-tipped bill; whitish legs. *Juv.:* finely feathered blackish head; all-dark bill; darker legs.

Voice. Typically silent. *When feeding:* a muffled *woof,* very much like a slightly disturbed dog. *In courtship:* short guttural hisses.

Habitat. Found in or over nearly every habitat except unbroken dense forest and open ocean. The vulture most likely to be found feeding in urban areas and on beaches. Nests in cavities in dead trees.

Distribution. Resident from s U.S. to s S.A.

Status in Belize. C to VC on mainland; occas. on Ambergris Caye.

References. *Identification:* Clark and Wheeler (1987); Wheeler and Clark (1995).

Turkey Vulture   FIGURE 13G,H; PLATE 5
Cathartes aura
OTHER NAMES. Buzzard (coll.), Doctor John Crow (C), so'sol (K), bosh ch'om (M), Sope (S).

Identification. 28″ (71 cm); wingspan 68½″ (174 cm). *Flight:* silvery gray remiges contrast with black body and wing coverts; longer wings and tail, and much slower, deeper wingbeats than Black; holds wings in distinctive dihedral when soaring (see Figure 13g,h), and typically rocks from side to side in soaring flight. *Ad.:*

unfeathered red head, white bill. *Juv.:* dark gray head and bill; brown feather edges; longer wings and tail than Black.

Voice. Silent.

Habitat. Found in or over nearly every terrestrial habitat, even occas. dense forest. Nests in cavities in dead trees.

Distribution. Partially migratory; breeds from s Can. to s S.A. Northern populations migrate, many as far s. as S.A., in winter.

Status in Belize. C to VC on mainland away from extensively forested areas; less C on Ambergris Caye and unrecorded from most other cayes.

References. *Identification:* Clark and Wheeler (1987); Wheeler and Clark (1995).

Lesser Yellow-headed Vulture

MAP 20; FIGURE 13G,H; PLATE 5

Cathartes burrovianus

OTHER NAMES. Savanna Vulture (arch.), John Crow (C), Sope (S).

Identification. 23″ (58.5 cm); wingspan 61½″ (156 cm). When perched, primaries project noticeably beyond tail, but only to or slightly beyond tail in Turkey. *Ad.:* predominantly yellow-and-orange head apparent even at a distance; white bill. *Juv.:* dusky head with thin pale collar on rear portion; yellowish swath across face; dark sooty brown plumage with narrow pale brown edges to remiges. *Flight:* similar to Turkey, but distinguished in flight by head color and white primary quills in upper wing; tends to soar lower; in a mixed group, usually found among the lowest-flying birds.

Voice. Silent.

Habitat. Open country, especially savannas, rice fields, and shrimp farms, usually in association with Turkey Vultures. Less likely to be found in populated areas than Black or Turkey.

Distribution. Resident from Oaxaca and Veracruz to c S.A.

Status in Belize. UC to FC resident in e. portion w. to sw OW, ne CA, occas. to nw CA and e. base of Maya Mtns.; absent from forested areas, including Mtn. Pine Ridge. Regularly seen on Ambergris Caye; unrecorded from other cayes. Contra Eitniear (1985), there is no indication that populations within Belize are migratory or seasonal.

King Vulture
FIGURE 13D; PLATE 5

Sarcoramphus papa

OTHER NAMES. King John Crow (C), yawa so'sol (K), ussi (M), Sope Real (S).

Identification. 30″ (76 cm); wingspan 72½″ (184 cm). *Ad.:* unmistakable; white with black flight feathers; multicolored featherless head. *Juv.:* larger than other vultures, with shorter, thicker bill; usually shows some white flecking on underparts. *Flight:* Flies on level or nearly level wings (Fig. 13d); appears front-heavy, with forebody and head carried below plane of wings. Wingbeats slow, deep, and labored, not rapid and shallow like Black. *Ad.:* patterned similarly to Wood Stork, but with much shorter neck, broader wings; feet do not project beyond tail tip. *Juv.:* Flight profile similar to much smaller Black, but has broader rectangular wings and lacks silvery gray patch in outer wing; has varying amounts of white mottling in underwing coverts, axillars, and belly.

Voice. Usually silent.

Habitat. Open country, patchy and contiguous woodland.

Distribution. Resident from Guerrero and s Veracruz to c S.A.

Status in Belize. Widespread but generally UC resident on mainland; most C in CA and w TO, less so in coastal areas.

FAMILY: PHOENICOPTERIDAE
(Flamingos)

World: 5. **New World:** 4. **Belize:** 1. Tropical and S. Temperate Zones throughout except se Asia and Aust. Their neck and legs are longer in proportion to body size than in any other group of birds, and their flight is rapid and direct, with outstretched neck and long legs trailing behind. Flamingos are highly gregarious, gathering in tight feeding groups of up to hundreds of thousands of birds, sometimes exceeding a million in one species. They inhabit large shallow alkaline or saline lakes, lagoons, and estuaries from sea level up to nearly 15,000 ft. (4,500 m). Flamingos' pink and red plumage comes from the food they eat, which is high in carotenoids. Special enzymes break down the carotenoids, converting them to pigments that are deposited in the developing feathers.

Greater Flamingo   PLATE 3
Phoenicopterus ruber
OTHER NAMES. American Flamingo (alt.).

Identification. 46½″ (118 cm). Extremely long, thin neck and legs; oddly shaped, bent, bicolored bill; black remiges. When foraging, sweeps head and bill side to side at an odd angle while walking in shallow water. *Flight:* long, spindly neck and legs extending fore and aft give it a unique appearance. *Ad.:* bright pink throughout; possible confusion with Roseate Spoonbill, but note black remiges in flight and very different bill and body proportions. *Juv.:* grayish buff, with pink cast on underparts. *Imm. (1st basic):* white, with only a hint of pink.
Voice. In flight, deep gooselike honking.
Habitat. Shallow coastal lagoons and estuaries.
Distribution. Locally resident in n Yucatán Pen., W.I., Galápagos Isl., s Eur., Afr., and c Asia. Some dispersal away from nesting colonies outside breeding season.
Status in Belize. Several records, but only one documented: two seen flying over Aguacaliente Lagoon TO, 28 Mar. 2001. Other reports: Birds Isle, Belize City, sometime in the 1970s; New R. between Carmelita and Guinea Grass OW, 20 Mar. 1991; four flying over Belize City, 25 Sept. 1992. Occas. reports from ne CO may also be valid.

FAMILY: ANATIDAE
(Ducks and Geese)
World: 157. **New World:** 75. **Belize:** 17. Worldwide except Antarctica and the great deserts of Afr. and Asia. A large and diverse group highly adapted for aquatic existence, ducks and geese have short, thick legs; feet with three forward-facing, webbed toes and a small, slightly elevated hindtoe; a thick layer of down feathers for insulation; and a highly developed oil gland for

waterproofing, which is accomplished by preening frequently. Most ducks have a laterally flattened bill with a nail at the tip, adapted for eating aquatic vegetation. All have lamellae near or at the lateral edges of the bill, well developed in plankton-filtering species and reduced to sharply serrated "teeth" in fish-eating species. The basic plumage of ♂s in the large subfamily Anatinae, referred to as "eclipse" plumage, is acquired in late summer and early autumn through molt of all flight feathers simultaneously, rendering the birds flightless while new feathers grow in. Flight feathers grow in first, reenabling flight before the strikingly patterned body feathers of alternate plumage are fully acquired. **Reference:** Madge and Burn (1988).

SUBFAMILY: DENDROCYGNINAE
(Whistling-Ducks)
Named for their high-pitched, whistling vocalizations, whistling-ducks are believed to be more closely related to geese than to ducks. They are recognized in flight by long legs that project beyond the tail, a slightly drooped head and neck, and blackish underwings. Wingbeats more rapid than in geese and Muscovy Duck, less rapid than in other ducks. In the 1960s the Black-bellied Whistling-Duck was rare in Belize and the Fulvous Whistling-Duck was unrecorded. Today the Black-bellied is locally common to abundant; Fulvous is fairly common in winter at Crooked Tree, the only place where it is seen regularly.

  Things to note: bill and leg color, location and pattern of white and black in plumage. *In flight,* underwing-belly contrast.

Black-bellied Whistling-Duck   PLATE 4
Dendrocygna autumnalis
OTHER NAMES. Black-bellied Tree-Duck (arch.), Whistling Duck (C), pijij (K), pato (M), Pijiji (S).

Identification. 19″ (48.5 cm). *Ad.:* red bill, pink legs/feet, large white wing patch, black belly. *Juv.:* gray bill and legs/feet; whitish belly; somewhat similar to Fulvous, but note gray head and pale dusky belly. *Flight:* broad white bar on upper wing; little (juv.) or no (ad.) contrast between underwing and belly.

Voice. Various high-pitched shrill whistles, repeated frequently. Spanish name "Pijiji" (pronounced "Pē-hē-hē") is onomatopoeic for a frequently given vocalization.

Habitat. Rice fields, coastal lagoons, other wet or ponded areas with emergent vegetation.

Distribution. Resident from nw Mex. and s Texas to c S.A.

Status in Belize. C to locally VC late summer and autumn visitor in many areas; smaller numbers in winter through early summer. Nests principally in north, locally in south. Abundance has increased dramatically in last 35 years, with only four records prior to 1965.

References. *Status:* Barlow et al. (1969, 1972); Wood and Leberman (1987).

Fulvous Whistling-Duck   MAP 21; PLATE 4

Dendrocygna bicolor

OTHER NAMES. Fulvous Tree-Duck (arch.).

Identification. 20″ (51 cm). From Black-bellied by all-dark upperwing surface, uniform pale tawny plumage, white flank stripes. Ad. and juv. similar. *Flight:* black underwings contrast sharply with pale tawny undersides; conspicuous white uppertail coverts.

Voice. Very hoarse, tinny, and nasal *hudeer,* like a tin horn, not piercing like that of Black-bellied.

Habitat. Large, marsh-lined lagoons and estuaries, rice fields.

Distribution. Resident in New World from nw Mex. and s U.S. to sc S.A.; in Old World from c and s Afr. to sc Asia.

Status in Belize. FC visitor to Crooked Tree BE, primarily from Nov. to May; small groups occas. seen at Blue Creek rice fields OW and Cox Lagoon BE; one record for s Ambergris Caye. Thus far, only a nonbreeding visitor, but may establish breeding population in near future. Unrecorded prior to 1986.

References. *Status:* Howell et al. (1992); Miller and Miller (1992).

SUBFAMILY: ANSERINAE
(Geese)

Most geese are long-distance migrants that breed in Arctic and high Temperate Zones and rarely migrate as far as the Tropics. They are marginally represented in Belize, with only three records of two species. Most feed on grain in fields, sometimes well away from water, but return to the safety of lakes and bays to roost at night. Their bill is not laterally flattened as in most ducks and is generally shorter and deeper based. Geese fly with slow, steady wingbeats. Although there are only three documented records, small flocks of unidentified geese are reported by locals occasionally in winter in CO.

Things to note (imm.): bill and leg color, scalloped or unscalloped plumage. *In flight,* contrast between tail and tail coverts.

Greater White-fronted Goose

FIGURE 10A,B

Anser albifrons

OTHER NAMES. White-fronted Goose (combined form).

Identification. 29″ (73.5 cm). Gray brown, with white lower belly and vent. *Ad.:* irregular black barring on underparts; white face (ring around base of bill); pale pinkish orange bill and orange legs/feet (pink in Snow). *Imm.:* lacks diagnostic features of ad.; distinguished from imm. blue-morph Snow by pale bill and legs/feet, dark tail with contrasting white uppertail coverts, and paler, scalloped plumage. *Flight:* distinguished from blue-morph Snow by conspicuous white uppertail coverts, black tail, and wing coverts that do not contrast lighter than rest of wing.

Voice. Nasal, high-pitched, laughing *ah-kook-a-loook.*

Habitat. Pastureland and agricultural fields, including rice fields.

Distribution. Nests in Arctic from Alaska to nc Can.; migrates to c Mex., s Eur., and sc Asia in winter.

Status in Belize. One record: Canton Farm 22 mi. (35 km) n.w. of Belize City, 15 Jan. 1973 (specimen).

Figure 10

Geese. Greater White-fronted Goose, *(a)* adult and *(b)* juvenile; Snow Goose, *(c)* white morph and *(d)* blue morph.

Snow Goose
FIGURE 10C,D

Chen caerulescens

OTHER NAMES. Blue Goose (blue morph only).

Identification. 27″ (68.5 cm). *Ad. white morph:* all white except for black primaries. American White Pelican is much larger, with distinctive pelican bill. *Imm. white morph:* resembles ad. except for pale gray-brown upperparts. *Ad. blue morph:* all dark, with white head and upper neck, light blue-gray wing coverts. *Imm. blue morph:* like ad. but with dark head; somewhat resembles imm. Greater White-fronted but with dark bill and dark pink legs/feet. *Flight:* White morph: black primaries only. Blue morph: white underwing linings; pale blue upperwing coverts contrast with black primaries; little contrast between uppertail coverts and tail.

Voice. Harsh, nasal *honk* and higher-pitched *heenk*.

Habitat. Pastureland and agricultural fields, including rice fields.

Distribution. Nests in New World Arctic; winters from c U.S. to c Mex.

Status in Belize. Two records: Big Falls Farm ne CA, Nov. 1975 (blue morph); white morph at Tres Leguas OW, 29 Jan. to 12 Feb. 1991 (white morph).

References. *Status:* Howell et al. (1992).

SUBFAMILY: ANATINAE
(True Ducks)

Tribe: Anatini (Surface-feeding Ducks)

The Anatini are the largest group of waterfowl in Belize, with eight species recorded, all but one migratory. Their common name reflects their habit of tipping in shallow water to feed on aquatic vegetation just below the surface. They also feed on land on grains and grasses. When flushed, they take off nearly vertically. The resident Muscovy Duck has a longer hindtoe, stronger claws, and legs set farther forward than in other ducks, enabling it to perch in trees, where it nests in cavities. It is frequently domesticated, but free-flying birds away from settlements are likely to be wild. Domesticated birds often have various amounts of white in their plumage. Males in the genus *Anas* have a highly distinctive alternate plumage, which is worn most of the year. The ♂ in eclipse plumage is mostly mottled and streaked in browns like the ♀. Only two, Blue-winged and Cinnamon Teal, present a major ID challenge.

Things to note (♂ eclipse and ♀): body size; bill size, shape, and color; face pattern (streaks or mottling vs. clear areas); pattern at base of tail. *In flight,* wing pattern (wing coverts, secondaries), belly color.

Muscovy Duck

PLATE 4

Cairina moschata

OTHER NAMES. Pats (K), pato (M).

Identification. 30″ (76 cm). Easily distinguished from other ducks by large, bulky size; black plumage; pinkish bill with black ring. *Ad.:* entirely white upperwing and underwing coverts. *Imm.:* much reduced white in wing coverts (sometimes absent). ♂: bare facial skin, shaggy crest, dark red to black knob at base of bill. ♀: feathered face; lacks crest and knob at base of bill. *Flight:* slow, steady wingbeats (faster in whistling-ducks); shorter, straighter neck than cormorant.

Voice. Generally silent. *In courtship:* ♂ occas. gives hissing sound, and ♀ a soft quack.

Habitat. Wooded margins and eddies of major river systems; wooded lagoons and swamps; marshes.

Distribution. Resident from w and ne Mex. to c S.A.

Status in Belize. UC to FC resident locally on mainland, except CA and w OW, where seldom seen; occas. on Ambergris Caye. Formerly more common, but numbers have been reduced by hunting.

Reference. *Conservation:* Jones and Vallely (2001).

American Wigeon

MAP 22; PLATE 4

Anas americana

OTHER NAMES. American Widgeon (arch.), Baldpate (arch.).

Identification. 18½″ (47 cm). Steep forehead, pale powder-blue bill with black tip. ♂ *alt.:* white crown; broad, metallic green postocular stripe. ♂ *eclipse:* roughly intermediate between ♂ alt. and ♀. *Ad.* ♀: pale salt-and-pepper gray head contrasts with brown body; dark smudge around and behind eyes sometimes appears as diffuse stripe. *Flight:* ad. ♂ has conspicuous white upper secondary coverts; ad. ♀ and, to a lesser extent, imm. ♂ have reduced white in greater coverts, but still show more white in forewing than other ♀ ducks; imm. ♀ often lacks white in wing.

Voice. ♂ gives nasal, sneezy *hur-whee-ha,* with emphasis on middle note; ♀ gives harsh *grouw* notes.

Habitat. Marshes, estuaries, lagoons, rice fields; farm ponds with shallow, standing water.

Distribution. Nests from Alaska to n and wc U.S.; winters from s Alaska and e U.S. to nw S.A.

Status in Belize. R to locally FC winter visitor in north, mid-Oct. to early Apr. Most records are from Crooked Tree BE and Blue Creek rice fields OW. One record for Ambergris Caye; unrecorded s. of Belize City.

Reference. *Status:* Jones et al. (2000).

Mallard

NOT ILLUSTRATED

Anas platyrhynchos

Identification. 21½″ (54.5 cm). ♂ *alt.:* all-green head and neck separated from chestnut brown breast by narrow white ring; pale body; mostly black posterior. ♀: mottled brown nearly throughout; paler neck and head with dark crown and eyestripe; white-edged tail and undertail coverts; bill orange with dark central spot. ♂ *eclipse:* like ♀ but with olive-yellow bill, reddish brown breast. *Flight:* blue secondaries bordered fore and aft with white.

Voice. Loud nasal *wack wack wack wack wack wack wack,* trailing off and speeding up toward end.

Habitat. Marshes, lagoons, rice fields; farm ponds with shallow, standing water.

Distribution. Nests in N.A. from n Can. s. to n Mex.; n. populations withdraw s. in winter.

Status in Belize. One record: Big Falls Farm ne CA, 25 Nov. 1976.

Reference. *Status:* Jones et al. (2002).

Blue-winged Teal

PLATE 4

Anas discors

OTHER NAMES. Duck (C), kok'rax i pats (K), pato (M), Pato Careto (S).

Identification. 15½″ (39.5 cm). ♂ *alt.:* distinctive white facial crescent, blue-gray head and neck. ♂ *eclipse and* ♀: mottled brown nearly throughout; darker crown and eyestripe set off paler supercilium; whitish throat and face (area at base of bill); broken white eye-ring. *Flight:* fast and direct; blue upper secondary coverts, brighter in ♂.

Voice. ♂: high-pitched, thin, toy-mouse-like *tseef* and *tseef-tuf* (♂ calls more frequently in spring). ♀: 1. weak, coarse, nasal *kack;* 2. rapid, nasal *quănh quănh quănh-quănh-quănh-quănh.*

Habitat. Most areas with shallow, standing, or slow-running water; most common in rice fields and other freshwater marshes.

Distribution. Nests from e Alaska and c Can. to c U.S.; winters from s U.S. to n S.A.

Status in Belize. C to locally VC winter visitor, early Aug. to mid-May. Most abundant at Crooked Tree BE and Blue Creek rice fields OW.

References. *Identification:* Kaufman (1988a); Jackson (1991).

Cinnamon Teal
PLATE 4

Anas cyanoptera

Identification. 15½" (39.5 cm). ♂ *alt.:* bright chestnut nearly throughout; eyes red; legs/feet yellow. ♀: very similar to ♀ Blue-winged but with longer, heavier, and slightly spatulate bill, more gently sloping forehead, more uniformly patterned face with less obvious eyestripe and eyering, reduced or absent pale facial area at base of bill, darker throat, and more diffuse markings on breast and sides; because of its rarity in Belize, ♀ Cinnamon should be IDed only under the most favorable of circumstances by someone thoroughly familiar with both species. ♂ *eclipse* (July to Oct.): similar to ♀ but with warm, slightly reddish brown plumage and red eyes.

Voice. Similar to that of Blue-winged; ♂ sometimes gives a low-pitched whistled *peep.* Generally silent in winter.

Habitat. Similar to that for Blue-winged Teal.

Distribution. Nests from sw Can. through w U.S. to Mex. plateau, and disjunctively in S.A.; winters from sw U.S., primarily on Pacific slope, to s S.A.

Status in Belize. R winter visitor, Sept. to Apr. Most records are from Nova Shrimp Farm BE and Blue Creek rice fields OW.

References. *Status:* Jones et al. (2000). *Identification:* Jackson (1991).

Northern Shoveler
PLATE 4

Anas clypeata

OTHER NAMES. Shoveller (arch.).

Identification. 18½" (47 cm). Larger than other teal, with large spatulate bill (longer than head). ♂ *alt.:* green head, white breast, chestnut belly, blue upper secondary coverts. ♂ *eclipse:* similar to ♀ but with mottled dusky head, white facial crescent (but not crisp like ♂ Blue-winged Teal), yellow eyes. ♀: mottled brown nearly throughout; bill much larger and more spatulate than in Cinnamon Teal; angle of bill and forehead nearly flat. *Flight:* slower, more lumbering than smaller teal; ♀ has gray, not blue, upper secondary coverts.

Voice. ♂: very hoarse, coarse *sheck-sheck.* ♀: less hoarse *chek-ka chek-ka.* Generally silent in winter.

Habitat. Marshes, lagoons, rice fields; farm ponds with shallow, standing water.

Distribution. Nests in Arctic and n Temperate Zones worldwide; winters from S. Temperate Zone to near the equator.

Status in Belize. UC and local winter visitor in north, late Sept. to mid-Apr.

Reference. *Status:* Jones et al. (2000).

Northern Pintail
MAP 23; PLATE 4

Anas acuta

OTHER NAMES. Common Pintail (arch.).

Identification. 21½" (54.5 cm). Longer neck and proportionately smaller head, smaller and thinner bill, and longer tail give it a sleeker look than other ducks. ♂ *alt.:* unmistakable with chocolate brown head, white neck stripe and breast, mostly gray body, and long, pointed central tail feathers; bill gray with black ridge and cutting edge. ♂ *eclipse:* grayish body with black mottling, pale brown and whitish head and neck, and gray-and-black bill; lacks extended central tail feathers. ♀: mottled brown nearly throughout; unmarked face lacking conspicuous eyestripe or supercilium; bill uniformly lead gray; tail longer, more pointed than in other ducks (except ♂ pintail). *Flight:* long neck; sleek body; nearly unmarked wings have gray underwing linings, not white as in other *Anas* ducks.

Voice. ♂: hollow *toot* notes. ♀: harsh *cack* notes. Generally silent in winter.

Habitat. Marshes, estuaries, lagoons; shallow, standing water in rice fields.

Distribution. Nests in Arctic and N. Temperate Zone worldwide; winters from c Temperate Zone to near the equator.

Status in Belize. VU winter visitor in n. half, Nov. to early May.

Green-winged Teal   PLATE 4
Anas crecca
OTHER NAMES. Common Teal (U.K.).

Identification. 14½″ (37 cm). Smallest teal with proportionately smaller bill. ♂ *alt.:* distinctive chestnut and iridescent green head, vertical white bar on side of breast, buff and black undertail coverts. ♂ *eclipse and* ♀: like other teal, mottled brown nearly throughout; smaller size apparent in direct comparison with ♂ eclipse and ♀ Blue-winged; also has shorter neck, more rounded head, steeper forehead, noticeably smaller and rather thin gray bill, bill often with small amount of yellow along sides of lower mandible, and slightly more prominent eyestripe and lores; throat and face do not contrast paler than rest of head; pale buff to whitish horizontal stripe along sides of undertail coverts; legs/feet fleshy gray (yellow in Blue-winged). *Flight:* compact body with short neck and narrow, pointed wings; rapid, twisting flight with abrupt changes in direction; iridescent green patch in secondaries (speculum); gray, not blue, upper secondary wing coverts; paler belly than Blue-winged, with fewer markings.

Voice. ♂: piping *krick* (♂ in autumn gives a hoarser call than in winter and spring). ♀: quacks much like other ♀ ducks, but call higher-pitched and thinner than most. Generally silent in winter.

Habitat. Marshes, lagoons, rice fields; farm ponds with shallow, standing water.

Distribution. Nests in Arctic and Temperate Zones worldwide; winters from c N.A., c Eur., and s Asia to s Mex., n Afr., and s Asia.

Status in Belize. R winter visitor, Dec. to Mar. Apparently more frequent formerly.

References. *Status:* Barlow et al. (1972). *Identification:* Jackson (1991); Kaufman (1988a).

Tribe: Aythyini (Bay Ducks)

Bay ducks are typically found in deeper water away from shore, where they dive beneath the surface for mollusks, crustaceans, aquatic insects, and rooted bottom vegetation. As an aid in swimming underwater, their legs are set farther back on body than in dabbling ducks, and their hindtoe is lobed. When flushed, the birds run across the water's surface to gain flight. Like dabbling ducks, the ♂ is boldly marked; the ♀ and eclipse-plumage ♂ are mostly brown. Most species also have a distinctive wing pattern, which aids in flight ID. Bay ducks, like dabbling ducks, are highly migratory, with most nesting at higher latitudes and few migrating as far south as the Tropics. Only two have been recorded in Belize.

Things to note: bill color and pattern, face pattern. *In flight,* extent of white, if any, in wing.

Ring-necked Duck   MAP 24; FIGURE 11D–F
Aythya collaris

Identification. 17″ (43 cm). Small, mostly dark duck with peaked to slightly crested head in profile. ♂ *alt.:* black back, pale gray sides and flanks, conspicuous white bar on side of breast, white ring on bill near tip. *Ad.* ♀: all brown except for gray side of head, small white patch on face at base of bill, white eye-ring, and (usually) a thin white postocular stripe; white ring around bill thin to absent. *Juv.:* like ♀ but lacks white in face and on bill; juv. ♂ may show traces of fine black-and-white barring on flanks of ad. ♂. *Flight:* gray remiges (lightest on secondaries) contrast with darker wing coverts; underwing pale gray. Lesser Scaup has white wing stripe.

Voice. Silent in winter.

Habitat. Open, deeper water in estuaries, lagoons, and ponds; occas. flooded rice fields.

Distribution. Nests from nc Can. to n U.S.; winters from n and c U.S. to n C.A.

Status in Belize. Small flocks regularly seen at Crooked Tree BE, late Oct. to early Apr. Seldom recorded elsewhere.

Reference. *Status:* Jones et al. (2000).

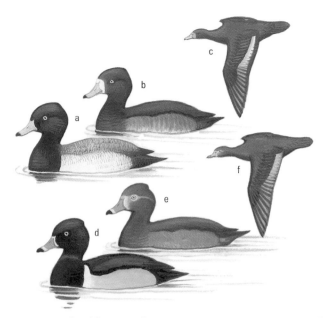

Figure 11

Bay Ducks. Lesser Scaup, *(a)* ♂, *(b)* ♀, and *(c)* ♀ in flight. Ring-necked Duck, *(d)* ♂, *(e)* ♀, and *(f)* ♀ in flight.

Lesser Scaup
Aythya affinis

MAP 25; FIGURE 11A–C

Identification. 16″ (40.5 cm). More rounded head than Ring-necked Duck. ♂ *alt.:* black fore and aft, with white midsection; pale bluish bill with black tip; back light gray (fine black-and-white barring); sides, flanks, and belly white. *Ad.* ♀: all brown like ♀ Ring-necked Duck but with side of face also brown; white facial patch at base of bill more conspicuous and usually more extensive than in Ring-necked Duck; bill lacks white ring near tip. *Juv.:* like ad. ♀ but with only trace of white patch in face at base of bill; on water, very similar to juv. Ring-necked Duck but has rounder head and browner face and lacks white eye-ring. *Flight:* broad white band in secondaries (pale gray in Ring-necked Duck), becoming gray in primaries; underwing linings white (pale gray in Ring-necked Duck).
Voice. Usually silent in winter.
Habitat. Open, deeper water in estuaries, lagoons, and shrimp farm ponds.
Distribution. Nests from Arctic to n U.S.; winters from n U.S. to C.A.

Status in Belize. Locally C winter visitor, mid-Oct. to early Apr., mostly in Shipstern Lagoon CO and Crooked Tree BE. R to VU elsewhere, including cayes.

Tribe: Mergini (Sea Ducks)

Sea ducks mostly nest in the Arctic and high Temperate Zones and winter at sea and, in the case of mergansers, on large lakes and bays. Only an occasional stray reaches the Tropics. Like bay ducks, they have a lobed hindtoe and run across the water's surface before taking flight. Mergansers have a long, narrow, rounded bill with the cutting edge (tomium) modified into saw-like serrations for grasping fish, their principal diet. As with other Anatinae, the ♂ is much more boldly patterned than the ♀. Most species have distinctive white wing patches. They fly with shallower wingbeats than other ducks.

Things to note: bill shape and color, neck-breast contrast, nature of crest. *In flight,* amount and pattern of white in wings.

Figure 12

Mergansers. Hooded Merganser, *(a)* ♀ and *(b)* ♂; *(c)* Red-breasted Merganser, ♀.

Hooded Merganser

FIGURE 12A,B

Lophodytes cucullatus

Identification. 17″ (43 cm). Small duck with crested head, very thin bill. Dives frequently, often escaping attention by diving rather than flying. ♂: unmistakable, with black-tipped white head fan, black-and-white bars on sides of breast, cinnamon flanks, and yellow eyes; head fan when lowered appears as broad white stripe behind eye; bill black. ♀: dark gray brown throughout with cinnamon-brown head fan; even when head fan is depressed, odd head shape with shaggy mane and thin bill readily distinguish it from other ducks; bill has orange base. *Flight:* slender duck with thin wings; rapid, shallow wingbeats; white in wings much reduced compared with Red-breasted.
Voice. Usually silent in winter, but wings produce high-pitched trill in flight.
Habitat. Freshwater ponds.
Distribution. Nests from se Alaska and c Can. to c U.S.; winters in w N.A. from se Alaska to U.S.-Mex. border and in e N.A. from New England to Florida and Texas, rarely to ne Mex.
Status in Belize. One record: Crooked Tree BE in 1990 or 1991.
References. *Distribution:* Ornat et al. (1989). *Status:* Jones et al. (2002).

Red-breasted Merganser

FIGURE 12C

Mergus serrator

Identification. 21½″ (54.5 cm). Noticeably larger than Hooded, with shaggy double-pointed crest at rear of crown (never fanned); longer bill, orangish in both sexes. ♂ *alt.:* dark green head; prominent white neck band; cinnamon-brown breast; black, gray, and white body. ♂ *basic and* ♀: orangish brown head merges with pale gray neck and body; white wing panel usually obscured. *Flight:* long, slender body; rapid, shallow wingbeats; ♂ has white across base of wings, split by two thin black lines; ♀ has white in secondaries only, split by one black line.
Voice. Usually silent in winter.
Habitat. Freshwater and brackish lakes and ponds, bays, and estuaries.
Distribution. Nests from Alaska and n Can. s. to wc Can. and Great Lakes; winters along both coasts to s Baja California and n Veracruz.
Status in Belize. Two records: 2 mi. (3 km) n. of Belize City, 1 Dec. 2000, and nearby Nova Shrimp Farm BE, 17 Dec. 2000 (two individuals).
Reference. *Status:* Jones et al. (2002).

Tribe: Oxyurini (Stiff-tailed Ducks)

The Oxyurini are small freshwater ducks with a longer tail than in other ducks and composed of stiff feathers that act as a rudder when diving. Their legs are set far back on the body to aid in propulsion under water. Like grebes, they can sink beneath the surface with hardly a ripple, as well as dive like other ducks. Their bill is more gooselike, not laterally flattened as in most other Anatinae. Only one member has reached Belize, and it is rare.

Masked Duck
Nomonyx dominicus

PLATE 4

Identification. 14″ (35.5 cm). Small duck with relatively long, pointed tail often held cocked. ♂ *alt.:* blue bill with conspicuous black tip; black head contrasts with chestnut neck and breast; body mottled chestnut and blackish. ♂ *basic,* ♀, *and juv.:* distinctive black-and-white-striped head; stripes broadest in ♂, narrowest in juv.; bill dull blue to gray. *Flight:* distinctive white wing patch.
Voice. Silent away from breeding areas.
Habitat. Marshes with mosaic of open water and dense emergent vegetation.
Distribution. Resident from w and s Texas and W.I. to sc S.A.
Status in Belize. R winter visitor; recorded Crooked Tree BE, Big Falls Farm BE/CA, and Cristo Rey CA, Dec. to Mar. Because of its skulking nature and marshy haunts, it is rarely seen and may be more common than the few records indicate.
References. *Status:* Howell et al. (1992); Jones et al. (2000).

FAMILY: ACCIPITRIDAE
(Hawks, Kites, and Eagles)
World: 235. **New World:** 71. **Belize:** 32. Nearly worldwide, absent only from Antarctica. The Accipitridae are characterized by powerful talons, a hooked bill used for catching and consuming prey, and a distinctive, often yellow cere (slightly swollen fleshy area around nostrils at base of upper mandible). Representatives are found in nearly all habitats and at all elevations. Those found in open country are expert gliders with broad wings adapted to soaring flight; those in forested areas have shorter wings and a longer tail for greater maneuverability. In some, the bill is specialized (e.g., snail eaters, such as Snail Kite and Hook-billed Kite, have an elongated hook). Wing shape varies widely, typically being long, broad, and rounded, but often relatively narrow and pointed.

Hawks present some of the most challenging ID problems, partly because the birds have so many different plumage forms. For example, imms. differ from ads., and many species go through several intermediate plumages; individual variation can be extensive in some species (many species even have two or more color morphs); and in some the ♂ and ♀ differ. To complicate matters, many imms. have a different flight shape from that of ads. (e.g., narrower wings, longer tail), and the ♂ and ♀ of the same species may differ significantly in size. **References:** Clark and Wheeler (1987); Ferguson-Lees and Christie (2001); Wheeler and Clark (1995).

SUBFAMILY: PANDIONINAE
(Osprey)
Cosmopolitan. Osprey is the only species in the subfamily Pandioninae, considered by some to be a separate family. It is taxonomically distinguished from other hawks by its reversible outer toe and spiny footpads for grasping fish. It also lacks bony ridges above its eyes, giving it a more round-headed appearance than that of other hawks. It plunges feetfirst into water after fish swimming near the surface.

Osprey
Pandion haliaetus

FIGURE 13A; PLATE 5

OTHER NAMES. Billy Hawk (C), Fishing Hawk (C), Jincho (S).

Identification. 24″ (61 cm); wingspan 64″ (163 cm). Large raptor with mostly white undersides and head. *Flight:* long wings with strong crook at wrist, all-white undersides, gray flight feathers, black patch at bend of underwing. Resident ssp. *ridgwayi:* immaculate white underparts, white head with thin black line through eyes. Migrant *carolinensis:* black flecking in upper breast, bold black band through eyes.
Voice. Piping, piercing *whew* to *kew* notes, singly, in a slow series, or in rapid succession (≈3 notes/sec).
Habitat. Most coastal and offshore areas with open water for feeding and trees or poles for perching; less commonly in vicinity of larger inland bodies of water. Nests on exposed platforms created by broken tree trunks, poles, old lighthouses, and other structures.
Distribution. Nests throughout most of N.A.

to n C.A. and W.I., through much of Eur., Asia, and Aust., and locally in Afr.; winters to c S.A., s Afr., and most of s Asia and Indonesia. **Status in Belize.** Caribbean *P. h. ridgwayi:* nests in cayes and coastal lagoons. Migratory *P. h. carolinensis:* UC to FC winter visitor in coastal lowlands and offshore cayes, where may be seen with *ridgwayi.* Occas. seen far from aquatic habitat.

SUBFAMILY: ACCIPITRINAE
(Accipiters)

Kites

The three species of forest kites in Belize— Gray-headed, Hook-billed, and Double-toothed —have broad, rounded wings with strongly barred remiges. All three occasionally soar above the forest canopy, Double-toothed less so than the other two. Hook-billed exhibits extraordinary plumage variation and pronounced seasonal movements. The remaining five kites in Belize are found in association with more open woodlands and unforested habitats. Except for the Snail Kite, these all have pointed wings, and all but the two *Ictinia* kites are easily IDed. Plumbeous and Mississippi can be difficult to ID in imm. plumages but do not overlap seasonally in Belize.

Things to note: head and face pattern, back color, size. *Ictinia* only, presence/absence of rufous in primaries, season of year. *In flight,* underwing pattern, rounded vs. pointed wings, tail length and shape, presence/absence and number of tail bands.

Gray-headed Kite

FIGURE 13C; PLATES 7, 10, 11
Leptodon cayanensis
OTHER NAMES. Cayenne Kite (arch.).

Identification. 19½″ (49.5 cm); wingspan 39″ (99 cm). Large, round-winged kite with fairly long tail, often seen soaring above canopy or perched in large tree. Black tail with three thin gray bands. *Ad.:* dark brownish gray upperparts, pale gray head, white underparts. Juv. has two distinctive plumage morphs, both dark brown

above with two or three broad, light gray tail bands. *Juv. light morph:* all-white head and underparts, black central crown patch; resembles stockier Black-and-white Hawk-Eagle, but with yellow, not black, lores; lacks white patch at bend of wing; more distinctly barred tail (two or three broad, light gray bands); black central crown feathers do not form a crest. *Juv. dark morph:* dark brown head, like rest of upperparts; lightly to boldly streaked underparts; two or three broad gray tail bands. *Flight:* Ad.: black underwing coverts, strongly barred black-and-white primaries and tail. Juv.: unlike ad., has white underwing coverts, but shares strongly black-and-white-barred underprimaries of ad. **Voice.** Emphatic catlike *raowwww!* to *e-raaoouu!* and *eee-yow!* **Habitat.** Typically, forested river edges, but may be seen in or over most heavily forested areas. **Distribution.** Resident from s Veracruz and Chiapas to c S.A. **Status in Belize.** UC resident on mainland. **Reference.** *Status:* Barlow et al. (1969).

Hook-billed Kite

MAP 26; FIGURE 13C,E; PLATES 7, 10, 11
Chondrohierax uncinatus

Identification. 16½″ (42 cm); wingspan 34½″ (87.5 cm). Extremely variable with at least seven plumage types. Both ad. and juv. have light, intermediate, and dark morphs, with some individual variation within each morph. Light-morph ad. ♂ and ♀ also differ. Common characters of all plumages: distinctive flight profile (see below); fairly long, slightly rounded tail; rather heavy, strongly hooked bill; yellow-green cere; yellow-orange supraloral spot; and yellow-orange to yellow legs/feet. Ad.'s eyes vary from white to pale green to bluish gray. Juv. has dusky eyes. *Ad. dark morph:* dark slate gray throughout, with one broad white tail band. *Juv. dark morph:* similar to dark-morph ad. but with pale gray to whitish barring in remiges, fine white flecks on undersides, two visible tail bands. *Ad. intermediate morph:* like dark morph but with fine white barring on underparts, white undertail coverts, bold black-and-white barring in pri-

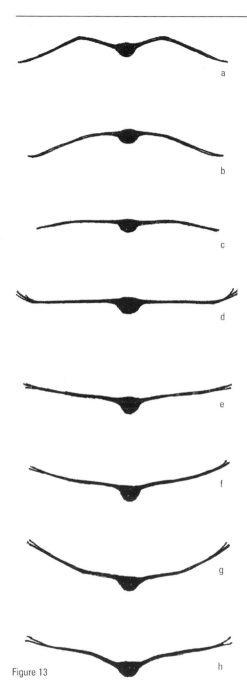

Hawks in flight.

(a) Osprey and Snail Kite soaring and gliding.

(b) Swallow-tailed, Mississippi, and Plumbeous kites and Cooper's Hawk gliding; Double-toothed Kite soaring and gliding; Swainson's Hawk gliding.

(c) Gray-headed, Swallow-tailed, Mississippi, and Plumbeous kites and Black-collared Hawk soaring; Hook-billed Kite and Broad-winged and Red-tailed hawks gliding; Crested Caracara, American Kestrel, Merlin, and Peregrine Falcon soaring and gliding.

(d) King Vulture and hawk-eagles soaring.

(e) Hook-billed Kite and Sharp-shinned, Cooper's, White, Gray, and Broad-winged hawks and black-hawks soaring; Black Vulture and Short-tailed Hawk gliding.

(f) Black Vulture and Short-tailed and Red-tailed Hawks soaring.

(g) Turkey and Lesser Yellow-headed vultures, White-tailed Kite, and Swainson's Hawk, White-tailed, Zone-tailed, and Roadside hawks soaring.

(h) Turkey and Lesser Yellow-headed vultures and Zone-tailed Hawk gliding; Northern Harrier soaring and gliding.

Figure 13

maries, two or three visible tail bands. *Juv. intermediate morph:* variable but basically dark brown above, white below with fine to coarse barring, white collar, three or four pale bands in tail. *Ad. ♂ light morph:* gray, with coarse gray-and-white or cinnamon-and-white barring underneath, boldly barred primaries, unbarred secondaries, two or three visible white bands in tail. *Ad. ♀ light morph:* gray face, rufous collar, coarse rufous barring underneath sometimes forming solid band across breast, boldly barred primaries and faintly barred secondaries, two or three visible white bands in tail. *Juv. light morph:* dark brown above, white to creamy white and unbarred below, all-white head and neck except for dark brown crown, three or four pale tail bands. *Soaring flight:* broad, rounded wings held slightly forward, sharply curved in at base posteriorly; outer primary tips well separated; tail spread and frequently twisted left and right for stability; holds wings flat, occasionally in slight dihedral. *Gliding flight:* tail compressed, wings bent at wrist and outer primaries compressed, sometimes to a point; distinguished from *Buteo* by strong notch where rear base of wing joins body, longer tail, more head projection, and large, deeply hooked bill. *Flapping flight:* slow, deep wingbeats.

Voice. Rapid nasal laugh: *cacaca-ca-ca-ca-ca ca ca ca ca ca ca,* slowing and dropping in pitch.

Habitat. Primary and old secondary forest; occas. forest edge; also may be seen soaring above forested areas.

Distribution. Generally resident from c Sinaloa and s Texas to c S.A., but pronounced seasonal movements occur throughout much of its range.

Status in Belize. Relatively UC resident in s. and w. portions; also in CO, where it may be present only in the breeding season. Large southbound migrating flocks occur along s. coast from mid-Oct. to mid-Nov. Recorded occas. on Ambergris Caye.

Reference. *Voice:* Moore (1992).

Swallow-tailed Kite

MAP 27; FIGURE 13B,C; PLATE 9

Elanoides forficatus

OTHER NAMES. Scissors-tail Hawk (C), tixerx (K), tihera nej (M).

Identification. 23" (58.5 cm); wingspan 49½" (125 cm). Striking black-and-white raptor with deeply forked tail, black back and flight feathers, white head and underparts. *Flight:* long, pointed wings; forked tail typically spread wide; graceful flight with occas. slow, moderately deep wingbeats.

Voice. Typically, *k-lee!* or *kree!* repeated several times. *In courtship:* series of *tew-whee* notes.

Habitat. Open broadleaf and pine forests, most common in upland areas.

Distribution. Nests in se U.S. and discontinuously from n C.A. to c S.A. Birds nesting in N.A. and C.A. migrate to S.A. in nonbreeding season.

Status in Belize. Locally FC summer resident in s. half, early Feb. to mid-Sept. Most C in Mtn. Pine Ridge; only an occas. migrant in n. half. Recorded twice in Sept. at Caye Caulker and once migrating across Bay of Honduras near Snake Cayes (69 individuals).

White-tailed Kite   FIGURE 13G; PLATE 9

Elanus leucurus

OTHER NAMES. Black-shouldered Kite (combined form).

Identification. 15½" (39.5 cm); wingspan 37" (94 cm). Mostly white with large black patch in upper wing. *Ad.:* gray back and wings; white head, underparts, and tail; small black area around eyes. *Juv.:* similar but with light rufous wash across breast, mottled gray and brown on crown and back. *Flight:* Large black patch in upperwing coverts. From below, all white except for black crescent in bend of wing. Much narrower wings and tail than White Hawk, and tail lacks black band. Flapping flight is erratic, with strong wingbeats. Hovers frequently while foraging.

Voice. Somewhat ospreylike *kerr,* but softer; juv. gives a more ospreylike *tew.*

Habitat. Open areas, including grasslands, pastures, wet meadows, rice fields, and marshes.

Distribution. Resident from nw and s U.S. to sc S.A.; s S.A. populations migrate n. in austral winter.

Status in Belize. FC and widespread resident on mainland; also several records from Ambergris Caye, where possibly resident.

Snail Kite MAP 28; FIGURE 13A; PLATE 9
Rostrhamus sociabilis
OTHER NAMES. Everglade Kite (arch.),
Welk's Hawk (C).

Identification. 19″ (48.5 cm); wingspan 44″ (112 cm). Readily IDed in any plumage by habitat, shape, manner of flight, and large white patch at base of tail. *Ad. ♂:* dark slate gray throughout (black at a distance) except for white tail base and tail coverts; cere, lores, eyes, eyering, and legs/feet red. *Ad. ♀:* blackish brown above; heavily streaked below; soft parts orange; same tail pattern as ♂. *Juv.:* similar to ad. ♀ but with mostly pale buff head; less heavily streaked below; gray cere; yellow legs/feet. *Flight:* buoyant; short tail; broad rounded wings; from Northern Harrier by shorter, bowed wings (not held in a dihedral), shorter tail, and more extensive white in tail region.

Voice. 1. Very raspy, nasal *ănh* given singly or repeated 5–10 times in a series;
2. similar, but run together into a cackle—a slow, raspy *a-a-a-anh* with a froglike or insectlike quality.

Habitat. Lagoons and freshwater marshes; less often, rice fields.

Distribution. Resident from s Mex. and Florida to sc S.A.; southernmost populations migrate n. in austral winter.

Status in Belize. FC to C resident in n. half. Especially C in lagoons along New R. and at Crooked Tree; less C s. of c BE, and only occas. seen as far s. as TO.

Double-toothed Kite
MAP 29; FIGURE 13B; PLATES 7, 11
Harpagus bidentatus

Identification. 13″ (33 cm); wingspan 27″ (68.5 cm). General aspect more like that of small accipiter than kite. Distinctive puffy white undertail coverts that spread to sides of rump are quite conspicuous and often project above folded wings on perched birds. Size and shape of Sharp-shinned Hawk but with different flight profile (see below) and longer wings. When perched, folded wings reach halfway down tail; in accipiters, they extend at most one-third of way down tail. Barred Forest-Falcon has longer tail and very short wings that do not extend past uppertail coverts. *Ad.:* heavy chestnut barring underneath, coalescing into band across breast; white throat split down middle with thin dark stripe (thus "double-toothed"); slate gray above, with brownish cast except on head; blackish tail with three thin whitish bands. *Juv.:* like ad. but browner; beneath, varies from white to buff and may be unstreaked, lightly streaked, or heavily streaked; those with streaked breasts have barred flanks and thighs, but all have puffy white undertail coverts. *Flight:* long wings; white underwings with barred remiges, most prominent in outer primaries; typically soars with wings bowed downward and tail compressed; accipiters have more heavily barred remiges and mottled, not immaculate, underwing coverts and soar on flat wings with tail slightly spread; Barred Forest-Falcon never soars above forest canopy.

Voice. Fairly loud, piercing *shreeea,* somewhat like sound of rusty hinge.

Habitat. Primary forest, occas. broken forest and second growth. Usually remains under forest canopy but occas. soars above canopy.

Distribution. Resident from s Veracruz to c S.A.

Status in Belize. UC resident away from coast, R near coast, except in n.e. Recorded occas. on Ambergris Caye where possibly resident.

Reference. *Status:* Howell et al. (1992).

Mississippi Kite   FIGURE 13B,C; PLATE 9
Ictinia mississippiensis

Identification. 14½″ (37 cm); wingspan 35″ (89 cm). Small kite with long, pointed wings, relatively long tail. Folded wings extend only slightly past tail tip. Similar to Plumbeous, but little if any seasonal overlap. *Ad.:* medium gray with contrasting pale gray to whitish head and white panel on upper wing (secondaries); near-black primaries and tail. *Subad.:* similar to ad., but head and panel in secondaries not pale. *Juv.:* streaked or mottled underparts; some pale mottling in upperparts; as in ad., primaries contrast darker than rest of plumage. *Flight:* Ad.: all gray, with darker primaries and tail; paler head. Subad.: underwing coverts mottled brown, two or three thin white bands visible in undertail; whitish base to primaries. Juv.: heavily mottled and streaked brown and gray; no rufous at base of primaries; two or three white bands in tail.
Voice. Silent in migration.
Habitat. Chiefly aerial when migrating.
Distribution. Nests in c and s U.S.; winters in c S.A.
Status in Belize. Occas. autumn transient principally along coast, mid-Sept. to late Oct. May occas. pass through s Belize in spring as well.
Reference. *Status:* Jones et al. (2002).

Plumbeous Kite   FIGURE 13B,C; PLATE 9
Ictinia plumbea

Identification. 14″ (35.5 cm); wingspan 35″ (89 cm). Similar to Mississippi, but has at least some rufous in primaries in all plumages; folded wings extend well past tail tip. In flight, outermost primary much shorter than next outermost. *Ad.:* uniformly gray throughout, including head and upper secondaries (whitish in Mississippi); primaries do not contrast darker. *Subad.:* like ad., but underparts mottled whitish; darker overall than Mississippi, with shorter tail and greater primary extension beyond tail tip. *Juv.:* streaked and mottled, especially on underparts. *Flight:* Ad.: conspicuous rufous primaries; two white bands in undertail (lacking in ad. Mississippi). Subad.: like ad., but underwing coverts mottled brown; from subad. Mississippi by ru-

fous base to primaries, bolder tail bands. *Juv.:* reduced rufous in primaries.
Voice. *At nest:* rapid, laughing *hee-h-h-h-he* with a ringing quality. Also, on occasion, thin, shrill whistles.
Habitat. Open forests, savannas, chopped second growth, milpas.
Distribution. Nests from s Tamaulipas and Yucatán Pen. to c S.A.; winters in S.A.
Status in Belize. Locally UC to FC summer resident on mainland, mid-Feb. to late Aug.

Black-collared Hawk
MAP 30; FIGURE 13C; PLATES 6, 10
Busarellus nigricollis
OTHER NAMES. Fishing Buzzard (arch.), Fishing Hawk (C), Chestnut Hawk (C).

Identification. 20″ (51 cm); wingspan 48½″ (123 cm). *Ad.:* large rufous-colored hawk with creamy white head, black band across upper breast. *Juv.:* only a hint of rufous on body and underwing; whitish head with streaked crown; partial breast band; rest of plumage barred and mottled.
Voice. 1. Very un-birdlike groan—a low, snarling *aaaanh* (1½ sec);
2. laughing *whee-whee-whee-whee*.
Habitat. Forested edges of sluggish rivers and lagoons.
Distribution. Resident from s Sinaloa and s Veracruz to c S.A.
Status in Belize. UC to FC resident locally on mainland w to c OW and s. to ne CA and ne SC.

Northern Harrier   FIGURE 13H; PLATE 9
Circus cyaneus
OTHER NAMES. Marsh Hawk (arch.), Hen Harrier (U.K.).

Identification. 20″ (51 cm); wingspan 42½″ (108 cm). Prominent white uppertail coverts in all plumages. *Ad. ♂:* gray, paler beneath, with black wingtips. *Ad. ♀:* brown, with heavily streaked underparts, barred dark-and-light brown tail. *Juv.:* rich cinnamon underparts in autumn, fading to buff by spring, by which time it shows streaking on breast (but not belly). *Flight:*

long, rounded wings; long tail; forages low over open habitats with wings held in dihedral.

Voice. Silent in winter.

Habitat. Rice fields, marshes, shrimp farms, estuaries, lagoons.

Distribution. Nests across most of N.A., Eur. and Asia; winters from U.S., c Eur., and c Asia to n S.A., n Afr., and s Asia.

Status in Belize. UC to VU winter visitor on mainland, late Sept. to early Apr., primarily in north; recorded occas. on Ambergris Caye and Caye Caulker. Ad. may be unrecorded in Belize.

Genus: Accipiter

Three *Accipiter* species occur in Belize, and none is common. The Bicolored Hawk is resident throughout and may be fairly common in some areas, but it is a seldom seen forest dweller. The other two, Sharp-shinned and Cooper's, are very uncommon migrants and winter visitors. Compared with most other hawks, accipiters have shorter, broader, more rounded wings and a longer tail; however, forest-falcons and Double-toothed Kite have similar profiles. In sustained flight, accipiters can almost always be told from other hawks by their characteristic straight-line flight with three or four rapid wingbeats followed by a brief glide.

Sharp-shinned and Cooper's can be especially difficult to tell apart. Juvs. have a distinctly different plumage pattern from that of ads. The sexes are nearly identical except that ♀s are larger; thus, ♀ Sharp-shinned may be nearly as large as ♂ Cooper's, making size comparisons alone risky. Bicolored is easily distinguished from other accipiters, although some juvs. can look remarkably like Collared Forest-Falcon. Many of the ID features of Sharp-shinned and Cooper's are relative and subtle and are not always apparent, even in closely observed birds. The more experience one has with accipiters, the easier they are to ID. Nevertheless, even the most experienced birders let some individuals go as simply "unidentified accipiter."

Things to note (Cooper's vs. Sharp-shinned): size, head shape, and crown-nape contrast. *In juv.,* prominence of supercilium, presence/absence of white mottling on back; extent and thickness of streaking underneath. *In flight,* relative size; wingbeat pattern; degree of head projection; shape of tail tip; amount of bend at wrist.

Sharp-shinned Hawk FIGURE 13E; PLATE 8
Accipiter striatus

Identification. ♂ 11½", ♀ 13½" (29–34.5 cm); wingspan 21–24" (53.5–61 cm). Small hawk with rounded wingtips and relatively long, barred tail. From Cooper's by smaller, more rounded head with little evident contrast between crown and neck. Tail more narrowly tipped white or gray. Never raises hackles. *Ad.:* gray above, barred rufous below; black-and-gray-barred tail. *Juv.:* brown above, streaked brown on white below; barred tail; from Cooper's by fairly conspicuous pale supercilium; heavier streaking of underparts. *Flight:* less head projection beyond leading edge of wings (wings are actually held slightly forward); often has more noticeable bend at wrist in routine flight, shallower and more rapid wingbeats, and more buoyant flight than Cooper's, square-tipped tail. *Note:* the shape of the tail tip can vary, depending upon the way it is held (flared when soaring vs. compressed when in direct flight), and the stage of feather growth if in molt, so it is a character that must be used with caution.

Voice. Silent in winter.

Habitat. Most wooded areas, usually in or near clearings, forest edge, and savannas. Migrates chiefly over coastal habitats.

Distribution. Nests from c Alaska and c Can. to mtns. of U.S. and Mex. plateau, disjunctively in W.I. Winters from s Can. to s C.A.

Status in Belize. UC transient and VU winter visitor on mainland and Ambergris Caye, early Oct. to at least early Mar.

References. *Status:* Howell et al. (1992). *Identification:* Kaufman (1990); Liguori (2000).

Cooper's Hawk FIGURE 13B,E; PLATE 8
Accipiter cooperii

Identification. ♂ 16", ♀ 19" (40.5–48.5 cm); wingspan 28–33" (71–84 cm). Similar to Sharp-shinned in all plumages, but larger. Has darker crown (especially in ♂) that contrasts sharply with paler neck and upperparts. Often raises hackles when perched, exposing white nape and increasing crown-nape contrast. Tail more broadly tipped white. *Ad.:* gray above, barred rufous below, barred black-and-gray tail. *Juv.:* brown above, streaked brown and white below; barred tail; from Sharp-shinned by less prominent supercilium, and thinner streaks underneath exposing more white and giving the underparts an overall paler appearance; often has at least some white mottling in upperparts (Sharp-shinned shows little or no white). *Flight:* rounded tail tip; heavier-bodied than Sharp-shinned, with head and neck projecting well in front of outstretched wings; usually shows less of a bend at wrist in routine flight; deeper, slower wingbeats and less buoyant flight; has prominent white undertail coverts that are especially noticeable in distant birds.

Voice. Silent in winter.

Habitat. Similar to that of the preceding species.

Distribution. Nests from s Can. to n Mex.; winters from n U.S. to C.A.

Status in Belize. VU transient and R winter visitor on mainland s. of CO, late Sept. to early Mar.

References. *Status:* Howell et al. (1992). *Identification:* Kaufman (1990); Liguori (2000).

Bicolored Hawk   PLATE 8
Accipiter bicolor

Identification. ♂ 14″, ♀ 18″ (36–46 cm); wingspan 25–30″ (63.5–76 cm). *Ad.:* striking, with its plain pale gray underparts and, when visible, rufous thighs; ♀ strikingly larger than ♂. *Juv.:* brown above, paler below—varying from rich cinnamon to creamy white—but never streaked as in other accipiters; paler juvs. very similarly patterned to some Collared Forest-Falcons, with full white collar and strong brown hook behind auriculars, but even ♀ is much smaller than smallest Collared Forest-Falcon; also has shorter, less rounded tail, longer wings that extend significantly past uppertail coverts, and more upright posture, whereas Collared Forest-Falcon typically perches hunched over.

Voice. 1. Nasal *ank* or *kank,* usually near nest, much like Cooper's Hawk;
2. sharp, nasal *kep!;*
3. harsh, rapid *ank-ank-ank-ank-ank-ank-ank-ank-ank.* Generally silent outside breeding season, but both members of pair can be quite vocal near nest.

Habitat. Primary and secondary broadleaf forest.

Distribution. Resident from s Tamaulipas to sc S.A.

Status in Belize. UC resident on mainland but not often reported, because it resides in dense forest and seldom vocalizes away from nest.

Reference. *Voice:* Delaney (1992).

Crane Hawk   PLATE 9
Geranospiza caerulescens
OTHER NAMES. Blackish Crane-Hawk (arch.), Black Crane-Hawk (I. Davis).

Identification. 19½″ (49.5 cm); wingspan 38½″ (98 cm). Slim, small-billed, small-headed, long-legged hawk with long tail and relatively short, rounded wings. No other hawk has similar body proportions. Dark grayish black with two white bands in black tail. Folded wings extend only halfway down length of tail. Quite agile when feeding, often climbing around on trunks and branches on "double-jointed" legs, with wings flapping for balance, in pursuit of small prey items in crevices and bromeliads. *Ad.:* red legs/feet, gray cere. *Juv.:* paler, with diffuse whitish face; white mottling and vermiculations underneath; orange legs/feet. *Flight:* narrow white band across the outer primaries of underwing; fairly rapid, deep wingbeats; seldom soars more than briefly.

Voice. Loud, clear, plaintive whistled *wheeeooo.*

Habitat. Forested streamsides, forest edges, savannas, roadsides. Often forages in large trees with bromeliads, typically near water.

Distribution. Resident from s Sonora and c Tamaulipas to sc S.A.

Status in Belize. UC resident in n. half; scarce in south. One record from n Ambergris Caye, where possibly resident.

White Hawk

MAP 31; FIGURE 13E; PLATES 6, 11

Leucopternis albicollis

OTHER NAMES. Sak i c'och (K), suc muhan (M).

Identification. 20½" (52 cm); wingspan 48½" (123 cm). *Ad.:* readily recognized by all-white plumage except for conspicuous black subterminal tail band, black primary tips, and fine black barring in inner primaries; some may also have black in secondaries and wing coverts. *Juv.:* broader black tail band; more black in remiges; barring extends to secondaries and greater secondary wing coverts.

Voice. Hoarse, shrill, piglike squeal: *eeeeeeah.*

Habitat. Primary and old secondary broadleaf forest and forest edge.

Distribution. Resident from s Veracruz to nc S.A.

Status in Belize. UC resident on mainland, mostly away from the coast, n to w BE and c OW.

Genera: Buteogallus *and* Harpyhaliaetus *(Black-Hawks and Solitary Eagle)*

The black-hawks, including the similarly plumaged Solitary Eagle, can be confusingly similar. The Solitary Eagle is rare in Belize and should be IDed with extreme care. Subtle plumage differences and body proportions are the best criteria for IDing the three species. The Solitary Eagle is considerably larger, but size can be deceptive, especially on birds in flight. On perched birds, it is important to learn the different body proportions exhibited by each, which hold true regardless of plumage or distance from the observer.

Things to note: overall size; relative size of bill, folded wing vs. tail length. *In ad.,* presence/absence of white bars in thighs; color of lores. *In juv.,* presence/absence of dark malar mark; streaked vs. mostly dark breast; color of thighs and flanks; color of cere and lores. *In flight,* overall size, length of tail, number of tail bands, color of uppertail coverts.

Common Black-Hawk

FIGURE 13E; PLATES 5, 10

Buteogallus anthracinus

OTHER NAMES. Lesser Black-Hawk (arch.), Crab Hawk (C), Chicken Hawk (C), k'ek i c'och (K), muhan (M).

Identification. 19½" (49.5 cm); wingspan 46½" (118 cm). Medium-sized hawk with broad, rounded wings and short tail. *Ad.:* dark slate gray (appears black at a distance) with one broad white band in tail; cere and lores yellow; wings extend to or nearly to tip of tail; may have very fine white barring on thighs, visible at close range but never as conspicuous as in Great. *Juv.:* brown above, boldly streaked below, mostly whitish head accentuated with dark eyestripe and malar stripe; flanks blackish brown; longer-tailed than ad.; tail may extend well beyond wingtips; usually 4–7 dark bands in tail (9–13 in Great), but number is variable and not always a reliable field mark; uppertail coverts dark, always at least partially white in Great; base of bill extensively pale; cere yellow. *Flight:* very broad wings and short tail that is usually spread in soaring flight; ad. shows one visible white tail band; juv. has multiple thin tail bands but usually shows darker band at tail tip; flight profile more like a *Buteo* in gliding flight; flies on level wings.

Voice. Loud, ringing *klee klee klee klee klee klee* (6–10), often preceded by a soft *cŭ cŭ cŭ,* and fading at the end.

Habitat. Typically, open wooded areas near water, forest edge, towns, and mangrove forests.

Distribution. Largely resident from sw U.S., c Tamaulipas, and W.I. to n S.A.; northernmost populations withdraw s. in winter.

Status in Belize. FC resident near coast and along major river systems, much less C in upland areas. Resident on Ambergris Caye, Caye Caulker, and several inshore cayes; recorded also from Half Moon Caye.

Reference. *Identification:* Clark and Wheeler (1995).

Great Black-Hawk

FIGURE 13E; PLATES 5, 10

Buteogallus urubitinga

OTHER NAMES. Chicken Hawk (C), k'ek i c'och (K), muhan (M).

Identification. 22″ (56 cm); wingspan 50½″ (128 cm). Similar to Common Black-Hawk in all plumages but differs in having tail that projects well beyond folded wings because of shorter primary extension, and by longer legs, thicker bill, and gray, not yellow, lores (but cere is yellow in both). *Ad.:* like Common but with white-tipped uppertail coverts (giving impression of extra tail band on upper surface in flight); fine white bars in thighs. *Juv.:* dark malar stripe of Common lacking or nearly so; this, along with finer dark streaks in crown and nape, give it a lighter-appearing head than the other two; flanks mostly pale (blackish brown in Common); tail pattern highly variable, generally with 9–13 thin dark bars, and with or without broad subterminal band; bill all dark. *1st basic* (Common attains ad. plumage with 1st molt): similar to juv. but with fewer and broader dark tail bands (4–7); most also have very broad subterminal band; uppertail coverts barred whitish, underparts less heavily streaked; malar region remains mostly pale. *2nd basic:* similar to ad. but body and underwing coverts usually flecked whitish; inner primaries usually pale, forming narrow wing panel; tail usually black, with 2–4 white bands. *Flight:* similar to Common but ad. has white-tipped uppertail coverts and partially exposed second white band at base of tail; juv. has less heavily streaked underparts; in all, tail longer than in Common and generally held less widely spread, and wings narrower and longer; like Common, flies on level wings.

Voice. Long, piercing whistle of uneven pitch, usually rising, then falling: *currleeeeeeeee-aah.*

Habitat. Generally found in more densely wooded areas than the preceding, often but not always near water; also feeds in rice fields and other open areas.

Distribution. Resident from s Sonora and c Tamaulipas to sc S.A.

Status in Belize. Found nearly throughout on mainland; generally less C near coast than the preceding species, but more frequent in inland and upland areas.

References. *Identification:* Clark and Wheeler (1995); Howell and Webb (1995).

Solitary Eagle

MAP 32; PLATES 5, 10

Harpyhaliaetus solitarius

OTHER NAMES. Black Solitary Eagle (alt.).

Identification. 28″ (71 cm); wingspan 67″ (170 cm). Larger version of black-hawks, with much thicker legs and heavier bill. Size of King Vulture; black-hawks are closer in size to Black Vulture. *Ad.:* blackish gray plumage, slightly paler and more blue gray than black-hawks (difference is subtle and may not be useful at a distance); tail with one broad white band; folded wings extend to or slightly beyond tail tip, similar to Common; cere, lores, and partial eye-ring yellow; often shows a bushy hindcrown, a good mark when visible. *Juv.:* like Common, has bold dark malar stripe; differs from both black-hawks in having unbarred dark thighs and incomplete dark breast band; tail pale dusky gray, with only faint barring and indistinct dark tip. *1st basic:* like juv. but tail gray and mostly unbarred, with broad dark subterminal band. *2nd basic:* similar to ad. but body and underwing coverts flecked with pale buff; broad gray, not white, tail band. *Flight:* profile most like much smaller Common Black-Hawk but has larger, more forward-projecting head; remiges of ad. dark gray, tipped black (remiges dark nearly throughout in black-hawks and thus do not show contrasting black tips); juv. distinguished by blackish thighs and sides of breast, unbarred remiges, and broad terminal tail band.

Voice. Short, rapid series of whistled notes: *ple ple ple ple ple . . . ,* usually given in flight. While perched, a long, loud whistled *keeeeeerlooooooo,* dropping in pitch about halfway through.

Habitat. Extensive tracts of primary broadleaf and pine forest in interior.

Distribution. R and local resident in highlands and foothills from n Mex. to s Andes.

Status in Belize. R apparent resident in Maya Mtns. and Mtn. Pine Ridge. Few adequately documented records.

References. *Status:* Eitniear (1986, 1991); Jones

et al. (2000). *Identification:* Howell and Webb (1995). *Voice:* Stiles and Skutch (1989). *Conservation:* Jones and Vallely (2001).

Genera: Asturina *and* Buteo *(Buzzards)*

Buzzards are small to medium-sized, compact hawks with rounded wings and a short to medium-length tail. All but one in Belize are in the genus *Buteo*. As ads., all are relatively easy to tell apart, but juvs. can be challenging.

Things to note: *In ad.,* color of upperparts, color and pattern on underparts, folded wing vs. tail length. *In juv.,* face pattern; pattern of bars and streaks underneath, if any; folded wing vs. tail length. *In flight,* streaks, bars, or solid color on breast; wings held horizontal, in dihedral or upturned at tips; rounded vs. pointed wingtips in soaring and gliding flight; contrast, if any, between wing coverts and remiges, and within remiges; tail length; number and color of pale tail bands; dark vs. white uppertail coverts.

Gray Hawk   FIGURE 13E; PLATES 6, 11
Asturina nitida

Identification. 17″ (43 cm); wingspan 34½″ (87.5 cm). Small buzzard, similar in all external characters to buteos and formerly placed in that genus. *Ad.:* medium gray above; finely barred gray and white below; tail black with two or three bold white bars. *Juv.:* brown above, white below, with dark streaking on breast and belly and barring on thighs; brown crown, eyestripe, and malar stripe set off distinct white supercilium and auriculars. *Flight:* underwings pale; only outer primaries tipped black; white-tipped uppertail coverts; soars with wings held nearly flat.
Voice. 1. High-pitched, descending *peeeeuur* to *kreeeeeah,* beginning forcefully and losing its thrust (purer tone than in Roadside Hawk); 2. nasal *aaaannnnnnh,* descending in pitch at end (but not rising in middle like Roadside); 3. clear hollow whistles, each ≈1 sec long with <1 sec pause between each. Much less vocal than Roadside Hawk.
Habitat. Forest edge, roadsides, open country with scattered large trees.

Distribution. Largely resident from sw U.S. to c S.A.; northernmost populations withdraw s. in winter.
Status in Belize. FC resident on mainland; occas. on Ambergris Caye.

Roadside Hawk   FIGURE 13G; PLATES 6, 11
Buteo magnirostris
OTHER NAMES. Large-billed Hawk (I. Davis), Chicken Hawk (C), xepi k'uch (K), muhan (M), Gavilan (S).

Identification. 14½″ (37 cm); wingspan 29″ (73.5 cm). The most common buzzard and also the smallest. *Ad.:* gray brown above, grayest on head; throat and breast diffusely streaked gray brown; barred rufous on belly and thighs; tail grayish, with four or five black bars; eyes pale yellow. *Juv.:* boldly streaked breast and barred belly (unique among hawks in Belize); mostly dark auriculars; indistinct supercilium; lacks conspicuous malar stripe. *Flight:* light brown underwings with rufous panel in innermost primaries; longer tail than other small buzzards, usually not fanned; typically flies low and direct on rapid, shallow wingbeats, seldom soaring high overhead like other buzzards; however, in courtship display, soars in circles with wings held in dihedral while calling constantly.
Voice. 1. Nasal, fairly high-pitched shrill *eeeeeeahhh,* usually higher-pitched in middle; 2. loud, shrill *cree cree cree . . . ;* 3. loud, laughing *anh anh anh . . .* (15–20); 4. *heh ha heh ha heh ha . . .* with the cadence of a flicker *(Colaptes).* A very vocal hawk.
Habitat. Widespread in broken woodland and forest edge, including roadsides and tree-lined rivers; occas. seen in forest interior at army ant swarms.
Distribution. Resident from n Tamaulipas and Jalisco to sc S.A.
Status in Belize. C resident on mainland; UC on Ambergris Caye.
Reference. *Voice:* Moore (1992).

Broad-winged Hawk

FIGURE 13C,E; PLATES 6, 11

Buteo platypterus

Identification. 16" (40.5 cm); wingspan 34" (86.5 cm). Longer primary extension than Gray or Roadside. Two morphs, but rare dark morph unrecorded in Belize. *Ad.:* brown above; conspicuous white throat; heavily barred rufous on breast (sometimes forming solid band), more sparsely on belly; black tail with two bold white bars, the innermost often partially obscured. *Juv.:* brown above; white below, with dark brown streaks; dark auriculars and lack of well-defined supercilium distinguish it from Gray Hawk. *Flight:* underwings pale, with dark trailing edge; white panel in primaries appears translucent when backlit; often soars with outer primaries compressed, giving a pointed look to its otherwise relatively broad, rounded wings; soars with wings held nearly flat; glides with wings angled slightly down.

Voice. Generally silent in winter.

Habitat. Forest edge and open country with scattered trees. Migrates over most terrestrial habitats, especially along the coast.

Distribution. Nests from s Can. to se U.S. and W.I.; winters from W.I. and s Mex. s. of Yucatán Pen. to c S.A.

Status in Belize. VU transient and R winter visitor, mid-Oct. to late Mar., mostly in s. half; recorded once each on Ambergris Caye and Caye Caulker.

Reference. *Status:* Howell et al. (1992).

Short-tailed Hawk

FIGURE 13E,F; PLATES 6, 10, 11

Buteo brachyurus

Identification. 17" (43 cm); wingspan 37" (94 cm). Small buzzard, like the three preceding species, and could be confused with any of the three, as well as with Zone-tailed, White-tailed, and Swainson's. Longer-winged than other small buzzards—when perched, wingtips reach to tip of tail. Two morphs; light morph ≈1½ to 2 times as common as dark morph. *Ad. light morph:* could be confused with ad. White-tailed and Swainson's; uniform dark brown above, includ-

ing auriculars and malar region; all white below; finely barred tail, with outer band distinctly broader; White-tailed has prominent black subterminal band; is mostly gray, not brown, above; and folded wings extend past tail tip; Swainson's has chestnut band across upper breast and similar wing:tail ratio. *Juv. light morph:* similar to ad. but with tail bands all of about equal width, indistinct streaks on sides of breast, streaked auricular patch. *Ad. dark morph:* brownish black throughout, with gray-and-black-banded tail; most like juv. Zone-tailed but smaller and browner (when seen in good light) and has different flight profile. *Juv. dark morph:* similar to ad. but with white flecks in plumage and narrower outermost tail band; also similar to juv. Zone-tailed Hawk but differs in same aspects as ad. *Flight:* longer-winged and shorter-tailed than most other buzzards, with wingtips often tapering to a point; soars with wings curved up toward tip, unlike most other buzzards. Light morph: gray secondaries and innermost primaries in underwing contrast with white underwing coverts and outer primaries; no other buzzard in Belize except Swainson's has a similar wing pattern, but Swainson's is larger, has complete chestnut band across upper breast, white uppertail coverts, and narrower wings; juv. Gray, Roadside, and Broad-winged have longer tail and no strong contrast between underwing coverts and remiges. Dark morph: blackish underwing coverts contrast with light gray remiges; outer three or four primaries distinctly paler, forming whitish oval in outer wing; Zone-tailed is larger, rocks side to side with wings held in distinct dihedral, has longer tail, has rounded wingtips in soaring flight, and lacks light primary panel; rare dark-morph Swainson's (unrecorded in Belize) has light undertail coverts (black in Short-tailed) and thinner wings, which appear to be longer.

Voice. 1. Clear, shrill, whistled *kreeeea,* repeated; 2. shrill *whee whee whee wheeu.*

Habitat. In or over most habitats from dense woodland to open savannas. Much more often seen in flight than perched.

Distribution. Resident from c Sonora, n Tamaulipas, and s Florida to c S.A.

Status in Belize. UC to FC resident on mainland.

Swainson's Hawk

FIGURE 13A,G; PLATES 6, 11
Buteo swainsoni

Identification. 20½″ (52 cm); wingspan 49½″ (126 cm). Long-winged hawk with wingtips that reach or slightly exceed tail tip when perched. Tail finely barred dark and light in all plumages. *Ad. light morph:* chestnut upper breast contrasts sharply with white throat and pale, virtually unstreaked underparts; upperparts uniformly brown, with no light feathers or patches other than white-tipped uppertail coverts. *Juv. light morph:* lightly to boldly streaked underparts, but streaks concentrated on upper breast (lower breast in Red-tailed); head boldly marked dark and light. *Ad. dark morph* (rare, and much less likely than light morph to be seen in Belize): the only dark buteo with pale undertail coverts; otherwise, all dark brown except for white-tipped uppertail coverts in some birds. *Subad. dark morph:* similar to ad. dark morph but with mottled pale buff underparts and head. *Juv. dark morph:* differs from juv. White-tailed in having pale leading edge to underwing, lacks white patch on upper breast, and has darker tail. *Flight:* slender hawk with long wings and relatively pointed wingtips (e.g., more so than Zone-tailed); flies with wings held in distinct dihedral (but does not teeter like Zone-tailed Hawk and Turkey Vulture); uppertail coverts tipped pale gray to white in all but the darkest birds, forming a distinct U. Light morph: wing coverts white (ad.) to pale buff (juv.) and unmarked, contrasting sharply with medium gray remiges; lacks dark carpal bar of Red-tailed. Dark morph: leading edge of underwing does not contrast darker, as it does in all but darkest Red-tailed.
Voice. Usually silent in migration and winter.
Habitat. Could be seen in flight over most open habitats. When perched, on fence posts or snags; on ground, in open fields, grassland, and savannas.
Distribution. Nests in w N.A. from w Can. to n Mex. and winters primarily in sc S.A.; migrates

through Mex. and Pacific slope of C.A. in Mar.–Apr. and Sept.–Oct.
Status in Belize. One documented record: subad. near Big Falls TO, 30 Nov. 2001.
Reference. *Status:* Jones (2002).

White-tailed Hawk

MAP 33; FIGURE 13G; PLATES 6, 10, 11
Buteo albicaudatus
OTHER NAMES. Sennett's White-tailed Hawk (arch.).

Identification. 21″ (53.5 cm); wingspan 51½″ (131 cm). Closely related to Swainson's Hawk and, like that species, takes two full years to mature, has long wings that taper to a near point, and holds its wings in a dihedral in flight. Differs in having broader wings that are pinched in at the base, giving it a distinctive flight profile. Inner primaries darker gray than secondaries and outer two primaries. When perched, wings project beyond tip of tail in all but juv. Only one morph. *Ad.:* gray above; white below; rufous scapular bar; white tail with black subterminal bar. *Juv.:* similar to rare dark-morph Swainson's, with its pale undertail coverts and long, narrow wings, which are less pinched in at base than in ad.; distinguished by white markings on head, white patch on upper breast, paler tail, and dark leading edge of underwing; many also have pale area behind eyes. *2nd year:* intermediate between juv. and ad.; looks most like juv. Red-tailed, with its dark head, white breast, and streaked upper belly, but lacks dark carpal bar of Red-tailed, has longer, more tapered wings and finer barring in remiges, and lacks pale panel in outer wing exhibited by many Red-taileds.
Voice. High-pitched laughing
kur*eeee k-hek k-hek k-hek . . . ;*
generally silent away from nest.
Habitat. Open country, primarily savannas and pastureland.
Distribution. Resident from Sonora and s Texas to sc S.A.
Status in Belize. UC resident on mainland s. to c CA and in coastal savannas, e. of Maya Mtns., s. to ne TO; strays to s TO.
References. *Identification:* Clark and Wheeler (1989). *Voice:* Sibley (2000).

Zone-tailed Hawk
FIGURE 13G,H; PLATES 5, 6, 10
Buteo albonotatus

Identification. 19″ (48.5 cm); wingspan 51″ (130 cm). Classic Batesian mimic of the Turkey Vulture. It is thought that the Zone-tailed is more successful at catching prey by mimicking the carrion-eating Turkey Vulture. It is patterned similarly and is the only buzzard that, like the Turkey Vulture, rocks side to side on wings held in a strong dihedral. Easily distinguished, however, by its barred remiges, yellow cere, yellow legs/feet, feathered head, and smaller size. *Ad.:* tail with one broad light band and one or two thinner bands (bands gray on upper surface, white on undersurface); has dark trailing edge of wing, lacking in vultures. *Juv.:* multiple narrow bands in tail, fine white speckling in body; juv. dark-morph Short-tailed is smaller, has more pointed wings held close to horizontal, and does not teeter.
Voice. Silent in winter.
Habitat. Open country, including pastureland, savannas, rice fields, and shrimp farms.
Distribution. Primarily resident from sw U.S. and n Mex. discontinuously through C.A. to c S.A.; n. populations migratory.
Status in Belize. VU winter visitor, mid-Oct. to mid-Apr. To some extent, may be overlooked because of its similarity to *Cathartes* vultures and some Short-tailed Hawks.
References. *Status:* Howell et al. (1992); Ornat et al. (1989).

Red-tailed Hawk
MAP 34; FIGURE 13C,F; PLATES 6, 11
Buteo jamaicensis

Identification. 21″ (53.5 cm); wingspan 50″ (127 cm). Species highly variable, but small resident Belize population apparently consists of all light-morph birds. Medium-sized buzzard with average-proportioned wings and tail, pale breast with streaks concentrated on belly, and dark leading edge of inner wing (carpal bar) on undersurface. Folded wings do not extend beyond tail tip. *Ad.:* unique rufous-red tail. *Juv.:* can be confused with several other species; best mark is dark carpal bar visible in flight. Ad. and most imms. have a dark hood except at center of throat, which is mostly white. Many have white flecking in upperparts.
Voice. Harsh scream: 1. screaming *kreeeur* or *kreeeaa;*
2. shorter, serial *kree kree kree . . .* , with each note ending abruptly.
Habitat. Submontane pine and mixed pine/broadleaf forest; occas. in lowlands.
Distribution. Nests from c Alaska and Can. s. to C.A. highlands and W.I.; n. populations withdraw s. in winter.
Status in Belize. UC resident in and near Mtn. Pine Ridge CA, and recently in n OW; also reported from w OW, Ladyville BE, Cockscomb Basin SC, and Payne's Creek TO.
Reference. *Status:* Wood and Leberman (1987).

Genera: Morphnus *and* Harpia *(Eagles)*

The Harpy Eagle, largest (by weight) and most powerful eagle in the world, was once widespread throughout much of C.A. and tropical S.A., but never common. The Crested Eagle, its underappreciated cousin, although quite spectacular in its own right, is neither as large nor as majestic. Until recently, it was thought to reside no farther north than Hon.; however, recent records from Guat. and Belize suggest otherwise. Rather than postulating a northern range expansion, it is more likely that this species, because of its rarity and close similarity to the Harpy, was simply overlooked. Most of the earlier Belize reports of Harpy Eagle did not adequately eliminate the possibility of Crested. Both of these rare species live deep within the rainforest and seldom soar above the canopy.

Things to note: *In ad.,* presence/absence of dark breast band; size of legs/feet and bill; single or double crest; extent of barring on thighs. *In juv.,* presence/absence of contrast between wing coverts and remiges; size of legs/feet and bill; length and shape of crest.

Crested Eagle

MAP 35; PLATE 5

Morphnus guianensis
OTHER NAMES. Guiana Crested Eagle
(arch.).

Identification. 31″ (78.5 cm); wingspan 66½″
(169 cm). Noticeably smaller and slimmer than
Harpy, with smaller bill and less massive legs/
feet. Two morphs. *Ad. light morph:* lacks Harpy's
black breast band and has single crest; fine cinnamon barring on underparts visible at close range.
Ad. dark morph (unrecorded in Belize): head and
breast dusky like rest of upperparts; lower underparts heavily barred. *Juv.:* in addition to different body proportions, hindcrown is crested, not
shaggy. *Older imm.:* attains ad. plumage in about
three years; back becomes dusky before lesser
and median wing coverts, so forewing contrasts
paler than back and hindwing; head, throat, and
upper breast pale gray (white in comparable-
aged Harpy); may average coarser black bars
in tail than Harpy. *Flight:* narrower wings than
Harpy; prominent barring in remiges.
Voice. Shrill high-pitched *peeeee,* sometimes
two-parted, with the second part higher.
Habitat. Undisturbed primary broadleaf forest;
stays beneath canopy.
Distribution. R and local resident from n C.A.
to c S.A. Because of extensive loss and frag-
mentation of its rainforest habitat throughout
much of its range, it is considered *Globally
Near Threatened.*
Status in Belize. R resident in remote areas of
w TO, s CA, and w OW.
References. *Status:* Jones et al. (2000); Miller
and Miller (1992). *Conservation:* Stattersfield and
Capper (2000); Jones and Vallely (2001).

Harpy Eagle

MAP 36; PLATE 5

Harpia harpyja

Identification. 38″ (96.5 cm); wingspan 80″
(203 cm). Very large, with large bill and massive legs and feet. *Ad.:* easily told by bold black
breast band, split crest, ruff of loose feathers,
and stocky build. *Juv.:* similar to juv. Crested
but with stockier build and larger bill, and
legs/feet; shaggy hindcrown. *Older imm.:* attains ad. plumage over about four years; other

than body dimensions, distinguished from light-
morph Crested by lack of contrasting pale wing
coverts and by white, not pale gray, head; tail
pattern variable, but may average fewer and thinner dark bars; attains uniform dusky blackish
upperparts of ad. sooner. *Flight:* broader wings
than Crested, with less prominent barring in
remiges.
Voice. Plaintive wailing *wheeeeoooooo.*
Habitat. Like the preceding, undisturbed primary broadleaf forest, including river-edge forest. Stays beneath canopy.
Distribution. R and local resident from s Mex.
to c S.A. Because of extensive loss and frag-
mentation of its rainforest habitat throughout
much of its range, it is considered *Globally
Near Threatened.*
Status in Belize. R resident in remote areas of
w and s TO and s CA.
References. *Status:* Eitniear (1986); Jones et al.
(2000) *Voice:* Peterson and Chalif (1973). *Conservation:* Stattersfield and Capper (2000); Jones
and Vallely (2001).

Genera: Spizastur *and* Spizaetus
(Hawk-Eagles)

Hawk-eagles are intermediate in size between
the smaller "hawks" and larger eagles. Distinguished from other hawks and eagles in Belize by
having feathered tarsi all the way to the toes. All
three in Belize are readily told from each other,
but each can be confused with other species.

Things to note: nature of crest, tail pattern,
underwing pattern, flight silhouette.

Black-and-white Hawk-Eagle

MAP 37; FIGURE 13D; PLATES 7, 11

Spizastur melanoleucus
OTHER NAMES. Black-and-white
Eagle-Hawk (arch.).

Identification. 22½″ (57 cm); wingspan 51″
(130 cm). Dark brownish black above, with white
head and underparts. Superficially resembles
light-morph juv. Gray-headed Kite but, in addition to feathered tarsi, has stockier build, shorter
tail, white crescent at bend of folded wings,
and black, rather than yellow, lores. *Flight:* lacks
boldly black-and-white-barred primaries in un-

derwing and has more and finer bars in tail than juv. Gray-headed Kite; has pure white underwing coverts (creamy white in juv. Gray-headed Kite); white leading edge of wing is evident when viewed from above; juv. Ornate Hawk-Eagle has dark flecking in underwing coverts, barred thighs, and longer tail, which is usually held compressed. Ages similar.

Voice. Hysterical, clear whistles at moderate pitch.

Habitat. Primary and old secondary broadleaf forest. Frequently seen flying above canopy.

Distribution. Resident from s Tamaulipas to c S.A.

Status in Belize. UC to VU resident away from coast n. at least to c OW and c BE; once in CO. Most numerous in s CA and Maya Mtns.

Reference. *Status:* Eitniear (1986).

Black Hawk-Eagle

FIGURE 13D; PLATES 7, 10, 11

Spizaetus tyrannus

OTHER NAMES. Tyrant Hawk-Eagle (arch.), Black Eagle-Hawk (arch.), kush kush tapi (M).

Identification. 26½″ (67.5 cm); wingspan 55½″ (141 cm). Large raptor with long legs and tail, bushy crest, and strongly barred thigh and tarsi feathers. *Ad.:* mostly sooty black plumage, with bushy black-and-white crest; tail broadly barred black and gray. *Juv.:* mottled dark brown and blackish above; barred and streaked black and white below; white throat, mostly white crown, and broad blackish auriculars. *Flight:* strongly barred remiges; three white tail bands; wings broad and rounded at tip, pinched in at base, held slightly forward of perpendicular, longer than in Ornate, and longer and narrower than in Black-and-white Hawk-Eagle.

Voice. Shrill whistled *wheeeeeur   wht-wht-wht wheeeeeur,* repeated; usually given in flight.

Habitat. Occupies wider range of habitats than other two hawk-eagles, including open forest and pine woodland. Often flies high above canopy.

Distribution. Resident from n Veracruz to c S.A.

Status in Belize. UC resident on mainland throughout. The most common hawk-eagle in most of Belize.

References. *Status:* Eitniear (1986). *Voice:* Moore (1992).

Ornate Hawk-Eagle

MAP 38; FIGURE 13D; PLATES 7, 10, 11

Spizaetus ornatus

OTHER NAMES. Crested Eagle-Hawk (arch.), Ornate Eagle-Hawk (arch.), Carasow (= Curassow) Hawk (C).

Identification. 24½″ (62 cm); wingspan 51″ (130 cm). *Ad.:* unmistakable; elongated central crown feathers often raised vertically; head, neck, and sides of upper breast rufous; throat white, bordered laterally by black line; heavily barred underparts. *Juv.:* resembles Black-and-white Hawk-Eagle but lacks white at bend of the wing and has longer crest, heavily barred thigh and tarsi feathers, and longer tail. *Flight (juv.):* black flecks in underwing coverts, barred thighs, and longer wings and tail than Black-and-white Hawk-Eagle.

Voice. Hysterical screaming *whaa whee whee whee whu-whu . . . ,* similar to that of Black-and-white Hawk-Eagle.

Habitat. Principally in primary broadleaf forest; occas. in pine forest. Soars above canopy.

Distribution. Resident from s Tamaulipas and Jalisco to c S.A.

Status in Belize. R to locally UC resident n. to c OW and c BE; active nest recently located in CO. Generally absent from coastal areas.

References. *Status:* Eitniear (1986); Miller and Miller (1992). *Voice:* Moore (1992). *Conservation:* Jones and Vallely (2001).

FAMILY: FALCONIDAE
(Caracaras and Falcons)

World: 62. **New World:** 25. **Belize:** 10. Worldwide. Found in most available habitats and at nearly all elevations. Externally, they differ little from the Accipitridae. Open-country falcons have extraordinary powers of flight, and the Peregrine Falcon is considered to be the fastest living bird, reaching speeds up to 120 mph (195 kph) when diving on prey. **Reference:** Ferguson-Lees and Christie (2001).

SUBFAMILY: MICRASTURINAE
(Forest-Falcons)

Unlike open-country falcons, which have slender, pointed wings, the more maneuverable forest-falcons have short, broad wings with rounded wingtips, as well as a long tail and long legs. The Collared Forest-Falcon can be found at the forest edge and will occasionally fly across clearings, but the Barred Forest-Falcon is strictly a forest interior bird. They never soar above the forest canopy.

Things to note: head pattern, size of head relative to body, length of tail, amount of primary extension in folded wing.

Barred Forest-Falcon   MAP 39; PLATE 7
Micrastur ruficollis

Identification. 14″ (35.5 cm); wingspan 21″ (53.5 cm). Small; size and shape of small accipiter. *Ad.:* gray above; finely barred black and white below; three thin white bands in tail; much thinner, longer-tailed, and longer-legged than Gray Hawk. *Juv.:* variable; brown above; white below, sometimes with brown barring; some have white auriculars bordered behind with dark crescent and white collar; unbarred juv. similar to some juv. Bicolored Hawks but has thinner pale gray bands in tail, shorter wings that do not project beyond uppertail coverts, unfeathered yellow lores and orbital ring, and more rounded head.
Voice. 1. Clear, slightly nasal, barking *ehr!* 2. nasal *cah-ah* and *cah-coe*.
Habitat. Primary broadleaf forest. Stays within canopy and subcanopy.
Distribution. Resident from n Veracruz and c Yucatán Pen. to c S.A.
Status in Belize. UC resident on mainland away from coast n. to n CA; also in w and c OW, locally in ne OW, and in CO.
References. *Status:* Wood and Leberman (1987). *Voice:* Moore (1992).

Collared Forest-Falcon   PLATE 7
Micrastur semitorquatus
OTHER NAMES. Toov (M).

Identification. ♂ 21½″ (54.5 cm), ♀ 24½″ (62 cm); wingspan 31–36″ (78.5–91.5 cm). Much larger and not closely similar to Barred Forest-Falcon. Long, rounded black tail with three or four narrow white bands; very long legs; short wings that do not extend beyond uppertail coverts; hunched-over posture. *Ad. light morph:* blackish above and either white or creamy buff below, with white or buff collar and white or buff auriculars bordered behind by black crescent; yellow cere, lores, and eye-ring; some juv. Bicolored Hawks are similarly patterned but much smaller, with longer wings, and have shorter tail with broad pale gray (not narrow white) bands, much shorter legs, dark lores, and more upright posture. *Juv. light morph:* brown above (paler than ad.); barred brown on white below; collar and postauricular crescent somewhat obscured by fine brown mottling; pale feather edges on upperparts give scalloped effect. *Ad. dark morph:* some are all black, with barred remiges; others also have barred underparts; best IDed by characteristic size, shape, and posture, along with unfeathered yellow lores and orbital ring characteristic of the genus. *Juv. dark morph:* similar to ad. dark morph but dark brown, with pale brown barring on underparts and occas. on wings.
Voice. Far-carrying, humanlike *oww!* (as in short for "ouch"). Also, *ä ä ä ä ä äw äw äw äw äww äww äwww äwww   äwww.*

Most often heard at dawn and dusk. Easily confused with Laughing Falcon (see Laughing Falcon account below).
Habitat. Primary and secondary broadleaf forest; occas. second-growth scrub, pine forest.
Distribution. Resident from s Sinaloa and s Tamaulipas to c S.A.
Status in Belize. UC to FC on mainland. Secretive; heard much more often than seen.
Reference. *Identification:* Wheeler and Clark (1995).

Crested Caracara

Figure 14

SUBFAMILY: CARACARINAE

(Caracaras)

Caracaras are characterized by an elongated head and a longer, heavier bill when compared with typical falcons. They are largely terrestrial scavengers.

Crested Caracara   FIGURES 13C, 14

Caracara plancus

OTHER NAMES. Audubon's Caracara (arch.).

Identification. 21″ (53.5 cm); wingspan 48½″ (123 cm). Black-and-white raptor with long, rounded wings; long neck for a raptor; and moderately long tail and legs. *Ad.:* pale blue bill; orange-red to pale blue cere and lores; black crown with shaggy hindcrown; rest of foreparts white with vermiculated black-and-white nape, upper back, and upper breast; finely banded black-and-white tail with broad black tip. *Juv.:* similar to ad. but body mostly dark brown, not black, and mottled with pale feather edges; fore-

parts and undertail coverts dirty white. *Flight:* primaries white with black feather tips, similar to Black Vulture; also white head and tail region; thus, white at all four corners.

Voice. 1. Rattling, harsh *ka-a-a-a-a-a*; 2. deep, hoarse *wuck*. Strays to Belize are likely to be silent.

Habitat. Open habitats such as savannas, rice fields, and pastureland.

Distribution. Resident from s U.S. and W.I. to s S.A.

Status in Belize. Only one adequately documented record: near San Felipe OW, 17 Dec. 2000. Several other inadequately documented reports from CO, OW, and near Dangriga span the period from mid-Dec. to early Mar.

Reference. *Status:* Jones et al. (2002).

SUBFAMILY: FALCONINAE

(True Falcons)

Except for the distinctive Laughing Falcon, the true, or typical, falcons are swift, barrel-chested birds with pointed wings and a long, usually compressed tail. Of these, American Kestrel is the least compact and the most likely to flare its tail. Most *Falco* falcons are rather easy to ID under ideal circumstances, but all can be difficult if seen briefly, in the distance, or under atypical conditions. The distinctive Laughing Falcon is the sole member of the genus *Herpetotheres*. It is typically seen on exposed perches, where it calls early in the morning, beginning often before first light, and again around dusk.

Things to note: relative size, head pattern, breast color and pattern, color of back. *In flight,* wing shape, manner of flight (fast or slow, straight or meandering, powerful or "soft" wing strokes).

Laughing Falcon   PLATE 9
Herpetotheres cachinnans
OTHER NAMES. Guaco (C), koej kampk (K), bac bac (M).

Identification. 20" (51 cm); wingspan 34" (86.5 cm). Readily told by pale buff head and underparts, with bold black patch through eyes to nape. Rest of upperparts dark brown with black-and buff-banded tail. *Flight:* broad cinnamon patch at base of primaries on upperwing surface. Flight direct on fairly rapid, shallow wingbeats; does not soar.
Voice. 1. Slow series of *ah!* notes.
2. *äww* calls similar to *oww* notes of Collared Forest-Falcon but without the human-voice quality.
3. pair often perform duet, their calls increasing in intensity until they reach a peak, at which point, one utters *ah* and the other immediately responds *ha;* thus the laughing sound *ah-ha,* repeated a number of times at ≈2 sec intervals.
Habitat. Most forested and semiforested habitats, including open woodland and savannas. Often perches on exposed branches.
Distribution. Resident from s Sonora and s Tamaulipas to c S.A.
Status in Belize. FC resident on mainland; UC on Ambergris Caye.
Reference. *Voice:* Moore (1992).

American Kestrel   FIGURE 13C; PLATE 8
Falco sparverius
OTHER NAMES. Sparrow Hawk (arch.).

Identification. 11" (28 cm); wingspan 25" (63.5 cm). The smallest *Falco.* Distinctive multi-patterned head. When perched, occas. pumps tail downward. ♂: unmistakable; black-tipped orange tail, blue-gray wings with black spots, rufous back, buff nape with black eyespot. ♀: not as colorful but same basic pattern; uniformly rufous brown above, with dark barring throughout, including tail; head pattern similar to ♂ but lacks buff nape; less distinct eyespot. *Flight:* more meandering, less deliberate than other *Falco species;* long, narrow wings often held sharply bent at wrist; slim body; long tail; hovers while foraging.
Voice. Shrill *klee klee klee klee klee* or *kree kree kree kree kree.*
Habitat. Open areas, including pastureland, agricultural fields, meadows, and towns. Frequently perches on power poles and lines.
Distribution. Nests from Alaska and c Can. discontinuously to s S.A. Northern populations migrate s. through Mex. and C.A.
Status in Belize. UC winter visitor, mid-Sept. to early Apr. More common in north than south.

Merlin   FIGURE 13C; PLATE 8
Falco columbarius
OTHER NAMES. Pigeon Hawk (arch.).

Identification. 11½" (29 cm); wingspan 26½" (67.5 cm). Slightly larger and distinctly more compact than American Kestrel. Uniformly gray or brown above, with banded tail and streaked underparts; faint to conspicuous "teardrop" below eyes, and indistinct pale supercilium. Like the kestrel, sexually dimorphic. Subspecies in Belize is *F. c. columbarius.* ♂: slate gray above, with two or three visible gray bands in black tail. ♀ *and juv.:* dark brown above with two or three visible light brown bands in dark brown tail. *Flight:* shorter and broader wings, shorter tail, and stockier body than kestrel; swift, direct flier; unlike kestrel, never hovers; slower, deeper wingbeats than Peregrine, and tail pattern differs in having fewer light bands, leaving more tail area black; similar-sized Bat Falcon has narrower, more swept-back wings, conspicuous white throat and upper breast, and black head.

Voice. Usually silent in migration and winter.

Habitat. Most open habitats, including forest edge, estuaries, lagoons, coastal beaches, and cayes.

Distribution. Nests in Arctic and N. Temperate Zone worldwide; winters from s Can., c Eur., and c Asia to n S.A., n Afr., and s Asia.

Status in Belize. UC to FC (cayes) transient and UC winter visitor, mid-Sept. to early May; found chiefly in coastal areas and the cayes, with few records from more than 20 mi. (30 km) inland.

Aplomado Falcon   MAP 40; PLATE 8
Falco femoralis

Identification. 16½″ (42 cm); wingspan 34½″ (87.5 cm). Nearly as large as Peregrine, but sleeker. *Ad.:* pale supercilium and auriculars set off dark postocular stripe; "teardrop" narrower than in Peregrine, more prominent than in Merlin; black lower breast band and sides finely barred with white; pale cinnamon belly, thighs, and undertail coverts. *Juv.:* similar to ad. but brown, not gray, above; streaked upper breast; solid dark lower breast band and sides; paler cinnamon-buff thighs and undertail coverts. *Flight:* similar in size to the Peregrine but with longer tail and longer, slimmer wings; shape and flight characteristics more like Plumbeous Kite than other falcons, and at a distance could be mistaken for that species.

Voice. 1. Screaming *kee kee kee kee . . . ;*
2. Barred Forest-Falcon–like sharp, oily *ehr!* (courtship only?).

Habitat. Savannas; occas. other open areas such as rice fields, shrimp farms, and agricultural fields. Unlike other *Falco* falcons, usually perches at midlevels on interior branches of trees, less often on exposed snags.

Distribution. Largely resident discontinuously from n Mex. to n C.A. and from Pan. throughout S.A.

Status in Belize. UC to locally FC resident in coastal savannas from n BE and e OW to ne TO;

occas. seen elsewhere, as in CO, w OW, Mtn. Pine Ridge, and s TO.

Bat Falcon   PLATE 8
Falco rufigularis

OTHER NAMES. Lion Hawk (C), lik lik (K, M).

Identification. 10″ (25.5 cm); wingspan 26½″ (67.5 cm). Smaller than kestrel and much more compact. Mostly dark, with prominent white throat. Larger Orange-breasted is virtual carbon copy, and the two can be easily confused at a distance when size difference is not readily apparent. *Ad.:* medium blue gray above; white throat and partial collar isolate black head; black-and-white barred breast; rufous thighs. Lacks orange breast of Orange-breasted; has proportionately smaller head, smaller bill, smaller legs/feet. *Juv.:* dark brown above (darker than ad.); may also have orange wash on upper breast, but not as extensive or well defined as in Orange-breasted; thin white bars in black vest, unbarred rufous thighs like ad. *Flight:* swift and direct, with rapid, shallow wingbeats and swept-back wings, narrower than in Orange-breasted and narrower at base than in Merlin; longer, less rounded tail; faster flight.

Voice. 1. Rapid *kea kea kea kea kea kea . . . ;*
2. single *kik* and *kiduh* notes.

Habitat. Widespread; most habitats, including buildings and communications towers in urban areas.

Distribution. Resident from s Sonora and c Tamaulipas to c S.A.

Status in Belize. FC resident on mainland; once on Ambergris Caye.

References. *Identification:* Howell and Whittaker (1995). *Voice:* Moore (1992).

Orange-breasted Falcon   MAP 41; PLATE 8
Falco deiroleucus

Identification. 14″ (35.5 cm); wingspan 33″ (84 cm). Very similar in plumage to much smaller Bat Falcon but differs in body proportions, with larger head, bill, and legs/feet. *Ad.:* distinct rufous-orange patch across upper breast; darker gray above than Bat Falcon, approaching black; thicker white bars in breast band; juv. Bat Falcon often has orangish diffusion on upper breast, so Orange-breasted should not be IDed by its orange breast alone, especially away from a known aerie. *Juv.:* other than size and body proportions, differs from Bat Falcon in having barred thighs, broader white bars in breast band, and a few fine dark streaks on rufous-orange breast. *Flight:* intermediate in size between Merlin and Peregrine, with stocky compact body, broad-based wings, and compressed tail; flies with slower, deeper wingbeats than both Peregrine and Bat Falcons; shorter, more rounded tail and broader wings than Bat Falcon.

Voice. Loud, ringing *că-că-că-că-că-că-că-că-că,* reminiscent of call of Lineated Woodpecker.

Habitat. Forested habitats, usually in vicinity of cliffs where it nests.

Distribution. Resident from s Veracruz and s Yucatán Pen. to sc S.A.

Status in Belize. R and local resident, largely confined to CA; seldom recorded elsewhere.

References. *Status:* Haney (1983); Howell et al. (1992); Miller and Miller (1992). *Identification:* Howell and Whittaker (1995). *Conservation:* Jones and Vallely (2001).

Peregrine Falcon FIGURE 13C; PLATE 8

Falco peregrinus

OTHER NAMES. Duck Hawk (arch.), Coot Hawk (C).

Identification. 17½″ (44.5 cm); wingspan 42½″ (108 cm). More compact and averages larger than Aplomado Falcon. Two identifiable subspecies occur in Belize: *F. p. anatum* and *F. p. tundrius. Ad. anatum:* dark slate gray above; white below; lower breast, belly, and thighs barred black and white; head black, with broad "teardrop" bordered posteriorly with small white slash (cheek patch). *Ad. tundrius:* smaller and paler than *anatum,* with thinner "teardrop" and larger white cheek patch; underparts with finer black bars, more white. *Juv. anatum:* brown above; bold brown streaking beneath, including throat, cheek patch, and undertail coverts. *Juv. tundrius:* much paler-headed, with whitish cheek patch behind much thinner "teardrop"; paler be-

neath, resulting from narrower brown streaking; head pattern similar to that of juv. Aplomado, but rest of plumage distinctly different. *Flight:* broad, tapered wings; heavy body; tail proportionately shorter than in both Merlin and Aplomado Falcon; unlike these two, flies with rapid, shallow wingbeats.

Voice. Squeally *crīīi* and *whee-check* cries usually during aerial encounters with other peregrines.

Habitat. Widespread; found primarily in open areas with exposed perches or poles. Most frequently seen near water.

Distribution. Cosmopolitan. Arctic and most N. Temperate populations are migratory.

Status in Belize. FC to C autumn and less C spring transient on cayes; UC transient and winter visitor on mainland; late Sept. to mid-May. Both *F. p. anatum* and *F. p. tundrius* occur in migration; probably only *anatum* in winter. Relative abundance of each in migration is not clear.

FAMILY: CRACIDAE
(Curassows and Guans)

World: 50. **New World:** 50. **Belize:** 3. New World Tropics and subtropics. Cracids are characterized by an elongated body with a small head, a long neck, and a long tail. Ground dwellers (curassows) are heavy-bodied, whereas primarily arboreal species (chachalacas, many guans) are more slender and lighter in weight. All have a chickenlike bill and short, broad, rounded wings; most have a crest of some sort. They have long, powerful legs and a fully developed hind-toe that is not elevated, an adaptation for perching in trees. Cracids have brightly colored areas of bare skin in or around the head and face. **Reference.** *Voice:* Moore (1992).

Things to note: relative size, head pattern, vocalizations.

Plain Chachalaca PLATE 12

Ortalis vetula

OTHER NAMES. Eastern Chachalaca (arch.), Cocrico (C), jeketso' (K), batch (M).

Identification. 19″ (48.5 cm). Less than half the mass of the other two cracids. Grayish brown above, paler below, with dusky cinnamon undertail coverts and darker tail tipped whitish. Like other cracids, has small head, long neck, and long tail. Red gular pouch visible when displaying.

Voice. *Call:* burry, nasal *chaa* to *churrr,* often repeated incessantly. Single birds and, more typically, pairs or groups engage in a cacophony of loud, rasping vocalizations that are reminiscent of its Creole name. Typically, ♂ and ♀ give overlapping sets of vocalizations in a duet: the ♂ a coarser, deeper *co-kri-co,* and the ♀ a higher-pitched, clearer *ca-kri-ca.*

Habitat. Forest floor to subcanopy within open woodland and scrub; forest edge. Gregarious.

Distribution. Resident on Gulf-Caribbean slope from s Texas discontinuously to nw C.R.

Status in Belize. C resident on mainland and n Ambergris Caye.

Crested Guan   PLATE 12

Penelope purpurascens

OTHER NAMES. Quam (C), pu'u (K), cosh (M), Cojolito (S).

Identification. 34″ (86.5 cm). Much larger and darker than chachalaca: blackish, with narrow white streaks and mottling on foreparts; red flap of skin on throat, blue-gray facial skin, and bushy crest that it raises and lowers; in good light, plumage shows green gloss.

Voice. 1. Loud, penetrating *kwänk!,* usually in series (reminiscent of a loud Tody Motmot), notes in series increasing in pitch at times;

2. audible wing flapping (by ♂ in courtship?) is a short series of flaps followed immediately by slightly longer, less intense series.

Habitat. Forested areas (broadleaf and pine); largely arboreal.

Distribution. Resident from c Sinaloa and s Tamaulipas to nw S.A.

Status in Belize. Locally UC in many areas on mainland, but increasingly scarce to absent near populated areas where hunted for food. Where protected from hunting, as in Cockscomb Basin Wildlife Sanctuary, FC and easily seen.

Reference. *Conservation:* Jones and Vallely (2001).

Great Curassow   PLATE 12

Crax rubra

OTHER NAMES. Central American Curassow (I. Davis), Carasow (C), chak mut (K), k'un bul (M), Faison (S).

Identification. 33″ (84 cm). As large as a guan, but unlike the other two, sexes differ. Both sexes have erect, curly feathers in the crown, a highly distinctive feature of this species. ♂: glossy black nearly throughout, with white undertail coverts and prominent butter yellow knob at base of bill. ♀ *dark morph:* dark blackish brown above; mottled with rufous in wing coverts; narrow white bars in secondaries and tertials; cinnamon brown below, becoming blackish on breast; head and neck finely scalloped black and white. ♀ *barred or gray morph:* paler and grayer; heavily barred on head, neck, breast, and upperparts.

Voice. 1. Medium-pitched sharp *whip!;*

2. extremely low-pitched *hmmmm* that is barely within the human auditory range;

3. loud, labored wing whooshing when flushed (and in courtship display?).

Habitat. Typically, forest floor within primary broadleaf forest interior; less often in secondary and fragmented forest. Roosts in trees.

Distribution. Resident from s Tamaulipas to w S.A. Because of extensive loss of its rainforest habitat, coupled with unchecked hunting pressure, is considered ***Globally Near Threatened.***

Status in Belize. Resident nearly throughout on mainland; now scarce or absent near populated areas where regularly pursued for food. Although FC in areas where it is protected (e.g., Rio Bravo Conservation and Management Area OW), it remains shy and retiring.

References. *Conservation:* Stattersfield and Capper (2000); Jones and Vallely (2001).

FAMILY: PHASIANIDAE
(Turkeys, Grouse, Pheasants, and Others)

World: 180. **New World:** 12 native; 12 non-native. **Belize:** 1 (native). Nearly worldwide, absent only from polar regions. The Phasianidae are a loose assemblage of chickenlike birds that have been variously classified. They are characterized by a large, rounded body with small head; the absence of a fully developed hindtoe; and an unserrated lower mandible.

Turkeys differ from others in the family by having a combination of long, strong legs; sparse feathering on the head, with prominent wattles and caruncles, especially in ♂s; and a broad tail. Males have a metatarsal spur on each leg. Like peafowl, ♂ turkeys in courtship raise and spread their elaborately decorated tail, puff out their chest, and withdraw their head. There are only two species of turkeys, one in N.A. and one restricted to the Yucatán Peninsula. Both are forest dwellers. **Reference:** Madge and McGowan (2002).

Ocellated Turkey   MAP 42; PLATE 12
Meleagris ocellata
OTHER NAMES. A' k'ach tzul (K), cutz mam (M), Pavo de Monte (S).

Identification. 42″ (107 cm). More gaudily patterned than its northern cousin the Wild Turkey. Bright blue featherless head with orange warts. ♂: body feathers blue black, tipped blue green and golden, accentuated by black subterminal bars; striking metallic coppery upperwing coverts; large blue-green and violet-blue eyespots in tail; uppertail coverts framed in black; inflatable protuberance above bill, hangs over bill when inflated. ♀: similar but with generally duller plumage; lacks forehead wattle.
Voice. 1. Guttural *tu-tu-tuk tuk tuk tuk tuk g-g-g-g-g-g-g-gk-gow;* starts softly, intensifies and speeds up, ending in an emphatic *gow!*
2. lower-pitched
boom boom boom boomboomboombooboobŏbŏ uh.
Habitat. Primary broadleaf and pine forest and forest clearings. Typically found on the ground during the day, but roosts in trees.
Distribution. *Yucatán Endemic.* Resident in Yucatán Pen. s. to n Guat. and w Belize. Because of its restricted range and severe hunting pressure in many areas, it is considered *Globally Near Threatened.*
Status in Belize. UC to locally C resident, restricted to w OW locally e. to near Hill Bank,

and in s half of CA; locally also in n CA. Only common in the few places where it is protected from persecution. Occasional reliable reports from e. of the Maya Mtns. suggest that it was once more widespread in Belize.
References. *Status:* Miller and Miller (1992). *Voice:* Moore (1992). *Conservation:* Stattersfield and Capper (2000); Jones and Vallely (2001).

FAMILY: ODONTOPHORIDAE (New World Quail)
World: 31. **New World:** 31. **Belize:** 3. New World Tropics and N. Temperate Zone. Once considered part of the Phasianidae, New World quail are now generally recognized as distinct at the family level. In addition to genetic differences, they are not known to hybridize with other Galliformes, a group known for its wide variety of hybrids, especially those produced in captivity. New World quail are small, plump, terrestrial birds with short, powerful legs, often found in dense undergrowth, where they are more likely to freeze than flush when alarmed, thus making them especially difficult to see. Most are highly gregarious. Many have some sort of head ornamentation or brightly colored crest. **References:** Madge and McGowan (2002). *Voice:* Hardy and Raitt (1995).

Black-throated Bobwhite
MAP 43; PLATE 12
Colinus nigrogularis
OTHER NAMES. Yucatán Bobwhite (alt.), Common Bobwhite (combined form), Quail (C), wor'ik (K).

Identification. 7¾″ (19.5 cm). The only quail found in open country and, consequently, the easiest of the group to see. Close relative of Northern Bobwhite *(Colinus virginianus),* with similar habits, haunts, plumage, and voice, and considered by some to be only a subspecies. ♂: intricately patterned gray, cinnamon brown, black, and white, with cinnamon brown the predominant color; black-and-white-striped head with black throat diagnostic; white feathers on underparts bordered with black give scalloped appearance. ♀: buff supercilium and throat;

brown, black, and white mottling of underparts, much like that of ♀ Northern Bobwhite.

Voice. 1. Loud clear *bob WHITE!* to *hurrWEET!;*
2. loud, whistled *hurrr!*

Habitat. Savannas and meadows; less common in secondary scrub bordering agricultural areas.

Distribution. Resident discontinuously in Yucatán Pen., Petén District of Guat., Belize, Hon., and n Nic.

Status in Belize. FC resident on mainland in e. half s. to ne TO; absent from e CO and ne BE.

References. *Status:* Ornat et al. (1989).

Spotted Wood-Quail   MAP 44; PLATE 12

Odontophorus guttatus
OTHER NAMES. Congo Bird (C), yab sik (K), koban ch'a qua (M).

Identification. 9½" (24 cm). Slightly larger and darker than other two, with distinctive crest. ♂: dusky cinnamon underparts, spotted with white; black throat, thinly streaked white; bright rufous orange revealed in raised crest. ♀: like ♂ but with gray-brown underparts; lacks orange in crest.

Voice. Burry, hollow *chōōō* notes often followed by a strident, explosive clear rhythmic *oh poor whip po'will's a widow,* repeated several times in rapid succession. Frequently uttered nearly simultaneously by two or more birds. Most often heard in the early morning and late afternoon.

Habitat. Ground dweller within primary broadleaf forest.

Distribution. Resident from s Veracruz and c Yucatán Pen. discontinuously to w Pan.

Status in Belize. UC to FC but seldom seen resident on mainland s. and w. of CO and BE, primarily away from coast.

Reference. *Voice:* Moore (1992).

Singing Quail   MAP 45; PLATE 12

Dactylortyx thoracicus
OTHER NAMES. Long-toed Partridge (I. Davis).

Identification. 8½" (21.5 cm). ♂: head mostly cinnamon, with narrow brown postocular line; faintly streaked grayish breast. ♀: very pale gray-

ish face and throat; cinnamon underparts lightly speckled white.

Voice. 1. Loud hollow whistles, increasing in tempo and volume, followed by a series of more complex phrases—roughly *chōō-ō-ō chōō-ō-ō chōō-ō-ō chōō-ō-ō chōō-chōō-chick-chrory-o chōō-chōō-chick-chrory-o chōō-chōō-chick-chrory-o;* similar to Spotted Wood-Quail vocalization but introductory notes wavering, phrases at end less complex.

2. simpler *toe-reo-reo toe-reo-reo toe-reo-reo . . . .*

Habitat. Ground dweller; primary n. semideciduous subtropical forest and second growth.

Distribution. Resident from sw Tamaulipas and Jalisco to E.S. and Hon.

Status in Belize. Seldom reported, but apparently a R resident in w CA. Also reliably reported in w OW and n Ambergris Caye. Reports from Maya Mtns. are undocumented.

References. *General:* Warner and Harrell (1957). *Status:* Howell et al. (1992); Miller and Miller (1992). *Voice:* Delaney (1992).

FAMILY: RALLIDAE
(Rails, Gallinules, and Coots)

World: 134. **New World:** 52. **Belize:** 13. Tropical and temperate regions worldwide. The Rallidae comprise two rather distinct groups: rails and crakes, which are more terrestrial, and gallinules and coots, which are more aquatic. Within the former, birds with a shorter bill are generally referred to as crakes; those with a longer bill, as rails. All species have short, broad, and rounded wings. Rails and crakes have long toes and a laterally compressed body for easy movement through dense marsh vegetation. Nearly all nervously flick their short tail when walking. Most have strongly contrasting undertail coverts (typically white) that are strikingly visible when the tail is raised. The largely aquatic coots often associate in large numbers with waterfowl, a group they superficially resemble. However, coots have a laterally compressed, not flattened, bill and lobed, not webbed, toes, much like grebes. Despite their short wings and reluctance to flush, rails have a remarkable dispersal ability and have colonized most of the world's archipelagos. On predator-free islands, many species evolved the loss of flight, which, with the occupation of humans, has made them vulnerable to predation by humans, cats, and rats. As a consequence, the Rallidae have the highest rate of extinction of any bird group—nearly 10% in the past 400 years. **References:** Taylor (1998). *Voice:* Hardy et al. (1996a).

Genus: Laterallus

Of the three species recorded in Belize, only one is common. They are no bigger than a Western Sandpiper and skulk beneath matted vegetation in areas of tall grass, making them almost impossible to see. They seldom fly. Fortunately, they vocalize frequently, and this is usually the only means by which their presence may be known. If seen, their plumages are distinctive.

Things to note: vocalizations, bill length and color, barred or unbarred flanks, back and nape color.

Ruddy Crake   PLATE 13
Laterallus ruber
OTHER NAMES. Red Rail (arch.), Ruddy Rail (I. Davis), Dodging Bull (C), ts'uhum ok' (K), oi oi (M).

Identification. 5¾″ (14.5 cm). *Ad.:* ruddy brown body, gray head, pale rufous throat, all-dark bill. *Juv.:* dark, dull gray brown throughout with paler throat; light brown bill.
Voice. *Call:* 1. single *chup* or *thuck* notes (like sound made by sucking tongue from roof of mouth);
2. *chk hrrr* and *chk chk chk hrrrr. Song:* harsh but slightly liquid rattle that descends the scale (2–3 sec).
Habitat. Weedy fields, grass-lined ditches, wet meadows, rice fields.
Distribution. Resident from n Veracruz and Colima to n Nic.
Status in Belize. FC to C resident on mainland; widespread in south but local and less C northward; UC on Ambergris Caye.

Gray-breasted Crake   MAP 46; PLATE 13
Laterallus exilis
OTHER NAMES. Gray-breasted Rail (I. Davis).

Identification. 5¾″ (14.5 cm). Dark olive-brown upperparts, with rufous nape, bright lime green bill with dark tip, plain gray face and breast, black-and-white-barred flanks and belly.
Voice. 1. *tk   tee tee tee tee tee tee* (6–12 *tee* notes, with a pause after the softer first note);
2. liquid, chattering rattle.
Habitat. Wet meadows, rice fields.
Distribution. Resident from Belize to c S.A.
Status in Belize. UC local resident in s TO; recorded also near Middlesex SC, Monkey Bay BE, and Gallon Jug OW.
References. *Status:* Howell et al. (1992); Russell (1966).

Black Rail   MAP 47; PLATE 13
Laterallus jamaicensis

Identification. 5¼″ (13.5 cm). Similar to Gray-breasted but with black-and-white-barred upperparts, black bill, darker gray head and breast, and chestnut brown nape.
Voice. 1. *ki-ki-jou* to *ki-ki-ki-jou;*
2. oily *chaa chaa chaa chaa chaa chaa chaa.*
Habitat. Seasonally flooded savannas.
Distribution. Nests very locally from nc U.S. to s S.A. N.A. populations migrate s. in winter. C.A. and S.A. (and some W.I.) populations appear to be resident. Perhaps never common, but extensive loss of suitable wetland habitat throughout its range has resulted in its being listed as ***Globally Near Threatened***.
Status in Belize. R and Local. Only five documented records, widely scattered, from OW to TO; four were in winter (Nov. to Mar.), but two individuals collected in ne TO 29–30 June 1963 were in breeding condition, suggesting that it may occasionally nest in Belize.
References. *Status:* Howell et al. (1992); Russell (1966). *Conservation:* Stattersfield and Capper (2000); Jones and Vallely (2001).

Clapper Rail   MAP 48; PLATE 13

Rallus longirostris

OTHER NAMES. Top-na-chick (C),
Chink-topnah (C).

Identification. 13½″ (34.5 cm). Long-billed
gray-brown bird; paler and tinged cinnamon buff
below, with gray-and-white-barred sides, flanks,
and belly; white throat; short white supraloral
line; bicolored gray-and-orange bill.
Voice. *Short call:* 1. rough *ch-dik;*
2. rough, throaty *chick chick chick chick . . . . Long
call:* loud, rough, throaty or chesty *kik-kik-kik-
kik-kik-kik-ki-ki-ki,* fading toward the end; one
calling bird often inducing several others to call.
Habitat. Mangrove forest.
Distribution. Resident, mostly in coastal areas,
from California and New England to Ecuador
and s Brazil.
Status in Belize. Locally C resident on cayes
and discontinuously along mainland coast s. to
n TO. Some seasonal movement is indicated by
occas. individuals seen away from nesting areas
or habitat.

Rufous-necked Wood-Rail

MAP 49; PLATE 13

Aramides axillaris

OTHER NAMES. Rufous-headed Wood-Rail
(I. Davis), Gallinola (S).

Identification. 12″ (30.5 cm). Smaller than Clapper Rail; rich rufous below; olive above, with
black rump and tail; gray saddle on upper back.
Relatively short greenish yellow bill and pinkish
red legs. Uniform Crake much smaller and rufous throughout; lacks gray saddle and has pale,
not black, undertail coverts.
Voice. 1. Short series of *kaowk!* or *kow!* notes, repeated at ≈2/sec; somewhat like that of Green
Heron, but notes clear and usually repeated
steadily.
2. random clucks and squawks.
Habitat. Mangrove forest.
Distribution. Resident discontinuously in
coastal areas from c Sinaloa and Yucatán Pen. to
n S.A.
Status in Belize. UC to FC and local on n cayes
and in a few places along mainland coast and

mangrove-lined cayes s. to s TO. Apparently,
only a winter visitor. A growing body of evidence
suggests that this species may be an altitudinal
migrant, nesting in the mountains (outside of
Belize) and wintering in mangrove forests along
the coast. All dated records from Belize are between mid-Sept. and late May.

Gray-necked Wood-Rail   PLATE 13

Aramides cajanea

OTHER NAMES. Cayenne Wood-Rail
(I. Davis), Top-na-chick (C), Cocoli (C),
konkolich (K, M), Gallinola (S).

Identification. 16″ (40.5 cm). Larger than Clapper Rail, greenish yellow bill, predominantly
gray head and neck, bright rufous primaries,
cinnamon-rufous underparts, black posterior,
and pinkish red legs/feet.
Voice. 1. Hollow, chickenlike clucks with occas.
higher-pitched notes;
2. loud *co-co-co-co-ri-ri;*
3. loud *o chucko weo weo,* repeated. Often several
birds call simultaneously.
Habitat. Widespread in wet areas, including
meadows, marshes, rice fields, open woodland.
Distribution. Resident from s Tamaulipas and
Oaxaca to sc S.A.
Status in Belize. FC resident on mainland
nearly throughout; once on Ambergris Caye.
Reference. *General:* Skutch (1994).

Uniform Crake   MAP 50; PLATE 13

Amaurolimnas concolor

OTHER NAMES. Uniform Rail (I. Davis).

Identification. 8½″ (21.5 cm). Similar to but
larger than Ruddy Crake (about the size of a
Sora) and found in different habitat. Note reddish, not grayish, legs/feet and longer, thinner
yellow-green bill; lacks Ruddy's gray face. From
much larger juv. Rufous-necked Wood-Rail by
shorter, thinner bill; shorter neck; and grayish, not black, posterior. *Ad.:* dull rufous brown
above, brighter below. *Juv.:* duller throughout.
Voice. Clear, whistled *torRY torRY torRY torRY
torRY,* reminiscent of Northern Barred-Woodcreeper's typical vocalization.

Habitat. Shallow water and drying pools within flooded forest.

Distribution. Resident locally from s Veracruz s. of Yucatán Pen. to c S.A.

Status in Belize. VU and rarely seen resident on mainland in s. half; also along New R. OW.

Reference. *Status:* Howell et al. (1992).

Sora
PLATE 13

Porzana carolina

Identification. 8¼″ (21 cm). *Ad.:* intensely yellow bill accentuated by black throat; face and underparts gray. *Juv.:* superficially resembles much smaller Yellow-breasted Crake but with pale greenish yellow bill, rather plain buffy brown face and breast without distinct supercilium.

Voice. 1. *sorrr-A!* usually repeated several times and often followed by

2. *tureep!;*

3. rapid series of descending liquid notes, slowing toward the end (reminiscent of a high-pitched horse's whinny).

Alarm call: 1. *keek!;*

2. *tik tik tik.* Often vocalizes in response to sharp, loud noises such as loud hand clapping.

Habitat. Freshwater marshes, rice fields, wet tall-grass meadows.

Distribution. Nests from nc Can. to c and sw U.S.; winters from s U.S. to n S.A.

Status in Belize. Locally C winter visitor, mid-Sept. to mid-Apr.

Yellow-breasted Crake
PLATE 13

Porzana flaviventer

OTHER NAMES. Yellow-breasted Rail (I. Davis).

Identification. 5¼″ (13.5 cm). Quite distinct from the three similar-sized *Laterallus* rails: yellow-buff nape and breast; whitish face; distinct white supercilium; mottled black, brown, and white upperparts; barred black-and-white flanks and belly. Legs yellow; bill dark gray.

Voice. Soft *chik* notes (Belize bird). W.I. birds:

1. scratchy *creek   creek;*

2. burry *turrr* or *turrur;*

3. rough *chuck chk-eek,* or simply *chk eek;*

4. shrill *wreek,* repeated;

5. cootlike *kek.*

Habitat. Freshwater marshes, rice fields.

Distribution. Resident locally from Guerrero, Veracruz, and W.I. to sc S.A.

Status in Belize. Three sight records, but only one documented: 4 mi. w. of Belize City, 27 June 1974; Big Falls Farm ne CA, 24 May 1984 (two individuals); Crooked Tree Wildlife Sanctuary BE, Dec. 1998–Feb. 1999 (photographed). As with other secretive rails, may be much more common than the few records indicate.

References. *Distribution:* Gatz et al. (1985). *Status:* Jones et al. (2000).

Spotted Rail
MAP 51; PLATE 13

Pardirallus maculatus

Identification. 10½″ (26.5 cm). *Ad.:* dark, nearly black plumage heavily spotted and barred with white; red legs/feet; medium-long bill, yellow green with red spot at base. *Juv.:* fewer white spots than ad. and dingier bill, lacking red spot.

Voice. 1. *whup   whup whp whp whpwhpwhpwhp,* reminiscent of small motor starting up;

2. harsh, grating *chuck cherrr,* repeated (Cuba);

3. *chik chik chik chdh* (Cuba);

4. shrill *peee dee* (Pan.);

5. harsh *chik chik chidik chik chidik,* etc. (Cuba).

Habitat. Freshwater marshes.

Distribution. Largely resident from Nayarit, Veracruz, and Cuba to sc S.A. Scattered extralimital records suggest that some populations may be migratory.

Status in Belize. Probably resident, at least locally in n. third, but few specific, dated records. Only three records from s Belize, all in TO: Punta Ycacos, June 1907; Blue Creek Village, 27 Jan. 1995; and near Big Falls, 19 Dec. 2001.

References. *Distribution:* Gatz et al. (1985); Scott et al. (1985). *Voice:* Raffaele et al. (1998).

Gallinules and Coots

Differ from other rails primarily in having heavier-set legs and the tendency to swim. Additionally, coots have lobed toes similar to those of grebes (but with lobes on each side of each toe, not just one side).

Things to note (juv.): Extent of white in undertail coverts; color of bill and frontal shield.

Purple Gallinule   MAP 52; PLATE 14
Porphyrio martinica
OTHER NAMES. American Purple-Gallinule (alt.).

Identification. 12½″ (32 cm). All-white undertail coverts, conspicuous on birds as they dash into cover. *Ad.:* one of the most colorful of all Belizean birds; head and underparts glossy bluish violet; back and rump green; primaries turquoise blue; bill red with yellow tip; frontal shield baby blue; legs/feet orange yellow. *Juv.:* basically brown, paler beneath, with greenish sheen on back and turquoise sheen in wings.
Voice. 1. Throaty or chesty *unk* and *kerk* notes;
2. *krē krē krē . . . ;*
3. squeaky, nasal *aonk   aok-aok-aok-aok;*
4. fast *chek-chek-chek-chek-chek-chek* sometimes followed by lower *unk-unk-unk-unk unk unk unk.*
Habitat. Freshwater marshes, rice fields.
Distribution. Largely resident from se U.S. to sc S.A., but most U.S. populations migrate s. in winter.
Status in Belize. Locally R to FC resident, perhaps throughout, but scarce and local in s. half, where nesting habitat is sparse. Migrants or strays occas. recorded on cayes.

Common Moorhen   PLATE 14
Gallinula chloropus
OTHER NAMES. Common Gallinule (alt.), Florida Gallinule (arch.).

Identification. 13½″ (34.5 cm). White undertail coverts with black central stripe; series of short white stripes on flanks. *Ad.:* lacks colorful plumage of Purple Gallinule but shares yellow-tipped red bill; red frontal shield; greenish yellow legs/feet; plumage dark blackish gray with olive-brown back. *Juv.:* brownish gray body, white barred flanks, and black central undertail coverts distinguish it from juv. Purple Gallinule.
Voice. *Call:* harsh, nasal *sherk* with a ringing quality, sometimes given in a series that slows

and ends with several nasal whining notes. Also, a variety of other grunts and clucks.
Habitat. Freshwater marshes, ponds with emergent vegetation, lagoons.
Distribution. Nests from n U.S., n Eur., and nc Asia to sc S.A., s Afr., s Asia, and Indonesia. N. populations migrate s. in winter.
Status in Belize. UC to locally FC winter visitor principally from early Sept. to early May, but occas. through summer; may nest locally or sporadically, at least in north. Migrants occas. seen on cayes.
References. *Status:* Barlow et al. (1969); Wood and Leberman (1987).

American Coot   PLATE 14
Fulica americana

Identification. 15″ (38 cm). Mostly black undertail coverts bordered laterally with white; lacks Moorhen's white flank stripes. *Ad.:* dark slaty gray body; black head and neck; white bill with dark reddish ring near tip; small red knob on forehead. *Juv.:* dull brownish gray throughout except for white lateral stripe on undertail coverts; pale gray bill; a few are still in juv. plumage when migrants arrive in Belize. *1st year:* similar to ad. but head not darker than rest of body; lacks red frontal shield and band near bill tip. *Flight:* white trailing edge to inner wing.
Voice. 1. Various grunts and croaks;
2. hoarse trumpetlike toots;
3. flat, throaty *koak, kek,* and *kek-kek* notes.
Habitat. Freshwater and brackish marshes, ponds, lagoons, rice fields with open water.
Distribution. Nests from nw and se Can. to nw C.R.; n. populations migrate s. in winter, some as far s. as n Colombia.
Status in Belize. UC to locally VC winter visitor primarily from Sept. to Apr.; a few occas. spend summer at Crooked Tree BE (where abundant in winter) and perhaps elsewhere.
Reference. *Voice:* Hardy et al. (1996a).

FAMILY: HELIORNITHIDAE (Sungrebes)

World: 3. **New World:** 1. **Belize:** 1. Tropics, including Afr., se Asia, C.A., and S.A. The Sungrebe differs in many ways from the two Old World species and may constitute a separate, monotypic subfamily. The Heliornithidae are superficially grebelike in appearance and habits. They have an elongate body with long neck, pointed bill, and relatively long, broad tail. Their toes are lobed, like those of grebes and coots, and their legs and feet are brightly colored or boldly patterned, perhaps as a warning signal to deter underwater predators. All three have longitudinal neck stripes, and all swim low in the water, especially when alarmed. They are adept at climbing into and concealing themselves in overhanging vegetation.

Sungrebe PLATE 14
Heliornis fulica
OTHER NAMES. American Finfoot (arch.).

Identification. 11″ (28 cm). Black-and-white-striped head and neck; legs/feet boldly barred black and white. Much longer-bodied than a grebe, with a moderately long tail, much longer than that of the virtually tailless grebe. ♀: auriculars tawny; bill pinkish, becoming mostly scarlet prior to breeding. ♂: lacks tawny auriculars of ♀; bill flesh-colored. *Flight:* rapid and direct, low over water.
Voice. Loud barking *k-wek k-wek wek wek.*
Habitat. Swamp forest, forest-lined streams.
Distribution. Resident from s Tamaulipas and Chiapas to c S.A. Absent from n Yucatán Pen.
Status in Belize. UC resident on mainland.

FAMILY: ARAMIDAE
(Limpkin)
World: 1. **New World:** 1. **Belize:** 1. New World Tropics and subtropics. Monotypic. In many ways the Limpkin is intermediate between rails and cranes but, based on recent genetic evidence, is thought to be most closely related to the Heliornithidae. It is an extraordinary vocalist characterized by long bill, neck, and legs and broad, rounded wings with a short, sickle-shaped outer primary that is clubbed at the end. It feeds primarily on the apple snail (genus *Pomacea*).

Limpkin PLATE 2
Aramus guarauna
OTHER NAMES. Clucking Hen (C), jọ chai (K), j'abb (M).

Identification. 24″ (61 cm). Dark brown, heavily spotted and streaked with white (most conspicuous on back and wing coverts); long, slightly downcurved bill. Heavier-set bill and legs than an ibis. *Flight:* outstretched neck held below horizontal; flies with sharp upstrokes and slower downstrokes; never flies high or for long distances.
Voice. 1. Loud, hysterical, penetrating *cooww!;* 2. longer, rolling *wāāāāāoo* screams; 3. drawn-out rolling guttural scream *uuuu-waa-a-a-a-aooo-o-o-o.* Typically calls at night and dawn.
Habitat. Freshwater marshes, lagoons, wet savannas; less common in wet meadows, roadside ditches.
Distribution. Resident from c Veracruz, Yucatán Pen., and Florida to sc S.A.
Status in Belize. FC to locally C resident on mainland nearly throughout but most plentiful in coastal lagoons; also recorded on n Ambergris Caye, where perhaps resident.

FAMILY: CHARADRIIDAE
(Plovers)
World: 66. **New World:** 18. **Belize:** 7. Worldwide away from the most arid deserts. For a relatively large family, plovers are remarkably uniform in appearance, showing little size variation compared with other related families, such as sandpipers. They are characterized by a short, pigeonlike bill with a slight bulge near the tip, relatively uniform leg-to-body ratio, rounded head, and vestigial hindtoe. Plovers feed by picking at the surface for small invertebrates and generally foraging in drier areas on firmer substrate than sandpipers. Many plovers feed at night as well as during the day, especially those dependent on tidal cycles for an accessible food source. Juvenal plumage consistently differs from ad. plumage only in having pale-edged contour feathers of upperparts. With feather wear, juvs. soon resemble ads. **Reference:** Hayman et al. (1986).

Genus: Pluvialis *(Tundra Plovers)*

Striking and unmistakable in alternate plumage. Most of the year, however, they are in basic or nonbreeding plumage and can look quite similar. Golden-plover passes through Belize only in spring, usually at inland sites, whereas Black-bellied is strictly coastal, where it may be common nearly year-round in suitable habitat.

Things to note: bill and body proportions; folded wing vs. tail length; vocalizations. *In basic and juv. plumage,* degree of crown/supercilium contrast, bars vs. streaks on flanks. *In flight,* presence/absence of white uppertail coverts, white wing stripe, and black axillars.

Black-bellied Plover   PLATE 15
Pluvialis squatarola
OTHER NAMES. Grey Plover (U.K.).

Identification. 11″ (28 cm). Larger than American Golden-Plover, with stockier build, larger head, and longer, thicker bill. Folded wings barely extend past tail, if at all. *Alt.:* finely patterned black-and-white back; mostly black underneath, with white vent and undertail coverts. *Basic:* Generally paler and grayer overall than golden-plover, but individual variation in both species precludes usefulness of this character by itself; supercilium contrasts less strongly with crown than in golden-plover; pale belly and unstreaked flanks contrast with darker, faintly streaked breast; in fresh plumage, has whitish edges to back feathers. *Juv.:* similar to basic, but with prominent white feather edges in back and wings; bright juvs. are browner, with light, yellowish brown feather edges, much like golden-plover. *Flight:* easily distinguished in all plumages by white uppertail coverts, conspicuous white wing stripe, and black axillars; flight calls of the two species are quite distinct.
Voice. Childlike, plaintive *ple-uh-ease* or *tree-oo-wee,* given in flight.
Habitat. Coastal beaches, mudflats, shrimp farms.
Distribution. Nests in Arctic; winters in coastal areas from sw Can., New England (U.S.), nc Eur., and Japan to s S.A., s Afr., and s Aust.
Status in Belize. UC to locally C winter visitor

on cayes and mainland coast, mid-July to early June; a few remaining through summer (or overlapping spring and autumn migrants?).
Reference. *Identification:* Paulson (1993).

American Golden-Plover   PLATE 15
Pluvialis dominica
OTHER NAMES. Lesser Golden-Plover (combined form).

Identification. 9¾″ (25 cm). Smaller than Black-bellied with longer neck, smaller head, and shorter, thinner bill; folded wings extend well past tail. *Alt.:* similar to Black-bellied, but dark feathers of upperparts tipped golden yellow, underparts mostly or entirely black. ♂ *alt.:* entirely black flanks, belly, and undertail coverts. ♀ *alt.:* white mottling in flanks and undertail coverts. *Basic:* similar to Black-bellied but averages slightly browner; whitish supercilium contrasts more with dark crown; faintly mottled underneath, with diffuse bars on flanks (usually plain in Black-bellied). *Flight:* lacks white rump and black axillars of Black-bellied; wing stripe much less conspicuous; flight calls distinctly different.
Voice. *Call:* soft, sweet to slightly tinny *turreep,* sometimes accented on 2nd syllable; typically given in flight or on takeoff.
Habitat. Newly planted rice fields, short-grass meadows, savannas.
Distribution. Nests in arctic Alaska and Can.; winters from c to s S.A.
Status in Belize. UC and local spring migrant, early Mar. to late May; unrecorded in autumn. Most records are from Blue Creek rice fields OW.
Reference. *Identification:* Roselaar (1990).

Genus: Charadrius *(Banded Plovers)*

All have at least one partial to complete dark band across the breast, and all but the Collared (!) have a white collar around the back of the neck. All have distinctive vocalizations, which can be recognized with a little practice.

Things to note: presence/absence of collar; number, thickness, color, and completeness of breast band(s) across breast; color of upperparts and legs/feet; length, thickness, and color of bill.

Collared Plover

MAP 53; PLATE 15

Charadrius collaris

Identification. 5¾″ (14.5 cm). Smallest of the plovers and one of the smallest of all shorebirds. Disproportionately long, flesh-colored legs and thin bill; small head. Ironically, the only banded plover in Belize that *lacks* a collar. *Ad.:* cinnamon crown and auriculars in all but very worn plumage; complete thin black breast band, white forehead, black forecrown and lores. *Juv.:* lacks black highlights in face but retains partial black breast band; has pale cinnamon-edged feathers on upperparts.

Voice. Rolling *t'dewp* or *t'dew;* in flight, *tip.*

Habitat. Shrimp farm dikes, sandflats and mudflats.

Distribution. Resident primarily in coastal areas from c Sinaloa, n Veracruz, and W.I. to s S.A. Some populations are migratory.

Status in Belize. VU migrant, winter visitor, and perhaps local resident on n. cayes and mainland coast. Nested at Nova Shrimp Farm BE in 1999.

Reference. *Status:* Jones et al. (2000).

Snowy Plover

PLATE 15

Charadrius alexandrinus
OTHER NAMES. Kentish Plover (U.K.).

Identification. 6¼″ (16 cm). Larger, squatter, and paler than Collared, with shorter, gray legs and white collar, broad white supercilium, pale lores, partial breast band. *Alt.:* black auricular patch and forecrown (may be dark brown in ♀). *Basic:* auriculars and forecrown sandy brown, like rest of upperparts. *Juv.:* fine pale feather tips give upperparts a scaled appearance.

Voice. 1. Soft, rough *prrip;*
2. louder *kriip.*

Habitat. Sandflats, beaches, drying shrimp farm ponds.

Distribution. Nests locally from wc and se U.S. and c Eurasia to s S.A., n Afr., and s Asia; winters primarily in coastal areas s. to Pan. (S.A. populations are sedentary), c Afr., and Indonesia.

Status in Belize. R winter visitor; few documented records.

Reference. *Status:* Jones et al. (2000).

Wilson's Plover

MAP 54; PLATE 15

Charadrius wilsonia
OTHER NAMES. Thick-billed Plover (arch.).

Identification. 7¼″ (18.5 cm). Larger than other single-banded plovers, with noticeably longer, thicker, all-black bill; broader breast band; and dull pinkish gray legs/feet. *Alt.:* black breast band, forecrown, and lores (dark brown in ♀). *Basic:* black areas replaced with same shade of brown as rest of upperparts. *Juv.:* fine pale edges to back and wing covert feathers.

Voice. 1. *pweet!;*
2. rolling, rough *terrorit;*
3. soft but rich *pik* or *kip;*
4. doubled *bi dik.*

Habitat. Sandflats and mudflats, shrimp farm dikes.

Distribution. Nests in coastal areas from nw Mex. and Virginia to n S.A.; winters along Atlantic and Pacific coasts from n Mex. and Florida to n Peru and c Brazil.

Status in Belize. UC winter visitor and local resident on inner cayes and mainland coast s. to n TO, occas. to Punta Gorda; nests on Ambergris Caye and perhaps a few other cayes, and locally along n mainland coast.

Semipalmated Plover

PLATE 15

Charadrius semipalmatus

Identification. 6¾″ (17 cm). Intermediate in size between Snowy and Wilson's. Much darker, richer brown than in Snowy, with full breast band and dark lores that offset white forehead; stubby bill; yellow-orange legs/feet. *Alt.:* orange bill with black tip; black breast band, forecrown, and auriculars. *Basic:* no black in plumage but retains full breast band; bill orange only at base of lower mandible. *Juv.:* fine pale feather edges give upperparts a scaled appearance; duller legs.

Voice. Squeaky *chur-it.*

Habitat. Sandflats and mudflats, shrimp farms; occas. rice fields.

Distribution. Nests in arctic and subarctic Alaska and Can.; winters primarily in coastal areas from California and N. Carolina to s S.A.

Status in Belize. FC to locally C migrant and less common winter visitor on cayes and mainland coast, mid-July to late May. A few occas. remain through summer. During migration, found in small to moderate numbers at a few inland localities (e.g., Blue Creek rice fields OW, Crooked Tree BE).

The **Piping Plover** *(Charadrius melodus)* has not been reported in Belize but is found in winter a short distance to the north in n Yucatán. Most like Semipalmated in all plumages but distinctly paler above (like Snowy), with pale, sandy brown auriculars, even in alt. plumage; partial to complete breast band, generally narrower than in Semipalmated; and pale lores. Differs from Snowy in having yellow to orange legs and shorter bill, which is bicolored in alt. plumage. *Flight:* broader white wing stripe than in Semipalmated; white uppertail coverts that accentuate dark tail.

Killdeer   PLATE 15
Charadrius vociferus

Identification. 9¾″ (25 cm). Most distinctive of the group. Much larger than others and found in much wider array of habitats—rarely on mudflats or sandflats. Has two black breast bands. Long tail extends well beyond wingtips; bright reddish orange rump and tail conspicuous in flight. Alt. and basic plumage, ♂, and ♀ all similar.
Voice. 1. Plaintive *kreee-EE* (or *kill-deer*); 2. shrill *deeet* notes.
Habitat. Many open short-grass habitats, including lawns, agricultural fields, and pastureland.
Distribution. Nests from s Alaska and c Can. to c Mex. and W.I., and disjunctively in w S.A. Winters from sw Can. and c U.S. to n S.A. Populations of W.I. and S.A. are sedentary.
Status in Belize. FC winter visitor, early Oct. to early Apr., occas. later.

FAMILY: HAEMATOPODIDAE
(Oystercatchers)
World: 11. **New World:** 4. **Belize:** 1. Worldwide except Indonesia, parts of se Asia and Afr., and the polar regions. Most are strictly coastal. All are either black or similarly patterned black and

white, are similar in size and shape, and have the same long, oddly swollen, bladelike red bill. Generally, those found on rocky shorelines are all black, and those found on sand or mudflats are pied. **Reference:** Hayman et al. (1986).

American Oystercatcher MAP 55; PLATE 16
Haematopus palliatus

Identification. 17″ (43 cm); bill 3–3½″ (7.5–9 cm). Distinctive. Blackish brown above, with black head, neck, breast, and flight feathers; bold white wing stripe, uppertail coverts, and underparts; long, bright orange-red bill, swollen in middle; yellow eyes; flesh-colored legs/feet.
Voice. Sharp, liquid *preet.* In encounters with others, a jacamar-like hysterical *pureet pureet preet pree-pree-pree-pre-pre-pr-pr-pr-pr.*
Habitat. Coastal sandy beaches.
Distribution. Resident to partially migratory along coast from nw Mex. and ne U.S. to s S.A.; summer only in ne U.S., and winter only in much of s Mex. and n C.A.
Status in Belize. R and local winter visitor, mid-July to mid-Apr. Majority of records are from Dangriga; also recorded from Belize City and Caye Chapel.
Reference. *Status:* Howell et al. (1992).

FAMILY: RECURVIROSTRIDAE
(Stilts and Avocets)
World: 10. **New World:** 4. **Belize:** 2. Tropical and Temperate Zones throughout much of the world wherever wetlands occur. All are slender-bodied, with a long neck, a long and thin bill, and spindly legs, and all are boldly patterned, primarily in blacks and whites. Avocets have a sharply upturned bill, bluish gray legs/feet, basal webbing between toes, and vestigial hindtoes. Stilts generally have straight or nearly straight bill; exceptionally long, reddish pink legs; and no hindtoe. They typically inhabit shallow ponds, marshes, mudflats and salt flats, and flooded fields. **Reference:** Hayman et al. (1986).

Black-necked Stilt

PLATE 16

Himantopus mexicanus

OTHER NAMES. Common Stilt (combined form), Black-winged Stilt (combined form).

Identification. 15″ (38 cm). Black above; white below, including white forehead and spot above eyes; exceptionally long, bright pink legs; straight, needlelike bill. ♂: black back. ♀: blackish brown back. *Juv.:* gray back; hindneck pale gray to whitish.

Voice. 1. Incessant, piercing, nasal *kip!;*
2. rougher, flatter, barking *kep!*

Habitat. Rice fields, lagoons, estuaries, shrimp farms.

Distribution. Mostly resident from sw Can., c and e U.S. to s S.A.; populations n. of s U.S. migrate s. in winter.

Status in Belize. FC to locally VC winter visitor, Aug. to May; a few nest at Crooked Tree and locally elsewhere in north. Population has increased significantly in past 30 years, with proliferation of rice and shrimp farming.

Reference. *Status:* Wood and Leberman (1987).

American Avocet

MAP 56; PLATE 16

Recurvirostra americana

Identification. 16½″ (42 cm). Uniquely black-and-white-patterned back and wings; white belly; long, thin, upturned bill; long, blue-gray legs. *Alt.:* foreparts bright rusty cinnamon. *Basic:* foreparts pale gray. ♀: sharply upturned bill. ♂: gradually upturned bill.

Voice. Ringing, strident *kreep!* notes, singly or repeated frequently.

Habitat. Estuaries, shrimp farms.

Distribution. Nests in w N.A. from s Can. to sw U.S. and Mex. plateau; winters from s U.S. to s Mex.

Status in Belize. Occas. winter visitor, mostly near coast, early Oct. to early Apr.

Reference. *Status:* Jones et al. (2000).

FAMILY: JACANIDAE
(Jacanas)

World: 8. **New World:** 2. **Belize:** 1. Tropics and subtropics worldwide. Although jacanas are superficially rail-like, morphological, biochemi-cal, and genetic evidence all suggest similarity to other shorebirds in Charadriiformes. They are characterized by long legs, with exceptionally long toes and claws for walking on floating vegetation. Most have a frontal shield or wattle, and the two New World species have bright yellow to greenish yellow remiges that are prominently displayed when flushed and upon landing, when their wings are briefly held high above their back. Jacanas are somewhat gregarious when not breeding, and highly vocal throughout the year.

Reference: Hayman et al. (1986).

Northern Jacana

PLATE 14

Jacana spinosa

OTHER NAMES. American Jacana (alt.), Georgie Bull (C), tz'ic ha's<u>a</u>b (K).

Identification. 9″ (23 cm). Striking bright yellow remiges and exceptionally long toes. *Ad.:* deep chestnut, with black foreparts glossed green in sunlight; bright yellow bill with pale blue cere and orange-yellow frontal shield. *Juv.:* streaked black-and-white head and white underparts.

Voice. 1. Series of moderately high-pitched *toot* and *canh* notes;
2. somewhat rough *krick krick krick krick krick krick krick;*
3. Clapper Rail–like *chah chah chah. . . . ,* speeding up slightly toward end;
4. *chidilik chidilik chidilik . . . ;*
5. clear *tik tik tik . . .* in flight;
6. *sheek sheek sheek;*
7. single *schick.*

Habitat. Freshwater marshes, rice fields, shallow ponds.

Distribution. Resident from s Sinaloa, c Tamaulipas, and W.I. to w Pan.

Status in Belize. Locally C resident on mainland.

FAMILY: SCOLOPACIDAE
(Sandpipers and Phalaropes)

World: 87. **New World:** 45. **Belize:** 26 (plus 1 provisional). Cosmopolitan. No other bird family shows such a wide range of bill lengths and shapes, and few exceed the sandpipers in variety of body sizes, foraging methods, and habitats used. Compared with plovers, sandpipers have smaller eyes, a more slender head, and a generally longer, slimmer, more tactile bill. All but the Sanderling have a small hindtoe. Sandpipers can be grouped according to four different feeding styles: ploverlike pecking at the substrate (Semipalmated Sandpiper), rapid pecking at the surface of the water (phalaropes), probing into soft substrate (dowitchers), and chasing small fish with bill submerged (yellowlegs). Those that probe locate food with tactile receptors in the bill tip. Sandpipers occupy a wide range of habitats from moist forest at one extreme to desert at the other, and from tiny seasonal ponds to open ocean. Many breed at inland sites and winter at coastal sites. Most species are long-distance migrants. **Reference:** Hayman et al. (1986).

For such a fascinating and diverse family, sandpipers are much underappreciated in Belize. Although most are restricted to rather narrowly defined wetland situations not present in much of the country, thousands congregate in areas with extensive shallow water and mudflats such as recently harvested rice fields, shrimp farms, and shallow lagoons. Smaller numbers congregate on sandy beaches.

SUBFAMILY: SCOLOPACINAE
(Sandpipers)

Includes all sandpipers in Belize except the phalaropes, a small but highly distinctive group that is sometimes placed in a separate family.

Tribe: Tringini

Most are long-legged and moderately long-billed. All bob either their foreparts or hindparts. The two yellowlegs are very similar in plumage but differ in body size and proportions. However, unless both species are present for direct comparison, these relative differences can be hard to discern. The other four species are more easily distinguished.

Things to note: overall size; bill length relative to head; bill thickness, shape, and color at base; leg color; vocalizations. *In flight,* pattern of white, if any, in wings, rump, and tail.

Greater Yellowlegs   PLATE 17
Tringa melanoleuca

Identification. 12″ (30.5 cm). Slender shorebird with long neck and bill and long, yellow legs/feet; larger than Lesser (no size overlap); bill thicker-based, usually slightly upturned, proportionately longer (1½ times length of head), and basal ⅓ typically paler. *Alt.:* bolder streaks on throat and neck than in Lesser; dark chevrons on breast, becoming sparser on belly and flanks and sometimes extending to undertail coverts. *Basic:* virtually identical to Lesser in plumage characters and should be separated using the relative differences in body size, bill, and calls; look for pale base to lower mandible on Greater. *Juv.:* from Lesser by whiter underparts, with distinct dark streaks on throat, breast, and sometimes sides; from ad. by neat white edges of all wing feathers (ad. has patchier pattern). *Flight:* less buoyant than Lesser; like Lesser, has white lower rump and mostly white tail; all-dark wings.

Voice. 1. Typically a clear, ringing *dear dear deur,* the last note usually a little softer and lower-pitched;

2. a faster *dear-dear-dear-dur.*

Habitat. Freshwater marshes, rice fields, shrimp farms, sandflats and mudflats.

Distribution. Nests in s Alaska and c Can.; winters from nw and ne U.S. to s S.A.

Status in Belize. FC to C winter visitor on mainland, less C on cayes, mid-July to mid-May, occas. through summer.

Reference. *Identification:* Wilds (1982).

Lesser Yellowlegs   PLATE 17
Tringa flavipes

Identification. 9¾″ (25 cm). Smaller version of Greater Yellowlegs, with thinner, straighter, all-dark bill that is proportionately shorter (1–1¼ times length of head). *Alt.:* densely finely streaked throat and neck; unbarred flanks. *Basic:* plumage virtually identical to that of Greater; best told by differences in body size, bill length and shape, and calls; bill dark throughout. *Juv.:* pale grayish beneath with diffuse streaking on throat and breast. *Flight:* more buoyant than Greater.

Voice. *Call:* flatter and lower-pitched than in Greater; typically a soft *tew tew;* but not as dry or rapid as in Short-billed Dowitcher.

Habitat. Similar to Greater Yellowlegs.

Distribution. Nests from n Alaska and nw Can. to s Alaska and sc Can.; winters from s U.S. to s S.A.

Status in Belize. FC to locally C winter visitor, mid-July to mid-May; infrequent on cayes.

Reference. *Identification:* Wilds (1982).

Solitary Sandpiper   PLATE 17
Tringa solitaria

Identification. 8¼″ (21 cm). Like small dark yellowlegs with contrasting dark shoulder, shorter olive legs, more compact body. From Spotted by longer neck, more upright posture, fine white spotting in upperparts; folded wings that project beyond tail tip, white eye-ring. When agitated, bobs foreparts up and down like yellowlegs, not rear end like Spotted. *Alt.:* fine streaking in head and neck. *Basic and juv.:* paler upperparts; head and neck smudgy, unstreaked. *Flight:* deep, powerful, somewhat erratic wingbeats, very different from Spotted; black-and-white-barred outer tail feathers and black central tail feathers; blackish underwings; lacks pale wing stripe; Yellowlegs have white uppertail coverts, a mostly white tail with fine black bars, and nearly white underwings.

Voice. 1. Clear, piercing *peat-eat!* and *peat-eat-eat;*

2. *weet! weet!*

Habitat. Freshwater marshes, rice fields, small ponds, streamsides.

Distribution. Nests from nc Alaska and c Can. to s Can.; winters from s Sonora, s Texas, and Cuba to sc S.A.

Status in Belize. FC winter visitor, late July to early May.

Willet   PLATE 17
Catoptrophorus semipalmatus

Identification. 13½″ (34.5 cm). Two recognizable subspecies: Eastern Willet (*C. s. semi-*

palmatus) and Western Willet (*C. s. inornatus*). Eastern is smaller, with relatively shorter bill and less white in wings. Western often wades in deeper water and has more white in forehead. *Alt.:* Eastern browner, more heavily barred and mottled with black. *Basic:* Eastern darker, slightly browner. *Juv.:* dusky wash extends across breast in Eastern; center of breast white in Western. *Flight:* boldly marked black-and-white wings.

Voice. *Call* (usually given when taking off):
1. clear, ringing *wee wit!;*
2. *klee lee!* to *klee-le-le!*

Habitat. Beaches, shrimp farms.

Distribution. Nests in interior from sc Can. to wc U.S. and on Atlantic coast from se Can. to ne Mex. Winters along coasts from nw and ne U.S. to n Chile and s Brazil.

Status in Belize. UC winter visitor on cayes and mainland coast, early July to mid-May. Once inland at Hill Bank OW, 30 Mar. 1955. On mainland, most often seen at shrimp farms, where sometimes FC during migration. Both *C. s. semipalmatus* and *C. s. inornatus* occur, but relative status of each is unclear.

Spotted Sandpiper   PLATE 17
Actitis macularia
OTHER NAMES. Shaky Batty (= Body) (C), tz'ic nik ha (K), sak i tuwiz ha'a (K).

Identification. 6¾″ (17 cm). Smaller, with less upright posture and shorter neck than Solitary; unspotted upperparts; fleshy-yellow legs/feet; pale supercilium; and long tail that projects beyond folded wings. When on the ground, continuously pumps its posterior like a waterthrush. *Alt.:* prominent black spots on clean white breast and belly. *Basic:* dusky smudge on sides of breast. *Juv.:* pale edges to wing covert feathers bordered subterminally with black. *Flight:* unique, with alternating rapid, shallow wingbeats and short glides; less prominent markings in tail than Solitary.

Voice. 1. *trē trē treet;*

2. *dreet dreet;*

3. *pee deep;*

4. *pi pi pi pi;*

5. *curry curry curry curry.* Calls softer, not as piercing as in Solitary Sandpiper.
Habitat. Rice fields, farm ponds, lagoons, streamsides, shrimp farms, mudflats and sandflats, beaches.
Distribution. Nests from n Alaska and nc Can. to c U.S.; winters from nw and s U.S. to sc S.A.
Status in Belize. C and widespread winter visitor, mid-July to early June.

Upland Sandpiper   PLATE 16
Bartramia longicauda
OTHER NAMES. Upland Plover (arch.).

Identification. 11½″ (29 cm). Small head; large eyes; long, thin neck; sleek body; long, graduated tail; and upright posture. Moderately short, thin orange-yellow bill with black tip, and orange-yellow legs/feet. *Ad.:* finely streaked and mottled throughout except for white belly and undertail coverts. *Juv.:* like ad. but with scaly pattern on upperparts. *Flight:* nearly black primaries and primary coverts contrast with rest of wing.
Voice. Loud, clear, liquid *hui huit!,* usually given when flushed.
Habitat. Drying rice fields, agricultural lands, pasturelands. Often perches on exposed tree snags and fence posts.
Distribution. Nests from e Alaska, nw and se Can. locally to c U.S.; winters locally in e S.A. from Suriname to c Argentina.
Status in Belize. Occas. spring and R autumn transient, mid-Mar. to mid- or late May; late July to early Oct.
Reference. *Status:* Wood and Leberman (1987).

Tribe: Numeniini (Curlews)

Large shorebirds distinguished by long, downcurved bill and brown plumage.
   Things to note: boldness of supercilium and eyestripe; length of bill; color of underwings; presence/absence of streaks on flanks.

Whimbrel   PLATE 16
Numenius phaeopus
OTHER NAMES. Hudsonian Curlew (arch.).

Identification. 15½″ (39.5 cm). Long neck; long, curved bill; relatively short legs; gray-brown plumage streaked with dark brown; barred flanks. Much shorter bill than all but a few juv. Long-billed Curlews. Dark brown crown and eyestripe separated by a whitish supercilium. Whitish lower belly and undertail coverts. *Flight:* dull pinkish cinnamon underwings heavily barred with dark brown. *Juv.:* from ad. by more prominently marked cinnamon buff feather edges on upperparts.
Voice. Loud, hysterical *kri-kri-kri-kri-kri-kri,* usually upon taking flight.
Habitat. Beaches, sandflats and mudflats.
Distribution. Nests in Alaska and n Can.; winters in coastal areas from California and N. Carolina to s S.A.
Status in Belize. UC and local winter visitor along mainland coast and cayes primarily from early July to mid-Apr.; occas. remaining through summer.

Long-billed Curlew   PLATE 16
Numenius americanus

Identification. 20½″ (52 cm). Similar to Whimbrel but with exceptionally long, curved bill (shortest in juv. ♂). Less prominent pale supercilium than Whimbrel. Cinnamon buff underparts streaked only on neck and breast; flanks unbarred; lacks whitish posterior underparts. *Juv.* (especially ♂): much shorter bill than ad., occas. no longer than longest-billed Whimbrels; from ad. by more prominently marked cinnamon buff feather edges on upperparts. *Flight:* unbarred bright cinnamon underwings.
Voice. 1. Shrill, clear *cur-leee;*
2. rapid, shrill *kwid-wid-wid-wid-wid.*
Habitat. Rice fields, freshwater and brackish marshes, wet meadows, shrimp farms.
Distribution. Nests in interior w N.A.; winters from California and s Texas to E.S. and n Yucatán Pen.
Status in Belize. R migrant and winter visitor, late Aug. to mid-May.

References. *Status:* Howell et al. (1992); Jones et al. (2000); Wood and Leberman (1987).

Tribe: Limosini (Godwits)

Unlike curlews, godwits have a long, upturned bill. Both N.A. species are rare in Belize and are quite different in appearance.

Things to note: color of underwing coverts; wing and tail pattern in flight.

Hudsonian Godwit   PLATE 16
Limosa haemastica

Identification. 15″ (38 cm). Large shorebird with long, slightly upturned, not decurved, bill. From Willet by longer, slightly upturned bill; slimmer appearance; darker legs/feet; and blackish tail. ♂ *alt.:* rich reddish chestnut underparts. ♀ *alt.:* chestnut-and-black scalloping on otherwise dull grayish buff underparts. *Flight:* readily distinguished from all other large shorebirds but Willet by boldly patterned black-and-white wings, from Willet by black tail and less white in more pointed wings.
Voice. In flight, a high-pitched *ka-weep!*, but usually silent in migration.
Habitat. Lagoons, rice fields, shrimp farms.
Distribution. Nests locally from w Alaska to n Ontario; winters in se S.A. Migrates long distances nonstop; seldom seen away from selected stopover points. Autumn migration mostly over Atlantic Ocean.
Status in Belize. Two records: Crooked Tree BE, 4 May 1986; Aqua Mar Shrimp Farm TO, 16 May 1999 (four individuals).
Reference. *Status:* Jones et al. (2000).

Marbled Godwit   PLATE 16
Limosa fedoa

Identification. 15½″ (39.5 cm). Large, long-legged, long-billed shorebird. Superficially like Long-billed Curlew; however, bill distinctively upturned, with basal ½ to 2/3 pinkish. ♂'s bill averages shorter than ♀'s. *Alt.:* finely barred underparts. *Basic and juv.:* unstreaked buffy underparts. *Flight:* bright cinnamon underwings.
Voice. 1. Nasal, laughing *ah-ha!;*

2. loud *ker-whit!*, sometimes given in rapid series, lower-pitched and hoarser than preceding vocalization.
Habitat. Shrimp farms, sandflats and mudflats, beaches.
Distribution. Nests in interior Can. and nc U.S.; winters in coastal areas from nw and se U.S. to s Mex., sporadically to n and w S.A.
Status in Belize. R winter visitor on mainland coast and cayes, Aug. to Mar.
Reference. *Status:* Jones et al. (2000).

Tribe: Arenariini (Turnstones)

Chunky shorebirds with short legs and short, peglike, slightly upturned bill used for turning over small shells, coral, seaweed, and debris. Boldly marked in blacks and whites. Frequent coastal shorelines almost exclusively.

Ruddy Turnstone   PLATE 17
Arenaria interpres

Identification. 8¾″ (22 cm). *Alt.:* strikingly black, white, and rufous, with bright red-orange legs/feet; head and breast pattern unique—white, with black mostly confined to face, collar, and sides of breast. *Basic:* duller, but with same basic pattern as alt. *Juv.:* like basic, but with feathers of upperparts edged pale yellowish brown; dull yellowish brown legs/feet. *Flight:* boldly black-and-white-striped wings, rump, and tail; rufous back and greater wing coverts in alt. plumage.
Voice. 1. Nasal to clear *chew* to *tew,* singly or run into a series;
2. *chow ch ch ch chow ch ch chow;*
3. Belted Kingfisher–like rattle, but squeaky and lower-pitched.
Habitat. Sandy beaches with seaweed or coral rubble; shrimp farms; occas. lagoons.
Distribution. Nests in Arctic; winters on coasts and islands worldwide from n U.S., nc Eur., and s Asia to s S.A., s Afr., s Aust., and N.Z.
Status in Belize. C winter visitor on cayes, locally FC winter visitor on mainland coast, early July to late May (a few year-round); recorded inland occas. at Crooked Tree in migration.

Tribe: Calidridini

Sandpipers in the genus *Calidris* (often referred to as "peeps") present one of the most complex ID challenges of any bird group. With practice, most can be IDed relatively easily; however, two —Semipalmated and Western—are especially difficult in basic plumage. Several species, including these two, in worn or faded plumage can also be confusing. A knowledge of plumage characteristics and the months they are worn can be very helpful in successful ID. Depending on the species, birds in juv. plumage are present roughly from July to Oct./Nov.; ads. in basic plumage from Sept. to Apr., and ads. in alt. plumage from Mar. to Sept.

Things to note: plumage (alt., basic, or juv.); overall size; length and shape of bill (thickness at base, tapered, curved, drooped, or straight); leg color; color and pattern of scapulars; conspicuousness of supercilium, if present; streaked or unstreaked flanks; folded wing vs. tail length; vocalizations. *In flight,* pattern of white, if any, in wings and uppertail coverts.

Red Knot
MAP 57; PLATE 18
Calidris canutus

Identification. 10¼" (26 cm). Nearly as large as Black-bellied Plover. Best IDed by plump build; relatively short, straight, moderately thick bill; dark legs/feet; and large size compared with other *Calidris*. *Alt.:* rich chestnut face, throat, neck, and breast. *Basic:* dirty gray above, white below, with fine spotting and flecking on breast and flanks. *Juv.:* underparts washed with light pinkish buff; feathers of upperparts finely edged dark gray (subterminally) and white (tip), giving the upperparts a neatly scaled pattern. *Flight:* pale gray tail and uppertail coverts, finely barred on coverts.
Voice. Soft, low-pitched *kuh* to slightly rough *kruh.*
Habitat. Shrimp farms, beaches.
Distribution. Nests in Arctic; winters locally in coastal areas from California, New Jersey, nc Eur., and se Asia to s S.A., s Afr., s Aust., and N.Z.
Status in Belize. UC and local migrant and winter visitor along c. mainland coast; once each on Caye Caulker and Ambergris Caye. Recorded only from early Sept. to early March. Most records are from shrimp farms and Dangriga.

Sanderling
MAP 58; PLATE 18
Calidris alba

Identification. 7¼" (18.5 cm). Larger than similar Western and Semipalmated, with medium-length straight black bill and black legs/feet; smaller and less chunky than Red Knot. *Alt.:* distinctive rufous head and breast, duller in ♀, diffusely streaked with dark brown. *Basic:* pale gray above, without brownish tones; white below; black at bend of wing. *Juv.:* boldly black-and-white-mottled back and scapulars with buff highlights in fresh plumage. *Flight:* bold white wing stripe, black primary coverts.
Voice. Barking *kip* notes.
Habitat. Sandy beaches, shrimp farms.
Distribution. Nests in Arctic; winters on coasts and islands worldwide from s Alaska, se Can., nc Eur., and s Asia to s S.A., s Afr., and s Aust.
Status in Belize. Locally FC winter visitor on cayes and mainland coast s. to ne TO, early Aug. to early May.

Semipalmated Sandpiper
PLATE 18
Calidris pusilla

Identification. 5¾" (14.5 cm). One of the smallest shorebirds, with short black legs and bill. Grayish to brownish above, mostly white beneath. Bill generally shorter than in Western; however, with some overlap (shortest-billed ♂ Western vs. longest-billed ♀ Semipalmated). Bill of both thick at base, but tapers to narrow tip in Western; variable in Semipalmated, tapered in some, relatively thick throughout in others. Bill of Least, by way of contrast, is relatively thin throughout. Western's bill usually has noticeable droop toward tip; in Semipalmated it rarely does. Semipalmated has webbing at base of toes, but this can be difficult to see in the field. *Alt.* (usually attained in Mar.): rather uniformly brownish gray above (paler, more uniformly distributed markings than Western), with fine streaking on underparts virtually confined

to the breast; Western has broad tawny rufous edges to scapular feathers, ear coverts, and sides of crown and has bold triangular spots on breast, sides, and flanks. *Basic* (July–Oct.): very difficult to tell from Western; generally, only birds with bill at the long (Western) and short (Semipalmated) extremes can be safely IDed; in direct comparison, Semipalmated appears warmer brown; thin black feather shafts in scapulars less distinct; also a darker, more contrasting face that sets off a thin but distinct white eye-ring; Western tends to be slightly grayer overall and to have a whiter face, offsetting prominent black eyes. *Juv.:* uniformly warm brownish gray above, with pale feather edges giving upperparts a scaled effect; in fresh plumage (July), may have bright buff breast band; Western tends to have more rufescent upperparts and paler head; in birds with rufescent cast to plumage, rufescent color is paler and more extensive than in Western; on Western, rufescent color restricted to back, inner scapulars, and tertials, which, along with its pale gray head and wings, gives it a strong two-toned pattern; juv. Western retains some rufescent-edged scapulars until late autumn—a useful character for separating many Westerns later in autumn.
Voice. Rolling *chrrup* or *cherk.* When flushed, sometimes a dry *chip-i-lip* note very similar to that of Western.
Habitat. Shrimp farms, rice fields, sandflats and mudflats.
Distribution. Nests in arctic Alaska and Can.; winters in coastal areas from s Mex. and W.I. to n Chile and c Argentina.
Status in Belize. Locally C autumn transient, FC spring transient, and occas. winter visitor in coastal lowlands, early Aug. to late May, but with few records between mid-Oct. and early Mar.; relatively few records from cayes. Most C in Aug., when it sometimes outnumbers Western. Because of its close similarity to Western, especially in basic plumage, birds seen in winter should be carefully documented.
References. *Identification:* Kaufman (1990); Veit and Jonsson (1984).

Western Sandpiper

PLATE 18

Calidris mauri

Identification. 6¼″ (16 cm). See Semipalmated, above. Typically feeds in deeper water than Semipalmated and Least and is more likely to probe than to pick at the surface.
Voice. 1. Liquid *jeet* or *cheep,* harsher and less shrill than that of Least, less harsh than that of Semipalmated (but birds in flocks may give calls indistinguishable from flock calls of Semipalmated);
2. *chip-i-lip,* as in Semipalmated.
Habitat. Shrimp farms, rice fields, sandflats and mudflats; occas. beaches.
Distribution. Nests in e Siberia and Alaska; winters mostly along or near coast from Washington State and New Jersey to n S.A.
Status in Belize. Locally C to VC autumn transient in coastal lowlands and cayes, less C in winter and spring; late July to mid-May. As with most other shorebirds, congregates at shrimp farms, where a thousand or more can be seen on some days in autumn. After Aug., generally outnumbers Semipalmated by one to two orders of magnitude.
References. *Identification:* Kaufman (1990); Veit and Jonsson (1984).

Least Sandpiper

PLATE 18

Calidris minutilla

Identification. 5½″ (14 cm). Smallest of the peeps and one of the smallest of all shorebirds. Generally darker and browner than others with yellowish to olive green, not black, legs (but muddy legs may appear black). Bill thinner throughout than preceding two; may appear slightly decurved like that of Western, but always thinner-based. Birds wading in mud can appear to have blackish legs. Hunched posture compared with Western and Semipalmated. Usually feeds on land, less often in shallow water. *Alt.:* darker and browner than Semipalmated, not two-toned like Western; some bright rufescent, others less bright; head and breast dingy, with heavy fine streaking on pale brown background. *Basic:* dull brownish gray above (darker than other small peeps), with complete dark breast band, rather plain face, and less conspicuous supercilium. *Juv.:* uniformly dark rufescent upperparts set it off in mixed flocks from Semipalmated and Western at any distance; in fresh plumage (July), has two conspicuous white lateral back stripes. *Flight:* browner and generally darker upperparts; light wing stripe not as prominent as in other small peeps; flocks rise nearly vertically on takeoff and fly off in a series of lurches; Semipalmated and Western usually flush more horizontally and fly directly away.

Voice. Distinctly different from Western and Semipalmated vocalizations; slightly rough, thin *treee* or *treep,* sometimes *tre-treep;* notes given singly or repeated several times.

Habitat. Shrimp farms, rice fields, sandflats and mudflats, lagoons, estuaries, beaches.

Distribution. Nests in Alaska and n Can.; winters from s U.S. (and Washington on w. coast) s. to c S.A.

Status in Belize. C transient and winter visitor in coastal lowlands and cayes, mid-July to late May, but UC and local in winter in interior.

Reference. *Identification:* Veit and Jonsson (1984).

White-rumped Sandpiper PLATE 18
Calidris fuscicollis

Identification. 7″ (18 cm). Larger and longer-winged than preceding three; most similar to Baird's, especially in juv. plumage. Both are very similar in size, shape, and wing length (folded wings extend well beyond tail). White-rumped has slightly decurved bill, tinged orangish at base. *Alt.:* contrasting rufous-and-gray upperparts; rufous in crown and auriculars; prominently streaked breast and flanks. *Basic* (unrecorded in Belize): mostly gray, with white belly, undertail coverts, and supercilium. *Juv.* (rare in Belize): upperparts more complexly patterned than in Baird's; back feathers dark with chestnut fringes; in fresh plumage, usually shows thin white V on sides of back; outer scapular feathers (closest to wing) black with white edges and pale bases, adding to complexity of pattern;

broad breast band of fine streaks on pale grayish or brownish background; usually has streaked or spotted flanks. *Flight:* readily distinguished from all other peeps by complete white uppertail coverts.

Voice. 1. Distinctive high-pitched, thin *cheep* to *chip,* almost insectlike; 2. lispy *tsip.*

Habitat. Rice fields, lagoons, shrimp farms.

Distribution. Nests in arctic Alaska and Can.; winters in se S.A.

Status in Belize. C spring transient in coastal lowlands and cayes, mid-Apr. to early June. One autumn record: 18 Oct. 1996, Nova Shrimp Farm BE. Numbers peak in mid-May after most other shorebirds have departed.

Reference. *Identification:* Alström (1987).

[Baird's Sandpiper] PLATE 18
Calidris bairdii

Identification. 6¾″ (17 cm). Most like White-rumped but differs in having all-black bill with no hint of a droop; clean white flanks; more uniformly patterned upperparts; and less conspicuous supercilium. Pale buffy breast band and face, including supercilium, showing less contrast than in White-rumped; unstreaked flanks. *Alt:* scapulars mostly pale but with contrasting black feather centers. *Ad. basic:* most like juv. but grayer. *Juv.:* buffier than adult; scaly-appearing back results from dark back and scapular feathers with distinct rounded, narrow white edges. *Flight:* from similar-sized White-rumped by brown central uppertail coverts with white on sides only.

Voice. Slightly gravelly or raspy *krrit.*

Habitat. Usually found in the drier, upper portion of marshes and mudflats with sparse low grasses, away from water.

Distribution. Nests in arctic e Siberia, Alaska, and Can.; winters in w and s S.A.

Status in Belize. Not yet confirmed but probably a VR spring (and autumn?) transient.

References. *Distribution:* Coffey (1960). *Status:* Jones (2002). *Identification:* Alström (1987).

Pectoral Sandpiper
Calidris melanotos

PLATE 18

Identification. ♂ 9″ (23 cm), ♀ 7¾″ (20 cm). Easily distinguished by dark breast streaks, ending abruptly and sharply cut off from white belly; yellow legs. Larger than other similar *Calidris,* especially ♂, which is much larger than ♀. *Alt.* (Mar.–Oct.): fine dark streaks on neck and breast, denser in male; upperparts dark brown with buffy feather edges, becoming rufous on crown, scapulars, and tertials. *Juv.:* head and breast buffier; upperparts rufous, with inner scapulars often outlined in white.
Voice. Distinctive *churr* or *churt,* usually given in flight.
Habitat. Rice fields, shrimp farms, marshes, lagoons.
Distribution. Nests in arctic Siberia, Alaska, and Can.; winters from c to s S.A.
Status in Belize. FC autumn and spring transient, mid-Aug. to early Oct. and early Mar. to late May.

Dunlin
Calidris alpina

PLATE 18

Identification. 8¼″ (21 cm). Distinguished from Stilt Sandpiper by shorter, black (not yellow) legs/feet; shorter neck; and slightly shorter bill. Larger than Western, with proportionately longer bill. Typically feeds hunched over and appears neckless. Stilt Sandpiper not hunchbacked when feeding and has distinct neck. *Alt.* (unrecorded in Belize): red back and scapulars, black central belly. *Basic:* much like large, dark Western; grayish with dull brownish wash. *Flight:* lacks Stilt Sandpiper's full white rump; more prominent white wing stripe than smaller *Calidris* (except Sanderling).
Voice. Harsh *dreeep,* like that of Least but lower-pitched, harsher.
Habitat. Beaches, shrimp farms, coastal lagoons.
Distribution. Nests in Arctic; winters in coastal areas from s Alaska, New England (U.S.), nc Eur., and Japan to Sinaloa, Tamaulipas, s Florida, c Afr., n India, and s China.
Status in Belize. Three acceptable records:

Commerce Bight near Dangriga SC, 21 Mar. 1990 (three individuals); Aqua Mar Shrimp Farm TO, 6 Jan. 1999; and Nova Shrimp Farm BE, 17 Dec. 2000.
References. *Status:* Howell et al. (1992); Jones et al. (2000).

Stilt Sandpiper
Calidris himantopus

PLATE 18

Identification. 8¼″ (21 cm). Long-legged shorebird with moderately long, drooped bill; yellow legs/feet; and spotted or barred undertail coverts (except in juv.). Wilson's Phalarope has thin, straight bill and shorter, black legs/feet. Typically seen wading and constantly probing in water. When feeding, posterior rises well above horizontal plane; larger, longer-billed dowitchers hold body nearly horizontal. *Alt.:* distinctive; heavily spotted and barred below, with rufous auriculars and crown separated by prominent whitish supercilium. *Basic:* much smaller than a dowitcher, with longer legs and shorter, slightly drooped bill. *Juv.:* warm buff wash on neck and breast; brown upperparts with pale buff-and-rufous feather edges. *Flight:* white band across uppertail coverts; lacks dowitchers' prominent white wedge through rump.
Voice. Low, soft *tu* or *tur,* in series or singly; not double- or triple-noted as in Lesser Yellowlegs or Short-billed Dowitcher; lower in pitch.
Habitat. Rice fields, shrimp farms.
Distribution. Nests in arctic Alaska and Can.; winters locally from se California and S. Carolina to w C.R. and n S.A.
Status in Belize. UC to locally FC transient and occas. winter visitor on mainland, mid-Aug. to mid-May. Occas. on Ambergris Caye.

Buff-breasted Sandpiper
Tryngites subruficollis

PLATE 16

Identification. 7½″ (19 cm). Easily distinguished under most circumstances. Uniformly buff-colored face and underparts, with prominent black eyes. *Ad.:* upperparts black and brown, with feathers edged in light buff; yellow legs/feet; short, straight, thin bill. *Juv.:*

paler below with white, not buff, feather edges on upperparts. *Flight:* immaculate white underwings.

Voice. *Flight calls:* 1. quiet *greet* (somewhat like Baird's);
2. *chup;* 3. *tik.*

Habitat. Newly planted rice fields, wet shortgrass meadows.

Distribution. Nests in arctic Alaska and Can.; winters in se S.A.

Status in Belize. Occas. spring and autumn transient; thus far recorded from late Aug. to late Sept. and mid-Apr. to early May. Migration period undoubtedly longer than indicated by the few dated records.

Reference. *Voice:* Sibley (2000).

Tribe: Limnodromini (Dowitchers)

Medium-sized shorebirds with very long, straight bill and relatively short legs; white wedge through uppertail coverts and rump to lower back. Feed in shallow water by probing rapidly into substrate. Although strikingly different from most other shorebirds, dowitchers are very similar to each other. Voice is easily the best way to separate the two dowitchers. With practice, almost any call can be assigned to one species or the other; however, in silent birds, plumage characters must be used. Both are very similar in basic plumage (Sept. to Apr.). In alternate plumage, the *hendersoni* race of Short-billed closely resembles Long-billed. Juveniles, on the other hand, are relatively easy to tell apart. Recognizing the plumage that a bird is in will facilitate its ID. Differences in bill length, wing length, and tail pattern are useful only in some, not all, individuals.

　Things to note: vocalizations, plumage (alt., basic, juv.), pattern of tertial feathers (juv.), barred or spotted vs. unmarked breast, color of belly, relative width of white bands in tail, folded wing vs. tail length (ad.), bill length relative to head.

Short-billed Dowitcher

PLATE 17

Limnodromus griseus

OTHER NAMES. Common Dowitcher (arch.).

Identification. 10¼″ (26 cm); bill 2–2½″ (5–6.5 cm). Very similar to Long-billed Dowitcher. For separation from Stilt Sandpiper, see account for that species. Bill averages shorter than in Long-billed, but there is extensive overlap; bird with bill 2 times length of head should be Long-billed; those with bill 1½ times length of head or less should be Short-billed; all others (the majority) are not safely separable using this character alone. Tail finely banded black and white; birds with black bands more than twice as thick as alternating white bands (tail looks darker) can be safely called Long-billed; those with white bands thicker than the black bands (tail looks paler) are Short-billed; all others not safely separable. *Ad.:* folded wings extend slightly beyond tip of tail; in Long-billed and all birds in their 1st year (through Dec.), primaries may not reach tail tip; if primaries project beyond tail tip, it is Short-billed, and if not, it could be either. *Alt.* (Apr.–Aug.): in fresh plumage, all but *hendersoni* are fairly easy to tell from Long-billed; however, as the plumage wears, both color and pattern change; Short-billed has orange to rufous throat and breast, and most (except *hendersoni*) have white belly, at least centrally and sometimes extensively, to include flanks and undertail coverts; breast densely spotted or scalloped with black (much less so in *hendersoni*); flanks unbarred to heavily barred; undertail coverts spotted (usually) or barred; dark dorsal feathers (back and scapulars) narrowly edged gray or narrowly to broadly edged rusty. *Basic* (Aug./Sept.–Apr.): very similar to Long-billed and often not safely separated in the field unless heard; other than wing length, bill length, and width of tail bands in some birds (see above), the two dowitchers can often be separated by Short-billed's tendency to have lighter gray throat, breast, and flanks, with fine dark streaks or speckles in breast, usually more concentrated or bolder on lower breast and often extending into white of upper belly; in Long-billed, throat and breast are usually unstreaked, and underparts are darker, with gray extending farther toward the belly and ending more abruptly; these differences are subtle and often hard to discern without direct comparison. *Juv.* (July–Nov.): brighter, orange-buff underparts, with gray, when present, confined to breast; strong buffy internal markings in tertials. *Caution:* both species in alt. plumage have internal rusty markings in tertials, so this character is useful only in the juv. Juv. tertials are among the last feathers to be molted and are often retained well into Dec., sometimes until Jan., thus enabling ID of some individuals well into winter.

Voice. *Call:* rapid *tu-tu* to *tu-tu-tu-tu,* typically given in flight; usually silent while feeding.

Habitat. Coastal lowlands: shrimp farms, estuaries, sandflats and mudflats; occas. marshes.

Distribution. Nests in subarctic from Aleutian Isl. (Alaska) to e Can.; winters primarily in coastal areas from California and Virginia to c Peru and c Brazil.

Status in Belize. UC to locally C transient and winter visitor in coastal areas and on the cayes, early July to late Apr. Often seen inland in migration; however, dowitchers seen away from the coast in winter are likely to be Long-billed.

References. *Identification:* Chandler (1998); Kaufman (1990); Pittaway (1992); Wilds and Newlon (1983).

Long-billed Dowitcher   PLATE 17
Limnodromus scolopaceus

Identification. 10¾″ (27.5 cm); bill 2¼–3″ (5.5–7.5 cm). See Short-billed account, above. *Alt.:* entirely salmon red underneath; foreneck finely spotted (unspotted in similar *hendersoni* race of Short-billed); in fresh plumage, breast, sides, and flanks barred black and white (black only in *hendersoni* and worn Long-billed); undertail coverts more often barred than spotted; light bands in the tail more likely to be pale cinnamon than white; dorsal feathers narrowly edged rusty, with some also tipped white in fresh plumage (Apr.–May). *Basic:* see Short-billed account. *Juv.:* gray beneath, with light rusty buff wash; tertials lack internal buffy bars

and fringes of juv. Short-billed (but see Short-billed account).

Voice. *Call: keek* or *kik,* higher-pitched than in Short-billed (almost always given as a single note or in erratic series). On takeoff, may give a rapid *ki-ki-ki-ki-ki-ki.* While feeding, gives sporadic *pit* notes.

Habitat. Freshwater marshes, mudflats.

Distribution. Nests in high Arctic from nw Can. to e Siberia; winters from w and s U.S. to n C.A.

Status in Belize. UC to locally FC winter visitor, late Aug. to late Apr.; most often seen at Blue Creek rice fields and shrimp farms, where shorebirds congregate in large numbers. This is the expected dowitcher at inland sites in winter.

References. *Status:* Jones et al. (2000). *Identification:* Chandler (1998); Kaufman (1990); Wilds and Newlon (1983).

Tribe: Gallinagini (Snipe)

Snipe have an excessively long bill and relatively short legs, and sloping forehead and eyes set high and back in the head give snipe a unique profile. They are cryptically colored and sit motionless, usually in short grass or reeds, where they are hidden and well camouflaged. They probe in soft mud for food, typically in areas with sparse to dense grass or reeds, making them that much more difficult to find. When flushed, they explode from underfoot and fly away in a rapid zigzag fashion.

Wilson's Snipe   PLATE 17
Gallinago delicata
OTHER NAMES. Common Snipe (combined form).

Identification. 10″ (25.5 cm); bill 2¼–2½″ (5.5–6.5 cm). Resembles dowitcher, but readily distinguished by characters mentioned above, as well as by dark stripe across base of auriculars and prominent light brown to whitish longitudinal stripes down back and scapulars. *Flight:* rapid with constant abrupt changes in direction; typically lands out of sight in short grass; lacks prominent white stripe up rump that is characteristic of dowitchers.

Voice. Distinctive, raspy, nasal *schap* in flight, especially when flushed.

Habitat. Wet drainage ditches, muddy pastures, marshes, rice fields, vegetated edge of mudflats.

Distribution. Nests from Arctic s. to c U.S., sc Eur., and c Asia; winters from se Alaska, s Can., nc Eur., and sc Asia to n S.A., c Afr., and s Asia.

Status in Belize. UC to locally FC winter visitor, mid-Sept. to early Apr.

SUBFAMILY: PHALAROPODINAE

(Phalaropes)

Unlike other shorebirds, phalaropes frequently swim. Wilson's swims less often than Red and Red-necked. Red (unrecorded in Belize) is usually seen at sea, seldom near or on shore; Wilson's is found in fresh or brackish water away from the sea; and Red-necked may be found in either. Wilson's is typically found with other shorebirds feeding on mudflats and in shallow water. In alternate plumage, all three are highly distinctive; and unlike in most birds, the ♀ is more brightly colored than the ♂.

Things to note: length and thickness of bill; plain white underparts; presence/absence of black ear patch, streaking or mottling in back.

Wilson's Phalarope   PLATE 16
Phalaropus tricolor

Identification. 8½" (21.5 cm). Longer-necked and longer-legged than other phalaropes, with longer, thinner bill. More likely to be confused with other shorebirds than with other phalaropes. Lacks wing stripe of other phalaropes. About the size of a Stilt Sandpiper, with similar white rump and pale gray tail; however, has straight bill and different manner of feeding. Picks at surface of water and mud, whereas Stilt Sandpiper probes with rapid and irregular motion, much like a dowitcher. Much smaller and paler than Lesser Yellowlegs, with shorter legs. ♀ *alt.:* striking head and neck pattern of black, blue gray, chestnut, and white; upperparts gray and dark chestnut. ♂ *alt.:* pattern on head, neck, and back much subdued. *Basic:* cleaner gray above than Stilt Sandpiper, with only slightly paler feather edges; clean white un-

derparts; white face; Stilt Sandpiper has faint mottling and light feather edges. *Juv.:* mottled brown-and-gray upperparts with pale feather edges like juv. Stilt Sandpiper, but with immaculate underparts.

Voice. *Flight call:* muffled, nasal *wurf.*

Habitat. Lagoons, shrimp farms.

Distribution. Nests in interior N.A. from c Can. to wc U.S. and Great Lakes region; winters in w and s S.A.

Status in Belize. R spring and autumn transient. Only three records: Nova Shrimp Farm TO, 20 Sep. 1997; Crooked Tree BE, 30 Apr. 1999 (three individuals); and Ambergris Caye, 14 May 1999.

Reference. *Status:* Jones et al. (2000).

Red-necked Phalarope   FIGURE 15
Phalaropus lobatus
OTHER NAMES. Northern Phalarope (arch.).

Identification. 7" (18 cm). Small gray-and-white shorebird with short, thin black bill. Sanderling has thicker, blunt-tipped bill. Unlike other shorebirds, usually seen swimming. ♀ *alt.:* mostly black head, chestnut neck, and white throat; gray-and-ochre back. ♂ *alt.:* duller head and neck pattern. *Basic:* white head with dark gray hindcrown and black auricular stripe; Sanderling has plain face with faint dark streaks and indistinct supercilium. *Flight:* similar in size to Sanderling, with similar prominent white wing stripe; however, with more black in underwing; if a flying bird or group lands on the water, it is not a Sanderling and warrants further investigation.

Voice. *Call:* short, sharp *kit* to *plik* (richer than that of Sanderling).

Habitat. Offshore waters; occas. lagoons and freshwater ponds.

Distribution. Nests in Arctic and subarctic; winters at sea off w S.A., in nw Indian Ocean, and w Pacific from Philippines to New Guinea. Migrates through continental interiors as well as at sea.

Status in Belize. One record: Cayo Rosario, Nov. 1993 and 4 Jan. 1994.

Reference. *Status:* Jones et al. (2000).

Figure 15

Red-necked Phalarope, basic plumage.

The **Red Phalarope** *(Phalaropus fulicarius)* is similar to the Red-necked and could also turn up in Belize. In basic plumage it has a plain gray back, whereas Red-necked has indistinct mottling and streaks in back. *Caution:* juv. Red-necked and Red, when molting (autumn and early winter), have strongly mottled upperparts. Red is best told by its thicker bill, which is yellow basally. Red also gives *keip* and *tink* calls, fuller than *kit* call of Red-necked.

FAMILY: LARIDAE
(Skuas, Gulls, Terns, and Skimmers)
World: 105. **New World:** 63. **Belize:** 24 (plus 1 provisional). Cosmopolitan. The systematics of the Laridae are complex. Some authors place only the gulls in the Laridae; others include the closely related terns as a subfamily (Sterninae) of Laridae. Still others include the skuas (Stercorariinae) and/or the skimmers (Rynchopinae). All are included here as part of the Laridae per AOU (1998). Skuas are the most pelagic, as well as the most northerly and southerly distributed of the group. Terns are the most widely distributed, being found on all major landmasses, usually in coastal areas, and most island groups. Gulls are absent from Antarctica and most islands within tropical latitudes. They reach their highest diversity in the N. Temperate Zone. Skimmers are restricted to coastal N.A., much of S.A. and Afr., and the Indian subcontinent. It is difficult to find common traits that characterize the Laridae in its broadest sense. All have webbed feet. Most gulls and terns share a plumage as ads. that is mostly gray and white or black and white. Many have a colorful bill and feet—usually yellow, orange, or red—and most

have similar breeding biology. Skuas are similar to gulls in that they have a plump body, a small head, a blunt bill, and slightly rounded wings. Like gulls, they take up to 4 years to reach maturity. Unlike gulls, they have two or more plumage morphs and are stronger fliers, and all are piratical. Outside the breeding season, they tend to be highly pelagic. Skimmers, on the other hand, are more closely related to terns, with their long, pointed wings and straight, pointed bill; however, their bill is highly modified for skimming food from the water's surface while in flight. Their lower mandible extends well beyond the upper mandible, is knifelike toward the tip, and is grooved along the cutting edge to the base for drawing tiny food items in the water up the bill and into the mouth. All but the skuas are highly gregarious.

SUBFAMILY: STERCORARIINAE
(Skuas and Jaegers)
Almost exclusively pelagic away from their breeding grounds; however, skuas and jaegers occasionally frequent populated coastal fishing communities such as Belize City, Dangriga, San Pedro, and Caye Caulker, where gulls congregate. ID of this group in most plumages can be extremely challenging. They take 3–4 years to mature (with different plumages at each stage of development), with as many as three color morphs at each stage, and light-morph ads. may have different basic and alternate plumages. The Great Skua is relatively easy to distinguish from the jaegers under most circumstances, but not from other skuas. **Reference:** Olsen and Larsson (1997).

Things to note: *In general,* overall size and robustness; relative bill size and head size. *In ad. and near ad.,* projection and shape of central tail feathers, extent of black in bill, extent of black in crown and face (light morph only), darkness of vent and undertail coverts. *In juv.,* presence/absence of barring in vent and tail coverts, back, and wings. *In flight,* presence/absence of barring in underwing, buoyancy of flapping flight, nature of extended central tail feathers when present.

Great Skua

FIGURE 16A

Stercorarius skua

OTHER NAMES. Northern Skua (arch.).

Identification. 22½" (57 cm); wingspan 53" (135 cm). Large, barrel-chested bird with proportionately larger head, shorter tail, and broader wings than smaller jaegers. Warm brown overall, with highly conspicuous white patch at base of primaries. Unlike in jaegers, white patch is equally prominent on upper surfaces and undersurfaces of wing. Unlike all but darkest imm. jaegers, has no prominent barring in plumage. Although only one morph is known, individuals may vary from rather pale to fairly dark. *Ad.:* warm brown, typically with paler back and upperwing coverts contrasting with darker remiges (contrast less evident in darker birds); darker birds have contrasting paler spots on wing coverts and scapulars; all ads. have darker crown and face that contrasts with paler, streaked neck and pale area behind eyes. *Juv.:* typically dark throughout except for prominent white wing patch; underparts usually washed with cinnamon; some have thin cinnamon feather edges in wing coverts and scapulars; differs from ad. in having smaller bill that is paler basally. *Flight:* slow, steady wingbeats in manner of Herring Gull; less agile than jaegers when pursuing prey; wings generally with less of an angle at bend than in jaegers.

Voice. Silent away from nesting areas.

Habitat. Offshore waters; nearshore, most likely to be near populated areas where gulls congregate.

Distribution. Nests in arctic Eur. and Iceland; winters in n Atlantic Ocean, primarily off Eur. and Afr., s. to the equator.

Status in Belize. One definite record: ad. found dead on beach near San Pedro, Ambergris Caye, 20 Mar. 1971. A skua species also was present in vicinity of Belize City, mid-Dec. 1976 to mid-Jan. 1977.

Reference. *Status:* Barlow et al. (1972).

Perhaps as likely as Great Skua to turn up in the future is the **South Polar Skua** *(Stercorarius maccormicki).* Unlike Great Skua, which has only one morph, it has *three morphs*—pale, intermediate, and dark. In all morphs, grayer or colder brown than Great, with no contrast between wing coverts and remiges. *Ad.:* dark birds have contrasting yellowish-hued nape, but it does not contrast as sharply with crown and face as in Great; light-morph birds have pale brownish gray head and underparts, contrasting sharply with back and wings. *Juv.:* paler and grayer than dark-morph ad.; juv. Great is very similar but tends to be warmer brown, and some Greats are further distinguished by contrasting pale cinnamon feather edges in wing coverts and scapulars.

Pomarine Jaeger

FIGURE 16B,C

Stercorarius pomarinus

OTHER NAMES. Pomarine Skua (U.K.).

Identification. 18½" (47 cm); wingspan 46" (117 cm). Smaller and slimmer than skuas, with thinner bill, longer tail, and reduced white at base of primaries, especially on upper surface, where only quills are white. Unlike Parasitic, most also have, in addition to white patch at base of primaries, a second white patch at base of primary coverts visible on underwing. Also larger, with broader wings and larger, rounder head. Bill pale on the basal half, dark on the distal half in all age classes and color morphs. *Ad. alt. light morph:* white beneath except for blackish vent and undertail coverts and dark upper breast band (some ♂s lack band); prominent black cap and face more extensive than in Parasitic, contrasts with pale base of bill; straw yellow nape; the two central tail feathers extend well beyond other rectrices and are twisted and round-tipped. *Ad. basic light morph:* central tail feathers barely, if at all, exceed other rectrices in length; same basic pattern as in alt., but breast, sides, flanks, and undertail coverts barred; straw-colored neck feathers may be partially or completely obscured by dusky wash. *Ad. dark morph:* entire body sooty black, but wings retain white pattern in primaries. *Juv.:* varies from nearly black to medium brown, averaging browner, less cinnamon than Parasitic; prominent white barring on tail coverts; rounded central tail feathers barely project, if at all. *2nd and 3rd year:* intermediate between juv. and ad.; most have at least some projection of the two central tail feath-

Figure 16

Skua and jaegers. *(a)* Great Skua; Pomarine Jaeger, *(b)* light-morph adult and *(c)* light-morph juvenile; Parasitic Jaeger, *(d)* light-morph adult and *(e)* light-morph juvenile.

ers, which are rounded but not twisted. *Flight:* less buoyant (steadier) than Parasitic, approaching that of the skuas; aerial pursuits are less acrobatic and usually not as prolonged as in Parasitic; juvs. (all morphs) have prominent white streaking on underwings.

Voice. Silent away from nesting areas.

Habitat. Offshore waters; nearshore, most likely to be near populated areas.

Distribution. Nests in Arctic; winters at sea primarily from Tropic of Cancer s. to s S.A., s Afr., and s Aust.

Status in Belize. Occas. winter visitor; seen most frequently at n cayes, Belize City, and Dangriga. Unfortunately, most records are undated,

so seasonal occurrence is not clear. The few dated records are from late Feb. to early May, but one in Puerto Barrios, Guat., 28 mi. (45 km) from Punta Gorda, 7–15 Oct. 1996, suggests an occas. autumn presence as well.

References. *Status:* Howell et al. (1992); Miller and Miller (1992). *Identification:* Kaufman (1990).

Parasitic Jaeger　　　　FIGURE 16D,E
Stercorarius parasiticus
OTHER NAMES. Arctic Skua (U.K.).

Identification. 17″ (43 cm); wingspan 41½″ (105 cm). Smaller and slimmer than Pomarine (not barrel-chested), with proportionately longer, narrower wings and smaller, flatter head. Bill varies from all dark (ad.) to bicolored (juv.), with the dark tip usually less pronounced and less extensive than in Pomarine. *Ad. alt. light morph:* same basic pattern as Pomarine; best separated by extended central tail feathers, which are pointed and not twisted; restricted dark crown does not extend behind eye or into malar region, as in Pomarine; vent and undertail coverts paler than in Pomarine. *Ad. basic light morph:* same basic pattern as ad. alt. but with barred flanks and undertail coverts and whitish, not straw-colored, nape; unlike Pomarine in basic plumage, usually retains extended central tail feathers. *Ad. dark morph:* similar to Pomarine but with smaller head; slimmer, all-dark bill; and pointed extended central tail feathers. *Juv.:* like Pomarine, exhibits much variation in color from nearly black (but usually with thin rusty-edged feathers) to medium rusty brown or grayish brown, but generally showing more of a warm cinnamon tone than Pomarine; intermediate and light morphs have finely streaked nape (unstreaked in Pomarine) and more conspicuous pale edges to back feathers and wing coverts; dark and intermediate morphs lack boldly barred tail coverts and vent of juv. Pomarine; usually has slightly extended, pointed central tail feathers. *2nd and 3rd year:* intermediate between juv. and ad.; most have at least some projection of the two pointed central tail feathers. *Flight:* more buoyant than Pomarine, more like Sooty or Bridled Tern than gull or skua; aerial pursuits generally longer and more acrobatic than in Pomarine; unlike Pomarine, lacks white base to primary coverts in underwing in all plumages; dark-morph juv. lacks prominent barring on underwing; intermediate and light morphs have underwing coverts irregularly streaked with cinnamon, not white, and thus exhibit less contrast between underwings and flanks than in juv. Pomarine.

Voice. Silent away from nesting areas.

Habitat. Offshore; nearshore, most likely to be near populated areas.

Distribution. Nests in Arctic; winters at sea primarily s. of the equator.

Status in Belize. Occas. transient, mostly in spring, and R winter visitor, early July to early June. Seen mostly around Belize City, but once each near San Pedro and Dangriga. Less likely beyond the reef than Pomarine.

References. *Status:* Howell et al. (1992); Miller and Miller (1992). *Identification:* Kaufman (1990).

SUBFAMILY: LARINAE
(Gulls)

Gulls dominate the coastal landscape in most N. Temperate areas; however, only the Laughing Gull is common as far south as Belize. Like jaegers, gulls take up to 4 years to mature (depending on the species), but they have only one plumage morph. ID of ads. is straightforward; however, non–Laughing Gulls that reach Belize are almost always imms. Because of their similar non-ad. plumages, individual variation, relatively large number of potentially occurring species, high incidence of hybridization, and tendency to turn up in unexpected places, imm. gulls can be among the most challenging bird groups to ID. Most species are colonial nesters and remain gregarious during winter months. **Reference:** Olsen and Larsson (2002).

Black-hooded Gulls

Gulls in this group have a dark hood as ads. in alt. plumage, although Franklin's has at least a partial hood in all plumages. Generally, only basic-plumage ads. and juvs. present an ID problem. Only the Laughing Gull is common.

Things to note: overall size; size and shape of bill, extent of dark gray or black in head (basic plumage), face and breast color (juv.), extent of black band in tail (juv.). *In flight,* wingtip pattern, presence/absence of contrast between underwing coverts and remiges.

Laughing Gull   MAP 59; PLATE 19
Larus atricilla
OTHER NAMES. Laughing Bird (C).

Identification. 16″ (40.5 cm); wingspan 40″ (102 cm). Size of Royal Tern but plumper, with shorter, less pointed wings; rounded, not forked, tail; and shorter, dark, blunt-tipped bill. *Ad. alt.:* all-black hood with broken white eye-ring; body white except for medium-dark gray mantle; trailing edge of wings white; bill and legs/feet deep dull red. *Ad. basic:* head white, with grayish smudges in auriculars and hindcrown, less extensive than in Franklin's. *Juv.:* dusky brown throughout except for rump, belly, and tail coverts; tail white, with broad black band at tip. *1st basic:* brown overtones in wings; more extensive black or sooty black in primaries than in ad.; little or no white in trailing edge of wing; black subterminal tail band; grayish back and gray smudge across nape and breast. *1st alt.:* mostly black hood. *2nd basic:* like ad. but with partial black tail band, grayish wash on nape and sides of breast. *Flight:* remiges contrast darker than underwing coverts.

Voice. 1. Nasal *ah-hah,* with both syllables equally emphasized;

2. nasal *caaoow,* repeated;

3. nasal *ă ă ă ă ă ă ă;*

4. loud *h h h h ha ha ha ha ha ha ha how how how how.* Young birds give high-pitched, piglike squeals. Generally silent away from nesting colony.

Habitat. Coastal areas, cayes, and offshore; occas. in migration at inland lagoons.

Distribution. Nests in coastal areas from nw Mex. and ne U.S. to n S.A.; winters in coastal areas from nw Mex. and se U.S. to s Peru and n Brazil.

Status in Belize. C winter visitor along coast and offshore; locally C in summer. Despite the relatively large number that remain through summer around Belize City, Dangriga, and populated cayes, nesting colonies in Belize are few and small, with nesting documented on only a few small cayes off TO and s SC. Inland, seen regularly at Crooked Tree BE and New R. OW in spring.

References. *Identification:* Kaufman (1990); Lehman (1994).

Franklin's Gull PLATE 19
Larus pipixcan

Identification. 14½″ (37 cm); wingspan 36½″ (92.5 cm). *Ad. alt.:* differs from Laughing in having smaller bill, white wingtips split by black subterminal band, and slightly paler mantle. *Ad.*

basic: like Laughing but remnants of hood more extensive and darker. *1st basic:* similar to Laughing but with well-defined partial hood, fewer brown overtones in wings, less sooty-black in primaries, and more conspicuous white trailing edge of wing; black tail band does not extend through outer web of outer tail feather. *1st alt.:* resembles ad. basic but lacks white subterminal band in wing; in this plumage, most closely resembles ad. basic Laughing Gull but has less extensive black in wingtips, more extensive black hoods. *Flight:* underwing entirely white except for wingtip.

Voice. Shrill *wheea* (usually silent in Belize).

Habitat. Coastal waters along and near beaches, estuaries, lagoons, shrimp farms.

Distribution. Nests in interior from wc Can. to wc U.S.; winters along w. coast of S.A., rarely n. to Mex.

Status in Belize. Occas. spring and autumn transient along coast (including Ambergris Caye), late Mar. to late May and mid-Oct. to early Dec.

References. *Status:* Jones et al. (2000). *Identification:* Kaufman (1990); Lehman (1983, 1994).

Bonaparte's Gull PLATE 19
Larus philadelphia

Identification. 13¼″ (33.5 cm); wingspan 33″ (84 cm). Distinctly smaller than Laughing or Franklin's, with paler gray mantle and more delicate bill. *Ad. alt.:* black hood; white outer primaries, but all primaries thinly tipped in black. *Ad. basic:* head white, with distinctive black spot behind eyes. *1st basic:* conspicuous dusky band in upper wing coverts; entire trailing edge of wing and portion of outer primaries and primary coverts black; black subterminal tail band; unlike Laughing and Franklin's, attains ad. plumage in its 1st spring. *Flight:* more buoyant than other, larger gulls.

Voice. Nasal, squealing, down-slurred *creeuh.*

Habitat. Coastal waters, especially near harbors; estuaries; lagoons.

Distribution. Nests in Alaska and w Can. e. to w Quebec; winters from nw U.S. and se Can. to Jalisco, Veracruz, and n W.I.

Status in Belize. R and irregular winter visitor

in north, late Dec. to early June. Recorded from Ambergris Caye, Belize City, Crooked Tree BE, and Hill Bank OW.
Reference. *Status:* Jones et al. (2000).

Pale-headed Gulls

Two pale-headed gulls, Ring-billed and Herring, occur regularly in Belize. Two other species have turned up once each, Black-legged Kittiwake from N.A. and Black-tailed Gull from Asia. A third, Great Black-backed Gull, has been reported twice but not confirmed, and at least two other species could turn up — Lesser Black-backed Gull and Kelp Gull. Of the two regularly occurring species, nearly all in Belize are imms. in their 1st basic plumage.

   Things to note: overall size; bill thickness, color, and pattern; eye color (ad.); leg color; head pattern; tail pattern. *In flight,* back/rump contrast (imm.); wingtip pattern (ad.).

Black-tailed Gull   NOT ILLUSTRATED
Larus crassirostris

Identification. 20½″ (52 cm); wingspan 47½″ (121 cm). Slightly larger than Ring-billed, with mostly black tail in all plumages and strongly bicolored bill, proportionately longer than in most gulls. *Ad.:* medium-dark gray mantle (darker than Ring-billed and Herring), yellow legs/feet, and black-and-red-tipped yellow bill. *1st basic:* unmottled gray-brown underparts sharply contrasting with white vent and undertail coverts; slightly paler and diffusely mottled upperparts; white rump; black tail; face and partial eye-ring white; strongly bicolored bill. *2nd basic:* intermediate between 1st basic and ad., with gray back and wing coverts; brownish smudge across nape and breast.
Voice. Nasal, catlike mewing.
Habitat. Coastal areas — beaches, nearshore waters.
Distribution. Nests in e Asia; winters s. to s China and Taiwan. VR, but reported with increasing frequency in N.A. from Alaska to California and from New England to Virginia.
Status in Belize. One record: Dangriga, 11 Mar. 1988 (ad. alt.).
Reference. *Status:* Howell and Webb (1995).

Ring-billed Gull   PLATE 19
Larus delawarensis

Identification. 18½″ (47 cm); wingspan 46½″ (118 cm). Similar to Herring but smaller (closer to size of Laughing Gull) and takes only 3 years to mature. *Ad.:* white body; medium-pale gray mantle; black primary tips with white spots; yellow eyes and yellow bill with black ring near tip; yellow legs/feet; brown mottling on nape in basic plumage. *Juv.:* mostly brown, with paler feather tips; some gray in wing coverts; whitish face, belly, and tail coverts; outer primaries all black; bill mostly or all black; eye dark. *1st basic:* most like 3rd basic Herring but smaller, tail band thinner, more complexly patterned brown-and-gray wings, dark eyes, and bill pinkish with black tip. *2nd basic:* similar to ad. but usually with thin black subterminal tail band; no white spots in black wingtips; bill usually pale yellowish (not bright yellow), with subterminal black band or all-black tip; legs/feet yellowish.
Voice. Squealing *keah* and *kow* notes.
Habitat. Beaches, harbors, lagoons.
Distribution. Nests from c Can. to n U.S.; winters from s Can. to s Mex.
Status in Belize. VU winter visitor s. to Ambergris Caye and Belize City, occas. to Punta Gorda, mid-Aug. to mid-Apr. Recorded once inland at Crooked Tree BE.
Reference. *Status:* Ornat et al. (1989).

Herring Gull   PLATE 19
Larus argentatus

Identification. 24½″ (62 cm); wingspan 57″ (145 cm). Noticeably larger and heavier-set than Laughing. *Ad.:* all-white body and tail with pale, diffuse streaking on nape, auriculars, and hind-crown (basic plumage only); mantle pale gray throughout, with white trailing edge to wing; black wingtips with white spots; pale yellow eyes; yellow bill with red subterminal spot on lower mandible; pinkish legs/feet. *1st basic:* mottled brownish throughout, including uppertail coverts, but head usually paler than body, sometimes markedly so; tail mostly blackish, with no distinct tail band; inner primaries paler than rest of wing; bill mostly or all dark. *2nd basic:*

gray inner primaries contrast sharply with mostly brown wings and black outer primaries; mostly white rump contrasts with black tail; strongly bi-colored bill pinkish basally; eyes may be dark or pale. *3rd basic:* much like ad. but without white spots in black wingtips, some brown mottling in wing coverts, and variable amount of black in tail; bill yellow, with black subterminal band (like ad. Ring-billed); lacks red spot of ad.

Voice. Slightly rough, trumpeting *gaa gaa gaa gaa gaa gaa gaa;* lower-pitched, more subdued laughing *gä-gä-gä.*

Habitat. Harbors, beaches.

Distribution. Nests from Arctic s. to s Can., e coastal U.S., sw Eur., and ne Russia; winters from s Alaska and se Can. s. to n C.A., n W.I., Spain, and s China, rarely farther. Both its breeding and wintering range are expanding.

Status in Belize. UC winter visitor along coast s. occas. to Punta Gorda; mid-Oct. to late Apr. Recorded once inland at Hill Bank OW.

Reference. *Identification:* Dubois (1997).

[Great Black-backed Gull] PLATE 19
Larus marinus

Identification. 28″ (71 cm); wingspan 62½″ (159 cm). Largest gull in the world; ≈⅓ larger than Herring Gull, with proportionately heavier bill. *Ad.:* white head, tail, and underparts; dark blackish gray mantle; black wingtips with conspicuous white spots; yellow bill with red spot; pale pinkish legs/feet. *1st basic:* distinctly mottled brown and whitish upperparts, with paler rump and inner tail; dark tail band; head mostly white; underparts white, finely mottled or streaked with brown; bill black. *2nd basic:* similar to 1st basic, but bill pale with black ring near tip or all-black tip; back mottled dark and light gray. *3rd basic:* similar to ad. but bill has black ring and lacks red spot; upperwing coverts have brownish wash.

Voice. Typically, a deep *gaw.*

Habitat. Coastal beaches, harbors.

Distribution. Nests on both sides of Atlantic from Labrador, s Greenland, Iceland, and n Eur. s. to N. Carolina and France; most n. populations withdraw in winter as far s. as Great Lakes, Florida, n W.I. (R), and s Spain. Breeding and winter ranges are expanding.

Status in Belize. 1st-winter bird seen and photographed in Belize City, 11–12 Jan. 1989, but photograph apparently lost before it could be critically examined, and no written description was taken. One reported at Caye Bokel, 24–25 Oct. 1983, had no accompanying documentation. With recent reports of the similar-appearing Kelp Gull in C.A. and the Gulf coast of U.S., including recent nesting records in Louisiana, and Lesser Black-backed Gull s to Yucatán Pen., any large black-backed gull in Belize should not be assumed to be Great Black-backed (see below).

References. *Status:* Howell et al. (1992); Jones (2002).

Kelp Gull *(Larus dominicanus)* and **Lesser Black-backed Gull** *(Larus fuscus),* two species that could potentially turn up in Belize, closely resemble either Great Black-backed or Herring Gull, depending on plumage. Kelp is size of Herring; Lesser Black-backed is slightly smaller. *1st basic:* both have all-dark bill; Herring usually has pale base to bill; Lesser Black-backed has slightly slimmer bill, Kelp a slightly thicker bill; both are lighter-bellied than most Herrings, with contrastingly darker upperparts. *2nd basic:* both have much darker gray back than Herring, and Kelp has darker back than most Lesser Black-backeds. *Ad.:* both have dark gray to nearly black mantle and could readily be confused with much larger Great Black-backed; ad. Kelp has nearly black mantles with only a tiny white spot near tip of outermost primary; ad. Lesser Black-backed usually has dark gray mantle, becoming black toward wingtips, and larger white spot near wingtips; legs/feet yellow green in Kelp, yellow to orange yellow in Lesser Black-backed; eye color variable, but Lesser Black-backed usually has paler eyes; in basic plumage, Lesser Black-backed has fine dusky mottling on head and neck, whereas Kelp and Great Black-backed have little or none.

Black-legged Kittiwake
NOT ILLUSTRATED
Rissa tridactyla

Identification. 17½″ (44.5 cm); wingspan 39″ (99 cm). Slightly larger than Laughing Gull with shorter bill, mostly white or all-white head and underparts, and mostly gray mantle. *Ad.:* white head, tail, and underparts; gray mantle, with black wingtips lacking white internal spots; dark gray smudge behind eyes in winter; bill yellow. *1st winter:* black collar; black spot or smudge behind eyes. *Flight:* buoyant, with rather stiff wingbeats; slightly notched tail; from above, 1st winter has black outer primaries and diagonal black band across wing coverts, forming a distinctive black V in each wing; trailing edge of wing behind V is mostly white; black-tipped tail; from below, underwings nearly all white, with narrow black wingtips; ad. has all-gray mantle and white underwing, with slightly more extensive black wingtips; Franklin's from below is similar but has slightly rounded (not notched) tail, more extensive black in wingtips, and partial hood.

Voice. Silent away from nesting colony.

Habitat. Open ocean, coastal beaches and harbors.

Distribution. Circumpolar. Nests in Arctic and N. Temperate Zone; irregular in winter at sea and in coastal areas s. to nw Mex., se U.S., n Afr., and Japan, rarely farther.

Status in Belize. One record: Caye Caulker, 9 Jan 2000 (ad.).

Reference. *Status:* Jones et al. (2002).

SUBFAMILY: STERNINAE

(Terns)

Distributed about equally in the Temperate Zone and the Tropics. Seven tern species breed, or once bred, in Belize, compared with only one gull species. Unlike in gulls, plumages of ad. and imm. terns do not differ greatly; however, ads. resemble one another more closely than do gulls. Most terns plunge into the sea after their fish prey, whereas gulls feed from the water's surface. Gulls are more omnivorous, with many species feeding as readily on carrion and garbage as on fish. Terns range more widely across habitats, with some, like the noddies and Sooty and Bridled terns, being largely pelagic, and others, like Caspian and Black, being found at inland as well as coastal sites. **Reference:** Wilds and DiCostanzo (2002).

Genus: Sterna

Terns in this genus can be divided into three basic types: large gray-and-white terns with shaggy crests, small gray-and-white terns without crests, and black-and-white terns. The three shaggy-crested terns are the ones most often encountered in Belize (Royal and Sandwich are the most common terns in Belize, both restricted to the coast and offshore waters). The two black-and-white terns are found offshore and are generally only seen near cayes where they breed. None of the smaller gray-and-white terns is especially common, and most are restricted to the coast and offshore waters.

Things to note: overall size and bulk; bill thickness, length, and color; leg color; extent and pattern of black in crown; presence/absence of shaggy hindcrown; folded wing vs. tail length; vocalizations. *In flight,* amount and pattern of black or dark gray in wingtips; amount of tail fork; back/rump/tail contrast; gull-like or buoyant flight; rapid vs. slow wingbeats. *Sooty vs. Bridled:* shape of white area in forehead; amount of white in underwing; crown-back contrast.

Gull-billed Tern   MAP 60; PLATE 20
Sterna nilotica

Identification. 13½″ (34.5 cm); wingspan 36½″ (92.5 cm). Differs from similar-sized Sandwich in having much shallower tail fork and shorter, thicker bill with no yellow tip; very pale gray upperparts, which appear nearly white under most field conditions. Lacks shaggy hindcrown. *Alt.:* all-black crown, usually acquired in Apr. *Basic:* all-white head, with dark gray line or smudge behind eyes. *Flight:* very pale overall; shallow tail fork; short bill; does not plunge-dive like other *Sterna* terns but picks at surface.

Voice. Nasal *k-weck,* often repeated; also *are ink.* In breeding season, a nasal laughing *ăk ăk ăk* given in an irregular series.

Habitat. Shrimp farms, lagoons, beaches.

Distribution. Nests from s Calif., s New York, s Eur., and c Asia s. to Mex. (Sinaloa and Veracruz, perhaps farther), W.I., disjunctively in S.A., w and n Afr., s Asia, and Aust. Winters from nw

Mex. and n Gulf of Mex. to sc S.A., c Afr., s Asia, Aust., and N.Z.

Status in Belize. UC winter visitor and locally FC migrant along and near mainland coast, mid-July to mid-May. Most common in spring at Crooked Tree BE; occas. transient on cayes.

References. *Identification:* Kaufman (1990); Vinicombe (1989).

Caspian Tern
MAP 61; PLATE 20

Sterna caspia

Identification. 21" (53.5 cm); wingspan 48½" (123 cm). Heavyset; almost gull-like proportions; broad (but pointed) wings; short tail, with shallow fork; thick, pointed red bill. *Alt.* (Apr.–June): complete black crown. *Basic:* black crown finely streaked white, occas. with all-white forehead. *Juv.:* dusky feather edges in back and wing coverts give upperparts a scaly effect. *Flight:* underside of outer primaries dusky, contrasting strongly darker than rest of underwing; steady, gull-like flight; Sandwich flies more like the smaller *Sterna* terns, and Royal is intermediate.

Voice. Ad. gives loud, harsh, nasal *aaaaow* or *aaaonk;* imm. gives high-pitched, piercing squeal.

Habitat. Shrimp farms, lagoons, estuaries.

Distribution. Nests locally from c Can., nc Eur., and c Asia s. to nw Mex., n Gulf of Mex., s Afr., s Aust., and N.Z. Winters primarily in coastal areas from s California, N. Carolina, s Eur., and s Asia to n C.A., s Afr., Aust., and N.Z.

Status in Belize. UC and local winter visitor along and near coast s. to Dangriga, rarely to n TO, primarily mid-Aug. to early May, occas. to mid-June, and perhaps through summer. Occas. on n cayes. Most common at Crooked Tree BE in spring.

Royal Tern
PLATE 20

Sterna maxima

OTHER NAMES. Large Seagull (C).

Identification. 18" (45.5 cm); wingspan 44" (112 cm). From Caspian by thinner, yellow to red-orange bill and more deeply forked tail. *Alt.* (seldom seen in Belize): complete black crown; red-orange bill. *Basic:* most of crown

white; black confined to postocular stripe and hindcrown; orange bill. *Juv.:* yellow bill; dusky feather tips in back; differs from ad. basic and from juv. Caspian in having dusky bar in secondaries and in lesser wing coverts (especially noticeable in flight). *Flight:* much less dusky in outer underwing (confined to perimeter of outer primaries); flight more buoyant and tern-like than Caspian's.

Voice. 1. Ringing *kreee* to *kreet;*
2. harsh, rolling *keerra;*
3. scratchy *toorrruk;*
4. harsh *kak.*

Habitat. Beaches, cayes, shrimp farms.

Distribution. Nests locally in coastal areas from s California and New Jersey s. to Sinaloa, Yucatán Pen., and n W.I.; also in n and se S.A. and w Afr. Winters in coastal areas from c Calif. and N. Carolina to Peru and n Argentina, and from nw to sw Afr.

Status in Belize. Year-round visitor on immediate coast and cayes. C in winter; local and generally uncommon in summer. Recorded once inland near La Democracia BE/CA. Seventeen banded birds recovered in Belize were all banded as nestlings on the U.S. Atlantic coast between Maryland and N. Carolina.

Sandwich Tern
MAP 62; PLATE 20

Sterna sandvicensis

OTHER NAMES. Cabot's Tern (arch.), Seagull (C).

Identification. 14" (35 cm); wingspan 35½" (90 cm). Smaller, slimmer than Royal; thin black bill (thinner than in Royal) with yellow tip. *Alt.* (typically seen only around breeding colony): complete black crown. *Basic:* forehead and forecrown white; black hindcrown and postocular stripe. *Juv.:* dusky feather tips in upperwing coverts and back; bill brownish (younger birds) to blackish, with much reduced yellow tip in 1st winter (hard to see in some individuals). *Flight:* flight behavior and profile more as in smaller *Sterna* terns than in Royal or Caspian; more deeply forked tail than in larger *Sterna* terns, but less than in smaller terns; lacks juv. Royal's broad dusky bar in secondaries. *Caution:* in distance, yellow bill tip may "disappear," making bill seem shorter, more like Gull-billed's.

Voice. 1. *kruhdee* to *keerik,* higher-pitched, more abrupt than in Royal;
2. scratchy *klee klee klee klee* repeated rapidly;
3. scratchy high-pitched *kreep* (young only).

Habitat. Beaches, cayes, shrimp farms.

Distribution. Nests in coastal areas discontinuously from Virginia and nc Eur. s. to s S.A., s Eur., and the Caspian Sea. Winters in coastal areas from Florida and n Gulf of Mex., s Eur., and s Caspian Sea s. to s S.A., s Afr. and Sri Lanka.

Status in Belize. C winter and FC summer resident on cayes and along mainland coast; less common at cayes; once inland at Lamanai OW. Small breeding colonies persist on several small cayes. Nonbreeding population in Belize has increased greatly since early 1960s. Four banded birds wintering in Punta Gorda were banded as nestlings on s.e. coast of N. Carolina.

References. *Status:* Barlow et al. (1972). *Identification:* Kaufman (1990). *Conservation:* Jones and Vallely (2001).

Roseate Tern

MAP 63; PLATE 20

Sterna dougallii

Identification. 12½″ (32 cm); wingspan 27″ (68.5 cm). Shortest wings and longest tail of the *Sterna* terns; thus, at rest, tail projects well beyond wingtips. In other respects, very similar to Common Tern. Inner webs of outer primaries silvery white, contrasting sharply with dark outer webs. Legs distinctly shorter than in Forster's, slightly shorter than in Common (noticeable when the two are seen together). Longer, thinner bill than Common and especially Forster's. *Alt.:* all-black crown and black bill; at height of breeding season, base of bill turns deep red, occas. orange red as in Forster's, and has pale rosy flush on breast. *Basic:* white forecrown; black hindcrown; lacks dusky carpal bar of Common; legs/feet dull dusky reddish (Common Tern's legs/feet in same plumage usually brighter). *Juv.:* thin black edges to most mantle feathers, giving upperparts a distinctly scaly appearance. *1st basic:* like ad. basic

but often with poorly defined carpal bar (less well developed than in Common). *Flight:* rapid, shallow wingbeats (resulting from shorter wings than other *Sterna*); powder white primaries, with thin dark leading edge visible on dorsal surface.

Voice. 1. *chup;*
2. harsh *chēēēh. At nesting colony:* harsh *chevik.*

Habitat. Small cayes, ocean; occas. coastal beaches.

Distribution. Nests discontinuously in New England (U.S.) and the Maritime Provinces (Can.); Florida Keys and W.I. to Venezuela; Belize and Bay Isl. (Hon.); Great Britain, Ireland, and w France; s and e Afr. and islands off e Afr.; Oman; s India and Sri Lanka; and Japan through Indonesia to n and w Aust. In the New World, winters from lesser Antilles to Brazil; in the Old World in the vicinity of breeding colonies, but Eur. and Azores birds migrate to equatorial w Afr.

Status in Belize. UC to locally FC summer visitor offshore, Apr. to late Sept., occas. to Nov.; R along mainland coast. Formerly more C, but most nesting colonies have been replaced by resorts and fishing camps. Nesting colony persists on Tobacco Caye off Dangriga; possibly other small colonies elsewhere.

References. *Status:* Udvardy et al. (1973). *Identification:* Hume (1993); Kaufman (1990). *Conservation:* Jones and Vallely (2001).

Common Tern

PLATE 20

Sterna hirundo

Identification. 12″ (30.5 cm); wingspan 31″ (78.5 cm). Folded wings project to or slightly beyond tip of tail. Folded primaries contrast darker than the rest of wing; in Roseate they do not. In direct comparison with Roseate, Common has shorter, stockier bill and darker mantle and stands slightly taller on longer legs. *Alt.:* black-tipped red bill; pale to medium gray breast sets off white face and throat. *Basic:* white forecrown; black hindcrown; dusky carpal bar (appears as horizontal bar in resting bird separating wing from scapulars), most prominent in 1st basic, less prominent in ad. (some Roseates in 1st basic also have indistinct carpal bar). *Flight:* similar to Roseate but with deeper, slower wingbeats; outer wing more extensively dusky, not just on leading edge, and darker mantle contrasts more with white rump and tail; thin black line in outermost tail feather.

Voice. Typically, harsh down-slurred *keearrr;* but usually silent in Belize.

Habitat. Offshore waters, coastal beaches, estuaries.

Distribution. Nests throughout the Holarctic from nc Can. and nc Eurasia s. to n U.S. (and on Atlantic Coast to S. Carolina), n Afr., and sc Eur. Winters in coastal areas from c Mex., Florida, nc Afr., and s Asia to s S.A., s Afr., and Aust.

Status in Belize. Seasonal distribution complex and not fully understood. Generally UC to VU transient and winter visitor offshore, at cayes, and along mainland coast; early Sept. (and probably Aug.) to late May. Occas. FC to C in migration, at least in spring. Unrecorded inland.

References. *Identification:* Hume (1993); Kaufman (1990); Wilds (1993).

Forster's Tern
Sterna forsteri

PLATE 20

Identification. 13″ (33 cm); wingspan 31½″ (80 cm). Rarest of the Roseate/Common/Forster's complex in Belize, the only one likely to be found inland, and the least likely to be found offshore. Folded wings generally fall slightly short of tail tip. Longer legs than in Common, decidedly longer than in Roseate; shorter, thicker bill and larger head than Roseate. *Alt.:* orange bill with black tip (which some Roseates also have); underparts white year-round, never with gray (Common) or with rosy flush (Roseate). *Ad. basic:* black postocular line contrasts with pale dusky hindcrown, giving appearance of thin black mask. *1st basic:* dusky wingtips similar to those of Common, but lacks dusky carpal bar. *Flight:* white rump isolated by pale gray mantle and gray central tail; outer wing pattern variable — in ad., upper surface of wingtips slightly paler than rest of wing, undersurface of primaries less extensively dusky; in imm., outer wing more like Common.

Voice. 1. Short, hard *tip* or *kip;*

2. very harsh, nasal *keurt* and *keurr;* not as drawn out as in Common.

Habitat. Lagoons, marshes, beaches.

Distribution. Nests from sc Can. s. locally to nw Mex., n Gulf of Mex., and N. Carolina. Winters mostly near coast from n California, n Gulf of Mex., and Virginia to E.S. and Yucatán Pen.

Status in Belize. Occas. transient and winter visitor, late Aug. to mid-Apr., mostly in north.

References. *Status:* Jones et al. (2000). *Identification:* Kaufman (1990); Wilds (1993).

Least Tern
Sterna antillarum

MAP 64; PLATE 20

OTHER NAMES. Little Tern (combined form).

Identification. 8½″ (21.5 cm); wingspan 20″ (51 cm). Smallest tern in Belize; moderate tail fork. Gray of mantle extends to rump and central tail feathers. *Ad. alt.:* yellow bill; clean white forehead contrasts sharply with black crown. *Ad. basic:* black bill; white of forehead extends into forecrown and lores. *Juv.:* dark feather tips on back and wings give scaly appearance; crown mottled black and white; black bill with pale base to lower mandible. *Flight:* bounding; because of small size and powerful wings, body bounces up and down in exaggerated fashion with each full wing stroke.

Voice. 1. Shrill *kli-deet!;*

2. flatter, squeaky *chitit.* The two often given in alternate sequence or by different individuals in a group.

Habitat. Coastal beaches, shrimp farms. Nests on isolated sandy beaches and dunes with patchy herbaceous vegetation.

Distribution. Nests along both coasts from c Calif. and New England, and along the Missouri and Mississippi Rivers from nc U.S. s. to s Mex. and Hon., Lesser Antilles, and Venezuela. Winters on Pacific coast from Nayarit to Pan. and on Caribbean coast primarily from Pan. to n Brazil.

Status in Belize. Locally FC summer resident on a few cayes and along mainland coast s. to n TO, mid-Mar. to early Oct.; occas. in winter.

Bridled Tern

MAP 65; PLATE 20

Sterna anaethetus

OTHER NAMES. Rocky Bird (C).

Identification. 13½" (34.5 cm); wingspan 32½" (82.5 cm). Paler back than Sooty (dark gray, not black). In poor light and at a distance, this distinction can be hard to discern. White forehead extends back in a point to just posterior of the eyes; in Sooty, it stops in front of the eyes, appearing more as a white triangle. *Alt.:* white forehead sharply delineated from crown and lores. *Basic:* crown-forehead separation less clearly defined. *Juv.:* very different from Sooty; entirely white beneath, with mostly white head; medium gray, not dark gray, above; feathers of back and wing coverts edged black subterminally and white terminally, giving intricately scaled pattern; head pattern reminiscent of other *Sterna* terns in basic plumage. *Flight:* underwing mostly white, with only distal portion of remiges darker; more extensive white in outer tail than in Sooty.

Voice. Generally, a single *ank,* sometimes doubled; has tin horn quality (very different from that of Sooty). On nesting grounds, a nasal *hanh!* followed by a rapid *hä-hä-hä-hä-hä-hä-hä-hä-hä-hä.*

Habitat. Offshore and isolated small cayes, where it nests in coral rubble, often with sparse vegetation.

Distribution. Nests discontinuously on offshore islands throughout Tropics except c Pacific, and in S. Temperate Zone to s Aust. Disperses out to sea after breeding season.

Status in Belize. Locally FC summer resident offshore. Small nesting colonies persist on several small cayes off c and s Belize. Rarely seen from mainland. Dates of spring arrival unclear, but nests with eggs present in early Apr. Not recorded after mid-Sept.

References. *Identification:* Harris (1988). *Conservation:* Jones and Vallely (2001).

Sooty Tern

MAP 66; PLATE 20

Sterna fuscata

OTHER NAMES. Wide Awake (C).

Identification. 14½" (37 cm); wingspan 35" (89 cm). Very similar to Bridled but with nearly black, not dark gray, mantle; triangular white forehead does not extend posteriorly over eyes. *Alt.:* white forehead sharply delineated. *Basic:* Forehead not as distinct; black-and-white-spotted collar separates black crown from black back. *Juv.:* very different from Bridled; blackish nearly throughout except for white lower belly and undertail coverts and sprinkling of white spots in upperparts. *Flight:* stronger flight on stiffer wings than Bridled; gray remiges in underwing contrast sharply with white underwing coverts; tail mostly black with narrow white outer tail.

Voice. Nasal *a-RA-na-rak,* or *I'm wide awake.*

Habitat. Offshore and isolated small cayes, where it nests in coral rubble beneath trees and shrubs.

Distribution. Nests on offshore islands throughout Tropics. Disperses out to sea after breeding season.

Status in Belize. Locally FC summer resident offshore, Feb. to mid-Aug. (occas. later). Moderate to large colonies bred historically on a few s cayes; now greatly reduced as cayes where it formerly bred have been developed for tourism or occupied as fishing camps. Only known remaining nesting colony is on Middle Snake Caye, and it is threatened by repeated human disturbance. Rarely recorded far inland after major storms. An emaciated bird recovered in inland SC on the unseasonable date of 26 Nov. 1997 had been banded in Florida on 6 June 1966—31½ years earlier!

References. *Identification:* Harris (1988). *Conservation:* Jones and Vallely (2001).

Black Tern

PLATE 20

Chlidonias niger

OTHER NAMES. Black Marsh-Tern (alt.).

Identification. 9½" (24 cm); wingspan 24½" (62 cm). *Alt.:* highly distinctive with medium gray upperparts; black head, breast, and belly; white vent and undertail coverts. *Basic:* superficially like Common Tern but with distinctly darker gray mantle and much shorter, only slightly forked, gray tail; black "teardrop" behind eyes; dark gray sides of upper breast form partial breast band. *Flight:* buoyant and erratic, with

Figure 17

Noddies. Black Noddy, *(a)* adult and *(b)* 1st year; Brown Noddy, *(c)* adult and *(d)* 1st year.

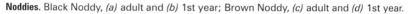

deep wingbeats; frequently dips at water surface; seldom dives; upperwings and underwings uniformly gray in all plumages, paler on undersurface.

Voice. Sharp *tseep* or *peep.*

Habitat. Offshore waters, large inland lagoons.

Distribution. Nests in interior N.A. from c and se Can. to c U.S., and in Eurasia from nc Eur. and wc Asia to s Eur. and sc Asia. In New World, winters in coastal regions from Nayarit to Peru on the Pacific side and Colombia to Surinam on Atlantic side. In Old World, winters on w. coast of Afr.

Status in Belize. FC to C autumn and occas. spring transient, early Aug. to early Nov. and late Apr. to late May. Most plentiful offshore in autumn, but also FC at times at shrimp farms and inland lagoons.

Reference. *Distribution:* Williams (1983).

Genus: Anous *(Noddies)*

All-dark terns with white crown. Brown Noddy is most likely to be seen in Belize; however, Black Noddy may be expected as a vagrant, especially following tropical storms and hurricanes originating in the e Caribbean. The two can be deceptively similar, especially when not seen together. Noddies dip at the water surface to feed.

Things to note: length and thickness of bill, degree of crown-nape contrast and back-tail con-trast, darkness of plumage, center of gravity at front of or under wings.

Brown Noddy   MAP 67; FIGURE 17C,D

Anous stolidus

OTHER NAMES. Common Noddy (alt.), Noddy Tern (arch.).

Identification. 15″ (38 cm); wingspan 33″ (84 cm). Larger and more robust than Black Noddy, with thicker bill slightly shorter than head. Little, if any, back-tail contrast. Plumage paler and browner overall but can appear black in poor light or in distance. Differs from juv. Sooty Tern primarily in having dark underwings, vent, and undertail coverts. *Ad.:* white cap blends gradually through hindcrown and nape to dark brown back. *1st summer:* white confined to forehead, extending posteriorly as short supercilium. *Flight:* shorter bill and longer tail than Black set center of gravity farther back.

Voice. At nesting colony: 1. harsh, grating *ca-a-a-a-a-uh*, dropping slightly at the end; 2. lower-pitched, grating *graaooww.*

Habitat. Open ocean; for nesting, predator-free cayes. Nests in trees and on ground.

Distribution. Offshore islands throughout most of Tropics; disperses out to sea outside breeding season.

Status in Belize. Occas. seen offshore, primarily mid-Apr. to mid-Sept., but recorded nearly year-round. Formerly nested on several cayes off central and s Belize, but now apparently extirpated as breeding species in Belize, as its former nesting sites are now developed or used as fishing camps.

References. *Conservation:* Jones and Vallely (2001).

Black Noddy
FIGURE 17A,B

Anous minutus
OTHER NAMES. White-capped Noddy (alt.).

Identification. 13″ (33 cm); wingspan 27½″ (70 cm). Smaller and slimmer than Brown Noddy, with longer, thinner bill as long as head. Tail contrasts paler than back. Darker overall than Brown (nearly black), but without direct comparison or good light, plumage shade can look deceptively similar in the two. *Ad.:* white cap blends less gradually with dark nape than in Brown Noddy. *Juv. and 1st summer:* full white crown sharply set off from black nape (Brown has white forehead only). *Flight:* longer bill and shorter tail than Brown place center of gravity farther forward.

Voice. At nesting colony: a harsh, grating *ca-a-a-a-a-a*.

Habitat. Open ocean; nests on predator-free cayes in trees.

Distribution. Nests on offshore islands in tropical Atlantic and Pacific oceans; disperses out to sea after breeding season.

Status in Belize. Extirpated. Formerly nested on Glovers Reef and probably Tom Owens Caye. Other than a sight record on 31 Oct. 1998, immediately following Hurricane Mitch, it has not been documented in Belize since 1907.

Reference. *Status:* Jones et al. (2000).

SUBFAMILY: RYNCHOPINAE
(Skimmers)

Odd-looking birds with noticeably longer lower mandible than upper mandible. Black Skimmer is the only one, of three worldwide, found in the New World. It is only occas. seen in Belize. **Reference:** Wilds and DiCostanzo (2002).

Figure 18

Black Skimmer

Black Skimmer
MAP 68; FIGURE 18

Rynchops niger

Identification. ♀ 17″, ♂ 18″ (43–45 cm); wingspan 47″ (119 cm). Relatively large bird with long, heavy bill and very long, pointed wings; dark above; white below. *Ad.:* black above; white below, with mostly white tail; black-and-red bill; white of underparts extends as broad band across forecrown and forehead; ♂ larger, with longer, deeper-based bill than ♀. *Alt.:* hindneck black like crown and back. *Basic:* hindneck whitish. *1st basic:* mottled brown-and-black upperparts but otherwise resembles ad. *Flight:* feeds by flying just above water's surface with wings held high above horizontal while lower mandible skims water surface like a boat's keel; bill grooved in such a way that when it encounters small prey items, they are directed toward the gullet; powerful, bounding flight when not feeding; when feeding, wingbeats are necessarily shallower.

Voice. Nasal barking *kap* and softer *kup* notes, often given alternately.

Habitat. Coastal beaches.

Distribution. Nests along Atlantic coast from New England to n Yucatán Pen. and locally along Pacific coast from c Calif. to Oaxaca. In S.A., nests in interior lowlands and locally along both coasts s. to Ecuador and Argentina. Winters from Calif. and se U.S. to s S.A.

Status in Belize. Occas. winter visitor along central mainland coast, Nov. to late Apr., once in June. Most often seen near Belize City and Dangriga, but recorded twice inland at Crooked Tree BE and Hill Bank OW.

Reference. *Status:* Barlow et al. (1972).

FAMILY: COLUMBIDAE
(Pigeons and Doves)

World: 308. **New World:** 69 native; 4 nonnative. **Belize:** 19 (2 non native). Nearly worldwide; absent only from high Arctic and Antarctica. Most are strong fliers, and many migrate long distances. Pigeons are usually larger and more robust than doves, with a broad, square-tipped tail, but "pigeon" and "dove" are loosely applied and have no taxonomic significance. Vocalizations of most a simple series of coos or hoots. All characteristically pump their head back and forward as they walk, presumably to gain perspective on the relative distances of objects. Most can be divided into those that eat seeds and those that eat fruit, with most of the fruit eaters found in the Old World. Except for flamingos, pigeons and doves are the only birds that feed their young on a milk-like substance produced in the crop. **References:** Gibbs et al. (2001). *Voice:* Hardy et al. (1989b).

Genus: Columba

Except for the distinctive Rock Dove, birds in this group can appear frustratingly similar, especially in rapid overhead flight or seen from below when flying above or through or above foliage. When seen well, they are usually differentiated by their distinctive head and bill pattern. As they call frequently and each has its own vocal signature, voice is easily the best way to distinguish them.

Things to note: bill length and color, head pattern, pale vs. dark undertail coverts, degree of contrast between tail and undertail coverts, presence/absence of scaling, vocalizations.

Rock Dove   FIGURE 19A
Columba livia
OTHER NAMES. Feral Pigeon, Domestic Pigeon, Rock Pigeon (all alt.).

Identification. 13″ (33 cm). Multitude of plumage types, including "wild type" (Figure 19a), which is medium gray, with darker head and neck and two broad black bars in wings. Found in urban settings or fields where other pigeons are not likely to be. *Flight:* unlike other *Columba* pigeons, flies with slow, steady wingbeats; glides with wings held high above horizontal.

Voice. Very deep, hollow *who-o-o* or *coo-o-o*.

Habitat. Urban areas and a few rural villages.

Distribution. Originally, Eur. to c and s Asia and n Afr. Introduced and domesticated in populated areas throughout most of the world except Arctic and Antarctic regions.

Status in Belize. Introduced to New World in early 17th century, but probably not established in Belize until after European occupation in the 18th century. FC to VC resident in most urban areas, but absent from most villages away from main roads. Small populations on Caye Caulker and Ambergris Caye.

Pale-vented Pigeon   PLATE 21
Columba cayennensis
OTHER NAMES. Rufous Pigeon (arch.), Cayenne Pigeon (I. Davis), Blue Pigeon (C), Red Mangrove Pigeon (C), palom (K), paloma (M, S).

Identification. 12½″ (32 cm). Larger and paler than Short-billed; vinaceous purple, with blue-gray head and rump, iridescent violet-green nape, and brownish wing coverts; paler undertail coverts. Upper surface of tail darker basally, with broad pale distal band. Bill all dark. *Flight:* uniform grayish plumage with paler undertail co-

Figure 19

(a) Rock Dove; *(b)* Eurasian Collared-Dove.

verts; when landing, bicolored tail is apparent; like most other *Columba* pigeons, often flies with short, quick downstroke, slower upstroke.

Voice. *Call:* 1. soft *wheoo;*
2. burry *whhhooooo.*
Song: 1. typically *good for yOOOuu!,* sometimes preceded by clear *oOOOooo;*
2. less typically an unaccented weak *good for you* to emphatic *GOOD FOR YOOOU.*

Habitat. Canopy of open and patchy broadleaf and pine forest, second growth, forest edge, mangroves, and littoral forest; also towns and villages.

Distribution. Resident from Tabasco and c Yucatán Pen., to sc S.A.

Status in Belize. C resident nearly throughout, including many nearshore cayes. Generally more numerous coastally than inland; absent from areas of contiguous forest. R to occas. nonbreeding visitor to outer cayes (e.g., Caye Caulker). Recorded from Ambergris Caye but possibly not resident.

Scaled Pigeon

PLATE 21

Columba speciosa
OTHER NAMES. Mountain Pigeon (C), pal<u>o</u>m (K), paloma (M, S).

Identification. 13″ (33 cm). Dark-tipped pale feathers of neck and underparts give bird a scaly appearance. Yellow-tipped red bill. ♂: purplish chestnut above. ♀: duller, brownish. *Flight:* from below, darker, browner plumage and noticeably darker tail than Pale-vented, and contrasting sharply with nearly white lower belly and undertail coverts.

Voice. *Call:* short, low-pitched growl. *Song,* lower-pitched than in other forest pigeons:
1. *whooOOO cooks-for-you;*
2. *who wh whooo.*

Habitat. Canopy of most broadleaf forest types; occas. pines.

Distribution. Resident from s Veracruz and all but nw Yucatán Pen. to sc S.A.

Status in Belize. Variously scarce to C resident in forested areas on mainland. Distribution is complicated by tendency of populations to move around seasonally and may be tied to fruiting seasons of certain preferred food trees. Absent from some areas of seemingly good habitat and common in others.

Reference. *Voice:* Moore (1992).

White-crowned Pigeon MAP 69; PLATE 21
Columba leucocephala

Identification. 14″ (35.5 cm). Uniformly dark slate gray. *Ad.:* conspicuous white crown, iridescent green nape, pale eyes. *Juv.:* white reduced to small patch on forehead; darker plumage than other pigeons. *Flight:* from below, all dark, with little tail–undertail coverts contrast.
Voice. *Call:* rolling *bwrrrrr* or *b bwrrrrrr bur.* *Song: ooooo* followed by a pause, then *you look so gooood* (*look* is short and higher-pitched); sometimes without introductory *ooooo.* Tone similar to White-winged Dove's, but less burry and with different pattern.
Habitat. Canopy within littoral forest.
Distribution. Largely resident on islands in Caribbean from Florida Keys and n Yucatán Pen. s. through W.I. to Pan. and Lesser Antilles. Local populations on islands near mainland C.A. move to adjacent mainland in winter.
Status in Belize. UC to C summer resident on cayes, including Ambergris, late Feb. to mid-Oct. Most birds leave cayes in winter and apparently move to adjacent mainland coast. The few mainland records may be explained by the fact that the total population is small and may be largely absorbed by the relatively vast coastal mainland. Recorded once inland in spring from Hill Bank. During the breeding season, birds on inner cayes may occas. commute to and from mainland (e.g., summer records from near Dangriga).
References. *Distribution:* Ornat et al. (1989). *Status:* Howell et al. (1992).

Red-billed Pigeon MAP 70; PLATE 21
Columba flavirostris

Identification. 13″ (33 cm). Readily distinguished by its two-toned plumage and nearly black tail. Dull purplish head, neck, breast, and scapulars contrast with blue-gray belly, undertail coverts, rump, and wing coverts. Pale bill with red base (similar to Scaled Pigeon). *Flight:* all dark, including undertail coverts, but nearly black tail stands out.
Voice. *Call:* 1. gruff growl with *ooo* at end; 2. gruff *er-rrrrr.* *Song:* similar to that of Pale-

vented but with middle note doubled—*cooks fo-or you,* often preceded by a rich *whooooo,* rising, then falling in pitch.
Habitat. Principally semi-deciduous and deciduous broadleaf forest, submontane pine forest.
Distribution. Resident from nc Sonora and s Texas to c C.R.
Status in Belize. Variously scarce to VC resident on mainland, most common in north and west, s. to c BE and c and s CA, occasionally farther s. Seldom seen, and apparently not resident, in TO. One record from Caye Caulker. Absent from Maya Mtns. With only one record for Belize as late as 1964, it has literally invaded the country in the past 40 years.
References. *Status:* Barlow et al. (1970); Erickson (1977); Wood and Leberman (1987).

Short-billed Pigeon PLATE 21
Columba nigrirostris
OTHER NAMES. Pasakuk (K), wortis coh poo (M), Tres Pesos Son (S).

Identification. 11½″ (29 cm). Smaller, more compact, and browner than other pigeons. Brown back and wings contrast with vinaceous gray head, neck, and underparts; bill uniformly dark. *Flight:* in overhead flight, appears all dark, including undertail coverts; no range overlap with larger White-crowned.
Voice. *Call:* soft *gururrrrr.* *Song:* different cadence and tonal quality than others'; a clear, low-pitched, hollow, slightly tinny *it FEELS so good!*
Habitat. Subcanopy and canopy interior of primary and secondary broadleaf forest and forest edge.
Distribution. Resident on Gulf-Caribbean slope from s Veracruz and se Yucatán Pen. to n Colombia and on Pacific slope to s C.A.
Status in Belize. C resident n. to n OW and possibly s CO; most common in south and interior.
Reference. *Voice:* Moore (1992).

Genera: Streptopelia *and* Zenaida

Smaller and sleeker than pigeons, with a small head and in most a longer tail. Not found in forest.
  Things to note: tail shape and pattern, wing pattern, presence/absence of nape markings.

Eurasian Collared-Dove   FIGURE 19B
Streptopelia decaocto
OTHER NAMES. Collared Dove (arch.),
Collared Turtle-Dove (U.K. alt.).

Identification. 12¼″ (31.5 cm). Closely resembles smaller domesticated **Ringed Turtle-Dove** *(Streptopelia "risoria"),* a caged bird occasionally seen in the wild in Belize. Collared-dove is pale sandy brown with pink-tinged buffy gray head and neck, dark primaries that contrast sharply with rest of body, and gray undertail coverts. Ringed Turtle-Dove is creamier and lacks pink tones; upperparts uniformly creamy brown, with only slightly darker primaries; undertail coverts white, not gray. Both have black-based white tail as seen from below; however, collared-dove shows thin black lateral spur on outer rectrix. Turtle-dove has mostly white undertail, with black visible only at the very base; lacks black spurs.
Voice. *Call:* harsh mew, given in flight and while landing. *Song:* slightly mournful, hollow, three-note *wha-whoo who* or *kuk-kooo-kook.*
Habitat. All strata within urban and populated rural landscapes.
Distribution. Originally, c and s Asia, and e Eur. Spread rapidly across Eur. in 19th century. Introduced into Bahamas in 1974 and now spreading rapidly across s N.A.
Status in Belize. Two recent records: Ambergris Caye, 20 Apr. 1996 and 28 Feb. 1999. Likely to become established in Belize in the near future as it continues its spread westward across the New World.
References. *Distribution and identification:* Romagosa and McEneaney (1999); Smith (1987). *Status:* Jones et al. (2000).

White-winged Dove   MAP 71; PLATE 21
Zenaida asiatica

Identification. 11¼″ (28.5 cm). Similar to Mourning Dove but larger and chunkier, with short, square-tipped tail. Conspicuous white line usually visible in folded wings, much more so in flight. Like Mourning Dove, a fast, direct flier.
Voice. *Song:* tinny, burry *grrrr* plus *who cooks   for youuu,* or *hoo-koo   hoo kōōō.*

Habitat. Pastureland, fallow fields, patchy second-growth scrub, towns, and villages.
Distribution. Nests from sw U.S. and W.I. to Pan.; some populations, especially in U.S. portion of range, are migratory. Introduced in Florida.
Status in Belize. Unrecorded prior to 1967, it is now a C resident in CO, ne OW, Ambergris Caye, and Caye Caulker. It disperses widely in autumn commonly to c OW and n BE, less C farther s. and w. UC to FC autumn transient in SC and TO (Oct. and Nov.); these birds may originate from n Belize and Yucatán Pen. where the species is partially migratory.
References. *Status:* Barlow et al. (1969); Miller and Miller (1992). *Systematics:* Barlow et al. (1970).

Mourning Dove   PLATE 21
Zenaida macroura
OTHER NAMES. American Mourning Dove (alt.).

Identification. 11″ (28 cm). Relatively small, sleek dove with thin, pointed tail and small head; black spots but no white in wing. Fast, direct flier.
Voice. *Song:* mournful
aah whOOoo who who who with rising inflection on long second note (rarely, if ever, sings in Belize). Wing flutter or whistling whir on take-off and sometimes on landing.
Habitat. Pastureland, fallow fields, savannas, towns, and villages.
Distribution. Nests from sc Can. to s Mex. plateau; winters from n U.S. to Pan.
Status in Belize. UC autumn transient and occas. winter visitor, primarily in n. half, mid-Oct. to late Mar.

Genus: Columbina *(Ground-Doves)*

Small, squat, short-tailed doves. All share a large rufous patch in the primaries that is especially visible in flight, as well as various amounts of spotting in the wings. All but the forest-dwelling Blue Ground-Dove are conspicuous birds of open country that spend much of their time on the ground, although the Blue also feeds on the ground in large clearings. Ground-doves have short, hollow calls, which may be repeated incessantly throughout the day. Each species has a distinctive signature vocalization that is easy to learn with a little practice. For example, the ever-optimistic Blue Ground-Dove repeatedly chants *hope,* whereas the equally pessimistic Ruddy bemoans *no hope.* The Common declares emphatically *NOO'ope* while the Plain-breasted simply says *nope.*

Things to note: color and distribution of spots in wing; extent of scaling, if present; body color; vocal pattern.

Inca Dove PLATE 22

Columbina inca

Identification. 8½″ (21.5 cm). Superficially similar to Common Ground-Dove, but longer tail has conspicuous white lateral edges and body feathers are thinly dark-edged throughout, giving it a heavily scaled appearance. Common Ground-Dove has scaling only on head and breast. Like other ground-doves, has rufous primaries but lacks dark wing spots.
Voice. *Song:* distinctive, burry *noah hope,* repeated at ≈1–1½ sec intervals.
Habitat. Open areas, roadsides, forest edge, plantations, towns, and villages.
Distribution. Resident from sw U.S. to C.R. except for Yucatán Pen. and much of Caribbean slope of C.A.
Status in Belize. One record: Punta Gorda, 8 Sept. 1996.
Reference. *Status:* Jones et al. (2000).

Common Ground-Dove MAP 72; PLATE 22

Columbina passerina
OTHER NAMES. Scaly Ground-Dove (I. Davis), Scaly-breasted Ground-Dove (arch.), Rosy Ground-Dove (arch.), Turtle Dove (C).

Identification. 6½″ (16.5 cm). Rufous patch in primaries, visible in flight, contrasts strongly with rest of plumage. Lacks reddish plumage of ♂ Ruddy; has prominent scaling on breast and head in all plumages, bicolored black-tipped pinkish red bill, and slightly shorter tail than Ruddy, with narrow white tail corners (best seen when tail is spread for landing). Also lacks Ruddy's scapular spots. ♂: vinaceous and bluish highlights on crown and nape; wing spots dark iridescent violet. ♀: grayer and more uniformly colored; duller bill; purplish chestnut wing spots.
Voice. Soft, hollow, slightly hoarse *ōōōup,* repeated endlessly. Notes slightly more drawn out than in Plain-breasted and given at rates of ≈1 note/sec.
Habitat. Ground and low perches in most well-drained unforested habitats. On mainland, found especially in pine and pine-oak-calabash savannas; also along roadsides and in fields.
Distribution. Resident from s U.S. to nc S.A.
Status in Belize. FC to C resident in coastal lowlands s. to s BE. Also, C on Ambergris Caye and Placencia Pen.; UC on Caye Caulker. In autumn and winter, occas. seen w. to c OW and n CA, and s. to Punta Gorda.
Reference. *Identification:* Dunn and Garrett (1990).

Plain-breasted Ground-Dove

MAP 73; PLATE 22
Columbina minuta
OTHER NAMES. Little Ground-Dove (I. Davis), Turtle Dove (C).

Identification. 5¾″ (14.5 cm). Smallest of the ground-doves. Both sexes lack scaling of Common and reddish plumage of ♂ Ruddy. More closely resembles ♀ Ruddy, but smaller, paler, and duller, with less rufous in wing panel and violet, not black, wing spots. ♂: head dull bluish gray, contrasting with gray-brown body. ♀: duller than ♂ and lacking blue-gray color in head.
Voice. Incessant soft, hollow *nō'up* or *wō'up* (≥1 note/sec).
Habitat. Ground and low perches. Throughout most of its range in Belize, closely tied to pine and pine-oak savannas, but outside this belt also found in fallow fields, pastureland, and other disturbed unforested landscapes.
Distribution. Resident locally from Jalisco and c Veracruz s. discontinuously to sc S.A.
Status in Belize. UC to C resident on mainland w. to c OW, ne CA, and e. base of Maya Mtns.

Ruddy Ground-Dove   PLATE 22
Columbina talpacoti
OTHER NAMES. Turtle Dove (C), cak i tut
(K), puru wok (M), Tortolita (S).

Identification. 6¾″ (17 cm). Black spots in
wings and scapulars; conspicuous rufous patch
in primaries visible in flight. Slightly longer-
tailed than Common and Plain-breasted, and
distinctly larger than the latter. ♂: rich ruddy
brown upperparts, paler ruddy vinaceous underparts, and mostly blue-gray head. ♀: duller grayish brown with ruddy tones lacking or confined
to rump and tail base; can be confused with
both ♀ Common and Plain-breasted ground-
doves (see accounts for those species).
Voice. Soft, hollow *no hope,* with slight emphasis
on 2nd syllable. As with other ground-doves, call
is repeated incessantly at the rate of ≈1 note/sec.
Habitat. Widespread; ground and low perches
in most well-drained unforested areas, including
roadsides, urban landscapes, and savannas.
Distribution. Resident from s Sonora and s
Tamaulipas to c S.A.
Status in Belize. C resident nearly throughout
on mainland; absent from Mtn. Pine Ridge and
Maya Mtns. Possibly a scarce winter visitor on
Ambergris Caye.
Reference. *Identification:* Dunn and Garrett
(1990).

Blue Ground-Dove   PLATE 22
Claravis pretiosa
OTHER NAMES. Blue Dove (C), rax i tut
(K), tut (M).

Identification. 8¼″ (21 cm). Largest and most
sexually dimorphic of the ground-doves with
pale brownish bill. ♂: unmistakably grayish blue,
with black wing spots and bars. ♀: earth brown,
with dark rufous wing spots and bars, uppertail
coverts, and central tail.
Voice. 1. Deep, hollow, clear *hope* or *'ope,* shorter
and more clipped than call of Gray-fronted
Dove;
2. deep, throaty *gope;* 3. deep, owl-like *who.*
Habitat. Typically subcanopy, but occas. lower
and on ground, primarily in broadleaf forest and
secondarily in pine forest. Usually solitary or in

pairs; occas. gathering in small groups or flocks
that feed on ground in clearings and at forest
edge.
Distribution. Resident from s Tamaulipas and
Chiapas to c S.A.
Status in Belize. UC to C on mainland nearly
throughout; scarce or absent in much of CO, but
progressively more C southward.
Reference. *Voice:* Moore (1992).

Genera: Leptotila *and* Geotrygon *(Forest
Doves)*

Found singly or in pairs on forest floor, often
in small clearings or along footpaths. Typically
call from low branches. When disturbed, nervously lower head and jerk tail upward. *Leptotila*
doves present one of Belize's toughest ID challenges. Not only are they difficult to see (typically, they flush suddenly from underfoot and
disappear quickly into the forest), but even when
they are seen reasonably well, in the deep forest shade their subtle color differences are not
always apparent. Although all four *Leptotila* have
varying amounts of white in the corners of their
tail, the slight differences are of limited use in
the field. All also have pale yellowish eyes, red
orbital ring, rufous underwings, and red to pinkish red legs. Habitats and ranges of all but Caribbean Dove overlap extensively in Belize. Best
told by vocal differences; however, Ruddy Quail-
Dove (genus *Geotrygon*), the easiest to ID visu-
ally, sounds remarkably like Gray-chested Dove
(genus *Leptotila*).
    Things to note: color and shading of crown,
face, and breast; presence/absence and color
of iridescence on nape; quality and length of
each vocalization; number of vocalizations per
minute. *In flight,* amount of white in tail corners.

White-tipped Dove   MAP 74; PLATE 22
Leptotila verreauxi
OTHER NAMES. White-fronted Dove
(arch.), Ground Pigeon (C), mukui (K), tzu
tzui (M).

Identification. 11½″ (29 cm). Little contrast
between crown and breast (both grayish vinaceous); white flanks and belly; iridescent purple
sheen on nape (not always apparent in deep

shade). Slightly more white in tail corners than Gray-fronted, noticeably more than Gray-chested.

Voice. Distinctly 2- or 3-parted: soft, low-pitched, lazy to mournful, hollow *whooo-youuuu?* to *who-ah-youuu?* Slaty-breasted Tinamou's vocalization somewhat similar but deeper, not mournful.

Habitat. Ground to mid-strata in deciduous and semi-deciduous broadleaf forests, second-growth scrub, pine woodland, and savannas. Absent from humid tropical forest.

Distribution. Resident from nc Sonora and s Texas to c S.A.

Status in Belize. FC and widespread resident on mainland s. to c CA and n TO.

References. *Status:* Wood and Leberman (1987). *Voice:* Moore (1992).

Gray-fronted Dove   MAP 75; PLATE 22

Leptotila rufaxilla

OTHER NAMES. Gray-headed Dove (is part of), Ground Pigeon (C), mukui (K), tzu tzui (M).

Identification. 10½″ (26.5 cm). Non-iridescent blue-gray crown and nape; warm brownish breast; white flanks and belly. More white in tail corners than Gray-chested, with which it overlaps broadly in range and habitat.

Voice. Deep, hollow, soft *woe;* somewhat as in Blue Ground-Dove, but much softer and fades slightly (in Blue Ground-Dove, emphatic, hollow, and abruptly cut off at end). Call much shorter (<1 sec) than in other *Leptotila* species and Ruddy Quail-Dove.

Habitat. Ground to mid-strata in broadleaf forests, including both primary and secondary forest, as well as patchy forest. Avoids pine forests and savannas.

Distribution. Resident primarily on Gulf-Caribbean slope from s Tamaulipas and c Yucatán Pen. to w Colombia and e. of the Andes to n Argentina.

Status in Belize. FC to C resident on mainland n. to e CO, but largely replaced by White-fronted Dove in north.

Reference. *Voice:* Moore (1992).

Caribbean Dove   MAP 76; PLATE 22

Leptotila jamaicensis

OTHER NAMES. White-bellied Dove (arch.), Jamaican Dove (arch.), Ground Pigeon (C).

Identification. 11½″ (29 cm). Similar in some ways to Gray-fronted, in others to White-tipped, but with more extensive white foreparts than either and iridescent rose-colored area on side of neck. Also has more extensive amount of white in tail corners and bright red, not reddish pink, legs. Little geographic overlap with other *Leptotila* in Belize.

Voice. Lazy, mournful, low-pitched *who-whooo wh-whoo,* quite unlike other *Leptotila* vocalizations.

Habitat. Ground to mid-strata in littoral forest and edge.

Distribution. Resident on Yucatán Pen. and adjacent islands, Bay Isl. (Hon.), Grand Cayman Isl., Jamaica, and Isla San Andres (off Nic.).

Status in Belize. FC resident in ne CO and on Ambergris Caye. Recorded on Caye Caulker but not resident; one record from near Ladyville BE.

Gray-chested Dove   MAP 77; PLATE 22

Leptotila cassini

OTHER NAMES. Cassin's Dove (arch.), Ground Pigeon (C), mukui (K), tzu tzui (M).

Identification. 10½″ (26.5 cm). Darkest of the *Leptotila* in Belize, and the only one with combination of brown crown and vinaceous gray breast, with gray extending through belly and becoming brownish gray on flanks; only under-tail coverts are white. No iridescence on hind-neck; least amount of white in tail corners.

Voice. Drawn-out, low, mournful *ooooooo.* Much like that of Ruddy Quail-Dove, but each note distinctly longer (1½–1¾ sec), spaced farther apart (1 note every 4½–6 sec), higher-pitched, and falling slightly in pitch and fading at the end. Much more drawn out than in Gray-fronted, with which it is often heard, and not multisyllabic as in White-tipped and Caribbean.

Habitat. Ground to mid-strata in primary and secondary humid broadleaf forest. Often found together with Gray-fronted but avoids the more open forests.

Distribution. Resident primarily on Caribbean slope from e Campeche and c Belize to nw Colombia.

Status in Belize. FC to C resident on mainland in s. half, n. in Maya Mtns. and foothills to sw BE and n CA.

Ruddy Quail-Dove   PLATE 22
Geotrygon montana
OTHER NAMES. Quail (C), cak i mukui (K), chuk tzu tzui (M).

Identification. 9½″ (24 cm). Unique profile, with steeply sloped forehead that forms virtually no angle with downward-pointing red bill. Eyes placed high and back on head. Louder wing whir when flushed than *Leptotila* doves. ♂: brownish rufous plumage with rufous-brown stripe across lower auriculars dividing otherwise buffy face; breast grayish vinaceous. White bar on side of breast at bend of wing. ♀: duller overall; brownish cinnamon face, with dusky bar across lower auriculars; breast grayish cinnamon.
Voice. Like that of Gray-chested Dove, but each note shorter (≈1 sec), lower-pitched, and more monotone (does not fade or drop in pitch); less spacing between calls (1 note every 3–4 sec).
Habitat. Ground and lower strata in most primary and secondary broadleaf forest.
Distribution. Resident from s Sinaloa, sw Tamaulipas, and W.I. to sc S.A.
Status in Belize. UC to locally C resident on mainland; recorded twice on Sapodilla Cayes.
References. *Status:* Jones et al. (2000). *Voice:* Moore (1992).

FAMILY: PSITTACIDAE
(Parrots)
World: 352. **New World:** 150 native; several additional Old World parrots introduced. **Belize:** 10. Tropics and S. Temperate Zone worldwide. Parrots are fairly uniform in appearance (but remarkably variable in size); all have characteristic deep-based hooked bill and, unlike birds of prey, a strongly upcurved lower mandible, a large head, a short neck, and legs with two fore-

pointing and two aft-pointing toes. Most in New World have at least some green in their plumage, and some are predominantly green. Parrots pair for life, and although they usually travel in flocks, pairs can usually be discerned within the flock. Most have a characteristic vocal signature, a distinctive note or expression uttered periodically, along with more generic squawks and gurgles. Many are also readily IDed by flight characteristics, e.g., wingbeats, grouping of birds, and tendency to fly straight or constantly twisting or changing direction. **Reference:** Juniper and Parr (1998).

Olive-throated Parakeet   PLATE 23
Aratinga nana
OTHER NAMES. Aztec Parakeet (alt.), Olive-throated Conure (alt.), Wood-lice Kiti (C), tzilon (K), pili (M).

Identification. 9″ (23 cm). Small, slender, green parrot with pointed tail, brownish olive throat and breast, and mostly blue remiges; whitish eye-ring. *Flight:* flies fast and low in tight groups, with frequent changes in direction.
Voice. Variable series of harsh, nasal *cree* and *creck* notes.
Habitat. Canopy of forest edge and second-growth scrub.
Distribution. Resident on Gulf-Caribbean slope from c Tamaulipas to nw C.R.; also in W.I.
Status in Belize. C resident on mainland and presumed resident on Ambergris Caye; regular winter visitor to Caye Caulker.
Reference. *Voice:* Moore (1992).

Scarlet Macaw   MAP 78; PLATE 23
Ara macao
OTHER NAMES. Guacamaya (C), mo' (K, M).

Identification. 35″ (89 cm). Unmistakable. Large, with massive bill and long, pointed tail. Plumage mostly scarlet red, with blue remiges, rump, and tail coverts and yellow greater wing coverts; featherless white face. *Flight:* direct on slow, steady wingbeats; usually traveling in pairs, or when in groups, often strung out one behind the other.

Voice. Loud raucous *rrrahk!* given in flight; notes usually softer, less raucous when perched.

Habitat. Canopy in primary broadleaf and, less often, pine forests in interior.

Distribution. Resident from e Campeche (formerly s Tamaulipas) discontinuously to Amazonian Brazil.

Status in Belize. UC within its restricted range; total population may not exceed 150 birds; range much reduced in last 30 years. Core population found in upper Raspaculo and Macal watersheds in se CA. Seasonally, much of the population moves e. across Maya Divide into sw SC (rarely n TO) in pursuit of seasonal food supplies. As many as 100 birds found in Red Bank SC every year, primarily from Jan. to Mar. Small numbers also reported in Cockscomb Basin SC.

References. *Status:* Miller and Miller (1992). *Conservation:* Jones and Vallely (2001).

Brown-hooded Parrot   MAP 79; PLATE 23
Pionopsitta haematotis
OTHER NAMES. Red-eared Parrot (arch.), rax i puyuch' (K), silon (M).

Identification. 8½″ (21.5 cm). Mostly green with blue-black remiges, pale bill, and eye-ring. *Ad.:* dark brown head. *Juv.:* lacks contrasting dark brown hood. *Flight:* rapid and direct on relatively deep, powerful wingbeats; typically flies just above canopy; even in relatively poor light, the red axillars and contrasting dark head are apparent.

Voice. Characteristic scratchy-clear *chirrup, creek,* and rolling *keereek* notes given frequently during raucous chatter. Vocalizations more liquid, not as harsh as in White-crowned.

Habitat. Canopy and subcanopy in primary and secondary broadleaf forest and forest edge.

Distribution. Resident on Gulf-Caribbean slope from c Veracruz and c Yucatán Pen. to nw Colombia and on Pacific slope from C.R. to Ecuador. Absent from most of Yucatán Pen.

Status in Belize. C resident on mainland n. to c OW and n BE, locally to n OW; most abundant in south and west; absent from Mtn. Pine Ridge.

References. *Identification:* Whitney (1996). *Voice:* Moore (1992).

White-crowned Parrot   PLATE 23
Pionus senilis
OTHER NAMES. White-capped Parrot (arch.), puyuch' (K), suc pol (M).

Identification. 9½″ (24 cm). More uniformly dark body and wings than Brown-hooded and lacks its red axillars. Violet-blue remiges, red tail coverts, and pale bill. *Ad.:* bronzy green, with bluish head and breast, white forecrown and throat. *Juv.:* lacks the bluish tones of ad.; white restricted to forehead; can be confused with White-fronted but lacks its red facial area. *Flight:* similar to Brown-hooded, but more often than not flies higher above canopy, and birds flying singly are more typical than in other species of parrots; when pairs fly together, they are often well separated.

Voice. Single or doubled harsh, shrill *krēak!* and *krēa!* mixed in with other harsh and shrill notes.

Habitat. Canopy and subcanopy in broadleaf and pine forest and forest edge.

Distribution. Resident on Gulf-Caribbean slope from sw Tamaulipas and c Yucatán Pen. to w Pan. and on Pacific slope in C.R. and w Pan. Absent from n Yucatán Pen.

Status in Belize. C resident on mainland nearly throughout. In north, more C than Brown-hooded; in south and west, often outnumbered by Brown-hooded.

References. *Identification:* Whitney (1996). *Voice:* Moore (1992).

Genus: Amazona

Characterized by large head; stocky, mostly green body; broad, rounded wings; square, yellow-tipped tail; and dark blue in remiges. Larger *Amazona* have red patch in secondaries; smaller ones, in primary coverts. *Amazona* parrots have a distinctive slow flight on rapid, very shallow or even fluttery, stiff wings. This distinctive flight easily distinguishes smaller *Amazona* from Brown-hooded and White-crowned at a distance. Distinguishing White-fronted and Yellow-lored from each other is more difficult. These two are unique among Belizean parrots in that the sexes differ. Most species have a characteristic vocal "signature."

Things to note: body size, head pattern, bill color or tone, vocalizations.

White-fronted Parrot   MAP 80; PLATE 23
Amazona albifrons
OTHER NAMES. White-fronted Amazon (alt.), Corn-eater (C), Corn Kiti (C), tut (M).

Identification. 10¾″ (27.5 cm). Small green parrot with short tail, mostly blue-violet remiges, red face, white forehead, and yellowish bill. ♂: red primary coverts in upper wing, white forehead and forecrown. ♀: green primary coverts, white restricted to forehead.
Voice. Characteristic *yak yak yak . . .* to *chak chak chak . . .* and squeaky, rolling *eah! eah! eah!* mixed in with other raucous chatter.
Habitat. Canopy and subcanopy within open second-growth scrub, forest edge, savannas. Flocks frequently descend on cultivated fields, especially cornfields, to feed.
Distribution. Resident from s Sonora and Tabasco to nw C.R.
Status in Belize. C to VC resident s. to c CA and c SC. Unrecorded from TO and cayes.
Reference. *Voice:* Moore (1992).

Yellow-lored Parrot   MAP 81; PLATE 23
Amazona xantholora
OTHER NAMES. Yellow-lored Amazon (alt.), Yucatán Parrot/Amazon (alt.), Corn-eater (C), Corn Kiti (C), tut (M).

Identification. 10½″ (26.5 cm). Similar to White-fronted but with yellow lores and blackish auricular patch. ♂: red greater primary coverts in upper wing; red area encircling eyes; white forecrown. ♀: lacks white forecrown, red around eyes, and red in greater primary coverts; reduced yellow in lores.
Voice. Similar to White-fronted, but with some notes more expressive and trumpetlike.
Habitat. Similar to that of White-fronted.
Distribution. *Yucatán Endemic.* Resident in Yucatán Pen. s. to c Belize.
Status in Belize. C to locally VC resident in CO, e OW, ne CA, and all but sw BE. UC and local in w OW, n CA, and n SC. Reliable informa-

tion on its occurrence and status in these more southern and western areas is sketchy because of its close similarity to the preceding species.

Red-lored Parrot   PLATE 23
Amazona autumnalis
OTHER NAMES. Red-lored Amazon (alt.), Yellow-cheeked Parrot/Amazon (alt.), Mangrove Parrot/Amazon (arch.), Mangro Parrot (C), cho cho' (K), chuk ni (M).

Identification. 13½″ (34 cm). Relatively large Amazon with bluish crown, red forehead, and yellow face. Distinctive head pattern is apparent, even at a long distance in good light.
Voice. Characteristic *quidick quidick so quick so quick* often preceded by several lower-pitched *choit* notes; also high, shrill *eek!* and *caw caw* notes mixed in with raucous squawks and chatter.
Habitat. Canopy and subcanopy in most forested habitats, including open pine savannas and patchy forest.
Distribution. Resident primarily on Gulf-Caribbean slope from n Tamaulipas and c Yucatán Pen. to nw S.A., with disjunct population in Amazonian Brazil.
Status in Belize. C and widespread resident nearly throughout on mainland, although UC in CO and absent at higher elevations in Maya Mtns.
Reference. *Voice:* Moore (1992).

Mealy Parrot   MAP 82; PLATE 23
Amazona farinosa
OTHER NAMES. Mealy Amazon (alt.), Blue-crowned Parrot (arch.), Watch-out Parrot (C), cho cho' (K), ya'ax tut (M).

Identification. 16″ (40.5 cm). Largest of the group; distinctive blue crown; large, pale orbital ring; gray bill; tail with more extensive yellow tip than in other large *Amazona*.
Voice. Typical raucous parrot squawks with characteristic *wat CHOUT!* or *got CHUH!* notes, along with melodious *keoww!* notes.
Habitat. Canopy and subcanopy within primary and tall secondary forest, gallery forest, forest edge.

Distribution. Resident primarily on Gulf-Caribbean slope from c Veracruz and s Yucatán Pen. to c and se Brazil.

Status in Belize. UC to locally C resident on mainland away from coast in primary forest n. to c OW and w BE; scarce or absent in areas of fragmented and second-growth forest.

Reference. *Voice:* Moore (1992).

Yellow-headed Parrot   MAP 83; PLATE 23

Amazona oratrix

OTHER NAMES. Yellow-headed Amazon (alt.), Yellow-crowned Amazon (combined form), Guatemalan Parrot/Amazon (arch.), Yellow-head (C), k'an y jolom cho cho' (K), kun pol tut (M).

Identification. 14½″ (37 cm). Size of Red-lored, which often shares the same habitat. *Ad.:* yellow face and crown, pale bill. *Juv.:* yellow restricted to forecrown, little or no red at bend of wing, bill dusky; gradually attains yellow crown, face, and auriculars; pale bill.

Voice. Distinctive rolling, rapid-fire gurgling notes.

Habitat. Canopy and subcanopy in pine savannas; occas. in other open forested habitats.

Distribution. Resident from Jalisco to Oaxaca and c Tamaulipas to nw Hon. Because of its restricted range globally, its popularity in the pet trade, and inadequate protection, it is considered *Globally Endangered*.

Status in Belize. UC to C resident of lowland pine savannas from n BE, e OW, and ne CA s. to s. limit of pines in ne TO, occas. farther s. Subspecies *belizensis* nearly endemic to Belize. Heavily persecuted for the pet trade and could easily be driven to extinction despite its present stable population in Belize if current efforts to protect it are not enforced.

References. *Systematics:* Lousada and Howell (1996); Monroe and Howell (1966); Parkes (1990a). *Identification:* Lousada and Howell (1996). *Conservation:* Jones and Vallely (2001); Stattersfield and Capper (2000).

Yellow-naped Parrot   PLATE 23

Amazona auropalliata

OTHER NAMES. Yellow-headed Parrot (Amazon) (combined form).

Identification. 14½″ (37 cm). Similar to Yellow-headed and thought by some authorities to be the same species. The subspecies in the Bay Isl. *(caribaea),* where the Belize birds likely originated, differs from Yellow-headed in having yellow restricted to the nape and forecrown, a prominent dark gray cere, gray-tipped bill, and pale gray eye-ring (whitish in Yellow-headed). *Juv.:* typically has reduced yellow in crown, no yellow in nape.

Voice. Low, far-carrying, raucous, rolled *h-rah h-rah h-rah . . . , rr-aah rrowh rr-aah rrowh . . . ,* etc. Less gurgling and more raucous than in Yellow-headed.

Habitat. In Bay Isl. and Mosquitia of Hon., pine savannas; on Calabash Caye, littoral scrub and forest.

Distribution. Discontinuously from s Mex. (Pacific slope) and Bay Islands, Hon. (Caribbean), to nw C.R.

Status in Belize. Three birds discovered on Calabash Caye in Turneffe Isl. shortly after Hurricane Mitch in late autumn or early winter 1998 and thought to be of wild rather than captive origin. One was shot, and the two remaining were still present as of early 2003.

References. *Status:* Jones et al. (2002). *Systematics and identification:* Lousada (1989); Lousada and Howell (1996); Parkes (1990a). *Voice:* Howell and Webb (1995).

FAMILY: CUCULIDAE
(Cuckoos and Anis)

World: 138. **New World:** 33. **Belize:** 8. Nearly cosmopolitan; absent only from Arctic, some subarctic regions, Antarctica, and deserts of n Afr. and Middle East. Cuckoos and their relatives are slender birds with long, graduated tail; laterally compressed, decurved bill; and zygodactyl feet (two toes directed forward, two backward). Some are secretive forest species; others are conspicuous open-country species. Many in the Old World and a few in the New World are nest parasites, laying their eggs in nests of other species rather than raising their own young. **Reference:** Hardy et al. (1987b).

SUBFAMILY: COCCYZINAE
(New World Cuckoos)

Uniformly brown or rufous above and pale below, most with at least some yellow in their bill; long, graduated tail, black-and-white or gray-and-white below. All in the genus *Coccyzus* are similar in appearance. Typically seen flying across openings and darting into dense foliage, where they sit motionless and can be difficult to see. When seen well, they are not especially difficult to ID, but birds in their first autumn can be tricky.

Things to note: undertail pattern; color of bill, eye-ring, and underparts. *In flight,* presence/absence of rufous patch in primaries.

Black-billed Cuckoo   PLATE 24
Coccyzus erythrophthalmus

Identification. 11¼″ (28.5 cm). Slender, long-tailed bird; gray brown above, white below, with slightly decurved, black-and-gray bill. Lacks rufous in primaries, but some individuals may show a dull rufous wash. *Ad.:* bright red to red-orange eye-ring; rectrices narrowly tipped with white, bordered subterminally with dark gray. *Juv.:* whitish underparts washed pale grayish buff on throat and breast; grayish buff to pale greenish eye-ring; undertail gray, with ill-defined whitish feather tips; narrow pale tips to wing covert feathers. Some have distinct pale (but not yellow) base to lower mandible. Undertail pattern in all plumages is best mark for separating Black-billed from the other two.
Voice. Silent in Belize.
Habitat. Midlevels to subcanopy within broadleaf forest.
Distribution. Nests e. of Rocky Mtns. from s Can. to c U.S.; winters in w S.A. from Colombia to Bolivia.
Status in Belize. Occas. spring and autumn migrant, mid-Apr. to mid-May and late Sept. to mid-Nov.
Reference. *Status:* Barlow et al. (1970).

Yellow-billed Cuckoo   PLATE 24
Coccyzus americanus

Identification. 11½″ (29 cm). Most like Mangrove Cuckoo. Bill black, with yellow lower mandible, often with yellow extending into upper mandible; eye-ring yellow. *Flight:* only Yellow-billed shows bright rufous patch in primaries (sometimes visible in folded wings). *Ad.:* underside of tail black, with extensive white tips to graduated tail feathers. *Juv.:* undertail less contrasting, gray with diffuse white feather tips; may have yellow only at base of lower mandible. *Caution:* some Black-billed, especially imms., have dull rufous tone in many wing feathers.
Voice. Usually silent outside breeding season. *Song:* c-c-c-c-c-c-cdow-cdow-cdow-cdow-cdow; not harsh like that of Mangrove.
Habitat. Midlevels to subcanopy in most forest habitats, including mangroves, forest edge, and second-growth scrub.
Distribution. Nests from n U.S. to c Mex., n Yucatán Pen., and n W.I.; winters in S.A.
Status in Belize. UC (mainland) to C (cayes) spring and autumn transient, mid-Apr. to early June and late Aug. to early Nov.

Mangrove Cuckoo   PLATE 24
Coccyzus minor

Identification. 12½″ (32 cm). Similar to Yellow-billed but lacks rufous patch in wings; has buff underparts, strongest on belly and undertail coverts; and has stouter bill, with yellow on lower mandible only. *Ad.:* distinctive black mask and gray crown; black undertail with bold white feather tips. *Juv.:* mask less distinct, upperparts browner; less contrasting gray tail with whitish feather tips.
Voice. *Song:* 1. very harsh, nasal froglike *caa caa caa caa caa caa caa caa caa caa oo-oo oo-oo oo-oo,* with *oo-oo* much lower-pitched;
2. much faster *că-că-că-că-că-că ōōō ōōō ōōō ōōō ōōō ōōō ōōō ōōō,* with abrupt change from high-pitched, nasal *că* notes to low-pitched *ōōō* notes.
Habitat. Littoral forest, mangroves, riverine forest, forest edge, and scrub.
Distribution. Resident from s Sonora, c Tamaulipas, s Florida, and Bahamas to n S.A.

Status in Belize. Status poorly known; at best, VU and local resident along coast and lowland waterways w. to New R. in n Belize. Formerly bred on a few n. cayes and still occurs as occas. migrant, but now apparently extirpated as breeding species on cayes. Nesting habitat has been steadily converted for residential and commercial development. A specimen from San Ignacio CA taken 8 Apr. 1926 is the only record away from coastal plain.

Squirrel Cuckoo   PLATE 24
Piaya cayana
OTHER NAMES. Pe-quam (C), pich' (K), chi'ix peech (M).

Identification. 18″ (45 cm). Much larger than *Coccyzus* cuckoos, with a spectacular long black-and-white tail, rufous upperparts, cinnamon-and-gray underparts, and yellow-green bill and eye-ring.
Voice. 1. *CHICK! warr;*
2. sharp *clar whip;*
3. *wip* repeated steadily at a rate of ≈18 times in 10 sec;
4. *pik!,* similar to *Picoides* woodpecker;
5. *chesh chesh chesh chesh peech.*
Habitat. Most broadleaf forests and forest edge; less common in pine forest.
Distribution. Resident from s Sonora and s Tamaulipas to sc S.A.
Status in Belize. FC resident on mainland and Ambergris Caye.
Reference. *Voice:* Moore (1992).

SUBFAMILY: NEOMORPHINAE
(Ground-Cuckoos)
Unlike the Coccyzinae, the ground-cuckoos are cryptically marked in various shades of browns and have a ragged crest. At least some of their time is spent on the ground.

Things to note: size and fullness of tail; presence/absence of streaking on breast and white spotting in plumage; habitat.

Striped Cuckoo   MAP 84; PLATE 24
Tapera naevia
OTHER NAMES. American Striped Cuckoo (alt.).

Identification. 11½″ (29 cm). Size of Yellow-billed Cuckoo. Ragged crest, yellow bill, white supercilium. *Flight:* whitish base to primaries. *Ad.:* buffy cinnamon-brown upperparts striped with black; unmarked pale buff underparts. *Juv.:* crown and upperparts with cinnamon spots; indistinct dusky bars or scaling on breast.
Voice. Clear resonant, plaintive. 1. *tree tree [tree tree] TREE tre,* the last note shorter, sometimes absent;
2. shorter, simpler *tree tree* and *tree tree tree.*
Habitat. Lower strata within open second-growth scrub and fallow fields. Sings from exposed perch.
Distribution. Resident from c Veracruz and se Yucatán Pen. to sc S.A.
Status in Belize. Locally FC resident in lowlands on mainland nearly throughout except for w OW. More often heard than seen.

Pheasant Cuckoo   PLATE 24
Dromococcyx phasianellus

Identification. 14½″ (37 cm). Noticeably larger than Striped (a little larger than an ani) with long, broad, bushy tail; thinner, darker bill; and ragged erectile chestnut crest. *Flight:* prominent pale base to primaries. *Ad.:* spotted breast, mottled upperparts. *Juv.:* unmarked breast, darker upperparts spotted buff.
Voice. *Song:* loud tremulous *tow tow toow tuh* or *durt durt durrrr duh,* the 3rd note more tremulous and on same pitch as other notes; much lower-pitched than in Striped Cuckoo. More rapid, higher-pitched, shorter, and less haunting than in Great Tinamou.
Habitat. Ground to subcanopy within primary and secondary broadleaf forest; dense second growth.
Distribution. Resident from w Oaxaca and c Veracruz to c S.A.
Status in Belize. R and local resident, with records from widely scattered localities in in-

terior from near sea level to 3,000 ft. (900 m) elevation. Poorly known in Belize.

References. *Status:* Howell et al. (1992). *Voice:* Moore (1992).

SUBFAMILY: CROTOPHAGINAE

(Anis)

Relatively large, black cuckoos with grotesquely large bill. Very similar in appearance, especially in juvenal plumage. Smooth-billed, however, is rare and reported from only a few cayes. They superficially resemble grackles but are easily distinguished by their large, thick-based bill and floppy flight.

Things to note: vocalizations. *In ad. only,* presence/absence of grooves on bill and hump at base of upper mandible, color of iridescence on head and nape. *In juv.,* shape of lower mandible.

Smooth-billed Ani   MAP 85; PLATE 24
Crotophaga ani

Identification. 13½" (35 cm). Noticeably larger than Groove-billed, with different vocal repertoire. Lacks grooves in bill at all ages; however, Groove-billed does not always have noticeable grooves in its bill (absent in imm.), and even if present, grooves can be difficult to see at a distance. *Ad.:* angle of bill (culmen) rises more steeply from tip to forehead and usually (but not always) has noticeable hump at base of upper mandible; crown slightly rounded, forming slight angle with bill at its base. Head and nape feathers edged with brownish bronze gloss, contrasting with glossy, green-edged back feathers (most apparent in strong sunlight). *Juv.:* lacks iridescence and hump at base of upper mandible; difficult to tell from Groove-billed; shape of lower mandible differs and can be a useful field mark at close range—mandible thickest in middle, narrows towards base in most individuals; best IDed by its distinctive vocalizations.

Voice. 1. Slurred, whining *ree-o-rink* to *ooo-rink;* 2. mewing, hawklike *teeeahh* or slurred *reee-ah.*

Habitat. Ground and lower strata along edge of second-growth scrub, fallow fields, littoral forest edge.

Distribution. Resident on islands off Yucatán

Pen., Bay Isl. (Hon.), s Florida, and W.I. and from C.R. to sc S.A.

Status in Belize. Occas. winter visitor to n. cayes where it may occas. remain to breed, at least on Ambergris Caye. Not recorded from mainland.

References. *Status:* Howell et al. (1992). *Identification:* Balch (1979); Mlodinow and Karlson (1999). *Voice:* Howell and Webb (1995).

Groove-billed Ani   PLATE 24
Crotophaga sulcirostris
OTHER NAMES. Wari Tick Blackbird (C), Cowboy Blackbird (C), ch'i quan (K), tz'ic bul (M).

Identification. 12½" (32.5 cm). Smaller than Smooth-billed. *Ad.:* two to three grooves in upper mandible, but not always easy to see, especially at a distance or in shade; bill rises more gradually from tip to forehead and lacks hump at base of upper mandible that is usually present in Smooth-billed; crown flatter than in Smooth-billed, thus no angle where bill joins forehead; feathers of head and back edged with glossy bluish green (brownish bronze in Smooth-billed). *Juv.:* similar to juv. Smooth-billed but smaller (only useful in direct comparison); lower mandible of uniform thickness throughout except near tip; best told from juv. Smooth-billed by vocalizations.

Voice. 1. Sharp *pit! choy* to *chick warry;* 2. liquid *shrip;* 3. when agitated, a series of *tee-ho tee-ho tee-ho* notes, often preceded by soft clucking notes.

Habitat. Ground and lower strata within second-growth scrub, fallow fields, forest edge.

Distribution. Resident from s Sonora and s Texas to Guyana and n Chile.

Status in Belize. C resident on mainland away from extensive forest and on Ambergris Caye; regular winter visitor to Caye Caulker and occas. transient on other cayes.

References. *Identification:* Balch (1979); Mlodinow and Karlson (1999).

FAMILY: TYTONIDAE
(Barn Owls)

World: 16. **New World:** 2. **Belize:** 1. Nearly cosmopolitan, but absent from Alaska, most of Can., Saharan Afr., and much of Asia. The only New World representative, Barn Owl, is one of the most widespread birds in the world. Barn Owls differ from true owls primarily in internal morphology. Externally, they are distinguished by their heart-shaped, monkeylike facial disk, and large head relative to body size. General characteristics of owls, including barn owls, are presented below under the Strigidae. **Reference:** *Voice:* Hardy et al. (1990).

Barn Owl   PLATE 25
Tyto alba
OTHER NAMES. Monkey Bird (C), quarom (K), bouh (M), Curujo (S).

Identification. 15″ (38 cm). Medium-sized pale buff, gray, and white owl, about the size of a Roadside Hawk, with disproportionately large head, thus appearing front-heavy. Dark eyes framed by heart-shaped white facial disk. At night, especially in the beam of a spotlight or car headlights, can appear all white.
Voice. 1. Loud, breathy hissing (1–1½ sec); 2. harsh, penetrating scream, dropping in pitch at end (2–4 sec); 3. metallic *click-click-click* . . . .
Habitat. Urban communities, agricultural areas, quarries.
Distribution. Resident in New World from n U.S. to s S.A.; in Old World, in Eur. s. of Scandinavia, throughout most of Afr. except Sahara Desert, in Middle East, and from India through se Asia to Aust. and islands of the Pacific.
Status in Belize. UC to locally FC resident on mainland.

FAMILY: STRIGIDAE
(Typical Owls)

World: 188. **New World:** 74. **Belize:** 12. Found worldwide except Antarctica. The Strigidae are a much larger family than the barn owls, and like the Tytonidae, they are nocturnal and predatory, resembling diurnal birds of prey, with their strongly hooked bill and sharp hooked talons. Unlike the Tytonidae, typical owls have a rounded facial disk. Most have cryptically patterned soft plumage. All owls have flight feathers covered with soft, velvety pile, which, along with their broad wings requiring less vigorous flapping, enables them to flush silently without the wing whir of other large birds. Contrary to popular belief, owls see quite well in daylight and cannot see well in extremely dark conditions (e.g., during the new moon). All in Belize are nocturnal, but a few smaller species are also active during daylight hours, mostly in the morning. The larger species do not vocalize during the day and are encountered only by chance. As with other nocturnal or secretive species, owls are best IDed by their vocalizations. **References:** König et al. (1999, 2002). *Voice:* Hardy et al. (1990).

Things to note: vocalizations, overall size, presence/absence of ear tufts, presence/absence of streaks or bars on breast, facial pattern and color, color of eyes.

Vermiculated Screech-Owl   PLATE 25
Otus guatemalae
OTHER NAMES. Guatemalan or Middle American Screech-Owl (is part of), Variable Screech-Owl (combined form), Monkey Bird (C), quarom (K), bouh (M).

Identification. 8½″ (21.5 cm). Small, grayish brown, short-tailed owl with short, inconspicuous ear tufts, yellow eyes, and green bill. Finely streaked and barred throughout, with prominent white scapular spots. Typical of the genus, it has short black stripes on underparts lined with fine wavy bars or vermiculations.
Voice. Slow, low-pitched trill that builds gradually in intensity, then fades. Similar to vocalization of marine toad *(Bufo marinus),* but much softer and shorter.
Habitat. Midlevel, primarily within broadleaf forest; secondarily, pine forest.
Distribution. Resident from s Sonora and s Tamaulipas to Colombia and Venezuela.
Status in Belize. UC to FC resident on mainland throughout.
References. *Voice:* Delaney (1992); Moore (1992).

Crested Owl   MAP 86; PLATE 25
Lophostrix cristata

Identification. 16″ (40.5 cm). Medium-sized, dark cinnamon-brown owl with finely barred underparts. Conspicuous long, white ear tufts and "moustache" stand in stark contrast to dark chestnut facial disks. Yellow eyes and yellowish bill.
Voice. Deep, throaty *w-w-w-w-WOOOO*, with emphasis on the longer final note.
Habitat. Subcanopy within mature broadleaf forest.
Distribution. Resident from c Veracruz s. of Yucatán Pen. to c S.A.
Status in Belize. UC resident in Maya Mtns. and foothills, including Vaca Plateau CA. Recorded first in 1990 at Caracol CA and subsequently near Rio Frio Caves CA, in several localities at mid- and upper elevations in s Maya Mtns. TO, and in Cockscomb Basin SC.
Reference. *Status:* Miller and Miller (1992).

Spectacled Owl   MAP 87; PLATE 25
Pulsatrix perspicillata
OTHER NAMES. Bubu te' (K), bouh (M).

Identification. 18″ (45.5 cm). Large owl with dark brown upperparts, head, and breast; pale unstreaked buffy belly; conspicuous white eyebrows, moustache, and throat bar; and yellow eyes.
Voice. Very deep, metallic, accelerating *whŭ whŭ whŭ whŭ-whŭ-whŭ-wh-wh,* fading toward the end. Quality similar to sound made by flexing a large saw blade.
Habitat. Subcanopy within primary and secondary broadleaf forest.
Distribution. Resident from c Veracruz s. of Yucatán Pen. to c S.A.
Status in Belize. UC and local resident in interior n. to w OW, n CA, and probably sw BE.

Great Horned Owl   MAP 88; PLATE 25
Bubo virginianus

Identification. 20½″ (52 cm). Largest owl in Belize, and only owl on the cayes. Prominent orange-cinnamon facial disks bordered laterally with black and around the bill and eyes with a white **X**. White throat bar with necklace of bold dark streaks beneath. Rest of body heavily mottled dark and light brown and reddish-buff. Yellow eyes.
Voice. Distinctive 5- to 6-part, deep, resonant *who wh-who   whoo whoo* (♂); higher-pitched *who wh-who   w-who whoo* (♀). Imm. gives short, harsh screams.
Habitat. Open forested and urban landscapes.
Distribution. Resident from Alaska and nc Can. to sc S.A.
Status in Belize. FC resident on Ambergris Caye; UC on mainland coast s. to s BE, once in c TO (sight record from Big Falls, possibly of a stray).
Reference. *General:* Houston et al. (1998).

Genus: Glaucidium *(Pygmy-Owls)*

Tiny owls lacking ear tufts. Both species in Belize cock and pump their tail, a characteristic of the genus. Although similar in appearance, they are readily distinguished by their vocalizations. They frequently vocalize during the day, especially in the morning, and thus are relatively easy to locate.

Things to note: presence/absence of scapular spots, spotted vs. striped crown, marked or unmarked nape, length of tail, pitch and number of notes in vocal series.

Central American Pygmy-Owl
MAP 89; PLATE 25
Glaucidium griseiceps
OTHER NAMES. Least Pygmy-Owl (combined form), ton ton (M).

Identification. 5¾″ (14.5 cm). Size of a wood-pewee; rich brown above; duller gray-brown nape and crown, with fine spots in crown (but not nape); indistinct spots in wing coverts and scapulars; dark brown tail with 3 or 4 visible white or nearly white bands on undersurface, 2 or 3 on upper surface.
Voice. Soft, hollow *toe* or *toot* notes, given at a rate of 2–4/sec, 2–9 in a series.
Habitat. Midlevels to subcanopy within primary and secondary broadleaf forest.

Distribution. Resident from c Veracruz s. of Yucatán Pen. to nw Colombia.

Status in Belize. UC to locally FC resident of mainland interior n. to n CA and sw BE; also in w OW and locally in e OW; unrecorded from coastal plain.

References. *Voice:* Delaney (1992); Moore (1992).

Ferruginous Pygmy-Owl

MAP 90; PLATE 25

Glaucidium brasilianum

OTHER NAMES. Ridgway's Pygmy-Owl (is part of), Screech Owl (C).

Identification. 7″ (18 cm). Size of an Olive-sided Flycatcher. Plumage highly variable: some are rich rufous brown above, and others dull gray brown, with various intermediate morphs. All have white streaks in crown and conspicuous white spots in wing coverts and scapulars. Tail pattern highly variable, from pale rufous to dark brown, with up to eight paler or darker bands or no bands at all. Birds with dark brown tail tend to have white or nearly white bands; those with pale brown or rufous tail tend to have darker brown bands. Some of the most richly colored birds have no bands in the tail. Duller birds have been mistaken for Northern (or Mountain) Pygmy-Owl *(Glaucidium gnoma),* which does not occur in Belize.

Voice. Hollow *what!* notes given at rate of 2–3/sec; usually >9 notes in a series, and often continuing for half a minute or more.

Habitat. Midlevels to subcanopy within deciduous and semi-deciduous broadleaf forest, submontane pine and broadleaf forest; also patchily distributed in urban areas. Occas. perches in the open, even on power lines.

Distribution. Resident from s Arizona and s Texas to sc S.A.

Status in Belize. Distribution complex: C resident in CO, all but s OW, and most of CA, including Belmopan and Mtn. Pine Ridge; less C in Maya Mtns. and foothills of w SC and TO. May occur locally in w BE. Absent from coastal plain s. of OW.

Burrowing Owl

PLATE 25

Athene cunicularia

Identification. 9½″ (24 cm). Small, long-legged, terrestrial owl; heavily spotted above and barred and spotted below; distinctive black-and-white band across lower throat/upper breast. Yellow eyes. Stands erect; exhibits frequent nervous bobs.

Voice. Shrill *SCREE,* followed immediately by a cackling *whk-whk-whk-whk-whk.*

Habitat. Open areas with clay, mud, or sand banks, dunes, or levees.

Distribution. Nests in w N.A. from s Can. to c Mex. and in Florida and W.I.; also resident in much of S.A. Western N.A. populations are migratory, wintering s. to n C.A.

Status in Belize. Two records: beach at mouth of Manatee R. BE, Jan. 1901; quarry site near Indian Creek TO, 8–9 Apr. 1998.

Reference. *Status:* Jones et al. (2000).

Mottled Owl

PLATE 25

Ciccaba virgata

OTHER NAMES. Mottled Wood-Owl (arch.), Screech Owl (C), quarom (K), bouh (M).

Identification. 14″ (35.5 cm). Medium-sized, dull brown owl streaked below, spotted and barred above. Deep brown eyes. *Light morph:* conspicuous whitish eyebrows and "moustache"; sparser, narrower streaking on pale underparts. *Dark morph:* less conspicuous facial markings, more heavily streaked brownish buff underparts.

Voice. 1. Low-pitched, sliding *whOa* or *awhOa,* with middle section strongly emphasized;

2. *wh whhh whoa;*

3. loud, harsh mammal-like wail, dropping in pitch (≈1½ sec).

Habitat. Midlevels to subcanopy within most forested landscapes, including forest edge.

Distribution. Resident from c Sonora and n Tamaulipas to c S.A.

Status in Belize. FC to C resident on mainland; apparently also resident on n Ambergris Caye but absent from other cayes.

Reference. *Voice:* Moore (1992).

Black-and-white Owl   MAP 91; PLATE 25
Ciccaba nigrolineata
OTHER NAMES. Black-and-white
Wood-Owl (arch.).

Identification. 15½″ (39.5 cm). Blackish gray above, white below, with fine black barring throughout; bright orange-yellow bill and feet; deep brown eyes set in dark gray facial disks.
Voice. 1. Low-pitched
ah-ah-ah-ah-ah-ah-ah WHOW [uh].
2. similar, but without accented note at end, much like variant Mottled Owl vocalization.
Habitat. Subcanopy within primary and secondary broadleaf forest.
Distribution. Resident from se San Luis Potosí to nw S.A.
Status in Belize. Distribution poorly known. UC to VU resident in w OW, locally in e OW, foothills of Maya Mtns., including Vaca Plateau s CA, and perhaps elsewhere. Once in Orange Walk Town.

Figure 20

Short-eared Owl

Stygian Owl   MAP 92; PLATE 25
Asio stygius

Identification. 16″ (40.5 cm). Medium-sized, mostly dark owl with yellow eyes. Smaller than Great Horned, with prominent white diamond on forehead, more closely set ear tufts, and prominent dark streaks throughout underparts. Lacks rich buff and cinnamon highlights of Great Horned and has blackish, not orange, facial disks.
Voice. 1. Very soft, brief *who* notes given ≈2–4 sec apart;
2. somewhat louder, higher-pitched *whoo.*
Habitat. Subcanopy within open pine forest.
Distribution. Resident discontinuously from s Sonora and W.I. to sc S.A.
Status in Belize. R resident probably throughout pine belt, but actual localities of record are few: Mtn. Pine Ridge, near Hill Bank OW, c and w BE, and ne TO.
References. *Status:* Howell et al. (1992); Wood and Leberman (1987).

Short-eared Owl   FIGURE 20
Asio flammeus

Identification. 16″ (40.5 cm). Tiny ear tufts, often not visible in the field; yellow eyes surrounded by black eye-patch; fewer bands in the tail (3 or 4) than in Striped (5–7). *Flight:* black greater primary coverts and primary tips isolate pale tawny buff inner primaries; buoyant or bouncy flight with deep wingbeats; forages low over open fields and marshes, where it may be seen at dawn and dusk. Northern Harrier has white uppertail coverts, and both harrier and Striped Owl lack pale tawny wing patch.
Voice. 1. Nasal bark *(wark!);*
2. thin, labored hiss. Usually silent away from breeding grounds.
Habitat. Freshwater and brackish marshes, meadows, fallow fields, estuaries.
Distribution. Nests from Arctic s. to c U.S. and c Eurasia; also resident populations in the n Andes and s S.A. Populations in the N. Hemisphere winter from s Can. to c Mex. and from c Eurasia to c Afr. and s Asia.

Status in Belize. One record: Aqua Mar Shrimp Farm TO, 4 Mar. 1999 (mummified carcass). **Reference.** *Status:* Jones et al. (2000).

Striped Owl   MAP 93; PLATE 25
Pseudoscops clamator
OTHER NAMES. Quarom (K), bouh (M).

Identification. 14″ (35.5 cm). Medium-sized, eared owl; much paler than similar-sized Stygian, with white facial disks outlined in black. Only eared owl in Belize with dark eyes. Prominent ear tufts and pale face distinguish it from vagrant Short-eared. Stripes on underparts lack fine crossbars of Stygian. *Flight:* lacks pale tawny buff wing patch of Short-eared; also, steadier flight, with shallow, rapid wingbeats; not likely to be seen foraging over open fields during daylight.
Voice. 1. Slightly rough *whōō,* dropping slightly at end;
2. much rougher, nasal *whaaa!,* somewhat like short Barn Owl screech;
3. high-pitched squealy *eeeaaah.*
Habitat. Open disturbed areas, marshes, meadows, and savannas with scattered trees.
Distribution. Resident from c Veracruz to sc S.A. Absent from Yucatán Pen.
Status in Belize. UC to locally FC resident e. of Maya Mtns. n. to s BE.

FAMILY: CAPRIMULGIDAE
(Nighthawks and Nightjars)
World: 89. **New World:** 44. **Belize:** 8. Worldwide except Arctic and Antarctica. Caprimulgids are characterized by very short legs; a large, usually flattened head; a tiny exposed bill with an enormous gape surrounded by stiff rictal bristles; large eyes that, unlike those of owls, are placed well back on the sides of the head. They also differ from owls in lacking facial disks; most have a longer tail and long wings that are narrow and pointed in those that forage primarily on the wing, broader and rounded in those that hunt primarily from a perch. These exclusively nocturnal birds can see about twice as well in extremely low light as other birds, including owls. Some, like Common Pauraque, are ground dwellers;

others perch readily in trees, usually facing parallel on a medium to large branch. All are insectivorous, and all are cryptically patterned to enable them to escape detection during daylight hours. **References:** Cleere (1998). *Voice:* Hardy et al. (1989a); Ranft and Cleere (1998).

SUBFAMILY: CHORDEILINAE
(Nighthawks)
Mostly aerial when active, feeding on the wing. Usually seen flying in dawn or evening sky, especially during migration. During the day they roost on the ground or lengthwise on a tree branch, where they are difficult to see because of their cryptic plumage. Short-tailed is rare, but both Common and Lesser can be seen together during migration. Common is a local summer resident; Lesser is a widespread migrant and winter visitor, occasionally remaining to breed. Nighthawk ID can be tricky, and flying and perched birds present a different set of ID challenges.

   Things to note: folded wing vs. tail length, back-scapular contrast, color of throat stripe. *In flight,* pointed vs. slightly rounded wingtips, manner of flight (bounding or batlike), presence/absence and position (between bend of wing and wingtip) of white wing band.

Short-tailed Nighthawk   PLATE 26
Lurocalis semitorquatus
OTHER NAMES. Semi-collared Nighthawk (alt.).

Identification. 8¼″ (21 cm). Very dark, with conspicuous white throat and noticeably shorter tail than the two *Chordeiles.* Also lacks white bar in wing, and flight profile and behavior are quite different. When perched, wings extend well beyond end of tail. *Flight:* very erratic and batlike; typically seen foraging along rivers just before dawn and just after dusk.
Voice. In flight, a sharp, slightly liquid *g'wick* and *whik whik whik* to *whik whik whik whik whik,* and a rougher *gwirrk.*
Habitat. Forest-lined rivers and streams.
Distribution. Resident discontinuously from e Chiapas to sc S.A.

Status in Belize. Three recent sight records: S. Stann Creek, Cockscomb Basin SC, 10 May 1998; S. Water Caye, 8 Sept. 1998; Caye Caulker, 25 Jan. 2000. The two records from cayes suggest that this species may be partially migratory or prone to wander in n. part of its range.
References. *Status:* Jones et al. (2000). *Voice:* Howell and Webb (1995).

Lesser Nighthawk   PLATE 26
Chordeiles acutipennis
OTHER NAMES. Texas Nighthawk (arch.), Trilling Nighthawk (arch.), xpuhuy (K), pou hoi (M).

Identification. 8½" (22 cm). Smaller than Common. Folded wings do not extend beyond tail; back and scapular feathers do not contrast darker than wing coverts. ♂: white band in primaries always visible in folded wings; has white subterminal tail band and white throat stripe. ♀: lacks white tail band; has buffy brown, not white, band across primaries and narrower brown barring across base of primaries; throat stripe buffy, not white. *Flight:* more rounded wingtips than in Common, the result of outermost primary being equal to or shorter than second outermost primary; distinctive white bar across outer wing in ♂ is ⅔ of the way from bend to wingtip and tapers posteriorly; buffy brown bar in ♀ may not be visible in flying bird in poor light or at a distance; typically flies with shallower, more rapid wingbeats; when foraging, generally flies straighter and closer to the ground; flight behavior differences are not absolute and should not be used alone in making an ID.
Voice. *In breeding season:* 1. long, slow trill; or 2. nasal, whining *waa-o-o-o-o-o*. Silent outside the breeding season.
Habitat. During day, perches on ground, usually in the open, or lengthwise on tree branches. Forages aerially at night; can be seen at dawn or dusk over almost any habitat, even urban areas.
Distribution. Nests from sw U.S. to c Mex., discontinuously through C.A., and in n. half of S.A. Northern populations migrate s. in winter.
Status in Belize. C transient and UC winter visi-

tor, early Sept. to mid-May, occas. remaining to breed. Resident locally in CO.
References. *Status:* Barlow et al. (1969). *Identification:* Czaplak and Wilds (1986); Eisenmann (1963).

Common Nighthawk   MAP 94; PLATE 26
Chordeiles minor
OTHER NAMES. Booming Nighthawk (arch.), xpuhuy (K), pou hoi (M).

Identification. 9¼" (23.5 cm). Larger than Lesser. When perched, wingtips extend beyond tip of tail; white bar in primaries usually covered by tertials; dark back and scapular feathers contrast with paler gray wing coverts; throat stripe white. ♂: basal color of belly and undertail coverts white (buffy in Lesser). ♀: like ♂, primary bar is white; belly, undertail coverts, and throat stripe buffy, as in Lesser. *Flight:* flight profile like Lesser's, but wings more pointed (outer primary usually longer than second outermost); greater angle at bend of wing than in Lesser; white bar in wing (♂ and ♀) halfway between bend and tip and broadening posteriorly; inner primaries lack contrasting brown bars of Lesser; typically flies with deeper, more languid wingbeats; when foraging, makes more sharp turns and abrupt mid-air hovering stops than Lesser.
Voice. Emphatic nasal *peeunt!* given frequently at dawn, dusk, and early evening on nesting grounds and during spring migration.
Habitat. During day, perches lengthwise on tree branches. Feeds on the wing at night; best seen at dawn and dusk. Nests on ground and flat gravel roofs of buildings.
Distribution. Nests from nc Can. to Pan.; winters in S.A. e. of the Andes.
Status in Belize. Summer resident, early Apr. to late Oct., in Mtn. Pine Ridge and locally in coastal lowlands (e.g., Hill Bank OW, Belize City, Payne's Creek TO). As a migrant, widespread throughout. Most frequent in autumn along coast and at cayes.
References. *Distribution:* Selander and Alvarez del Toro (1953). *Identification:* Czaplak and Wilds (1986); Eisenmann (1963).

SUBFAMILY: CAPRIMULGINAE
(Nightjars)

Seldom seen nocturnal birds, far more often IDed by their distinctive vocalizations. Unlike nighthawks, never seen in sustained overhead flight. Depending on the species, may be seen perched on the ground or in a low shrub or even on a high tree branch. Occas. encountered during the day as they flush from underfoot and quickly disappear in the forest.

Things to note: vocalizations, face and throat pattern, color of nape, folded wing vs. tail length. *In flight,* pattern and extent of white or buff, if any, in tail; presence/absence of white band in wing.

Common Pauraque   PLATE 26
Nyctidromus albicollis
OTHER NAMES. Pauraque (alt.), White-collared Cuejo (I. Davis), Hoo-yoo (C), pu ju yuk (K), puiyero (M), Tapacamino (S).

Identification. 11½" (29 cm). Easily the most common and widespread of the nightjars in Belize. Large, long-tailed species seen most often in headlight beams on road at night, but occas. in daytime when flushed from underfoot. Plumage variable, ranging from gray to extensively rufous, especially in crown and back. ♂: white bar in primaries and lateral white stripes in tail visible when bird flushes. ♀: thinner, buff-colored wingbar; white in tail reduced to small patch at each corner; because both wing and tail patches are inconspicuous, ♀s flushed at night may appear to be all dark.
Voice. 1. Burry *wh-what* . . . × 4–6, often followed by a burry, explosive *P'WEEOO!* (or less emphatic *p'weull!*);
2. emphatic *wheo* or *wiull,* slightly more drawn out than call of Yucatán Poorwill;
3. clear *hear you.*
Habitat. Ground and low branches at forest edge, second-growth scrub, roadsides.
Distribution. Resident from s Sinaloa and s Texas to sc S.A.
Status in Belize. C resident on mainland and Ambergris Caye. Unrecorded from other cayes.
Reference. *Voice:* Moore (1992).

Yucatan Poorwill   MAP 95; PLATE 26
Nyctiphrynus yucatanicus

Identification. 8¼" (21 cm). Smallest of the group. Warm-brown bird like Chuck-will's-widow, but less mottled or vermiculated and considerably smaller. Tail feathers, except central pair, tipped white. When perched, holds unmarked breast feathers out from body in the fashion of a bib.
Voice. *Song:* soft, burry *will.* Less emphatic than frequently given single note of Common Pauraque.
Habitat. Deciduous and semi-deciduous forest and forest edge. Primarily found in trees.
Distribution. *Yucatán Endemic.* Resident in Yucatán Pen. s. to n Guat. and n Belize.
Status in Belize. UC to locally FC resident s. to c BE and c CA.
References. *Status:* Howell et al. (1992). *Voice:* Pierson (1986).

Chuck-will's-widow   PLATE 26
Caprimulgus carolinensis

Identification. 12" (30.5 cm). Lacks white marks in wings and tail of Common Pauraque. Also darker and richer brown, with dark brown, not rufous, auriculars. *Ad.* ♂: white inner webs to tail feathers (lacking in 1st year ♂s). ♀: lacks white in tail.
Voice. *Song:* soft *chuck* (not audible at a distance) followed immediately by clear, hollow *whido whido.* Most likely to be heard in spring.
Habitat. Branches in low to mid-strata, less often on ground; forest, forest edge, scrub.
Distribution. Nests in se U.S.; winters from s Tamaulipas, s Florida, and W.I. to n S.A.
Status in Belize. Seldom reported except on small cayes and as tower kills in autumn, which indicate that it is an UC or even FC autumn migrant. Apparently much less frequent in winter and spring (Dec. and Apr. records only). Seldom vocalizes while in Belize, making it far more difficult to detect.
Reference. *Status:* Jones et al. (2000).

Yucatan Nightjar

MAP 96; PLATE 26

Caprimulgus badius

OTHER NAMES. Tawny-collared Nightjar (combined form), Salvin's Nightjar (combined form), Yucatán Will (I. Davis), xpuhuy (K).

Identification. 9¾″ (25 cm). Smaller and shorter-tailed than Chuck-will's-widow and Common Pauraque. Conspicuous tawny collar; prominent white spots or flecks on breast; eyeshine green, not red or orange as in other nightjars. ♂: similar to ♂ Whip-poor-will, but shape of white in tail broad and triangular, wrapping around tail corners; from beneath, undertail appears all white. ♀: similar to ♀ Whip-poor-will but browner overall, with more extensive tawny collar; undertail brown and streaked.

Voice. *Song:* clear whistled *toe reo-a-reo,* similar to song of Chuck-will's-widow but with different cadence.

Habitat. Low to mid-strata at forest edge.

Distribution. *Yucatán Endemic.* Nests in Yucatán Pen. s. to n Belize; winters s. occas. to nw Hon.

Status in Belize. Poorly understood: recorded primarily in winter, mid-Oct. to late Apr., but recent summer records from Shipstern CO and New R. OW suggest breeding, at least locally, in north. Locally FC in CO and OW in winter and perhaps elsewhere, with records scattered throughout s. to Punta Gorda and on Ambergris and Half Moon cayes.

References. *Distribution:* England (2000). *Identification:* Howell (1997). *Voice:* Pierson (1986).

Whip-poor-will

PLATE 26

Caprimulgus vociferus

OTHER NAMES. Eastern Whip-poor-will (is part of), Northern Whip-poor-will (is part of).

Identification. 9¼″ (23.5 cm). Similar to Yucatan Nightjar but lacks or nearly lacks tawny collar and lacks conspicuous white spots on breast. ♂: white in tail corners more extensive toward the center of the tail than in outermost feathers. ♀: grayer than Yucatan Nightjar with tawny collar reduced or absent.

Voice. *Call:* soft *prik. Song:* rapidly repeated clear *whip-poor-will,* or, more accurately, *whip!-po-o-whea!*

Habitat. Ground to mid-strata within forest and at forest edge.

Distribution. Nests in e N.A. from s Can. to s U.S. and disjunctively in highlands from sw U.S. to Hon. Winters from n Mex. and Florida s. to w Pan.

Status in Belize. Few confirmed records, all of tower kills and mist-netted birds in Oct. early Nov., and early Mar.; likely more frequent than the few records indicate. Presence in midwinter unknown.

FAMILY: NYCTIBIIDAE (Potoos)

World: 7. **New World:** 7. **Belize:** 1 (plus 1 provisional). Neotropical. Potoos are nocturnal, owl-like aerial feeders with an exceptionally large head and eyes and long wings and tail. As in nightjars, their eyes are placed on the side of the head rather than facing forward. Potoos differ from nightjars in perching upright and having their mouth, eyes, head, wings, and tail even larger relative to body size. They are remarkably well camouflaged during the day, when perched at the end of a branch or post with their head extended upward, eyes closed, and tail pressed against the perch, appearing very much like an extension of their perch. At night, their eyeshine is easily picked up in vehicle headlights or with the aid of a searchlight. **References:** Cleere (1998). *Voice:* Hardy et al. (1989a); Ranft and Cleere (1998).

Things to note: vocalizations, overall size, relative size of head, presence/absence of malar stripe, extent of mottling in plumage, non-reflected (daytime) eye color.

[Great Potoo]

FIGURE 21A

Nyctibius grandis

OTHER NAMES. Grand Potoo (arch.).

Identification. 21″ (53.5 cm). Very pale plumage and nearly immaculate head, with no malar stripe. Much larger than Northern Potoo; however, size can be quite deceptive for a bird in the beam of a searchlight at night. Eye color dark brown (but reflected eyeshine at night bright reddish orange, as in Northern).

Voice. Very rough, hoarse *gwaaaaaaow*, descending at the end.

Habitat. Mid-strata, openings in forest, savannas; not likely to be seen in cleared areas near villages and towns.

Distribution. Resident from e Chiapas and c Guat. to c S.A.

Status in Belize. Several reports, but none confirmed. Most, but perhaps not all, are likely mis-IDed Northern Potoos resulting from confusion with their respective vocalizations.

References. *Distribution:* Rangel-S. and Vega-R. (1991). *Status:* Jones (2002).

Northern Potoo   FIGURE 21B; PLATE 26
Nyctibius jamaicensis
OTHER NAMES. Common Potoo (combined form), Jamaican Potoo (alt.), Six-month Bird (C).

Identification. 16″ (40.5 cm). Much smaller than Great Potoo, with relatively smaller head and more dark markings on head (including prominent malar stripe), breast, and scapulars than Great. Eye color yellow; reflected eyeshine bright reddish orange.

Voice. Rough, hoarse *gwaaaaaaah gwa gwa gwa gwa,* with long note higher-pitched than in Great Potoo and not descending at end. The short series of notes at the end, lacking in Great, are weaker and lower-pitched than the long introductory note and may be inaudible, even at a relatively close range, thus sounding more like Great. The Common Potoo *(Nyctibius griseus),* once thought to be the same species as Northern, and depicted as that in older commercial tape recordings, sounds very different. Northern sounds much more like Great than it does Common.

Habitat. Mid-strata; forest clearings and edge, second growth and other disturbed habitats, rural communities.

Distribution. Resident from s Sinaloa and s Tamaulipas to C.R.; also in Jamaica and Hispaniola.

a   b

Figure 21

Potoos. *(a)* Great Potoo; *(b)* Northern Potoo.

Status in Belize. UC to locally FC resident on mainland; recorded twice from Ambergris Caye, where possibly resident.

Reference. *Status:* Miller and Miller (1992).

FAMILY: APODIDAE
(Swifts)

World: 98. **New World:** 30. **Belize:** 6. Cosmopolitan, absent only from polar regions and high Temperate Zone. Swifts are truly aerial, spending all waking hours in flight, except when at the nest. Their flight is fast and powerful. On clear days, swifts often fly higher than the unaided eye can see. Their remiges are designed for speed, producing a powerful forward force, with only the short secondaries providing lift. Swifts are second only to the Peregrine Falcon in maximum flight speed, and exceed even it in sustained flight. Swifts have a unique manner of flight: unlike other birds, which flap their wings in a horizontal plane, swifts rapidly tilt the plane of their flapping wings counterclockwise, then clockwise. When they are viewed head-on, their flight appears similar to a seesaw in superfast motion. This manner of flight enables swifts, with their long, powerful wings relative to body size, to maintain level flight without their body bobbing strongly up and down with each wing stroke. Despite the small size of their tarsi and feet, they have a strong grip and sharp claws, which, along with stiff tail quills, enable them to perch securely on vertical surfaces. As in nightjars and potoos, their gape is very large and surrounded by rictal bristles to assist in aerial capture of insect prey. Most give high, thin twittering notes in flight. Because swifts are small dark birds typically seen against a bright, pale sky, often in rapid flight, ID can be a real challenge, even under the best of circumstances. **Reference:** Chantler (2000).

Things to note: overall size; shape of tail; manner of flight (flap to glide ratio, rapidity of wingbeats); pattern of white, if any, in plumage; presence/absence of chestnut in plumage.

White-chinned Swift
FIGURE 22D
Cypseloides cryptus
OTHER NAMES. Zimmer's Swift (arch.).

Identification. 5¾″ (14.5 cm). All-dark swift, extremely difficult to ID under all but the most ideal circumstances. Lacks white markings of larger White-collared and smaller Lesser Swallow-tailed and chestnut breast and collar of Chestnut-collared. Does not have slightly paler throat of Chimney or Vaux's and is distinctly larger than either. White edges to tiny chin feathers are all but impossible to see under field conditions. The absence of a useful field character is thus problematical. Unless conditions are ideal (good light, close range, bird seen against a dark background such as a distant hill), claiming a swift to be all dark is at best tentative. And even if it can be determined that the bird is truly all black, the possibility of its being a stray Black Swift *(Cypseloides niger)* cannot be discounted. *Flight:* shorter tail than both Black and Chestnut-collared, but this difference is subtle; has a more fluttery flight than Black Swift, with little or no gliding; both Black and Chestnut-collared glide frequently, often for extended periods (up to several seconds in the former).

Voice. Apparently a hard, buzzy chatter, unlike vocalizations of other swifts in Belize.

Habitat. Aerial.

Distribution. Little-known swift with scattered records from w Mex. to n S.A. Some populations may be migratory.

Status in Belize. One definite record: vicinity of Southern Lagoon BE, 9 Aug. 1931 (4 collected). Also, 14 or more swifts seen at Hidden Valley Falls, Mtn. Pine Ridge, 19 Mar. 1991, were likely this species. Possibly a R but seldom detected resident (summer only?) in c and perhaps s Belize.

References. *Status:* Howell et al. (1992). *Voice:* Howell and Webb (1995).

Chestnut-collared Swift
FIGURE 22C
Streptoprocne rutila

Identification. 5¼″ (13.5 cm). Similar in size and shape to the equally rare White-chinned but has

Figure 22

Swifts. White-collared Swift, *(a)* juvenile and *(b)* adult; *(c)* Chestnut-collared Swift; *(d)* White-chinned Swift; *(e)* Lesser Swallow-tailed Swift; *(f)* Chimney Swift; *(g)* Vaux's Swift.

deep chestnut breast and collar. *Flight:* most like that of Chimney, but with more gliding and tail spreading, a trait not typical of White-chinned.
Voice. Buzzy crackling chatter: *zzchi zzchi zzchi . . .* with occas. screechy notes; similar to the crackling noise of high-voltage electric power lines.
Habitat. Aerial.
Distribution. Resident from s Durango and Sinaloa s. of Yucatán Pen. to c Andes.
Status in Belize. Two records: Cockscomb Basin Wildlife Sanctuary SC, 15 Mar. 1993 (4 with Vaux's Swifts); Monkey Bay BE, 22 Mar. 1996.
References. *Status:* Vallely and Aversa (1997). *Voice:* Howell and Webb (1995).

White-collared Swift

MAP 97; FIGURE 22A,B
Streptoprocne zonaris
OTHER NAMES. Kusal (M).

Identification. 8¼″ (21 cm). Largest swift in Belize. Tail clearly notched; wings long and relatively broad. White collar not always easy to see in fast-flying birds and does not extend across breast in young birds, thus resulting in potential confusion with even larger, broader-winged White-naped Swift *(Streptoprocne semicollaris),* a w Mex. endemic. White-naped has square-tipped tail, but tail of White-collared may also appear square-tipped when spread. *Flight:* fast and powerful compared with flight of other Belize swifts; often glides for long periods (many seconds).
Voice. Thin, wiry *peep peep peep . . .* or *seep seep seep . . . ;* somewhat like begging sounds of a small nestling. Flocks of birds make a whooshing sound as they race past in tight formation at high speed.
Habitat. Aerial; found over most landscapes but primarily near or over forested areas.
Distribution. Resident from s Tamaulipas, Guerrero, and W.I. through C.A. s. of Yucatán Pen. and discontinuously to sc S.A.
Status in Belize. UC to C resident n. regularly to s OW and c BE, occas. to c OW and n BE. Most common in interior; unrecorded from cayes.

References. *Identification:* Howell (1993a); Semo and Booher (2002).

Genus: Chaetura

Chimney and Vaux's swifts represent a classic ID challenge, compounded by the fact that resident Vaux's has darker throat and breast than migrant N.A. birds—as dark as those of many Chimney Swifts.
Things to note: overall size, wing-to-body length, flap-to-glide ratio.

Chimney Swift   FIGURE 22F
Chaetura pelagica

Identification. 4¾″ (12 cm). Larger than Vaux's, with darker rump (no back-rump contrast). Seldom seen together, so relative size by itself is not especially useful; but, as result of size difference, body proportions and flight characteristics differ. Chimney is Cliff Swallow size and has proportionately longer wings than Vaux's. *Flight:* glides rather frequently, with wings noticeably drooped below horizontal.
Voice. Usually silent in migration. May occas. give liquid twittering notes in spring, which are louder and not as thin as in Vaux's.
Habitat. Migrates and forages over most habitats; however, unlike resident Vaux's, not likely to be seen flying low over forested streams or circling over forest clearings.
Distribution. Nests in e N.A. from s Can. to Gulf of Mex.; winters in w S.A.
Status in Belize. FC autumn transient, late Sept. to early Nov., mostly along or near coast, less often above ridgelines in interior; status in spring less clear but apparently an UC transient, late Mar. to late Apr. Occas. recorded at cayes.
Reference. *Identification:* Devillers (1970).

Vaux's Swift   FIGURE 22G
Chaetura vauxi
OTHER NAMES. Dusky-backed Swift (arch.), kusal (M).

Identification. 4¼″ (11 cm). Smaller than Chimney, with paler rump contrasting with darker back and wings. Noticeably smaller than Cliff Swallow and with proportionately shorter wings than Chimney Swift. *Flight:* more hurried, faster, slightly stiffer wingbeats, pausing only briefly for short glides.

Voice. Thin, high-pitched twitter without thin shrill notes of Lesser Swallow-tailed; faster, more run-together, and higher-pitched than in Chimney Swift.

Habitat. Aerial; mostly over forested and semi-forested areas as well as both small and large clearings, including expansive agricultural areas, but generally away from coastal plain.

Distribution. Nests in w N.A. from se Alaska to c Calif., and from Durango and s Tamaulipas to Venezuela. N.A. population winters from Mex. to Hon.; C.A. population is sedentary.

Status in Belize. FC to C resident in interior, less C near coast; unrecorded from cayes. Migrant subspecies from N.A. *(C. v. vauxi),* with paler throat and breast, has not been documented in Belize.

Reference. *General:* Bull and Collins (1993).

Lesser Swallow-tailed Swift

MAP 98; FIGURE 22E

Panyptila cayennensis

OTHER NAMES. Cayenne Swift (arch.).

Identification. 5¼″ (13.5 cm). Small and slim, with white throat and breast. Often mistaken for similarly patterned White-throated Swift *(Aeronautes saxatalis),* a resident species in N.A. and the highlands of Mex. and n C.A. White-throated has white throat extending as broad line through belly nearly to undertail coverts. In Lesser Swallow-tailed, white stops abruptly at upper breast. Both have white patch on flanks, but patch is more extensive in White-throated. *Flight:* long, thin, swept-back wings and slim, needlelike tail (tail is actually forked, but typically held with the feathers pressed close together).

Voice. High-pitched, thin twitter; sweeter and shriller than in Vaux's.

Habitat. Aerial; may be seen over most landscapes, but usually near or over forests.

Distribution. Resident from c Veracruz s. of Yucatán Pen. to c S.A.

Status in Belize. FC resident n. locally to n OW

and n BE, occas. n. to CO. Unrecorded from cayes.

FAMILY: TROCHILIDAE
(Hummingbirds)

World: 335. **New World:** 335. **Belize:** 22 (plus 1 provisional). Primarily Neotropical, but with a few species found as far north as s Alaska and Can. and as far south as Tierra del Fuego. Hummingbirds constitute a large and diverse family, second only to tyrant flycatchers in total number of species. Like swifts, they have elongated outer wings and tiny tarsi; otherwise they are like no other birds in the world. The Bee Hummingbird *(Mellisuga helenae)* is the world's smallest bird, weighing only 1.6 g. Hummingbirds flap their wings faster than any other bird —up to an incredible 200 times/sec in courtship flights of some smaller species. They are the only birds that can fly backward. They also rank among the world's most colorful birds, with their array of neon-bright iridescent greens, reds, and purples. All are highly adapted nectivorous feeders, with a tubular, sucking tongue, and many have a bill that closely matches in length and shape the corolla tube of the flower type most often visited. All supplement their diet with protein-rich insects, which they capture either by hawking or gleaning. **References:** Howell (2001); Johnsgard (1997); Williamson (2001).

SUBFAMILY: PHAETHORNITHINAE
(Hermits)

Characterized by their greatly reduced number of iridescent feathers, pendent nests, and tendency not to hold a territory. Most have a long, curved bill, a striped face, and graduated tail feathers, sometimes with the central pair extended. Some species form leks where ♂s gather to sing. Males have complex songs and pump their tail vigorously while singing and hovering. Wing whir while hovering is louder than in most other hummingbirds. Hermits are inquisitive birds, often flying directly up to human "intruders" to investigate.

Things to note: overall size, color of breast and throat, tail pattern, length of central tail feathers.

Band-tailed Barbthroat   MAP 99; PLATE 27

Threnetes ruckeri

OTHER NAMES. Rucker's Hermit (I. Davis).

Identification. 4½″ (11.5 cm). Rufous breast; broad white band at both base and tip of its wedge-shaped tail; blackish throat outlined in white.
Voice. *Call: swick!,* lower-pitched and buzzier than in hermits. *Song:* high-pitched, with 1st part buzzy, 2nd part squeaky; repeated.
Habitat. Lower strata within broadleaf forest and forest edge.
Distribution. Resident primarily on Caribbean slope from s Belize to nw S.A.
Status in Belize. UC resident in interior lowlands and foothills of TO and SC n. to Cockscomb Basin; absent from higher elevations.
References. *Distribution:* Land and Kiff (1965). *Status:* Howell et al. (1992); Wood and Leberman (1987). *Voice:* Howell and Webb (1995).

Long-billed Hermit   MAP 100; PLATE 27

Phaethornis longirostris

OTHER NAMES. Long-tailed Hermit (combined form), Western Long-tailed Hermit (alt.), tz'unun (K), tzunon (M).

Identification. 6½″ (16.5 cm). Large hummingbird with long, white, extended central tail feathers and long, decurved bill. Black-and-white-striped face; cinnamon rump and uppertail coverts.
Voice. *Call:* 1. *sweeup* (louder, more emphatic than Stripe-throated's), typically given in rapid flight;
2. *sweea sweea chuchuchu,* typically given during chases;
3. soft *chp* while feeding. *Song* (given in leks): coarse or raspy *squee,* repeated incessantly.
Habitat. Broadleaf forest edge and clearings; second-growth scrub.
Distribution. Resident from Nayarit and c Veracruz s. of Yucatán Pen. to nw S.A.
Status in Belize. C resident n. to c OW and nc BE; unrecorded from cayes.

Stripe-throated Hermit   PLATE 27

Phaethornis striigularis

OTHER NAMES. Little Hermit (combined form), Boucard's Hermit (arch.), tz'unun (K), tzunon (M).

Identification. 3¾″ (9.5 cm). Readily told from other hermits by its small size, cinnamon underparts, and pointed tail with only slight extension of central tail feathers; tail feather tips pale cinnamon, not white. In courtship display, hovers with tail cocked and spread wide, bill pointed skyward, periodically pivoting abruptly 180°, wings producing loud hornetlike buzzing.
Voice. *Call:* 1. *swea* (softer than in Long-billed), typically given in rapid flight;
2. soft *chp* given while feeding. *Song* (usually given in leks): high-pitched insectlike squeaks (like squeaky Orange-billed Sparrow song but more rhythmic).
Habitat. Lower levels within broadleaf forest and forest edge, clearings, second-growth scrub.
Distribution. Resident primarily on Gulf-Caribbean slope from c Veracruz s. of Yucatán Pen. to nw S.A.
Status in Belize. C resident, progressively less C farther n. and perhaps absent from most of CO; unrecorded from cayes.
Reference. *Voice:* Moore (1992).

SUBFAMILY: TROCHILINAE
(Typical Hummingbirds)

Highly diverse group comprising 90% of the family. Most have iridescent feathers on at least a portion of their body and build nests supported beneath by a branch or leaf. Both ♂s and ♀s vigorously defend foraging territories, and ♂s do not form leks. Most hummingbirds have a large and often confusing vocal repertoire, although specific elements of their songs and calls are rather simple. Both sexes give simple one- to several-note calls. Longer series of notes uttered in rapid succession are given during aggressive encounters, usually chases. Many also have an advertising song given by the ♂ only. These are typically an uneven series of high and low notes emitted in an uneven or rhythmic cadence. Songs are given from an exposed perch, and whether a simple one-note "song" (Brown Violet-ear) or a complex sputtering (Wedge-tailed Sabrewing), they are usually repeated over and over, often for many minutes at a time.

Things to note: overall size; bill length, color, and curvature, if any; color of throat and crown; presence/absence of white spot or stripe behind eye; tail shape; presence/absence and pattern of white in tail.

Scaly-breasted Hummingbird

MAP 101; PLATE 28

Phaeochroa cuvierii

OTHER NAMES. Cuvier's Hummingbird (arch.), tz'unun (K), tzunon (M).

Identification. 4¾″ (12 cm). Rather non-descript, medium-sized, green hummingbird with straight black bill, tiny white postocular spot, conspicuous white tail corners, and dusky cinnamon belly. Greenish throat and breast appear mottled or scaled, but this character is subtle and not always apparent.

Voice. *Call:* metallic *tik* or *tink,* like weak Blue Grosbeak call. *Song:* dry, high-pitched series of well-separated notes; for example, *spit spit spee see spit see . . . ,* and *sweet sweet sweet what chip chip what sweet chip swee . . . ,* etc.; louder, with more distinctly separated notes than in other hummers (e.g., White-bellied Emerald).

Habitat. Midlevel strata at broadleaf forest edge, clearings.

Distribution. Resident from n Guat. and s Belize primarily on Caribbean slope to n Colombia.

Status in Belize. UC to FC resident away from coast n. to c OW and w BE.

Reference. *Voice:* Moore (1992).

Wedge-tailed Sabrewing

MAP 102; PLATE 27

Campylopterus curvipennis

OTHER NAMES. Tuxtla Sabrewing (arch.), tz'unun (K), tzunon (M).

Identification. 5″ (12.5 cm). Medium-sized, with slightly decurved bill; broad, pointed tail; plain pale gray underparts; and small white postocular

spot. In direct sunlight, forecrown glistens violet. ♂: tail distinctly wedge-shaped; lacks white tip. ♀ *and imm.:* tail feathers tipped white, and tail less wedge-shaped; imms. of both sexes have duller crown and cinnamon-washed underparts.

Voice. *Call:* metallic *kip* or *chip* notes, given singly or in an irregular series reminiscent of Red Crossbill. *Song:* rich, euphonia-like sputtery warble—a thin, rapid jumble of chips and sputters.

Habitat. Low to mid-strata in broadleaf and submontane pine forest clearings and edge.

Distribution. Resident in mtns. from s Tamaulipas to n Oaxaca and on Yucatán Pen.

Status in Belize. Distribution complex and discontinuous; UC to C resident locally in interior throughout much of country, but ranges to coast in CO.

Reference. *Status:* Wood and Leberman (1987).

Violet Sabrewing

MAP 103; PLATE 27

Campylopterus hemileucurus

OTHER NAMES. DeLattre Sabrewing (arch.), tz'unun (K), tzunon (M).

Identification. 5¾″ (14.5 cm). Unmistakable in any plumage. Strong sexual dimorphism. ♂: vivid deep violet nearly throughout (appears black in the shade), with prominent white tail corners and small white postocular spot. ♀: blue violet only on throat, but its large size, downcurved bill, and large flashes of white in tail distinguish it.

Voice. 1. High-pitched, sharp chipping, sometimes run into a rattle;

2. in flight, single hard *chip. Song:* repetitious *swit* notes plus an occas. *spi-dee,* possibly by a second bird.

Habitat. Low to mid-strata in broadleaf forest; especially common near streams.

Distribution. Resident from Guerrero and c Veracruz s. of Yucatán Pen. to w Pan.

Status in Belize. UC to FC resident in Maya Mtns. and foothills of TO, CA, and SC; UC and local in Mtn. Pine Ridge. Most plentiful at higher elevations.

White-necked Jacobin   MAP 104; PLATE 27

Florisuga mellivora

OTHER NAMES. Tz'unun (K), tzunon (M).

Identification. 4½" (11.5 cm). ♂ *and some ♀s:* unmistakable; head, throat, and breast violet blue; white lower nape; white tail (mostly concealed in perched birds by elongated green uppertail coverts). *Other ♀s and imm.:* similar to Scaly-breasted Hummingbird but lack white postocular spot and are strongly scalloped with dusky green to violet beneath (much more so than Scaly-breasted).

Voice. *Call:* 1. squeaky *chimp,* not unlike call of Wilson's Warbler;

2. insect-like *tk.*

Habitat. Midlevels to subcanopy at broadleaf forest edge and clearings; frequently seen hovering over wooded streams and ponds.

Distribution. Resident from c Veracruz s. of Yucatán Pen. to c S.A.

Status in Belize. FC resident n. to c OW and nc BE. Unrecorded from cayes.

Brown Violet-ear   MAP 105; PLATE 27

Colibri delphinae

Identification. 4¼" (11 cm). Unlike most hummingbirds, has predominantly gray-and-brown plumage. Broad violet postocular stripe (appears black in the shade), bordered below by pale dusky malar stripe and iridescent green throat. Tail broad, square-tipped, and bronzy green, with black subterminal band; uppertail coverts strongly accentuated with cinnamon; bill short and straight.

Voice. *Call:* 1. short dry *chip;*

2. slurred *tsip;*

3. dry rattling chatter. *Song:* short series of sharp, liquid *swit* notes, repeated incessantly.

Habitat. Mid-strata in tropical moist broadleaf forest, mostly in uplands.

Distribution. Resident on Caribbean slope from s Belize to n and w S.A.

Status in Belize. UC and local resident in Maya Mtns.; lowland records from near Southern Lagoon BE on 28 July 1905 and Hill Bank

OW on 25 Nov. 1956 suggest that this species is prone to wander seasonally.

Reference. *Voice:* Stiles and Skutch (1989).

Green-breasted Mango   PLATE 27

Anthracothorax prevostii

OTHER NAMES. Prevost's Mango (arch.), tz'unun (K), tzunon (M).

Identification. 4¾" (12 cm). Medium-sized hummingbird, iridescent green with deep purplish black tail and fairly long downcurved bill. ♂: black throat outlined in iridescent blue green, which extends as a line down center of breast to belly. ♀: differs in having white-tipped tail and deep blue-green stripe along the median line of its otherwise mostly white underparts from bill to vent. *Imm.:* much like ♀ but with cinnamon flecks along sides of throat and breast.

Voice. *Call:* 1. *tsip;*

2. thin *see;*

3. repetitive *ship ship ship . . .* to *chip chip chip . . . . Chase call:* shrill squeaky twitter. *Song:* thin buzzy, rhythmic *zizick-zizee zizick-zizee zizick-zizee . . . .*

Habitat. Midlevels to subcanopy within littoral forest, second-growth scrub, broadleaf forest edge, cultivated areas, towns, and villages.

Distribution. Resident from s Tamaulipas and s Guerrero to n Venezuela and Peru.

Status in Belize. C resident on many cayes; less C on mainland coast, where may be seasonally absent in some areas. UC and local inland, and scarce in much of w OW and nw CA.

Black-crested Coquette

MAP 106; PLATE 28

Lophornis helenae

OTHER NAMES. Helena's Coquette (I. Davis).

Identification. 2¾" (7 cm). Tiny, with short, straight, needlelike red bill with black tip. Conspicuous white band across rump; green spots on undersides. *Ad. ♂:* long, showy crown and gorget plumes; glittering green throat. *Imm. ♂:* plumes shorter, throat white. ♀: lacks crown and gorget plumes; throat pale, with dark flecks;

contrasting blackish auriculars. The remarkably similar, but distinctly smaller, diurnal bumble-bee moth (*Aellopos* spp.) shares the coquette's diagnostic white rump band, and when it is nectaring, its protruded tongue can be mistaken for a hummingbird's bill.

Voice. Generally silent. *Call:* 1. slightly metallic *teek* when feeding;

2. chase call a high-pitched twittering. *Song?:* clear, upward *tsuweee.*

Habitat. Low to mid-strata at broadleaf forest edge and clearings.

Distribution. Resident primarily on Gulf-Caribbean slope from c Veracruz s. of Yucatán Pen. to C.R.

Status in Belize. R to UC resident in w TO and s CA; recorded twice on Placencia Peninsula SC.

Reference. *Voice:* Howell and Webb (1995).

Canivet's Emerald   MAP 107; PLATE 28

Chlorostilbon canivetii

OTHER NAMES. Fork-tailed Emerald (combined form), Blue-tailed Emerald (combined form), tz'unun (K), tzunon (M).

Identification. 3½" (9 cm). ♂: glittering green plumage and deeply forked black tail. ♀: tail un-forked with white feather tips; similar to Ruby-throated, but with white also toward the base of the outermost rectrices; white postocular stripe.

Voice. *Call:* 1. short, dry *bzzzt;*

2. short, harsh, dry rattle.

Habitat. Low levels in deciduous and semi-deciduous forest edge, second-growth scrub, savannas, cultivated areas.

Distribution. Resident from s Tamaulipas to n Guat. and Belize.

Status in Belize. UC to C resident of lowlands s. to c CA and ne TO, occas. s. to Punta Gorda; absent from Maya Mtns. FC on Amber-gris Caye; recorded once on Caye Caulker.

Reference. *Status and systematics:* Howell (1993b).

Violet-crowned Woodnymph

MAP 108; PLATE 27

Thalurania colombica

OTHER NAMES. Purple-crowned Woodnymph (alt.), Crowned Woodnymph (alt.), Common Woodnymph (combined form), Colombian Woodnymph (I. Davis).

Identification. 4¼" (10.5 cm). ♂: brilliant green gorget, violet-blue forecrown and upper back, deep blue-black forked tail. ♀: all-dark tail with white at corners; lacks white postocular mark; has slightly decurved bill and green flanks.

Voice. Dry, hard, rattling chips, sometimes running into chatters.

Habitat. Tropical moist broadleaf forest.

Distribution. Resident on Caribbean slope from s Belize and e Guat. to nw S.A.

Status in Belize. UC and local resident in w and c TO; most records are from Bladen Reserve and Columbia River Forest Reserve. Recorded once at Douglas da Silva, Mtn. Pine Ridge.

References. *Status:* Wood and Leberman (1987). *Systematics:* Escalante-Pliego and Peterson (1992). *Voice:* Howell and Webb (1995).

Blue-throated Goldentail   PLATE 28

Hylocharis eliciae

OTHER NAMES. Blue-throated Sapphire (alt.), Elicia's Goldentail (arch.).

Identification. 3¼" (8.5 cm). Bright golden tail, red bill. ♂: blue-violet throat. ♀: blue-speckled throat; less red on bill. Superficially resembles Rufous-tailed Hummingbird, but Rufous-tailed is larger, with green throat and rufous tail.

Voice. *Chase call:* high-pitched squeaky chippering. *Song* (given only during the dry season): piercing *tseee* followed by an alternating series of single and double notes or short trills and short pauses: *tseee sa se sa se sasese seet twosip twosip twosip,* etc.

Habitat. Forest edge, cultivated areas.

Distribution. Resident from c Veracruz and c Guat. to n Colombia.

Status in Belize. Two records: near Beaver Dam Creek CA, 19 Apr. 1987; and near San Pedro Columbia TO, 3 Apr. 1994. Possibly a scarce resident.

References. *Status:* Mills and Rogers (1988); Vallely and Aversa (1997). *Voice:* Howell and Webb (1995); Stiles and Skutch (1989).

White-bellied Emerald   PLATE 28

Amazilia candida

OTHER NAMES. Tz'unun (K), tzunon (M).

Identification. 3½″ (9 cm). Somewhat resembles other hummingbirds with white underparts; however, combination of black-and-red bill and square-tipped, gray-green tail distinguish it. Although tail has dark subterminal band and paler corners, it lacks prominent black-and-white markings of similar ♀ Ruby-throated Hummingbird and Canivet's Emerald, and the prominent postocular stripe of the latter. Also has green, not dusky, auriculars.

Voice. *Contact call:* fairly high-pitched *thip. Chase calls:* 1. very dry rattly *d-d-d-d-d-d-t* repeated frequently;
2. rapid twitter, more metallic than in Rufous-tailed.
Song: 1. *chibit chibit chee chee . . . ,* repeated (quality of nestling songbird);
2. very high-pitched, thin *ch-bet seet seet . . . ,* repeated;
3. *t-whee sŭwee . . . ,* repeated; etc.

Habitat. Most strata within broadleaf forest and forest edge.

Distribution. Resident from se San Luis Potosí to n Nic.

Status in Belize. UC to C resident on mainland.

Reference. *Voice:* Moore (1992).

Azure-crowned Hummingbird

MAP 109; PLATE 28

Amazilia cyanocephala

OTHER NAMES. Red-billed Azurecrown (arch.).

Identification. 4¼″ (11 cm). Similar to but larger than White-bellied Emerald, with blue crown (nearly lacking in imm.), more red in bill, dusky sides, and plain brownish tail.

Voice. *Call:* 1. harsh *zeup* to *zeep,* repeated;
2. twitter or dry chatter;
3. soft *tup* while feeding.

Habitat. Midlevels to subcanopy in pine wood-land and savanna, broadleaf forest, and forest edge from sea level to highest elevations in Mtn. Pine Ridge and Maya Mtns.

Distribution. Resident from s Tamaulipas s. of Yucatán Pen. to n Nic.

Status in Belize. UC to C resident in a broad wedge across Belize from c BE and c TO s.w. and w. to s CA and w TO. Also in ec OW. Absent from CO, most of OW, n CA, s TO, and cayes. Although found in a wide variety of habitats and elevations within this zone, it is absent from these same habitats in areas outside this zone. Clearly, something other than macrohabitat or elevation is the limiting factor in its distribution.

Rufous-tailed Hummingbird   PLATE 28

Amazilia tzacatl

OTHER NAMES. Rieffer's Hummingbird (arch.), tz'unun (K), tzunon (M).

Identification. 4¼″ (11 cm). Belize's most common and widespread hummer. Mostly iridescent green, with deep rufous tail, dark cinnamon-rufous undertail coverts, white leg tufts, and black-tipped red bill. ♂: brilliantly iridescent green throat and breast, dull grayish cinnamon belly. ♀: less red in bill, less green iridescence on throat and breast, and paler belly.

Voice. *Contact call:* harsh *thek,* singly or repeated incessantly at ≈3/sec. *Chase call:* rapid, sharp, staccato to musical twitter, usually dropping in pitch at end (e.g., *tseee tseee tseee see seeseeseesee*). *Other calls:* 1. thin, high-pitched, almost liquid trill *t-t-tsee-ee-ee-ee-ee-ee-ee* (8–10 notes/sec), often dropping in pitch or tapering off at end;
2. thin *eeeeeea. Song* (given mostly very early in morning): long irregular series, *sip sip see see sip see me slip see me . . . .*

Habitat. Low to mid-strata. Nearly ubiquitous, but absent in interior of extensively forested areas.

Distribution. Resident primarily on Gulf-Caribbean slope from c Veracruz and nc Yucatán Pen. to nw S.A.

Status in Belize. C to VC resident nearly throughout, but UC to scarce at higher elevations in Maya Mtns. and outnumbered by Buff-bellied in CO. Recorded occas. from Ambergris

Caye and Caye Caulker, where apparently not resident.

Reference. *Voice:* Moore (1992).

Buff-bellied Hummingbird

MAP 110; PLATE 28

Amazilia yucatanensis

OTHER NAMES. Fawn-breasted Hummingbird (arch.), Yucatán Hummingbird (arch.).

Identification. 4″ (10 cm). Similar to Rufous-tailed, but with brighter cinnamon belly and undertail (little contrast between belly and undertail coverts); tail is mostly green distally. ♀: similar to ♂ but with less red in bill.
Voice. *Call:* 1. grating *dzik,* much harsher than that of Rufous-tailed.
2. fairly hard chips, sometimes run into a rattle.
Habitat. Low to mid-strata in pinelands, arid scrub, and open second growth; absent from areas with high annual rainfall and dense forest.
Distribution. Resident on Gulf-Caribbean slope from s Texas to n Guat. and Belize.
Status in Belize. C resident in CO; progressively less C w. and s. to sw OW, ne CA, and se SC. Unrecorded from TO and cayes.
Reference. *Status:* Wood and Leberman (1987).

Cinnamon Hummingbird

MAP 111; PLATE 28

Amazilia rutila

Identification. 4¼″ (11 cm). Readily distinguished from other hummingbirds by its rich cinnamon underparts. Tail mostly rufous. ♀: less red in bill.
Voice. *Call:* 1. harsh *chit* to *jit* to *j-dit,* often strung together in irregular series, much drier than in Rufous-tailed;
2. sharp *thk* notes in irregular rhythm;
3. high-pitched, clear *peep,* repeated incessantly. *Chase call:* high-pitched, thin *seet seet seet-seet-seet . . . ,* usually speeding up, sometimes close to a trill. *Song:* shrill *see see see see see.*
Habitat. Low to mid-strata in littoral forest and forest edge, mangroves, cultivated areas.
Distribution. Resident from c Sinaloa and n Yucatán Pen. to C.R.

Status in Belize. C resident on many cayes, and on mainland coast s. to c TO. North of s BE recorded inland in e OW and most of CO.

Stripe-tailed Hummingbird

MAP 112; PLATE 28

Eupherusa eximia

Identification. 3¾″ (9.5 cm). Small hummingbird with all-black bill, rufous panel in secondaries, and white inner webs of outer two tail feathers. From above, white visible only in spread tail; from below, white predominates, even in folded tail. ♂: glittering green below. ♀: pale gray below with more extensive white in tail.
Voice. *Call:* 1. sharp, rolled *d-d-d-d-t d-d-t* while foraging;
2. rapid, dry twitter (chase call?). *Song:* slow, dry, insectlike trill.
Habitat. Midlevels within interior of submontane tropical moist broadleaf forest.
Distribution. Resident mostly in highlands from c Veracruz and n Oaxaca to w Pan.
Status in Belize. C to VC resident at higher elevations in Maya Mtns.; less C and local in foothills.
References. *Status:* Howell et al. (1992); Wood and Leberman (1987).

Purple-crowned Fairy   MAP 113; PLATE 27

Heliothryx barroti

OTHER NAMES. Barrot's Fairy (arch.), tz'unun (K), tzunon (M).

Identification. 5″ (12.5 cm). Not likely to be mistaken for any other hummingbird. Even in silhouette it has a unique shape with its long, tapered tail and medium-length, arrow-straight bill. Gleaming white below from throat to tail tip; black mask. *Ad.* ♂: iridescent violet forecrown and ear spot. ♀: noticeably longer tail than ♂; lacks violet. *Imm.:* cinnamon highlights on upperparts; sparsely spotted on throat.
Voice. Generally silent. *Call:* 1. loud squeak;
2. thin, dry, slightly metallic *tssit;*
3. rapid series of high-pitched *tsit* notes.
Habitat. Mid- to upper strata within broadleaf forest and forest edge.

Distribution. Resident from e Chiapas, n Guat., and Belize to w S.A.

Status in Belize. UC to FC resident n. to c CA and w SC; also in w and c OW; absent from coastal areas n. of s TO. Recorded once on Caye Caulker, 15 Aug. 1999.

Long-billed Starthroat   FIGURE 23
Heliomaster longirostris

Identification. 4¾″ (12 cm). Easily distinguished from other Belizean hummingbirds by its long, straight bill (nearly twice the length of its head), bold white malar stripe, and small white postocular spot on an otherwise dark head, white tufts on flanks that usually project above the folded wings, and white central rump patch. *Ad. ♂ and some ♀s:* iridescent turquoise-blue forecrown and rose-pink throat.

Voice. Sharp *pik* or *peek.*

Habitat. Forest edge and clearings, plantations.

Distribution. Resident from Guerrero and c Veracruz s. of Yucatán Pen. to c S.A.

Status in Belize. Three records: Beaver Dam e CA, 21 Sept. 1999; Big Falls TO, 29 July 2000; 7 mi. (11 km) s. of La Democracia BE, 24 May 2001 (two individuals).

Reference. *Status:* Jones et al. (2002).

[Sparkling-tailed Hummingbird]
NOT ILLUSTRATED
    Tilmatura dupontii
    OTHER NAMES. Sparkling-tailed Woodstar (alt.), Dupont's Hummingbird (alt.).

Identification. ♂ 3¾″ (9.5 cm), ♀ 2¾″ (7 cm). Small hummingbird, green above, with short, straight bill and prominent white slash on sides of lower rump. *Ad. ♂:* very long, deeply forked tail with prominent white spots, iridescent blue to blue-violet throat set off by white upper breast. *Imm. ♂:* some similar to ad. ♂ but with shorter tail, blue and green flecks in otherwise white throat; others resemble ♀ except for green mottling on underparts, white tail corners. *♀:* cinnamon underparts, including throat and auriculars; short, square-tipped tail with creamy-white tail corners; small white postocular spot.

Voice. Usually silent.

Figure 23

Long-billed Starthroat

Habitat. Lower strata to subcanopy in humid to semiarid broadleaf forest and forest edge, second-growth woodland, and scrub.

Distribution. Resident in mtns. and foothills (seasonally to near sea level) from c Sinaloa and c Veracruz s. to c Nic.

Status in Belize. A ♂ was closely studied near Tres Leguas OW on 23 Feb. 2002. Most, but not all, field marks were adequately described.

Ruby-throated Hummingbird   PLATE 28
Archilochus colubris

Identification. 3½″ (9 cm). Small hummingbird with medium-length, straight, all-black bill. ♂: brilliant red gorget set off by gleaming white upper breast; deeply notched black tail. ♀: similar to Canivet's Emerald but tail mostly green, bordered by black distally and white in tail corners only; small white postocular spot; whiter lower underparts.

Voice. Squeaky *chup* and *chup-chup* notes; squeaky twitter in chases, usually with introductory high note followed by lower notes.

Habitat. Most strata; forest edge and clearings, second-growth scrub, landscaped yards in towns and villages.

Distribution. Nests in e N.A. from s Can. to the Gulf of Mex.; winters from s Sinaloa to C.R.

Status in Belize. UC autumn transient and winter visitor and FC spring transient, early Oct. to late Apr.

Reference. *General:* Robinson et al. (1996).

FAMILY: TROGONIDAE
(Trogons)

World: 39. **New World:** 25. **Belize:** 4. Nearly pantropical, with representatives in C.A. and S.A., Afr., and s and se Asia. Trogons are characterized by soft, dense, brightly colored plumage (most with either red or yellow underparts); short legs and neck; a short, thick bill with a strongly curved culmen; strongly arched, rounded wings; a moderately long, graduated, square-tipped tail; and two toes directed backward. They perch upright and remain motionless, with their tail pointed directly downward. Typical vocalizations are simple notes given singly or in a short to moderately long series. They feed by hover-gleaning fruits, insects, and small vertebrates from branch and leaf tips. **References:** Johnsgard (2000). *Voice:* Hardy et al. (1987b); Moore (1992).

Things to note: color of belly, bill, and eye-ring; pattern of black and white on under tail.

Black-headed Trogon   PLATE 29
Trogon melanocephalus
OTHER NAMES. Citreoline Trogon (combined form), Ramatutu (C), k'an i kok (K), ko'ko' (M), Peche Amarillo (S).

Identification. 10¾" (27.5 cm). Yellow underparts, powder-blue eye-ring (both sexes), unmarked wings, graduated tail feathers broadly tipped white (visible on underside only). ♂: black head and breast, blue-green back, bluish violet rump. ♀: uniformly dark gray above and on breast; less extensive white tips to undertail feathers. *Imm.:* like ♀ but with black-and-white barring at the base of the outermost tail feathers.
Voice. *Call:* 1. *chonk* to *tonk;*
2. rolling, guttural *brrrrret,* sometimes followed by series of *chonk* notes. *Song:* rapid, somewhat liquid *cuh-cuh-cuh . . . × 10–20;* starts slowly, gradually speeding up and rising in pitch.
Habitat. Midlevels to subcanopy in broadleaf and, to a lesser extent, pine forest, forest edge, and broken forest with scrub; seldom found in extensive tracts of primary forest. Most likely trogon in open, patchy forest and scrub, urban edge.

Distribution. Resident from c Veracruz to nw C.R.
Status in Belize. C resident on mainland; UC (resident) on Ambergris Caye; occas. in winter on Caye Caulker.

Violaceous Trogon   PLATE 29
Trogon violaceus
OTHER NAMES. Gartered Trogon (I. Davis), Ramatutu (C), k'an i kok (K), ko'ko' (M), Peche Amarillo (S).

Identification. 9¾" (25 cm). Smaller, shorter-tailed trogon than Black-headed, a useful key to its ID, even in flight. Yellow underparts; graduated tail feathers narrowly barred black and white, with less extensive white tips than in Black-headed. ♂: incomplete or split yellow eye-ring; green back and rump, black head with violet highlights; peppered black-and-white wing coverts. ♀: white partial eye-ring; finely barred black-and-white wings; less extensive barring on undertail. *Note:* imm. Black-headed has limited black-and-white barring at base of outermost tail feathers.
Voice. *Call:* 1. *chonk* to *tonk* similar to vocalization of Black-headed;
2. rolling *churrr,* less hollow than in Black-headed, and a similar rolling *brrrt,* often repeated;
3. liquid *whu-whu-whu-whut. Song:* nasal, liquid down-slurred *keo keo keo keo . . .* to *cyow cyow cyow cyow . . . ,* usually with 8–20 notes in a series.
Habitat. Midlevels to subcanopy in broadleaf and, to a lesser extent, pine forest, forest edge, and broken forest with scrub. More likely than Black-headed to be in forest interior, less likely to be near urban areas.
Distribution. Resident from se San Luis Potosí to c S.A.
Status in Belize. FC to C resident on mainland.

Collared Trogon
MAP 114; PLATE 29

Trogon collaris

OTHER NAMES. Ramatutu (C), cak i kok (K), chuk ko' ko' (M).

Identification. 11″ (28 cm). Yellow bill; white band separating breast from red belly. ♂: underside of tail black, with fine white bands (broader in imm.); iridescent green hood and upperparts; black face; red eye-ring. ♀: head, breast, and upperparts non-iridescent brown; underside of tail gray, with thin white feather tips bordered subterminally with black; less extensive yellow in bill; partial white eye-ring.

Voice. *Call:* 1. rolling *brrrrrow;*

2. liquid *drrrrr* or *tchrrrrr,* similar to that of Tawny-winged Woodcreeper but less nasal. *Song:* clear, hollow, nasal *cow cow;* occas. 3 notes in series, rarely one; responds readily to imitation of its call.

Habitat. Midlevels to subcanopy in primary broadleaf forest and forest edge.

Distribution. Resident from Guerrero and se San Luis Potosí to c S.A.

Status in Belize. UC to FC resident in most of TO, and in w SC n. to n CA; also in w OW and locally in e OW (New R.).

Slaty-tailed Trogon
MAP 115; PLATE 29

Trogon massena

OTHER NAMES. Massena Trogon (arch.), Ramatutu (C), cac i kok (K), chuk ko'ko' (M).

Identification. 13½″ (34.5 cm). Largest Belize trogon; red underparts; lacks white breast band of Collared; bill and eye-ring orangish red; undertail all dark gray (partially barred white in imm.). ♂: mostly iridescent green above; salt-and-pepper wing coverts. ♀ *and imm.:* mostly dark gray, with red confined to lower belly and undertail coverts.

Voice. *Call:* rapid-fire, low-pitched *dur-r-r-r-r-r-r-r-r-r-r.* *Song:* 1. loud, barking crow-like *cah* or *caw* notes;

2. softer hawklike notes, nasal *ah ah ah ah . . . ,* given at various speeds.

Habitat. Midlevels to subcanopy in primary broadleaf forest and forest edge.

Distribution. Resident from c Veracruz and c Yucatán Pen. to n S.A.

Status in Belize. FC to C resident n. to ne SC and nc CA; also in w and c OW.

FAMILY: MOMOTIDAE
(Motmots)

World: 10. **New World:** 10. **Belize:** 3. Neotropical. Motmots are characterized by a relatively large head; small, weak feet; a fairly long, stout, slightly decurved bill; and a graduated tail. Their plumage is often green, with blue and rufous highlights, a boldly marked head, and 1 or 2 black breast spots. All but the Tody Motmot have elongated central rectrices, which in most species are racket-tipped, the result of loosely attached feather barbs near the tip that soon fall off in emerging feathers during preening. These arboreal forest dwellers sit motionless, sometimes slowly wagging their tail sideways like a pendulum. Motmots sally out to catch prey. Vocalizations typically are clear to hoarse hoots given mainly at dawn.

Things to note: vocalizations, presence/absence of racket-tipped tail, head pattern and colors, broadness of bill as seen from below.

Tody Motmot
MAP 116; PLATE 29

Hylomanes momotula

OTHER NAMES. Kwaren kosh (M).

Identification. 6¾″ (17 cm). Much smaller than other motmots, with short tail that lacks elongated racket-tipped central tail feathers; has rufous crown and nape, turquoise "brow," black auricular patch, and two white stripes on side of throat (unique among motmots). Like other motmots, sits motionless and is hard to detect. Habit of wagging tail slowly from side to side often reveals its presence.

Voice. 1. Loud, penetrating, hollow *whoop!* repeated at ≈1½ sec intervals;

2. faster Ferruginous Pygmy-Owl–like *whut whut whut . . .* (can be low- or moderately high-pitched);

3. series of gruff hoots *(quah quah quah quah . . .).* Most often heard at the first light of dawn.

Habitat. Midlevels to subcanopy within primary broadleaf forest interior.

Distribution. Resident from c Veracruz and c Yucatán to w Colombia.

Status in Belize. FC resident on mainland in s and w TO, w SC, and s. two-thirds of CA; also in w OW and locally in e OW.

References. *Voice:* Delaney (1992); Moore (1992).

Blue-crowned Motmot   PLATE 29
Momotus momota
OTHER NAMES. Lesson Motmot (I. Davis), Good Cook (C), hut hut (K, M).

Identification. 16″ (40.5 cm). Long, racket-tipped tail; red eyes; black central crown broadly bordered in turquoise blue; black lower auricular stripe outlined in turquoise; two central breast spots that form an inverted black chevron. Sits motionless and occasionally wags tail slowly back and forth. Seen singly or in pairs.

Voice. Soft, deep, owl-like *hoop hoop,* occasionally *hoop hoop hoop.* Calls most frequently at dawn but may occas. be heard well into the morning, especially on overcast days and in the breeding season. Responds readily to imitation of its call.

Habitat. Midlevels to subcanopy in primary and secondary broadleaf forest interior; occas. pine forest.

Distribution. Resident from c Nuevo Leon and c Tamaulipas to c S.A.

Status in Belize. FC to C resident on mainland. Much more often heard than seen.

Reference. *Voice:* Moore (1992).

Keel-billed Motmot   MAP 117; PLATE 29
Electron carinatum
OTHER NAMES. Hom (K).

Identification. 12½″ (32 cm). Smaller than Blue-crowned and much less widespread. Broad-based bill is convex in outline when viewed from below (Blue-crowned has narrow straight-sided bill). Also distinguished by green crown, rufous forehead, turquoise brow that does not extend to the hindcrown, and dark amber, not red, eyes. ♂: green breast. ♀: mustard-colored breast.

Voice. Hoarse, nasal *ohhnng* notes, usually given singly, 4–6 sec apart.

Habitat. Midlevels to subcanopy; primary moist tropical broadleaf forest interior with an abundance of lianas.

Distribution. Resident on Gulf-Caribbean slope from s Veracruz and e Oaxaca s. of Yucatán Pen. to C.R. Extirpated from much of its former range. Because of extensive loss of its primary rainforest habitat, it is considered *Globally Vulnerable.*

Status in Belize. UC to FC resident in Maya Mtns., in Vaca Plateau CA, and Tapir Mtn. Nature Reserve nc CA. Belize is one of the last outposts where this species is relatively common.

References. *Status:* Miller and Miller (1992, 1996). *Voice:* Gilardi (1997). *Conservation:* Jones and Vallely (2001); Stattersfield and Capper (2000).

FAMILY: ALCEDINIDAE
(Kingfishers)

World: 93. New World: 6. Belize: 5. Nearly cosmopolitan, with the great majority of species found in the Old World. Kingfishers are characterized by a long, daggerlike, disproportionately large bill and short legs, with two of three forward-facing toes partially joined. Most, including all in the New World, are primarily blue gray or green, and all but one in Belize have a crest. Only in Belted is the ♀ decorated more extensively with rufous than the ♂. Calls are simple rattles or harsh single notes. All New World kingfishers, and many Old World species, plunge into the water for prey, usually fish. **Reference:** Fry et al. (1992).

Things to note: overall size; blue vs. green plumage; presence/absence of breast band and white spots in wings; extent of rufous, if any, on underparts.

Ringed Kingfisher   PLATE 30
Ceryle torquata
OTHER NAMES. Ch'ej chem (K, M), Martin Pescado (S).

Identification. 15½″ (39.5 cm). Similar to Belted, but noticeably larger, with more massive bill. Steady, deliberate flight with slower wing-beats than Belted. ♂: entirely rufous breast and belly; white undertail coverts. ♀: broad, blue-gray breast band separated from rufous belly by white band; rufous undertail coverts.

Voice. *While perched:* loud, slow mechanical rattle (6–8/sec); much slower and lower-pitched than in Belted Kingfisher. *In flight:* loud *chdak* to *shack.*

Habitat. Widespread; found in open areas with Belted, as well as forested streams, swamps, and rivers; flies high over large open areas, revealing its presence with its occas. loud call.

Distribution. Resident from s Sinaloa, s Texas, and Lesser Antilles to s S.A. Absent from n. half of Yucatán Pen.

Status in Belize. FC to C resident on mainland; occas. seen on Ambergris Caye.

Reference. *Voice:* Moore (1992).

Belted Kingfisher   PLATE 30
Ceryle alcyon
OTHER NAMES. Ch'ej chem (K, M), Martin Pescado (S).

Identification. 12½″ (32 cm). Noticeably smaller than Ringed and flies with more rapid wing-beats; bill proportionately smaller. Ragged double-peaked crest. ♂: blue-gray breast band on otherwise white underparts. ♀: like ♂ but with the addition of rufous band across lower breast, extending to flanks.

Voice. Loud, dry to slightly liquid rattle of ≈8–15 notes in rapid succession (duration <1–2 sec), never a single note as in Ringed.

Habitat. Roadside ditches and creeks, coastal lagoons, mangrove swamps, rice fields, power lines near water; avoids forested rivers and creeks.

Distribution. Nests from c Alaska and nc Can. to s U.S.; winters from s Alaska and n U.S. to n S.A.

Status in Belize. C winter visitor, primarily mid-Aug. to late Apr.; occas. reported in May, June, and July.

Amazon Kingfisher   MAP 118; PLATE 30
Chloroceryle amazona
OTHER NAMES. Amazon Green-Kingfisher (I. Davis), ch'ej chem (K, M), Martin Pescado (S).

Identification. 11¼″ (28.5 cm). Slightly smaller than Belted, with proportionately larger bill and single-peaked crest. Glossy green instead of blue gray (reflects blue green at certain angles). Seldom seen flying across extensive open areas or above the forest canopy. ♂: rufous breast band. ♀: green breast band (often incomplete).

Voice. Loud, squeaky accelerating and descending rattle: *turee turee turee tree tre tr tr tr.*

Habitat. Primarily forested rivers, streams, and lagoons, but occas. in open areas such as edges of rice fields, roadside ditches.

Distribution. Resident from s Sinaloa and s Tamaulipas to sc S.A. Absent from n. two-thirds of Yucatán Pen.

Status in Belize. UC to FC resident n. to c OW and c BE, locally to ne OW and possibly CO; absent from cayes.

Green Kingfisher   PLATE 30
Chloroceryle americana
OTHER NAMES. Little Green-Kingfisher (I. Davis), ch'ej chem (K, M), Martin Pescado (S).

Identification. 7¾″ (20 cm). Small version of Amazon with less prominent crest, white spots in wings, and mostly white outer tail feathers that are conspicuous in flight. Like the preceding three, has a bold white collar. ♂: broad rufous breast band. ♀: two green bands, one across breast and one across upper belly.

Voice. 1. Harsh, flat *zeet* or *jeet;* 2. dry *titik* to *tititik;* 3. harsh, grating *bru breet breet breet breet.*

Habitat. Wood-lined streams and rivers.

Distribution. Resident from se Arizona and c Texas to sc S.A.

Status in Belize. FC to C resident on mainland, occas. reported on Ambergris Caye and Caye Caulker.

Reference. *Voice:* Moore (1992).

American Pygmy Kingfisher PLATE 30

Chloroceryle aenea
OTHER NAMES. Pygmy Kingfisher (alt.),
Least Green-Kingfisher (I. Davis), ch'ej
chem (K, M), Martin Pescado (S).

Identification. 5¼″ (13.5 cm). Smallest of the
New World kingfishers (body size of Plain
Xenops, with a long bill). Extensive rufous underparts, becoming pale to rich cinnamon on
throat, pale cinnamon to near white on collar,
and white on lower belly and undertail coverts.
Less prominent wing spots than in Green; Green
and Pygmy kingfishers genuflect nervously and
flick tail sharply upward. ♀: dark green breast
band flecked with white. ♂: lacks breast band.
Voice. *Call:* 1. dry, hummingbird-like *tk;*
2. dry *d-d-d-dit;* 3. accelerating *tk tk tk t-t-t-t-t.*
Habitat. Quiet pools, swamps, backwaters,
heavily vegetated lagoon margins; generally
avoids faster-flowing streams.
Distribution. Resident from c Veracruz to c
S.A.
Status in Belize. UC to locally C resident on
mainland; recorded once on s Ambergris Caye
and twice on Caye Caulker.

FAMILY: BUCCONIDAE
(Puffbirds)

World: 33. **New World:** 33. **Belize:** 2. Neotropical. Puffbirds are characterized by a disproportionately large head and eyes, a swollen bill,
and short legs, wings, and tail. Their thick but
lax plumage gives them a plump appearance—
hence the name "puffbird." Most have a stout,
hooked bill that may be straight or decurved,
and tapered toward the tip. All perch motionless for long periods but remain alert, search-
ing for insect prey, which they hawk flycatcher-
like from the air. Their flight is swift and direct.
Like most in the group, the two in Belize are frequently overlooked because of their infrequent
activity. They are generally quiet; even when calling, their vocalizations are soft and high-pitched,
easily going undetected.

White-necked Puffbird PLATE 29

Notharchus macrorhynchos

Identification. 9¾″ (25 cm). Large-headed,
squat, black-and-white bird with relatively short
tail and swollen, blunt-tipped, slightly hooked
bill. White forehead, broad white collar, and
black breast band further distinguish it.
Voice. Occas. a mournful, descending *peeeur,*
but usually silent. In breeding season, a long,
bubbling trill, sometimes rising and falling
slightly.
Habitat. Mid-strata to canopy along forest edge
or in semi-open to open country with scattered
trees; sits motionless on exposed branches.
Distribution. Resident from n Oaxaca to c S.A.
Absent from nw Yucatán Pen.
Status in Belize. UC resident on mainland in
north; less common in south.
Reference. *Voice:* Howell and Webb (1995).

White-whiskered Puffbird
MAP 119; PLATE 29

Malacoptila panamensis
OTHER NAMES. Panama Softwing
(I. Davis), tonto tz'ic (M).

Identification. 7¾″ (19.5 cm). Somewhat similar in shape to Tody Motmot but larger, with
shaggy white facial feathers, loose plumage,
streaked underparts, spotted upperparts, and
stockier bill. ♂: cinnamon-brown foreparts. ♀:
gray-brown plumage with more distinct pale
spotting above.
Voice. A rather insignificant high-pitched, thin,
slightly lisping *tseeeeer* with slight downward
pitch. Usually silent.
Habitat. Midlevels within broadleaf forest interior and edge.
Distribution. Resident primarily on Gulf-
Caribbean slope from e Chiapas and e Tabasco
to nw S.A.
Status in Belize. UC to FC resident on mainland away from coast n. to n CA and sw BE (possibly to c BE); also in w and c OW.
References. *Voice:* Delaney (1992); Moore (1992).

FAMILY: GALBULIDAE
(Jacamars)

World: 18. **New World:** 18. **Belize:** 1. Neotropical, mostly confined to S.A., with only one found n. of C.R. Jacamars are characterized by a long, narrow, straight bill; a strongly graduated, fairly long tail; short legs; and short, rounded wings. Like puffbirds, they sit motionless for long periods, occasionally darting out to catch a butterfly, dragonfly, bee, or wasp. Their long bill can grasp a butterfly's body while pinning its wings and can keep the dangerous stinger of a wasp at bay. While perched, they hold their bill above horizontal. In contrast to puffbirds, jacamars are very noisy, especially around the nest.

Rufous-tailed Jacamar
MAP 120; PLATE 29

Galbula ruficauda

OTHER NAMES. Black-chinned Jacamar (arch.).

Identification. 9″ (23 cm). Iridescent golden green above and across breast; cinnamon belly, undertail coverts, and tail, except for green central tail feathers. With its long, needle-thin bill, reminiscent of a giant hummingbird. ♂: white throat. ♀: pale cinnamon-buff throat.
Voice. *Call:* 1. shrill, piercing *pweeup!;* 2. slightly less emphatic *kea!,* similar to call of Royal Flycatcher; 3. squeaky, piercing *wheuh wheuh . . . . Song:* fast, hysterical, penetrating series, speeding up and becoming a fast rattle at end—*pweee pweee pwee pwe we we we we-we-e-e-e-e-e-e-e-e.*
Habitat. Low to mid-strata in broadleaf forest interior and edge.
Distribution. Resident primarily on Gulf-Caribbean slope from c Veracruz and c Yucatán Pen. to c S.A.
Status in Belize. UC to FC resident on mainland away from coast n. to ne OW.
Reference. *Voice:* Moore (1992).

FAMILY: RAMPHASTIDAE
(Toucans)

World: 41. **New World:** 41. **Belize:** 3. Neotropical. Toucans are among the world's most spectacular birds with their grotesquely large, colorful, laterally compressed, mostly hollow bill with overlapping plates, and serrated cutting edge. Despite its immense size, the bill is very light and used primarily for eating small berries, occasionally for robbing other birds of their eggs and small young. Toucans are further characterized by a bare area of often brightly colored facial skin, rounded wings, and a fairly long, graduated tail. They live in social groups most of the year. The Keel-billed Toucan is Belize's national bird and one of the birds most sought after by tourists. For all their gaudiness, toucans have rather unspectacular calls. They fly on rapid, shallow wingbeats alternating with long glides, typically traveling single-file in loose groups across a trail, river, or forest opening, with each bird in the group waiting until the preceding bird has crossed the opening before venturing across. **References:** Short and Horne (2001). *Voice:* Hardy et al. (1996a).

Emerald Toucanet
MAP 121; PLATE 30

Aulacorhynchus prasinus

OTHER NAMES. Rax i selepan (K), ya'ax pun (M).

Identification. 13½″ (34.5 cm). Emerald green, with large black-and-yellow bill, unfeathered gray eye-ring, and chestnut undertail coverts.
Voice. 1. *wuk wuk wuk . . . ,* often repeated incessantly at rate of ≈2½/sec; 2. similar *wank wank wank . . .* notes given at irregular intervals and loudness (a group sounds like chorus of frogs); 3. harsh, rolling *drrrrrr,* somewhat jaylike but lower-pitched and ending abruptly; 4. down-slurred, rolling froglike *br-r-rup.*
Habitat. Mid-strata to subcanopy, submontane and foothill broadleaf forest interior and edge; less often in submontane pine forest.
Distribution. Resident from Guerrero and se San Luis Potosí to w S.A.
Status in Belize. C resident in Maya Mtns., less C in Vaca Plateau CA and Mtn. Pine Ridge; seasonal breeding visitor in w OW. Disperses occas. at end of rainy season to lower elevations in se OW and in w BE and interior SC and TO. Unrecorded from CO.
Reference. *Status:* Wood and Leberman (1987).

Collared Aracari
PLATE 30

Pteroglossus torquatus

OTHER NAMES. Pillis (C), pi chik (K, M), Medio Pito (S).

Identification. 16″ (40.5 cm). Black above, with red face and rump; yellow below, with red-and-black patches. Bill black below, warm gray above. Ad. has pale yellow eyes and pupil that appears oddly oblong.
Voice. Loud, metallic *perdeet!* to *kldeek!*
Habitat. Midlevels to subcanopy in broadleaf forest and forest edge.
Distribution. Resident from c Veracruz to n S.A.
Status in Belize. FC to C resident on mainland; formerly on Ambergris Caye.
Reference. *Voice:* Moore (1992).

Keel-billed Toucan
PLATE 30

Ramphastos sulfuratus

OTHER NAMES. Belizean Bill Bird (C), Big-bill Pillis (C), selepan (K), pun (M), Pito Real (S).

Identification. 21½″ (54.5 cm). Striking black plumage, extensive yellow throat and breast, unfeathered green eye-ring, white uppertail coverts, and red undertail coverts. Enormous green bill with maroon tip, and orange and turquoise flashes.
Voice. Froglike. 1. *troik troik troik . . . ;*
2. rolling *brrret brrret brrret . . . ;*
3. harsher, rolling *breeup breeup breeup . . . .*
Quality varies from nearly clear to burry to harsh.
Habitat. Subcanopy to canopy in broadleaf forest and forest edge.
Distribution. Resident from se San Luis Potosí to n S.A.
Status in Belize. FC to C resident on mainland.
Reference. *Voice:* Moore (1992).

FAMILY: PICIDAE
(Woodpeckers)

World: 217. **New World:** 121. **Belize:** 11. Worldwide except Aust. and N.Z. Most are arboreal. Woodpeckers are characterized by a moderately short tail with stiff, pointed central rectrices for supporting the weight of the body while perched or climbing on a vertical tree trunk, and by a powerful, chisel-like bill used to drill holes in the trunk to extract food and to excavate a nest cavity. They have a long, tubular harpoonlike tongue with backward-slanting barbs at the tip, used for extracting insect larvae from drillings. Most have feet with two toes facing fore and two aft, lending added support for the body. In many species, both sexes hammer their bill against a resonant tree trunk or branch in a distinctive rhythm or cadence, known as drumming, to advertise their territory and secure a mate. This serves much the same function as song in other birds. With practice, many species can be distinguished by their specific drumming "signature." All but one woodpecker in Belize are resident.
Reference: Winkler et al. (1995).

Acorn Woodpecker
MAP 122; PLATE 31

Melanerpes formicivorus

OTHER NAMES. Ant-eating Woodpecker (I. Davis).

Identification. 8¾″ (22 cm). Resembles no other woodpecker. Black and white, with red crown, white face becoming pale yellow on lower throat and upper breast, black forehead and chin, and black breast streaked white. White eyes and oddly patterned face give this species a clownish look. One of the few truly social woodpeckers, typically found in groups. ♂: all-red crown. ♀: red hindcrown separated from white forecrown by a black band. *Flight:* large white wing patches, white rump.
Voice. 1. Distinctive, harsh, nasal *wack-wack;*
2. lengthier *wanka-wanka-wanka . . .* , and various other noisy, nasal chattering calls. *Drumming:* evenly paced, ≈12 notes (almost slow enough to count the individual taps).
Habitat. Midlevels to subcanopy in pine and pine-oak forest. Dependent on oaks, which have a distribution similar to that of Caribbean pine *(Pinus caribaea);* thus its close ties to Mtn. Pine Ridge and lowland pinelands. Stores acorns in small holes it drills in tree trunks, later feeding on larval insects that infest the rotting acorn.
Distribution. Resident from Oregon (U.S.) to n Colombia. Absent from Yucatán Pen.

Status in Belize. FC to C resident in Mtn. Pine Ridge and coastal plain from n OW s. to ne TO.

Black-cheeked Woodpecker

MAP 123; PLATE 31

Melanerpes pucherani

OTHER NAMES. Pucheran's Woodpecker (arch.), tzen tse'rej (K), kolon te' (M), Checo (S).

Identification. 7¼" (18.5 cm). Similar to Golden-fronted in size, shape, vocalizations, and habits. However, plumage characters and preferred habitat differ. Distinguished by black face and auricular patch, short white postocular stripe, yellow forehead, black-and-white-barred central tail feathers, and black-barred sides and flanks. *Flight:* conspicuous white rump. ♂: red crown and nape. ♀: red only on nape.

Voice. *Call:* most often, a rapid, slightly liquid, 4- to 6-syllable rattle very similar to but slightly less nasal and lower pitched than that of Golden-fronted.

Habitat. Midlevels to subcanopy in broadleaf forest edge and clearings within forest.

Distribution. Resident from c Veracruz s. of Yucatán Pen. to nw S.A.

Status in Belize. FC resident n. to nc CA and c BE, perhaps discontinuously in w and c OW.

Reference. *Voice:* Moore (1992).

Red-vented and Golden-fronted Woodpeckers

Closely similar species with red crown (♂) and nape, finely barred back, and pale grayish brown face and underparts.

Things to note: length of bill relative to head, length of tail, color of feather tufts at base of bill, vocalizations.

Red-vented Woodpecker

MAP 124; PLATE 31

Melanerpes pygmaeus

OTHER NAMES. Yucatán Woodpecker (alt.), Red-crowned Woodpecker (combined form), Golden-fronted Woodpecker (combined form).

Identification. 6¾" (17 cm). Closely resembles Golden-fronted but smaller, with very short tail

and bill (the latter barely half the length of its head) and rounder head, which give it a squat appearance, unique among American woodpeckers and noticeable even in flight. More often seen foraging on outer limbs and foliage than Golden-fronted. Ironically, in Belize, it is Red-vented, not Golden-fronted, that has tuft of golden yellow feathers at base of bill. Both species have reddish wash on vent. *Flight:* conspicuous white rump, very short tail. ♂: red extends from forecrown through nape. ♀: red only on nape.

Voice. *Call:* harsh *cheh-heh-heh-heh-heh* with squirrel-like quality. *Rattle:* similar to Golden-fronted's but somewhat burry and squirrel-like.

Habitat. Midlevels to subcanopy in most open forest types, including broadleaf and pine. Often found with Golden-fronted.

Distribution. *Near Yucatán Endemic.* Resident in Yucatán Pen. s. to c Campeche, n Belize, and Bay Isl. (Hon.).

Status in Belize. UC to FC resident in CO, e and c OW, extreme ne CA, and all but sw BE; also on Ambergris Caye and Caye Caulker.

Reference. *Status:* Wood and Leberman (1987).

Golden-fronted Woodpecker   PLATE 31

Melanerpes aurifrons

OTHER NAMES. Uxmal Woodpecker and Santacruz Woodpecker (I. Davis), Carpenter (C), che'ko' (K), kolon te' (M), Checo (S).

Identification. 9¼" (23.5 cm). Similar in plumage to Red-vented and in vocalizations to Black-cheeked. Pale grayish buff face and underparts, all-black central tail feathers, and fine white bars in otherwise black upperparts distinguish it from Black-cheeked. Differs from Red-vented in larger size and disproportionately longer bill and tail. Populations in Belize have red, not golden, tuft at base of bill. *Flight:* conspicuous white rump and medium-length tail. ♂: red extends from nape through crown. ♀: red only on nape and hindcrown.

Voice. *Call:* 1. *check;*

2. *check-a,* usually repeated several times;

3. rolling *chrrr;*

4. rapid, nasal rattle of 4–6 syllables, very simi-

lar to that of Black-cheeked (individual notes are hard to count.

Habitat. Midlevels to subcanopy at forest edge and most open areas with trees; frequents mango trees and coconut palms, among others. The common woodpecker around towns.

Distribution. Resident from s Oklahoma (U.S.) to n Nic.

Status in Belize. C to VC resident away from extensive forest, including Ambergris Caye, Caye Caulker, Turneffe Isl., and Moho Caye off Placencia.

Yellow-bellied Sapsucker   PLATE 31
Sphyrapicus varius

Identification. 7¾″ (19.5 cm). Black-and-white-barred plumage nearly throughout, with conspicuous white wing patch. *Ad. ♂:* red crown and throat, both bordered by black; underparts washed with yellow. *Ad. ♀:* like ad. ♂ but with white throat. *Juv.:* upperparts washed brownish; underparts dingy pale yellowish, with diffuse dusky streaking; much less distinct head pattern than in ad., lacking bold black and red markings. *Flight:* conspicuous white wing patches and rump.

Voice. *Call:* whining, nasal *ănnnnh,* similar to that of Roadside Hawk but softer, shorter, not explosive.

Habitat. Midlevels to subcanopy in broadleaf and pine forest, forest edge. Sapsuckers drill small holes in parallel rows around tree trunks to extract sap. These characteristic drillings, which persist as long as the tree stands, are a near permanent sign of the historical occurrence of sapsuckers in an area.

Distribution. Nests from e Alaska and c Can. to n U.S.; winters from se U.S. to W.I. and Pan.

Status in Belize. UC winter visitor, mid-Oct. to late Apr.; at times FC on cayes in migration.

Ladder-backed Woodpecker
MAP 125; PLATE 31
Picoides scalaris

Identification. 7″ (18 cm). Heavily barred black and white above, with black-and-white-pat-terned head (white auriculars outlined in black) and dingy brownish underparts with fine black bars and spots. Lacks white rump of other similar woodpeckers and white wing patches of somewhat similar juv. Yellow-bellied Sapsucker. ♂: red hindcrown. ♀: lacks red hindcrown. *Juv.:* mostly black crown with red flecks.

Voice. 1. Sharp *pik;*
2. rapid shrill chatter;
3. rhythmic *kee-ki-kurr kee-ki-kurr kee-ki-kurr . . . .*

Habitat. Midlevels to subcanopy in open pine woodlands.

Distribution. Resident from sw U.S. to w Nic.

Status in Belize. UC to locally FC resident in coastal plain from e OW and n BE s. to ne TO, including extreme ne CA; absent from cayes.

Smoky-brown Woodpecker   PLATE 31
Veniliornis fumigatus
OTHER NAMES. Brown Woodpecker (arch.), tzen tse'rej (K), kolon te' (M), Checo (S).

Identification. 6¼″ (16 cm). Small size; dull brown nearly throughout; brighter, tawny brown on back, with dull brownish buff face. ♂: red in crown and nape. ♀: lacks red.

Voice. *Call:* 1. rough *kip* to slightly slurred *tsip,* occas. repeated incessantly like Couch's Kingbird call but slightly rougher;
2. very nasal, rapid *anh-anh-anh . . .* (20–25 notes);
3. scratchy, nasal laugh or rattle (≈8/sec), usually preceded by a *chip!;*
4. liquid *choit choit choit choit choit choit. Drumming:* thin, with rapid, even tempo (up to 1 sec long).

Habitat. Lower levels to subcanopy in broadleaf forest interior and edge, scrub.

Distribution. Resident from Nayarit and sw Tamaulipas s. to the Andes.

Status in Belize. FC resident on mainland.

Reference. *Voice:* Moore (1992).

Golden-olive Woodpecker   PLATE 31

Piculus rubiginosus
OTHER NAMES. Green Woodpecker
(I. Davis), tzen tse'rej (K), kolon te' (M),
Checo (S).

Identification. 8½″ (21.5 cm). Olive-green back,
bronzy wings, brown tail, and barred olive-and-
creamy-yellow underparts; gray crown, red nape,
and pale grayish buff face. ♂: red malar stripe and
thin red line extending from nape along sides of
crown to bill. ♀: red restricted to nape.
Voice. *Call:* 1. loud *kia!;*
2. loud *kurr* or *turr;*
3. fairly long, dry *brrrrrrrr* on an even pitch
(2½–3/sec);
4. squeaky *whit chek!*
Habitat. Midlevels to subcanopy in pine and
broadleaf forest and forest edge.
Distribution. Resident from c Veracruz to n and
w S.A.
Status in Belize. UC to locally C resident on
mainland nearly throughout; most plentiful in
Mtn. Pine Ridge.
Reference. *Voice:* Moore (1992).

Chestnut-colored Woodpecker   PLATE 31

Celeus castaneus
OTHER NAMES. K'an i corochech (K),
kolon te' (M).

Identification. 9″ (23 cm). Chestnut plumage
barred with black, pale ochre head, prominent
shaggy crest, and greenish yellow bill. ♂: irregular red patch below and behind eyes. ♀: no red
in face.
Voice. *Call:* burry *cow* or *keur;* sometimes immediately followed by a short *wanh-wanh.* At a
distance, similar to single note of Collared Trogon (which typically gives a 2-note *cow cow*),
but at close range woodpecker's call is distinctly burry. *Drumming:* even tempo and pitch
(≈1/sec); lower-pitched than in Smoky-brown.
Habitat. Midlevels to subcanopy within broadleaf forest interior.
Distribution. Resident on Gulf-Caribbean
slope from c Veracruz to w Pan.

Status in Belize. UC to locally FC resident on
mainland.
Reference. *Voice:* Moore (1992).

Tribe: Campepherini

Despite belonging to different genera, these two
species are very similar in size, appearance, and
behavior. Both are about equally common in
most parts of the country and are often found
in the same habitats. Both are predominantly
black, with long neck and crested head, which is
mostly or all red. Both have pale bill. Vocalizations and drumming of each are quite different.

Things to note: face pattern, shape of crest,
vocal differences, drumming.

Lineated Woodpecker   PLATE 31

Dryocopus lineatus
OTHER NAMES. Father Red-cap (C), tzen
tse'rej (K), kolon te' (M).

Identification. 13″ (33 cm). Large, mostly black
woodpecker with mostly red head. Both sexes
have black auriculars and white extending from
neck through lower auriculars to bill. Crest more
pointed than in Pale-billed. White lateral line on
each side of back stops at base of tertials. Both
species are heavily barred beneath. ♂: crest red
throughout, red malar stripe. ♀: black forecrown
and malar stripe.
Voice. *Call:* 1. *kree kree kree . . .* series;
2. ringing *wick wick wick . . . ;*
3. squirrel-like rolling *cheurrrr;* also variously
4. *pk brrrrr;*
5. *chalk;* and
6. *kip! Drumming:* rapid series of ten or so taps,
usually slowing and losing intensity.
Habitat. Midlevels to subcanopy in most areas
with large trees, including primary and secondary broadleaf forest, open areas with scattered
large trees, pines, and towns and villages.
Distribution. Resident from s Sonora and c
Nuevo León to c S.A.
Status in Belize. FC to C resident on mainland
and n Ambergris Caye.

Pale-billed Woodpecker   PLATE 31
Campephilus guatemalensis
OTHER NAMES. Guatemalan Ivory-bill (arch.), Flint-billed Woodpecker (arch.), Father Red-cap (C), tzen tse'rej (K), kolon te' (M).

Identification. 14½" (37 cm). Similar to but larger than Lineated, with more extensive red in head. Lateral white line on either side of body runs from neck through scapulars to lower back, where they nearly join. ♂: entirely red head. ♀: black forecrown and throat.
Voice. *Call:* 1. nasal, squeaky *[wht wht] wht-hehdek, hehdek-hehehehdek;*
2. rapid, laughing, nasal *ankkank* or *ankankank.* Notes are more nasal and squeaky than that of Lineated. *Drumming:* distinctive double rap.
Habitat. Found in much the same areas as Lineated, but less frequent in pines and in towns and villages.
Distribution. Resident from s Sonora and s Tamaulipas to w Pan.
Status in Belize. FC resident on mainland.
Reference. *Voice:* Moore (1992).

FAMILY: FURNARIIDAE
(Ovenbirds)
World: 240. **New World:** 240. **Belize:** 6. Neotropical. Large family confined primarily to S.A. Ovenbirds are perhaps the most diverse family in the New World Tropics in outward appearance, habits, nest structure, and breeding biology. Most come in various shades of browns and grays, and most live on or near the ground in the forest interior and nest in burrows or holes. Many species in S.A. build a domed nest that resembles a clay oven.

Rufous-breasted Spinetail   PLATE 33
Synallaxis erythrothorax
OTHER NAMES. Rufous-breasted Synallaxis (I. Davis).

Identification. 6¼" (15.5 cm). Small, slim, relatively long-tailed dark brown bird with rufous wings and breast and black throat with white spots in upper throat. Pointed rectrices give tail tip a spiny look.

Voice. Very distinctive, somewhat nasal *[wack] wack wack wack oh.* Often heard but seldom seen.
Habitat. Dense tangles, especially along roadsides and riverbanks.
Distribution. Resident from c Veracruz to nw Hon. and E.S.
Status in Belize. UC to locally C resident on mainland nearly throughout, but scarce or absent in much of CO.
References. *Voice:* Delaney (1992); Moore (1992).

Scaly-throated Foliage-gleaner
MAP 126; PLATE 32
Anabacerthia variegaticeps
OTHER NAMES. Spectacled Foliage-gleaner (alt.), Scaly Foliagegleaner (I. Davis).

Identification. 6½" (16.5 cm). Smaller than Buff-throated with shorter bill, gray head with prominent ochraceous buff eye-ring and postocular stripe (spectacles). Pale cream-colored throat and upper breast with fine dark feather edges give the appearance of scales at close range. Forages in mosses, bromeliads, and other epiphytes throughout the forest strata in much the same fashion as a xenops.
Voice. *Call:* sharp, explosive *squeezk! Song:* rapid series of sharp, high-pitched *tsee* notes, accelerating toward the end, often preceded by a buzzy sneeze.
Habitat. Midlevels to subcanopy within broadleaf forest interior.
Distribution. Resident discontinuously from Guerrero, Puebla, and s Veracruz s. of Yucatán Pen. to nw S.A.
Status in Belize. Found only on Doyle's Delight TO/CA, Belize's highest peak, where apparently FC. Discovered in Belize in Aug. 1989.
References. *Status:* Howell et al. (1992). *Voice:* Howell and Webb (1995).

Buff-throated Foliage-gleaner

MAP 127; PLATE 32

Automolus ochrolaemus

OTHER NAMES. Buff-throated Automolus (arch.).

Identification. 7¾" (19.5 cm). Mostly brown above, with rufous tail. Larger than Scaly-throated, with larger bill and different behavior and habitat; ochraceous buff eye-ring and postocular stripe give spectacled appearance, as in Scaly-throated; however, ochraceous buff of throat extending laterally onto sides of neck readily distinguishes it, especially when feathers are flared out in courtship.

Voice. *Call:* 1. slightly rough, slightly liquid *pik!* to *prik!;*
2. *piquick. Song:* liquid trill that slows and drops in pitch (≈1 sec).

Habitat. Understory within primary and secondary broadleaf forest and forest edge.

Distribution. Resident primarily on Gulf-Caribbean slope from c Veracruz s. of Yucatán Pen. to c S.A.

Status in Belize. FC resident in interior n. to nc CA and possibly sw BE; also in much of w and c OW.

References. *Voice:* Delaney (1992); Moore (1992).

Plain Xenops   PLATE 33

Xenops minutus

OTHER NAMES. Little Xenops (arch.).

Identification. 4¾" (12 cm). Small brown bird with short, wedge-shaped bill, rufous-and-black flight feathers, pale buff supercilium, and conspicuous white malar stripe. Feeds by creeping along branches and the bases of leaf clusters, much like a chickadee (*Poecile* sp.).

Voice. *Call:* squeaky *tseip,* similar to that of Yellow-bellied Flycatcher. *Song:* rapid, sputtery, dry trill, dropping in pitch at end; drier and more intense than trill of Rufous-tailed Hummingbird; very similar to that of Olivaceous Woodcreeper but averages drier and higher-pitched.

Habitat. Midlevels to canopy within broadleaf forest interior and edge.

Distribution. Resident primarily on Gulf-Caribbean slope from c Veracruz to c S.A.

Status in Belize. FC resident on mainland.

Reference. *Voice:* Moore (1992).

Tawny-throated Leaftosser

MAP 128; PLATE 32

Sclerurus mexicanus

OTHER NAMES. Tawny-throated Leafscraper (arch.), Mexican Leafscraper (arch.).

Identification. 6½" (16.5 cm). Squat, short-tailed bird with rather long, nearly straight bill. Dark brown, with rich tawny rufous throat and upper breast and chestnut rump. Uses its long, thin bill to flip through leaf litter on forest floor in search of insect larvae.

Voice. *Call:* loud *piat! Song:* descending, slowing series, typically of 3–9 rich, plaintive notes, *squee squee . . . .*

Habitat. Ground and understory within primary broadleaf forest.

Distribution. Resident in highlands from Hidalgo to c S.A.

Status in Belize. UC resident above 3,000 ft. (900 m) in Maya Mtns.; thus far recorded from Doyle's Delight TO/CA, Little Quartz Ridge TO, and Mt. Margaret CA, but likely to reside on other high peaks and ridges as well.

References. *Status:* Jones et al. (2000). *Voice:* Howell and Webb (1995).

Scaly-throated Leaftosser

MAP 129; PLATE 32

Sclerurus guatemalensis

OTHER NAMES. Scaly-throated Leafscraper (arch.), Guatemalan Leafscraper (arch.).

Identification. 7" (17.5 cm). Similar to Tawny-throated but has shorter bill, diffusely mottled brown-and-whitish throat and upper breast, and dark brown, not chestnut, rump. Like other leaftossers, uses its long, thin bill to flip through leaf litter on forest floor in search of insect larvae.

Voice. *Call:* 1. sharp, explosive *sweeik!;*
2. low, gruff *chuck. Song:* series of high-pitched, penetrating *wht!* and *wheet!* notes that variously slow down and speed up and rise and drop in pitch, eventually with notes run together at end:

. . . wht wht wheet wheet wheet w-w-w-w-w-w-w-w-w.

Habitat. Ground and understory within primary and secondary broadleaf forest.

Distribution. Resident primarily on Gulf-Caribbean slope from e Oaxaca and s Yucatán Pen. to nw S.A.

Status in Belize. UC to FC resident below 2,600 ft. (800 m) away from coast n. to nc CA, and probably sw BE; also in w OW and locally in e OW.

References. *Voice:* Delaney (1992); Moore (1992).

FAMILY: DENDROCOLAPTIDAE (Woodcreepers)

World: 51. **New World:** 51. **Belize:** 9. Neotropical. Woodpecker-like tree climbers, woodcreepers use their stiff tail for support, but lack the powerful chisel-shaped bill of woodpeckers, have a longer tail, and have three forward-pointing toes and one hindtoe. They do not drum; nor can they drill holes in wood. Most are brown, with a rufous rump and tail, often with gray or olive plumage highlights, and with or without streaks, spots, or bars. Their bill is highly variable, long and curved in some species, short and chisel-like in others. Some habitually follow army ant swarms. **Reference:** *Voice:* Hardy et al. (1991).

Things to note: overall size; length, thickness, and shape of bill; streaked, barred, or plain back and underparts; presence/absence of supercilium.

Tawny-winged Woodcreeper   PLATE 32
Dendrocincla anabatina
OTHER NAMES. Tawny-winged Woodhewer (arch.), letz letz (K), tuk tuk cheh (M).

Identification. 7¼″ (18.5 cm). Conspicuous bright tawny remiges, pale supercilium and throat, chestnut tail, shaggy crown. Frequently flicks each wing alternately.

Voice. *Call:* clear, nasal *tcherr* to *chew,* the latter slightly whiny. *Song:* long, slow, liquid trill (≈6 notes/sec), sometimes continues for a minute or more.

Habitat. Understory to subcanopy within primary and secondary broadleaf forest, forest edge, and high scrub. Frequents army ant swarms.

Distribution. Resident on Gulf-Caribbean slope from c Veracruz to w Pan.

Status in Belize. FC resident on mainland.

Reference. *Voice:* Moore (1992).

Ruddy Woodcreeper   PLATE 32
Dendrocincla homochroa
OTHER NAMES. Ruddy Woodhewer (arch.), letz letz (K), tuk tuk cheh (M).

Identification. 7¾″ (19.5 cm). Bright ruddy plumage with deeper rufous in wings, chestnut in tail; featherless gray eye-ring and lores; bushy forecrown and forehead. Like Tawny-winged, flicks one wing, then the other.

Voice. *Call:* 1. squeaky, nasal *kew* or *tew,* somewhat like Blue-gray Tanager call but louder, fuller;

2. *twit* × 4. *Song:* squeaky trill, starts high, immediately drops an octave and continues at that pitch (≈3½ sec); *twit twit twit . . .* × 14–15.

Habitat. Similar to habitat for Tawny-winged. Also frequents army ant swarms.

Distribution. Resident from n Oaxaca to nw S.A.

Status in Belize. UC to locally FC resident on mainland.

Olivaceous Woodcreeper   PLATE 32
Sittasomus griseicapillus
OTHER NAMES. Olivaceous Woodhewer (arch.), Mexican Woodhewer (I. Davis), letz letz (K), tuk tuk cheh (M).

Identification. 6¼″ (16 cm). Slightly larger than Wedge-billed, with thinner-based, slightly longer, slightly decurved bill. Gray head and underparts, olive-brown back and forewings, and rufous tertials, rump, and tail. *Flight:* conspicuous pale wing stripe formed by light tawny base of remiges.

Voice. Rapid trill very similar to that of Plain Xenops but usually lower-pitched and not as dry; starts low, proceeds higher and faster, then lower and slower at end (≈1½ sec).

Habitat. Midlevels within primary and secondary broadleaf and pine forest and forest edge.

Distribution. Resident from Jalisco and sw Tamaulipas to c S.A.

Status in Belize. FC resident on mainland.

Reference. *Voice:* Moore (1992).

Wedge-billed Woodcreeper

MAP 130; PLATE 32

Glyphorynchus spirurus

OTHER NAMES. Wedge-billed Woodhewer (arch.), Wedge-bill (arch.), letz letz (K), tuk tuk cheh (M).

Identification. 5¾″ (14.5 cm). Slightly smaller than Olivaceous, but with brown head and underparts; speckled face, throat, and breast; pale supercilium; and short, chisel-shaped bill. *Flight:* like Olivaceous, has conspicuous light tawny wing stripe.

Voice. *Call:* harsh, dry, emphatic *chip!* or *chic!,* similar to but louder than Orange-billed Sparrow's call. *Song:* up-the-scale trill that slows at end (≈2 sec); the only species in Belize with a trill that both ascends and slows. *Dusk song: whtu ×* many.

Habitat. Midlevels to subcanopy within primary and secondary broadleaf forest and forest edge.

Distribution. Resident on Gulf-Caribbean slope from s Veracruz s. of Yucatán Pen. to c S.A.

Status in Belize. FC resident on mainland n. to n CA and s BE; also in w OW and locally in e OW.

Reference. *Voice:* Moore (1992).

Strong-billed Woodcreeper

MAP 131; PLATE 32

Xiphocolaptes promeropirhynchus

OTHER NAMES. Strong-billed Woodhewer (arch.), Guatemalan Woodhewer (I. Davis), letz letz (K), tuk tuk cheh (M).

Identification. 12″ (31 cm). Noticeably larger than Northern Barred-Woodcreeper, with long, thick-based bill that tapers toward tip. Finely streaked on head, back, and breast; contrasting white throat. Should not be confused with smaller Ivory-billed, which is more prominently and extensively streaked (including belly) and has slender, ivory white, not gray, bill.

Voice. *Call:* loud *t-tarrrrrr WHIP!* *Song:* loud up-slurred series,

tōōōWIP!   tōōōWIP!   tōōōWIP! . . . , gradually lessening in intensity.

Habitat. Midlevels to subcanopy within broadleaf forest interior and clearings.

Distribution. Resident from se San Luis Potosí s. of Yucatán Pen. to c S.A.

Status in Belize. Local and UC resident discontinuously in w OW, perhaps locally along New R. in e OW, and from sw CA to w TO.

References. *Status:* Miller and Miller (1992). *Voice:* Moore (1992).

Northern Barred-Woodcreeper   PLATE 32

Dendrocolaptes sanctithomae

OTHER NAMES. Barred Woodcreeper (combined form), Barred Woodhewer (arch.), letz letz (K), tuk tuk cheh (M).

Identification. 10½″ (26.5 cm). Large and dark. Heavily, but thinly, barred black on brown head, back, and underparts; most conspicuous on slightly paler breast; bars otherwise hard to see in deep forest shade. In profile, can be told by long, nearly straight bill with gradual taper. Lower mandible pale only at base. Flicks wings nervously.

Voice. *Call:* soft *wh-whee.* *Song: torrr-Y   torrr-Y   torrr-Y   torrr-y   torrr-y   torrr-y;* starts slowly, speeds up. Generally calls only for a short period at dawn.

Habitat. Midlevels to subcanopy within broadleaf and pine forest interior; occas. forest edge.

Distribution. Resident from Guerrero and c Veracruz to nw S.A.

Status in Belize. UC to FC resident on mainland.

Reference. *Voice:* Moore (1992).

Ivory-billed Woodcreeper   PLATE 32

Xiphorhynchus flavigaster

OTHER NAMES. Ivory-billed Woodhewer (arch.), letz letz (K), tuk tuk cheh (M).

Identification. 9½″ (24 cm). Hindparts rufous; foreparts heavily streaked with white and pale buff; unstreaked buff throat and supercilium; bill pale throughout, with nearly straight lower mandible. Often confused with smaller Streak-headed, as the only clear difference in the two is their size. Ivory-billed has proportionally larger, paler bill. Although ≈1½ times as large as Streak-headed, size differences per se can be very deceptive when observing a lone bird.

Voice. *Call:* 1. loud nasal *cheuw!;*
2. *tweo!;*
3. *whip!;*
4. short liquid laugh, *hee ha-ha-haw,* similar to one call of Bright-rumped Attila.
Song: 1. clear, melodious, slow, rising, then descending series, *wha-wha-whee-whee-whee-whuh whō whō whō whō whō whō;*
2. short, slow trill that slows and ends with high, then low, notes.

Habitat. Most forested areas and forest edge, including pines; midlevels to subcanopy.

Distribution. Resident from s Sonora and s Tamaulipas to nw C.R.

Status in Belize. FC to C resident on mainland.

Reference. *Voice:* Moore (1992).

Spotted Woodcreeper   MAP 132; PLATE 32
Xiphorhynchus erythropygius
OTHER NAMES. Spotted Woodhewer (arch.), letz letz (K), tuk tuk cheh (M).

Identification. 9¼" (23.5 cm). Only woodcreeper in Belize with spotted rather than barred plumage. Distinctly bicolored bill, gray above, pale below. In profile, bill is shorter than that of Ivory-billed. Confined to higher elevations.

Voice. *Song:* well-spaced *keeoo   keeo   keeo   [keeo],* the first note louder, the next 2 or 3 softer and lower-pitched; 1–2 sec pause between notes.

Habitat. Midlevels to subcanopy within broadleaf forest interior.

Distribution. Resident in highlands from se San Luis Potosí to sw S.A.

Status in Belize. FC resident in Maya Mtns. above 2,300 ft. (700 m).

Reference. *Status:* Miller and Miller (1992).

Streak-headed Woodcreeper
MAP 133; PLATE 32
Lepidocolaptes souleyetii
OTHER NAMES. Thin-billed Woodhewer (arch), letz letz (K), tuk tuk cheh (M).

Identification. 7¾" (19.5 cm). Plumage very similar to that of Ivory-billed; ⅓ smaller, with thinner, slightly decurved bill, with gray upper mandible. Vocalizations quite different. As a general rule, if there is any doubt as to whether a bird is small enough to be Streak-headed, it is probably an Ivory-billed.

Voice. *Song:* rapid, liquid, almost blubbery trill that sounds a little like wet lips flapping together; drops slightly in pitch immediately after first few notes (more liquid than in Ruddy Woodcreeper; lower-pitched and usually shorter than in Long-billed Gnatwren).

Habitat. Midlevels to subcanopy within broadleaf and pine forest and forest edge.

Distribution. Resident from Guerrero and c Veracruz s. of Yucatán Pen. to nw S.A.

Status in Belize. UC to locally FC resident on mainland n. to nc OW and n BE.

References. *Status:* Wood and Leberman (1987). *Voice:* Delaney (1992); Moore (1992).

FAMILY: THAMNOPHILIDAE (Antbirds)
World: 207. New World: 207. Belize: 9. Neotropical. The antbird family is nearly as diverse as the ovenbird family. No single external character typifies the antbirds, and despite their English names, relatively few antbird species, and none in Belize, routinely follow army ant swarms. Antbirds come in various combinations of blacks, grays, and browns; none are gaudily colored. They typically inhabit broadleaf forests, where they may be found at the forest edge in dense tangles, or inside the forest from the ground and understory to the canopy.

Great Antshrike   MAP 134; PLATE 33
Taraba major
OTHER NAMES. Oro ich (M).

Identification. 8" (20 cm). Large crested antshrike, uniformly dark above, white below, with disproportionately large bill and red eyes. Lives in dense tangles and can be very difficult to see. ♂: black above with white wingbars. ♀: dull rufous above, without wingbars.

Voice. *Call:* 1. growling *rrrrr,* repeated frequently;
2. louder, rolling trogonlike *brrrro,* repeated several times at ≈2 calls/sec. *Song:* hollow, accelerating trill *wha   wha   wha   wha   wha   wha   wha wha-wha-wha-wha-wha-wha-wha-wa-wa-wa-wa-wa,* typically with a soft, rough *grǎǎǎa* at the end that is audible only at close range. Song similar to that of Plain Antvireo. Frequently heard but seldom seen.

Habitat. Dense tangles, second-growth scrub, forest edge, and occas. understory within forest interior.

Distribution. Resident primarily on Gulf-Caribbean slope from s Veracruz and ne Oaxaca s. of Yucatán Pen. to sc S.A.

Status in Belize. FC resident generally away from coast n. to n CA and c BE, and locally in vicinity of New R. e OW.

Reference. *Status:* Wood and Leberman (1987).

Barred Antshrike   PLATE 33
Thamnophilus doliatus
OTHER NAMES. Rakax i tzu̱l (K), to ko we (M).

Identification. 6¾" (17 cm). Smaller than Great Antshrike, with proportionately smaller bill, pale yellow eyes. ♂: finely barred black and white throughout (brown and buff in imm.); prominent crest mostly white with black feather tips. ♀: rufous above, ochraceous buff below, with stripes only on auriculars and nape.

Voice. *Call:* 1. nasal crowlike *cǎǎǎǎ* to *grǎǎǎ;* 2. nasal, down-slurred *wheur* × 3–6; 3. mournful, slow, nasal *wanh* × 6–10, slowly descending the scale but not speeding up. *Song:* series of ≈20–25 nasal *wanh* notes, gradually speeding up like a bouncing ball, ending with an abrupt *wank!*

Habitat. Dense tangles, second-growth scrub, understory to midlevels within broadleaf and pine forest edge.

Distribution. Resident from s Tamaulipas to sc S.A.

Status in Belize. C resident on mainland; recorded twice recently on Ambergris Caye.

Reference. *Voice:* Moore (1992).

Western Slaty-Antshrike
MAP 135; PLATE 33
Thamnophilus atrinucha
OTHER NAMES. Slaty Antshrike (combined form).

Identification. 5¾" (14.5 cm). Vocally similar to the Barred Antshrike, but strikingly different plumage, smaller size, and lacking crest. ♂: slate gray with black central crown and central back, black wings with white feather tips, and white-tipped black tail; note plain gray face. ♀: olive brown above and buffy brown below, with tawny brown crown and rufous tail; blackish wings with pale buff feather tips.

Voice. *Call:* 1. nasal *wänk;*
2. emphatic, nasal *änh!* followed immediately by a short nasal trill;
3. nasal, somewhat scratchy *aow* to *aow aow,* not unlike song of Collared Trogon but notes less clear. *Song:* slow nasal trill, speeding up and ending with abrupt *wank!,* very similar to that of Barred Antshrike but lower-pitched.

Habitat. Understory to subcanopy within broadleaf forest interior and forest edge.

Distribution. Resident on Caribbean slope from s Belize and e Guat. to nw S.A.

Status in Belize. FC to locally C resident in coastal plain of TO n. to Monkey R.

Russet Antshrike   MAP 136; PLATE 33
Thamnistes anabatinus
OTHER NAMES. Tawny Antshrike (arch.).

Identification. 6" (15 cm). Smaller and, other than bill shape, unlike the two *Thamnophilus* antshrikes. Similar in size and shape to a vireo, and with a distinctive pale buff supercilium, also suggestive of a vireo, but larger bill, rufous wings and tail, and rich buff underparts are unlike any vireo. Sexes similar.

Voice. *Song:* 1. rich *sweet   sweet   sweet sweet sweet sweet* (typically 4–6 notes);
2. *sweea sweea sweea sweea sweea.*

Habitat. Vines and tangles in subcanopy to canopy within primary broadleaf forest interior.

Distribution. Resident from s Veracruz and ne Oaxaca to n and w S.A.

Status in Belize. UC (lower elevations) to FC (higher elevations) resident in Maya Mtns. and foothills of w TO and s CA.

Plain Antvireo   MAP 137; PLATE 33
Dysithamnus mentalis
OTHER NAMES. Slaty-capped Antvireo (arch.), Olivaceous Antvireo (I. Davis).

Identification. 4½″ (11.5 cm). Superficially resembles a vireo; however, has shorter tail, different bill shape, and plumage differences. ♂: olive gray, with pale yellowish belly and whitish throat, thin white wingbars, and distinctive dark auricular patch. ♀: olive brown above and across breast, with rufous crown, whitish eye-ring, and thin pale buff wingbars; lacks contrasting dark auriculars of ♂; may be confused with similar-sized Tawny-crowned Greenlet, but greenlet has smaller bill and longer tail and lacks eye-ring and wingbars.

Voice. *Call:* 1. nasal *wank* or *wanh;* 2. *chet chet. Song:* very squeaky laughing cackle or slow trill of ≈20 notes, speeding up and falling in pitch (2¼–2½ sec); similar to Great Antshrike song.

Habitat. Midlevels to subcanopy within primary broadleaf forest.

Distribution. Resident from ne Chiapas and s Campeche primarily on Caribbean slope to c S.A.

Status in Belize. UC to locally FC resident in w OW, most of CA s. of Belize R., and Maya Mtns. and foothills of w SC and nw TO.

Reference. *Voice:* Moore (1992).

Slaty Antwren   MAP 138; PLATE 33
Myrmotherula schisticolor

Identification. 4¼″ (10.5 cm). Resembles miniature Dusky Antbird, with short tail and thinner bill. ♂: slate gray, with black throat and breast and small white wing covert tips that form rows of spots. ♀: olive brown above, tawny brown below, with paler throat; lacks spots in wings.

Voice. *Call:* nasal, up-slurred *reeah. Song:* quiet, whistled *weep weep weep weep weep.*

Habitat. Midlevels to subcanopy within primary broadleaf forest.

Distribution. Resident from e Chiapas, c Guat., and s Belize on Caribbean slope to n and w S.A.

Status in Belize. UC to FC resident at higher elevations in Maya Mtns. in sw TO and probably adjacent CA.

References. *Status:* Jones et al. (2000). *Voice:* Howell and Webb (1995).

Dot-winged Antwren   MAP 139; PLATE 33
Microrhopias quixensis
OTHER NAMES. Boucard Antwren (I. Davis).

Identification. 4½″ (11.5 cm). Strongly graduated, medium-length tail, with broad white feather tips. Usually holds tail slightly spread. Travels through forest in small groups. ♂: except for white-tipped wing coverts and tail corners, jet black. ♀: gray above and rich rufous below, with same wing and tail pattern as ♂.

Voice. *Call:* series of unevenly spaced squeaky *tew* notes given by all birds in group. *Song:* melodious trill, rising then falling, *dt dt dt dt-dt-dtdtdtdtdtdtdt dew dew dew dew dew.* Shortened song similar to that of Tropical Gnatcatcher but slower.

Habitat. High understory to subcanopy within broadleaf forest interior and forest edge.

Distribution. Resident from n Oaxaca and se Yucatán Pen. to c S.A.

Status in Belize. FC to C resident on mainland, mostly in interior n. to ne CA, nc OW, and locally to s CO.

References. *Voice:* Delaney (1992); Moore (1992).

Dusky Antbird   MAP 140; PLATE 33
Cercomacra tyrannina
OTHER NAMES. Tyrannine Antbird (arch.), Tyrannine Antwren (I. Davis).

Identification. 5¼″ (13.5 cm). Similar to, but larger than, Slaty Antwren with longer tail; different habitat. ♂: uniformly dark gray, including throat and breast; thin white edges to wing coverts. ♀: richer tawny underparts than ♀ Slaty Antwren, and not paler on throat and lores.

Voice. *Call:* 1. sharp, squeaky *kick;* 2. loud wrenlike *churr* to *chair;* 3. *brrt;* 4. clear *tur* to *teur;* 5. wrenlike *d-d-d-t;* 6. rough *breey. Song:* hollow *chew chew chew* . . . (typically 8–10 notes), rising in pitch and speeding up; ♀'s song higher-pitched than ♂'s.

Habitat. Dense second-growth scrub, tangles, understory of forest edge.

Distribution. Resident from n Oaxaca and se Yucatán Pen. to c S.A.

Status in Belize. FC to C resident n. to n OW and n BE.

Reference. *Voice:* Moore (1992).

Bare-crowned Antbird   MAP 141; PLATE 33
Gymnocichla nudiceps

Identification. 6″ (15 cm). Larger than Dusky Antbird, with unfeathered blue facial skin. ♂: black, with thin white feather tips in wing coverts and unfeathered blue forecrown and face. ♀: grayish brown above, with cinnamon-rufous underparts and wingbars; unfeathered blue skin restricted to broad area around eyes and lores.

Voice. *Song:* ≈13–15 loud, clear, whistled *sweea* notes delivered with quickening pace; cadence of Dusky Antbird song, but quality much sweeter, purer.

Habitat. Understory and ground within broadleaf forest interior and forest edge.

Distribution. Resident from s Belize and e Guat. primarily on Caribbean slope to n Colombia.

Status in Belize. VU and sparsely distributed resident at low elevations along the base of Maya Mtns. in TO, s SC, and s CA.

Reference. *Status:* Howell et al. (1992).

FAMILY: FORMICARIIDAE
(Antthrushes)

World: 62. **New World:** 62. **Belize:** 1. Neotropical. Antthrushes were formerly placed in the antbird family but now are considered by most to warrant status as a separate family. They are more robust than antbirds, with long legs, a very short tail, and exclusively ground-dwelling habits. They typically walk with their tail cocked high.

Black-faced Antthrush   PLATE 33
Formicarius analis

OTHER NAMES. Mexican Antthrush (is part of), ch'uluk (K), tulin nuche' (M).

Identification. 7¼″ (18.5 cm). Plump, short-tailed, long-legged ground bird with black face and throat, pale blue eye-ring, and rufous-chestnut band across upper breast. Otherwise, brown above and sooty gray below, with chestnut uppertail coverts and pale cinnamon undertail coverts. Walks on forest floor with short tail cocked.

Voice. *Call: b-drrrt,* louder and more liquid than similar note of Ochre-bellied Flycatcher. *Song:* distinctive, clear *dot   doe doe doe* . . . × 10–15; one of the more characteristic forest sounds. Often heard but seldom seen.

Habitat. Ground and understory of broadleaf forest interior.

Distribution. Resident primarily on Gulf-Caribbean slope from c Veracruz to c S.A.

Status in Belize. FC to C resident on mainland.

References. *Voice:* Moore (1992). *Systematics:* Howell (1994b).

FAMILY: TYRANNIDAE
(Tyrant Flycatchers)

World: 402+. **New World:** 402+. **Belize:** 50 (plus 1 provisional). The largest family of birds in the New World, and the largest in the world under some taxonomic schemes. The tyrant flycatchers are a highly diverse assemblage of species with few traits in common. Although found from subarctic N.A. to the southern tip of S.A., the vast majority are found in the Tropics. Most species in Belize perch upright in vegetation, have a small hook at tip of a flattened bill, with rictal bristles at the base, and catch insects on the wing as they sally forth from exposed perches. A few glean insects from foliage in the fashion of a vireo or warbler, and a few eat fruit seasonally. In most, the sexes are similar; however, in a few the ♀ is recognizably different. Some of the most difficult ID challenges in the avian world (e.g., *Contopus, Empidonax,* and *Myiarchus*) are found in this family. Four subfamilies are recognized: the Elaeniinae, with 8 species in Belize; the Platyrinchinae, with 6; the Fluvicolinae, with 16; and the Tyranninae, with 20.

SUBFAMILY: ELAENIINAE
(Tyrannulets and Elaenias)
Small to medium-sized, non-migratory species, mostly lacking bold field marks. To the neotropical neophyte, many can be frustratingly difficult to ID, because of their overall greenish aspect with varying amounts of whitish to yellowish wing feather edgings and indistinct facial markings. But once their behavioral patterns and vocalizations are learned, they are not so difficult. An exception is the Yellow-bellied Tyrannulet, which is boldly marked and has a much shorter tail than the others.

Things to note: vocalizations; behavior (tail pumping, wing flicking, sallying vs. gleaning); posture (upright vs. horizontal, tail down vs. tail cocked); bill size and width across the base; color and nature of markings in the wings; presence/absence of eye-ring, supercilium, and crest.

Yellow-bellied Tyrannulet
MAP 142; PLATE 34
Ornithion semiflavum

Identification. 3½″ (9 cm). Distinctively marked but easily overlooked high in the canopy, where it typically resides. Its stubby tail, tiny bill, all-yellow underparts, and broad white supercilium are all easy to see, even in the treetops, making this species the easiest in the group to ID.
Voice. *Call:* 1. *peeuh;*
2. strident *tree tree tree tree tree tree;*
3. squeaky-mouse *squee-uh. Song:* emphatic, strident *peeuh   pee pee pee pit!* Vocalizations are more intense and rapidly paced than in Northern Beardless-Tyrannulet.
Habitat. Canopy and subcanopy within broadleaf forest and forest edge.

Distribution. Resident primarily on Gulf-Caribbean slope from c Veracruz s. of Yucatán Pen. to C.R.
Status in Belize. UC to C resident n. to c OW and n BE, possibly to s CO.
References. *Voice:* Delaney (1992); Moore (1992).

Northern Beardless-Tyrannulet
MAP 143; PLATE 34
Camptostoma imberbe
OTHER NAMES. Beardless Flycatcher (arch.).

Identification. 4″ (10 cm). Except for its bright orange lower mandible, one of the drabbest of a drab group of flycatchers. Small, olive-gray, short-billed flycatcher with rather inconspicuous supercilium, eye-ring, and wingbars, and a hint of yellow on belly. On the other hand, quite vocal, and possessing a unique manner of gleaning insects quite un-flycatcher-like from foliage while constantly pumping its tail and frequently erecting and lowering its bushy crest. Will sometimes hang upside down while gleaning insects from the tips of branches.
Voice. *Call:* variously, lazy to emphatic *perr it* to *peeewit!* to *purrrWIT!*, sometimes followed by a short, rapid burry jumble. *Song:* 1. strident *PEEE   pee pee pee pee,* not as fast or lively as Yellow-bellied Tyrannulet song;
2. *beetlit beetlit peee peee peee;* sometimes with burry notes mixed in between phrases;
3. less often a rapid, clear, metallic *pe pe pe pe pe pe pe. Dawn song: per per per PEE-dit.*
Habitat. Open pine forest and savanna, broadleaf forest edge, second-growth scrub.
Distribution. Resident from se Arizona and s Texas to C.R. Populations in nw Mex. and Arizona are migratory.
Status in Belize. FC to C resident on mainland s. to ne CA and ne TO; UC and local to nw CA and s TO.

Greenish Elaenia PLATE 34

Myiopagis viridicata

OTHER NAMES. Placid Flycatcher
(I. Davis), tunt (K).

Identification. 5½″ (14 cm). Small greenish fly-catcher with yellow belly and yellow feather edges in wings. Told from Yellow-olive Fly-catcher by small, narrow, pointed bill; smaller, flatter, olive-gray head; more distinct supercilium; and less contrast between grayish head and greenish back. Told from Paltry Tyrannulet by upright stance, longer bill, less distinct supercilium, and slightly longer tail. Never perches horizontally with tail cocked, almost always perching more vertically with tail held in straight line with body or slightly depressed. Yellow central crown feathers are usually concealed.

Voice. 1. Forced, thin whistled *cheeeuh;*
2. slow, forced *cheeeu weeeu.*

Dawn song: 1. repetitious, slightly plaintive *chew-ee-ee'u* to *chewee-eeu;*
2. thin, whistled *chea wea wit.*

Habitat. Midlevels to subcanopy within broadleaf and pine forests, forest edge, and tall second growth; also parks and urban areas with large shade trees.

Distribution. Resident from s Durango and s Tamaulipas to c S.A.

Status in Belize. FC to C resident on mainland; recorded once on s Ambergris Caye.

Reference. *Voice:* Moore (1992).

Caribbean Elaenia MAP 144; PLATE 34

Elaenia martinica

OTHER NAMES. Lesser Antillean Elaenia
(I. Davis).

Identification. 5¾″ (14.5 cm). Small-headed, nondescript flycatcher with small, rather narrow bill. Frequently hops from branch to branch unlike most flycatchers, which remain motionless between sallies. Similar to Northern Beardless-Tyrannulet, but larger, darker, grayer, and with a longer bill. Broad pale lemon edges to secondaries form a pale wing panel. Little, if any, geographical overlap in Belize. Like beardless-tyrannulet, has pinkish orange lower mandible, but its crest, when raised, reveals white basal feathers, which are lacking in beardless-tyrannulet. From wood-pewee by grayish throat (no contrast with breast), small rounded head, narrow bill, and behavior. The solitary Caribbean differs from the gregarious Yellow-bellied in having duller plumage and no eye-ring and in seldom raising its crest.

Voice. Distinctive clear *wheeur* to *peeur* or even *keeea!* (varying degrees of intensity of the same basic call); not hoarse or nasal, as in Yellow-bellied Elaenia.

Habitat. Littoral forest.

Distribution. Mostly resident in W.I. and islands in w and s Caribbean.

Status in Belize. FC resident on Caye Caulker; also recorded in winter on Ambergris Caye, and at least once each on Lighthouse Reef, Glovers Reef, and mainland near Belize City.

References. *Status:* Howell et al. (1992); Ornat et al. (1989).

Yellow-bellied Elaenia PLATE 34

Elaenia flavogaster

OTHER NAMES. Tunt (K), ya (M).

Identification. 6¼″ (16 cm). Resembles Caribbean Elaenia but has brighter yellow belly, pale eye-ring, and prominent crest, which it holds erect most of the time. A raucous, somewhat gregarious bird with two to several in a group frequently bursting forth with simultaneous calling. Has habit of leaning forward on perch and peering inquisitively from side to side. Superficially resembles small *Myiarchus* flycatcher, but note white basal feathers in crest, eye-ring, and lack of rufous in wings and tail.

Voice. 1. Hoarse, breathy *wheeeur;*
2. explosive burry chatter,
whrrrr t-whrrrr t-whrrrr . . . usually given by a group of birds, not as shrill as in Social Flycatcher. *Dawn song:* harsh, burry *pwi ti tee* and occas. *purrr tee!*

Habitat. Midlevels to subcanopy at forest edge, most pine woodlands, and most open areas with scattered trees, including towns and villages.

Distribution. Resident from c Veracruz to c S.A.

Status in Belize. C resident on mainland and

Ambergris Caye; R seasonal visitor to other cayes.

Ochre-bellied Flycatcher PLATE 35
Mionectes oleagineus
OTHER NAMES. Oleaginous Pipromorpha (arch.), tunt (K).

Identification. 5¼″ (13.5 cm). No prominent plumage features other than ochre-yellow belly and undertail coverts on an otherwise drab olive body with gray lores and throat, faintly streaked breast. Dark eyes stand out in plain face. Hover-gleans insects from leaf tips. Moves about more actively than related Sepia-capped and often leans forward on its perch and peers. It and the Sepia-capped have a curious habit of periodically raising or flashing one wing.
Voice. Usually silent. *Call:* 1. *pee-ik* to *p-lik;* 2. plaintive *cheu. Song:* liquid *whick* to *trick* notes (similar to Melodious Blackbird vocalization) interspersed with series of emphatic nasal *hdet!* to *bdet!* notes.
Habitat. Midlevels within broadleaf forest interior and clearings.
Distribution. Resident from se San Luis Potosí to c S.A.
Status in Belize. FC to C resident on mainland.
References. *Status:* Wood and Leberman (1987). *Voice:* Delaney (1992); Moore (1992).

Sepia-capped Flycatcher
MAP 145; PLATE 34
Leptopogon amaurocephalus
OTHER NAMES. Brown-capped Leptopogon (arch.).

Identification. 5¼″ (13.5 cm). Olive brown, paler below, becoming lemon yellow on belly. Distinguished by sepia-brown crown, dark post-auricular crescent, and small "teardrop" that give it a unique facial expression. Differs from Ochre-bellied in having ochre wingbars and tawny yellow secondary and tertial edges. Perches nearly vertically, often motionless, making it difficult to detect. Like Ochre-bellied, periodically raises one wing.
Voice. *Song:* rapid, liquid, burry trill (1¼–1½ sec). Starts softly and immediately builds in in-

tensity, initially rising, then descending in pitch; somewhat woodcreeper-like, but distinct tone and pattern are quickly learned.
Habitat. Midlevels within broadleaf forest interior.
Distribution. Resident primarily on Gulf-Caribbean slope from c Veracruz and se Yucatán Pen. to c S.A.
Status in Belize. UC to FC resident on mainland, mostly in interior, n. to c CA and w SC; also in w OW and locally in e OW.
References. *Voice:* Delaney (1992); Moore (1992).

Paltry Tyrannulet MAP 146; PLATE 34
Zimmerius vilissimus
OTHER NAMES. Mistletoe Tyrannulet (alt.).

Identification. 4½″ (11.5 cm). Similar in appearance to Greenish Elaenia and Yellow-olive Flycatcher, but with stubbier bill and more conspicuous supercilium that extends prominently behind the eyes. Frequently perches horizontally with tail slightly cocked. Vocalizations most like otherwise dissimilar Yellow-bellied Tyrannulet.
Voice. *Call:* 1. clear, plaintive *peeu* to *peeeup,* longer and more strident than Yellow-bellied Flycatcher call; 2. *peeuh peeuh peeuh peeuh peeuh,* somewhat similar to, but not as strident as, in Yellow-bellied Tyrannulet.
Habitat. Midlevels to subcanopy within broadleaf forest and forest edge; also plantations and edges of villages.
Distribution. Resident from e Chiapas to n S.A.
Status in Belize. UC resident in s TO up to ≈2,500 ft. (≈750 m) in Maya Mtns.
Reference. *Status:* Jones et al. (2000).

SUBFAMILY: PLATYRINCHINAE
(Tody-Tyrants and Flatbills)
Characterized by a broad, flattened bill. Some, like the spadebills and the flatbills, have an exceptionally short, wide bill. The Yellow-olive Flycatcher also has a wide-based bill, but not exaggeratedly so. The exception is the Northern Bentbill; however, in plumage characters it resembles other members of this group. Plumage varies from nondescript (Eye-ringed Flatbill) to

bold (Common Tody-Flycatcher). The Platyrin-chinae are non-migratory.

Things to note: bill width and shape, eye color, posture, behavior, vocalizations.

Northern Bentbill   PLATE 34

Oncostoma cinereigulare
OTHER NAMES. Bent-billed Flycatcher (arch.), Gray-throated Bentbill (I. Davis).

Identification. 4″ (10 cm). Similar to Slate-headed Tody-Flycatcher in both plumage pattern and some vocalizations, but has uniquely downward-bent bill and less prominent wingbars, lacks white "spectacles," and has more upright posture.
Voice. *Call:* 1. *brrrrrt* rising in pitch; 2. *pt burrr* to *tp-prrr,* very much like that of Slate-headed Tody-Flycatcher. *Song:* burry *burrrrrrrrr* on one pitch.
Habitat. Understory to subcanopy within broadleaf forest, forest edge, second-growth scrub; less often, dense roadside and riverbank tangles.
Distribution. Resident from c Veracruz to w Pan.
Status in Belize. FC to C resident on mainland.
Reference. *Voice:* Moore (1992).

Slate-headed Tody-Flycatcher

MAP 147; PLATE 34
Poecilotriccus sylvia

Identification. 3¾″ (9.5 cm). Tiny green-and-yellow flycatcher with gray head, pale eyes, white "spectacles," prominent yellow wingbars, and straight, laterally flattened bill. Horizontal posture. Plumage pattern and vocal repertoire similar to those of Northern Bentbill.
Voice. *Chup* notes with occas., blubbery *chp-burrr.*
Habitat. Dense tangles along roadsides and riverbanks and at broadleaf forest edge.
Distribution. Resident primarily on Gulf-Caribbean slope from c Veracruz to n S.A.
Status in Belize. UC to locally FC resident on mainland n. to at least n OW and n BE, but apparently absent in CO.

Common Tody-Flycatcher

MAP 148; PLATE 34
Todirostrum cinereum
OTHER NAMES. Northern Tody-Flycatcher (arch.), White-tipped Tody-Flycatcher (I. Davis), pilitit (M).

Identification. 3¾″ (9.5 cm). Although they have a similar spatula-shaped bill, Slate-headed and Common Tody-Flycatchers are quite different in plumage, habitat, behavior, and vocal repertoire. Common has white eyes set in a jet black face, entirely yellow underparts, and interesting habit of wagging or swishing its tail from side to side.
Voice. *Call:* an emphatic *tik* given singly or at a rate of ≈2/sec. *Song:* loud, slightly tinny *d-d-d-dt,* with quality of Tropical Kingbird's most typical vocalization, but shorter, more emphatic, with no variation in cadence. Sometimes two birds will duet, with one bird calling repeatedly, *tik tik tik tik tik . . . ,* while the other bursts forth with several loud *d-d-d-dt* rattles.
Habitat. Understory to subcanopy in open areas with scattered large trees, including plantations, orchards, towns, and villages; also forest edge, but not in forest interior or in dense tangles.
Distribution. Resident from c Veracruz to c S.A.
Status in Belize. C resident nearly throughout on mainland and Ambergris Caye, but scarce or absent in most of CO.

Eye-ringed Flatbill   PLATE 35

Rhynchocyclus brevirostris
OTHER NAMES. Short-billed Flatbill (I. Davis).

Identification. 6½″ (16.5 cm). Medium-sized olive-green flycatcher with short, laterally flattened, broad-based bill and large, round head; large black eyes in a plain face, further emphasized by bold white eye-ring. Characteristically perches motionless, with tail slightly drooped. Its weak song, infrequently given, is barely noticeable.
Voice. Very high-pitched *zueeeee,* rising in pitch, faint *zit* at end.

Habitat. Midlevels to subcanopy within broadleaf forest interior.

Distribution. Resident from Guerrero and c Veracruz to Pan.

Status in Belize. UC to locally FC resident in interior; scarce to absent in coastal areas, including most of CO. Unrecorded on cayes.

Reference. *Voice:* Moore (1992).

Yellow-olive Flycatcher   PLATE 34

Tolmomyias sulphurescens

OTHER NAMES. White-eyed Flycatcher (arch.), Sulphury Flatbill (arch.), tunt (K).

Identification. 5¼″ (13.5 cm). Although a flatbill, it much more closely resembles the elaenias and tyrannulets. Gray head contrasts with olive-green back; yellowish below, with yellow highlights in wings. Larger, rounder head and longer, broader bill than Paltry Tyrannulet and Greenish Elaenia and lacks prominent supercilium of the tyrannulet (supercilium barely extends past the eye). Stance usually intermediate between more vertical posture of Greenish Elaenia and horizontal posture of Paltry Tyrannulet and does not cock tail like the tyrannulet. Ad. has whitish eyes detectible at close range. All three have distinctly different vocalizations.

Voice. Very high-pitched, forced *sss sss sss sss,* with ≈1 sec pause between each note.

Habitat. Midlevels to canopy within broadleaf, forest and forest edge; less frequently in pine forest.

Distribution. Resident from c Veracruz to c S.A.

Status in Belize. C resident on mainland.

Reference. *Voice:* Moore (1992).

Stub-tailed Spadebill   PLATE 34

Platyrinchus cancrominus

OTHER NAMES. White-throated Spadebill (combined form), Mexican Spadebill (I. Davis).

Identification. 3½″ (9 cm). Unlike the larger flatbill, the tiny Stub-tailed Spadebill is a bundle of energy. It calls frequently and is constantly sallying from its perch in aerial pursuit of insects. Its oddly complex facial pattern, short tail, and large, flat bill readily ID it.

Voice. *Song:* rapid, squeaky *speed-d-de-dunk.*

Habitat. Sparse understory within broadleaf forest interior.

Distribution. Resident from c Veracruz to nw C.R.

Status in Belize. FC resident on mainland.

References. *Voice:* Delaney (1992); Moore (1992).

SUBFAMILY: FLUVICOLINAE

Composed of a few resident tropical species and an array of migratory species that are in Belize only seasonally. Perhaps the most heterogeneous subfamily, the Fluvicolinae includes a few strikingly colored or adorned species like Vermilion and Royal flycatchers; however, the relatively undistinguished *Empidonax* and *Contopus* groups constitute the bulk of the subfamily in Belize. No single visible morphological characters typify this group.

Royal Flycatcher   PLATE 35

Onychorhynchus coronatus

OTHER NAMES. Northern Royal-Flycatcher (is part of), Mexican Royal-Flycatcher (I. Davis), tunt (K).

Identification. 6¾″ (17 cm). Spectacular red crest (yellow orange in the ♀) tipped with blue violet is seldom raised. Normally folded crest and long bill give this species a hammerhead appearance. Note also, pale tawny rump, cinnamon-colored tail, pale spotted wingbars, and prominent rictal bristles.

Voice. *Call: eonk!,* somewhat like short note of Rufous-tailed Jacamar. *Song:* mournful, thin, descending

duh whew   whew   whew   whew   whew.

Habitat. Midlevels to subcanopy within broadleaf forest and forest edge.

Distribution. Resident from c Veracruz to c S.A.

Status in Belize. UC to locally FC resident on mainland, except possibly CO.

References. *Voice:* Delaney (1992); Gilardi (1997); Moore (1992).

Ruddy-tailed Flycatcher

MAP 149; PLATE 34

Terenotriccus erythrurus

OTHER NAMES. Cinnamon Terenotriccus (arch.).

Identification. 4″ (10 cm). Tiny and inconspicuous flycatcher of the forest interior. Head and back grayish olive; underparts, tail, and wing feather edges cinnamon. Thin, pale eye-ring sets off black eyes in plain face. Typically perches erect, with tail slightly drooped. Its weak, simple call and habit of perching quietly make it easy to overlook.
Voice. *Song:* thin but emphatic *pia cheet!*
Habitat. Midlevels within broadleaf forest interior.
Distribution. Resident primarily on Caribbean slope from ne Chiapas and s Campeche to c S.A.
Status in Belize. UC and local resident n. to ec CA and w SC; also w OW and locally in e OW.
Reference. *Voice:* Moore (1992).

Sulphur-rumped Flycatcher

MAP 150; PLATE 34

Myiobius sulphureipygius

OTHER NAMES. Sulphur-rumped Myiobius (I. Davis), tunt (K).

Identification. 5″ (12.5 cm). Distinguished by prominent pale yellow rump offset by nearly black tail; ochre breast; large, beady black eyes set in plain face; and prominent bristles at base of bill.
Voice. Hard, flat buntinglike *spk* or *pk*.
Habitat. Understory to midlevels within broadleaf forest interior.
Distribution. Resident primarily on Gulf-Caribbean slope from c Veracruz to nw S.A.
Status in Belize. FC resident on mainland n., mostly in interior, to n OW and w BE; not recorded from CO.
Reference. *Voice:* Moore (1992).

Genus: Contopus *(Pewees)*

Pewees are small to medium-sized brownish flycatchers. The two larger species, Olive-sided Flycatcher and Greater Pewee, are rather distinctive. The three smaller pewees, on the other hand, are notoriously difficult to ID, even in the hand, but can usually be IDed by their characteristic vocalizations. Plumage differences among the three are average differences only and should be used along with vocal differences in making a definitive ID. This is especially important in documenting a Western Wood-Pewee or an out-of-season Eastern Wood-Pewee. The smaller pewees can be confused with some of the *Empidonax,* but the former are slightly larger and browner, lack a clear eye-ring, have longer wings and shorter legs, generally have a darker breast, have dark smudges in undertail coverts, and do not flick their tail. *Note:* some Willow Flycatchers also lack a distinct eye-ring and on average are browner than the other *Empidonax.* Conveniently, all three pewees vocalize frequently, and migrant Eastern and Western sing year-round.

Things to note: vocalizations, primary extension, absence of eye-ring, breast pattern, lower mandible color and extent.

Olive-sided Flycatcher   PLATE 36

Contopus cooperi

Identification. 7″ (18 cm). Dark grayish sides, flanks, and breast split down the center by a white band connecting white throat and belly. At times, white body feathers high on flanks peer through above the folded wings, adding to this species' distinctive appearance. Has peaked head but not the full crest of Greater Pewee and has shorter tail.
Voice. *Call: pip pip pip pip* or *kip kip kip kip.*
Habitat. Exposed snags in canopy at forest edge. In migration, found also in more open habitats but rather consistently on snags high in a tree.
Distribution. Nests from Alaska and nc Can. s. in West to mtns. of nw Baja Calif. and in East to n U.S. Winters from sc Mex. s. of Yucatán Pen. to c S.A.
Status in Belize. Relatively UC transient, mid-Aug. to early Nov. and late Apr. to late May; UC to FC winter visitor locally at higher elevations, occas. at lower elevations.

Greater Pewee
MAP 151; PLATE 36

Contopus pertinax

OTHER NAMES. Coues' Flycatcher (arch.).

Identification. 7¼″ (18.5 cm). Similar to Olive-sided but darker overall, with rather uniform darkish gray underparts, paler only on throat and belly, which is pale yellowish. Prominent crest; bright yellow-orange lower mandible.

Voice. *Call:* 1. similar to Olive-sided's, *pip pip* or *kip kip,* sometimes 3 or 4 to a series; 2. slow, rolling trill *pt pt pt pt prreeerrrr-prreeerrr,* quality of a Killdeer call. *Song:* slow, lazy whistled *José Marie* to *José Maria.*

Habitat. Exposed snags at midlevels to canopy in pine forest and forest edge.

Distribution. Largely resident in highlands from c Arizona to nc Nic.; northernmost populations migratory.

Status in Belize. Local resident in Mtn. Pine Ridge.

Western Wood-Pewee
NOT ILLUSTRATED

Contopus sordidulus

OTHER NAMES. Western Pewee (alt.).

Identification. 5¾″ (14.5 cm). Under most circumstances not safely separable from Eastern Wood-Pewee in the field except, with experience, by voice. Lower mandible ≈½ to ⅔ black with pinkish orange base; breast and sides dark, usually no lighter than upperparts; less olive above on average than in Eastern; wingbars average more dusky, not white (but varies with plumage wear). Dusky feather centers in undertail coverts usually more prominent than in Eastern and Tropical. Longer primary extension than in Tropical but not Eastern. These are average differences only, with some overlap in all.

Voice. Burry *bzyeeer;* sometimes a slurred, plaintive *peeuuu* and a slightly disyllabic *pee-irr,* approaching the common *peee-ur* call of Eastern Wood-Pewee, but somewhat burry, not as clear.

Habitat. May be found in most habitats with scattered to moderately dense tree cover, but perhaps more likely in pine forest.

Distribution. Nests from e Alaska and w Can. in mtns. to Hon.; winters in S.A. s. to Peru and Bolivia.

Status in Belize. One record: two in separate localities in Mtn. Pine Ridge, 25 Oct. 1998.

References. *Status:* Jones et al. (2000). *Identification:* Kaufman (1990).

Eastern Wood-Pewee
PLATE 36

Contopus virens

OTHER NAMES. Eastern Pewee (alt.), tunt (K).

Identification. 5¾″ (14.5 cm). Pinkish orange on at least the basal half of the lower mandible; however, individuals vary widely in the extent of the pale base, resulting in a significant amount of overlap with both Tropical and Western. Typically paler than Western, especially on breast and sides, with a slightly more olive back; wingbars whitish in ad. in fresh plumage but soon wear thin. Dark centers to undertail coverts not as prominent as in Western. Longer primary extension than in Tropical.

Voice. *Call:* usually a soft to fairly emphatic *wit,* somewhat similar to call of Least or Willow Flycatcher. *Partial song:* whistled, mournful *pee-aaah* or a softer *peee-ur,* occas. interspersed with slow, sweet, up-slurred *purree* or more drawn-out *puuweee. Full song:* drawn-out, clear, whistled *pee-ah-weeee.* Sings in both spring and autumn.

Habitat. Widespread; in migration found at nearly all levels and in nearly all habitats with woody vegetation.

Distribution. Nests in e N.A. from s Can. to Gulf of Mex. Winters in S.A. s. to Bolivia and w Brazil.

Status in Belize. VC autumn transient, mid-Aug. to mid-Dec., and C spring transient, mid-Mar. to early June.

References. *Voice:* Moore (1992). *Identification:* Kaufman (1990).

Tropical Pewee
PLATE 36

Contopus cinereus

Identification. 5½″ (14 cm). Generally, entire lower mandible pinkish orange, but occas. with dark tip. Shorter primary extension and slightly darker, more crested crown than in Eastern or Western wood-pewee. In fresh plumage has a distinct yellowish wash on belly, often extending up center of breast, contrasting with dusky olive sides.

Voice. *Call:* fairly soft *pe-wit* or *pe-it,* reminiscent of Northern Beardless-Tyrannulet call but less emphatic. *Song:* 1. short rattling trill that drops in pitch and slows; 2. short, rolling *p-r-r-r,* somewhat similar to vocalization of Dusky-capped Flycatcher. *Dawn song: peeeur per eat!*

Habitat. Midlevels to subcanopy in open broadleaf forest and forest edge, less often in pines; occas. in more open habitats with scattered trees.

Distribution. Resident from c Veracruz to c S.A.

Status in Belize. FC resident on mainland.

Reference. *Voice:* Moore (1992).

Genus: Empidonax

Most species in this genus can be notoriously difficult to ID. Six species occur in Belize, all as either transients or winter visitors. With experience, all can be readily told by their songs and, in most cases, by their calls. Fortunately, all *Empidonax* species sing, at least occasionally, while in Belize, simplifying to some extent the ID challenges. In order to safely ID most noncalling *Empidonax*—especially in autumn migration— it helps to know the degree of feather wear (fresh or worn plumage) and the bird's age (juv. or ad.) and to be cognizant of the lighting (color differences are subtle and can be perceived differently in strong sunlight, haze, and shade). Few plumage and structural characters are absolute; most are *average* differences between species; thus, the ID of an individual bird is rarely based on one character or even two but on a combination of several characters that may point strongly to one species. The best approach to learning the *Empidonax* is to study positively IDed birds (calling or singing birds) under natural conditions in the field, noting as many plumage, structural, and behavioral characters as possible while the bird is in sight.

Things to note (season and habitat): Yellow-bellied and Least are the only empids likely to be encountered between Nov. and Mar. Yellow-bellied in forest interior and edge; Least in open woodland and scrub. White-throated, a rare winter visitor, prefers edges of marshes. These three can be separated by plumage characters alone in winter. Habitat preferences, however, break down during migration, and the presence of migrant empids (Acadian, Alder, and Willow) in spring and autumn complicates the picture. Birds in both juvenal and worn adult plumage in autumn further complicate ID.

Things to note (vocalizations): *For calls,* tone, pitch, loudness, number of syllables. Single note (short, soft *wit* to *whit* or higher-pitched, sharper *pip*); 2 syllables (up-slurred *peip,* down-slurred *peup*); or rough, flat, and drawn out *(r-reeah). For songs,* richness, pattern, number and emphasis of syllables (1. short, dry, harsh 2-syllabled *che-BEK* or *che-bunk;* 2. clear, explosive *seeuh-KEET!;* 3. scratchy 2-syllable *fitz-beuw* or 3-syllable *rree-bee-ah;* or 4. drawn-out, burry *bree-uh*).

Things to note (plumage, structural, and behavioral characters): *Bill (from beneath)*— length vs. width at base, overall size, extent of pale coloration on lower mandible. *Throat*— color, degree of contrast between throat and side of head. *Eye-ring*—lacking, thin, or bold; even width throughout or thicker posteriorly; white or yellow. *Back*—predominant hue gray, brown, or green. *Wings*—degree of contrast with back; color of wingbars (white to yellow buff to cinnamon buff); primary projection (short, medium, or long). *Behavior*—upward tail flick, wing flick.

Yellow-bellied Flycatcher   PLATE 36
Empidonax flaviventris

Identification. 5¼″ (13.5 cm). Relatively small, round-headed *Empidonax* with moderate primary projection and relatively short bill. Only *Empidonax* with yellow throat (in fresh and moderately worn plumage only). Greater wing-back contrast than in others (black wings, green back); greener above than all but Acadian; yellowish eye-ring usually broadest posteriorly (Acadian has thin, even-width eye-ring). In heavily worn plumage (ads. Aug. to Oct.), can lack yellow tones, including on throat. These are best told from Least by greener back and longer primary projection. 1st basic plumage duller, with pale yellow-olive throat and relatively broad, bright yellow-buff wingbars. In most plumages, most closely resembles Acadian. Birds without yellow throats (worn plumage) told from Acadian by a combination of characters: more rounded head with steeper forehead, smaller bill, shorter tail, less primary extension, broader eye-ring of uneven thickness, darker breast (stronger throat-breast contrast), and stronger throat-face contrast.

Voice. *Call:* most typical, especially in winter, is downwardly inflected *peeup,* sometimes given every few seconds incessantly. In migration, gives a wider variety of calls, with some approaching those of Acadian, for example, a higher-pitched, shrill *peeip! Song:* dry *che-bunk* to *je-berk,* with neither syllable accented. Harsher, lower-pitched, less emphatic than in Least. Sings much less frequently than Least while in Belize.

Habitat. Low to mid-strata in forest interior and less often at forest edge. Ranges over wider range of habitats in migration.

Distribution. Nests from nc Can. to s Can. and ne U.S.; winters from s Tamaulipas to Pan.

Status in Belize. FC to C winter visitor, late Aug. to late-May.

References. *Identification:* Kaufman (1990); Whitney and Kaufman (1985a, 1986b).

Acadian Flycatcher PLATE 36
Empidonax virescens

Identification. 5½″ (14 cm). Large, greenish *Empidonax* with pale underparts; less contrast between pale grayish to whitish throat and side of head than in other empids. Less wing-back contrast than in Yellow-bellied in fresh plumage; distinct but relatively narrow pale yellowish eye-ring, bolder than in many Alder/Willow (= Traill's), thinner than in most Least and Yellow-bellied. Longest primary extension on average of all empids; longer, broader-based bill than in most similar Yellow-bellied; flatter forehead than Yellow-bellied and Least, usually with slightly more of a peak on rear crown. Unlike other *Empidonax,* molts before migrating s.; thus

birds in worn plumage in autumn not likely to be Acadian.

Voice. *Call:* Variously *peeip!, seeip!, weeip!,* and *sweep!,* similar to Yellow-bellied call but usually more emphatic and slightly more drawn out, typically rising in pitch or dropping only slightly. *Song:* explosive *seeuh-KEET!,* occas. given in spring but apparently not in autumn.

Habitat. Low to mid-strata at forest edge and in open woodland and second-growth scrub.

Distribution. Nests in e U.S. from Great Lakes and s New England to Gulf of Mex.; winters from e Nic. to nw S.A.

Status in Belize. FC autumn transient, late Aug. to early Nov.; UC spring transient, mid-Mar. to early May.

References. *Identification:* Kaufman (1990); Whitney and Kaufman (1985a, 1986b).

Alder Flycatcher PLATE 36
Empidonax alnorum
OTHER NAMES. Traill's Flycatcher (combined form).

Identification. 5½″ (14 cm). Willow and Alder flycatchers are virtually indistinguishable by plumage characters and are discussed together here as Traill's Flycatcher, the old name for the combined form. More like the little-known White-throated (see below) than other *Empidonax* in Belize. Similar in size and structure to Acadian, but with shorter primary extension on average. These two also average browner than Acadian, although some Alders can be nearly as green. Darker breast band on average than Acadian; distinct contrast between white throat and side of head.

Voice. *Call:* sharp *pip* to *peep. Song:* breathy or scratchy *phwe-BE-ah.* Sings in spring and occas. in autumn.

Habitat. Low to mid-strata at forest edge and in open woodland and second-growth scrub.

Distribution. Nests from Alaska and nc Can. to sw Can. and ne U.S.; winters in S.A., but limits of winter distribution are poorly known.

Status in Belize. FC autumn transient from at least early Sept. to late Oct., especially on cayes; less C inland. Status in spring unclear.

No definite spring records, but some silent Alder/Willow-type flycatchers observed in spring may pertain to this. Alder/Willow-type flycatchers have been recorded in autumn from late Aug. to early Nov. and in spring from late April to early June.

References. *Identification:* Kaufman (1990); Whitney and Kaufman (1985a, 1986a).

Willow Flycatcher   PLATE 36
Empidonax traillii
OTHER NAMES. Traill's Flycatcher (combined form).

Identification. 5½″ (14 cm). See preceding species account. Differs slightly from Alder in averaging browner or grayer and may have paler face with less throat-face contrast. Eye-ring averages thinner, nearly absent in some birds.
Voice. *Call:* emphatic *whit,* varies in intensity but usually more emphatic than in Least. *Song:* scratchy *fitz-beuw.* Occas. sings in autumn.
Habitat. Low to mid-strata at forest edge and in open woodland and second-growth scrub.
Distribution. Nests from s Can. to s U.S.; winters from s Mex. and Hon. to Pan.
Status in Belize. FC autumn transient from at least late Aug. to mid-Oct., especially on cayes; less C in spring, late April to early June. Abundance relative to Alder not clear, for much is still to be learned about these two species in Belize.
References. *Identification:* Kaufman (1990); Whitney and Kaufman (1985a, 1986a).

White-throated Flycatcher   PLATE 36
Empidonax albigularis
OTHER NAMES. Light-throated Flycatcher (I. Davis).

Identification. 5¼″ (13.5 cm). Structurally similar to Alder/Willow but warmer brown, with contrastingly brighter tawny rump and uppertail coverts, ochre wash on flanks, and buffy cinnamon, not white, wingbars in fresh plumage. White on throat often extends as pale area behind auriculars. Call and song very different.
Voice. *Call:* rough or scratchy *r-reeah,* very unlike calls of other *Empidonax. Song?:* similar to call, a rough *bree-uh.*

Habitat. Principally along edge of freshwater marshes; may be more widespread in migration.
Distribution. Nests in highlands from sw Chihuahua and sw Tamaulipas to w Pan.; winters in lowlands from Nayarit and Veracruz to Pan.
Status in Belize. Poorly known, but appears to be a R and local winter visitor, at least in north. Timing of arrival in and departure from wintering areas in Belize is not known. Other *Empidonax* have been mis-IDed as this in the literature, farther confusing its true status.
References. *Status:* Miller and Miller (1992); Wood and Leberman (1987). *Voice:* Delaney (1992); Howell and Webb (1995).

Least Flycatcher   PLATE 36
Empidonax minimus

Identification. 5″ (12.5 cm). Relatively large, round head; short, wide bill; and short tail. Shorter primary extension than in other *Empidonax.* Dull brown above, with little or no olive tone; little contrast between head color and back color, and wings do not contrast significantly darker than back. On the other hand, has stronger contrast between white throat and dark face and breast than Acadian and Yellow-bellied do. The most active *Empidonax,* generally flicking wings and tail more often than others. Readily told from Yellow-bellied in all but most worn plumage by white throat, less wing-back contrast, and duller, browner plumage; from Alder and Willow by bolder eye-ring, smaller size and distinctly smaller bill, shorter primary extension, more rounded head, and shorter tail; from Acadian by duller, browner plumage; whiter throat contrasting more with dark face; smaller bill; short primary extension; and shorter tail.
Voice. *Call:* soft *pit* or *wit. Song:* staccato *chēbek* to *chi-d-bek,* sharper, faster, and higher-pitched than in Yellow-bellied. Occas. sings in autumn.
Habitat. Most widespread of the *Empidonax* in Belize, found at low to mid-strata in most habitats with woody vegetation except broadleaf forest interior. Most common at woodland and second-growth edge.
Distribution. Nests from nc Can. to n U.S.;

winters from Sinaloa, Nuevo Leon, and Tamaulipas to C.R.

Status in Belize. C winter visitor, late Aug. to early May.

References. *Identification:* Kaufman (1990); Whitney and Kaufman (1985a,b).

Genus: Sayornis *(Phoebes)*

Larger than *Empidonax* and wood-pewees. Flick tail sharply downward (*Empidonax* flick tail up; pewees do not flick tail).

Black Phoebe
MAP 152; PLATE 35

Sayornis nigricans

Identification. 6½″ (16.5 cm). All black except for sharply contrasting white belly; pale feather edges in wing. Flicks tail downward.

Voice. Emphatic clear single notes, varying from *chip* to *cheur* and a softer *chur*. *Song:* rich, alternating *pēter* and *pētra* with ≈1½ sec separating the two.

Habitat. Fast-flowing forest-lined streams.

Distribution. Resident from sw U.S. to w S.A. Absent from Yucatán Pen.

Status in Belize. Local resident in interior n. to n CA and nc BE, rarely to c OW.

[Eastern Phoebe]
PLATE 35

Sayornis phoebe

Identification. 6½″ (16.5 cm). Dark olive gray above; darker on head; pale underparts with dusky on sides only; wings have pale feather edges but lack wingbars. Bill all dark. Constantly flicks tail downward like Black Phoebe. Pewees have wingbars (sometimes indistinct), head does not contrast darker than rest of upperparts, dusky wash extends across breast, lower mandible is at least partly orangish, and they do not flick tail. *Ad.:* mostly whitish underparts. *Juv.:* pale yellow belly.

Voice. *Call:* liquid *chip;* sharper, not as rich as Black Phoebe's.

Habitat. Low to mid-strata at forest edge, and in open areas with scattered trees.

Distribution. Nests e. of Rocky Mtns. from c Can. to se U.S.; winters from se U.S. to s Mex.

Status in Belize. Two unconfirmed reports. Has

been recorded in s Quintana Roo, Mex., near the Rio Hondo.

Reference. *Status:* Jones (2002).

Vermilion Flycatcher
MAP 153; PLATE 35

Pyrocephalus rubinus

OTHER NAMES. Robin Redbreast (C), tzala te' (M), El Diablito (S).

Identification. 5½″ (14 cm). The only tyrant flycatcher in Belize exhibiting strong sexual dimorphism. All but ad. ♂ have whitish supercilium. Flicks its tail sharply up, then down. *Ad.* ♂: vivid red head and underparts; dark brown of upperparts extending to the nape, auriculars, and lores. In courtship rises straight up from perch on rapidly fluttering wings while constantly singing. *Ad.* ♀: paler gray brown above and mostly white below, with streaked breast and pink vent and undertail coverts. *Imm.* ♂: similar to ad. ♀ but with red belly and red mottling in breast and crown. *Imm.* ♀: yellowish vent and undertail coverts. *Juv.:* speckled breast and white vent and undertail coverts.

Voice. *Call:* short, metallic *peen* or *peep*. *Song:* 1. short, dry ascending trill that speeds up *te-te-t-t-t-reet;*

2. rolling *dt dt drrreo. Dawn song: pt pt pt pt pur-r-r-reeet.*

Habitat. Savannas, fallow fields, pastureland, and agricultural areas; also in parks and other landscaped areas in towns and villages.

Distribution. Largely resident from sw U.S. to ne Nic. and disjunctively in S.A. s. to n Chile, c Argentina, and Uruguay.

Status in Belize. FC to C resident from CO and e OW s. to n CA (n. of Mtn. Pine Ridge) and e. of Maya Mtns. to ne TO. Recorded occas. in w OW, on Ambergris Caye, and on Caye Caulker.

SUBFAMILY: TYRANNINAE
(Kingbirds and Allies)

Includes both resident and migratory species. Among them are some of the largest members of the family and some of the showiest. No one outward morphological trait characterizes this subfamily.

Bright-rumped Attila   PLATE 35
Attila spadiceus
OTHER NAMES. Polymorphic Attila (arch.),
belix (K).

Identification. 8¼″ (21 cm). Strangely propor-
tioned flycatcher with large head and prominent
bristles at base of oddly shaped bill: straight culmen with hooked tip, and lower mandible that
curves upward near tip, give bill a unique upturned appearance. Brown above; pale below,
becoming pale yellow on belly and undertail coverts. Diffusely streaked throat and breast; pale
supercilium; red eyes. Characteristically holds
wings and tail drooped, exposing bright golden
yellow lower rump and uppertail coverts. Occasionally flicks tail up sharply. Although often
noisy, can be hard to see because of its tendency
to sit motionless for long periods.
Voice. *Call:* 1. loud, shrill, laughing *ah heh heh
heh heh;*
2. rapid, shrill *wheh-wheh-whe-whe-whuh,* similar to call of Ivory-billed Woodcreeper but more
shrill;
3. shrill *wee-dee-duh* to a softer *heh-h-heh;*
4. rapid *whi-d-dt,* like loud Stub-tailed Spadebill
song.
Song: 1. loud, clear, whistled *quick quick grab-it
grab-it grab-at-it grab-at-it graaaahb-it!;*
2. whistled *weed-it weed-it weed-it weed-it weed-
it* that builds in intensity, a pause, and then a
sighed *wheeeuw;*
3. rapid, loud, shrill *whahda whee whee whee whee
whee whee whuh whuh.*
Habitat. Midlevels to canopy within broadleaf
and pine forests; less often at forest edge.
Distribution. Resident from n Sinaloa and c
Veracruz to c S.A.
Status in Belize. FC to C resident on mainland.
Reference. *Voice:* Moore (1992).

Rufous Mourner   MAP 154; PLATE 35
Rhytipterna holerythra
OTHER NAMES. Ch'en hix (K).

Identification. 8″ (20.5 cm). Closely similar to
Rufous Piha, although only distantly related.
Both are uniformly rufous and about the same
shape, but piha is ⅓ larger. Mourner has thin-

ner bill and lacks piha's thin gray eye-ring, paler
throat, and tuft of bushy feathers at base of
bill. Both sit motionless, hidden in the foliage
inside the rainforest, and can be very difficult
to locate; however, each has a highly distinctive
song. Usually heard before seen.
Voice. *Song:* clear, whistled, drawn-out
whireeep   peewwww.
Habitat. Canopy and subcanopy within broadleaf forest interior.
Distribution. Resident primarily on Gulf-
Caribbean slope from n Oaxaca s. of Yucatán
Pen. to nw S.A.
Status in Belize. UC to locally FC resident away
from coast n. to c CA; also in w OW and locally
in e OW; probably also in sw BE.
References. *Voice:* Delaney (1992); Moore (1992).

Genus: Myiarchus

Genus of closely similar flycatchers, some of
which are notoriously difficult to tell apart. From
other flycatchers by brownish olive upperparts,
modest crest, medium to pale gray throat and
breast, pale to bright lemon yellow belly and
undertail coverts, moderately long bill, and at
least some rufous on inner webs of flight feathers. Yellow-bellied Elaenia is similar in pattern
but lacks rufous in plumage, has white feathers
at base of crest, and has a smaller bill.
   Things to note: vocalizations; overall size;
extent of rufous in rectrices; shade of gray on
throat and face; intensity of yellow on underparts; color of wingbars, tertial edges, and base
of lower mandible.

Yucatan Flycatcher   MAP 155; PLATE 36
Myiarchus yucatanensis

Identification. 7¼″ (18.5 cm). Most like similar-
sized Dusky-capped, but with face paler and
grayer, especially around eyes and lores; paler,
grayer wingbars and whitish-edged tertials; and
a less well defined crest, a trait useful in combination with other characters but not by itself.
Easily distinguished by vocal differences.
Voice. Whistled *uurrrrrreep* rising abruptly in
pitch at the end, somewhat like first note of Rufous Mourner's song. *Dawn song:*

1. *doe ree-bee* and a more drawn out *duuuur-reebee;*

2. *duuuuuurree deuurr.*

Habitat. Midlevels within open woodland habitats and forest edge, including both broadleaf and pine.

Distribution. *Yucatán Endemic.* Resident on Yucatán Pen. s. to n Guat. and n Belize.

Status in Belize. UC to locally C resident on mainland s. to s OW and c BE; several sight records suggest that it is also an UC resident on Ambergris Caye.

References. *Voice:* Moore (1992). *Identification:* Howell (1994a).

Dusky-capped Flycatcher   PLATE 36

Myiarchus tuberculifer
OTHER NAMES. Olivaceous Flycatcher (arch.), b'it i cuc (K).

Identification. 6¾″ (17 cm). Closely similar to Yucatan Flycatcher, but with darker brown head (face nearly as dark as crown); dull brownish wingbars; and pale cinnamon–edged tertials. More well-defined crest than Yucatan; distinctly different vocalizations.

Voice. 1. Soft, mournful *whuurrrrr* to *wheeurr,* occas. interspersed with *wh-dt* and *pe-dit chick!* calls and a rolling *pddddddr;*

2. soft *wuurrrrr* followed by a rolling trill. *Dawn song:* distinctive, mournful *wheeoooo,* often with *whick, ch-breer,* and other burry notes. Vocalizations are lazier and more subdued than those of Brown-crested.

Habitat. Midlevels within broadleaf and pine forest interior and forest edge and second-growth scrub.

Distribution. Mostly resident from se Arizona to c S.A.; northernmost populations migratory.

Status in Belize. C resident on mainland and Ambergris Caye; has also nested on Caye Caulker.

References. *Voice:* Moore (1992). *Identification:* Howell (1994a).

Great Crested Flycatcher   PLATE 36

Myiarchus crinitus
OTHER NAMES. Crested Flycatcher (arch.).

Identification. 8½″ (21.5 cm). Most like Brown-crested, but differs in having medium-gray throat and breast sharply contrasting with rich lemon yellow belly and undertail coverts, and flesh-colored base to lower mandible. Much more extensive cinnamon rufous on inner webs of rectrices than smaller Dusky-capped and Yucatan. Distinctive vocalizations.

Voice. Emphatic *wheep!* or *wheeip!* with rising inflection.

Habitat. Canopy and subcanopy within broadleaf forest interior. In migration, much more widespread.

Distribution. Nests in e N.A. from s Can. to Gulf of Mex.; winters from c Veracruz to n S.A.

Status in Belize. C transient and UC to FC winter visitor, mid-Sept. to late May; absent from most cayes in winter.

Reference. *Identification:* Howell (1994a).

Brown-crested Flycatcher   PLATE 36

Myiarchus tyrannulus
OTHER NAMES. Wied's Crested Flycatcher (arch.), Mexican Flycatcher (I. Davis).

Identification. 8½″ (21.5 cm). From Great Crested by much paler underparts, with less contrast between pale gray breast and pale lemon belly; gray extending to upper belly; nearly all-black bill with flesh color, when present, confined to a small area near the chin. From Dusky-capped and Yucatan by more extensive rufous in wings and tail, larger size, and heavier bill; distinctive vocalizations.

Voice. *Call:* 1. clear *prik!;*

2. rough *r-r-r-ur. Song:* complex series of *whit* calls mixed with burry notes; e.g., *ch-beer ch-b-b-durr erip! pewhit-d-d-deer,* etc.

Habitat. Midlevels to subcanopy within broadleaf and pine forest interior and forest edge.

Distribution. Three distinct populations, possibly representing different species: 1. nests from se Calif., c Arizona, and s Texas to Hon., and winters primarily on the Pacific slope from

Oaxaca to E.S.; 2. resident in w Nic. and nw C.R.; and 3. resident in n and c S.A.

Status in Belize. C summer resident on mainland and Ambergris Caye, early Mar. to late Aug.; may also breed on Caye Caulker. A few overwinter.

References. *Voice:* Moore (1992). *Identification:* Howell (1994a).

Genera: Pitangus, Megarynchus, *and* Myiozetetes *(Kiskadees)*

All similarly patterned: olive above and yellow below, with black-and-white head; mostly concealed yellow feathers in central crown. All are known as "kiskadee" in Creole.

Things to note: overall size, bill size, presence/absence of rufous in wings, vocalizations.

Great Kiskadee PLATE 37

Pitangus sulphuratus

OTHER NAMES. Kiskadee Flycatcher (arch.), Derby Flycatcher (arch.), Kiskadee (C), k'il kej (M), ch'il kay (M).

Identification. 9½" (24 cm). Larger than a kingbird, with larger bill, black-and-white head, bright yellow underparts, and rufous in primaries that is especially conspicuous in flight. **Voice.** 1. Hoarse, slightly shrill *deeee;* 2. nasal *kis-ka-dee!,* often shortened to simply *kis-ka!* **Habitat.** Midlevels to subcanopy within most open habitats and forest edge, including broadleaf and pine, second growth, fields, and marshes with scattered trees, parks, towns, and villages. **Distribution.** Resident from s Sonora and s Texas to sc S.A. **Status in Belize.** VC resident on mainland; FC resident on Ambergris Caye and regular winter visitor to Caye Caulker.

Boat-billed Flycatcher PLATE 37

Megarynchus pitangua

OTHER NAMES. Kiskadee (C), k'il kej (M), ch'il kay (M).

Identification. 9¼" (23.5 cm). Similar in size and pattern to kiskadee but lacks rufous in pri-

maries and has a bulbous bill, convex in shape both from the side and from below. Kiskadee has narrower, nearly straight-sided bill. **Voice.** *Call:* 1. rolling, squeaky *cheeeurr;* 2. clear, liquid *rrrr;* 3. raspy *chee churur whit;* 4. squeaky, but rough *ch-choit* or *choit choit ch-choit,* with 2nd part rolled. *Song:* very scratchy but liquid *ch-e-e-e-e-e-e-it.* *Dawn song:* rolling, burry *churrr,* sometimes followed by *cheowit!* **Habitat.** Most common inside broadleaf forests near rivers, streams, and natural clearings and along forest edge. Absent from expansive open areas and low second-growth forest. **Distribution.** Resident from s Sinaloa and sw Tamaulipas to c S.A. **Status in Belize.** FC to C resident on mainland. **Reference.** *Voice:* Moore (1992).

Social Flycatcher PLATE 37

Myiozetetes similis

OTHER NAMES. Vermilion-crowned Flycatcher (arch.), Giraud's Flycatcher (I. Davis), Kiskadee (C), k'il kej (M), ch'il kay (M).

Identification. 7" (18 cm). Distinctly smaller than the other two, with proportionately smaller head and much smaller bill, no rufous in primaries, and dark gray-and-white, not black-and-white, head pattern. More gregarious than the other two. **Voice.** *Call:* 1. shrill *kea!;* 2. *brrrr brrrr brrrr . . . ,* but not breathy as in Yellow-bellied Elaenia. *Song:* shrill *kea kea kea ch-kea ch-kea kea kea,* etc. Typically, several birds will simultaneously burst into song. **Habitat.** The most wide-ranging of the kiskadees: broadleaf and pine forest and forest edge, second growth, open country with scattered trees, and towns and villages. **Distribution.** Resident from s Sonora and sw Tamaulipas to c S.A. **Status in Belize.** VC resident on mainland and Ambergris Caye. **Reference.** *Voice:* Moore (1992).

Genera: Myiodynastes *and* Legatus
(Streak-breasted Flycatchers)

All three are summer-breeding visitors, departing in autumn for S.A. Typically arrive in Mar. and depart in Sept. Sulphur-bellied is common, but similar Streaked is uncommon. Piratic is smaller, with much smaller bill. All three have yellow basal feathers in the central crown that are usually not visible.

Things to note: overall size, bill size, chin color, thickness of lateral throat stripe, color of belly and tail, extent of streaking underneath, presence/absence of streaks in back.

Streaked Flycatcher   PLATE 37
Myiodynastes maculatus

Identification. 8½" (21.5 cm). Similar to much more common Sulphur-bellied but has larger bill, with basal ½ to ⅔ of lower mandible pale flesh-colored, less bold lateral throat stripe, and white chin; belly, supercilium, and lower auricular region very pale lemon yellow; breast and flanks less coarsely streaked than in Sulphur-bellied.
Voice. *Call:* 1. sharp woodpecker-like *bek;*
2. *tchevoo*, starts abruptly, trails off (similar to Rose-throated Becard). *Song:* series of woodpecker-like but squeaky *pik!* notes (≈2/sec) periodically followed by a sharp, squeaky *p-teurr.*
Habitat. Midlevels to canopy within broadleaf (and pine?) forest interior and edge.
Distribution. Two populations: 1. nests from sw Tamaulipas to w Hon., and winters from C.R. to c S.A.; 2. resident from C.R. to sc S.A., with southernmost populations migrating n. to n S.A.
Status in Belize. Local and generally UC summer resident in interior, mid-Mar. to Sept.
References. *Status:* Wood and Leberman (1987). *Voice:* Moore (1992).

Sulphur-bellied Flycatcher   PLATE 37
Myiodynastes luteiventris
OTHER NAMES. Wilix (K).

Identification. 8" (20.5 cm). Differs from Streaked in having smaller, all-black bill and black chin that bridges black lateral stripe on either side of throat. Also has more heavily streaked pale sulfur-yellow belly and white supercilium and lower auriculars.
Voice. *Song:* shrill, toy mouse–like *squeea-toe.* *Dawn song:* somewhat melodious *tureet t-d* to *pea-twit-it.*
Habitat. Midlevels to canopy within broadleaf and pine forest interior and edge, open habitats with scattered large trees.
Distribution. Nests from se Arizona and n Tamaulipas to C.R.; winters in S.A. from e Ecuador to n Bolivia.
Status in Belize. C summer resident, mid-Mar. to late Sept., occas. to mid-Oct., and rarely through the winter. Recorded occas. in migration on cayes.
Reference. *Voice:* Moore (1992).

Piratic Flycatcher   PLATE 37
Legatus leucophaius
OTHER NAMES. Striped Flycatcher (I. Davis).

Identification. 6½" (16.5 cm). Less similar and smaller than preceding two, with much smaller bill; unstreaked olive-gray back and crown, and more diffuse streaking underneath. Trace of a lateral throat stripe.
Voice. Rapid, clear, soft *wh-ti-ti-tit* (≈1 sec), periodically followed by a piercing, clear *wheeuh.* Also, a rapid *ca-ca-ca-ca-ca-ca*, which sometimes precedes its typical song.
Habitat. Subcanopy and canopy within broadleaf forest interior and edge.
Distribution. Nests from se San Luis Potosí to c S.A. Populations of Mex. and C.A. winter in S.A.
Status in Belize. FC but somewhat local summer resident, late Feb. to mid-Sept. Unrecorded from cayes.
Reference. *Voice:* Moore (1992).

Genus: Tyrannus *(Kingbirds)*

Kingbirds perch on exposed tree limbs, power lines, and fences, from which they sally out for insects that they catch on the wing before returning to the same or nearby perch. Unlike most other passerines, kingbirds are diurnal migrants.

This is especially evident in autumn, when thousands of Eastern Kingbirds may be seen daily in Sept. and early Oct. flying south along the coast.

Two virtually indistinguishable species of yellow-bellied kingbirds, Tropical and Couch's, are common in Belize. They even occupy the same habitats and are often seen together, but they have distinctly different vocalizations. Two other similar species, Cassin's Kingbird and Western Kingbird, are vagrants. All kingbirds have a bright yellow, orange, or red central crown patch that is usually concealed but exposed during mating and aggressive displays. When sporting their full-length tail, the Scissor-tailed Flycatcher and Fork-tailed Flycatcher are unmistakable. Males of both species have a longer tail than ♀s, and ads. have a longer tail than juvs.

Things to note: bill size; extent and shade of gray in face and throat (where applicable); deeply forked, notched, or square-tipped tail; pattern of black and white in tail (where applicable); color of back, breast, belly, and tail; presence/absence of pale tertial and wing covert edges; vocalizations.

Tropical Kingbird   FIGURE 24C; PLATE 37
Tyrannus melancholicus

Identification. 8½″ (21.5 cm). Gray head with dark lores and auricular patch (mask); upperparts olive; underparts yellow, with white throat and dusky wash across upper breast. Wing coverts and tertials have prominent pale feather edges. Tail notched. Almost identical in plumage and structure to Couch's; silent birds are perhaps not safely separable in the field.
Voice. 1. Rapid-fire, harsh *prt-it-t-t-t* . . . rising and falling slightly in pitch; may give this vocalization at various speeds, often alternating slow and fast;
2. rapid *dit-dit-ddddd* to *d-d-d-d-dt,* somewhat like that of common Toady-Flycatcher but higher pitched, more shrill.
3. *uhde-de-de-de-de-de.* Trills often preceded by burry *wheet-EET-eet* to *vuhdee duh dee,* especially at dawn.
Habitat. Open areas, wherever exposed perches are available.

Distribution. Mostly resident from se Arizona and n Tamaulipas to sc S.A. Populations in nw Mex. and Arizona withdraw s. in winter.
Status in Belize. VC resident throughout, including larger cayes.
References. *Identification:* Kaufman (1992); Pyle (1997).

Couch's Kingbird   FIGURE 24C; PLATE 37
Tyrannus couchii
OTHER NAMES. Tropical Kingbird (combined form).

Identification. 8¾″ (22 cm). Almost identical to Tropical Kingbird (see preceding account). Couch's bill is slightly shorter and broader, a difference that may be discernible on some birds in direct comparison with Tropical. Couch's averages brighter overall, including greener back, and has slightly paler wings that show less contrast with pale feather edges.
Voice. *Call:* sharp *kip!* to *pik! Song:* variously
1. *whit whit whit whitcheer!;*
2. *puwhit puwhit picheeur!;*
3. *kip ke-wheer;*
4. burry *treeer* to *breeur,* higher and thinner than in Cassin's;
5. *pik beer* to *chi-breer. Dawn song: dimeet dimeet diMEEtreo.*
Habitat. Similar to that of Tropical, but with an inclination toward drier areas such as upland pine savannas, Mtn. Pine Ridge, where relative numbers of this species are greater.
Distribution. Resident from s Texas to n Guat.
Status in Belize. C resident on mainland, Ambergris Caye, Caye Caulker, and perhaps the Turneffe Isl. Generally only 1 in 5 to 1 in 10 is Couch's, but in a few pine savanna areas Couch's may be as common as Tropical.
References. *Status:* Wood and Paulson (1988). *Identification:* Kaufman (1992); Pyle (1997). *Voice:* Moore (1992).

Cassin's Kingbird   FIGURE 24A
Tyrannus vociferans

Identification. 8½″ (21.5 cm). Darker, grayer back than other yellow-bellied kingbirds, with darker gray wash across breast and throat, set-

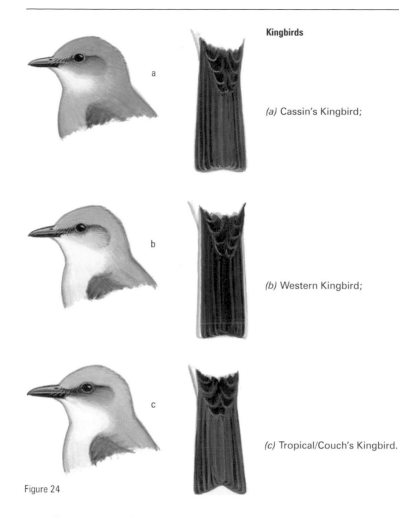

Kingbirds

(a) Cassin's Kingbird;

(b) Western Kingbird;

(c) Tropical/Couch's Kingbird.

Figure 24

ting off contrastingly white malar area. Shows no obvious mask in its all-dark head. In fresh plumage, has pale tip to unnotched tail, but this becomes obscured with feather wear (some birds by late spring). Wing covert and tertial feather edges contrast lighter than rest of wing, as in Tropical/Couch's but not Western. Cassin's has noticeably smaller bill than Tropical/Couch's.

Voice. Emphatic 1. *k-dear;*
2. *ch-beeur!;* lower-pitched and often more emphatic and raucous than that of Couch's.

Habitat. Open areas with scattered large trees, including fields, pastures, parks, towns, and villages.

Distribution. Nests from w U.S. to Oaxaca; winters from sw Calif. and Sonora to w Guat.

Status in Belize. One confirmed record: Gallon Jug OW, 22 Dec. 1999 to 2 Mar. 2000.

References. *Status:* Lasley et al. (2000). *Identification:* Kaufman (1992).

Western Kingbird   FIGURE 24B
Tyrannus verticalis
    OTHER NAMES. Arkansas Kingbird (arch.).

Identification. 8″ (20.5 cm). Palest overall of the group, with smallest bill. Typically has less distinct auricular patch, grayer (less olive) back, and paler, grayer breast than Tropical/Couch's, with almost no throat/breast contrast. Wing coverts lack contrasting paler edges of Cassin's and Tropical/Couch's. Square-tipped tail black, with thin white outer edges. *Note:* white edges may be mostly worn away in birds in worn plumage prior to molting (early autumn).

Voice. 1. Sharp *pik* to *kit,* often run together into slow, short trill;

2. sharp *whick!;*

3. more varied *whidik pik whidi pik pik pik pik.*

Habitat. Open areas with exposed perches.

Distribution. Nests in w N.A. from s Can. to nw Mex. and s Texas; winters on the Pacific slope from s Mex. to C.R. and in s Florida.

Status in Belize. Two documented records: Punta Gorda, 30 Oct. 2001, and s. of San Ignacio, 27 Feb. 2002 (two).

References. *Status:* Howell (1994a). *Identification:* Kaufman (1992).

Eastern Kingbird   PLATE 37
Tyrannus tyrannus

Identification. 8″ (20.5 cm). Dark gray and black above; white below, with pale dusky smudge across breast. Black head contrasts with dark gray back. Broad white band across tip of tail. Flame-colored central crown patch is usually concealed. *Flight:* underwing mostly dark gray.

Voice. *Call:* thin, buzzy *kzeer. Song:* thin, wiry swiftlike twitter, occas. given in migration.

Habitat. Low level to canopy in most wooded areas (forest interior and edge) and to a lesser extent open areas with exposed perches.

Distribution. Nests in N.A. in and e. of Rocky Mtns. from c Can. to Gulf of Mex.; winters in S.A. from w Amazonia to n Argentina.

Status in Belize. VC autumn migrant along coast, mid-Aug. to early Nov.; less common in spring, mid-Mar. to late May. Less C in interior. This diurnal migrant can be seen flying south along and near coast in Sept. and early Oct.

Gray Kingbird   PLATE 37
Tyrannus dominicensis

Identification. 8½″ (21.5 cm). Resembles Eastern Kingbird but has slightly notched tail, lacking white band at tip. Lighter gray above, with contrasting dark gray auriculars. White below, with faint lemon wash on flanks; lacks dusky

smudge across breast. Bill noticeably longer and thicker than in Eastern. *Flight:* underwing coverts whitish (dark in Eastern).

Voice. 1. Sharp *peet;*

2. *burr;*

3. loud, emphatic *pi-tirr;*

4. slow, high-pitched twitter or rattle *pi-ti-reee pi-ti-rro,* rougher than that of Tropical.

Habitat. Forest edge, second growth, towns; most areas with exposed perches.

Distribution. Nests in Florida and W.I.; winters in c and s W.I., occas. w. to coast of Yucatán Pen. and Belize.

Status in Belize. Occas. transient and R winter visitor on n cayes and mainland coast s. to c SC, July to mid-May. Recorded twice well inland: El Cayo CA, 22 Mar. 1960; and La Milpa OW, 20 Apr. 1999. Most records are from spring.

References. *Status:* Jones et al. (2000). *Voice:* Raffaele et al. (1998).

Scissor-tailed Flycatcher   PLATE 37
Tyrannus forficatus
OTHER NAMES. Scissor-tailed Kingbird (I. Davis).

Identification. 13″ (33 cm) with full-length tail. Pale gray and white, with darker wings and long, forked, black-and-white tail. *Ad.:* rose-pink sides, underwing coverts, and undertail coverts; strikingly long tail. *Juv.* (seen in autumn before molting into first basic plumage): much shorter tail and pale salmon to pinkish yellow flanks and undertail coverts.

Voice. *Call:* sharp *pik* to *perk* to *prik.*

Habitat. Fence lines, power lines, and trees along edges of open fields and pastures.

Distribution. Nests in sc U.S. from Kansas and Missouri to ne Mex.; winters primarily on the Pacific slope from Guerrero to w Pan., and increasingly on Gulf-Caribbean slope from s Veracruz to Belize.

Status in Belize. Locally UC to FC winter visitor on mainland and occas. transient and winter visitor on cayes, late Sept. to early May. Numbers have increased steadily in the past two decades.

Reference. *Status:* Jones et al. (2000).

Fork-tailed Flycatcher MAP 156; PLATE 37

Tyrannus savana

OTHER NAMES. Swallow-tailed Flycatcher
(I. Davis), Scissors-tail (C).

Identification. 15″ (38 cm) with full-length tail.
Highly gregarious species usually found in loose
flocks. Black head set off by white throat and
pale gray back; extremely long, forked black tail
edged in white. Immaculate white beneath, lacking pink highlights of Scissor-tailed. *Juv.:* black
mask; much shorter tail that, when held closed,
may not appear to be forked. Could be mistaken
for Loggerhead Shrike *(Lanius ludovicianus).*
Voice. *Call:* while perched, a hard warblerlike
tik or *chik. Chase call: whirr. Other calls (song?)
usually given in flight:* grating *d-d-d-d-drrrt* and
gr-gr-gr-gr-gr.
Habitat. Pine and pine-oak savannas; pastureland.
Distribution. Resident from c Veracruz and n
Belize to s S.A. Populations in s S.A. migrate to
c and n S.A., rarely to N.A.
Status in Belize. C resident from n OW and n
BE s. to c CA and e. of Maya Mtns. to ne TO;
occas. seen elsewhere.

GENERA: *INCERTAE SEDIS*

(Genera of Uncertain Affinities)

Taxonomists have long debated the taxonomic
relationships of the tyrant flycatchers, becards,
tityras, cotingas, and manakins. The American Ornithologists' Union (AOU, 1998) decided
that, for now, it was better to leave seven genera
(six represented in Belize) in taxonomic limbo
than to venture what would amount to an arbitrary decision and place them in one or more
of several existing families. Taxonomic studies
of these species have produced inconclusive and
often conflicting evidence as to their relationships. Even the latest technology using DNA has
done little to advance our understanding of this
challenging group.

Genus: Schiffornis

The Thrush-like Schiffornis has in the past been
placed with the manakins (Thrush-like Manakin) in the Pipridae, and with the "mourners"

(Thrush-like Mourner) variously in the Cotingidae and Tityridae. For more than a century it
has been placed in the genus *Schiffornis,* and
its current English name, unlike "Manakin" and
"Mourner" before, does not suggest any affinities
above the level of genus.

Thrush-like Schiffornis PLATE 35

Schiffornis turdinus

OTHER NAMES. Thrush-like Mourner,
Thrush-like Manakin, Brown Mourner
(I. Davis), xuxb tz'ic (K).

Identification. 6¾″ (17 cm). Rather plump,
brownish olive bird with moderately short tail
and conspicuous black eyes in a plain face. Although nondescript, does not closely resemble
any other species in Belize. Rufous Mourner is
warm rufous brown, with longer tail and bill.
Female ant-tanagers are larger and have richer
brown tones, thicker bill, and longer tail.
Voice. Very distinctive clear, whistled *to weeea
duh wheet eat!* or *Oh where be me feet, Pete?*
Habitat. Low to mid-strata within broadleaf
forest.
Distribution. Resident from s Veracruz to c S.A.
Status in Belize. FC to C resident on mainland.
References. *Voice:* Delaney (1992); Moore (1992).

Genera: Lipaugus *and* Laniocera

The taxonomic relationships among the Rufous
Piha, Speckled Mourner, and Rufous Mourner
(genus *Rhytipterna* in the Tyrannidae) are unclear. The AOU (1998) and Sibley and Monroe (1990) both placed Rufous Mourner in
the Tyrannidae. The AOU kept the Speckled
Mourner and Rufous Piha together but left them
incertae sedis. Sibley and Monroe, on the other
hand, placed all of the genera *incertae sedis* of the
AOU, as well as the tityras, becards, cotingas,
and manakins, in subfamilies of the Tyrannidae
but show the Rufous and Speckled mourners as
closely related, with the Rufous Piha in with the
cotingas. Neither set of authors considered the
Rufous Mourner and Rufous Piha to be close
relatives.

Things to note: overall size; presence/absence
of thin eye-ring, bushy feathers at base of bill,

pale throat, yellow slash at bend of wing, or fine scalloping in plumage; shade of color on throat; bill size and shape; vocalizations.

Rufous Piha
MAP 157; PLATE 35

Lipaugus unirufus

OTHER NAMES. Tz'ic ul chakou (K).

Identification. 9¾" (25 cm). Closely resembles Rufous Mourner. Both are uniformly rufous brown and similarly shaped; however, piha is ≈⅓ larger and has heavier bill, thin gray eye-ring, paler throat, and tuft of feathers at base of bill. Both sit motionless, hidden among the foliage inside the rainforest, and can be very difficult to locate. Each has a loud, distinctive song; thus usually heard before seen.

Voice. *Call:* 1. rolled, squirrel-like *bdrup   bdrup   bdrup;* 2. loud, rolling *d-r-r-r-r-r-r-r.* *Song:* loud, explosive *P-WEOOO!*

Habitat. Midlevels to subcanopy within broadleaf forest.

Distribution. Resident primarily on Gulf-Caribbean slope from n Oaxaca s. of Yucatán Pen. to nw S.A.

Status in Belize. UC to FC resident in interior n. to sw BE and nc CA; also w OW and locally in e OW. Most plentiful in Maya Mtns.

References. *Voice:* Delaney (1992); Moore (1992).

Speckled Mourner
MAP 158; PLATE 35

Laniocera rufescens

Identification. 8¼" (21 cm). Most closely resembles unrelated Rufous Mourner but fairly easily distinguished when seen well. Has thicker bill, pale yellow patch on sides (often concealed by folded wings), mottled brown and rufous wing coverts, and finely scalloped breast. Voice softer than that of Rufous Mourner. Could be confused with larger Rufous Piha, but piha lacks any markings in plumage.

Voice. *Song:* clear whistled *derriere,* somewhat similar to one song of White-breasted Wood-Wren.

Habitat. Midlevels to subcanopy within primary broadleaf forest.

Distribution. Resident on Gulf-Caribbean slope from n Oaxaca s. of Yucatán Pen. to nw S.A.

Status in Belize. Scarce local resident in interior, primarily in Maya Mtns. and foothills, but also w OW and locally in se OW.

Reference. *Voice:* Belize Zoo (n.d.).

Genus: Pachyramphus *(Becards)*

The becards have been placed in the cotinga family or, along with the cotingas, in the tyrant flycatcher family. Recent evidence, however, suggests that they may not be as closely related to the cotingas as once thought, and the AOU has for the moment left them in limbo, pending further study. All in Belize are in the genus *Pachyramphus,* and all but Cinnamon Becard are strongly sexually dimorphic.

Things to note: presence/absence of supraloral stripe, eye-ring, wingbars, scapular bar, crown-neck contrast, graduated tail feathers, or pale tips to rectrices.

Cinnamon Becard
MAP 159; PLATE 38

Pachyramphus cinnamomeus

Identification. 5¾" (14.5 cm). Rufous above, paler ochraceous tawny below. Resembles ♀ Rose-throated but lacks dark crown and has pale supraloral stripe and graduated tail. Rufous Mourner is much larger, lacks the pale supraloral stripe and dark lores, has longer tail, and has rufous rather than ochraceous underparts.

Voice. *Song:* plaintive whistled 1. *teww to to tew tew tew;* 2. *tewww tew tew tew;* etc.

Habitat. Midlevels to canopy within broadleaf forest and forest edge.

Distribution. Resident on Gulf-Caribbean slope from s Veracruz s. of Yucatán Pen. to nw S.A.

Status in Belize. UC to FC resident in interior n. to n CA; also w OW and locally in e OW.

Reference. *Voice:* Moore (1992).

White-winged Becard MAP 160; PLATE 38
Pachyramphus polychopterus
OTHER NAMES. Black-backed Becard
(I. Davis).

Identification. 5¾″ (14.5 cm). Similar in size
and shape to Gray-collared, and both have wingbars in all plumages. Strongly sexually dimorphic, and ♂ exhibits different juv., imm., and
ad. plumages. *Ad. ♂:* black and gray, with strong
white markings in wings and scapulars; darker
gray underneath than Gray-collared and lacks
pale gray supraloral stripe. Gray on sides of neck
does not extend around nape. *Imm. ♂:* similar to
brownish olive ♀, but with paler, yellowish wing
markings and grayish throat and breast. Unlike Gray-collared in any plumage, has whitish
spectacles, has no head/nape contrast, and lacks
white scapular bar. ♀: brownish olive above; pale
lemon yellow below, palest on throat; bright cinnamon edges to wing feathers; pale yellowish underparts; conspicuous pale spectacles. *Juv.:* like
ad. ♀.
Voice. *Song:* 1. clear whistled *cho cho cho cho* to
2. *che che cho cho cho cho,* the latter similar to
Green-backed Sparrow song but notes softer,
more musical;
3. *chew-y chew-y chew-y chew-y;*
4. *i-choy choy choy chĕ;*
5. more varied *cho cho cho cho-ur-che cher cher
cher,* sometimes accelerating into a trill:
chrchrchrchrchrchr;
6. *cho churl churl churl churl.*
Habitat. Midlevels at broadleaf forest edge, in
second growth, and in open areas with scattered
trees.
Distribution. Resident on Caribbean slope
from Belize and Guat. to sc S.A. e. of the Andes;
southernmost populations are migratory.
Status in Belize. UC to FC resident n. recently
to c OW and n BE. Since first recorded in 1970
in TO, has spread steadily n., most likely in response to deforestation.
Reference. *Status:* Jones et al. (2000).

Gray-collared Becard PLATE 38
Pachyramphus major
OTHER NAMES. Mexican Becard (I. Davis).

Identification. 5¾″ (14.5 cm). Similar to White-
winged and, like that species, strongly age and
sexually dimorphic, all with black crown and
pale supraloral stripe. *Ad. ♂:* black and pale
gray, with strong white markings in wings and
scapulars. Paler underneath than White-winged,
with gray collar extending around nape. *Imm.
♂:* much like ad. ♂ but with cinnamon-brown
back and rump and pale yellow-buff underparts and wing markings. ♀: cinnamon brown
above, paler cinnamon buff below, black-and-
cinnamon wings, graduated tail with broad cinnamon feather tips, especially noticeable on underside. ♀ Rose-throated lacks pale supraloral
stripe and has unmarked wings and tail and
ochraceous buff underparts.
Voice. *Song:* 1. soft, forced, nasal *tew tew tew*
(sometimes a longer series).
2. bluebirdlike chortling *tew tewtew; tew tew
tewtewtew.*
Habitat. Midlevels within broadleaf and pine
forest and forest edge.
Distribution. Resident from c Sonora and c
Nuevo Leon to n Nic.
Status in Belize. R to locally UC resident on
mainland, perhaps throughout.
References. *Status:* Wood and Leberman (1987).
Voice: Delaney (1992).

Rose-throated Becard PLATE 38
Pachyramphus aglaiae

Identification. 6¾″ (17 cm). Lacks wingbars,
pale facial markings, and tail spots in all plumages. Tail not graduated. ♂: dark gray above;
paler below. Most birds in north have rose-
colored throat; whereas most birds in south lack
rose color or have it restricted to feather bases.
♀: dark rufous brown above, paler ochraceous
below, with distinctly blackish crown.
Voice. *Call:* 1. thin, *teeeuurr,* which begins
abruptly and drops in pitch;
2. Rose-breasted Grosbeak–like *tink,* but softer.
Song: 1. short, thin, rapid, squeaky, accelerating
rattle ending in *speee;*

2. squeaky, buzzy *wha-chee* repeated 3 or 4 times.
Habitat. Midlevels to subcanopy within deciduous to evergreen broadleaf forest and forest edge; second-growth scrub.
Distribution. Resident from se Arizona and n Tamaulipas to w Pan. Northernmost populations withdraw s. in winter.
Status in Belize. Resident on mainland; C in CO, progressively less C southward; recorded on Ambergris Caye, where possibly a R resident or a stray.
References. *Status:* Wood and Leberman (1987). *Voice:* Moore (1992).

Genus: Tityra *(Tityras)*

Tityras, like becards, have been placed in taxonomic limbo by the AOU because of their uncertain affinities with other groups. Tityras are highly conspicuous black-and-white birds of forest edge and openings.

Things to note: color of face, color and thickness of bill, shape of dark face/crown patch, presence/absence of pale forehead.

Masked Tityra   PLATE 38

Tityra semifasciata
OTHER NAMES. White Woodpecker (C), so choj (K), sur ko cho (M).

Identification. 8¾″ (22 cm). ♂: mostly white, with black primaries and distal wing coverts; broad black band in tail. Featherless, pinkish red face and bill (except for tip) broadly bordered posteriorly with black. ♀: brownish gray wash on upperparts; less distinct head pattern.
Voice. Very nasal, scratchy *oink* and *wanka* notes (very un-birdlike). *In flight only:* very harsh *zit,* similar to Dickcissel call but harsher and louder.
Habitat. Open to closed broadleaf forest interior and edge; open areas with scattered trees; pines.
Distribution. Resident from s Sonora and sw Tamaulipas to c S.A.
Status in Belize. C resident on mainland; UC resident on n Ambergris Caye.
Reference. *Voice:* Moore (1992).

Black-crowned Tityra   PLATE 38

Tityra inquisitor
OTHER NAMES. Black-capped Tityra (arch.), White-collared Tityra (I. Davis).

Identification. 7¾″ (19.5 cm). Black-and-white body pattern of Masked, but has much slimmer bill and lacks red in face and bill. ♂: crown and bill all black. ♀: different head pattern than in ♀ Masked; black cap, whitish forehead, and chestnut facial patch.
Voice. 1. Very nasal, scratchy *oink,* similar to Masked's;
2. harsh *sheka sheka sheka . . . ,* with quality of Band-backed Wren vocalization;
3. harsh, grinding *cha cha cha;*
4. in flight, very harsh *zit,* like Masked's.
Habitat. Open to closed broadleaf forest interior and edge; open areas with scattered trees; pines.
Distribution. Resident from se San Luis Potosí to c S.A.
Status in Belize. UC to locally FC resident on mainland. Often seen with Masked, although invariably less common.
Reference. *Status:* Wood and Leberman (1987).

FAMILY: COTINGIDAE (Cotingas)

World: 58. **New World:** 58. **Belize:** 1. Neotropical; confined primarily to S.A. Cotingas closely related to tityras, becards, pihas, Speckled Mourner, and perhaps Thrush-like Schiffornis, all of which have been placed in the Cotingidae at one time or another. Male cotingas are among the most beautiful of all birds. Cotingas are found exclusively in forested areas, where they frequent fruiting trees. **Reference:** Snow (1982).

Lovely Cotinga   MAP 161; PLATE 38

Cotinga amabilis

Identification. 7¼″ (18.5 cm). Plump, rounded body, with small, rounded head and short tail. Strongly sexually dimorphic. ♂: unmistakable with its turquoise blue plumage accentuated with large deep purple patches on throat and belly. ♀: gray-brown upperparts, heavily scalloped with white; whitish underparts heavily mottled and spotted with gray.

Voice. Generally silent. Occas. gives dry fluttering rattles in flight.

Habitat. Mid- to upper strata within broadleaf forest interior; early in the morning often perches on exposed branches protruding above canopy.

Distribution. Resident on Gulf-Caribbean slope from c Veracruz s. of Yucatán Pen. to C.R.

Status in Belize. VU to R resident in interior n. to c CA and (discontinuously?) in w OW; once at Lamanai c OW.

Reference. *Voice:* Howell and Webb (1995).

FAMILY: PIPRIDAE
(Manakins)

World: 49+. **New World:** 49+. **Belize:** 2. Neotropical. Manakins are small, short-tailed, big-headed birds with a fascinating courtship ritual. In most species, the ♂ is strikingly colored and the ♀ is uniformly brown or green. Manakins are frugivorous and usually found in the vicinity of fruiting trees in the forest and forest edge. Males of the two species in Belize do not present an ID challenge; however, ♀s can be difficult to tell from other small, nondescript passerines, but once their general shape and mannerisms are learned, they are easily recognized.

Things to note (♀s): color of legs, bill, and belly.

White-collared Manakin
MAP 162; PLATE 38
Manacus candei
OTHER NAMES. Cande's Manakin (arch.), Cohune Popper (C), t'otz bayal (K), hur hur (M).

Identification. 4¾″ (12 cm). Small plump bird with large head, very short tail. ♂: striking black, white, and yellow, with olive rump and extendable throat feathers. ♀: mostly olive, with yellow belly and undertail coverts and bright orange legs; ♀ Olive-backed Euphonia is similar in size, shape, and color, but with gray legs, red (not yellow) undertail coverts, and much thicker bill.

Voice. 1. Loud toy-machine-gun-like burst of ≈5 or 6 hard, dry notes (≈⅓ sec);
2. in display, ♂ makes a sharp snap or pop with the wings, followed by buzzy calls similar to call #1;
3. distinctive wing whir in flight (♂ only)—*brrr brrr brrr brrr;*
4. rough *cheuur* to *cheuur wit;*
5. squeaky *cheerie.*

Habitat. Understory and midlevel strata within broadleaf forest and forest edge; second-growth scrub.

Distribution. Resident on Gulf-Caribbean slope from n Oaxaca s. of Yucatán Pen. to w Pan.

Status in Belize. C resident on mainland n. to c OW and n BE; UC and local to n OW and e CO.

Reference. *Voice:* Moore (1992).

Red-capped Manakin
PLATE 38
Pipra mentalis
OTHER NAMES. Yellow-thighed Manakin (arch.), cak i t'otz bayal (K), chuk pol hur hur (M).

Identification. 4¼″ (11 cm). Small chunky bird with large head and very short tail; smaller than White-collared. ♂: jet black, with red head, white eye, and yellow "thighs." ♀: undistinguished, but combination of small size, short tail, short grayish tarsi (orange in White-collared), large head, and uniformly dull olive plumage eliminate other similar species.

Voice. *Call:* 1. sputtery *pit!* to *plt!* to *put!;*
2. loud, raspy *dzeet! Song:* thin
pt pt pt peeeeeeeeeeur pit!
In display, 1. hard buzzy *zzzzrk;*
2. rapid snapping *kak-kak-kak-kak-kak;*
3. sharp *lik-lik,* etc.

Habitat. Midlevels to canopy within broadleaf forest, sometimes at forest edge. Found in more mature forest than White-collared.

Distribution. Resident primarily on Gulf-Caribbean slope from c Veracruz to nw S.A.

Status in Belize. FC resident on mainland.

References. *Voice:* Howell and Webb (1995); Moore (1992).

FAMILY: VIREONIDAE
(Vireos)

World: 52. **New World:** 52. **Belize:** 15. Exclusive to New World. Vireos were once thought to be closely related to wood-warblers; however, recent evidence suggests that vireos are more closely related to shrikes (Laniidae). They are characterized by a thicker, more rounded bill than in wood-warblers, with a slight hook at the tip, and slower, more deliberate foraging behavior, moving through the foliage more methodically, with fewer hops and short flights as they forage among the leaves and branches. Many twist their head curiously, as if gazing skyward. Some in the genus *Vireo* characteristically cock their tail; most warblers do not. Vireos are active singers on their breeding grounds, often singing throughout the day. **Reference:** *Voice:* Barlow (1990).

Genus: Vireo *(Those with Wingbars)*

Most vireos can be divided into two groups, those with wingbars and eye-rings or spectacles and those with eyestripes and no wingbars. ID of vireos with wingbars is straightforward. White-eyed and Mangrove are closely allied but differ significantly in their vocalizations and plumage characteristics.

Things to note: presence/absence and, if present, color of spectacles; placement and richness of yellow and white in underparts.

White-eyed Vireo
PLATE 39

Vireo griseus

Identification. 4½" (11.5 cm). Only vireo with combination of yellow spectacles, creamy white wingbars, and whitish throat and breast. Quite vocal. *Ad.:* white eyes. *Imm.:* dark eyes, as in Mangrove Vireo.
Voice. *Call:* 1. House Wren–like nasal scold *chǎ-chǎ-chǎ* . . . , varies from fast chatter to slow and irregular series;
2. *cheo;*
3. repeated honeycreeper- or gnatcatcher-like mews. *Song:* variations on the theme *Chick, see the vireo, chick!* Sings occas. throughout winter.

Habitat. Second-growth scrub, roadside tangles, mangroves, forest edge, occas. forest interior.
Distribution. Nests in e N.A. from s Great Lakes and s New England to Gulf of Mex.; winters from Gulf states to n W.I. and Hon.
Status in Belize. C transient and FC winter visitor, late Sept. to mid-Apr.
References. *Identification:* Pyle (1997). *Voice:* Moore (1992).

Mangrove Vireo
MAP 163; PLATE 39

Vireo pallens
OTHER NAMES. Petén Vireo (is part of).

Identification. 4½" (11.5 cm). Similar to White-eyed but with bold yellow loral spot not continuing around the eyes; dark eyes; and yellowish underparts. Color of upperparts varies from yellowish olive to grayish olive, the latter more like White-eyed. Like White-eyed, an active singer.
Voice. *Call: drrrrēt.* Scold: *cheooooo* or *che che che che cheooo cheooo. Song:* almost always consists of a slow trill or short series of nasal, usually somewhat harsh notes. Examples: 1. moderately low-pitched, slow trill (often the same individual will give alternate songs of different pitches or tempos);
2. rough *tree tree tree* . . . ;
3. strident *chee chee chee* . . . ;
4. *cheo cheo cheo* . . . ;
5. *churr churr churr* . . . ;
6. *chevy chevy chevy* . . . ;
7. *droi droi droi* . . . .
Habitat. Second-growth scrub, roadside tangles, forest edge. Although occas. found in mangroves, it is more common in a variety of other scrubby habitats both near the coast and well inland. In winter when White-eyed is present, the two are often found together.
Distribution. Two populations, possibly representing separate species: 1. resident along Pacific coast from s Sonora to C.R.; 2. resident on Caribbean slope from Yucatán Pen. to n Nic.
Status in Belize. C resident at lower elevations on mainland nearly throughout; also on Ambergris Caye and Turneffe Isl.
References. *Voice:* Moore (1992). *Systematics:* Parkes (1990b).

Yellow-throated Vireo
PLATE 39

Vireo flavifrons

Identification. 5¼″ (13.5 cm). Unmistakable: bright yellow throat, breast, and spectacles; green head and back; blue-gray wings, rump, and tail; white wingbars and belly. Yellow-breasted Chat is larger, has white spectacles, lacks wingbars, and inhabits dense tangles.

Voice. *Call:* emphatic, somewhat nasal, scolding *chih cheh cheh cheh cheh cheh cheh,* usually accelerating and descending slightly. *Song* (heard occas. in spring): liquid, but distinctly burry, slurred series containing various *cheerio, cheerup,* and *three-eight* notes spaced ≈3 sec apart.

Habitat. Mid- to upper strata in mature and old second-growth broadleaf and pine forests and forest edge; less frequently in younger second-growth forest.

Distribution. Nests in e N.A. from Great Lakes and s New England to Gulf of Mex.; winters from sw Tamaulipas to n S.A.

Status in Belize. UC to FC winter visitor, early Sept. to late Apr.; more widespread in migration.

Reference. *Identification:* Pyle (1997).

Plumbeous Vireo
MAP 164; PLATE 39

Vireo plumbeus

OTHER NAMES. Solitary Vireo (combined form).

Identification. 4¾″ (12 cm). All gray above, white below, with conspicuous white spectacles, wingbars, and tertial edges; olive wash on rump and wings; and hint of yellow buff on sides and flanks. Smaller than Yellow-throated and Blue-headed; closer in size to Philadelphia.

Voice. *Call:* similar to that of Yellow-throated but less emphatic. *Song* (sings nearly year-round): an alternating series of sweet, clear *chur-ee, ree-ship,* and *ree-chorry* notes. The pause between notes is longer than in Red-eyed or Yellow-green, and the phrases tend to be clearer (less burry) than in Yellow-throated.

Habitat. Subcanopy to canopy in mature pine, broadleaf, and mixed forests.

Distribution. Nests from U.S. Great Basin and Rocky Mtns. through highlands of c Mex. to

Hon.; n. populations winter in Mex.; s. populations are resident.

Status in Belize. FC resident in Mtn. Pine Ridge and above 2,000 ft. (600 m) in Maya Mtns.; also discontinuously in coastal plain in ec SC. The small subspecies in Belize, *V. p. notius* may be an endemic or near endemic, but the subspecific affinities of this and nearby populations in Guat. and Chiapas are still unclear. It is intermediate in plumage characters between other races of Plumbeous Vireo and Cassin's Vireo *(Vireo cassinii).* It is likely to be more closely related to Plumbeous Vireos in the nearby C.A. highlands than to the Cassin's Vireo, which nests no closer to Belize than Baja California, Mex.

References. *Status:* Phillips (1991). *Identification:* Heindel (1996); Pyle (1997).

Blue-headed Vireo
PLATE 39

Vireo solitarius

OTHER NAMES. Solitary Vireo (combined form).

Identification. 5¼″ (13.5 cm). Striking bird noticeably larger than Plumbeous (size of Yellow-throated), with bolder white spectacles and wingbars; bright green back; blue-gray head contrasting sharply with white throat and green back; bright yellowish buff on sides and flanks.

Voice. Calls and song similar to Yellow-throated Vireo's, but song more liquid, not burry, and with slightly shorter interval between phrases (≈2½ sec). May be slightly richer than song of Plumbeous.

Habitat. Mid- to upper strata in mature trees both within forested areas and in parks. In migration, could turn up in almost any wooded habitat.

Distribution. Nests across c and s Can. and ne U.S.; winters from se U.S. s. in highlands to n Nic.

Status in Belize. Two records: Belmopan, 25–26 Dec. 2000, and Mtn. Pine Ridge CA, 5 Mar. 2002. Until recently, considered conspecific with Plumbeous Vireo, and no distinction was made by most observers. Blue-headed should be expected occas. in Belize in migration or winter. Any Solitary seen outside the range of the resident Plumbeous may well be a Blue-headed and should be examined closely.

References. *Status:* Jones et al. (2002). *Identification:* Heindel (1996); Pyle (1997).

Genus: Vireo *(Those without Wingbars)*

Not as strikingly marked as vireos with wingbars, these species present more of an ID challenge. Like other vireos, they are told from wood-warblers by their blunt-tipped bill and sluggish behavior.

Things to note: placement and intensity of yellow (if present) and white on underparts, color of upperparts, characteristics of super-cilium, dark or pale lores.

Warbling Vireo   PLATE 39
Vireo gilvus
OTHER NAMES. Eastern Warbling-Vireo (is part of).

Identification. 5″ (12.5 cm). Among the most nondescript of vireos; grayish olive above, with no wingbars, indistinct whitish supercilium, and whitish breast, becoming pale yellow buff on belly. Dark line through eyes does not extend to bill, leaving area around base of bill whitish. Tennessee Warbler is smaller, with a relatively smaller head, and has thin and pointed bill, bright green back, and thin, pale yellow wing-bar; yellow, when present, is on breast, not belly. Also, much more active than vireos and often travels in groups. Philadelphia Vireo has dark lores and yellow wash on breast.
Voice. *Call:* 1. soft, rough *fit* to *fet;*
2. less typically, soft but harsh nasal mew. *Song:* mellow jumble of high and low notes, typically ending on a high note.
Habitat. Mid- to upper strata within broadleaf forest; more widespread in migration.
Distribution. Nests from nw and ec Can. to s U.S. and in Mex. highlands to Oaxaca; winters from s Sonora and se San Luis Potosí to Pacific slope of Hon. Populations in e and w N.A. are considered by some authorities to represent separate species.
Status in Belize. Two believable sight records: Union Camp near Little Quartz Ridge TO,

4 Apr. 1992; Crooked Tree BE, 21 Mar. 1999. Other reports lack convincing documentation.
References. *Status:* Parker et al. (1993). *Identification:* Kaufman (1990); Pyle (1997); Terrill and Terrill (1981). *Voice:* Barlow (1990).

Philadelphia Vireo   PLATE 39
Vireo philadelphicus

Identification. 4½″ (11.5 cm). Olive green above, becoming gray on crown; supercilium more prominent than in Warbling, especially in front of eyes, where set off below by thin dark lores. Differs from Tennessee in having duller green back; pale yellow, not white, undertail coverts; more diffuse face pattern; larger head; thicker bill; and more sluggish behavior. Some Warbling have pale yellowish wash on sides and flanks, never on breast. Warbling has grayer back, with little head-back contrast. *Alt.:* faint yellowish wash on throat and breast. *Juv. and basic:* yellowish wash brighter.
Voice. *Call* (seldom heard): an undistinguished, nasal, scratchy *reh. Song:* similar to but slower than Red-eyed song (≈1 phrase every 2 sec); however, not known to sing in Belize.
Habitat. Various, including scrub, orchards, yards, and early successional and mature broad-leaf forest (midlevels to subcanopy).
Distribution. Nests e of Rocky Mtns. across c and s Can.; winters from s Veracruz to n Colombia.
Status in Belize. FC transient and UC winter visitor, early Oct. to late May.
References. *Identification:* Kaufman (1990); Pyle (1997); Terrill and Terrill (1981).

Red-eyed Vireo   PLATE 39
Vireo olivaceus

Identification. 5¾″ (14.5 cm). Olive green above and white below, with red eyes (ad. only), creamy-buff undertail coverts. Prominent gray crown set off below by thin black border; bold white supercilium; black eyestripe. Yellow-green has brown, not red, eyes; yellow sides, flanks, and undertail coverts; yellower green upperparts; and crown not outlined in black. Also has longer, deeper bill and more extensively pale lower mandible than Red-eyed.

Voice. *Call:* nasal *chwănh. Song* (occas. given in spring migration): alternating *chir-r-ep* and *chir-e-up* notes (≈1 every 1½–2 sec), similar to song of Yellow-green but notes generally are richer, not clipped; less spacing between notes than Plumbeous or Yellow-throated songs and not as full or rich as either.

Habitat. Mid- to upper strata of tall second growth and forest edge; less often in mature forest.

Distribution. Nests from nc Can. to nw and se U.S.; winters in Amazon Basin.

Status in Belize. VC autumn and C spring transient, early Aug. to late Nov. and late Mar. to late May.

References. *Identification:* Pyle (1997); Terrill and Terrill (1981). *Voice:* Moore (1992).

Yellow-green Vireo   PLATE 39
Vireo flavoviridis

OTHER NAMES. Red-eyed Vireo (combined form).

Identification. 5¾″ (14.5 cm). Similar to Red-eyed but with yellow sides, flanks, and undertail coverts; brighter green upperparts; dark brown eyes; and no thin black border to gray crown. Distinctly larger than Philadelphia, with noticeably longer, heavier bill; throat and breast white, not yellow. Yellow-green Vireos reported in winter in Belize are likely mis-IDed Philadelphias.

Voice. *Call:* high nasal *twanh. Song:* 1. alternating *chirlip* and *churup* notes, clipped and less musical than Red-eyed song (at a distance, notes are surprisingly like song of House Sparrow, but cadence is different);

2. richer, alternating *cheerip* and *cheerup* notes, more like those of Red-eyed Vireo but generally less musical and phrases delivered ≈1–1½ sec apart.

Habitat. Broadleaf forest, tall second growth, forest edge, open woodland with scattered large trees; usually in canopy, occas. lower.

Distribution. Nests from s Sonora and n Tamaulipas to Pan.; winters in w Amazon Basin.

Status in Belize. C summer resident on mainland (except higher elevations?) and Ambergris Caye, early Mar. to mid-Oct.; occas. seen in migration on other cayes. Has been considered in the past to be conspecific with Red-eyed Vireo.

References. *Identification:* Pyle (1997); Terrill and Terrill (1981). *Voice:* Moore (1992).

Black-whiskered Vireo   PLATE 39
Vireo altiloquus

Identification. 5¾″ (14.5 cm). Closely related to Red-eyed but has lateral throat stripe that varies in intensity from fairly bold to thin and indistinct. Also has distinctly longer and slightly deeper bill than even the Yellow-green. Habits much like those of Red-eyed and Yellow-green.

Voice. *Call:* 1. thin *tzit;*

2. sharp, nasal *yeeea.*

Habitat. Forest and scrub.

Distribution. Nests in Florida and W.I.; winters in c and s W.I. and in S.A. e of the Andes.

Status in Belize. Two records: Half Moon Caye, 22 Mar. 1926, and Ambergris Caye, 13–18 May 2002.

Reference. *Identification:* Pyle (1997).

Yucatan Vireo   MAP 165; PLATE 39
Vireo magister

Identification. 6″ (15 cm). Largest of the genus; uniformly olive brown above and whitish below, with dusky flanks; exceeded only by Warbling in drabness. Distinguished from other vireos by broad, creamy white supercilia that meet or nearly meet across forehead. Supercilium set off below by bold dark eyestripe extending through lores to base of bill. Has brownish, not gray, crown. Bill as long as Black-whiskered's, but deeper and with pale gray base to lower mandible. Legs/feet blue gray, bluest in spring.

Voice. *Calls and scolds:* 1. harsh *chk-chk-chk* to *ch-ch-ch-ch-ch;*

2. harsh, rapid *sque-sque-sque-sque;*

3. low-pitched liquid *bik-bik,* frequently repeated;

4. woodpecker-like *wick.*

Song: 1. *chur chur chuweet churwee wheo,* etc., with phrases evenly paced;

2. periodic *chuwee-chuwee* and *chea-chea* notes given within a rather varied song sequence;
3. liquid *choree* and *cheo-cho* with *cho-cho* and *chow-chow* variations mixed in.

Habitat. Mangroves and littoral forest.

Distribution. *Near Yucatán Endemic.* Resident along Caribbean coast of Yucatán Pen., Bay Isl. (Hon.), and Cayman Isl.

Status in Belize. C to VC resident on cayes s. to Snake Cayes (formerly Sapodillas); generally less C along immediate mainland coast s. to c TO.

Reference. *Identification:* Morgan et al. (1985).

Genus Hylophilus *(Greenlets)*

Although more active and superficially warbler-like than other vireos, greenlets should not present an ID challenge once their distinctive field marks are learned.

Things to note: color of crown, eyes, throat, and underparts.

Tawny-crowned Greenlet   PLATE 39
Hylophilus ochraceiceps
OTHER NAMES. Tawny-crowned Hylophilus (arch.), wa wa (K).

Identification. 4¾″ (12 cm). Distinctive tawny crown, often with a ruffled look; pale yellow eyes; gray face and throat; ochre breast. More likely to be confused with ♀ Plain Antvireo than with any of the true vireos, but has different shape, with its smaller bill and longer tail. Also lacks Plain Antvireo's dark eyes and white eye-ring and has no hint of wingbars. Typically associates with mixed-species feeding flocks, often in close association with ant-tanagers.

Voice. *Call:* nasal, whiny *twă twă twă twă* to *toy toy toy toy. Song:* clear, whistled *deeeeee,* quite unlike that of other vireos.

Habitat. Understory and midlevels within mature and old second-growth broadleaf forest interior.

Distribution. Resident from c Veracruz to nc S.A.

Status in Belize. C resident on mainland nearly throughout; less C in CO.

Reference. *Voice:* Moore (1992).

Lesser Greenlet   PLATE 39
Hylophilus decurtatus
OTHER NAMES. Gray-headed Greenlet (arch.); Gray-headed Hylophilus (arch.).

Identification. 4¼″ (11 cm). Tiny; shorter-tailed than other vireos, with gray head, green upperparts, white underparts, yellowish wash on sides and flanks, and white eye-ring. More warblerlike in its behavior than other vireos, moving about foliage with frequent short flights and hops, even hanging upside down and hover-gleaning at leaf tips. Frequently associates with mixed-species feeding flocks. Superficially resembles Tennessee Warbler or Nashville Warbler, but the former has a white eyeline, not an eye-ring, and a longer tail, and the latter (which is rare in Belize) is yellow underneath, including the throat.

Voice. *Call:* 1. *ji-jit* and *ji-ji-jit;*
2. short *chee,* sometimes repeated;
3. nasal scold, *chĕ chĕ chĕ . . . ;*
4. raspy, slightly musical *che cheh cheh che. Song:* somewhat similar to that of Yellow-green Vireo, but repertoire is more varied and delivered faster; frequently gives two or three similar phrases in a row during singing bouts; phrases also tend to be of 3 syllables, whereas in Yellow-green Vireo, phrases are typically 2-syllabled. Examples: 1. thin, but melodious *cher-d-lee cher-d-lee cher-d-lee;*
2. double *chi-di-leep chi-di-leep;*
3. thin, rapidly repeated *check-a-chee check-a-chee check-a-chee;*
4. thin *cher weet churwee;*
5. *cheet churweet.* Often repeats song endlessly and, as with other resident vireos, sings throughout the day.

Habitat. Canopy and subcanopy of tall second-growth to mature broadleaf forest. Forages higher in forest than Tawny-crowned.

Distribution. Resident from se San Luis Potosí to nw S.A.

Status in Belize. C resident on mainland.

Reference. *Voice:* Moore (1992).

Genera: Vireolanius *and* Cyclarhis *(Shrike-like Vireos)*

The heavy-billed Green Shrike-Vireo and Rufous-browed Peppershrike were once placed in their own families, Vireolaniidae and Cyclarhidae, respectively. Recent DNA evidence, however, shows them to be very closely allied with other vireos. Both are readily identifiable, and both are more often heard than seen.

Things to note: head pattern and color.

Green Shrike-Vireo   MAP 166; PLATE 39
Vireolanius pulchellus
OTHER NAMES. Emerald Shrike-Vireo (arch.), qu'iche' raxon (K).

Identification. 5½″ (14 cm). Green color and sluggish behavior make it difficult to detect in forest canopy. *Ad.:* green throughout except for yellow throat and turquoise blue crown; has plain face with contrasting black eyes; stout bill with hooked tip. *Juv.:* yellow eyeline and yellow malar.
Voice. *Call:* 1. harsh, squeaky *chik;* 2. short, nasal, squeaky chatter, *enh-enh-enh-enh-enh. Song:* rich, clear *dear dear dear dear,* repeated frequently throughout the day.
Habitat. Canopy and subcanopy within primary broadleaf forest interior.
Distribution. Resident from c Veracruz to Pan. Possibly some seasonal movement locally.
Status in Belize. C dry-season resident in interior n. to n CA; also in w and c OW. Conspicuous when singing (late Dec. to early June), but recorded much less frequently in rainy season when not singing. It is unclear whether this hard-to-see canopy dweller partially withdraws from Belize in the rainy season or is simply overlooked.
References. *Voice:* Delaney (1992); Moore (1992).

Rufous-browed Peppershrike
MAP 167; PLATE 39
Cyclarhis gujanensis
OTHER NAMES. Mexican Peppershrike (arch.).

Identification. 6¼″ (16 cm). Green above and yellow below, with gray head, bold rufous supercilium and forecrown, and very stout bill. Found in open second growth, where it has a knack for staying just out of sight in foliage; typically remaining motionless while singing, moving to nearby perch or tree only between singing bouts.
Voice. *Call:* 1. *check;* 2. mournful *waa waa waa waa* reminiscent of one Barred Antshrike vocalization. *Song:* clear and distinctive whistled series of alternating high and low notes, almost a jumble. Examples: 1. clear, whistled *dimētrideo;* 2. *teuh toe tee tee toe;* 3. *tŭ weetle tu too e o;* 4. *whidido whidido whidē o,* lower-pitched and richer than in Spot-breasted Wren. Each individual has its own song type, which it repeats endlessly. *Alternate song?:* whistled *turea turea turea turea turea turea turea turea turea turea* slowly descending the scale, reminiscent of song of Canyon Wren *(Catherpes mexicanus).*
Habitat. Open country with scattered trees and shrubs, roadside brush, forest and second-growth edge, pinelands, and occas. mangroves; typically in drier regions.
Distribution. Resident from s Tamaulipas to sc S.A.
Status in Belize. FC resident on mainland w to c OW and s. through ne CA to ne TO, rarely to s TO. UC resident on Ambergris Caye, but absent from other cayes.
References. *Status:* Coffey and Coffey (1990); Wood and Leberman (1987).

FAMILY: CORVIDAE
(Jays, Crows, and Magpies)
World: 117. **New World:** 52. **Belize:** 3. Nearly cosmopolitan; absent from Antarctica and N.Z. Ravens (related to crows) are the largest of all passerines. The Corvidae are characterized by a relatively thick, powerful bill; stout legs; and strongly grasping feet. Most are omnivorous, eating everything from young birds and eggs to carrion, fruit, nuts, and seeds. Most tropical species are forest dwellers, although many in temperate regions are found in grasslands, deserts, and tundra far from the nearest forest. Nearly all are highly vocal. Sexes alike. **References:** Madge and Burn (1994). *Voice:* Hardy (1990).

Things to note: for determining age, color of bill and head, presence/absence of eye-ring, color of eyes.

Green Jay   PLATE 40

Cyanocorax yncas
OTHER NAMES. Inca Jay (arch.),
Cling-cling (C).

Identification. 11¼″ (28.5 cm). Unmistakable; green above and yellow below, with yellow lateral edge to tail and complexly patterned black-and-blue head. *Ad.:* yellow eyes. *Juv.:* brown eyes.
Voice. Series typically of 3–8 notes, all notes in the series the same, but one series may be very harsh and the next clear and hollow: 1. very harsh, nasal *chĕ chĕ chĕ* . . . to *chă chă chă* . . . , higher-pitched and more nasal than in Yucatan Jay;
2. tinny and clear to hoarse *clea clea clea;*
3. rapid, staccato *de-de-de-de-de-de-de-de do-o-o-o-o-o-o-o;*
4. *anhk anhk;* etc. Individuals or groups may vocalize some or all of these sequences during one vocal session.
Habitat. Midlevels within broadleaf and pine forest interior and forest edge.
Distribution. Resident from Nayarit and s Texas to nw Hon. and in nw S.A.
Status in Belize. UC to FC resident on mainland away from coast. Most plentiful in Mtn. Pine Ridge.
References. *Voice:* Hardy (1990); Moore (1992).

Brown Jay   PLATE 40

Cyanocorax morio
OTHER NAMES. White-tipped Brown-Jay and White-tipped Jay (color morph, formerly thought to be separate species), Piam-piam (C), pap (K), pa'ap (M).

Identification. 16″ (40.5 cm). Large; dark dull brown above, becoming white on belly and undertail coverts. Graduated tail feathers tipped white. *Ad.:* black bill. *1st year:* yellow bill and eye-ring, becoming black in 2nd year.
Voice. 1. Loud, nasal *pam!* or *pyam!,* repeated frequently;
2. *jay!,* also repeated frequently;
3. hysterical, much repeated *caaaa!;*
4. hoarse *[c]reeah.* Vocalizations often have a guttural popping sound at the beginning.

Habitat. Midlevels to canopy within most forest types, usually near forest edge (absent from interior of larger forest tracts); open country with scattered trees.
Distribution. Resident on Gulf-Caribbean slope from s Texas to w Pan.
Status in Belize. C to VC resident on mainland; possibly resident also on n Ambergris Caye, where seen occas.
Reference. *Voice:* Moore (1992).

Yucatan Jay   MAP 168; PLATE 40

Cyanocorax yucatanicus
OTHER NAMES. Black-and-blue Jay (arch.), Blue Piam-Piam (C).

Identification. 13″ (33 cm). *Ad.:* blue above, with black head and underparts. *Juv.* (July to Sept.): entirely white head and underparts, yellow eye-ring, yellow bill. *Imm.:* white body feathers replaced with jet black feathers of ad.; eye-ring and bill remain yellow until 3rd year.
Voice. *Call:* 1. very harsh *chă chă chă* . . . , similar to Green Jay vocalization but louder and lower-pitched;
2. clear *chuduk;*
3. clear, nasal *whyy-why* and *wee wee;*
4. Golden-fronted Woodpecker–like *chrrr;*
5. *wä wänk,* with humanlike quality;
6. clear *wik-wedek;* etc. Groups may give some or all of these notes.
Habitat. Midlevels within semi-deciduous and deciduous broadleaf forest, pine and pine-oak forest, forest edge.
Distribution. *Yucatán Endemic.* Resident in Yucatán Pen. s. to w Tabasco, n Guat., and n Belize.
Status in Belize. C to VC resident in CO, progressively less C s. to s OW, ne CA, s BE, and extreme ne SC; also resident on n Ambergris Caye. Recorded once each on Placencia Pen. SC and near Silk Grass SC, indicating occas. southward dispersal.
References. *Status:* Miller and Miller (1992). *Voice:* Moore (1992).

FAMILY: HIRUNDINIDAE
(Swallows)

World: 90. **New World:** 34. **Belize:** 10. Cosmopolitan, absent only from the polar regions. Two, Barn Swallow and Bank Swallow (known as Sand Martin in the Old World), are among the world's most wide-ranging birds, being found on all continents except Australia and Antarctica. Superficially they resemble swifts, with their long, pointed wings; short, weak legs/feet; tiny bill; and wide gape adapted for aerial pursuit of insects. However, among other things, they do not have a shortened forewing, they have different flight characteristics and a greater variety of plumage colors and patterns, and their breeding biology is profoundly different. Martins are typically larger than other swallows. Most temperate-latitude species are highly migratory and are one of only a few groups of passerines that migrate during daylight hours. **Reference:** Turner and Rose (1989).

Genus: Progne *(Martins)*

In flight, martins can be told from other swallows by their tendency to fly in a relatively straight line, with long glides between flapping flight. They have broader-based wings that taper to a point and noticeably more head projection than other swallows. In sustained flapping flight, they somewhat resemble a Bat Falcon. Except for ♂ Purple, martins in Belize can be difficult to separate, especially in flight. Even perched birds can be challenging, especially birds in molt during autumn passage. Both Purple and Gray-breasted are seasonally abundant in Belize; however, Snowy-bellied has been recorded only once in Belize, and little is known of its distribution away from its limited nesting areas.

Things to note: color of forehead and collar, color and shade of throat, presence/absence of blue-black flecking on underparts, degree of breast-belly contrast, streaked or unstreaked undertail coverts.

Purple Martin
Progne subis
OTHER NAMES. Kusal (M).

PLATE 41

Identification. 7¾" (19.5 cm). Largest of the swallows in Belize. *Flight:* direct, with frequent gliding; long, pointed, broad-based wings. *Ad. ♂:* all dark glossy blue black. *Ad. ♀:* glossy blue black restricted to upperparts; throat and breast dark sooty gray, becoming splotchy on belly and undertail coverts; gray forehead and collar distinguish it from Gray-breasted. *Juv.:* like ad. ♀ but with mostly white belly and undertail coverts and mostly brown upperparts. *Year-old ♂:* lacks pale forehead and partial collar, but has scattered blue-black feathers in throat, breast, sides, and flanks.
Voice. *Call:* liquid, burry *chur* and *che-chur* notes, singly or in series. Usually silent in Belize.
Habitat. Primarily aerial, generally over open country; perches on power lines and tall dead trees in open areas.
Distribution. Nests from c and s Can. to highlands of c Mex.; winters in S.A. e. of the Andes.
Status in Belize. C autumn transient, less C in spring; late June (Belize's earliest autumn migrant) to late Oct., and early Feb. to mid-Apr. The martin seen most frequently on the cayes.
Reference. *Status:* Dickerman et al. (1980).

Snowy-bellied Martin
Progne dominicensis
OTHER NAMES. Caribbean Martin (is part of), Sinaloa Martin (is part of).

PLATE 41

Identification. 7" (18 cm). Intermediate in size between Purple and Gray-breasted. ♂: striking blue black, with sharply contrasting white belly to undertail coverts; 1st-summer ♂ Purple somewhat similar but with uneven (blotchy) distribution of blue-black feathers on undersides. ♀: dark dusky throat and breast; less breast-belly contrast than in ♂ but more than in Gray-breasted or Purple. Most closely resembles 1st year ♂ Purple and may not always be safely told in flight. In close view, both Purple and Gray-breasted have finely streaked flanks and undertail coverts; these are unstreaked in Snowy-bellied.
Voice. Caribbean sounds much like Purple and

Gray-breasted; voice of Sinaloa apparently undescribed, but probably similar.

Habitat. Likely to be found in the same areas as other martins in migration.

Distribution and Taxonomic Status. This "superspecies" comprises both the Caribbean Martin *(P. [dominicensis] dominicensis)* and the very similar Sinaloa Martin *(P. [dominicensis] sinaloae),* which are virtually indistinguishable in the field. Some authorities consider the complex to represent one species; others, two. Caribbean Martin nests in W.I.; its winter range is unknown (probably S.A.). Sinaloa Martin nests in highlands of w Mex. from ne Sonora to Michoacan; it also is thought to winter in S.A.

Status in Belize. One record: Belize City, late Aug. 1962 (several seen flying out to sea with migrating Purple Martins). Given that Caribbean and Sinaloa martins seen in the field are essentially indistinguishable, which type actually seen is not known. Thus, the name "Snowy-bellied Martin," which encompasses both the Caribbean and the Sinaloa martins when treated as subspecies, is used here for convenience.

References. *Systematics and distribution:* American Ornithologists' Union (1998); Holt (1926); Howell and Webb (1995); Moore (1945); Turner and Rose (1989).

Gray-breasted Martin   PLATE 41
Progne chalybea
OTHER NAMES. Kusal (M).

Identification. 6¾″ (17 cm). Slightly smaller than Purple, but size difference useful only in direct comparison of perched birds. All plumages, including ad. ♂, are similar to ♀ and juv. Purple. Lacks gray collar and forehead of ♀ Purple; however, the absence of these characters can be difficult to determine in overhead and distant flying birds. *Note:* in some molting ♀ Purples, the gray collar and forehead can be mostly obscured; thus, failure to see these features does not necessarily eliminate Purple. *Flight:* much like that of Purple; can be confused with Rough-winged Swallow, but size and different manner of flight usually distinguishes it. Rough-winged also has light wing panel.

Voice. *Call:* 1. liquid, rolling *chĕr* to a drier *tchur* and a harsher, more emphatic *cheor;*
2. rough *pēŭo.* *Song:* burry, rolling chirps and chips; for example, *churrr   chip chip chip chip.*

Habitat. Open country; nests in tree cavities and in crevices in buildings and other structures.

Distribution. Nests from c Sinaloa and c Nuevo Leon to sc S.A. Populations on Gulf-Caribbean slope from Belize and n Guat. migrate s. in winter.

Status in Belize. C to VC dry-season resident, late Dec. (Belize's earliest spring migrant) to late Sept. No confirmed records from outside this period. In July and Aug., large flocks of migrating martins of both species gather in certain areas, especially along coast. Generally, much less C than Purple on cayes in migration.

Reference. *Status:* Jones et al. (2000).

Genus: Tachycineta

Tachycineta swallows are dark above and gleaming white below. Two occur in Belize; one, Tree Swallow, is a winter visitor, and the other, Mangrove Swallow, is a permanent resident.

Things to note: presence/absence of white eyebrows and tertial edges. *In flight,* color of rump and underwing coverts.

Tree Swallow   PLATE 41
Tachycineta bicolor
OTHER NAMES. Christmas Bird (C), kusal (M).

Identification. 5½″ (14 cm). *Ad.:* metallic dark blue or greenish blue above (appears black in all but the best light), white below. *Imm. and some ad. ♀s:* brown or mottled brown and greenish blue above. *Caution:* juvs. have brownish wash across upper breast and partial whitish collar similar to, but not as bold as in, Bank Swallow; however, by the time Tree Swallows reach Belize (end of Oct.), most juvs. should have already molted into 1st basic plumage. *Flight:* uniform dark underwings contrast with snow-white underparts.

Voice. *Call:* 1. liquid *churdle-churdle;*
2. dry, somewhat rough *chee* notes, sometimes given in rapid succession.

Habitat. Primarily aerial. Likely to be found over open areas; often congregates over wetlands; perches on power lines, dead snags.

Distribution. Nests from n Alaska and nc Can. to sc U.S.; winters from s U.S. to Cuba and Pan.

Status in Belize. C to locally VC winter visitor along and near mainland coast in north, less C to south and inland. Found in winter on Ambergris Caye, but primarily a transient on other cayes. One of the last N.A. migrants to arrive in autumn (late Oct.) and one of the first to leave (early Apr.).

Reference. *Identification:* Lethaby (1996).

Mangrove Swallow
PLATE 41

Tachycineta albilinea
OTHER NAMES. Kusal (M).

Identification. 4½″ (11.5 cm). Similar to Tree but smaller, with white rump, white supraloral stripe (eyebrow), and white tertial edges. *Ad.:* metallic blue green above. *Juv.:* grayish brown above. *Flight:* from Tree by white underwing coverts.

Voice. *Call:* somewhat rough *treep.*

Habitat. Lagoons, coastal areas, rivers; more widely dispersed outside the nesting season.

Distribution. Resident from c Sonora and s Tamaulipas to Pan. and in Peru.

Status in Belize. Locally C resident on mainland, Ambergris Caye, and Caye Caulker.

Two other related species could turn up in Belize and should be looked for. **Violet-green Swallow** *(Tachycineta thalassina)* has white on sides of rump only. Folded wings greatly exceed length of tail; not so in Tree and Mangrove. *Ad ♂ and some ad. ♀s:* emerald green back and crown contrast sharply with deep violet uppertail coverts, wings, and tail; white of underparts extends up behind eyes. *Juv. and some ad. ♀s:* sides of head dusky. *Caution:* white on Tree Swallow's flanks can extend up onto sides of rump. **Blue-and-white Swallow** *(Notiochelidon cyanoleuca)* is much like Tree Swallow but with more deeply forked tail and black, not white, undertail coverts. Southernmost populations of this S.A. species migrate n. during the austral winter (roughly May–July) and have been recorded at least once in both Guat. and s Mex. Any Tree Swallow seen in summer should be studied carefully—it may be a Blue-and-white.

Genus: Stelgidopteryx *(Rough-winged Swallows)*

The taxonomic relationship of the rough-winged swallows *(Stelgidopteryx)* is extremely complex. For the purposes of this field guide, they are divided into those that migrate to Belize from the north in winter (Northern Rough-winged Swallow), and those that are resident (Ridgway's Rough-winged Swallow), although this division is not entirely accurate. Some Northern Rough-winged also breed in Belize (for example, in Cockscomb Basin), and these have plumage characters that are intermediate between migratory Northern and resident Ridgway's. Taxonomists are divided as to whether Northern and Ridgway's constitute one or two species, but because they are separable in the field at close range, more useful information on this group can be obtained if observers record both forms in their field notes whenever possible rather than simply calling everything "rough-winged."

Location and time of year are helpful in determining which of the two forms is present. Generally, rough-winged swallows seen along forested streams in the interior, especially in hilly areas with caves, are likely to be Ridgway's. Those in open country, especially in coastal areas and in the interior over farmland and rice fields, are likely to be migratory Northern, which are in Belize between late Sept. and Apr.

Things to note: overall darkness of plumage; if present, extent of dark feathers in undertail coverts; presence/absence of white forehead spot; location and season.

Northern Rough-winged Swallow
PLATE 41

Stelgidopteryx serripennis
OTHER NAMES. Rough-winged Swallow (combined form), kusal (M).

Identification. 5¼″ (13.5 cm). Brownish above and mostly white below, with dusky throat and breast fading to white on belly. Paler above than

Ridgway's; lacks white forehead spot and has all-white or nearly all-white undertail coverts. Resident and migratory Northern Rough-winged are very similar; however, resident populations approach Ridgway's in some plumage characters, thus complicating the taxonomic picture. For example, undertail coverts of resident Northern Rough-winged have dark centers but are not entirely dark like Ridgway's. This character is apparent only on perched birds at close range. *Flight:* broad-based wings and lazy, loping flight distinguish it from other swallows, except Tree; in overhead flight, can be distinguished from martins by flight behavior and pale panel in wing created by pale bases of remiges. Martins have straighter, more deliberate flight and uniformly dark underwings. Tree Swallow has entirely white underparts (but may have dusky smudge on upper sides) and uniformly dark underwings.

Voice. *Call:* flat, sputtering *frit* and slightly richer *breet*.

Habitat. Resident populations are found in forest clearings and perhaps elsewhere, but distribution and habitat preferences relative to those of Ridgway's are unclear. N.A. migrants may be found in most open areas, especially along coast and over lagoons, agricultural fields, orchards, pastureland, and roadways.

Distribution. Nests from wc and se Can. to nw Mex. and Gulf of Mex.; winters from extreme s U.S. to Pan. Resident populations occur from s Sonora and s Nuevo Leon s. of Yucatán Pen. to C.R.

Status in Belize. Complex and not fully understood. Those from N.A. winter in Belize (late Sept. to mid-Apr.). Resident populations are found at scattered locations in the interior.

References. *Identification:* Lethaby (1996). *Systematics:* Paynter (1957).

Ridgway's Rough-winged Swallow

MAP 169; PLATE 41

Stelgidopteryx [serripennis] ridgwayi
OTHER NAMES. Northern Rough-winged Swallow (combined form).

Identification. 5¼″ (13.5 cm). Darker above than both migrant and resident Northern Rough-wingeds with tiny white spot on forehead, and dark brownish distal undertail coverts. White forehead spot best seen on birds flying directly at observer, and on perched birds at close range. *Flight:* dark undertail coverts give impression of squared-off tail base, as opposed to Northern's wedge of white in underside of tail.

Voice. Similar to that of Northern Rough-winged.

Habitat. Forest clearings and wooded streams in karst limestone areas, where it nests in caves.

Distribution. *Near Yucatán Endemic.* Resident on Yucatán Pen. s. to n Guat. and Belize and w. to c Veracruz.

Status in Belize. C resident in Maya Mtns. and karst limestone hills in TO, SC, and CA, n. to sw BE; reported also in w OW.

Reference. *Systematics:* Phillips (1986).

Bank Swallow   PLATE 41

Riparia riparia
OTHER NAMES. Sand Martin (U.K.), kusal (M).

Identification. 5″ (12.5 cm). Like Rough-winged, brown above and white below but with distinct brown band across breast delineating clean white throat and partial white collar. *Flight:* smaller than Rough-winged, with narrower-based wings and fairly direct flight with quick, brief wingbeats between short glides; Rough-winged has lazy, less direct flight with slower wingbeats.

Voice. *Call:* 1. harsh sputtering *zit* to *bzit;* 2. *churt* to *churdut.* Seldom vocalizes in Belize.

Habitat. Most open areas, but concentrations occur only along coast. Some also migrate along ridgelines in interior.

Distribution. Nests from n Alaska, nc Can., and n Eurasia to sc U.S., ne Mex., s Eurasia, and ne

Afr. Winters in S.A. (occas. n. to s Mex.), Afr., and s Asia.

Status in Belize. FC to locally C autumn and less C spring transient, primarily along coast; mid-Aug. to mid-Nov. and mid-Mar. to late May; occas. in winter.

Reference. *Identification:* Lethaby (1996).

Genus: Petrochelidon

Cliff and Cave swallows have a square-tipped tail; relatively broad-based, short wings; and flight that is slower and less deliberate than that of Barn and Bank, with sweeping turns and more gliding (more like Rough-winged). The pale rump on Cliff and one subspecies of Cave is also readily apparent on all birds but those directly overhead.

Things to note: color of throat and forehead, color and extent of contrast between rump and back and between crown and neck, face, and forehead.

Cliff Swallow   PLATE 41
Petrochelidon pyrrhonota
OTHER NAMES. Kusal (M).

Identification. 5¼″ (13.5 cm). Chunky swallow with short, broad-based wings; square-tipped tail; dark throat; and pale rump. *Ad.:* blue-black crown and chestnut throat and auriculars contrast sharply with whitish collar and underparts; back deep blue black, with thin white streaks; those that pass through Belize have pale buff forehead (Mex. populations with dark chestnut forehead have not been reported in Belize). *Juv.:* lacks white back streaks, and forehead generally not as pale; small percentage have pale throat like Cave, but auriculars remain dark.

Voice. *Call:* harsh *churt;* fuller and more drawn out than that of Bank. Mostly silent in Belize.

Habitat. Open areas; concentrates along coast, but also found over interior wetlands and occas. elsewhere. Some migrate along ridgelines in interior.

Distribution. Nests from n Alaska and nc Can. to sc Mex.; winters in se S.A.

Status in Belize. C autumn and less C spring transient, especially along coast, mid-Aug. to early Nov. and early Mar. to mid-May.

Cave Swallow   PLATE 41
Petrochelidon fulva
OTHER NAMES. Cinnamon-throated Swallow (is part of).

Identification. 5¼″ (13.5 cm). Two distinctive subspecies groups (possibly representing distinct species). Representatives of both groups have been recorded in Belize. *Ad., pallida group:* pale cinnamon rump, throat, and auriculars, becoming duller across nape; pale collar and face isolate dark blue-black crown and rufous-cinnamon forehead; little contrast between throat and rest of underparts. *Ad., fulva group:* similar to *pallida* group, but with deep chestnut rump and forehead, and richer cinnamon throat, auriculars, and nape (= collar); less contrast between rump and rest of upperparts. *Juv.* (both groups): duller; lacks cinnamon and rufous colors of ad. and white streaks in back.

Voice. *Fulva group:* soft, nasal *sweik* or *whiet. Pallida group:* calls richer, more like those of Barn Swallow, not as nasal or cracking as in *fulva.* Seldom vocalizes in Belize.

Habitat. Most likely to be seen migrating along coastline, but also found over wetlands and other large, open areas in interior.

Distribution. Partially migratory populations in se New Mex., w and s Texas, and ne Mex. (*pallida* group), and largely resident populations in Chiapas, n Yucatán Pen., s Florida, and n W.I. (*fulva* group). Seasonal movements in both groups are poorly understood.

Status in Belize. *Pallida* group: VU autumn migrant along coast, mid-Sept. to mid-Nov. *Fulva* group (probably *P. f. citata* from nearby Yucatán Pen.): one record, Blue Creek rice fields OW, 30 Mar. 1999.

References. *Status:* Jones et al. (2000). *Voice:* Howell and Webb (1995). *Systematics:* Smith et al. (1988).

Barn Swallow   PLATE 41
Hirundo rustica
OTHER NAMES. Swallow (U.K.), kusal (M).

Identification. 5¼″ (13.5 cm). Common seasonally throughout most of the world and, as such, one of the most familiar of all birds. It is unmistakable, with its long, forked tail; glossy blue-black upperparts and rufous throat. *Ad.:* long tail (averages shorter in ♀) and cinnamon-orange underparts (averages paler in ♀). *Juv.:* much shorter tail, paler throat and underparts. *Flight:* fast, with frequent changes in direction; flaps wings steadily, with partial wing fold every few seconds; soars less than other swallows. White flashes in spread tail.

Voice. *Call:* 1. *trip* to *twit;*
2. *fweck;*
3. *pi-deep. Song:* thin, squeaky screeches, chirps, and sputters.

Habitat. Nearly ubiquitous, but concentrations occur along coast and offshore, and in interior over wetlands, farms, and pastures.

Distribution. Nests from nc Can., n Eur., and nc Asia to c Mex., n Afr., and sc Asia; winters from c Mex., c Afr., and s Asia to s S.A., s Afr., and Indonesia.

Status in Belize. C to VC transient, early Mar. to early June, and mid-July to late Nov.; UC to locally FC in winter.

FAMILY: TROGLODYTIDAE (Wrens)

World: 79. **New World:** 79. **Belize:** 9. Except for one Holarctic species, wrens are restricted to the New World. They reach greatest species diversity in C.A., with fewer in S.A. and fewer still in N.A. Wrens are characterized by a thin, slightly decurved bill; short, rounded wings; and brownish plumage. Most are small and have bars somewhere in their plumage, typically in the flight feathers or undertail coverts, and some have spots, wingbars, and stripes. The tail, which varies in length from almost nonexistent to moderately long, is frequently held cocked in many species. Wrens are known for their loud, bubbly, often melodious, and occasionally harmonic songs. **References:** Brewer (2001). *Voice:* Hardy and Coffey (1998).

   Things to note: overall size; habitat; tail length; presence/absence of bars in undertail coverts, tail, wings, or back; presence/absence of white supercilium or streaked auriculars.

Band-backed Wren   MAP 170; PLATE 42

Campylorhynchus zonatus
OTHER NAMES. Banded Cactus Wren (arch.).

Identification. 7¾″ (19.5 cm). Large wren with prominent supercilium and long, banded tail. *Ad.:* strongly barred upperparts, spotted breast, cinnamon belly. *Juv.:* streaked back, lacks spots in breast, has pale cinnamon-buff belly.

Voice. *Call:* harsh *check* and *sheck* notes. *Song:* very harsh, nasal *bedenk brewink,* often repeated (quality similar to that of tityras). Typically, two or more birds burst into song together, producing an unmistakable loud, raspy chatter.

Habitat. Forages among bromeliads in large trees within broadleaf forest and forest edge.

Distribution. Resident from n Veracruz s. of Yucatán Pen. to nw S.A.

Status in Belize. UC to locally FC, but somewhat nomadic, resident away from coast n. to n CA and sw BE. One record from Lamanai OW and possibly from near Belize City.

Spot-breasted Wren   PLATE 42

Thryothorus maculipectus
OTHER NAMES. Katy-yu-baby-di-cry (C), man sik kan sukuya'a (K), bolich (K), tulin (M).

Identification. 5¼″ (13.5 cm). Medium-sized wren with white supercilium, barred tail and undertail coverts, unbarred wings, and cinnamon-brown flanks and belly. *Ad.:* heavily spotted breast and face. *Juv.:* lacks prominent spots of ad. and can be confused with both Plain and Carolina; note dull grayish rather than white underparts, and indistinct spotting on breast.

Voice. *Call:* 1. rolling *trrrrruueeet* that ascends the scale (sounds like someone running fingertips through a comb);
2. staccato trill *ddddd-d-d-d-d d d d* on an even pitch or with sharp rise and fall in pitch near beginning. *Song:* repertoire typically 5 or more notes (song of White-breasted Wood-Wren usually 4 or fewer notes). Examples: loud, clear *toe wea du wobegone, toe teuh toe tuweo, wha cheer do we che dee we o, cheer what chee doe du wee, duh wheeta whea who, te we tuh wea toe,*

etc. The Creole name, Katy-yu-baby-di-cry, is roughly onomatopoeic.

Habitat. Forest edge, second-growth scrub, roadside tangles, vines; also forest interior, but to a lesser extent than White-breasted Wood-Wren.

Distribution. Resident from c Nuevo Leon and c Tamaulipas to n C.R.

Status in Belize. C resident on mainland.

Reference. *Voice:* Moore (1992).

Carolina Wren

MAP 171; PLATE 42

Thryothorus ludovicianus

OTHER NAMES. White-browed Wren (is part of).

Identification. 4¾" (12 cm). Rufous-brown upperparts; bold white supercilium; dark eyeline; barring in tail, undertail coverts, wings, and auriculars/neck. Similar in size and appearance to Spot-breasted, but with plain white underparts and barred remiges. Vocalizations are quite different.

Voice. *Call:* 1. liquid *pr-di-rit* or *pretty bik* (rolled "r's");

2. loud, harsh scold similar to call of Red-throated Ant-Tanager;

3. clear, hollow *p-r-r-r-r-t* or downward rolling, liquid *teurrrrrr* followed by second bird's dry *chăăăă* or *d-d-d-d-d-d-d-d;*

4. hollow, Morse code–like *d-d-dit.*

Song: clear ringing roll of 3–6 notes, repeated rapidly. 1. *deedwoe deedwoe deedwoe deedwoe;*

2. *churvy churvy churvy churvy churvy.*

Habitat. Understory within low, semi-deciduous and deciduous forest and forest edge; also locally in streamside trees and brush within savannas.

Distribution. Resident in e N.A. from Great Lakes and s New England to ne Mex., and discontinuously in Yucatán Pen. and nw Nic. Populations from Yucatán Pen. and Nic. are considered by some authorities to be a separate species, White-browed Wren (*T. albinucha*).

Status in Belize. Resident in three widely separated areas: sw OW, e OW near Lamanai, and w CA. Reports from elsewhere are not documented.

References. *Status:* Howell et al. (1992). *Voice:*

Moore (1992). *Systematics:* Lowery and Berrett (1963).

Plain Wren

MAP 172; PLATE 42

Thryothorus modestus

OTHER NAMES. Modest Wren (I. Davis).

Identification. 5¼" (13.5 cm). Brown above, whitish below, with white supercilium, faint eyeline, unstreaked auriculars and neck, and unbarred cinnamon flanks and undertail coverts. Carolina has bold eyeline and barred auriculars/neck and undertail coverts.

Voice. *Call:* dry *chut* to *ch-ch-chut. Song:* 1. short, slurred *s-l-lip;*

2. longer *see slippy de slip* to *see spiddly spee.*

Habitat. Understory within submontane pine forest; locally, broadleaf forest.

Distribution. Resident from e Oaxaca s. of Yucatán Pen. to Pan.

Status in Belize. UC and local resident in Mtn. Pine Ridge; also recorded in hills n.w. of San Ignacio in nw CA.

House Wren

PLATE 42

Troglodytes aedon

OTHER NAMES. Southern House-Wren (*musculus* group, is part of), Tropical House-Wren (arch.), House Bird (coll.), tulin (M).

Identification. 4½" (11.5 cm). Unmarked brown back and crown; paler, buffish brown below, with finely barred wings, tail, and undertail coverts. Lacks prominent supercilium.

Voice. *Call:* 1. breathy, rough *chăă;*

2. fast series of dry, scratchy *chĕ* notes;

3. short *chă* notes in a slow series (≈2/sec). *Scold:* grinding *d-d-d-d-d-d-d. Song:* bubbly, explosive jumble with rapid alternating series of high- and low-pitched notes, usually preceded by a few high, thin, squeaky notes.

Habitat. Towns and villages, orchards, open country with scattered trees and brush; less commonly in open pine forest and savanna.

Distribution. Nests from wc and se Can. to s S.A. Populations in Can. and most of U.S. migrate s. in winter.

Status in Belize. Locally C resident on mainland.
Reference. Moore (1992).

Sedge Wren   MAP 173; PLATE 42
Cistothorus platensis
OTHER NAMES. Short-billed Marsh-Wren (arch.), Slender-billed Grass-Wren (arch.).

Identification. 4¼″ (11 cm). Heavily streaked back and crown; heavily barred wings and tail; unbarred undertail coverts. Dips constantly when agitated; cocks its tail strongly upward.
Voice. *Call:* sharp, dry *chp. Song* (quite varied but always harsh): 1. dry *chp chp cheedle cheedle channh;*
2. *chp chp channh* (the *channh* is a nasal rattling scold);
3. *shick shick shick shick cheeee;*
4. harsh rattle plus *cheeee;*
5. dry, rolling chatter;
6. rough nasal insectlike *ăăăă* or *chăăă.*
Habitat. Seasonally flooded lowland savannas and well-drained hillside meadows.
Distribution. Nests in e N.A. from c and se Can. to ec U.S.; winters from s U.S. to ne Mex. Also, numerous disjunct resident populations from c Mex. to s S.A.
Status in Belize. C resident in ne TO and se SC, and FC but local resident at higher elevations in Mtn. Pine Ridge. The ssp. *russelli* is endemic to Belize.
Reference. *Systematics:* Dickerman (1975).

White-bellied Wren   MAP 174; PLATE 42
Uropsila leucogastra

Identification. 4¼″ (11 cm). Similar to Plain Wren and Carolina Wren but smaller, with a much shorter tail and white, not dark, lores. Lacks cinnamon-brown flanks and undertail coverts of Plain Wren, and undertail coverts are barred.
Voice. *Call:* 1. soft *tup* or *chuk,* often given in an irregular series of ≈1/sec;
2. squeaky *chip. Scold: d-d-d-d-d-d-d-d-d-d-d-d,* much like that of Spot-breasted or House wren. *Song:* clear, liquid, and low-pitched; variously *dibleo, diblideo,* and *de duh d diblideo.*

Habitat. Understory within broadleaf forest, forest edge, and second-growth scrub.
Distribution. Resident from Jalisco and sc Tamaulipas to Belize, discontinuously in n Hon.
Status in Belize. C resident s. to c BE and w. of Maya Mtns. to s CA. Reports from e. of Maya Mtns. are unconfirmed.
Reference. *Voice:* Moore (1992).

White-breasted Wood-Wren   PLATE 42
Henicorhina leucosticta
OTHER NAMES. Lowland Wood-Wren (arch.), tun tulin (K), tulin (M).

Identification. 4¼″ (11 cm). Short stubby tail, white supercilium, strongly barred black-and-white face, gray sides, cinnamon flanks and undertail coverts. Often found in association with Spot-breasted Wren. *Ad.:* white throat and breast. *Juv.:* grayish throat and breast, less distinct barring in face; similar to Gray-breasted Wood-Wren *(Henicorhina leucophrys),* which is not found in Belize.
Voice. *Call:* most diagnostic are frequently repeated *klink* and *bleet. Scold:* harsh, rapid *dt-dt-dt-dt-dt-dt. Song:* highly varied repertoire usually consists of 4 or fewer clear, whistled notes, typically with high and low notes more or less alternating.
Examples: 1. *tuh woe tu weet* or *let's go to eat;*
2. loud clear *tēuh-toe;*
3. *a-whe-te-u;*
4. *dee day doe;* etc. Example of a dueting pair: first bird whistles *eat eat* and second bird responds immediately *too weak to eat.*
Habitat. Understory within broadleaf forest interior and forest edge. More often in forest interior and less often in second-growth scrub than Spot-breasted Wren.
Distribution. Resident primarily on Gulf-Caribbean slope from se San Luis Potosí to n S.A.
Status in Belize. UC (n.e.) to C resident on mainland.
References. *General:* Dickerman (1973). *Voice:* Moore (1992).

Nightingale Wren MAP 175; PLATE 42
Microcerculus philomela
OTHER NAMES. Northern Nightingale-
Wren (alt.), Dark-throated
Nightingale-Wren (arch.).

Identification. 4¼″ (11 cm). Bird of deep broadleaf forest with only a stub for a tail. Dark gray
brown nearly throughout, only slightly paler on
throat; pale tips to wing covert feathers, and
darker, scalelike feather edgings on underparts.
No trace of a supercilium. Hardest of all the
wrens in Belize to see, but its distinctive lazy
song given at dawn and dusk reveals its presence.
Voice. *Call:* raspy *chik,* about halfway between
those of Ovenbird and Orange-billed Sparrow.
Song: short whistled notes (≈1/sec), many off-
key, given on randomly different pitches in
nearly endless series. Quite unique.
Habitat. Understory within foothill and montane broadleaf forest interior.
Distribution. Resident on Gulf-Caribbean
slope from w Oaxaca s. of Yucatán Pen. to C.R.
Status in Belize. FC resident in Maya Mtns. and
karst limestone hills in interior TO and SC, e
and s CA, and possibly sw BE.
Reference. *Status:* Wood and Leberman (1987).

FAMILY: SYLVIIDAE
(Old World Warblers, Gnatcatchers, and Gnatwrens)
World: 294. **New World:** 15. **Belize:** 3. Nearly
worldwide, but most are confined to the Old
World. The Sylviidae are highly variable; most
are small insectivorous birds with a thin bill, thin
legs, and predominantly gray, brown, or olive
plumage.

Long-billed Gnatwren PLATE 42
Ramphocaenus melanurus
OTHER NAMES. Long-billed Antwren
(I. Davis).

Identification. 5″ (12.5 cm). Long, daggerlike
bill as in a diminutive jacamar, and a moderately long, disjointed tail. Has broad white tips
to underside of rectrices somewhat like those of
a gnatcatcher, but is gray brown above and cinnamon below, more like a wren. Like the wrens,
stays within tangles and vines where it can be
difficult to see.
Voice. *Call:* soft irregular *chp* notes. *Song:* lazy,
liquid trill that initially drops in pitch, then remains constant; usually with 1 or 2 short introductory notes: *tp tur-rrrrrrrrrr* or *tp d-d-d-d-d-d-
d-d-d-d-d-d;* sometimes rises in pitch again at the
end. Notes are more melodious, not blubbery,
and not as separable as those of Streak-headed
Woodcreeper.
Habitat. Vines and tangles at forest edge;
second-growth scrub.
Distribution. Resident from c Veracruz to c
S.A.
Status in Belize. FC to C resident on mainland.
Reference. *Voice:* Moore (1992).

Genus: Polioptila *(Gnatcatchers)*

Gnatcatchers are small blue-gray, black, and
white birds with a long tail. The two species in
Belize are found in very different habitats: Blue-
gray in pine woodlands, and Tropical in broadleaf forests. However, the relatively few migrant
Blue-grays that winter in Belize may be seen in
almost any habitat, including broadleaf forest.
Both species flick and pump their tail constantly
while foraging for insects in the outer foliage.
The ♀s of both species and the ♂ Blue-gray are all
similar, especially when seen from below, which
is often the case in tall broadleaf forest. Both
species have similar mewing calls but very different songs.

    Things to note: presence/absence of well-
defined gray or black crown, supercilium, or eye-
ring.

Blue-gray Gnatcatcher MAP 176; PLATE 40
Polioptila caerulea

Identification. 4¼″ (11 cm). Blue gray above and
white below, with mostly white undertail. Plain
face with black eyes set off by white eye-ring. ♂
alt.: thin black lateral crown stripe. ♀: slightly
duller than ♂; lacks black lateral crown stripe.
Voice. *Call:* 1. thin, wiry, nasal *peeee* to *peee-pēnt,*
higher-pitched and thinner than calls of Tropical
Gnatcatcher and Red-legged Honeycreeper;
2. faster nasal series *peee peee peee* (usually 2–4

notes). *Song:* high-pitched, nasal *skeet* and *squea squu squeet* notes.

Habitat. Resident population restricted to pine and pine-oak woodland and savannas, locally in calabash-palmetto savannas without pines. Migrants may be found in any wooded habitat.

Distribution. Nests from cw and ne U.S. to Belize and n Guat.; winters from s U.S. to Hon. and Cuba. Populations s. of U.S. are resident.

Status in Belize. C resident in ne CO and n OW, more widespread from e OW and most of BE s. (e. of Maya Mtns.) to ne TO; also FC in Mtn. Pine Ridge. Resident population supplemented with migrants from N.A. in winter (Sept. to Apr.).

Reference. *Status:* Wood and Leberman (1987).

Tropical Gnatcatcher   PLATE 40
Polioptila plumbea
OTHER NAMES. White-browed Gnatcatcher (I. Davis).

Identification. 4″ (10 cm). Blue gray above and white below, with underside of tail mostly white, as in Blue-gray. ♂: distinctive black crown and thin black postocular stripe outline white supercilium. ♀: similar but with gray crown and postocular stripe, which are slightly darker than the back; more well-defined supercilium than in Blue-gray and lacks white eye-ring.

Voice. *Call:* 1. thin nasal *wăah* similar to that of Blue-gray Gnatcatcher and Red-legged Honeycreeper, but shorter and lower-pitched than the former and not quite as buzzy as the latter;
2. thin nasal *dweee;*
3. rough, nasal *tweh,* usually repeated in series, like Yellow-green Vireo call but higher-pitched, repetitious.
Song: 1. thin, high-pitched, descending trill, stopping abruptly about halfway down the scale;
2. less frequently, a thin, short, *Euphonia*-like warble.

Habitat. Midlevels to canopy within broadleaf forest interior and edge.

Distribution. Resident from s Veracruz to c S.A.

Status in Belize. FC resident on mainland in south, becoming increasingly UC and local northward.

Reference. *Voice:* Moore (1992).

FAMILY: TURDIDAE
(Thrushes)

World: 175. **New World:** 65. **Belize:** 9. Virtually worldwide. Thrushes are a large, moderately diverse, and widespread family with representatives on all continents but Antarctica, and on many oceanic islands. Most are characterized by a medium-length, thin, blunt-tipped bill; a chunky body; an upright posture; and relatively long legs. Many forage on or near the ground, others from the ground to the treetops, and still others exclusively in trees. Thrushes are among the most accomplished songsters in the world. Some solitaires and nightingale-thrushes have complex, harmonic songs that defy description, and the Slate-colored Solitaire is arguably the most accomplished singer in Belize. **References:** Clement (2000). *Voice:* Hardy and Parker (1985).

Eastern Bluebird   MAP 177; PLATE 43
Sialia sialis

Identification. 6¾″ (17 cm). No other bird in Belize resembles the Eastern Bluebird: blue above, rufous and white below. ♂: sky blue above, with rufous throat and breast and white belly. ♀: grayer above except for rump, tail, and portion of wings, which are blue; underparts, especially throat, are paler, giving it a more washed-out appearance than ♂.

Voice. *Call:* 1. clear *turlee;*
2. harsh *pridik.*
Song: rich, burry 1. *chortle chertle;*
2. *cho chor chortle chur;* etc.

Habitat. Midlevel strata within submontane pine forest clearings and edge.

Distribution. Nests in e N.A. from s Can. to Gulf of Mex.; also, resident populations in highlands from se Arizona to nw Nic. N.A. populations are partially migratory.

Status in Belize. UC resident in Mtn. Pine Ridge.

Genus: Myadestes

Solitaires are marvelous songsters, and their melodious fluty notes fill the air wherever they occur. The Slate-colored Solitaire is the only one that occurs in Belize, and it is restricted to higher elevations.

Slate-colored Solitaire MAP 178; PLATE 43

Myadestes unicolor

OTHER NAMES. Xalau (K), ki'yon (M).

Identification. 7¾″ (19.5 cm). *Ad.:* slate gray throughout except for conspicuous white eye crescents and mostly white outer tail feathers. *Juv.:* heavily scalloped, with thin black feather edges on all but wings and tail. *Flight:* conspicuous pale buff base to remiges. The similar Brown-backed Solitaire *(Myadestes occidentalis),* which has been reported in Belize, probably erroneously, has distinctive brown cast to upperparts, less conspicuous eye-ring, and prominent white malar mark outlined below with black (Slate-colored may have a faint malar line). The two species have very different vocalizations.

Voice. *Call:* 1. rough, nasal *draank;* 2. buzzy *zrink. Song* (characteristic sound of the Maya Mtns.): rich, clear, harmonic, flute-like *weedoe teee wheeowee doe doe whit whit whit whit whit; doe-whip! de-e-e-e-e teedle-o chup chup chup chup (de-e-e-e-e-e* is a harmonic trill). *Other song endings:* clear, resonant *too wee do wee do* or *whip!-do-do-do-do-do.*

Habitat. Midlevels to canopy within montane broadleaf forest.

Distribution. Resident in highlands from sc San Luis Potosí to nw Nic.

Status in Belize. C resident above 2,000 ft. (600 m) in Maya Mtns.; occas. at lower elevations in winter.

References. *Status:* Howell et al. (1992). *Voice:* Delaney (1992).

Genera: Catharus *and* Hylocichla
(Spot-breasted Thrushes)

Of the four thrushes in Belize with spotted breasts, three present an ID challenge. All are brown to rufous above and faintly to boldly spotted beneath. ID of the larger, boldly spotted Wood Thrush (genus *Hylocichla*) is straightforward, but the other three are best told by their vocalizations and subtle differences in color and in face and breast patterns. All live on or near the ground in wooded or semiwooded habitats.

Things to note: presence/absence of distinct eye-ring; color of upperparts, face, and flanks; extent and distinctiveness of spots on breast; vocalizations.

Veery PLATE 43

Catharus fuscescens

OTHER NAMES. Wilson's Thrush (I. Davis).

Identification. 7¼″ (18.5 cm). Brown to rufous brown above, with buff wash on throat and breast and pale grayish flanks, creating more contrast in color between breast and belly than either of the other two *Catharus.* Further distinguished from Swainson's by only a hint of an eye-ring. Differs from Gray-cheeked in having brownish, not gray, auriculars and more diffuse spotting on breast. Represented in Belize by two fairly distinct subspecies, *C. f. fuscescens,* which is rufous brown above, with diffuse spotting on the breast, and *C. f. salicicola,* which has little rufous above and a more distinct cluster of spots on the breast and is thus closer in appearance in many aspects to both Gray-cheeked and Swainson's than to nominate *fuscescens.* Nevertheless, some individuals with intermediate characteristics may not be safely distinguished in the field.

Voice. *Call:* burry, down-slurred *vyur;* softer, more down-slurred than that of Gray-cheeked. *Song:* descending buzzy, fluty series of 5 or 6 drawn-out rolling notes (rarely heard in Belize).

Habitat. Understory and ground within most broadleaf forest types.

Distribution. Nests from sc Can. to nc U.S.; winters in c S.A.

Status in Belize. UC to FC autumn and spring transient, mid-Sept. to late Nov. and mid-Apr. to late May. Most often seen on cayes. Both the more eastern *fuscescens* and western *salicicola* ssp. pass through Belize, with *salicicola* generally more frequent.

References. *Status:* Wood and Leberman (1987). *Identification:* Lane and Jaramillo (2000b).

Gray-cheeked Thrush PLATE 43

Catharus minimus

Identification. 6¾″ (17 cm). Distinguished more by its *lack* of field marks than by any diagnostic character. Dull brown above, with no hint of rufous; grayish face with indistinct

whitish eye-ring (most apparent behind the eye). More boldly spotted than most Veeries, and with darker, more olive flanks; only a hint of buff on breast, but not on throat or face.
Voice. *Call:* slightly burry *PEEur,* similar to Veery's but more emphatic and nasal and less down-slurred. *Song:* thin, buzzy, slightly fluty series of 5 or 6 notes on different pitches; not as rich as Veery's. Rarely heard in Belize.
Habitat. Understory and ground within most broadleaf forest types.
Distribution. Nests in e Siberia, Alaska, and n Can.; winters in S.A. e. of Andes.
Status in Belize. UC autumn and spring transient, late Sept. to mid-Nov. and mid-Apr. to late May.
References. *Status:* Wood and Leberman (1987). *Identification:* Knox (1996); Lane and Jaramillo (2000c).

Swainson's Thrush PLATE 43
Catharus ustulatus
OTHER NAMES. Olive-backed Thrush (arch.).

Identification. 7″ (18 cm). Dull gray brown to olive brown above, generally lacking any rufous tones; strong buff wash across breast and throat, which, unlike in the other two, extends to the auriculars; conspicuous buff eye-ring. Breast distinctly spotted as in Gray-cheeked, more so than even in western Veery *(salicicola);* flanks light olive, not grayish. *Caution:* western Swainson's *(C. u. ustulatus),* which may occur infrequently in Belize, has rufous tones in upperparts, much like western Veery.
Voice. *Call:* 1. soft to sharp *perk;*
2. flatter *what;*
3. soft *prt.* *Flight call:* flat, clear *queep. Song:* thin, fluty series of notes that ascend the scale; given occas. in spring.
Habitat. Understory and ground within most broadleaf forest types.
Distribution. Nests from nc Alaska and Can. to sw and ne U.S.; winters mostly in highlands from Nayarit and s Tamaulipas to s Mex. and in lowlands from Guat. and s Belize to c S.A.
Status in Belize. FC to C autumn and spring transient, mid-Sept. to early Nov. and late Mar.

to late May; occas. remaining through winter, primarily in south.
Reference. *Identification:* Lane and Jaramillo (2000b).

Wood Thrush PLATE 43
Hylocichla mustelina
OTHER NAMES. Tolocok (K), pi pish (M).

Identification. 7½″ (19 cm). Larger and more robust than the *Catharus* thrushes; rich rufous above, except for olive-brown rump and tail. Snow-white below, boldly spotted with black.
Voice. *Call:* 1. scolding *whit-whit-whit-whit;*
2. short, rapid, low-pitched, laughing *tŭ-tŭ-tŭ-tŭ-tŭ;*
3. burry *jur* to *jer,* given during migration both during the day and at night while migrating. *Song:* rich, fluty, bouncy series of 3 or 4 notes. Examples: *chree odalee, pree-duleet, prettily-o-o-o, prit-ole-e-e-e.* Song phrases variously end on high or low note or a short fluty trill. Heard occas. in spring.
Habitat. Understory and ground within most broadleaf forest types.
Distribution. Nests in e N.A. from s Can. to Gulf of Mex.; winters from se San Luis Potosí to n Colombia.
Status in Belize. C winter visitor, late Sept. to early May.
References. *Identification:* Lane and Jaramillo (2000a). *Voice:* Moore (1992).

Genus: Turdus *(Robins)*

Two are resident, and a third is a vagrant. Robins are larger than the spot-breasted thrushes and have a yellow bill.
Things to note: body color, throat pattern, color of legs, presence/absence of eye-ring.

Clay-colored Robin PLATE 43
Turdus grayi
OTHER NAMES. Clay-colored Thrush (alt.), Gray's Thrush (arch.), Gray's Robin (arch.), Brown Cusco (C), k'o k'ob (K), ko ko ta' (M).

Identification. 9¾″ (25 cm). Clay brown above, tawny buff below, streaked throat, yellowish bill, and pinkish flesh-colored legs. Frequently seen on the ground, where it alternately runs short distances and pauses with an upright posture, occas. picking at the ground for insect larvae.

Voice. *Call:* 1. drawn-out burry to clear *tueorreet;* 2. drawn-out, burry *drreeeo;* 3. muffled *chuck-chuck-chuck-chuck-chuck;* 4. nasal *chau-chau-chau-chau-chau;* 5. thin *seeeee.* *Song:* burry series of melodious, usually 2-syllable notes, some down-slurred, some up-slurred. Frequently given phrase is *churry-churro tureet-tureet.* Rich, but not as harmonic as song of White-throated Robin; different cadence than that of Yellow-tailed Oriole, and not as repetitious as either.

Habitat. Ground to subcanopy within most broadleaf forest types, usually at or near edge, seldom deep within interior; also parks, towns, and other open areas with scattered trees.

Distribution. Resident from n Nuevo Leon and n Tamaulipas to n Colombia.

Status in Belize. C resident at low and mid-elevations on mainland; occas. on Ambergris Caye.

Reference. *Voice:* Moore (1992).

White-throated Robin MAP 179; PLATE 43
Turdus assimilis

OTHER NAMES. White-throated Thrush (alt.).

Identification. 9½″ (24 cm). Dark slaty gray above, slightly lighter below, with black-streaked white throat and unstreaked white band across lower throat/upper breast. Further distinguished from Clay-colored by bright yellow to orange-yellow bill, eye-ring, and legs. Little elevational overlap with Clay-colored.

Voice. *Call:* 1. buzzy *dzurt;* 2. buzzy, grating *zureep!;* 3. burry *rank;* 4. thin *see;* 5. Clay-colored Robin–like *deorreeet.* *Song:* mockingbird-like, and like the mockingbird, an expert mimic. Phrases are simpler, more repetitious, and faster than Clay-colored's, often very harmonic, taking on the quality of Slate-colored Solitaire's. Example: *chur-chur wheo wheo t-wur t-wur whe-e-e-e.*

Habitat. Midlevels to subcanopy within montane and foothill broadleaf forest interior and forest edge.

Distribution. Largely resident at mid- to high elevations from s Sonora and sw Tamaulipas to nw S.A.; some populations exhibit altitudinal migration.

Status in Belize. C resident at mid- and high elevations in Maya Mtns.; less C in the hills of w OW; occas. in lowlands in winter.

Reference. *Voice:* Moore (1992).

American Robin FIGURE 25
Turdus migratorius

Identification. 9½″ (24 cm). Dark gray upperparts, with contrastingly dark head and broken

Figure 25

American Robin

white eye-ring, rufous breast, black-and-white-streaked throat, and white belly and undertail coverts.

Voice. *Call:* 1. emphatic, squeaky *kip* or *kiup,* sometimes followed by *wick-wick-wick-wick;* 2. soft *tut-tut-tut-tut;* 3. very high-pitched, waxwing-like *seeeer,* but more drawn out and dropping slightly in pitch.

Habitat. Open country with scattered to moderately dense tree cover.

Distribution. Nests from n Alaska and n Can. to s U.S. and in Mex. plateau to Oaxaca; winters from n U.S. to c Mex.

Status in Belize. Two records: Hill Bank OW, 5 Jan. 1981, and Crooked Tree Village BE, 23 Mar. 2000.

Reference. *Status:* Howell and Webb (1995).

FAMILY: MIMIDAE
(Thrashers)

World: 35. **New World:** 35. **Belize:** 3. Restricted primarily to N.A. and C.A.; however, with several species in S.A. Mimids are slender birds with a medium to fairly long, straight to decurved bill; short, rounded wings; fairly long legs; and a long, moderately graduated tail. They are noted for their melodious, sometimes intricate, song phrases, and some are excellent mimics of other birds—thus the English name "mockingbird." Only the northernmost species are migratory.
References: Brewer (2001). *Voice:* Hardy et al. (1987a).

Gray Catbird   PLATE 40
Dumetella carolinensis
OTHER NAMES. Northern Catbird (arch.), chi chi sa'a (K), re'ish (M).

Identification. 8¼″ (21 cm). Medium-dark slate gray with a black crown that does not extend laterally to the eyes, and with chestnut undertail coverts.

Voice. *Call:* 1. catlike, whining nasal *aaaaaa,* rising slightly in pitch in middle; 2. rough *whut;* 3. soft *chit* and *chidit* given frequently during migration; 4. when agitated, a harsh *j-j-j-jit. Song* (rarely

heard in Belize): similar to, but more liquid than, that of mockingbird with phrases run together.

Habitat. Understory to midlevel strata at forest edge (occas. interior); second-growth scrub. Frequents fruiting trees, where often seen in canopy as well as other strata.

Distribution. Nests from s Can. to wc and se U.S.; winters from se U.S. to Pan.

Status in Belize. C winter visitor, late Sept. to early May.

Reference. *Voice:* Moore (1992).

Black Catbird   MAP 180; PLATE 40
Melanoptila glabrirostris

Identification. 7¾″ (19.5 cm). Similar in shape and behavior to Gray Catbird, but slightly smaller in size; glossy black throughout. A small portion of the populations on Ambergris Caye, and more recently on Caye Caulker, are partially to completely white (leucistic).

Voice. *Call:* 1. hard *tik,* much like Northern Cardinal's; 2. *chong;* 3. nasal, rough *cheow;* 4. nasal, rough *breep;* 5. *cho tōk;* 6. rough *chĕwhēē;* 7. short *mew,* shorter than in Gray Catbird and not whining. An individual will give many of these notes in random sequence with several to many seconds in between. *Scold:* nasal *chaa* more or less as in Red-throated Ant-Tanager. *Song:* fluty, harmonic, burry *lik wrr t-we* and various flat, sputtery notes, including a rattly *t-t-t-t-t.* Also, an inquisitive *you bring your key?* and a variety of clear whistles, grinds, and sputters.

Habitat. On cayes, understory and midlevels within littoral forest; on mainland, semi-deciduous to deciduous forest interior and edge.

Distribution. *Yucatán Endemic.* Resident in Yucatán Pen. s. to sw Campeche, n Guat., and n Belize. Because of its restricted range and the vulnerability of its habitat to development, it is considered ***Globally Near Threatened.***

Status in Belize. C resident on Ambergris Caye and Caye Caulker; UC to locally C on mainland w. to e OW and s. to c Belize, once each near Gallon Jug OW and Monkey R. TO. Formerly resident on Lighthouse and Glovers Reefs. Numbers may be increasing locally on mainland. **References.** *Status:* Miller and Miller (1991). *Conservation:* Jones and Vallely (2001); Stattersfield and Capper (2000).

Tropical Mockingbird   MAP 181; PLATE 40
Mimus gilvus
OTHER NAMES. Graceful Mockingbird (I. Davis), Nightingale (C), Chicas (S).

Identification. 9½″ (24 cm). Gray above and white below, with white wingbars and broad white tips to all but the central tail feathers. Eyes yellowish. Curious habit of running a short distance on the ground, then stopping and slowly raising or stretching its wings.
Voice. *Call:* 1. very harsh *aaaaaaa;* 2. loud, flat *chip! Song:* large vocal repertoire. A typical singing bout is a string of short phrases (usually in sets of three), with each set different from the last. Additionally, frequently mimics other birds. Notes range from clear (mostly) to burry to harsh. Example: *chipper chipper chipper niño niño niño whea whea whea chureep chureep cheeto cheeto,* etc. May sing for long periods without pause, and often sings on moonlit nights.
Habitat. Most open country, including towns and villages, open pine woodland, savannas, pastureland, orchards, and other areas with scattered shrubs and trees.
Distribution. Resident from s Veracruz and e Oaxaca to Hon.; also in n and e S.A. and in the Lesser Antilles. Some postbreeding dispersal is evident in C.A. populations.
Status in Belize. Distribution complex. On mainland, C resident in CO, all but w OW, throughout BE, ne CA, n and e SC, and ne TO. In autumn and winter, small numbers disperse into sw OW, w CA, and s TO. C resident on Ambergris Caye, Caye Caulker, and Turneffe Isl.; strays (or formerly resident?) at Lighthouse Reef and Glovers Reef.

FAMILY: MOTACILLIDAE
(Pipits and Wagtails)
World: 62. **New World:** 12. **Belize:** 1. Primarily Old World, although a few are confined to the New World, mostly in the Andes. Nearly all are slender, ground-dwelling species inhabiting various open-country habitats. Many pump their tail, and many also have white tail markings usually confined to the outer rectrices. All have a relatively short, thin bill, moderate to long tail and legs, and long hind claw. **Reference:** Alström et al. (2002).

American Pipit   FIGURE 26
Anthus rubescens
OTHER NAMES. Water Pipit (combined form).

Identification. 6″ (15 cm). Somewhat resembles a waterthrush, but larger and grayer and with longer tail. Also found in more open habitats. *Basic:* brownish gray and faintly streaked above, indistinct pale supercilium and malar, darker gray lateral throat stripe, unstreaked

Figure 26

American Pipit

throat, prominently streaked breast, indistinct pale brownish wingbars, and white outer tail feathers conspicuous in flight. Walks, rather than hops or runs, while constantly pumping tail. *Flight:* strongly undulating; frequently calls in flight; when flushed, may fly in high, wide circles, then land in same or nearby area.

Voice. High, thin, lispy or squeaky *sip, si-sip,* or *si-si-sip* given upon flushing and in flight.

Habitat. Short-grass meadows, lawns, wet ditches and swales, and shorelines of ponds, lagoons, and seacoast.

Distribution. Nests from n Alaska, n Can., and c Greenland to U.S. Rocky Mtns., s Hudson Bay, and Newfoundland; winters from c U.S. to s Mex.

Status in Belize. Two records, both from Punta Gorda: 3 Nov. 1999 and 5 Nov. 2001.

FAMILY: BOMBYCILLIDAE
(Waxwings)

World: 3. **New World:** 2. **Belize:** 1. Small N. Temperate family with one Holarctic, one Nearctic, and one Palearctic representative, all similar in appearance. Waxwings are so named for extended red tips to their secondaries that resemble drops of sealing wax. Each species has a prominent yellow or red tip to its tail and a prominent crest. All are highly gregarious, highly migratory, and irruptive, in that they travel much farther south in some winters than in others, seeking highly variable seasonal berry supplies.

Cedar Waxwing   PLATE 43
Bombycilla cedrorum

Identification. 6½" (16.5 cm). Prominent crest, brownish body with vinaceous cinnamon cast on head and breast, dull yellowish belly, small black mask thinly outlined in white, and blue-gray rump and tail with black subterminal band and broad yellow tip. Usually seen in small groups, rarely singly.

Voice. Very high-pitched, thin *seeeee,* sometimes doubled or tripled.

Habitat. Most wooded habitats, usually in canopy. Feeds on berries.

Distribution. Nests from c Can. to c U.S.; winters from s Can. to Pan.

Status in Belize. Irregular winter visitor, mid-Dec. to early May. Never C, and in some winters may be absent.

FAMILY: PARULIDAE
(Wood-Warblers)

World: 116. **New World:** 116. **Belize:** 46 (plus 1 provisional). Exclusively New World. Wood-warblers are small, insectivorous, active songbirds with a thin, pointed bill; a slightly flattened head; short wings with only nine primaries; and a moderate-length tail. Their songs range from buzzy and simple (Blue-winged Warbler) to melodious and complex (Gray-crowned Yellowthroat). Along with the tanagers, grosbeaks, and buntings, they are sometimes placed in the Emberizidae, making that the largest family of birds. However, the more conventional treatment is to retain the wood-warblers as a separate family. About half breed north of Mex.-U.S. border and migrate to C.A. and S.A. in winter. Of the 46 species recorded in Belize, 40 are migrants from N.A.

Wood-warbler plumages vary, sometimes considerably, between ♂ and ♀, ad. and imm., spring (alt.) and autumn (basic). While the ♂s of most species are among Belize's most attractive birds, the ♀s and autumn imms. are among the most confusing. However, unlike some flycatchers and sandpipers, seldom are two species of warblers so similar in appearance that they are truly difficult to separate under field conditions. The ID challenge lies more in their small size, the sheer number of species and plumages involved, and the complex combinations of field characters they share. In addition to knowing which ones do or do not have wingbars, eyestripes, ear patches, tail spots, or streaked breasts, it is important to become familiar with their characteristic behavior patterns and call notes. The habitat in which they are found is less important, because outside of the breeding season, and especially during migration, most species may be seen in a wide array of habitats. **References:** Curson et al. (1994); Dunn and Garrett (1997). *Voice:* Borror (1990).

Genus: Vermivora, *in Part (Blue-winged and Golden-winged Warblers)*

Differ from *Dendroica* warblers in generally lacking tail spots and having a finer, more pointed bill. Blue-winged and Golden-winged warblers, despite striking differences in plumage, are very closely related. Their breeding ranges overlap extensively, and hybrids are relatively frequent, although not sufficiently frequent to warrant combining the two into one species. Because each is very different in appearance, hybrids between the two are quite easy to recognize. And because both first-generation hybrids and backcross hybrids are recognizable in the field, hybridization in these two species has been extensively studied. As would be expected from two closely related species, their size, behavior patterns, and vocalizations are all very similar.

Things to note: face pattern, color of wingbars, amount of yellow (if present) on underparts.

Blue-winged Warbler PLATE 44
Vermivora pinus

Identification. 4½″ (11.5 cm). Yellow head and underparts (except for white undertail coverts), blue-gray wings with conspicuous white wingbars, thin dark line through eyes. ♂: most of head yellow; only nape is green; line through eyes is black. ♀: green extends into hindcrown and auriculars; line though eyes is dusky.
Voice. *Call:* mostly silent, but occas. gives a sharp, slightly musical, but not especially loud, *chip. Flight note:* high-pitched, buzzy *tzii,* either as a single note or doubled. *Song:* typically dry, buzzy *beez-bizzz.* Seldom sings in Belize.
Habitat. Midlevel strata; forest edge, second-growth scrub.
Distribution. Nests in e N.A. from Great Lakes and s New England to n Gulf states; winters from sw Tamaulipas to c Pan.
Status in Belize. UC to FC transient and UC winter visitor, early Sept. to late Apr.
Reference. *Status:* Wood and Leberman (1987).

Golden-winged Warbler PLATE 44
Vermivora chrysoptera

Identification. 4½″ (11.5 cm). White head with dark patches; yellow forecrown; white underparts; yellow wingbars. ♂: bold black throat and auriculars; large yellow patch in wing coverts. ♀: gray throat and auriculars; two broad yellow wingbars.
Voice. *Calls and flight notes:* indistinguishable from those of Blue-winged. *Song:* dry, buzzy *zeee buzz-buzz-buzz.* Seldom sings in Belize.
Habitat. Midlevels to subcanopy; forest edge and interior.
Distribution. Nests in e N.A. from s Can. s. in Appalachian Mtns. to n Georgia; winters from Chiapas and s Belize to nw S.A.
Status in Belize. UC to FC transient and VU winter visitor on mainland, mid Aug. to early May; UC transient on cayes.

Blue-winged × Golden-winged Warbler PLATE 44
Vermivora pinus × *Vermivora chrysoptera*

All first-generation hybrids (produced by Blue-winged mating with Golden-winged), are the **Brewster's** type. Many hybrids that then mate with a pure Blue-winged or Golden-winged also look similar to the first-generation Brewster's. Only some hybrids that mate with a Golden-winged or Blue-winged have offspring that are referred to as **Lawrence's**. Thus, Brewster's type considerably outnumbers Lawrence's type. See below.

Identification. 4½″ (11.5 cm). **Brewster's Warbler.** Variable, but always with black line through eyes and with yellow wingbars. *1st-generation* ♂: mostly white below, with yellow breast and greenish back. *1st-generation* ♀: similar to Blue-winged but duller, with yellowish wingbars; easily overlooked. *2nd-generation* ♂: all white underneath, gray back. *2nd-generation* ♀: mostly or all white underneath; duller than ♂; others with various amounts of yellow underneath and green in back. **Lawrence's Warbler.** All have at least ghost of gray or black auriculars and throat. ♂: black throat and auriculars; yellow forecrown, breast, and belly; white wingbars; greenish back.

♀: very dingy; washed-out grayish throat and auriculars, yellowish wingbars, dingy olive back.

Habitat. Same as parental types.

Distribution. May be found anywhere within the broad range of overlap between the two parental species.

Status in Belize. Typical Brewster's may be seen occas. in both spring and autumn. Typical Lawrence's has been recorded only twice: Cahal Pech CA, 4–8 Oct. 1992, and Lamanai Outpost Lodge OW, winter of 1998–1999.

References. *Status:* Howell et al. (1992). *Genetics:* Dunn and Garrett (1997).

Genus: Vermivora, *in Part (Tennessee and Orange-crowned Warblers)*

These two species are among the most undistinguished of all wood-warblers. In both, the ♂ looks much like the ♀, and neither has much in the way of distinguishing characters. Tennessee, however, is one of Belize's most common wood-warblers in migration, whereas Orange-crowned has been documented in Belize only once. Any suspected Orange-crowned Warbler in Belize should be thoroughly studied.

Things to note: color of undertail coverts and back; presence/absence of full supercilium, lower eye crescent, faint streaks on breast, or single thin wingbar.

Tennessee Warbler   PLATE 47
Vermivora peregrina

Identification. 4½″ (11.5 cm). Small warbler with bright olive-green back; thin pale tips to greater, and sometimes median, wing coverts; thin supercilium; and yellowish to white underparts with white undertail coverts. Orange-crowned is similar but duller and has yellow undertail coverts (see next account). Philadelphia Vireo is larger and chunkier, with more rounded head and blunt-tipped bill; does not have bright green back or thin buff wingbar; like other vireos, it is much less active than warblers. Tennessee flicks wings and sometimes pumps tail downward; feeds on nectar of small flowers at tips of outer branches, and on flower stalks of coconut palm. The most gregarious of the

wood-warblers; often seen in groups of up to 20 individuals in migration. ♂ *alt.:* gray crown contrasting with bright olive-green back; nearly pure white underparts. ♀ *alt.:* greenish crown, yellow-buff wash across throat and breast. *Imm.:* yellower underneath, greener crown than in ad.

Voice. *Call:* 1. weak *tsit* and *seet* notes;
2. rich *chip,* softer than and not as rich as in Yellow Warbler;
3. softer *chit. Flight note:* thin, short *tsee,* not buzzy. Does not sing in Belize.

Habitat. Midlevels to canopy; forest edge, high second-growth scrub.

Distribution. Nests from c Can. to s Can. and ne U.S.; winters from c Mex. s. of Yucatán Pen. to nw S.A.

Status in Belize. C transient and UC winter visitor, early Sept. to late May.

References. *Status:* Wood and Leberman (1987). *Identification:* Kaufman (1990).

Orange-crowned Warbler   PLATE 47
Vermivora celata

Identification. 4¾″ (12 cm). Duller than Tennessee, with yellow, not white, undertail coverts; olive-gray to dull olive-green upperparts; indistinct supercilium; small but distinct lower eye crescent; and faint streaks on breast. Lacks Tennessee's thin wingbar. ♂: bright orange base to central crown feathers, but hard to see unless feathers are raised or disheveled. ♀ *and 1st winter:* similar but without orange in crown. ♀ Black-throated Blue has white undertail coverts and *usually* has white patch at base of primaries and distinctive olive-drab color (not olive gray or olive green). Imm. ♀ Mangrove Warbler has distinctive yellow edges to all flight feathers.

Voice. *Call:* distinctive, hard, somewhat liquid *tzik* or *chik;* reminiscent of weak Hooded Warbler call. *Flight note: seep;* not as thin as in Tennessee.

Habitat. Midlevel; forest edge, second-growth scrub.

Distribution. Nests from n Alaska and nc Can. to sw U.S. and se Can.; winters from s U.S. to Guat.

Status in Belize. One documented record: 5 mi.

(7.5 km) w. of Gracie Bank BE, 16 Dec. 2001 (mist-netted). Several other reports, all undocumented.

Reference. *Identification:* Kaufman (1991).

Genus: Vermivora, *in part (Nashville and Virginia's Warblers)*

Characterized by complete white eye-ring, gray head, and, in the ♂, red base to central crown feathers, which is seldom seen. Both species (except for e. subspecies of Nashville) pump their tail in the manner of a Palm or Prairie Warbler. Both are rare in Belize, and all records should be thoroughly documented.

Things to note: color of throat, vent, undertail coverts, and back; tail pumping.

Nashville Warbler
PLATE 47

Vermivora ruficapilla

Identification. 4½″ (11.5 cm). Gray head with thin, complete white eye-ring. Green back, wings, and tail; mostly yellow below. *Ad. ♂:* brightest, with most extensive yellow underneath. ♀: duller; dullest in imm.; some imm. ♀s have pale yellow, but never pure white, throat like Virginia's and always have mostly green wings. Nashville Warblers in e N.A. (*V. r. ruficapilla*) differ from those in w N.A. (*V. r. ridgwayi*) in having more yellow underneath and brighter green back. Although imms. of both subspecies may have whitish lower belly and vent, even the ad. ♂ *ridgwayi* has some white on belly. *Ridgwayi* also has duller grayish green on back, with brighter green uppertail coverts, providing contrast that is lacking in eastern birds. Most notably, *ridgwayi* pumps its tail almost constantly, much like Palm Warbler; eastern *ruficapilla* only occas. pumps its tail. Superficially similar Lesser Greenlet always has white throat. Virginia's Warbler has gray back and yellow restricted to undertail coverts and a patch on its breast.

Voice. *Call:* emphatic, slightly metallic *pink,* similar to call of Indigo Bunting. *Flight note: tsip* to *seet* without buzzy tones, similar to that of Tennessee but louder.

Habitat. Low and midlevel; forest edge, secondgrowth scrub, fallow fields, roadside brush.

Distribution. Nests from sc Can. e of Rocky Mtns. s. to s Great Lakes and New England, and discontinuously from s British Columbia to sw Calif. Winters from s Sonora and s Texas to Guat.

Status in Belize. Occas. winter visitor, early Oct. to late Apr. Two recent Oct. records are thought to pertain to *ridgwayi;* subspecies of other records not determined.

Reference. *Status:* Jones et al. (2000).

Virginia's Warbler
PLATE 47

Vermivora virginiae

Identification. 4½″ (11.5 cm). Similar to Nashville but extensively white underneath, with yellow only on upper breast and undertail coverts; gray, not green, back and wings, and contrasting yellow-green rump. Easily confused with some imm. ♀ Mangrove Warblers, but Mangrove Warbler in all plumages has pale yellow edges to all wing feathers and yellow inner webs to its tail feathers. Virginia's Warbler pumps its tail in the fashion of a Palm Warbler, Mangrove does not.

Voice. *Call: chink,* given frequently; slightly more emphatic and rougher than in Nashville.

Habitat. Fallow fields, savannas, roadside brush.

Distribution. Breeds in U.S. Great Basin; winters from Nayarit to Oaxaca.

Status in Belize. Recorded five or six times between mid-Dec. and early May.

Reference. *Status:* Jones et al. (2000).

Genus: Parula

Two species occur in Belize: one a resident with limited distribution, the other a migrant. They are distinctive in most plumages and differ in aspect from most other warblers in being smaller and shorter-tailed, with a bicolored bill.

Things to note: presence/absence of eye crescents, extent of wingbars and yellow on underparts.

Northern Parula
PLATE 44

Parula americana

OTHER NAMES. Parula Warbler (arch.).

Identification. 4¼″ (11 cm). Mostly blue gray above, with green patch in back; bold white wingbars; yellow throat and breast; white belly and undertail coverts; white eye crescents; pale lower mandible. ♂ *alt.:* brightest, with conspicuous rufous breast band, often bordered black anteriorly. *Basic* ♂ *and ad.* ♀*:* duller overall, but with some rufous in breast. *Imm.* ♀*:* dullest, with extensive olive-green wash on upperparts, no rufous breast patch, and less distinct eye crescents. Imm. ♀ Magnolia is larger and has faint streaking on flanks, full eye-ring, contrasting yellowish rump, and outer half of tail is black.

Voice. *Call:* soft, dry to liquid *chip* to *chick,* similar to Tennessee Warbler call (softer, less rich than in Yellow Warbler); drier notes similar to those of Green-breasted Mango. *Flight note:* high-pitched, weak, nasal, descending *tsif,* sometimes repeated frequently. *Song:* insectlike *z-z-z-z-z-z-z-zip.* Seldom sings in Belize.

Habitat. Midlevels to canopy; forest interior and edge, tall second-growth scrub.

Distribution. Nests in e N.A. from s Can. discontinuously to Gulf of Mex.; winters from ne Mex. to Hon. and in W.I.

Status in Belize. FC to C winter visitor on cayes and n.e. mainland, late Aug. to early May, becoming less C s. to n CA and s SC; scarce on mainland farther s.

Tropical Parula   MAP 182; PLATE 44
Parula pitiayumi
OTHER NAMES. Olive-backed Warbler (arch.), Sennett's Warbler (arch.), Pitiayumi Warbler (arch.).

Identification. 4¼″ (11 cm). Local resident. Easily distinguished from all Northern Parulas by black face lacking white eye crescents, thinner wingbars, and more extensive yellow underparts. ♂: may or may not have diffuse orange wash across breast. ♀: duller overall.

Voice. *Call:* similar to Northern Parula's. *Song:* less buzzy than in Northern Parula.

Habitat. Canopy and subcanopy; broadleaf forest interior and edge.

Distribution. Largely resident from nw Mex. and s Texas to sc S.A. Absent from Yucatán Pen.

Status in Belize. Locally FC resident at middle and higher elevations in s Maya Mtns. of TO,

CA, and perhaps SC and in Vaca Plateau CA. Recorded once in Mtn. Pine Ridge.

Reference. *Status:* Jones et al. (2000).

Yellow Warbler Complex

Despite their striking plumage differences, the Yellow Warbler and the Mangrove Warbler are considered to be one species. Although this may seem surprising, it becomes clearer when one examines the complex array of Yellow Warblers throughout the New World (see discussion under Mangrove Warbler account, below). Because the two forms that occur in Belize are easily distinguished in most plumages, they are treated separately.

Things to note: yellow edges to all wing feathers, plain face.

Yellow Warbler   PLATE 46
Dendroica petechia (aestiva group)

Identification. 4¾″ (12 cm). Mostly yellow in all but dullest plumages: yellow green above; yellow below; plain yellow to greenish yellow face with no trace of supercilium, and thus black eyes are set off in plain yellow face; wing feathers tipped or edged with yellow; tail feathers yellow on inner webs, appearing all yellow from below. Exhibits frequent shallow, but sharp, tail flicking. ♂: red streaks on breast. ♀: duller, unstreaked or faintly streaked breast (but not red). Dullest imm. ♀s are mostly brownish except for pale yellow to whitish eye-ring and yellow undertail coverts and edges to flight feathers.

Voice. *Call:* loud, emphatic, liquid *chip;* varies in intensity. *Flight call: zeet,* more emphatic than, for example, in most *Vermivora* warblers. *Song:* similar to that of Mangrove Warbler (see next account), but seldom sings full song in Belize.

Habitat. Second-growth scrub, forest edge, fallow fields, roadside brush, open country with scattered woody vegetation, towns and villages.

Distribution. Nests from n Alaska and nc Can. to sc U.S. and c Mex.; winters from s Sonora and s Tamaulipas to n S.A.

Status in Belize. C winter visitor, late July to late May.

Reference. *Identification:* Kaufman (1991).

Mangrove Warbler
MAP 183; PLATE 46

Dendroica petechia (*erithachorides* group)

OTHER NAMES. Yellow Warbler (combined form).

Identification. 4¾″ (12 cm). *Ad. ♂:* full chestnut hood, fine chestnut streaks on breast. *Imm. ♂:* chestnut patches in head, chestnut streaks on breast. *Ad. ♀:* diffuse or no streaking on breast, but often has small amount of chestnut flecking in head, especially on crown. *Imm. ♀:* duller, often with considerable amount of gray in plumage; some individuals have yellow confined to undertail coverts, feather edges in wings, inner webs of rectrices, and center of breast (see Virginia's Warbler account). Brighter individuals, on the other hand, may be indistinguishable from some migrant Yellow Warblers.

Voice. *Call:* loud, liquid *chup* to *chip,* usually richer and lower-pitched than in migrant Yellow; approaching call of Kentucky Warbler but richer and fuller. Calls incessantly when agitated (≈2 notes/sec). *Song:* typically a distinctive, clear *sweet sweet sweet sweeter than sweet,* richer and lower in pitch than in migrant Yellows, and often with additional syllables. Sings nearly year-round, although only sporadically in autumn.

Habitat. Mangroves; rarely elsewhere in winter.

Distribution. *Erithachorides* group — including *D. p. bryanti,* the subspecies in Belize — is resident from nw and ne Mex. to w S.A. *Petechia* group (Golden Warbler), which is not found in Belize, is resident from extreme s Florida and W.I. w. to Cozumel Isl. and s. to Venezuela. The taxonomic grouping of Yellow Warblers is very complex, because populations vary considerably throughout the species' range. Although the Mangrove Warbler in Belize may look quite different from migrant Yellow Warblers from the north, rangewide these chestnut-headed birds do not fit into a neat, easy-to-differentiate package.

Status in Belize. VC resident on cayes and on mainland coast s. to c TO; occas. seen away from mangroves in winter, but never far from coast.

Reference. *Voice:* Mennill (2001).

Chestnut-sided Warbler
PLATE 45

Dendroica pensylvanica

Identification. 4¾″ (12 cm). Frequently holds tail cocked. *♂ alt.:* yellow crown, uniquely black-and-white-patterned face, chestnut sides and flanks, boldly streaked back, bold cream-colored wingbars. *♀ alt.:* similar but with less chestnut and narrower wingbars. *Basic:* both sexes have lime green upperparts, pale gray underparts, pale cream-colored wingbars, and plain face with conspicuous white eye-ring; ♂ retains some chestnut in flanks.

Voice. *Call: chip* very similar to Yellow Warbler's; not slurred as in American Redstart, usually not as rich as in Yellow-throated. *Flight note:* very burry *breeet. Song* (given occas. in Apr. and May): similar to that of Yellow Warbler but more consistently with an accented, down-slurred last note. Typically, *pleased pleased pleased to meet you,* and variations, usually ending in *meet you.*

Habitat. Second-growth scrub, midlevels at forest edge.

Distribution. Nests e. of Rocky Mtns. from e Alberta to Nova Scotia s. to ne U.S. and s Appalachian Mtns.; winters from s Veracruz, primarily s. of Yucatán Pen., to Pan.

Status in Belize. C migrant throughout and UC (n.e.) to FC (s. and w.) winter visitor, early Sept. to late May.

Magnolia Warbler
PLATE 45

Dendroica magnolia

Identification. 4¾″ (12 cm). Yellow lower rump, conspicuous white wingbars, and rectangular black-and-white tail pattern distinguish it from all other species. *Flight:* white bar across tail, broken in center. *♂ alt.:* black-streaked yellow underparts often coalescing into black band across upper breast; black auriculars; mostly or all-black back. *♀ alt.:* thinner black streaking does not coalesce into band across breast; auriculars gray; back green, with black streaks. *Imm. ♀:* dullest; underparts have faint streaks only on flanks; thin white wingbars; thin pale gray band separates throat and breast; lacks strong head pattern. Imm. ♀ can be confused with imm. ♀ Northern

throated Green but lower-pitched, not as sharp. *Flight note:* similar to that of Black-throated Green.
Habitat. Midlevel; forest edge, second-growth scrub.
Distribution. Nests in w N.A. from sw British Columbia to nw Mex.; winters from sw U.S. to Oaxaca.
Status in Belize. One record: s Ambergris Caye, 1 Apr. 1990 (ad. ♂).
Reference. *Status:* Jones et al. (2000).

Golden-cheeked Warbler   FIGURE 27C
Dendroica chrysoparia

Identification. 5″ (12.5 cm). Narrow black eye-line in otherwise all-yellow patch on side of head; no green in auriculars as in Black-throated Green, and lacks yellowish wash across vent (between legs). *Ad. ♂:* black upperparts, including central crown, throat, and streaks on sides; no green in plumage. *Ad. ♀:* dull green back and central crown streaked black; chin and upper throat yellow. *Imm. ♀:* most like Black-throated Green but lacks green auriculars (green eyeline only); lacks yellow wash across vent; back duller green.

Voice. *Call and flight note:* like those of Black-throated Green.
Habitat. Canopy and subcanopy in pine-oak and pine-broadleaf forest. As a stray, could turn up in any habitat.
Distribution. Nests in c Texas; winters in highlands of extreme s Mex., Guat. and Hon. to nw Hon. ***Globally Endangered.***
Status in Belize. One convincing record: Caves Branch CA, 6 Nov. 2001 (ad. ♂). Other reports not fully documented.
Reference. *Distribution:* Braun et al. (1986). *Status:* Jones (2002).

Black-throated Green Warbler   PLATE 45
Dendroica virens

Identification. 4¾″ (12 cm). Distinctive yellow face outlining a green auricular patch; bright green unstreaked back. *Flight:* conspicuous white in outer tail feathers. *Ad. ♂:* black throat and breast, boldly streaked sides and flanks. *Ad. ♀:* similar but with white throat. *Imm. ♀:* black reduced to diffuse streaking along sides and flanks. Green auricular patch, yellowish wash across vent, and brighter green back distinguish it in all plumages from the rare Golden-cheeked.

Figure 27

Rare warblers. *(a)* Hermit Warbler, adult ♂; *(b)* Black-throated Gray Warbler, adult ♂; *(c)* Golden-cheeked Warbler, adult ♂; *(d)* Townsend's Warbler, adult ♂.

Voice. *Call:* distinctive sharp, dry *tip. Flight note:* high-pitched, sweet *see. Song:* distinctive buzzy *zee zee zur zur zee* or a faster *zee-zee-zee-zur-zee,* occas. given in Apr. and May.

Habitat. Canopy and subcanopy; pine and broadleaf forest interior and forest edge.

Distribution. Nests e. of Rocky Mtns. from wc Can. to Newfoundland and ne U.S., s. to s Great Lakes, s Appalachian Mtns., and disjunctively in coastal Carolinas. Winters from ne Mex., s Florida, and W.I. to Pan.

Status in Belize. FC to locally C winter visitor, mid-Sept. to early May.

Townsend's Warbler
FIGURE 27D
Dendroica townsendi

Identification. 4¾″ (12 cm). Like Black-throated Green but with distinctive dark auriculars and yellow lower eye crescent; yellow breast and sides streaked black; and green back streaked with black. *Ad. ♂:* crown, auriculars, and throat black; sides boldly streaked black. *Ad. ♀:* crown and auriculars dark dull green; chin and upper throat yellowish; back mostly unstreaked. *Imm. ♀:* no black in throat; streaking on breast and sides diffuse; no streaks in back. Yellower throat, lack of yellow in vent, and darker, well-defined auricular patch distinguish it from Black-throated Green.

Voice. *Call and flight note:* like those of Black-throated Green.

Habitat. Canopy and subcanopy, broadleaf forest. In migration, almost any terrestrial habitat with trees.

Distribution. Nests in nw U.S., w Can., and se Alaska; winters on Pacific slope of w U.S. and at mid- to high elevations in Mex. and C.A.

Status in Belize. One record: hills near San Felipe TO, 19–21 Dec. 2001.

Hermit Warbler
FIGURE 27A
Dendroica occidentalis

Identification. 5″ (12.5 cm). Unlike others in group, lacks streaks on sides and has gray back. *Ad. ♂:* bold black throat and otherwise all-yellow head. *Ad. ♀:* black restricted to lower throat; has mostly yellow face, including forehead, but greenish crown and auricular patch. *Imm. ♀:* dullest plumage; like dull imm. Black-throated Green but with dull brownish olive back, plain dirty buff underparts with no streaks, and more diffuse green and yellow in head.

Voice. *Call and flight note:* like those of Black-throated Green.

Habitat. Canopy and subcanopy; pine and broadleaf forest interior and forest edge.

Distribution. Nests in w N.A. from Washington to Calif.; winters on Pacific slope from nc Mex. to Nic.

Status in Belize. Three records: Bermudian Landing BE, 28 Dec. 1991 (ad. ♂); Hidden Valley Falls CA (Mtn. Pine Ridge), 13 Mar. 2000 and 20 Feb. 2001 (both ad. ♂). The latter two records likely pertain to the same individual.

Reference. *Status:* Jones et al. (2000).

Blackburnian Warbler
PLATE 45
Dendroica fusca

Identification. 4¾″ (12 cm). ♂ *alt.:* fiery orange throat, only slightly paler on neck and supercilium; black upperparts, with bold white wing patch and pale stripe down each side of back. ♀ *alt.:* similarly patterned but duller overall; bold white wingbars do not form panel of white. *Imm. ♀:* dullest plumage; lacks orange. Note pale streak down each side of back, bold supercilium, distinct auricular patch, and bold white wingbars.

Voice. *Call:* rich *chip,* but less liquid or full than in Yellow. *Flight note:* buzzy *zzee,* sometimes doubled. Not known to sing in Belize.

Habitat. Canopy and subcanopy, broadleaf forest interior and edge.

Distribution. Nests from wc Can. to w Newfoundland s. to s Great Lakes and s Appalachian Mtns.; winters from C.R. to nw S.A.

Status in Belize. FC spring and UC autumn transient, mid-Mar. to late May and late Aug. to early Nov.

Yellow-throated Warbler
PLATE 45
Dendroica dominica

Identification. 5″ (12.5 cm). Unlike most other wood-warblers, similar in all plumages. Blue gray above, with black-and-white face pattern, bold white patch on side of neck, conspicuous white wingbars, yellow throat and breast, and streaked sides and flanks. ♀: differs only in having mostly blue-gray crown without lateral black border, and dull brownish wash on flanks. *Imm.* ♀: slight brownish cast to upperparts. Two subspecies are found in Belize: *D. d. albilora* has all-white supercilium; *D. d. dominica,* from the se U.S., has yellow fore-half of supercilium.

Voice. *Call: chip,* usually richer than in Yellow Warbler and sharper than in American Redstart. *Flight note:* clear, high-pitched *see. Song:* rich buntinglike *swee swee swee swee swee so so set,* but ending is variable. Seldom sings in Belize.

Habitat. Midlevels to canopy; open areas with scattered trees, including towns and villages; pine forest and broadleaf forest edge. Most often found in coconut palms and pines and around eaves of houses.

Distribution. Nests in e N.A. from s Great Lakes to Gulf of Mex.; winters from Florida and s Texas to C.R.

Status in Belize. Ssp. *albilora:* FC to C winter visitor, early July to late Apr. Ssp. *dominica:* occas. migrant on cayes.

Grace's Warbler   MAP 184; PLATE 45
Dendroica graciae

Identification. 4¾″ (12 cm). Like Yellow-throated, similar in all plumages. Lacks black mask and white neck patch of Yellow-throated; has short, mostly yellow supercilium. ♂: black forecrown. *Ad.* ♀: all-gray crown. *Imm.* ♀: brownish cast to upperparts, diffuse streaking on sides (ad. has bold streaking).

Voice. *Call:* 1. rich *chip,* softer and drier than in Yellow-throated and Yellow warblers; 2. *tup,* softer than in Kentucky Warbler. *Flight note:* very high-pitched, thin *sip. Song:* varied in pattern but always a thin, liquid trill; it may slow and drop in pitch at end, and it may have 1, 2, or 3 parts; example: *sit-sit-sit-sit-chchchchch.*

Habitat. Found exclusively in pine woodlands.

Distribution. Resident primarily in highlands from Rocky Mtns. of sw U.S. to Nic.

Status in Belize. C resident from e OW and n BE s. to ne TO and in Mtn. Pine Ridge.

Prairie Warbler   PLATE 46
Dendroica discolor

Identification. 4½″ (11.5 cm). Green above and yellow below (including undertail coverts), with dark and pale areas around eyes, and yellowish wingbars. Pumps tail like Palm Warbler (waterthrushes pump entire rear of body, not just tail). *Flight:* conspicuous white in outer tail feathers. *Ad.* ♂: rufous streaks in back; bold black streaks on sides and face; yellow supercilium and lower eye crescent. *Ad.* ♀: lacks rufous back streaks; has less strongly patterned face and more diffuse streaking underneath. *Imm.* ♀: lacks most of ad. pattern; grayish head, with whitish partial supercilium and broad whitish lower eye crescent; faint streaks on sides; small dark smudge on side of upper breast.

Voice. *Call:* 1. flat, hummingbird-like *chik;* like Palm Warbler vocalization but sharper. *Flight note:* thin *seep,* not buzzy. Does not sing in Belize.

Habitat. Ground and low-level strata; open disturbed areas, fallow fields, second-growth scrub.

Distribution. Nests in e N.A. from s Great Lakes and s New England to Gulf of Mex.; winters in s Florida and W.I. w to Caribbean coast of n C.A.

Status in Belize. FC transient and UC winter visitor on n cayes, late Aug. to mid-Apr.; UC transient on s cayes; scarce on mainland.

Palm Warbler   PLATE 46
Dendroica palmarum
OTHER NAMES. Western Palm Warbler (is part of), Yellow Palm Warbler (is part of).

Identification. 4¾″ (12 cm). Dull brownish gray, with contrasting yellow undertail coverts, yellow-olive rump, prominent supercilium, and streaked underparts. *Flight:* conspicuous white flashes in tail corners. A ground dweller that walks instead of hopping, while constantly pumping tail up and down. Two distinguishable subspecies occur in Belize: the common Western Palm Warbler *(D. p. palmarum)* and the rare Yellow Palm Warbler *(D. p. hypochrysea). Alt. Western:* yellow throat, central breast, and anterior portion of supercilium; rufous crown; prominent streaks underneath. *Basic Western:* yellow only in undertail coverts; lacks rufous in crown; diffuse streaking underneath. *Alt. Yellow:* entirely yellow underneath, with all-yellow supercilium; extensive rufous in crown; rufous streaks underneath. *Basic Yellow:* similar to Western, but with extensive yellow wash on underparts, yellow supercilium, and richer, more orangish brown above.

Voice. *Call:* distinctive slurred, flat *thik* or *thip;* slightly more drawn-out and slurred than in Prairie. *Flight note:* high-pitched, light *seet* or *see-seet.* Does not sing in Belize.

Habitat. Ground to midlevel strata; open disturbed areas, fallow fields, pine savanna.

Distribution. Nests e. of Rocky Mtns. from c and e Can. to n Great Lakes and n New England; winters from se U.S. to n W.I. and Caribbean coast of Mex. and n C.A.

Status in Belize. Ssp. *palmarum:* C winter visitor on n cayes, late Sept. to late Apr.; UC transient on s cayes; relatively UC winter visitor on n. mainland, w. and s. to e OW, ne CA, and s SC; scarce in TO. Ssp. *hypochrysea:* s Ambergris Caye, 26 Feb. 1996 and 8 Dec. 2000 (photograph).

"Baypoll" Warbler Complex

Strikingly different in spring, the Bay-breasted and Blackpoll warblers are confusingly similar in autumn. Bay-breasted is a trans-Gulf migrant, passing from Florida and the Gulf states to se Mex. and the Yucatán Pen. and on to S.A., reversing its route in spring. Blackpoll, on the other hand, migrates far to the east, passing through the e W.I. to ne S.A. Thus, Bay-breasted is an expected migrant in Belize, whereas Blackpoll is not. In spring, Blackpoll migrates north farther to the west but still well east of C.A.; thus there are only a handful of records from Belize.

Things to note (autumn): color of legs, undertail coverts, and sides of neck; wing-back contrast; boldness of wingbars; presence/absence of streaking in back and on sides.

Bay-breasted Warbler
PLATE 45
Dendroica castanea

Identification. 5″ (12.5 cm). Bold white wingbars and dark gray legs in all plumages. ♂ *alt.:* deep chestnut crown, throat, sides, and flanks; black face; conspicuous creamy buff patch on neck; gray-and-black-streaked upperparts; bold white wingbars. ♀ *alt.:* lacks strongly patterned black-and-chestnut head pattern; chestnut duller and restricted to sides and flanks; has pale neck patch of ♂. *Basic ♂:* similar to alt. ♀ but with chestnut restricted to flanks, pale neck patch less distinct, crown and back bright green, and wing coverts and scapulars contrastingly grayish. *Imm.♀:* underparts mostly buffy, including undertail coverts; bright green unstreaked upperparts, paler and brighter on sides of neck; indistinct supercilium; contrasting dark wings with bold white wingbars. Imm. Bay-breasted in Belize have been erroneously IDcd as Pine Warblers, a species that has not been reliably reported s. of n Mex.

Voice. *Call:* 1. high-pitched, thin, but fairly loud *tseet;*
2. loud, slurred *chip. Flight note:* loud, sharp buzzy *zeee.* Seldom sings in Belize.

Habitat. Canopy and subcanopy; broadleaf forest interior and edge.

Distribution. Nests e. of Rocky Mtns. from c Can. s. to n Great Lakes and n New England; winters from Pan. to nw S.A.

Status in Belize. FC spring and UC autumn transient, mid-Apr. to late May and late Sept. to early Nov., rarely to early Dec.

References. *Identification:* Hough (1996); Kaufman (1990).

Blackpoll Warbler
PLATE 45
Dendroica striata

Identification. 5″ (12.5 cm). Streaked back, white wingbars, white undertail coverts, and pale legs/feet in all plumages. ♂ *alt.:* most like Black-and-white Warbler, but with solid-black crown, all-white face, black lateral throat stripe, and white throat; streaked black and white underneath and black and gray on back; white wingbars; yellow legs/feet. ♀ *alt.:* predominantly brownish gray above and paler below, with streaked back, head, and underparts. *Basic* ♂: like alt. ♀ but with greenish wash on upperparts and pale, dull yellowish on throat and breast; retains thin dark lateral throat stripe; legs/feet duller. *Imm. (especially ♀):* duller than corresponding plumage in Bay-breasted, with faint streaks on back and sides of breast; grayish, not greenish, on sides of neck, white undertail coverts, less wing-back contrast, and less prominent wing-bars; feet and rear portion of legs yellowish.

Voice. *Calls and flight notes:* similar to those of Bay-breasted.

Habitat. Canopy and subcanopy; broadleaf and littoral forest interior and edge.

Distribution. Nests from n Alaska and c Can. s. to sc Can. and n New England; winters in n half of S.A.

Status in Belize. R spring transient on cayes, late Apr. to mid-May; one, perhaps two, credible autumn records (Oct.).

References. *Status:* Eisenmann (1955); Jones et al. (2000). *Identification:* Hough (1996); Kaufman (1990).

Cerulean Warbler   PLATE 45
Dendroica cerulea

Identification. 4½″ (11.5 cm). *Ad.* ♂: sky blue and white, with thin dark breast band, streaked sides and flanks, and white throat and wingbars. *Ad.* ♀: similar in pattern to ♂, but blue green above and lacks breast band; often has pale buff wash on underparts. *Imm.* ♀: dullest plumage; aqua green above, bold white wingbars, broad pale creamy yellow supercilium and creamy yellow underparts, white undertail coverts; similar to imm. ♀ Blackburnian but aqua green above; lacks pale lateral back stripes and distinct auricular patch.

Voice. *Call:* rich *chip* similar to that of Yellow or Chestnut-sided. *Flight note:* buzzy *zzee,* similar to that of Bay-breasted and Blackburnian. Seldom sings in Belize.

Habitat. Canopy and subcanopy; broadleaf forest interior; occas. second-growth scrub.

Distribution. Nests in e N.A. from Great Lakes and New England to n Gulf states; winters in w S.A.

Status in Belize. Apparently a C spring transient, at higher elevations in Maya Mtns., but relatively scarce in lowlands, late Mar. to late Apr.; UC to VU autumn transient, early Aug. to early Oct.

Reference. *Status:* Parker et al. (1993).

Black-and-white Warbler   PLATE 47
Mniotilta varia

Identification. 4¾″ (12 cm). In all plumages has heavily streaked black-and-white upperparts. ♂ *alt.:* black throat and auriculars, boldly streaked underparts. ♀ *and some basic* ♂s (especially imms.): white throat, limited streaking on undersides. *Imm.* ♀: like ad. ♀, but with suffusion of buff on undersides and face. Among the warblers, Black-and-white is also unique in its habit of climbing along trunks and branches in the fashion of a nuthatch (family Sittidae). The similar Black-throated Gray Warbler (one Belize record) has a uniformly gray back in all plumages and does not creep along branches.

Voice. *Call:* 1. sharp, very dry *chip* or *jit,* sometimes run into a harsh, dry rattle; 2. (also its flight note) high-pitched, short *seet* or *seet-seet. Flight note:* like call 2. *Song:* high-pitched, thin *see-suh see-suh see-suh see-suh,* much like that of Orange-billed Sparrow; however, seldom sings in Belize.

Habitat. Tree trunks and limbs, midlevels to subcanopy; broadleaf and pine forest interior and edge.

Distribution. Nests e. of Rocky Mtns. from c Can. s. to se U.S.; winters from nc Baja California, se Texas, and Florida to nw S.A.

Status in Belize. C winter visitor, late July to mid-May.

American Redstart   PLATE 47
Setophaga ruticilla

Identification. 5″ (12.5 cm). Unlike most wood-warblers, takes 2 years to mature. Redstarts have unique habit of holding tail cocked and spread to emphasize bright tail patches. *Ad.* ♂: jet black, with bold red-orange highlights in tail, wings, and sides; white belly. *Ad. ♀ and 1st basic ♂:* olive back; gray head; white below, with yellow highlights in tail, wings, and sides (some imm. ♂s have orange-yellow sides). *1st alt. ♂:* like ad. ♀, but with yellow-orange sides and black lores; some have black flecking on head and breast. *Imm. ♀:* lacks or nearly lacks yellow in wings.

Voice. *Call:* fairly loud, rich, slightly slurred *chip,* similar to, but generally not as sharp as that of Yellow, Yellow-throated, or Chestnut-sided. *Flight note:* clear, penetrating *seep* or rising *sweet. Song:* highly variable and easily confused with that of a number of other species (Magnolia, Chestnut-sided, and even Black-and-white). Typical songs are *see see see see seeoo,* sometimes clear, other times slightly buzzy. The ending may be emphasized *(SEE-oo; SEE SEE-oo)* or not *(see-oo),* or lacking altogether. Beginning notes can be very similar to those of Black-and-white *(see-suh see-suh see-suh . . .).* Sings occas. in Apr. and May before departing.

Habitat. Widespread; low levels to subcanopy; broadleaf and pine forest interior and edge, second-growth scrub, open areas with scattered woody vegetation.

Distribution. Nests from c Can. s. to wc and se U.S.; winters from nw and e Mex. and W.I. to nw S.A.

Status in Belize. C winter visitor, early Aug. to late May.

Prothonotary Warbler PLATE 44
Protonotaria citrea

Identification. 5¼″ (13.5 cm). Striking golden yellow bird with green back, blue-gray wings and tail, and white lower underparts. *Flight:* conspicuous white inner webs of tail feathers. *Ad. ♂:* entire head golden yellow, accentuating its black eyes and bill. *Ad. ♀:* like ♂ but with greenish hindcrown and nape. *Imm. ♀:* green extends into crown and face.

Voice. *Call:* 1. soft to fairly loud, metallic *zit* or *chit;*

2. sharp metallic *chink* like Hooded Warbler's call. *Flight note:* distinctive long, clear *seeep* or *zeeet. Song:* rich *sweet sweet sweet sweet sweet sweet.* Seldom sings in Belize.

Habitat. Low levels within swamp forest, river and stream edge, mangrove forest.

Distribution. Nests in e N.A. from s Great Lakes to Gulf of Mex.; winters from coastal Yucatán Pen. to nw S.A.

Status in Belize. C autumn and UC spring transient, mostly in coastal areas and cayes, late July to early Nov. and early Mar. to late Apr.; occas. in winter.

Worm-eating Warbler PLATE 47
Helmitheros vermivorus

Identification. 5″ (12.5 cm). Uniformly olive brown above, without wingbars; black-and-buff-striped head; rich buff underparts, brightest on breast; dusky-fringed undertail coverts; thickset bill (for a warbler); relatively short tail. Little seasonal or age variation. Often first detected by the noise it makes picking at dead clumps of foliage.

Voice. *Call:* 1. slightly rough, dry *chit;*

2. emphatic *zit* or *zeet,* sometimes repeated 2 or 3 times;

3. occas. a rough liquid *chip* with quality of Kentucky Warbler's. *Flight note:* like call #2. Rarely sings in Belize.

Habitat. Low levels to subcanopy; broadleaf forest interior and edge. Often forages in hanging clumps of dead leaves.

Distribution. Nests in e N.A. from Missouri, Ohio R., and s New England s. to near Gulf of Mex.; winters from ne Mex. and W.I. to Pan.

Status in Belize. FC transient and relatively UC winter visitor, early Aug. to late Apr.

Swainson's Warbler PLATE 47
Limnothlypis swainsonii

Identification. 5¼″ (13.5 cm). Flat-headed warbler with relatively long, spikelike bill. Differs from Yucatán Vireo in having warm brown crown, spikelike bill, flesh-colored rather than bluish legs, and different habits. Superficially resembles a waterthrush but does not pump rear end and is unstreaked below. Little seasonal or age variation. Can be very difficult to locate in the dense undergrowth.

Voice. *Call:* 1. distinctive sweet, loud *chip;*

2. more prolonged, slurred *sship;*

3. flatter *chup,* more like Kentucky's call. Not known to sing in Belize.

Habitat. Ground and understory within broadleaf forest interior, especially swamp forest and littoral forest.

Distribution. Nests in e N.A. from s Missouri and West Virginia to Gulf of Mex.; winters in Yucatán Pen. and n W.I.

Status in Belize. UC and seldom seen winter visitor s. to SC, rarely to TO, early Sept. to mid-Apr. Most often seen on cayes.

Reference. *Status:* Wood and Leberman (1987).

Ovenbird   PLATE 47
Seiurus aurocapilla

Identification. 5½" (14 cm). Olive brown above, boldly streaked black and white below, with orange central crown stripe bordered by black, and dark eyes set off with complete white eye-ring in an otherwise plain face. Ages and sexes similar. Walks rather than running or hopping, usually with its tail cocked.

Voice. *Call:* 1. sharp *tsick* to *tsip,* similar to, but not as dry as, Orange-billed Sparrow's call; 2. dry, slightly rough *chip,* singly or, when agitated, incessantly at ≈1 call/sec. *Song* (occas. heard in spring): distinctive, loud repetitious *TEA-cher* or *tea-CHER* 8–10 times, increasing in intensity.

Habitat. Ground and understory; broadleaf forest interior.

Distribution. Nests e. of Rocky Mtns. from c Can. to n Gulf states; winters from Sinaloa, ne Mex., and Florida to Pan. and n Venezuela.

Status in Belize. C transient and FC winter visitor, mid-Aug. to mid-May.

Waterthrushes

Easily distinguished from other warblers but difficult to tell from each other, waterthrushes superficially resemble *Catharus* thrushes but are smaller and have streaked, not spotted, underparts and a bold supercilium. Ages and sexes are similar. They teeter constantly, much like a Spotted Sandpiper, and dash about in short spurts when foraging. Almost always seen near water.

Things to note: width of supercilium behind eye; color of supercilium, throat, breast, and flanks; presence/absence of streaks in throat; density of streaks across breast.

Northern Waterthrush   PLATE 47
Seiurus noveboracensis
OTHER NAMES. Sakil (K), ukul chi'kan (M).

Identification. 5½" (14 cm). Brown above; heavily streaked below; bold supercilium. Slightly smaller than Louisiana, with proportionately shorter, thinner bill. Generally, but not always, washed with yellowish buff underneath. Supercilium thinner posteriorly, and pale yellowish to near white; breast streaks denser and darker (black) than in Louisiana, usually extending into throat.

Voice. *Call:* loud, sharp, metallic *teenk!* or *cheenk! Flight note:* buzzy *zeet,* increasing in intensity at end. *Song* (occas. given in late spring): typically a loud, rich *chip chip chip chory chory chory chory.*

Habitat. Ground and low-level strata; mangroves, woody streamsides, wooded estuary shorelines, swamp forests.

Distribution. Nests from n Alaska and nc Can. s. to n U.S.; winters from n Mex. and s Florida to n S.A.

Status in Belize. C winter visitor, late Aug. to late May.

References. *Identification:* Binford (1971); Kaufman (1990).

Louisiana Waterthrush   PLATE 47
Seiurus motacilla
OTHER NAMES. Sakil (K), ukul chi'kan (M).

Identification. 5¾" (14.5 cm). Slightly heavier-bodied than similar Northern Waterthrush, with pure white supercilium that does not taper behind eyes. Background color of underparts white except for pinkish buff wash on flanks. Streaks dark brown, not black, and not as dense on upper breast as in Northern; throat usually unstreaked. In spring, it has pinker legs. Teeters more slowly than Northern, and more prone to wag the rear half of its body side to side, as well as up and down. Call notes slightly different.

Voice. *Call: tink!;* similar to Northern Water-thrush call but drier, less metallic, and lacking some of its ringing quality. *Flight note:* high-pitched *zeet,* similar to that of Yellow Warbler but louder. *Song:* loud series beginning with several clear, sweet slurred *SWEEU* notes followed by a disjointed jumble of weaker notes. Sings occas. before leaving in early spring and upon autumn arrival in July.

Habitat. Similar to Northern Waterthrush but, in winter, restricted to wooded areas with flowing streams (ranges more widely in migration).

Distribution. Nests in e N.A. from c Great Lakes s. to near Gulf of Mex.; winters from n Mex. and W.I. to Pan.

Status in Belize. FC migrant and locally FC winter visitor, mid-July to mid-Apr. In winter, confined primarily to interior where, at higher elevations, ' it outnumbers Northern Water-thrush. Arrives and departs about 5 weeks before Northern.

References. *Status:* Wood and Leberman (1987). *Identification:* Binford (1971); Kaufman (1990).

Genus: Oporornis

Except for Kentucky Warbler, members of the genus *Oporornis* can be confusingly similar, especially in autumn. Only two, Kentucky and Mourning, have been definitely recorded in Belize. Connecticut has been reported but not confirmed, and while MacGillivray's has never been reported, it should be looked for. Mourning migrates through Belize in both spring and autumn but is never especially common. Connecticut migrates through the Caribbean well east of Belize, especially in autumn, and has never been adequately documented in n C.A. or Mex. MacGillivray's winters in highlands and along the Pacific slope of C.A.

Things to note (except Kentucky Warbler): gait (walking vs. hopping); presence/absence of eye crescents or eye-ring; if eye-ring present, its completeness and thickness; color and completeness of hood; color of throat; degree of contrast between lores and surrounding area; length of undertail coverts vs. tail length; call notes.

Kentucky Warbler   PLATE 46
Oporornis formosus

Identification. 5″ (12.5 cm). Uniformly olive green above, entire underparts yellow. In all plumages, has prominent yellow spectacles. *Ad.:* irregular black patch below spectacles, slightly more extensive and better defined in ♂, which also has more black in crown than ♀. *Imm.* (especially ♀): black highlights in face reduced to nearly lacking, but retains the distinctive yellow spectacles.

Voice. *Call:* moderately dry to fairly rich *chep* to *chup;* lower-pitched and flatter than in other forest understory species; lacks metallic quality of Hooded and waterthrush calls. *Flight note: dzit,* louder, harsher, and lower-pitched than in most warblers. Rarely sings in Belize.

Habitat. Ground and understory; broadleaf forest interior.

Distribution. Nests in e N.A. from s Great Lakes to Gulf of Mex.; winters from ne Mex. to Pan.

Status in Belize. C transient on mainland; C winter visitor in south, less C in north; UC to FC transient on cayes. Recorded early Aug. to late Apr.

[Connecticut Warbler]   PLATE 46
Oporornis agilis

Identification. 5¼″ (13.5 cm). Larger than Mourning. Bold white, uniform-width eye-ring in all plumages; long undertail coverts that extend nearly to tail tip; slightly paler and duller yellow underparts than Mourning; loral area no darker or lighter than rest of hood. Imm. Mourning has pale supraloral area and dark lores. Mourning Warbler hops; Connecticut walks, an important distinction. *Ad.* ♂: uniformly gray hood. *Ad.* ♀: hood washed brownish on crown and neck. *Imm.:* brownish hood, with paler throat.

Voice. Usually silent.

Habitat. Ground and understory; broadleaf forest interior.

Distribution. Nests in s Can. from w Alberta to w Quebec; winters from Venezuela to c Brazil.

Status in Belize. One closely observed, but

insufficiently described, on Half Moon Caye, 7 May 1958.

References. *Status:* Eisenmann (1955); Jones (2002); Russell (1964). *Identification:* Gustafson (1988); Pyle and Henderson (1990).

Mourning Warbler
PLATE 46
Oporornis philadelphia

Identification. 5″ (12.5 cm). Green above and mostly yellow below; relatively short tail and long undertail coverts. *Ad. ♂:* distinctive gray hood; lower portion of hood (upper breast) black, sometimes extending to throat; no eye-ring. *Ad. ♀:* hood paler gray than in ♂ with whitish throat and no black; either lacks eye-ring or has thin white eye-ring, usually slightly broken in front. *Imm.* (especially ♀): grayish olive of head extending as partial band across breast, thus forming an indistinct partial hood; throat and supraloral spot yellowish; usually has thin, broken whitish eye-ring, never bold; similar to ♀ Common Yellowthroat, but has diffuse partial breast band, shorter tail, and underparts yellow throughout from breast through undertail coverts and never has bright yellow throat sharply set off against darker face.

Voice. *Call:* distinctive, scratchy *chit* or *vit. Flight note:* thin, sharp, buzzy *zeep.* Does not sing in Belize.

Habitat. Understory; forest edge, second-growth scrub.

Distribution. Nests e. of Rocky Mtns. from c Can. to s Great Lakes and n New England; winters from s Nic. to nw S.A.

Status in Belize. FC spring and UC autumn transient, mid-Apr. to early June and mid-Sept. to mid-Oct. Most frequently seen on cayes.

Reference. *Identification:* Pyle and Henderson (1990).

Although **MacGillivray's Warbler** (*Oporornis tolmiei*) has not been observed in Belize, it likely occurs as a vagrant. Ad. ♂ differs from Mourning in having black lores and more extensive black on throat and breast, white eye crescents, longer tail, and shorter undertail coverts. Ad. ♀ is very similar to ad. ♀ Mourning but has distinct eye crescents, not a thin, nearly complete eye-ring (or no eye-ring). Imm. ♀ is even more similar,

but MacGillivray's has whitish, not yellowish, supraloral spot and throat, and stronger separation between head and breast. A few, however, have a yellow throat, so this characteristic alone is insufficient to tell the two apart. The two have different calls: MacGillivray's gives a sharp *tzik* or *fick* call somewhat similar to that of Common Yellowthroat but without the raspy edge, and a softer, slightly rough *tip.*

Common Yellowthroat
PLATE 46
Geothlypis trichas

Identification. 4¾″ (12 cm). Olive above; yellow throat, breast, and undertail coverts; whitish belly; and brownish flanks. Lacks eye-rings or crescents; does not have elongated undertail coverts. *Ad. ♂:* black mask bordered above with white. *Imm. ♂:* partial grayish or blackish mask lacking white dorsal border. *♀:* lacks mask of ♂ but has the same pattern of yellow, white, and brownish on underparts; yellow throat sharply set off from darker, olive face.

Voice. *Call:* distinctive flat, harsh *tchik* or *djik. Flight note:* dry, buzzy *dzeet. Song* (seldom heard in Belize): bouncy, but not especially musical series of 3-part notes—*wichity wichity wichity wich* to *wee-wichy wee-wichy wee-wichy we-wichy.*

Habitat. Understory; second-growth scrub, fallow fields, marshes, seasonally wet and dry savannas, roadside brush.

Distribution. Nests e. of Alaska from c Can. to s U.S. and Mex. Plateau; winters from s U.S. to Pan.

Status in Belize. C winter visitor, mid-Sept. to late May.

Gray-crowned Yellowthroat
MAP 185; PLATE 46
Geothlypis poliocephala
OTHER NAMES. Long-tailed Chat (arch.), Ground-Chat (arch.), Gray-headed Ground-Chat (I. Davis).

Identification. 5½″ (14 cm). Larger and longer-tailed than Common Yellowthroat, with heavier bill; green above and yellow below. Black restricted to lores and, in the ♂, immediately below eyes. Thin, broken white eye-ring. ♂: gray crown. ♀: no gray on head, black in lores only.

Voice. *Call:* variously 1. *crea crea;*

2. *cheereo* to *cherdleo;*

3. *tē-cher;*

4. rough *cheedree;*

5. softer, sweeter *ch dreer;*

6. *chimmy chorry;* and

7. buzzy *dreer* or *zeuur* much like, but richer than, Blue-black Grassquit song.

Song: 1. slow, sweet warble, very Indigo Bunting–like;

2. *chippy chippy chorry chorry chip chip chip,* slower and richer than in Rufous-capped Warbler.

Habitat. Understory; open pine forest, pine and pine-oak savannas, wooded edge of marshes.

Distribution. Resident from c Sinaloa and sc Tamaulipas to w Pan.

Status in Belize. C resident on mainland s. to c CA and in coastal savannas to c TO, locally to s TO. Most C in coastal plain; UC resident on Ambergris Caye; recorded once on Caye Caulker.

Hooded Warbler
PLATE 46

Wilsonia citrina

Identification. 5″ (12.5 cm). Green above, yellow below. Frequently fans tail to flash conspicuous white inner webs of tail feathers. In all plumages has a yellow forecrown and conspicuous black eyes in a plain yellow face. *Ad. ♂:* striking yellow mask framed in a black hood. *Ad. ♀:* variable; some with complete black hood like ♂; others with black reduced to lateral crown, extending around posterior border of yellow auriculars. *Imm. ♀:* lacks black altogether, but yellow face and forecrown sharply set off from green hindcrown and neck. Wilson's Warbler is smaller and has shorter tail with no white, and yellow of its face merges gradually with green auriculars and neck.

Voice. *Call:* hard, metallic *chick* to *chink,* similar to Blue Bunting call but not as rich. *Flight note:* soft, buzzy *zrrt,* seldom given. *Song:* clear, rich *sweeta sweeta swee-SWEET-ah.* Rarely sings in Belize.

Habitat. Understory; broadleaf forest interior.

Distribution. Nests in e N.A. from s Great Lakes and s New England to Gulf of Mex.; winters from sw Tamaulipas and Cuba to w Pan.

Status in Belize. C winter visitor, late July to late Apr.

Wilson's Warbler
PLATE 46

Wilsonia pusilla

OTHER NAMES. Pileolated Warbler (arch.).

Identification. 4½″ (11.5 cm). Smaller, with shorter tail than Hooded and lacking its white tail flashes, as well as having different habitat and behavior. As in Hooded, dark eyes surrounded by plain yellow face. Often cocks, and sometimes flicks, tail. *Ad. ♂:* glossy black patch in central crown. *Ad. ♀:* black usually less extensive, less glossy, and sometimes restricted to the forecrown. *Imm. ♀:* green crown, sometimes with blackish fore-edge; from imm. Yellow Warbler by darker upperparts and plain green wings without yellow feather edges. When viewed from below, told from Yellow Warbler by dusky, not yellow, undertail.

Voice. *Call:* very distinctive, slightly nasal *chimp* to *thnk* and *ink. Flight note:* sharp, slurred *tsip.* Does not sing in Belize.

Habitat. Midlevels to subcanopy; forest interior and edge; second-growth scrub.

Distribution. Nests from n Alaska and nc Can. to s Can., and in w N.A. to sw U.S.; winters from nw Mex. and Louisiana to w Pan.

Status in Belize. UC (coastal areas and cayes) to FC (inland) winter visitor, mid-Sept. to early May.

Reference. *Identification:* Kaufman (1991).

Canada Warbler
PLATE 46

Wilsonia canadensis

Identification. 5″ (12.5 cm). Gray above and yellow below, with conspicuous white eye-ring, yellow supraloral spot, and white undertail coverts. ♂ *alt.:* blue gray above; black forecrown, lores, and lower auricular region; prominent necklace of black streaks. *Basic ♂:* duller. *Ad. ♀:* paler, with less distinct necklace. *Imm. ♀:* washed with olive above; faint grayish necklace.

Voice. *Call:* sharp *tchup,* somewhat like that of Lincoln's Sparrow.

Habitat. Understory and low-level strata; broadleaf forest interior and edge.

Distribution. Nests e. of Rocky Mtns. from c Can. to s Great Lakes, New England, and s Appalachian Mtns.; winters in w S.A.

Status in Belize. UC autumn and scarce spring transient on cayes, few records from mainland; late Aug. to mid-Oct., 26 Apr. 1956 and 2 May 2002 (both from Hunting Caye).

Reference. *Status:* Jones et al. (2000).

Golden-crowned Warbler

MAP 186; PLATE 44

Basileuterus culicivorus

OTHER NAMES. Lichtenstein's Warbler (I. Davis).

Identification. 5″ (12.5 cm). Grayish olive above and yellow below, with tawny to dull yellow central crown stripe bordered in black; pale supercilium (yellow anteriorly) and yellow lower eye crescent.

Voice. *Call:* 1. short, uneven series of wrenlike *tzit* notes;

2. harsh wrenlike *chat,* sometimes repeated two or three times;

3. harsh ticking run together in short series (scold?).

Song: 1. sweet whistled warble ending on 2 high notes, *chu chu cho chwe teet;*

2. *see s-so so se-wit.*

Habitat. Understory to subcanopy; mature broadleaf forest interior.

Distribution. Resident from Nayarit and c Nuevo Leon to se S.A.

Status in Belize. C resident in interior n. to nc CA; also in forested portions of OW.

References. *Voice:* Hardy et al. (1994); Moore (1992).

Rufous-capped Warbler

MAP 187; PLATE 44

Basileuterus rufifrons

OTHER NAMES. Salvin Warbler (I. Davis).

Identification. 5″ (12.5 cm). Olive above and yellow below, with rufous crown and auriculars, white supercilium, and black eyeline. Frequently cocks tail high over back like a wren.

Voice. *Call: pik* or *pk* given irregularly; cadence is reminiscent of that of Red Crossbill. *Song:* 1. sweet *whea whea whea te tee tee tee,* somewhat Indigo Bunting–like, but often more jumbled and given at various speeds and pitches;

2. long Nashville Warbler–like series of chips with one or two changes in pitch and tempo; drier and more emphatic than in Grace's Warbler, and longer, drier, and faster than in Gray-crowned Yellowthroat.

Habitat. Understory; pine forest interior and edge, second-growth scrub, broadleaf forest edge.

Distribution. Resident from n Sonora and c Nuevo Leon to nw S.A.

Status in Belize. C resident in Mtn. Pine Ridge, s. locally in broadleaf forest to vicinity of Las Cuevas CA; UC and local resident disjunctively in pine and broadleaf woodland along foothills of Maya Mtns. in SC and TO.

Reference. *Voice:* Hardy et al. (1994).

Yellow-breasted Chat

PLATE 47

Icteria virens

Identification. 6¾″ (17 cm). Largest and most tanager-like of all the wood-warblers; easily told by its white spectacles, thick bill, lack of wingbars, bright yellow throat and breast, and white belly and undertail coverts. Stays in dense tangles and can be very difficult to see; however, its often repeated, distinctive call usually reveals its presence. ♂: black lores. ♀: gray lores.

Voice. *Call:* 1. rough, nasal *chew* to *chow;*

2. softer *chuck* and *chuck-chuck.* Much more often heard than seen. Does not sing in Belize.

Habitat. Understory; second-growth scrub, forest edge.

Distribution. Nests from sw Can. and s Great Lakes to c Mex. and n Gulf of Mex.; winters from ne Mex. to Pan.

Status in Belize. C transient and FC winter visitor, mid-Sept. to late Apr.

Gray-throated Chat

MAP 188; PLATE 44

Granatellus sallaei

Identification. 5¼″ (13.5 cm). Only distantly related to Yellow-breasted, and quite different in appearance. Relatively short, thick bill for a warbler. Habitually cocks, fans, and flicks tail up. ♂: slate gray above and on the throat and upper breast; red lower breast through midline of belly to undertail coverts; white flanks; bold white partial supercilium from above eyes to nape; white-tipped outer tail feathers. ♀: brownish gray above, with pale buff supercilium, plain grayish buff face setting off dark eyes, and buff throat and breast.

Voice. *Call:* 1. sharp *chit;*

2. softer *wit,* reminiscent of Least Flycatcher call, but harsher, more emphatic, and with a wrenlike quality;

3. low, burry woodcreeper-like trill on an even pitch, preceded with soft *duh* note. *Song:* various, clear, slightly plaintive whistled notes, with the next-to-last note on a lower pitch, and a drawn-out final note—*please tell me that you care* and a more lengthy *Jenny Jenny tell me now that you care.*

Habitat. Understory, deciduous and semideciduous forest, flooded and swamp forest interior and edge; less often, nonflooded tropical moist forest.

Distribution. Resident from c Veracruz through Yucatán Pen. to c Guat. and s Belize.

Status in Belize. FC resident on mainland in north, becoming very local and generally scarce s. of c CA and c BE.

References. *Status:* Wood and Leberman (1987). *Voice:* Delaney (1992); Hardy et al. (1994); Moore (1992).

FAMILY: COEREBIDAE
(Bananaquit)

World: 1. **New World:** 1. **Belize:** 1. Neotropical. The Bananaquit is variously placed in its own monotypic family (Coerebidae), in a small family that includes the honeycreepers (Coerebinae within the Coerebidae), in the Parulidae, in a larger family that also includes the tanagers (Thraupidae), and together with the tanagers, wood-warblers, sparrows, grosbeaks, and buntings in the Emberizidae. Regardless of how it is treated, it is enough different to warrant separation at least at the subfamily level. Here, it is placed in its own family in accord

with the American Ornithologists' Union (1998). Like honeycreepers, the Bananaquit has a sharp-pointed, moderately decurved bill, which it uses to probe into smaller flowers and pierce larger ones near the base of the corolla tube for nectar. It also pierces fruits for their juice. But it differs in many subtle ways from its nearest relatives—the honeycreepers, warblers, and tanagers—and its nesting habits are also quite different. The Bananaquit has at least 40 recognized subspecies throughout its range, demonstrating its remarkable adaptability and genetic plasticity. Its radiation must be fairly recent, given that it has yet to evolve any forms different enough to be classified as separate species.

Bananaquit
MAP 189; PLATE 50
Coereba flaveola

OTHER NAMES. Mexican Bananaquit (is part of), Cozumel Bananaquit (is part of).

Identification. 4″ (10 cm). No other bird in Belize has a combination of decurved bill, white supercilium, mostly yellow underparts, and yellowish rump. *Flight:* short tail, yellow lower rump, small white patch at base of primaries. Two subspecies are represented in Belize: gray-throated mainland form *(C. f. mexicana)* found from Mex. to Pan., and white-throated, darker-backed, mostly insular form *(C. f. caboti)* restricted to coastal Quintana Roo and offshore islands from Cozumel Isl. to n Belize cayes.

Voice. *Call:* 1. High-pitched, thin, hummingbird-like *seet;*

2. thin, rapid *d-d-d-d-de-e-e-e-uh,* repeated. *Song:* high-pitched, thin *see see seeta see seeta see;* similar to Yellow-faced Grassquit song but more complex, not a simple trill.

Habitat. Midlevels to canopy, broadleaf forest interior and edge.

Distribution. Resident from c Veracruz, ne Yucatán Pen., and W.I. to c S.A.

Status in Belize. Ssp. *mexicana:* UC to locally FC resident in lowlands and VC resident in Maya Mtns. n. to ne CA and c BE. Ssp. *caboti:* FC resident on Ambergris Caye (n. of San Pedro) and C resident on Caye Caulker. *Caboti* was unknown in Belize prior to the 1980s. It may have recently colonized Ambergris Caye and Caye Caulker from farther n., or it may have been previously overlooked.

References. *Status:* Jones et al. (2000); Ornat et al. (1989); Wood and Leberman (1987).

FAMILY: THRAUPIDAE
(Tanagers)

World: 256. New World: 256. Belize: 25. New World, primarily Neotropical. The tanagers comprise a large, moderately heterogeneous family, with only a few reaching the Temperate Zones, and include some of the world's most colorful species. As a group, they are characterized by a small "tooth" on the cutting edge of the upper mandible, and most have a short, moderately thick bill. Honeycreepers are an exception, with their thin, sharp-pointed, decurved bill. Most eat fruits, but many supplement their diet with insects. None are especially accomplished singers. Most are sedentary; however, those that breed in N. Temperate latitudes migrate to C.A. and S.A. in winter.

Reference: Isler and Isler (1999).

Common Bush-Tanager

MAP 190; PLATE 48

Chlorospingus ophthalmicus

OTHER NAMES. Brown-headed Chlorospingus (arch.), Dwight's Chlorospingus (is part of, I. Davis).

Identification. 5½″ (14 cm). Rather undistinguished small tanager. Olive above and mixed yellow and pale gray below, with sooty head and short white postocular stripe. Short, dark gray bill and a relatively short tail.

Voice. *Call:* 1. *chit,* given singly or in a short, rapid, accelerating series *chit chit chit chidudududuw;*

2. junco-like twittering. *Song: che-che-che* followed by sputtery notes.

Habitat. Midlevels to canopy; submontane broadleaf forest interior and edge.

Distribution. Resident in highlands from Guerrero and se San Luis Potosí to w S.A.

Status in Belize. VC resident above 2,300 ft. (700 m) in Maya Mtns. of CA, SC, and TO.

References. *Status:* Howell et al. (1992); Wood and Leberman (1987).

Gray-headed Tanager   PLATE 48

Eucometis penicillata

Identification. 6¾″ (17 cm). Green above and yellow below, with gray hood and peaked or slightly crested head; relatively thin bill for a tanager; constantly flashes tail. An ant follower seldom seen away from army ant swarms.

Voice. *Call:* 1. soft Ruby-throated Hummingbird–like *chep;*

2. high, thin *cheet;*

3. flat metallic cardinal-like *tk* or *tsk*. Combination of 1–3 often given in short, irregular series. *Song:* high-pitched, piercing, slurred *tsip tsip tsip tsip tsip.*

Habitat. Understory and low-level strata; broadleaf forest interior and edge.

Distribution. Resident from s Veracruz to c S.A.

Status in Belize. UC to C resident at low and mid-elevations on mainland.

References. *Voice:* Delaney (1992); Moore (1992).

Black-throated Shrike-Tanager

MAP 191; PLATE 48

Lanio aurantius

OTHER NAMES. Great Shrike-Tanager (arch.).

Identification. 8″ (20.5 cm). Relatively large tanager with hooked bill. ♂: oriole-like; black hood, wings, and tail; thin white scapular stripe; yellow back, rump, and underparts. ♀: brownish gray hood, tawny brown upperparts, and yellow underparts.

Voice. *Call (and song?):* 1. clear, whistled *peer!;*

2. *CHE-cup* to *WHEET-chu,* usually given in irregular series;

3. *chi-c-c-c-c-cup;*

4. rapid, Wood Thrush–like *whick-whick-whick-whick.*

Habitat. Subcanopy and canopy; mature broadleaf forest interior.

Distribution. Resident from c Veracruz s. of Yucatán Pen. to nw Hon.

Status in Belize. UC to C resident in interior n.

to s and ec CA; also in w OW and locally along New R. in e OW.

References. *Voice:* Delaney (1992); Moore (1992).

Genus: Habia *(Ant-Tanagers)*

Very similar in appearance and habits. Red-crowned is more common in forest interior, especially at higher elevations; Red-throated, in high second-growth forest and forest edge, primarily at lower elevations. Calls and songs of the two are markedly different and, once learned, are the most reliable way to tell them apart, especially in the deep shade of the forest interior.

Things to note: bill size, presence/absence of pale lores, crown pattern and color. *In ♀,* throat-breast contrast, color of lower mandible.

Red-crowned Ant-Tanager

MAP 192; PLATE 48

Habia rubica

OTHER NAMES. Kio kio kin (K), has has (M).

Identification. 7½″ (19 cm). Lores slightly paler than rest of face, bill shorter than in Red-throated. ♂: dark dull brick red, with red central crown stripe outlined laterally in blackish red. ♀: dull rufous brown, with dull tawny central crown stripe, pale lower mandible, and relatively darker throat that contrasts less with adjacent face and breast than in Red-throated.

Voice. *Call:* 1. *eurnh eurnh eurnh eurnh;*

2. *er er er;*

3. squeaky *ch ch ch;*

4. *chat.* All call types given frequently by birds in a group.

Song: 1. burry, robinlike *kurr kurr kurr kurr;*

2. clear *peter peter peter* to *peterer peterer peterer,* etc. (much lower-pitched and notes more widely spaced than in Green Shrike-Vireo);

3. slow, clear *peah-toe peah-toe peah-toe;*

4. hesitant liquid *cheery chorry churry cherry,* reminiscent of Buff-throated Saltator song.

Habitat. Understory to subcanopy; broadleaf forest interior and forest edge.

Distribution. Resident from Nayarit and sw Tamaulipas to c S.A.

Status in Belize. UC to FC resident at lower elevations in interior, C at higher elevations, n. to s and e CA and sw BE; also in nw CA, w and c OW, and locally in e and ne OW. May be absent in CO.

References. *Ecology:* Willis (1961). *Voice:* Moore (1992).

Red-throated Ant-Tanager

PLATE 48

Habia fuscicauda

OTHER NAMES. Dusky-tailed Ant-Tanager (arch.), kio kio kin (K), has has (M).

Identification. 8″ (20.5 cm). Slightly larger than Red-crowned, with longer bill. Both sexes have dark lores and all-black bill. ♂: like the preceding, but with slightly brighter red throat; crown not outlined in black. ♀: differs from Red-crowned in having paler throat that contrasts with darker breast and all-dark bill; lacks tawny central crown stripe.

Voice. *Call:* 1. loud, very harsh, nasal *cha cha cha . . . ;*

2. harsh, scolding *chanh.*

Song: repetitious rich, bubbly, rhythmic phrases.

1. *wheea toe wheea* and *toe toe wheea,* repeated;

2. more complex *toe toe wit toe o wit toe tu-wit toe;*

3. *chu heo tur cheet,* repeated, more or less like song of Yellow-tailed Oriole, but intensity does not increase with each phrase.

Habitat. Understory and midlevels; broadleaf forest interior and forest edge.

Distribution. Resident from sw Tamaulipas to n Colombia.

Status in Belize. C to VC resident on mainland; least C at higher elevations, where it is outnumbered by Red-crowned.

References. *Ecology:* Willis (1961). *Voice:* Moore (1992).

Genus: Piranga *(Those without Wingbars)*

Largest tanager genus in Belize. All are strongly sexually dimorphic. Four species lack wingbars. Males are readily IDed; ♀s are much more similar.

Things to note: color, size, and shape of bill. *In ♂,* tone of red, color of auriculars. *In ♀* (except Rose-throated), tone and pattern of greens and yellows; color of underside of tail, undertail coverts, and auriculars.

Rose-throated Tanager

MAP 193; PLATE 48

Piranga roseogularis

Identification. 6¼″ (16 cm). Medium-sized tanager with prominent white eye-ring. ♂: rosy throat and undertail coverts; red crown and uppertail coverts; duller red wings and tail, the former with bright red feather edges. ♀: red areas of ♂ replaced with yellow olive, and rosy throat and undertail coverts replaced with yellow.
Voice. *Call:* 1. harsh, nasal *annh,* somewhat like short Gray Catbird call but lower-pitched; 2. harsh bluebirdlike call. *Song:* somewhat hesitant, clear, sweet whistled *please tell me all, tell me all, Odie,* sometimes without *Odie* at the end.
Habitat. Subcanopy and canopy; deciduous and semi-deciduous seasonally flooded broadleaf forest interior.
Distribution. *Yucatán Endemic.* Resident in Yucatán Pen. s. to n Guat. and n Belize.
Status in Belize. UC to locally FC resident on mainland s. to n CA and c BE. One record each for Shipstern Caye and Ambergris Caye.
References. *Voice:* Delaney (1992); Moore (1992).

Hepatic Tanager

MAP 194; PLATE 49

Piranga flava

OTHER NAMES. Pepper Bird (C).

Identification. 7¾″ (19.5 cm). *Ad.* ♂: dull scarlet, brighter on crown and throat; dusky auriculars; dark gray bill. ♀ *and imm.:* dusky olive above, ochraceous yellow below; similar to some ♀ Summer Tanagers but never with orange or pink plumage highlights, and with dusky auriculars, dark gray bill, and darker, duller upperparts.
Voice. *Call:* variously soft *chip, cherk,* and drier *chuck* notes. *Song:* melodious series of high and low clear, melodious notes. Example: *chevy chuck cho twit ch'be choey chit.*
Habitat. Subcanopy and canopy; pine forest.
Distribution. Largely resident primarily in highlands from sw U.S. to nw S.A. U.S. populations withdraw s. in winter.
Status in Belize. C resident in coastal lowlands

from c BE to ne TO and in Mtn. Pine Ridge; inexplicably scarce in seemingly suitable habitat in n BE and e OW.

Summer Tanager

PLATE 49

Piranga rubra

OTHER NAMES. Cak i tz'ic (K), chuc ya'ax kinnil chi'ich (M).

Identification. 6¾″ (17 cm). Bill noticeably longer than in Scarlet. *Ad.* ♂: bright red throughout; pale brownish to reddish bill. ♀ *and imm.:* typically yellow olive above, brighter than in Scarlet, and yellow to mustard yellow beneath; some individuals have plumage with a pinkish to orangish suffusion, and a few are orange throughout; underside of tail green (grayish in Scarlet). *Imm.* ♂: many in 1st spring have red confined to head and breast, or may be mottled red and green. These have been confused with Red-headed Tanager *(Piranga erythrocephala),* a w. Mex. endemic that is not found in Belize.
Voice. *Call:* dry, rolling *pit-a-tuk* and *pit-a-tatuk. Flight note:* soft, wheezy *verree. Song:* rich series of 2- or 3-syllable notes, *cheerio chirup cheeriup chiburrr* etc., with robinlike quality.
Habitat. Midlevels to canopy; broadleaf and pine forest interior and edge; open country with scattered trees. Frequents fruiting trees.
Distribution. Nests from c and sw U.S. to n Mex.; winters from c Mex. to nc S.A.
Status in Belize. C winter visitor, early Sept. to mid-May.
References. *Identification:* Kaufman (1988c). *Voice:* Moore (1992).

Scarlet Tanager

PLATE 49

Piranga olivacea

Identification. 6¾″ (17 cm). Smaller bill than in Summer. ♂ *alt.:* brilliant scarlet red, with jet black wings and tail. *Basic* ♂: retains black wings and tail, but red body feathers are replaced with yellow olive, paler and yellower below, yellowest on undertail coverts. *Imm.* ♂: similar to ad. ♂ but with dark brown, not black, remiges. ♀: pale olive above, greenish yellow to yellow beneath, brightest on undertail coverts (undertail coverts of Summer do not contrast brighter); wings and tail dusky olive; underside of tail gray (green in Summer). *Flight:* underwing coverts strikingly white.

Voice. *Call:* emphatic *chick zwurr,* the second note nasal and drawn out. *Flight note:* clear *puwee.* Not known to sing in Belize.

Habitat. Subcanopy and canopy; broadleaf forest interior and edge.

Distribution. Nests in e N.A. from s Can. to n Gulf states; winters in w S.A.

Status in Belize. C autumn transient and FC spring transient, mid-Sept. to late Oct. and late Mar. to early May.

Reference. *Identification:* Kaufman (1988c).

Genus: Piranga *(Those with Wingbars)*

Three *Piranga* tanagers in Belize have prominent white wingbars, and all are easily distinguished. None are widespread. Western is a rare winter visitor, Flame-colored is found only on one mountain peak, and White-winged is found primarily in the Maya Mtns.

Things to note: size, shape, and color of bill; color of lower wingbar; pattern of white in tertials. *In ♂,* color of face, presence/absence of auricular mark. *In ♀,* streaked or unstreaked back, color of wings and wingbars, intensity of yellow underneath, degree of contrast between head and throat.

Western Tanager
PLATE 49
Piranga ludoviciana

Identification. 6¾″ (17 cm). ♂ *alt.:* strikingly marked black and yellow, with mostly red head; wings with yellow median wing coverts, white bar on greater coverts, and white-edged tertials. *Basic ♂:* most or all red in head obscured by yellow feather tips; black back tipped olive; body feathers are not molted in spring, but the pale feather tips of the face and back gradually wear off, revealing the red face and all-black back of "alt." plumage. *Ad. ♀:* variable. Brighter birds have olive head, nape, and rump, contrasting grayish olive back, and dark gray wings and tail; underparts yellowish, brightest on undertail coverts; upper wingbar yellowish, lower wingbar white. Duller birds are grayish, with little yellow except on rump and tail coverts.

Voice. *Call:* fast rattle, *br-d-d-dt* rising in pitch (Summer's call drops in pitch).

Habitat. Midlevels to canopy; forest interior and edge; frequents fruiting trees.

Distribution. Nests in w N.A. from wc Can. to Mex. border; winters from nc Mex. s. of Yucatán Pen. to C.R.

Status in Belize. Few records, mostly undated and none fully documented. Recorded in OW, BE, and TO.

Reference. *Identification:* Kaufman (1988c).

Flame-colored Tanager
MAP 195; PLATE 49
Piranga bidentata
OTHER NAMES. Stripe-backed Tanager (alt.).

Identification. 7¼″ (18.5 cm). Diagnostic dusky crescent on posterior edge of auriculars; gray bill. ♂: bright orange red, with black wings and tail and boldly streaked back, two conspicuous white wingbars, and broadly white-tipped tertials. ♀ *and imm.:* yellow head and underparts, black-streaked olive back; wings and tail dark brown; white wingbars and tertial tips. *Imm. ♂:* usually has some orange in plumage.

Voice. *Call:* fast *chit-o-wee. Song:* short vireo-like series of three or four phrases. Example: burry *chuwee cheerio chururee.* Not as full or rich as in Yellow-throated Vireo, burrier than in Plumbeous Vireo.

Habitat. Midlevels to canopy; montane broadleaf forest.

Distribution. Resident primarily in highlands from n Sonora and c Nuevo Leon to w Pan.

Status in Belize. Small resident population above 3,000 ft. (900 m) elevation on Mt. Margaret CA.

References. *Status:* Jones et al. (2000). *Identification:* Benesh (1997).

White-winged Tanager
MAP 196; PLATE 49
Piranga leucoptera

Identification. 5½″ (14 cm). Smaller than Western and Flame-colored, with much smaller bill. ♂: bright red, with broad black loral area, wings, and tail; bold white wingbars. ♀: similar to ♀

Western but darker and uniformly olive above, brighter and more uniformly yellow below, with darker wings and tail and two prominent white wingbars; bill dark, not pale.

Voice. *Call:* 1. high-pitched, clear *swee* or *si-wee;* 2. up-slurred *sweet* to *wi-seet;* 3. sharp *chick see. Song:* high-pitched squeaky, simple, short warble *si si-see-see chu.*

Habitat. Midlevel; montane and foothill broadleaf forest edge.

Distribution. Resident in highlands from s Tamaulipas to c Andes.

Status in Belize. FC resident at mid- and high elevations in Maya Mtns., Vaca Plateau CA, and broadleaf forest within Mtn. Pine Ridge; UC and perhaps seasonal in w. interior CA and OW.

Reference. *Voice:* Howell and Webb (1995).

Crimson-collared Tanager

MAP 197; PLATE 49

Ramphocelus sanguinolentus

OTHER NAMES. Mayor (K), police chi'ich (M).

Identification. 7¾" (19.5 cm). *Both sexes:* mostly black, with crimson red lower rump and tail coverts, hindcrown, collar, and upper breast; bluish white bill.

Voice. *Call:* 1. shrill, slightly buzzy *seeur,* to *seeurt;* 2. thin *seeeit.*

Song: 1. high-pitched, squeaky *see si ssiip s-s-sip . . . ;* 2. series of various *chick, teek, whit,* and *per-it* notes.

Habitat. Second-growth scrub, roadside brush and tangles.

Distribution. Resident on Gulf-Caribbean slope from c Veracruz s. of Yucatán Pen. to w Pan.

Status in Belize. FC resident on mainland n. to se OW and sc BE; reported once on Ambergris Caye.

Passerini's Tanager

MAP 198; PLATE 49

Ramphocelus passerinii

OTHER NAMES. Scarlet-rumped Tanager (alt.), tzib tzob (K).

Identification. 7" (18 cm). Bluish white bill. ♂: all black, with vivid scarlet rump and uppertail coverts. ♀ *and imm.:* gray head; tawny brown back, wings, and tail; bright tawny rump and tawny ochre breast; throat and belly paler and duller.

Voice. *Call:* 1. fairly harsh *check* or *sheck* (somewhat like soft Golden-fronted Woodpecker call); 2. *chat* (somewhat like that of Yellow-breasted Chat); 3. thin *seet,* often given in alternating series with *chat. Song:* dry, squeaky *chick ch-chuk ch-chuk,* etc.

Habitat. Second-growth scrub, roadside brush and tangles.

Distribution. Resident on Gulf-Caribbean slope from s Veracruz s. of Yucatán Pen. to w Pan.

Status in Belize. C resident on mainland n. to se OW and c BE.

Blue-gray Tanager

PLATE 48

Thraupis episcopus

OTHER NAMES. Blue Tanager (arch.), Bluebird (C), raxon tzul (K).

Identification. 6½" (16.5 cm). Unmistakable pale grayish blue and darker on back, with bright turquoise blue wings and tail.

Voice. *Call:* 1. forceful *tseeu;* 2. high, thin, slightly squeaky *eeeant,* singly or in a rapid irregular series; 3. in flight, a squeaky *see. Song:* forced series of alternating thin, higher-pitched and squeaky, lower-pitched notes, *see suh see suh see suh seee seee seeee.*

Habitat. Midlevels to canopy; open areas with scattered trees, towns and villages, parks, orchards, forest edge. Frequents fruiting trees.

Distribution. Resident from n Hildalgo and n Veracruz s. of Yucatán Pen. to nc S.A.

Status in Belize. C resident on mainland, increasingly less C northward, becoming scarce in n OW and CO. Occas. seen on Ambergris Caye.

Yellow-winged Tanager
MAP 199; PLATE 48
Thraupis abbas
OTHER NAMES. Abbott's Tanager
(I. Davis).

Identification. 7¼″ (18.5 cm). A play in pastel lilac blues and olive greens, with sharply contrasting jet black tail and hindwings, the latter accentuated with yellow patch at base of primaries. Head lilac blue, becoming dusky lemon-olive on underparts and dusky bluish on back; yellow green greater wing coverts; black lores.
Voice. *Call:* 1. high, thin *seea* to *seee* (shorter and not as high-pitched as in Bronzed Cowbird); 2. thin *wheet*. *Song:* soft to loud rolling trill that speeds up, then slows and drops slightly in pitch at end; quality varies from sweet to dry.
Habitat. Subcanopy and canopy; forest edge; open areas with scattered trees; towns and villages. Frequents fruiting trees.
Distribution. Resident from n Hidalgo and n Veracruz to Nic.
Status in Belize. C resident on mainland n. locally to s CO.
References. *Voice:* Gilardi (1997); Moore (1992).

Genus: Euphonia *(Euphonias)*

These tiny, brightly colored tanagers can be surprisingly hard to spot, even while singing, as they sit motionless in the foliage. All have complex song repertoires, making assignment of song types to specific species difficult. To ID an unseen individual, listen for species-characteristic notes or elements uttered periodically during the singing bout. Scrub, Yellow-throated, and White-vented euphonias are all similar; ♂s are glossy blue black, with a yellow forehead and mostly to entirely yellow underparts. ♀s are various combinations of olive, yellow, gray, and white, each species with a different pattern and thus relatively easy to ID. Elegant and Olive-backed are quite different in appearance from the others and each other.
   Things to note: *In ♂,* color of forecrown/forehead, underparts, and undertail coverts; presence/absence of full hood. *In ♀ (except Olive-backed),* color of crown and throat; pattern of yellow and white underneath.

Scrub Euphonia
PLATE 50
Euphonia affinis
OTHER NAMES. Lesson Euphonia
(I. Davis).

Identification. 4″ (10 cm). ♂: glossy blue black above, complete black hood; yellow breast, belly, and undertail coverts. ♀: mostly olive, becoming yellow on lower belly and undertail coverts and gray on crown and nape; underside of tail mostly or all dark.
Voice. *Call:* penetrating, high-pitched *dee dee dee*. *Song:* thin, rapid jumble of notes; reminiscent of Wedge-tailed Sabrewing song.
Habitat. Subcanopy and canopy; second-growth scrub, pine woodland and pine-oak savannas, broadleaf forest edge.
Distribution. Resident from s Sonora and sw Tamaulipas to nw C.R.
Status in Belize. FC resident in north, UC in s. third; occas. visitor or UC resident on Ambergris Caye, once on Caye Caulker.
Reference. *Voice:* Moore (1992).

Yellow-throated Euphonia
PLATE 50
Euphonia hirundinacea
OTHER NAMES. Bonaparte's Euphonia
(I. Davis).

Identification. 4¼″ (11 cm). ♂: like Scrub but entirely yellow underparts, with yellow extending through throat to bill. ♀: yellow confined to sides, flanks, and undertail coverts; pale gray throat.
Voice. *Call:* in flight and while foraging, a soft, metallic *tink,* often given repeatedly at irregular intervals. *Song:* complex and varied, often a continuous sputtery jumble of warbles, chips, etc. Examples of some more distinctive phrases:
1. buzzy-squeaky *teah-it, t-teach-it,* and *tea ch cha dit;*
2. rapid-fire *d-d-d-d-dt;*
3. *wheet wheet* followed by a harsh *ch-ch-ch-ch-ch-ch;*
4. clear *deet-deet-deet;*
5. clear *towē towē;*
6. *bdlp;*
7. squeaky-clear *pt t twee oo;*
8. *bleet ti, bi di di dit* followed by *choy choy;*

9. *chucka chucka cheezit* and *chick chicka cheo.* Some phrases are reminiscent of chickadee vocalizations (family Paridae), and some of its chattering sequences are reminiscent of Lesser Goldfinch calls.

Habitat. Midlevels to canopy; broadleaf forest edge; open areas with scattered trees, including towns and villages. Frequents flowering and fruiting trees, bromeliads.

Distribution. Resident from s Tamaulipas to w Pan.

Status in Belize. C resident on mainland.

Reference. *Voice:* Moore (1992).

Elegant Euphonia   MAP 200; PLATE 50
Euphonia elegantissima
OTHER NAMES. Blue-hooded Euphonia (combined form).

Identification. 4¼″ (11 cm). ♂: distinctive dark blue black with turquoise blue crown and nape, chestnut forehead, and ochraceous orange breast, belly, and undertail coverts. ♀: olive above and paler below, but retains the ♂'s blue crown and nape and chestnut forehead and has a cinnamon throat.

Voice. *Call:* 1. slightly nasal *chih chu;* 2. nasal *ehnk* to *djeht;* 3. clear *teu* to *teu teu. Song:* very rapid jumble of notes; lower-pitched than in Wedge-tailed Sabrewing. Reminiscent of a gurgling brook.

Habitat. Canopy and subcanopy; submontane and foothill broadleaf forest interior and edge.

Distribution. Resident from s Sonora and c Nuevo Leon s. of Yucatán Pen. to w Pan.

Status in Belize. UC and local resident in Maya Mtns. and the Vaca Plateau CA; recently near Gallon Jug OW.

Reference. *Status:* Howell et al. (1992). *Voice:* Howell and Webb (1995).

Olive-backed Euphonia
MAP 201; PLATE 50
Euphonia gouldi
OTHER NAMES. Gould's Euphonia (arch.).

Identification. 4¼″ (11 cm). Mostly olive. ♂: yellow forehead and chestnut central belly through undertail coverts. ♀: chestnut forehead and undertail coverts, but otherwise olive, becoming yellow olive on belly.

Voice. *Call:* varied, but typically with occas. dry, nasal *deh-deh-deh* notes. *In flight:* soft, sweet *pit. Song:* 1. quite varied, like that of Yellow-throated Euphonia, but characterized by periodic harsh, nasal *deh-deh-deh* and a squeaky *p d d deet* interspersed with high-pitched *peek!* and other notes. 2. soft, rapid jumble, possibly given only by the ♀.

Habitat. Canopy and subcanopy; broadleaf forest interior and edge. Frequents bromeliads.

Distribution. Resident primarily on Gulf-Caribbean slope from c Veracruz s. of Yucatán Pen. to w Pan.

Status in Belize. C resident on mainland n. to n OW and n BE.

Reference. *Voice:* Moore (1992).

White-vented Euphonia
MAP 202; PLATE 50
Euphonia minuta

Identification. 3¾″ (9.5 cm). Smallest of the group. ♂: like Scrub, has complete black hood, but breast and belly orangish yellow and undertail coverts white. ♀: well-defined pale gray throat; yellow breast and flanks; white vent through undertail coverts and underside of tail.

Voice. *Call:* 1. soft, slightly sharp *schik* or *s-wik;* 2. short, warbled phrases such as *t-burble t-burble. In flight:* high-pitched *sip sip. Song:* varied warble, often with periodic chip notes.

Habitat. Canopy and subcanopy; broadleaf forest interior and edge.

Distribution. Resident, perhaps discontinuously in C.A., from c Guat. and s Belize to nc S.A.

Status in Belize. UC resident in Maya Mtns. and foothills n. to se CA and sw SC; also in coastal s TO. One record from near Belize City.

References. *Distribution:* Phillips and Hardy (1965). *Voice:* Howell and Webb (1995).

Golden-hooded Tanager

MAP 203; PLATE 50

Tangara larvata

OTHER NAMES. Golden-masked Tanager (alt.), Masked Tanager (alt.).

Identification. 5¼″ (13.5 cm). Small tanager with short, conical bill. Black, mauve, and blue face framed in brilliant golden hood set off from jet black body; body highlighted with turquoise rump and shoulder patch and purple and turquoise flanks. Relatively small, conical bill for a tanager.
Voice. *Call:* soft, harsh *chet* to *chit,* repeated frequently. *Song:* dry rattling trill, *chat chat cha a a a a a a a a a* to *chip chip chip de-de-de-de-de.*
Habitat. Canopy and subcanopy; pine and broadleaf forest interior and edge.
Distribution. Resident primarily on Gulf-Caribbean slope from n Oaxaca s. of Yucatán Pen. to nw S.A.
Status in Belize. FC to C resident n. to sw OW, ne CA, and sw BE; also locally in e OW.
Reference. *Voice:* Moore (1992).

Genera: Chlorophanes *and* Cyanerpes *(Honeycreepers)*

Honeycreepers have often been placed, along with the Bananaquit, in the family Coerebidae, but recent studies support the premise that honeycreepers are tanagers that have evolved a thin, decurved bill adapted for feeding on nectar. Males are brightly colored; ♀s are more subdued in olive colors. Of the three species in Belize, the Green Honeycreeper stands apart. Shining and Red-legged are more closely related and similarly colored. Honeycreeper songs are rarely heard but have been described from C.R. as a long series of thin, high-pitched notes, with some variations in notes or cadence, depending on the species.
Reference: Stiles and Skutch (1989).

  Things to note: shape, length, and color of bill; color of legs. Additionally, *in ♂ Shining and Red-legged,* color of back, crown, and throat. *In ♀,* color of breast streaks, if any; presence/absence of blue malar stripe; dark or pale lores.

Green Honeycreeper   MAP 204; PLATE 50

Chlorophanes spiza

Identification. 5½″ (14 cm). Distinctly larger than the other two honeycreepers. ♂: glossy blue green, with red eyes enclosed in a partial black hood; mostly yellow bill. ♀: paler, non-iridescent green, with black eyes and less yellow in bill.
Voice. *Call:* 1. thin sharp *tsiip,* given in flight; 2. sharp *tchiip!,* sometimes repeated incessantly.
Habitat. Canopy and subcanopy; broadleaf forest interior.
Distribution. Resident primarily on Gulf-Caribbean slope from n Oaxaca s. of Yucatán Pen. to c S.A.
Status in Belize. UC to FC resident in TO (except ne), w SC, and s half of CA and disjunctively in w OW.

Shining Honeycreeper   MAP 205; PLATE 50

Cyanerpes lucidus

Identification. 4¼″ (11 cm). Both sexes have yellow legs and shorter bill and tail than in Red-legged. ♂: black throat, mask, wings, and tail; rest of plumage blue. ♀: mostly olive green, with streaked face, pale lores, blue malar stripe, and blue-and-green stripes underneath.
Voice. *Call:* 1. high-pitched, fairly sharp *chit;* 2. thin, somewhat liquid twittering.
Habitat. Canopy and subcanopy; broadleaf forest interior and edge. Frequents flowering trees.
Distribution. Resident from e Chiapas and s Belize to extreme nw Colombia.
Status in Belize. FC resident at higher elevations in Maya Mtns. of CA, SC, and TO; local and generally scarce in foothills (e. g., Cockscomb Basin).
References. *Status:* Howell et al. (1992). *Voice:* Howell and Webb (1995).

Red-legged Honeycreeper   PLATE 50

Cyanerpes cyaneus

OTHER NAMES. Blue Honeycreeper (arch.).

Identification. 4½″ (11.5 cm). Longer bill and tail than in Shining; legs red. ♂ *alt.:* predominantly blue and black; differs from Shining in having black back and nape, turquoise crown, and blue throat. ♀: olive green above; diffusely streaked yellow on underparts; dark lores and pale partial supercilium; legs dull red to pinkish, never yellow. *Basic ♂:* resembles ♀ in being mostly olive green, with paler, faintly streaked breast; however, retains black wings and tail. *Flight:* both sexes distinguished by bright yellow underwings.

Voice. *Call:* 1. nasal *ănnh* similar to mew notes of gnatcatchers, but shorter and ends more abruptly;

2. high-pitched *tsee,* much like typical wood-warbler flight call;

3. *dreep.*

Habitat. Canopy and subcanopy; broadleaf forest interior and edge (less often, pine forest); open areas with scattered trees. More widespread than other honeycreepers. Frequents flowering and fruiting trees.

Distribution. Largely resident from se San Luis Potosí to c S.A., but populations n of Belize and Guat. migrate s. in winter.

Status in Belize. UC to seasonally C on mainland nearly throughout. Mostly resident, but present only from Apr. to Sept. in CO and numbers diminished elsewhere in winter.

Reference. *Voice:* Moore (1992).

FAMILY: EMBERIZIDAE
(Seedeaters and Sparrows)

World: 321. **New World:** 279. **Belize:** 21. Primarily New World, with most representatives in the N. Temperate Zone. Absent from Aust., N.Z., and Antarctica. The taxonomic boundaries between this group and other groups, some seemingly very different, are far from distinct. Because of species that are transitional between groups, many taxonomists have included the Cardinalidae, tanagers, Bananaquit, and wood-warblers in this family. Even in the narrow sense (seedeaters, grassquits, sparrows, etc.), this is one of the largest bird families. The Emberizidae are characterized by a strong, conical, thick-based bill adapted to cracking and eating seeds (although many also eat insects); short, rounded wings with 9 primaries; and a moderate-length tail. Most live in open country, but a few, like the Orange-billed Sparrow, live on the forest floor and are rarely seen in the open. **References:** Byers et al. (1995); Rising (1996).

Grassquits, Seedeaters, and Seed-Finches

Seven species occur in Belize. Most are resident, but two, Slate-colored Seedeater and Blue Seedeater, are highly nomadic and may occur in an area from a few weeks to several years before moving on. Their movements are based, at least in part, on seasonal food supplies.

Things to note: body size, bill size and shape, habitat. *In ♂,* plumage color and whether glossy or flat; presence/absence of white patch at base of primaries or on underwing. *In ♀,* tone of brown (rich, dull, dark, pale); presence/absence of wingbars or streaks on breast.

Blue-black Grassquit   PLATE 51
Volatinia jacarina
OTHER NAMES. Rice Eater (C), comitz (M).

Identification. 4¼″ (11 cm). Small, conical bill with straight culmen. ♂ *alt.:* black, with deep blue gloss (quite evident in sunlight); lacks small white patch at base of primaries but has white axillars (visible only in flight). *Basic ♂:* feathers broadly tipped brown and buff, with otherwise blue-black feathers largely concealed; in fresh plumage (autumn) appears mostly brown, with fine black scaling, but as brown feather tips wear away through the winter, the underlying blue-black plumage becomes evident. ♀: brown above; paler below; only one in group with streaked breast.

Voice. *Call:* 1. thin, dry *chip;*

2. sharp, thin *dzit;*

3. sharp *cheek. Song:* forced *tseeeur* given by ♂, often while "bouncing" up in short aerial courtship flight from perch.

Habitat. Rice fields, fallow fields, roadside brush, and low second growth.

Distribution. Resident from s Sonora and s Tamaulipas to sc S.A.

Status in Belize. C to VC resident on mainland, becoming less C in n. third.

Slate-colored Seedeater

MAP 206; PLATE 51

Sporophila schistacea

Identification. 4¼″ (11 cm). Short, thick-based bill with curved culmen. ♂: gray, with white belly and white flashes in base of primaries, lesser wing coverts, and posterior malar region; distinctive pale orange-yellow bill; sits motionless while singing, often making it difficult to locate. ♀: olive brown above and pale brownish buff beneath, becoming pale yellow on belly and undertail coverts; dark gray bill. Differs from ♀ Variable Seedeater in being paler, browner above and buffier below, with pale throat and belly. *Imm.* ♂: resembles ♀ but has a pale yellow bill.

Voice. *Call:* 1. buzzy, nasal *shih* and *shih-shih;* 2. high-pitched lisping *ssik*. *Song:* high-pitched rapid twittering trill that speeds up and intensifies.

Habitat. Canopy and subcanopy; broadleaf forest edge.

Distribution. Largely resident, but nomadic, from Belize to nw S.A.

Status in Belize. Discovered in s TO in Jan. 1989 and sw OW in Mar. 1991. Seen with increasing frequency in these two areas since. Multiple observations of paired, territorial birds suggest that it nests in Belize, at least occasionally.

References. *Status:* Howell et al. (1992); Miller and Miller (1992).

Variable Seedeater

MAP 207; PLATE 51

Sporophila americana

OTHER NAMES. Wing-barred Seedeater (arch.), Black Seedeater (arch.), comitz (M).

Identification. 4¼″ (11 cm). Short, thickset bill with curved culmen. *Flight:* conspicuous white underwing coverts. ♂: glossy black, with small white patch at base of primaries (not always visible). ♀: brownish olive, slightly paler on throat and belly. Smaller and paler than Thick-billed Seed-Finch, with smaller, more curved bill and shorter tail.

Voice. *Call:* typically, a nasal *chih* to *chee*. *Song:* complex series of sweet melodic notes. Example: *sweeta-sweeta sweeta teu teu chur chur chur chur ti ti ti ti,* sometimes ending in a jumble.

Habitat. Fallow fields and low second-growth scrub, roadside brush, orchards, broadleaf and pine forest edge.

Distribution. Resident primarily on Gulf-Caribbean slope from n Oaxaca s. of Yucatán Pen. to c S.A.

Status in Belize. C to VC resident on mainland n. to c BE and s OW, locally to ne OW.

White-collared Seedeater   PLATE 51

Sporophila torqueola

OTHER NAMES. Morrelet Seedeater (arch.), Sharpe's Seedeater (arch.), Ricey (C), Grassy Bird (C), kok k'eke' sit (K), comitz (M).

Identification. 4¼″ (11 cm). Closely related to Variable Seedeater and has similar bill shape. ♂ *alt.:* boldly patterned black and white—note white throat, black breast band, and white wingbars and rump. *Basic* ♂: black back feathers obscured by olive-gray feather tips; sides and flanks rich buff; as feathers wear, back becomes black, sides and flanks white (= alt. plumage). ♀: olive brown, with light brown to whitish wingbars. *Imm.* ♂: like ♀ but brighter, with black-and-white wings.

Voice. *Call:* 1. clear *tew;* 2. clear *chea;* 3. nasal *ink*.

Song: 1. several sets of clear whistled notes, each set on a different pitch or of different quality, ending with 1–6 buzzy notes. Example: *sweet sweet brady brady bray bray tew tew tew wheet wheet wheet wheezzzzz.*

2. long, complex canary-like warbling—several clear, *sweet* notes followed by buzzy notes, and then a complex array of notes on different pitches, often ending with a wheezy *cheeeee cheeeee cheeee.*

Habitat. Fallow fields and low second-growth scrub, roadside brush, orchards, broadleaf and pine forest edge.

Distribution. Resident from c Sinaloa and s Texas to w Pan.

Status in Belize. VC resident on mainland and Ambergris Caye; UC on Caye Caulker.

Reference. *Voice:* Moore (1992).

Thick-billed Seed-Finch

MAP 208; PLATE 51

Oryzoborus funereus

OTHER NAMES. Lesser Seed-Finch (combined form), Lesser Rice Grosbeak (arch.), Thick-billed Seedeater (I. Davis), comitz (M).

Identification. 4¾″ (12 cm). Large, thick-based conical bill with no angle between straight culmen and forehead. Has longer tail, slimmer body, and smaller bill than Blue-black Grosbeak. *Flight:* conspicuous white underwing coverts. ♂: black throughout except for small white patch at base of the primaries (not always visible). ♀: rich dark brown, tending toward deep rufous on underparts.

Voice. *Call:* clear liquid *chirp. Song:* 1. typically begins with a short series of liquid *sweet sweet sweet* or slurred *ship ship ship* notes, followed by clear, thin, whistled notes at a variety of pitches and intervals, sometimes descending toward the end into a jumble of buzzy notes. Example: clear *su su swee swee tu swee su we su su swee . . .* , followed by buzzy *squee chee see chee see see . . . .* 2. less structured jumble of clear, liquid notes and buzzy *jeez* notes.

Habitat. Most common in open pine forest and savannas; also broadleaf forest edge, second-growth scrub, roadside brush.

Distribution. Resident primarily on Gulf-Caribbean slope from c Veracruz s. of Yucatán Pen. to nw S.A.

Status in Belize. FC to C resident on mainland n. locally to n OW and, perhaps, s CO.

References. *Voice:* Delaney (1992); Moore (1992).

Blue Seedeater   MAP 209; PLATE 51

Amaurospiza concolor

Identification. 5″ (12.5 cm). Larger than Variable Seedeater, with bill longer, not as thick-based, and with only a slightly curved culmen. ♂: flat blue-black plumage (no gloss), the blue being evident even in strong shade. ♀: uniformly rich cinnamon brown. Similar to but smaller than ♀ Blue Bunting, with smaller, more rounded, gray, not black, bill.

Voice. *Call:* 1. high-pitched sharp, slightly metallic *tswik* or *sik;* 2. thin twittering. *Song:* high-pitched, slightly tinny to sweet warble suggesting song of Indigo Bunting, *see-see-wee-see si-si-wee* to *seet see-wee-see si-si-wee-su.*

Habitat. Riverside bamboo thickets.

Distribution. Resident, but somewhat nomadic, from Chiapas and Belize to nw S.A.

Status in Belize. Small breeding populations at Monkey Bay (Sibun R.) BE and vicinity of Bermudian Landing (Belize R.) BE. Recently found also at Hill Bank OW. First found in Belize in Feb. 1991.

References. *Status:* Howell et al. (1992); Vallely and Aversa (1997). *Voice:* Howell and Webb (1995).

Yellow-faced Grassquit

MAP 210; PLATE 54

Tiaris olivacea

OTHER NAMES. Olive Grassquit (I. Davis), comitz (M).

Identification. 4¼″ (11 cm). Olive green above, with yellow forehead, supercilium, eye crescent, and throat. Small conical bill like that of Blue-black Grassquit. ♂: black foreparts frame yellow facial markings. ♀: duller throughout, lacks ♂'s black foreparts, and has paler, restricted areas of yellow in face.

Voice. *Song:* rapid, high-pitched, tinny *ti-ti-ti-ti . . .* consisting of ≈10 notes/sec, lasting 1–2 sec; insectlike.

Habitat. Roadside thickets, orchards, second-growth scrub.

Distribution. Resident from c Nuevo Leon and W.I. to nw S.A.

Status in Belize. Relatively recent colonist from Petén District, Guat. First recorded in late 1970s or early 1980s, and now locally C to VC in s. half of country away from coast and mtns. Recently reported from Gallon Jug in sw OW. The pattern of occurrence and chronology of records suggest that it spread into Belize along at least two fronts, the Western Highway in w CA and the San Antonio Road in w TO.

References. *Status:* Howell et al. (1992); Miller and Miller (1992).

Grassland Yellow-Finch

MAP 211; PLATE 54
Sicalis luteola
OTHER NAMES. Mexican Yellow-Finch
(I. Davis).

Identification. 4¼" (11 cm). Small, relatively short-tailed sparrow, yellow green above, with darker streaks in crown and back. Superficially resemblēs ♀ Lesser Goldfinch but has streaked upperparts, yellow rump, no white highlights in wing, and slightly larger, more rounded bill. Travels in small to large flocks. *Flight:* strongly undulating; in courtship flight, hovers or flies slowly on quivering wings while singing, reminiscent of courtship flight of Sky Lark *(Alauda arvensis).* ♂: bright yellow below, with yellow rump and yellow in face. ♀: duller on head and face, and has duller yellow underparts.

Voice. *Flight call:* double- to triple-noted 1. *kidit* to *kidilit* and

2. *kip-kip. Song.* long, complex series of canary-like buzzes and trills, often with many birds singing at once.

Habitat. Seasonally flooded savannas, fallow fields.

Distribution. Resident locally and discontinuously from vicinity of Mexico City and c Veracruz to nc S.A.

Status in Belize. Locally C resident, but to some degree nomadic. Two, possibly three, distinct population centers: c BE to extreme ne CA; se SC to ne TO; and possibly nc OW near Blue Creek, where a flock was recorded on one occas. One record of dispersing juv. at Punta Gorda, 3 Nov. 2001. More exploration of grassland savannas and fallow fields in other areas may well turn up additional populations. Discovered in Belize in 1971 and, until recently, known only from two small areas n. and w. of Belize City. It is not known if the species is expanding its range or is only now being found in long-established areas seldom visited by birders until recently.

Reference. *Status:* Wood and Leberman (1987).

Orange-billed Sparrow

MAP 212; PLATE 52
Arremon aurantiirostris
OTHER NAMES. tzub hin pur (K), tzi'ki puur (M).

Identification. 6¼" (16 cm). Related to the *Arremonops* sparrows (below), but bright orange bill, boldly marked black-and-white head, black breast band, and bright yellow patch at bend of wing make it unmistakable. *Juv.:* dusky gray bill and sooty plumage; paler only on throat and supercilium; bears little resemblance to ad.

Voice. *Call:* sharp, dry *tsik,* somewhat like call of Blue-black Grosbeak call but drier or flatter. *Song:* high, thin, squeaky *see-seet-uh-seet-seet-seeta-seet . . . ,* similar to song of Black-and-white Warbler but more varied.

Habitat. Ground and understory; broadleaf forest interior.

Distribution. Resident primarily on Gulf-Caribbean slope from n Oaxaca s. of Yucatán Pen. to nw S.A.

Status in Belize. C resident on mainland n. to n CA and s BE; once at Lamanai OW.

Genus: Arremonops

The Olive and Green-backed sparrows, along with the more southern Black-striped Sparrow *(Arremonops conirostris),* form a complex group of closely related species or subspecies. Much work remains to be done on this group in order to better understand the taxonomic relationships of the various populations. In Belize, Olive and Green-backed sparrows are distinctly different in most areas, but hybrids may occur in the northeast. They are often found together in many areas where the two overlap, with no indication of hybridization. Yet, in a few areas, birds with intermediate characters occur. Except for possible intermediates, the two are relatively easy to tell apart when seen well or heard. Their songs, although similar, have a different cadence. All *Arremonops* south of extreme northern Stann Creek District should be Green-backed.

Things to note: vocalizations; richness of green in upperparts; color of head stripes, undertail coverts, and flanks; degree of contrast between primaries and rest of wing.

Olive Sparrow   MAP 213; PLATE 52

Arremonops rufivirgatus

OTHER NAMES. Schott's Sparrow (I. Davis).

Identification. 6″ (15 cm). Gray head, with dark brown eyestripe and dark rufous-brown lateral crown stripe, the latter often mottled with black and sometimes entirely black in front of the eyes. Dull grayish olive upperparts; pale brownish gray underparts, with darker flanks and pale buff undertail coverts. Primaries contrast brighter olive than rest of upperparts.

Voice. *Call:* 1. Cardinal-like *tik;*

2. hummingbird-like *chp,* repeated;

3. thin *seeeh.*

Song: accelerating series of 4–6 clear notes, 1. sweet, liquid *chiuw chiuw chiuw chiuw-chiuw-chiuw-chuw-chuw-chuw;*

2. drier *chip   chip   chip chip chip-chip-chip-chipchipchip.*

Habitat. Arid and semiarid broadleaf and pine forest edge, second-growth scrub.

Distribution. Resident from c Sinaloa and s Texas to n Guat. and n Belize; disjunctively in C.R.

Status in Belize. FC to C resident on mainland s. to nw and se OW, ne CA, sw BE, and ne SC. Records from farther s. and w. should be carefully documented. Some birds in n OW (and elsewhere?) appear to be hybrids between this and Green-backed Sparrow. Further study is needed.

References. *Status:* Wood and Leberman (1987). *Systematics:* Monroe (1963); Parkes (1974). *Voice:* Hardy and Wolf (1993).

Green-backed Sparrow   PLATE 52

Arremonops chloronotus

OTHER NAMES. Black-striped Sparrow (arch.).

Identification. 6¼″ (16 cm). Olive-green upperparts (brighter and greener than in Olive Sparrow), with primaries not contrastingly brighter; flanks grayish yellow; undertail coverts brighter and yellower than in Olive. Gray head with all-black lateral crown stripe and eyestripe.

Voice. *Call:* 1. thin Orange-crowned Warbler–like *dzik;*

2. high, thin *seeee* to *seet seet seet.*

Song: 1. loud, clear *tsee tsee chonk chonk chonk chonk chonk;*

2. thin, sliding *suweet suweet toe toe toe toe;*

3. clear whistled *cho cho cho cho cho cho;*

4. *tur chip tur chip tur chip . . .* (8–10 paired notes in series). Song does not accelerate as in Olive Sparrow, and introductory notes are often of different quality and pitch than rest of song.

Habitat. Lower strata of relatively mesic broadleaf second growth woodland, thickets, and forest edge. Within the range of Orange-billed Sparrow, restricted to forest edge and second growth; outside range of Orange-billed Sparrow, also found in broadleaf forest interior. This species is also found with the similar Olive Sparrow in open pine woodland and second growth, where it is not uncommon to see the two together.

Distribution. *Near Yucatán Endemic.* Resident from e and c Yucatán Pen. to Tabasco, c Guat., and nw Hon.

Status in Belize. FC to C resident on mainland. May hybridize with Olive Sparrow in n Belize.

References. *Systematics:* Monroe (1963). *Voice:* Moore (1992).

Botteri's Sparrow   MAP 214; PLATE 53

Aimophila botterii

OTHER NAMES. Yellow-carpalled Sparrow (is part of; arch.), Petén Sparrow (arch.).

Identification. 5¾″ (14.5 cm). Most closely resembles Grasshopper Sparrow, but larger, longer-tailed, and grayer underneath. *Ad.:* dusky gray above, boldly streaked with rufous and black; grayish, not buff, face with dark rufous post-ocular stripe; lacks ochre-yellow supraloral area and pale central crown stripe of Grasshopper Sparrow; bold blotchy spots on sides of upper breast and on flanks; breast and flanks washed darker and browner, especially on flanks, than rest of underparts. *Juv.:* streaked underneath and much like juv. Grasshopper in other respects as well; however, Botteri's larger size, longer tail, and larger bill should distinguish it. Both species typically sing from an exposed perch; however, non-singing birds spend most of their time on or near the ground in the grasses, where they are difficult to see. When flushed, Botteri's often flies to a low perch; Grasshopper typically drops back down in the grass.

Voice. *Call:* sharp, high-pitched *zit* to *tit,* sometimes doubled. *Song:* variations on a rapid, dry, thin, sputtery *spit spit spit spit che up spit che up chee chee smack-smack-smack-smack-smack,* often drawn out to nearly 20 sec.

Habitat. Open pine and pine-oak-calabash savannas.

Distribution. Resident from se Arizona and s Texas s. to s Mex. and locally to nw C.R.

Status in Belize. UC to FC resident from n and e OW s.e. to c BE and extreme ne CA. A bird collected "17 mi. NW Monkey River" on 19 June 1963 may represent a separate (perhaps now extirpated) population center, as recent searches for this species in this area have failed to locate it.

Reference. *Voice:* Hardy and Wolf (1993).

Rusty Sparrow   MAP 215; PLATE 53
Aimophila rufescens

Identification. 7¼" (18.5 cm). Although in the same genus as Botteri's, the two share few plumage characteristics. *Ad.:* rufous tail and wings, thinly streaked back, relatively large bill, well-defined lateral throat stripe, and rich brownish buff to cinnamon-buff underparts. *Juv.:* streaked nearly throughout, somewhat reminiscent of Savannah or Lincoln's Sparrow (both rare) but much larger, with proportionately larger bill, and lacks distinct auricular patch. Larger, more rufous than juv. Botteri's, with proportionately larger bill and conspicuous lateral throat stripe.

Voice. *Call:* 1. wrenlike *chump* or *chup;*
2. soft *chank;*
3. clear *zeeer.* *Song:* loud, rich, and bubbly.
Examples: 1. *slip sliddle teetle* or *slip little beetle;*
2. *trip treedle;*
3. *schlip   che che che where.*

Habitat. Understory and low-level strata; pine forest edge; less often, open broadleaf woodland edge.

Distribution. Resident from ne Sonora s. of Yucatán Pen. to nw C.R.

Status in Belize. C resident in Mtn. Pine Ridge

and coastal plain from ec SC to ne TO. Recorded once at Jalacte TO on Belize-Guat. border, where a small disjunct population may exist.

Reference. *Voice:* Hardy and Wolf (1993).

Genus: Spizella

The *Spizella* are small sparrows with a relatively small, conical bill. Other than three records of Clay-colored, the Chipping Sparrow is the only *Spizella* in Belize. It is a resident of pine woodlands and savannas and is rarely seen elsewhere.

Things to note: color and pattern of crown; color of lores, nape, and rump; presence/absence of conspicuous lateral throat stripe.

Chipping Sparrow   MAP 216; PLATE 53
Spizella passerina

Identification. 5¼" (13.5 cm). *Alt.:* diagnostic rufous crown, white supercilium, black eyestripe; lacks or nearly lacks dark lateral throat stripe. Black-and-brown-streaked back, gray rump, and thin white wingbars. *1st basic (imm.) and basic ad.:* key features are gray rump and dark lores; crown streaked dark and light brown, usually with narrow whitish stripe down center of forecrown; face grayish buff, with darker auriculars; faint lateral throat stripe; nape and underparts dirty brown (imm.) to grayish (ad.). *Juv.:* streaked breast. Molts into first basic plumage by Sept.

Voice. *Call:* high-pitched, dry, sharp *dzit* to *dzip. Song:* very dry to fairly liquid (and usually slower) trill; faster and drier than in Grace's Warbler (separate notes barely discernible) and nearly always on one pitch.

Habitat. Ground to subcanopy; pine woodland.

Distribution. Nests from e Alaska and nc Can. to Gulf of Mex. and s. in C.A. s. of Yucatán Pen. to nw Nic. N.A. populations winter from s U.S. to c Mex.; C.A. populations are resident.

Status in Belize. FC to C resident from e OW s. to ne TO and in Mtn. Pine Ridge. One spring and one autumn sight record for Half Moon Caye. These may pertain to N.A. migrants rather than strays from the mainland, given that there are no other records in Belize away from nesting areas.

References. *Identification:* Kaufman (1990); Pyle and Howell (1996).

Clay-colored Sparrow PLATE 53
Spizella pallida

Identification. 5″ (12.5 cm). Most likely to show up in Belize in imm. plumage (streaked juv. molts before migrating). *Imm.:* closely resembles imm. Chipping, but with pale brown rump, pale lores, gray nape contrasting with buffy breast, more extensive pale central crown stripe, pale malar stripe, and conspicuous dark lateral throat stripe; prominent auriculars framed with dark brown.
Voice. *Call:* dry *dzit,* very much like call of Chipping Sparrow but slightly higher-pitched and weaker.
Habitat. Ground and low-level strata; open areas with scattered woody vegetation.
Distribution. Nests in c N.A. from c Can. (e British Columbia to e Great Lakes) s. to n U.S.; winters from n Mex. and s Texas to s Mex.
Status in Belize. Three records: c Ambergris Caye, 25 Sept. 1996; s Ambergris Caye, 21–22 Oct. 1996; Payne's Creek TO, late Sept. or early Oct. 2001.
References. *Status:* Jones et al. (2000). *Identification:* Kaufman (1990); Pyle and Howell (1996).

Vesper Sparrow PLATE 53
Pooecetes gramineus

Identification. 5¾″ (14.5 cm). Pale sandy brown above, with distinctive head pattern and white outer tail feathers. Note thin but distinct white eye-ring; white supraloral area; bold white malar framed below by dark lateral throat stripe and above by dark auriculars with pale center; cleanly streaked brown and gray back; and evenly streaked breast and sides. Rufous lesser wing coverts distinctive but usually concealed. Savannah Sparrow is smaller, has yellow supraloral, and lacks distinctive eye-ring. Lincoln's Sparrow is darker and browner overall, with rufous-and-gray head and rich buff malar and underparts. Imm. Dickcissel has larger bill, yellow supraloral area, unmarked auriculars, thinner lateral throat

line, whitish stripe down each side of back, and fainter streaks below. All three lack distinctive white outer tail feathers.
Voice. *Call:* thin *tssit.*
Habitat. Grasslands, fallow fields, brush.
Distribution. Nests in N.A. from c Can. s. to c U.S.; winters from s U.S. s. to s Mex., occas. to n C.A.
Status in Belize. One record: Punta Gorda, 26 Aug. 2001.

Lark Sparrow PLATE 53
Chondestes grammacus

Identification. 6¼″ (16 cm). Highly distinctive; boldly marked black-and-white head accentuated with chestnut auricular patch and lateral crown stripe. Underparts unmarked except for black central breast spot. Tail black, with bold white corners that are quite conspicuous in flight.
Voice. *Call:* slightly lispy *tsip.*
Habitat. Ground to canopy; open habitats, usually with scattered trees.
Distribution. Nests in w N.A. from s Can. s. to nc Mex. and e. to Tennessee; winters from s U.S. to s Mex., occas. to n C.A.
Status in Belize. Occas. autumn transient (Sept., Oct.); once in winter at Crooked Tree BE, 27 Feb. 1998.
Reference. *Status:* Jones et al. (2000).

Savannah Sparrow PLATE 53
Passerculus sandwichensis

Identification. 5¼″ (13.5 cm). Small and relatively short-tailed like Grasshopper Sparrow, but with notched tail, strongly streaked underparts, and bold auricular patch and lateral throat stripe. Background color of head is near white, with pale yellow supraloral spot. Streaks on breast often coalesce into ragged central breast spot.
Voice. *Call:* high, thin *tseet* and shorter *tsit* or *tsip.*
Habitat. Ground and understory; fallow fields, flooded and dry meadows.
Distribution. Nests from Alaska and n Can. s. to c and sw U.S., nw Mex., and the highlands of c Mex.; winters from c U.S. to s Mex. and Belize.

Status in Belize. Occas. winter visitor; late Oct. to early Apr.

Reference. *Status:* Erickson (1977).

Grasshopper Sparrow MAP 217; PLATE 53
Ammodramus savannarum

Identification. 4¾″ (12 cm). Large head and short, slightly rounded tail. *Ad.:* yellow-buff face with gray-tinged auriculars and pale eye-ring, yellow-ochre supraloral, dark crown and post-ocular stripe, and pale central crown stripe. Nape blue gray, finely streaked with dark rufous; more complex pattern of streaks on back and scapulars. Wing feathers dark brown with broad light brown and buff edges. Underparts buff, strongest on breast and flanks; streaks on sides and flanks only. *Juv.:* finely streaked breast, less buff in head and underparts; similar to juv. Botteri's (see Botteri's account, above). Migratory birds from N.A. are paler, with brighter head and breast than resident *A. s. cracens* and with yellow-buff, not grayish, auriculars and few or no streaks on sides and flanks.

Voice. *Call:* 1. sharp *tik* similar to that of Fork-tailed Flycatcher;
2. thin *seet. Song:* very high-pitched, dry, insect-like *tp tipit zzzzzzzzzzzzzzzz,* often followed with a thin warbling trill or jumble, somewhat like that of Grassland Yellow-Finch.

Habitat. Ground and, for singing, low bushes; savannas. Migrants may be found in any open weedy habitat.

Distribution. Nests from s Can. to s U.S. and disjunctively to Pan. and c W.I.; winters from s U.S. and Cuba to s Mex., and on Pacific slope to E.S. and s Hon. Populations s. of the U.S. are resident.

Status in Belize. Locally C resident in coastal plain from e OW and n BE s. to ne TO, locally in Mtn. Pine Ridge. Migrants from N.A. occas. seen mid-Oct. to late Apr. Any bird seen outside the pine belt is likely to be a N.A. migrant.

Lincoln's Sparrow PLATE 53
Melospiza lincolnii

Identification. 5½″ (14 cm). Head with peaked rufous-brown crown, broad gray supercilium, rufous-brown eyestripe, thin white eye-ring, buffy malar stripe, and black lateral throat stripe. Thin, even black streaks on ochraceous buff breast and flanks. Savannah Sparrow has bolder, more uneven streaking on whitish underparts, often coalescing into an irregular central breast spot; brown and white, not rufous and gray, head; and pale yellow supraloral area.

Voice. *Call:* 1. sharp, sucking *tchup* to *thip;*
2. *zeet,* not quite as high-pitched or thin as in Savannah Sparrow, and with less abrupt beginning.

Habitat. Understory; fallow fields, roadside brush, low second growth, forest edge.

Distribution. Nests from c Alaska and nc Can. s. to sw and ne U.S.; winters from nw and sc U.S. to s Mex., and in C.A. highlands to Hon.

Status in Belize. Occas. transient and R winter visitor, mid-Oct. to mid-Apr.

Reference. *Status:* Howell et al. (1992).

White-crowned Sparrow PLATE 54
Zonotrichia leucophrys

Identification. 6½″ (16.5 cm). Unstreaked breast, distinctively striped head. *Imm.:* plain grayish buff underneath, with brownish buff flanks; head light grayish brown, with rich brown lateral crown stripe and eyestripe; bill pinkish to orangish; more likely than ad. to turn up in Belize. *Ad.:* unmistakable black-and-white-striped head, pink to orange bill, and plain gray underparts.

Voice. *Call:* 1. thin *seep;*
2. emphatic, rich *cheep!*

Habitat. Ground and low-level strata; open areas with scattered trees, fallow fields.

Distribution. Nests from Alaska and n Can. s. in west to Great Basin and Pacific SW and in east to c Can.; winters from sw Can. and nc U.S. to c Mex.

Status in Belize. One record: Ambergris Caye, 28 Oct. 1988.

Reference. *Status:* Howell et al. (1992).

FAMILY: CARDINALIDAE
(Saltators, Grosbeaks, and Buntings)
World: 43. **New World:** 43. **Belize:** 12. New World, mostly Tropics and subtropics. Some-

times placed as a subfamily in the Emberizidae, the Cardinalidae are characterized by a strong, thick-based bill adapted for crushing seeds, even larger and stouter than in most emberizids. Many have rich, elaborate songs.

Genus: Saltator *(Saltators)*

Found in second-growth vegetation and forest edge scrub. The three in Belize are similarly patterned, with a white supercilium, pale throat, greenish upperparts, and grayish underparts. Unlike most other members of this family, which have a conical bill, saltators have a somewhat longer bill adapted more for eating fruit than for eating seeds. Buff-throated and Black-headed are most similar and are frequently found together, especially at fruiting trees.

Things to note: crown-back contrast, color of central throat, presence/absence of black band separating throat and breast, extent of supercilium behind eye.

Grayish Saltator   PLATE 52
Saltator coerulescens
OTHER NAMES. Lichtenstein's Saltator (I. Davis), John Smith Kill a Bird (C), tzi tzob (K), ta'an tzin tzo' (M).

Identification. 9″ (23 cm). Olive gray above, grayish buff below, becoming pale cinnamon on lower underparts; white throat with blackish lateral throat stripe; lacks black border between throat and breast of other saltators, has more extensive white supercilium, and auriculars do not contrast with nape and back. Vocal repertoire distinctly different.
Voice. *Call:* 1. sharp, high-pitched *seet!;*
2. squeaky *ink!* (higher-pitched, thinner, not as sharp as in Rose-breasted Grosbeak).
Song: 1. raucous, bouncy ditty with shark *peek!* notes interspersed throughout;
2. clear, whistled *chur chit ch-chur-weeeee* and a simpler *chick chō chō weeee,* the last note drawn out and strongly up-slurred. The Creole name "John Smith Kill a Bird" is roughly onomatopoeic.
Habitat. Midlevel strata; open habitats with scattered brush or trees; edges of towns and villages.

Distribution. Resident from s Sinaloa and s Tamaulipas to sc S.A.
Status in Belize. FC to C resident on mainland; occas. seen on Ambergris Caye but absent from other cayes.

Buff-throated Saltator   MAP 218; PLATE 52
Saltator maximus
OTHER NAMES. Tzi tzob (K), tzin tzo' (M).

Identification. 8½″ (21.5 cm). Cinnamon-buff central throat, bordered extensively with black. Head dark gray, becoming olive gray on nape and gradually merging with yellow-olive upperparts. Usually does not travel in groups and is much quieter than Black-headed; thus it is more easily overlooked.
Voice. *Call:* high-pitched, thrush-like *seeep. Song:* 1. short, soft, melodious, and robinlike *t-seet cher-rer-o cher-rer-o* to *chererer churero see churur* to *t-seet chero cherRY;*
2. weak *choro choro chuwea choro choro,* etc.
Habitat. Midlevels to subcanopy; broadleaf forest edge.
Distribution. Resident primarily on Gulf-Caribbean slope from c Veracruz, mostly s. of Yucatán Pen., to c S.A.
Status in Belize. FC to C resident on mainland n. to n CA and c BE, once in e OW (New R.).

Black-headed Saltator   PLATE 52
Saltator atriceps
OTHER NAMES. Tzi tzob (K), tzin tzo' (M).

Identification. 10½″ (26.5 cm). White central throat outlined in black. Unlike in Buff-throated, black extends through auriculars and hindcrown to form a black hood that contrasts sharply with golden olive neck and upperparts. Gregarious and noisy; their raucous chatter quickly alerts the observer to their presence.
Voice. *Call:* very harsh; variously 1. *chaa,*
2. *check,*
3. *chiat!,* and
4. squeaky *cheurk. Song:* explosive chips, chatters, and squawks ending in a rapid-fire, nasal rattle; usually preceded by several harsh call notes. Typically, two or more birds explode into song simultaneously.

Habitat. Midlevels to canopy; broadleaf forest edge; second-growth scrub. Frequents fruiting trees.

Distribution. Resident from sw Tamaulipas and Guerrero to Pan.

Status in Belize. C resident on mainland and Ambergris Caye.

Reference. *Voice:* Moore (1992).

Black-faced Grosbeak MAP 219; PLATE 52
Caryothraustes poliogaster
OTHER NAMES. Bishop Grosbeak (arch.), kix hrir (K).

Identification. 7¼″ (18.5 cm). Highly distinctive; green above, with yellow head and breast and sharply contrasting black face. Gray scapulars, rump, tail coverts, and belly. Sexes similar.

Voice. *Call:* 1. harsh, sharp *pink;*
2. cardinal-like *tik.*
3. dry *zeet* to *feent. Song:* emphatic mixture of high- and low-pitched squeaky notes and sputters.

Examples: 1. harsh, sputtery *spt* followed immediately by a clear, buzzy *preet preet preet;*
2. slurry *dreet dru droy droy;*
3. *tup tip tu chow chow;*
4. *che che ch-chu chuh chuh.*

Habitat. Midlevels to canopy; broadleaf and pine forest interior; forest edge; occas. weedy scrub.

Distribution. Resident on Gulf-Caribbean slope from c Veracruz s. of Yucatán Pen. to c Pan.

Status in Belize. C resident on mainland, mostly away from coast, n. locally, and perhaps discontinuously, to ne OW and perhaps s CO.

Reference. *Voice:* Moore (1992).

Northern Cardinal MAP 220; PLATE 52
Cardinalis cardinalis
OTHER NAMES. Red Cardinal (arch.).

Identification. 8½″ (21.5 cm). Prominent crest, black face, large red-orange bill. ♂: except for black face, bright red throughout. ♀: red crest and red-orange bill; otherwise brownish gray above and warmer brown below.

Voice. *Call:* 1. metallic *tk;*

2. flat *smk.*

Song: 1. rich, liquid *warick warick whadick whadick whadick whadick dwick dwick wick wick wick wick;*

2. *whick cheer cheer cheer cheer cheer,* often without the introductory note.

Habitat. Understory to midlevels; broadleaf and pine forest edge, second-growth scrub.

Distribution. Resident from se Can. and sw U.S. to s Mex., n Guat., and n Belize.

Status in Belize. UC to FC resident on mainland s. to nw and se OW, ne CA, and s BE.

Rose-breasted Grosbeak PLATE 52
Pheucticus ludovicianus
OTHER NAMES. Black-hooded Grosbeak (combined form).

Identification. 7¼″ (18.5 cm). Seasonally and sexually dimorphic, but highly distinctive in most plumages. ♂ *alt.:* striking black-and-white bird with large rose-red triangle on breast; large, conical whitish bill. *Basic ♂:* black-and-white pattern largely obscured by pale brown feather edges, but rose-red breast still conspicuous. ♀: boldly patterned brown-and-white-striped head; conspicuous white wingbars; pale brownish breast, with conspicuous streaks on flanks, sides, and breast. *Flight:* ♂ in all plumages has red underwing coverts and bold white patch at base of primaries; ♀ has yellow-buff to pale salmon underwing coverts, and no noticeable white at base of primaries.

Voice. *Call:* loud, squeaky *ink!* Probably does not sing in Belize.

Habitat. Midlevels to canopy; broadleaf forest edge; open space with scattered trees.

Distribution. Nests e. of Rocky Mtns. from sc Can. to c U.S.; winters from c Mex. to nw S.A.

Status in Belize. C transient and UC to locally FC winter visitor, mid-Sept. to early May.

Reference. *Identification:* Morlan (1991).

Black-headed Grosbeak

NOT ILLUSTRATED

Pheucticus melanocephalus

OTHER NAMES. Black-hooded Grosbeak (combined form).

Identification. 7½″ (19 cm). Seasonally and sexually dimorphic. Ad. ♂ unmistakable, but ♀ and imm. easily confused with similar-plumaged Rose-breasted. *Alt.* ♂: mostly or all black head, burnt orange neck and underparts, becoming yellow on central belly and vent; wings boldly marked black and white; barred black-and-brown back; orange rump. Much shorter, thicker-based bill than any oriole. *Basic* ♂: similar but with more orange in head, especially in supercilium and throat. *Imm.* ♂: like ♀ but usually with solid (unstreaked) orangish neck and underparts. *Ad.* ♀: similar to ♀ Rose-breasted but with sparser streaking on undersides, rarely extending across breast; upper mandible darker than lower mandible (bill all pale in Rose-breasted). *Imm.* ♀: most similar to ♀ Rose-breasted and sometimes perhaps not safely separable in the field. Averages finer streaking on underparts and streaks do not extend prominently across breast; thinner white markings in wings, slight to strong buffy wash across breast, darker upper mandible. *Flight:* all, including ad. ♂ have lemon-yellow underwing coverts.

Voice. *Call:* similar to but less rich or squeaky than Rose-breasted.

Habitat. Like that of Rose-breasted.

Distribution. Nests from sw Can. w. of Great Plains to mtns. of s Mex.; winters almost entirely in Mex.

Status in Belize. One record: Pook's Hill CA, 23 Jan. 2003 (ad. ♂).

Reference. *Identification:* Morlan (1991).

Blue-black Grosbeak   MAP 221; PLATE 51

Cyanocompsa cyanoides

Identification. 7″ (18 cm). Grotesquely large, triangular bill and robust body give this species a much different shape from that of the sleeker, longer-tailed Thick-billed Seed-Finch. ♂: deep glossy blue black throughout; ♂ seed-finch is flat

black and has small white patch at the base of its primaries; Blue Bunting is smaller, with distinctly smaller bill and bright blue highlights on face, shoulder, and rump. ♀: deep rich brown, closest in color to ♀ Thick-billed Seed-Finch, but readily distinguished from this and other similar species by much larger bill.

Voice. *Call:* 1. harsh, squeaky *pink!* or *pick!*, harsher than in Rose-breasted Grosbeak, louder and richer than in Orange-billed Sparrow; 2. harsh, sharp *chi-chick.*

Song: lazily whistled 1. *pē purr purr pē purr purr pē-pē*, generally descending the scale, but with higher notes interspersed, and

2. *pee pee purr purr puree puree,* disintegrating into a short jumble at end.

Habitat. Understory; broadleaf forest interior and edge; second-growth scrub.

Distribution. Resident primarily on Gulf-Caribbean slope from c Veracruz s. of Yucatán Pen. to c S.A.

Status in Belize. FC to C resident on mainland n. to s CO.

Reference. *Voice:* Moore (1992).

Blue Bunting   MAP 222; PLATE 51

Cyanocompsa parellina

OTHER NAMES. Rice Bird (C).

Identification. 5¼″ (13.5 cm). Smaller than Blue Grosbeak and Blue-black Grosbeak, with much smaller bill; darker than Indigo Bunting, with larger bill. ♂: easily distinguished by bright blue highlights in face, bend of wing, and rump, which contrast sharply with otherwise dark blue-black plumage. ♀: uniformly warm brown above; slightly paler and cinnamon brown below, with no hint of streaking; all-black bill (Indigo Bunting and Blue Grosbeak have pale lower mandible).

Voice. *Call:* rich *chip,* about halfway between calls of Black Phoebe and Hooded Warbler (not as sweet as the former; not as flat as the latter). *Song:* clear, whistled, melodious 1. *tutwe du weet* and

2. *wheo weo to we to we,* etc.; similar to song of *Passerina* buntings but typically weaker and shorter.

Habitat. Understory to midlevels; deciduous and semi-deciduous forest edge.

Distribution. Resident from c Sinaloa and c Nuevo Leon to n Nic.

Status in Belize. FC resident on mainland s. to c BE and w. of Maya Mtns. to s CA.

Reference. *Voice:* Moore (1992).

Blue Grosbeak   PLATE 51
Passerina caerulea

Identification. 6¾″ (17 cm). Thickset bill. Characteristically raises crown feathers, giving impression of a ragged crest; frequently flicks tail when agitated. *♂ alt.:* blue nearly throughout; much bluer than Blue-black Grosbeak, not glossy, and with black face and conspicuous chestnut wingbars. *Basic ♂:* brown edges to blue feathers. ♀: warm brown above, paler below, with pale buffy brown wingbars, gray rump, and pale lower mandible; ♀ Blue Bunting is uniformly dark brown throughout, with deeper-based, all-dark bill; Indigo Bunting smaller, with much smaller bill and less prominent wingbars.

Voice. *Call:* 1. sharp, metallic *pik!* to *tink!,* louder and more metallic than Northern Waterthrush call;

2. slightly rough, less metallic *chick!;*

3. short, harsh *zeet* as in Indigo Bunting, but louder and lower-pitched. *Song:* rich but slightly burry warble of high and low notes, lower-pitched and richer than song of Indigo Bunting or Gray-crowned Yellowthroat. Seldom sings in Belize.

Habitat. Fallow fields, roadside brush, rice fields.

Distribution. Nests from nc U.S. to c Mex., and on Pacific slope to C.R.; winters from nw and ne Mex. to w Pan.

Status in Belize. C transient and UC winter visitor, early Sept. to late Apr., with peak numbers in Oct. and early Apr.

Reference. *Identification:* Kaufman (1989).

Indigo Bunting   PLATE 51
Passerina cyanea

Identification. 5″ (12.5 cm). Small bunting with relatively small bill. Frequently pumps tail downward. *♂ alt.:* bright blue, with darker flight feathers; smaller in size and smaller-billed than Blue Grosbeak, and lacks chestnut wingbars. ♀: variously dull gray brown to fairly rich cinnamon brown, with varying amounts of faint to fairly distinct streaks on breast and thin, inconspicuous pale wingbars; duller and paler brown than ♀ Blue Bunting, with paler throat, faintly streaked breast, and pale lower mandible. *Basic ♂:* like ♀ but with varying amounts of blue in plumage, ranging from blue uppertail coverts and lesser wing coverts only (some 1st-winter birds), to all-blue rump and patches of blue on head and breast (some ads.).

Voice. *Call:* 1. sharp *pink!;*

2. softer, flat *tink! Typical flight note* (also given while perched): distinctive emphatic, buzzy *zee. Song:* lazy random series of rich *sweet* and *tew* notes; similar to Blue Grosbeak song, but not as rich or burry, and higher-pitched. Seldom sings in Belize.

Habitat. Rice fields, fallow fields, roadside brush, second-growth scrub, forest edge.

Distribution. Nests in e N.A. from s Can. to sw U.S. and Gulf of Mex.; winters from c Mex. to Pan.

Status in Belize. VC transient and FC to C winter visitor, mid-Sept. to mid-May. Peak numbers are present in Oct. and first half of Apr.

Reference. *Identification:* Kaufman (1989).

Painted Bunting   PLATE 51
Passerina ciris

Identification. 5″ (12.5 cm). *Ad. ♂:* vivid blue head with red eye-ring; yellow-green back; brilliant red underparts. Many consider the ♂ Painted Bunting to be one of the most beautiful birds in the world; and unlike the Indigo Bunting, it retains its colorful plumage throughout the year. *Ad. ♀ and 1st basic ♂:* green above and yellow green below, with narrow but distinct pale eye-ring; the only truly green bunting in Belize. *1st basic ♀:* duller, grayish olive above, pale yellowish gray below; distinguished from Indigo by plain face, no trace of a supercilium or wingbars, and thin pale eye-ring.

Voice. *Call:* 1. loud, rich *chip;*

2. liquid *plik;* both quite unlike Indigo Bunting call.

Habitat. Fallow fields, roadside brush, second-growth scrub.

Distribution. Nests disjunctively in sc U.S. to n Mex. and in se U.S.; winters from w and ne Mex. and s Florida to Pan.

Status in Belize. UC to locally FC transient and occas. winter visitor, early Oct. to late Apr.

Dickcissel   PLATE 54
Spiza americana

Identification. 6″ (15 cm). Relatively small, short-tailed, gregarious bird with conical bill, streaked brown back with one distinctly paler stripe on each side, grayish head with white throat, black lateral throat stripe, pale malar stripe, and pale supercilium. ♂ *alt.:* chestnut shoulder patch; distinctive black V on upper breast, surrounded below by yellow; supercilium and malar bright yellow anteriorly, white posteriorly. *Ad.* ♀: less distinctive, but with enough of the head pattern for recognition as a Dickcissel; lacks black V on breast. *Imm.* ♀: streaked breast and flanks; yellow confined to supraloral spot; somewhat similar to ♀ House Sparrow but with larger bill and dark lateral throat stripe. *Imm.* ♂: similar to imm. ♀ but brighter overall. *Flight:* undulating, with constant shifting of position of birds within the flock—a good way to ID birds migrating high overhead.

Voice. *Call:* 1. in flight and perched, very harsh *zank* reminiscent of Masked Tityra call but less emphatic;

2. loud, dry *zunt;* 3. emphatic slightly rough *whit!,* much like Willow Flycatcher call.

Song: 1. dry, buzzy *dick dick see-you see-you see-you;*

2. *dick cle-cle-cle-cle;*

3. *dur-dur-dur zeee.* Occas. sings during both spring and autumn migrations.

Habitat. Rice fields, fallow fields, second-growth scrub.

Distribution. Nests in c U.S. from Can. to Mex. border; winters primarily on Pacific slope from s Sinaloa through C.A. and on Caribbean slope in n S.A.

Status in Belize. FC to locally VC spring transient, late Mar. to mid-May, and locally C autumn transient, at least along coast, mid-Aug. to mid-Nov.

FAMILY: ICTERIDAE
(Blackbirds)

World: 97. **New World:** 97. **Belize:** 20 (plus 1 anticipated). Exclusively New World. All but three icterids found in Belize are resident. "Blackbird" is a poor choice of names for this highly diverse group, given that relatively few are mostly or all black. Aside from that, a common thrush in the Old World is called Eurasian Blackbird *(Turdus merula)*. But, for lack of a more accurate moniker, "blackbird" is now the well-entrenched English name for Icteridae. Members of the family are characterized by a short to medium-length, straight to slightly decurved bill that tapers to a sharp point. Many, such as the orioles, are brightly colored, especially the ♂, or have a brightly colored feature such as the red and yellow epaulets of the ♂ Red-winged Blackbird, the mostly yellow tail of the oropendolas, and the yellow-buff nape of the ♂ Bobolink. Many have an elaborate courtship display, and many build an intricately woven, pendulous nest. They inhabit many habitats, from open grasslands and marshes to the forest interior. Some are strictly arboreal, others strictly terrestrial. Most are gregarious outside the breeding season, and some, like oropendolas and the Red-winged Blackbird, are colonial nesters as well. **References:** Jaramillo and Burke (1999); Orians (1985). *Voice:* Hardy et al. (1998).

Bobolink   PLATE 55
Dolichonyx oryzivorus

Identification. 6½″ (16.5 cm). Unique among blackbirds, resembling no other species in the family. Small, with short, spiny-tipped tail and finchlike bill. ♂ *alt.:* black body with yellow-buff nape and white scapulars and rump. *Imm. and basic ad.:* quite different from ♂ alt., with streaked upperparts (except for nape), mostly unstreaked head and underparts, and pale stripe down each side of back; richer brownish buff

on head and underparts than in ♀ Red-winged Blackbird or any comparable sparrow; streaks in head confined to blackish brown lateral crown stripe and postocular stripe; birds in autumn are richer yellow buff on head and underparts. ♀ *alt.:* duller, with buff confined primarily to nape and breast.
Voice. *Call:* distinctive, emphatic *prink!*
Habitat. Fallow fields, weedy areas.
Distribution. Nests from sc Can. to c U.S.; winters in c S.A.
Status in Belize. UC spring and autumn transient on cayes, R on mainland; early Apr. to early June and early Sept. to late Oct.

Red-winged Blackbird MAP 223; PLATE 55
Agelaius phoeniceus
OTHER NAMES. Soldier Bird (C), Nancy Swasey (C).

Identification. 9″ (23 cm). *Ad. ♂:* unmistakable, with its bright red epaulettes (shoulders) bordered posteriorly with pale yellow on otherwise all-black body; in fresh plumage (autumn, early winter), feathers of head and back edged rufous. ♀: unlike other blackbirds, heavily streaked both above and below; its larger size and daggerlike bill distinguish it from the streaked sparrows. *Imm. ♂:* much like ♀ but darker, with trace of the red epaulettes; however, these are often hidden by overlapping contour feathers; some may be mostly black like ad. ♂ but with pale supercilium and less red in shoulder.
Voice. *Call:* 1. dry *chuck* to *check;*
2. nasal *ent* to *chent;*
3. *tchurrr. Song:* musical, but scratchy *odaleeee* to *okleee,* sometimes followed by a rough trill, which can sound remarkably like song of Marsh Wren *(Cistothorus palustris).*
Habitat. For nesting, freshwater marshes; for foraging, fallow fields, recently plowed agricultural land, pastures.
Distribution. Nests from e Alaska and c Can. to nw C.R. Populations in Can. and n U.S. migrate s. in winter.
Status in Belize. C resident on mainland s. and w. to c OW, ne CA, and s BE, occas. or locally to c CA and ne SC.

Eastern Meadowlark MAP 224; PLATE 55
Sturnella magna
OTHER NAMES. Common Meadowlark (arch.), Bob-White (C).

Identification. 9″ (23 cm). As its name implies, lives in fields and meadows and resembles a large lark. Readily IDed by bright yellow throat and breast split by distinctive black V, daggerlike bill, flat head, short tail, and heavily streaked upperparts. In fresh basic plumage, V is partially obscured by pale feather tips. *Flight:* conspicuous white outer tail feathers.
Voice. *Call:* 1. dry rattle;
2. *seeep* or *sreep;*
3. phoebe-like *chip. Song:* melodious, but thin and scratchy; variously *ch-cheery-cheerio, cheero-cheero-cheerio, chuh ch-cheerio cheerio,* etc.
Habitat. Savannas, farmland, mowed fields.
Distribution. Largely resident from se Can. and sw U.S. to n S.A.; northernmost populations withdraw s. in winter.
Status in Belize. C resident in lowlands on mainland from n OW and n BE w. to c OW and n CA and s. through e SC to ne TO. Apparently unrecorded from CO.

Yellow-headed Blackbird
NOT ILLUSTRATED
Xanthocephalus xanthocephalus

Identification. 9½″ (24 cm). *Ad. ♂:* unmistakable; black, with bright yellow head and breast, black loral patch, and white primary coverts. ♀: yellow on head and breast duller, much reduced; body dark brown, not black; upper belly streaked; lacks white in primary coverts. *Imm. ♂:* like ♀ but with white-tipped primary coverts; dark loral patch; deeper yellow to orangish face, throat, and breast; and unstreaked upper belly.
Voice. Soft, but rough *ch-ruk* to *truck.*
Habitat. Open country, including pastures, fallow fields, savannas, marshland.
Distribution. Nests in w and c N.A.; winters to c Mex., occas. to s Mex.
Status in Belize. One record of likely wild origin: an imm. ♂ on Caye Caulker, 23 Sept.–1 Oct. 2001. Three previous records were possible escaped cage birds: ad. ♂ on Ambergris Caye,

31 Aug. 1997; ♀ at a Belize City market in ≈1978, with frayed string attached to one leg; ad. ♂ on Long Caye s. of Caye Chapel (date unknown) that persistently went into open parrot cage for food.

Melodious Blackbird   PLATE 55

Dives dives

OTHER NAMES. Sumichrast's Blackbird (I. Davis), Singing Blackbird (arch.), Blackbird (C), ch'i quan (K, M).

Identification. 10¼″ (26 cm). Black throughout, including black bill and nearly black eyes. Distinctly larger than Bronzed Cowbird; smaller than Great-tailed Grackle, with shorter tail that lacks ♂ grackle's keel. Most closely resembles Giant Cowbird, especially the ♀, which lacks the ♂'s ruff; however, Melodious Blackbird lacks red eyes and has smaller, thinner bill with straight culmen. Constantly flicks tail up, unlike both Giant Cowbird and Great-tailed Grackle.

Voice. Vocalizations are loud and varied. *Call:* 1. loud *quick!* to *twik!;* 2. clear, down-slurred *dreur;* 3. more drawn-out *teeuuuuuuur.* *Song:* clear whistled 1. *whoit whoit whoit whit cheer!,* 2. *wait HERE!,* 3. *T-Rex T-Rex t-rex,* 4. *teek war* to *tic wary,* interspersed with single *dreur* notes, and 5. *chu-wheet!,* etc.

Habitat. Ground to canopy; most open areas with scattered trees, forest edge, clearings within forest interior. Forages occas. in fields away from trees.

Distribution. Resident from s Tamaulipas formerly to Nic., but with clearing of land has recently spread s. well into C.R.

Status in Belize. C to VC resident on mainland; also recorded from Ambergris Caye but possibly not resident.

Reference. *Voice:* Moore (1992).

Great-tailed Grackle   PLATE 55

Quiscalus mexicanus

OTHER NAMES. Boat-tailed Grackle (combined form), Blackbird (C), tz'ic i par (K), moshi ne' bosh chich (M).

Identification. ♂ 16″ (40.5 cm), ♀ 11½″ (29 cm). Abundant, highly gregarious, and highly (some would say excessively!) vocal bird. Grackles lose most or all of their tail feathers simultaneously when molting in late summer. *Ad. ♂:* all-black plumage, with long, keel-shaped tail; yellow eyes; and long, black bill with curved culmen. *Ad. ♀:* brown, with shorter, unkeeled tail; pale brown supercilium; and yellow eyes. *Juv.:* resembles ad. ♀ but has dark eyes.

Voice. *Calls/songs:* a seemingly endless variety of grating, raspy notes, clear notes, and penetrating shrieks, squeaks, chips, clacks, whistles, and screeches, often given repeatedly in various combinations: 1. *chuck;* 2. clear *ruck ruck ruck ruck e e e e e;* 3. *errrreeet!* to *tureet!* to *torreeeeee!;* 4. *turet tur-tur-tur-tur;* 5. clear penetrating *cree cree cree cree;* 6. harsh *crick crick crick crick;* 7. nasal *renk renk renk renk renk;* 8. sliding *twannnh twannnh,* often preceded by high-pitched grating *sheet-t-t-t-t;* 9. Yucatan Jay–like *cho-cho-cho-cho;* etc. *Flight call:* dry *check.*

Habitat. Nearly all open areas, including rice fields, pastureland, and plowed fields; less common in wooded habitats such as open pine forest and mangroves.

Distribution. Resident from wc U.S. to nw S.A.

Status in Belize. VC resident throughout, including all inhabited and many uninhabited cayes. Colonized both Belmopan CA and Gallon Jug OW shortly after they were established deep within continuous rainforest, and colonized remote cayes following the arrival of humans.

Reference. *Voice:* Moore (1992).

Genus: Molothrus *(Cowbirds)*

Cowbirds are the New World equivalent of the Eurasian cuckoos in that they mostly lay their eggs in the nests of other species. Since they feed

Rare Cowbirds. Brown-headed cowbird, adult ♀ *(a);* Shiny Cowbird, adult ♀ *(b)* and adult ♂ *(c).*

Figure 28

seasonally in open meadows and prairies, cowbird populations have proliferated throughout the New World with the replacement of forests by pastureland. The concomitant increase in nest parasitism has resulted in serious declines in some species that are especially vulnerable to cowbird parasitism.

Things to note: body size, bill shape, eye color. *In* ♂, presence/absence of neck ruff, color of feather gloss. *In* ♀, darkness/lightness of plumage; presence/absence of pale supercilium, pale throat, pale base to lower mandible, or indistinct streaks on breast.

[Shiny Cowbird]   FIGURE 28B,C
Molothrus bonariensis

Identification. ♂ 7¼″ (18.5 cm), ♀ 6¾″ (17 cm). Somewhat similar to Bronzed and Brown-headed cowbirds, as well as Melodious Blackbird, but much closer in appearance to Brown-headed Cowbird, which has stubbier, stout-based bill. Bronzed has larger bill with curved culmen. *Ad. ♂:* all black; smaller than Bronzed Cowbird and lacks ruff and red eyes, has purple-blue rather than greenish bronze sheen, and has shallower-based bill with straight culmen; significantly smaller than Melodious Blackbird, with proportionately shorter bill and tail, and lacks habit of constantly flicking tail. *Ad. ♀:* warm brown throughout, with faint supercilium and pale throat. *Juv.:* similar, but with faint

streaks below. ♀ and juv. closely resemble ♀ and juv. Bronzed but are paler, with faint supercilium and distinctly paler throat, as well as differently shaped bill that is all black. Ad. ♀ lacks faint breast streaks of ♀ Brown-headed and is warmer brown. Juv. best told by narrower daggerlike bill. ♀ Bronzed is much darker with different bill shape.

Voice. *Call:* 1. harsh *chick;* 2. rattling *bl-bl-bl-bl-bl-bl-bl-bl. Song:* high-pitched *see see cha cha tik tik blt blt blt blt blt.*

Habitat. Most disturbed open areas, including forest edge, agricultural fields and pastureland, towns and villages.

Distribution. Resident throughout most of S.A. n. to e Pan. Beginning in late 19th century, following habitat modification for agriculture, began spreading n. through W.I., reaching Cuba in the early 1980s, the Florida keys in 1985, Jamaica in 1993, the Cayman Isl. in 1995, and Yucatán Pen. in 1996. By the end of the 20th century, had spread n. and w. through the se U.S., as far n. as Maine and as far w. as Oklahoma.

Status in Belize. Not yet recorded, but likely to reach Belize in the near future.

References. *General:* Pranty (2000); Raffaele et al. (1998). *Distribution:* Smith and Sprunt (1987); Kluza (1998). *Identification:* Pranty (2000); Smith and Sprunt (1987).

Bronzed Cowbird
PLATE 55

Molothrus aeneus

OTHER NAMES. Red-eyed Cowbird (alt.), tsa eki tz'ic (K), hotz arroz (M).

Identification. ♂ 8¼″ (21 cm), ♀ 7¾″ (19.5 cm). Proportionately larger, flat head; red eyes; and no angle between bill and forehead. Similar to, but smaller and stockier than, Giant Cowbird. ♂: shiny black, with glossy greenish bronze head, breast, and back; distinctive "swollen" nape ruff. ♀: similar, but dull brownish black, lacking gloss; lacks swollen ruff. *Imm.:* unstreaked dark brown, much smaller than juv. Great-tailed Grackle, and with shorter tail and bill. (See Shiny Cowbird and Brown-headed Cowbird accounts.)

Voice. *Call:* very high-pitched, thin *seeeur* and *surree*. *Song:* thin, high-pitched wheezing and trills.

Habitat. Fallow fields, pastureland and agricultural fields, brush and second growth, open areas with scattered trees.

Distribution. Largely resident from sw U.S. to c Pan.; some populations, especially in U.S. and n Mex., withdraw s. in winter. Spread n. from Mex. into the U.S. in early 19th century and still spreading e. into Gulf states.

Status in Belize. C resident in CO, n BE, and Ambergris Caye, less C s. in interior to w TO; more widespread in winter. Formerly only a winter visitor; first documented nesting in Belize in 1968 at Rockstone Pond (Altun Ha) BE.

References. *Status:* Barlow et al. (1969); Erickson (1977).

Brown-headed Cowbird
FIGURE 28A

Molothrus ater

Identification. 6¾″ (17 cm). Similar in size to Shiny Cowbird; smaller than Bronzed. Differs from both in having stubby, stout-based bill. *Ad. ♂:* all-black body with greenish gloss; chocolate brown head. *Ad. ♀:* dull gray brown, with faint streaks below, pale throat, and faint supercilium. *Juv.:* like ad. ♀ but with bolder streaking below, scaly back, and light brown wingbars.

Voice. 1. high-pitched *see eep!;*
2. short, harsh rattle.

Habitat. Open fields, agricultural fields, and pastureland.

Distribution. Nests from c Can. to interior s Mex.; partially migratory; birds in Mex. winter mostly in lowlands near nesting areas.

Status in Belize. One record: Gallon Jug OW, 1 Mar. 2000.

Reference. *Status:* Jones et al. (2002).

Giant Cowbird
MAP 225; PLATE 55

Molothrus oryzivorus

OTHER NAMES. Tick Bird (C), ts'ok (K).

Identification. ♂ 13″ (33 cm), ♀ 11½″ (29 cm). Looks more like Melodious Blackbird than a cowbird, but has red eyes and heavier-set bill with slightly curved culmen and does not flick tail. *Ad. ♂:* disproportionately small head, which appears even smaller when neck ruff is expanded; hunchback appearance, even in flight. *Ad. ♀:* noticeably smaller than ♂ and lacks ruff. *Juv.:* pale yellowish white bill; eye color varies from brown to pale gray; similar to Yellow-billed Cacique but heavier-set bill and different behavior, with no habitat overlap. *Flight:* typically flies with long, sweeping dips on folded wings, following a short series of wing flaps; wings make distinctive whirring sound in flight.

Voice. *Call:* 1. nasal *chehk, chehk-chik;*
2. very raspy *creck;*
3. sharp *chrrik-rrik-rrik-rrik-rrik-rrik;*
4. grating *t-t-t-t-t-t. Song: quok* plus high, thin *sheet* notes.

Habitat. Nests in oropendola colonies in open areas with isolated large trees. Forages in plowed fields and other fields with sparse or low herbaceous vegetation.

Distribution. Resident primarily on Gulf-Caribbean slope from c Veracruz s. of Yucatán Pen. to c S.A.

Status in Belize. UC to locally C resident on mainland n. to c OW and n BE; occas. or locally to n OW and possibly s CO.

References. *Voice:* Hardy et al. (1998); Howell and Webb (1995).

Genus: Icterus *(Orioles)*

Orioles present an underappreciated ID challenge. Males are bright and showy, and their ID is *usually* straightforward. Females and imms., on the other hand, can be quite difficult to distinguish. The migratory Orchard Oriole and sedentary Hooded Oriole are very similar in all but ad. ♂ plumage. Some ♀ Black-cowled superficially resemble Yellow-backed and the Mex. endemic Audubon's Oriole. Hooded and Altamira also are similar in appearance.

Things to note: size and shape of bill; pattern of white (and other) markings in wing. *In ♂,* orange vs. yellow; pattern and extent of black in head, back, wings, and tail; tail pattern. *In ♀ and imm.,* pattern and extent of black (if any) in head, face, and throat; color of back; orange vs. yellow underparts. *In Hooded vs. Orchard,* length and curvature of bill, overall size, call notes.

Black-cowled Oriole PLATE 56

Icterus prosthemelas
OTHER NAMES. Lesson Oriole (arch.),
Banana Bird (C), k'an i tz'ic (K).

Identification. 7¾″ (19.5 cm). Shallow-based, slightly decurved bill. ♂: black hood, back, wings, and tail, with yellow rump, underparts, and shoulder; black hood separated from yellow underparts by thin chestnut band. ♀: highly variable; many, especially in south, virtually identical to ♂; others have yellowish green back, usually, but not always, mottled or flecked with black. Amount of black on head of ♀ varies considerably. At one extreme, black is restricted to face, chin, and throat. These individuals resemble imm. Yellow-backed Oriole, but black usually includes auriculars, and bend of wing is yellow, not black. Other ♀ Black-cowled (and molting imm. ♂s) have nearly entire head black and greenish yellow back. These individuals differ from Audubon's Oriole *(Icterus graduacauda),* which does not occur in Belize, in having a greenish yellow, not pure yellow, back and a thinner, more decurved bill. *Imm.:* differs from ad. ♀ by having dark brown, not black, wings and tail.

Voice. *Call:* 1. soft *churt-churt* to *chow-chow,* the latter reminiscent of House Sparrow call; 2. clear, emphatic, less varied *creek creek tut tut;* 3. *derr ch-cheet ch-cheet ch-cheet,* similar to one call of Yellow-backed Oriole. *Song:* soft euphonia-like jumble of clear and scratchy notes.

Habitat. Midlevels to canopy; broadleaf, pine, and palm forest interior and edge; open areas with scattered trees, especially coconut palms.

Distribution. Resident on Gulf-Caribbean slope from c Veracruz, Yucatán Pen., and W.I. to w Pan.

Status in Belize. C resident on mainland and n Ambergris Caye; absent from the other cayes.

Reference. *Voice:* Moore (1992).

Orchard Oriole PLATE 56

Icterus spurius
OTHER NAMES. Banana Bird (C).

Identification. 6½″ (16.5 cm). Smallest of the orioles, with short, straight bill. ♂: black hood, back, wings, and tail; deep chestnut red rump, shoulder, and underparts; white lower wingbar. ♀: very similar to ♀ Hooded but smaller, with shorter, straighter bill, slightly shorter tail, and different calls; never has orange hue in undertail coverts. *Imm. ♂:* center of throat and loral area black; differs from imm. ♂ Hooded in same ways as ad. ♀. Hooded has restricted range in Belize; Orchard is widespread when present.

Voice. *Call:* 1. *chuck* (occas. *ch-chuck*); 2. *chĕh,* singly or run together into a chatter (less nasal, more evenly paced than Baltimore). *Song:* rapid bouncy ditty with sweet and buzzy notes mixed together.

Habitat. Low level to canopy; broadleaf and pine forest edge; open areas with scattered trees, second-growth scrub, and fallow fields, including rice fields. Frequents flowering and fruiting trees.

Distribution. Nests in e N.A. from n U.S. to n and w Gulf of Mex. and highlands of c Mex.; winters from Sinaloa and Veracruz to nw S.A.

Status in Belize. UC (cayes) to VC (mainland) transient and C winter visitor, early Aug. to late Apr. Peak numbers pass through from late Aug. to mid-Sept. and again in early Apr.

References. *Identification:* Kaufman (1987b); Lehman (1988).

Hooded Oriole   MAP 226; PLATE 56
Icterus cucullatus
OTHER NAMES. Banana Bird (C), chin i tz'ic (K).

Identification. 7½" (19 cm). Relatively slim, decurved bill. ♂: unmistakable; mostly orange body with black face, throat, back, wings, and tail; white shoulder patch and lower wingbar; very similar to much larger Altamira Oriole, which has deep-based, straighter bill; orange shoulder; and small white patch at base of primaries. ♀: yellow olive above and yellow below, becoming orange yellow on undertail coverts; wings grayish, with two white wingbars; similar ♀ Orchard is smaller, with shorter tail, yellow undertail coverts and shorter, straighter bill, and calls are different. *Imm.* ♂: like ad. ♀ but with mostly yellow head and black face and throat; imm. ♂ Orchard is smaller, with shorter tail and shorter, straighter bill; ♀ Orange Oriole also has straighter bill, as well as yellower upperparts, less black in face, and black, not grayish, wings.
Voice. *Call:* 1. musical *wheet;*
2. flat *check;*
3. clear *peu;*
4. harsh *ch-ch-ch-ch-ch-ch-ch-ch.* *Song:* fairly brief series of liquid whistles and warbles.
Habitat. Open areas with scattered trees, especially palms and flowering and fruiting trees.
Distribution. Nests from sw U.S. to s Baja Calif., Sinaloa, and on Gulf-Caribbean slope to Belize. N. populations migrate to sw Mex.; s. populations are sedentary.
Status in Belize. C resident on mainland s. to ne SC and w. to c OW and ne CA, locally or irregularly w. to San Ignacio. C resident on larger cayes s. to the Turneffe Isl.
References. *Identification:* Kaufman (1987); Lehman (1988).

Yellow-backed Oriole   MAP 227; PLATE 56
Icterus chrysater
OTHER NAMES. Underwood Oriole (I. Davis), Banana Bird (C), k'an i tz'ic (K).

Identification. 8¾" (22 cm). Thick-based, straight bill. ♂: mostly yellow body with black face, throat, wings, and tail; black in face does not include auriculars. ♀: like ♂ but with head, back, and upper breast washed brownish orange; some ♀ Black-cowled Orioles are similar but have black auriculars, yellow shoulder, and thinner, more decurved bill. *Imm.:* head and back washed olive.
Voice. *Call:* 1. clear *chert,* given singly or repetitively, at the rate of <2/sec;
2. harsh *ch-chert-chi-chert chi-chert;*
3. mournful *doe WHIT doo,* repeated;
4. burry *tray tray tray tray* and *tr tray tray.* *Song:* slow mournful series of clear whistles on different pitches. Example: clear, whistled, slow *ko kou ko too . . . ,* etc. Pattern is reminiscent of Nightingale Wren song, but slower and much lower-pitched.
Habitat. Midlevels to canopy; primarily in pines, but also locally in open broadleaf forest and forest edge.
Distribution. Resident from Yucatán Pen. and Chiapas to nw S.A.
Status in Belize. Locally FC on mainland nearly throughout, but absent from nw CO, n OW, Vaca Plateau, Maya Mtns., and all but ne TO; C on Ambergris Caye, but absent from other cayes.
Reference. *Status:* Howell et al. (1992).

Yellow-tailed Oriole   PLATE 56
Icterus mesomelas
OTHER NAMES. Banana Bird (C), k'an i tz'ic (K).

Identification. 8¾" (22 cm). Fairly long, slightly decurved bill, thick at base; yellow bar across inner wing; yellow outer tail feathers. *Ad.:* yellow body with black wings, back, tail, face, and central throat; tertials edged white; the only black-and-yellow oriole in Belize with combination of mostly yellow head and black back. *Imm.:* back, rump, and central tail feathers green; back usually mottled with black; duller wings; yellow in outer tail feathers confined to inner webs. *Juv.:* similar, but lacks black in face and throat.

Voice. *Call:* 1. *chow,* given singly or in sets of two to several (louder than in Black-cowled Oriole); 2. *ch-chow ch-chow,* etc. *Song:* short, slightly mournful phrases, each repeated at regular intervals. Examples: 1. burry *woe choo towea t'woe;* 2. clear to burry *peah toe c'woe t'weer;* 3. burry *whay toe piggle-wiggle.* Song is often a duet involving both birds of a pair. When only one bird is singing, the phrases are usually of only 2 notes. Singing bouts often start softly (and sound deceptively distant) and become progressively louder with each successive phrase.

Habitat. Midlevels to canopy; broadleaf forest edge, often along edges of streams; less often, open areas with scattered trees around towns and villages.

Distribution. Resident on Gulf-Caribbean slope from nc Veracruz to nw S.A.

Status in Belize. FC to locally C resident on mainland.

Orange Oriole   MAP 228; PLATE 56
Icterus auratus
OTHER NAMES. Banana Bird (C).

Identification. 7¼″ (18.5 cm). Straighter, deeper-based bill than Hooded. *Ad. ♂:* orange body, including back, with black wings and tail; black lores, chin, and central throat; bold white patch at shoulder; thin lower wingbar; broken white patch at base of primaries; Hooded has black back, lacks white patch at base of primaries. ♀ *and imm.:* closely resemble young ♂ Hooded but with brighter, yellower head and underparts, less black in face, black wings, and broken white patch at base of primaries; ad. ♀ has black tail; imm. has olive tail.

Voice. *Call:* 1. low, dry chatter; 2. fairly hard, nasal *nyehk;* 3. clear *choo;* 4. slightly nasal, drawn-out *wheet. Song: peet* followed by a pause, then *chur* and a rapid, rich *chert-chert-chert-chert,* the latter often repeated several times (as in Mangrove Vireo, but lacking nasal quality).

Habitat. Midlevels to subcanopy; deciduous and semi-deciduous forest edge and open areas with scattered trees.

Distribution. *Yucatán Endemic.* Resident in Yucatán Pen. s. to c Campeche, s Quintana Roo, and ne Belize.

Status in Belize. Small population resident in ne CO; a few also on Ambergris Caye, but apparently only in winter (Oct. to Apr.).

References. *Voice:* Delaney (1992); Howell and Webb (1995).

Altamira Oriole   MAP 229; PLATE 56
Icterus gularis
OTHER NAMES. Lichtenstein's Oriole (arch.), Black-throated Oriole (arch.), Banana Bird (C), chin i tz'ic (K).

Identification. 9½″ (24 cm). Although similarly patterned, it is one-third larger than Hooded, with a straight, deep-based bill. *Ad.:* orange, not white, bar at bend of wing; and white patch at base of primaries. *Juv.:* from imm. ♂ Hooded by larger size, different bill, and lack of green on nape and crown; attains yellow shoulder patch in 2nd year, black-and-orange ad. plumage by end of 2nd year.

Voice. *Call:* 1. harsh rail-like *chet,* repeated several times; 2. muffled *chow;* 3. nasal *yenk* to *yenk yenk;* 4. *chirty chirty chirty . . .* repeated several to many times. *Song:* 1. soft, whistled *toe tee tu toe tee,* etc., and similar variations; 2. rapid whistled *tee-toe tee-toe tree tuh-tuh-tuh-tuh-tuh-chee* to a more varied *toe-tit toe-ti-ti-ti-ti TEE tuh toe tuh teet,* with all notes on a different pitch (like a fast Yellow-backed Oriole song).

Habitat. Midlevels to canopy; broadleaf forest edge, open areas with scattered trees.

Distribution. Resident from s Texas and Guerrero to Nic.

Status in Belize. UC to FC resident on mainland s. locally to e OW and n BE; occas. to n CA and s BE. Also recorded on Ambergris Caye, mostly in winter.

Reference. *Identification:* Kaufman (1987).

Baltimore Oriole   PLATE 56

Icterus galbula

OTHER NAMES. Northern Oriole
(combined form), Banana Bird (C), chin i
tz'ic (K).

Identification. 7½" (19 cm). Relatively thin,
straight bill, as in Orchard. *Ad. ♂:* unmistakable,
with black hood and back, mostly black wings
and tail, and orange underparts, rump, shoulder,
and tail corners; white lower wingbar and tertial
edges. *Ad. ♀:* variable; generally similar to ♂ but
with at least some green feather edges in head
and back, more yellow-orange below, and with
two bold white wingbars; other ♀s mostly green
above, but even the dullest have enough of the
♂ pattern to be easily recognizable. *Imm.:* olive
to grayish olive above, with pale brownish head
and scapulars, mostly yellow orange to orangish yellow below (in some imm. ♀s, underparts
are nearly yellow), often with broad pale grayish
wash across belly and vent (especially in ♀), and
two distinct white wingbars; face and throat lack
black of other similar species.
Voice. *Call:* 1. *check;*
2. harsh, dry, slightly uneven *cheh-cheh-cheh-
check;*
3. rapid dry *cheh-eh-eh-eh-eh-eh* (more nasal than
in Orchard);
4. clear *huree. Song* (occas. given in both spring
and autumn): clear, sweet, hollow series of notes,
sometimes interspersed with call notes.
Habitat. Subcanopy and canopy; broadleaf forest interior and edge; open areas with scattered
trees. In migration, also in second-growth scrub
and roadside brush. Frequents flowering and
fruiting trees.
Distribution. Nests e. of Rocky Mtns. from s
Can. to s Gulf states; winters from Jalisco, ne
Mex., Florida, and e Carolinas to nw S.A.
Status in Belize. C transient and winter visitor,
early Sept. to mid-May.
References. *Identification:* Kaufman (1987); Lee
and Birch (1998).

Although the **Bullock's Oriole** (*Icterus bul-
lockii*) has not been found in Belize, it could
turn up. It is similar to Baltimore, but in all
plumages, its bill is more extensively gray, including part of upper mandible. *Ad. ♂:* unmistakable, with bold white wing patch and mostly
orange head with black crown, eyestripe, and
central throat. *Ad. ♀:* grayish back, yellow face
and breast, pale gray belly. *Imm. ♂:* usually with
black face and throat and partial black eyeline of
ad. ♂, but olive back, and underparts with extensive grayish wash. *Imm. ♀:* can be confusingly
similar to imm. ♀ Baltimore; however, generally
lacks orange in plumage, averages grayer above
and paler below; most have trace of pale supercilium (lacking in Baltimore) and yellow auriculars and neck concolorous with throat (Baltimore has olive auriculars and neck that contrast
with yellow-orange throat).

Yellow-billed Cacique   PLATE 55

Amblycercus holosericeus

OTHER NAMES. Prevost's Cacique (arch.),
Bamboo Cracker (C), otz otz (K, M).

Identification. 9¼" (23.5 cm). *Ad.:* all black,
with distinctive pale yellow eyes and bill. *Juv.:*
dusky eyes, which become yellow rather rapidly
after fledging.; juv. Giant Cowbird is larger, with
heavier bill, different behavior, and no habitat
overlap.
Voice. *Call:* 1. nasal *wank,* sometimes repeated
several times;
2. soft *wok* to *uhwok. Song:* typically, ♂ will give
two to four clear notes repeatedly, and nearby ♀
will respond a few seconds later.
Examples: 1. ♂, clear, whistled *to we to wer,* repeated several times; ♀ response,
wheerrr drrrrrrrrrrrr, the first note clear, the second rough and drawn out.
2. ♂, clear *here here* or *cheo cheo;* ♀, *drrrrrrrrrr.*
Habitat. Understory; broadleaf and pine forest
interior and edge, second-growth scrub.
Distribution. Resident from s Tamaulipas to nc
S.A.
Status in Belize. C resident on mainland and
Ambergris Caye.

Genus: Psarocolius (*Oropendolas*)

Oropendolas are distinguished by blackish body
and mostly yellow tail (the Creole name for

the oropendola is Yellow-tail); they are highly colonial, building long, hanging nests suspended from the outer branches of large, isolated trees; and they have a fascinating courtship display in which the ♂ leans forward on a branch until it is nearly upside down, then emits a hollow gurgling sound (louder in Montezuma). Oropendolas have a steady, flapping flight with relatively slow wingbeats and often travel in loose, widely strung-out flocks, much in the manner of crows (*Corvus* spp.). Chestnut-headed is distinctly smaller than Montezuma; however, the ♀ is noticeably smaller than the ♂ in both species; thus, ♀ Montezuma can be nearly as small as ♂ Chestnut-headed.

Things to note: body size, color and pattern of bill and face.

Chestnut-headed Oropendola

MAP 230; PLATE 55
Psarocolius wagleri
OTHER NAMES. Wagler's Oropendola (arch.), Yellow-tail (C), ak'un kubul (K), ts'ok kubul (K), kobul cheh (M).

Identification. ♂ 13½″ (34.5 cm), ♀ 10¼″ (26 cm). Black body, with mostly yellow tail (especially when viewed from below), chestnut undertail coverts, pale greenish yellow bill, and pale blue eyes. At close range, head and breast show deep purplish chestnut cast. *Flight:* narrower and proportionately longer wings than Montezuma; faster, deeper wingbeats.
Voice. *Call:* relatively soft *wäcka. Song:* soft bubbly, gurgling, sputtery, and scratchy notes; conversational, not explosive as in Montezuma Oropendola.
Habitat. For nesting, canopy of large trees in broadleaf forest clearings and open areas near forest. At other times, canopy of broadleaf forest interior.
Distribution. Resident from c Veracruz s. of Yucatán Pen. to nw S.A.
Status in Belize. Local and generally UC resident in s and w TO, w SC, and s CA.

Montezuma Oropendola   PLATE 55
Psarocolius montezuma
OTHER NAMES. Yellow-tail (C), kubul (K), kobul (M).

Identification. ♂ 19″ (48.5 cm), ♀ 15½″ (39.5 cm). Like large version of Chestnut-headed, but with complex face and bill pattern. Deep chestnut body color appears black at a distance. Bill blue black, with orange distal half; facial skin pale blue, bordered above by gray and below by pale pink; dark eyes. In the distance, Montezuma's pale face and dark bill distinguish it. *Flight:* direct, with slow, deep, rowing wingbeats; broader, shorter wings than Chestnut-headed.
Voice. *Call:* 1. soft barking *hrup* or *wuk;* 2. loud, hollow, far-carrying *twop! Song:* ♂ gives eerie vocalization that begins with a few high-pitched thin notes followed by a sound like the crumpling of brittle paper, and ending with an explosive, rich, hollow gurgling *o-du-le-woe* sound, which carries a considerable distance. ♀ emits forced, nasal *wannnh* cries and grunts during ♂'s singing bouts.
Habitat. For nesting, canopy of isolated trees (typically the cotton tree, *Ceiba pentandra*). Otherwise, canopy and subcanopy of most broadleaf forest interior and edge, relatively open areas with scattered large trees. Frequents fruiting trees.
Distribution. Resident from se San Luis Potosí and s Yucatán Pen. to c Pan.
Status in Belize. C resident on mainland nearly throughout, but local and somewhat seasonal in northeast. Has nested on Ambergris Caye.
Reference. *Voice:* Moore (1992).

FAMILY: FRINGILLIDAE (Finches)

World: 134. **New World:** 31. **Belize:** 3. Primarily Old World, with a few representatives in Nearctic and n Neotropical regions. Only three occur in Belize, each with restricted distribution. This diverse family includes not only many of the world's birds with "finch" in their name (the word "finch" is applied to birds in several families), but crossbills, siskins, serins, canaries, redpolls, and many of the grosbeaks. All are characterized by a relatively short, thick-based bill used for cracking seeds. Most have a short, notched or forked tail, and many have a strongly undulating flight. Unlike the similar-appearing Emberizidae and Cardinalidae, and most other passerines, the Fringillidae have 10 primaries instead of 9. Crossbills are unique among birds in having a hook at the tip of both the upper and the lower mandibles, and these hooks cross over in the closed bill, a feature that aids them in extracting conifer seeds. **Reference:** Clement et al. (1993).

Red Crossbill   MAP 231; PLATE 54
Loxia curvirostra
OTHER NAMES. Common Crossbill (U.K.).

Identification. 6″ (15 cm). Broad-based, rounded bill with overlapping hooked mandible tips. Short, notched tail. Almost always seen in groups, and highly nomadic. ♂ *red variant:* reddish throughout, brightest on rump, palest on belly; wings and tail darker. ♂ *yellow variant:* red replaced with dull yellow to orange yellow. ♀: grayish olive to yellow olive, with bright olive-yellow rump and pale gray throat. *Juv.:* heavily streaked.
Voice. *Call:* series of irregularly spaced, hard, dry to liquid *kip* to *jip* notes. *Song:* series of thin, liquid *kip* and *kyip* notes mixed with buzzy *dree* notes and doubled to tripled *to-kip* and *tipity* notes.
Habitat. Canopy to ground; pine forest.
Distribution. Highly nomadic; nests from c and se Can., n Eur., and c Asia s. to Nic., nw Afr., and locally to se Asia; s. populations are mostly montane. The systematics of the Red Crossbill complex are poorly known, and a number of closely related species may be involved.
Status in Belize. UC resident in Mtn. Pine Ridge with isolated records from near the Belize Zoo BE and Hill Bank OW.

Black-headed Siskin   MAP 232; PLATE 54
Carduelis notata

Identification. 4¼″ (11 cm). Small bird with short, notched tail and small conical bill. *Ad.:* black hood, wings, and tail; yellow olive (♂) to olive (♀) back; yellow rump and underparts;

large yellow patch in wing; and yellow at base of tail. *Imm.:* lacks black hood but otherwise similar to ad. *Flight:* strongly undulating; prominent yellow bar in wing.
Voice. *Call:* 1. goldfinch-like *peuw;* 2. thin, nasal *jeeen;* 3. scratchy *ji-ji-jit. Song:* varied, rapid, twittering warble interspersed with occas. nasal and metallic notes; phrases often repeated in prolonged series.
Habitat. Canopy and subcanopy; pine forest interior and edge.
Distribution. Resident, mostly in highlands, from se Sonora and sw Tamaulipas to n Nic.
Status in Belize. C resident in Mtn. Pine Ridge; once at Monkey Bay BE.
Reference. *Voice:* Howell and Webb (1995).

Lesser Goldfinch   MAP 233; PLATE 54
Carduelis psaltria
OTHER NAMES. Dark-backed Goldfinch (alt.), Arkansas Goldfinch (arch.).

Identification. 4¼″ (11 cm). Small, siskinlike bird with shorter bill and white, not yellow, wing patches. ♂: black above and yellow below, with prominent white patch at base of primaries; (♂ Yellow-throated Euphonia has yellow forehead and blue-black upperparts and lacks white wing patch.) ♀: varies from olive above and yellow below to grayish olive above and pale, dingy yellow below; wings and tail black, with white wingbars, tertial edges, and patch at base of primaries; greener birds somewhat similar to Grassland Yellow-Finch but with unstreaked back, greenish (not yellow) rump, plain face, white wing markings, and conical bill (yellow-finch has curved culmen). *Flight:* strongly undulating; prominent (♂) to less conspicuous (♀) white patch at base of primaries.
Voice. *Call:* 1. nasal *zweeir;* 2. plaintive *tew;* 3. slightly rough, dry chatter *ch-ch-ch-ch-ch. Song:* complex and varied series of sweet and harsh twittering warbles, incorporating into the sequence its calls and, being a mimic, those of other species as well.
Habitat. Low level to canopy; most open areas,

including fallow fields, towns and villages, second-growth scrub.

Distribution. Resident from nw U.S. to c Texas, and through C.A. to nw S.A.

Status in Belize. Small, recently established resident population in vicinity of Trinidad, August Pine Ridge, and Carmelita in n OW. First reported in 1998.

Reference. *Status:* Jones et al. (2002).

FAMILY: PASSERIDAE
(Old World Sparrows)

World: 35. **New World:** 2, both non-native. **Belize:** 1. Except for introduced populations in New World, exclusively Old World; confined to Eurasia and Afr. Like the Fringillidae and Emberizidae, members of this family also have a short, thick-based bill adapted for eating seeds; and like the Fringillidae, they have 10 primaries. In most, the ♂, and sometimes the ♀, has a black throat. Although most are non-migratory, a few are short-distance migrants. Two species, House Sparrow and Eurasian Tree Sparrow *(Passer montanus),* have been widely introduced around the world. **Reference:** Clement et al. (1993).

House Sparrow
MAP 234; PLATE 54

Passer domesticus

OTHER NAMES. English Sparrow (arch.).

Identification. 5¾″ (14.5 cm). ♂: distinctive head pattern with gray crown and chestnut nape; black lores, throat, and upper breast; pale gray cheeks; back chestnut brown, streaked with black; rump grayish; prominent white upper wingbar; bill black in breeding season, otherwise pale yellowish brown. ♀: brownish gray head with pale brown partial supercilium; upperparts lighter, duller brown than in ♂; pale dirty brown to brownish gray underparts; bill light yellowish brown; pale supercilium, pale stripe on each side of back, and absence of lateral throat stripe distinguish ♀ from all other species in Belize.

Voice. *Call:* 1. liquid, rolled *chirrp* to *chirrip;* 2. *tree!;* 3. rapid *tre-tre-tre-tre-tre-tre;* 4. more subdued *cheh* and *cheh-cheh.* Groups of birds often spontaneously burst into frenzied chirping. *Song:* somewhat musical series of *chirrp* and *chirrip* notes, not unlike song of Yellow-green Vireo.

Habitat. Urban; nests under eaves in buildings.

Distribution. Resident originally in the Old World from n Eur. and nc Asia s. to n Afr., Sinai Pen., India, and Burma. Introduced to New York City and elsewhere in ne U.S. in early 1850s; from hence it has spread throughout N.A. s. of Arctic, and more recently, through much of C.A. Aided by additional introductions, it has colonized most of tropical S.A. from Ecuador and e Brazil to Tierra del Fuego. Also introduced in s Afr., Aust., N.Z., and locally in se Asia.

Status in Belize. Small resident populations in Punta Gorda (since at least mid-1980s), Dangriga (since mid-1990s), and Pomona/Alta Vista SC (since late 1990s). Also reported occas. in Belmopan, San Ignacio, and Belize City.

References. *Distribution:* Thurber (1972). *Status:* Howell et al. (1992).

Alström, P. 1987. The identification of Baird's and White-rumped sandpipers in juvenile plumage. *Birding* 19(2):10–13.

Alström, P., Mild, K., and Zetterström, B. 2002. *Pipits and Wagtails of Europe, Asia, and North America*. Christopher Helm, London.

American Ornithologists' Union. 1998. *The A.O.U. Check-list of North American Birds* (7th ed). Allen Press, Lawrence, Kans.

———. 2000. 42nd supplement to the A.O.U. Check-list of North American Birds. *Auk* 117:847–858.

———. 2002. 43rd supplement to the A.O.U. Check-list of North American Birds. *Auk* 119:897–906.

Balch, L. G. 1979. Identification of Groove-billed and Smooth-billed anis. *Birding* 11(6): 295–297.

Barlow, J. C. 1990. *Songs of the Vireos and Their Allies*. Ara Records, Gainesville, Fla. Audiocassette.

Barlow, J. C., Dick, J. A., Baldwin, D. H., and Davis, R. A. 1969. New records of birds from British Honduras. *Ibis* 111:399–402.

Barlow, J. C., Dick, J. A., and Pendergrast, E. 1970. Additional records of birds from British Honduras (Belize). *Condor* 72:371–372.

Barlow, J. C., Dick, J. A., Weyer, D., and Young, W. F. 1972. New records of birds from British Honduras (Belize), including a skua. *Condor* 74:486–487.

Beletsky, L. D. 1998. *Belize and Guatemala: The Ecotravellers' Wildlife Guide*. Wildlife Conservation Society. Academic Press, New York.

Belize Audubon Society Newsletter. 1969–2002. [Numerous short articles and notes.]

Belize Zoo. n.d. *A Tribute to Ted Parker: A Project of the Belize Zoo for the Ted Parker Foundation*. Belize Zoo and Tropical Education Center, Belize. Audiocassette.

Benesh, C. D. 1997. Intraspecific variation in adult male Flame-colored Tanagers: the lesson of Bog Spring. *Birding* 29(5):417–419.

Binford, L. C. 1971. Identification of Northern and Louisiana waterthrushes. *Calif. Birds* 2(1):1–10.

Bond, J. 1954. Birds of Turneffe and Northern Two Cays, British Honduras. *Notulae Naturae* 260.

Borror, D. L. 1990. *Songs of the Warblers of North America*. Cornell Univ., New York. Two audiocassettes.

Braun, M. J., Braun, D., and Terrill, S. B. 1986. Winter records of the Golden-cheeked Warbler *(Dendroica chrysoparia)* from Mexico. *Amer. Birds* 41:564–566.

Brewer, D. 2001. *Wrens, Dippers, and Thrashers*. Yale Univ. Press, New Haven, Conn.

Byers, C., Curson, J., and Olsson, U. 1995. *Sparrows and Buntings: A Guide to the Sparrows and Buntings of North America and The World*. Houghton Mifflin, Boston.

Chandler, R. J. 1998. Dowitcher identification and ageing: a photographic review. *Brit. Birds* 91(3):93–106.

Chantler, P. 2000. *Swifts: A Guide to the Swifts and Treeswifts of the World*. 2nd ed. Pica Press, Sussex, England.

Chapple, J. 1985. Some birds of Belize. *Army Birdwatching Soc. Bull.* 1985(1):B3.

———. 1989. Shipstern Wildlife Reserve: bird species checklist. *Army Birdwatching Soc. Bull.* 1989(2):B27, B36.

Cherry, K. R. 1989. Report from Belize. Exercise King Vulture 3. *Army Birdwatching Soc. Bull.* 1989(2):E1–E7.

Clark, W. S., and Wheeler, B. K. 1987. *A Field Guide to Hawks of North America*. Peterson Field Guide Series. Houghton Mifflin, Boston.

———. 1989. Field identification of the White-tailed Hawk. *Birding* 21(4):190–195.

———. 1995. Field identification of Common and Great black-hawks in Mexico and Central America. *Birding* 27(1):33–37.

Cleere, N. 1998. *Nightjars: A Guide to the Nightjars, Nighthawks, and Their Relatives*. Yale Univ. Press, New Haven, Conn.

Clement, P. 2000. *Thrushes*. Princeton Univ. Press, Princeton, N.J.

Clement, P., Harris, A., and Davis, J. 1993. *Finches and Sparrows: An Identification Guide.* Princeton Univ. Press, Princeton, N.J.

Clements, J. F. 2000. *Birds of the World: A Checklist.* 5th ed. Ibis Publishing Co., Vista, Calif.

Coffey, B. B. 1960. Late North American spring migrants in Mexico. *Auk* 77:288–297.

———. 1961. Some shorebird records from Mexico. *Wilson Bull.* 73:207–208.

Coffey, B. B., Jr., and Coffey, L. C. 1990. *Songs of Mexican Birds.* Ara Records, Gainesville, Fla. Two audiocassettes.

Conway, C. J., and Baird, S. J. 1995. Ornithology report for the Doyle's Delight expedition, Maya Mountains, Belize, 3–13 December 1993. In *Expedition to Doyle's Delight, Southern Maya Mountains, Belize* (S. Matola, ed.), Occasional Series no. 5, Forest Planning and Management Project, Ministry of Natural Resources, Belmopan.

Counsell, D. 1988. The RAFOS Expedition to Belize: Feb.-Mar. 1986. *Royal Air Force Ornithol. Soc. J.* 18:17–63.

Crease, A. J. 1990. Exercise King Vulture 3. British Army Birdwatching Society Expedition to Belize February—March 1989. *Adjutant* 20:4–17.

Curson, J., Quinn, D., and Beadle, D. 1994. *New World Warblers.* Christopher Helm, London.

Czaplak, D., and Wilds, C. 1986. Washington's November Nighthawk: a cautionary tale. *Birding* 18(6):169–173.

Davis, L. I. 1972. *A Field Guide to the Birds of Mexico and Central America.* Univ. of Texas Press, Austin.

Davis, Jr., W. E. 1999. Black-crowned and Yellow-crowned night-herons. *Birding* 31(5): 410–415.

Delaney, D. 1992. *Bird Songs of Belize, Guatemala, and Mexico.* Laboratory of Natural Sounds, Cornell Laboratory of Ornithology, Ithaca, N.Y. Audiocassette.

del Hoyo, J., Elliott, A., and Sargatal, J. (eds.). 1992–2002. *Handbook of the Birds of the World.* Vols. 1–7. Lynx Edicions, Barcelona.

[Nonpasserines; vols. 8–16 will cover the Passerines.]

Devillers, P. 1970. Chimney Swifts in coastal southern California. *Calif. Birds* 1(4):147–152.

Dickerman, R. W. 1960. Further notes on the Pinnated Bittern in Mexico and Central America. *Wilson Bull.* 84:90.

———. 1973. The Least Bittern in Mexico and Central America. *Auk* 90:689–691.

———. 1974. Review of the Red-winged Blackbirds *(Agelaius phoeniceus)* of eastern, west-central and southern Mexico and Central America. *Novitates* 2538.

———. 1975. Revision of the Short-billed Marsh-Wrens *(Cistothorus platensis)* of Central America. *Novitates* 2569.

———. 1985. Taxonomy of the Lesser Nighthawks *(Chordeiles acutipennis)* of North and Central America. In *Neotropical Ornithology* (P. A. Buckley et al., eds.). Ornithological Monographs 36, American Ornithologists' Union.

Dickerman, R. W., and Phillips, A. R. 1970. Taxonomy of the Common Meadowlark *(Sturnella magna)* in central and southern Mexico and Caribbean Central America. *Condor* 72:305–309.

Dickerman, R. W., Zink, R. M., and Fry, S. L. 1980. Migration of the Purple Martin in southern Mexico. *Western Birds* 11:203–204.

Dittmann, D. L., and Cardiff, S. W. 1999. Identification and hints to locate Louisiana's sulids. *Louisiana Ornithol. Soc. Newsletter* 185:8–13.

Dubois, P. J. 1997. Identification of North American Herring Gull. *Brit. Birds* 90(8):314–324.

Dunn, J. L., and Garrett, K. L. 1990. Identification of Ruddy and Common ground-doves. *Birding* 22(3):138–145.

———. 1997. *A Field Guide to Warblers of North America.* Peterson Field Guide Series, Houghton Mifflin Co., Boston.

Edwards, E. P. 1998. *A Field Guide to the Birds of Mexico and Adjacent Areas: Belize, Guatemala, and El Salvador.* Univ. of Texas Press, Austin, Tex.

Eisenmann, E. 1955. Status of the Black-polled, Bay-breasted, and Connecticut warblers in Middle America. *Auk* 72:206–207.

———. 1962. Notes on nighthawks of the genus *Chordeiles* in southern Middle America, with a description of a new race of *Chordeiles minor* breeding in Panama. *Novitates* 2094.

———. 1963. Breeding nighthawks in Central America. *Condor* 65:165–166.

Eitniear, J. C. 1984. Status of the King Vulture in Mexico and adjacent Central America. *Vulture News* 12:22–24.

———. 1985. The distribution and relative abundance of the Lesser Yellowheaded Vulture in Mexico and Belize, Central America. *Vulture News* 13:4–7.

———. 1986. Status of the large forest eagles of Belize. *Birds of Prey Bull.* 3:107 110.

———. 1991. The Solitary Eagle *Harpyhaliaetus solitarius*: a new threatened species. *Birds of Prey Bull.* 4:81 85.

Elliott, L., Stokes, D., and Stokes, L. 1997. *Stokes Field Guide to Bird Songs: Eastern Region.* Time Warner Audio Books. Audiocassette.

Ellis, D. H., and Whaley, W. H. 1981. Three Crested Eagle records for Guatemala. *Wilson Bull.* 93:284–285.

Emmons, K. M., Horwich, R. H., Kamstra, J., Saqui, E., Beveridge, J., McCarthy, T., Meerman, J., Silver, S. C., Pop, I., Koontz, F., Pop E., Saqui, H., Ostro, L., Pixabaj, P., Beveridge, D., and Lumb, J.n.d. *Cockscomb Basin Wildlife Sanctuary: Its History, Flora, and Fauna for Visitors, Teachers, and Scientists.* Producciones de la Hamaca, Caye Caulker, Belize, and Orangutan Press, Gays Mills, Wis.

England, M. 2000. The landbird monitoring programme at Lamanai, Belize: a preliminary assessment. *Cotinga* 13:32–43.

Erickson, R. 1977. First record of a Knot *Calidris canutus,* and other records, from Belize (British Honduras). *Bull. B.O.C.* 97:78–81.

Escalante-Pliego, P., and Peterson, A. T. 1992. Geographic variation and species limits in Middle American woodnymphs (*Thalurania*). *Wilson Bull.* 104:205–219.

Ferguson-Lees, J., and Christie, D. A. 2001. *Raptors of the World.* Houghton Mifflin, Boston.

Friesner, J. 1993. *The Burdon Canal Nature Reserve: A Preliminary Report.* Forest Planning and Management Project, Ministry of Natural Resources, Belmopan.

Fry, C. H., Fry, K., and Harris, A. 1992. *Kingfishers: Bee-eaters and Rollers.* Christopher Helm, London.

Gatz, T., Gent, P., Jakle, M., Otto, R., Otto, W., and Ellis, B. 1985. Spotted Rail, Brant, and Yellow-breasted Crake—records from the Yucatan. *Amer. Birds* 39:871–872.

Gibbs, D., Barnes, E., and Cox, J. 2001. *Pigeons and Doves: A Guide to the Pigeons and Doves of the World.* Yale Univ. Press, New Haven, Conn.

Gilardi, J. 1997. *Songs from a (Vanishing) Belizean Rainforest.* Songs for Gaia, Port Townsend, Wash. CD.

Greenberg, R. 1987. Seasonal foraging specialization in the worm-eating warbler. *Condor* 89(1):158–168.

Gustafson, M. 1988. Point/counterpoint: *Oporornis* eyerings. *Birding* 20(2):96–98.

Hallchurch, T. T. 1982. Exercise King Vulture, Belize, 23 February–16 March 1982. *Adjutant* 12:3–36. [Includes as Annex A, "Ringing Activities in Belize—1982," by Chris Mead, which was also apparently published in *Army Birdwatching Soc. Bull.* 1982(3):E1–E10.]

Hancock, J. 1999. *Herons and Egrets of the World: A Photographic Journey.* Academic Press, New York.

Hancock, J., and Kushlan, J. 1984. *The Herons Handbook.* Croom Helm, London.

Haney, J. C. 1983. First sight record of Orange-breasted Falcon for Belize. *Wilson Bull.* 95:314–315.

Hardy, J. W. 1983. *Voices of Neotropical Birds.* Ara Records, Gainesville, Fla. Audiocassette.

———. 1990. *Voices of the New World Jays, Crows, and Their Allies.* Ara Records, Gainesville, Fla. Audiocassette.

Hardy, J. W., and Coffey, Jr., B. B. 1988. *Voices of the Wrens.* Ara Records, Gainesville, Fla. Audiocassette.

Hardy, J. W., and Parker, T. A., III. 1985. *Voices of the New World Thrushes.* Ara Records, Gainesville, Fla. Audiocassette.

Hardy, J. W., and Raitt, R. J. 1995. *Voices of the New World Quails.* Ara Records, Gainesville, Fla. Audiocassette.

Hardy, J. W., and Wolf, L. L. 1993. *Voices of Mexican Sparrows.* Ara Records, Gainesville, Fla. Audiocassette.

Hardy, J. W., Barlow, J. C., and Coffey, Jr., B. B. 1987a. *Voices of All the Mockingbirds, Thrashers, and Their Allies.* Ara Records, Gainesville, Fla. Audiocassette.

Hardy, J. W., Reynard, G. B., and Coffey, Jr., B. B. 1987b. *Voices of the New World Cuckoos and Trogons.* Ara Records, Gainesville, Fla. Audiocassette.

———. 1989a. *Voices of the New World Nightjars and Their Allies.* Ara Records, Gainesville, Fla. Audiocassette.

———. 1989b. *Voices of the New World Pigeons and Doves.* Ara Records, Gainesville, Fla. Audiocassette.

Hardy, J. W., Coffey, Jr., B. B., and Reynard, G. B. 1990. *Voices of the New World Owls.* Ara Records, Gainesville, Fla. Audiocassette.

Hardy, J. W., Parker, T. A., III, and Taylor, T. 1991. *Voices of the Woodcreepers.* Ara Records, Gainesville, Fla. Audiocassette.

Hardy, J. W., Vielliard, J., and Straneck, R. 1993. *Voices of the Tinamous.* Ara Records, Gainesville, Fla. Audiocassette.

Hardy, J. W., Coffey, Jr., B. B., and Reynard, G. B. 1994. *Voices of Neotropical Wood Warblers.* Ara Records, Gainesville, Fla. Audiocassette.

Hardy, J. W., Reynard, G. B., and Taylor, T. 1996a. *Voices of the New World Rails.* Ara Records, Gainesville, Fla. Audiocassette.

Hardy, J. W., Parker, T. A., III, and Taylor, T. 1996b. *Voices of the Toucans.* Ara Records, Gainesville, Fla. Audiocassette.

Hardy, J. W., Reynard, G. B., and Taylor, T. 1998. *Voices of the Troupials, Blackbirds, and Their Allies.* Ara Records, Gainesville, Fla. 2 audiocassettes.

Harris, A. 1988. Identification of adult Sooty and Bridled terns. *Brit. Birds* 81(10):525–530.

Harrison, P. 1985. *Seabirds: An Identification Guide.* Rev. ed. Houghton Mifflin, Boston.

———. 1987. *Seabirds of the World: A Photographic Guide.* Princeton Univ. Press, Princeton, N.J.

Hayman, P., Marchant, J., and Prater, T. 1986. *Shorebirds: An Identification Guide.* Houghton Mifflin, Boston.

Heindel, M. T. 1996. Field identification of the Solitary Vireo complex. *Birding* 28(6):458–471.

Holt, E. G. 1926. On a Guatemalan specimen of *Progne sinaloae* Nelson. *Auk* 43:550–551.

Hough, J. 1996. Pine and "Baypoll" warblers: plumage variation and identification problems. *Birding* 28(4):284–291.

Howell, S. N. G. 1989. Short-tailed Nighthawk (*Lurocalis "semitorquatus"*) in Mexico. *Aves Mexicanas* 2(89-2):9–10.

———. 1990. *Songs of Mexican Birds,* by B. B. and L. C. Coffey. Review. *Wilson Bull.* 102:184–185.

———. 1993a. Photo spot: White-naped and White-collared swifts. *Euphonia* 2:66–68.

———. 1993b. Taxonomy and distribution of the hummingbird genus *Chlorostilbon* in Mexico and northern Central America. *Euphonia* 2:25–37.

———. 1994a. Field identification of *Myiarchus* flycatchers in Mexico. *Cotinga* 2:20–25.

———. 1994b. The specific status of Black-faced Antthrushes in Middle America. *Cotinga* 1:21–25.

———. 1995. A critique of Walters' (1993) new bird records from Belize. *Bull. B.O.C.* 115(3):177–180.

———. 1997. Yucatan Nightjar *Caprimulgus badius. Cotinga* 8:86–88.

———. 2001. *Hummingbirds of North America.* Academic Press, New York.

Howell, S. N. G., and de Montes, B. M. 1989. Status of the Glossy Ibis in Mexico. *Amer. Birds* 43:43–45.

Howell, S. N. G., and Webb, S. 1995. *A Guide to the Birds of Mexico and Northern Central America.* Oxford Univ. Press, New York.

Howell, S. N. G., and Whittaker, A. 1995. Field

identification of Orange-breasted and Bat falcons. *Cotinga* 4:36–43.

Howell, S. N. G., Dowell, B. A., James, D. A., Behrstock, R. A., and Robbins, C. S. 1992. New and noteworthy bird records from Belize. *Bull. B.O.C.* 112:235–244.

Hume, R. A. 1993. Common, Arctic, and Roseate terns: an identification review. *Brit. Birds* 86(5):210–217.

Humphrey, P. S., and Parkes, K. C. 1959. An approach to the study of molts and plumages. *Auk* 76:1–31.

———. 1963. Comments on the study of plumage succession. *Auk* 80:496–503.

Isler, M. L., and Isler, P. R. 1999. *The Tanagers*. 2nd ed. Smithsonian Institution, Washington, D.C.

Jackson, G. D. 1991. Field identification of teal in North America: female-like plumages. Part 1: Blue-winged, Cinnamon, and Green-winged teal. *Birding* 23(3):124–133.

Jaramillo, A., and Burke, P. 1999. *New World Blackbirds: The Icterids*. Princeton Univ. Press, Princeton, N.J.

Jenkins, P. G. 1983. The Royal Air Force Ornithological Society Belize Expedition 1981. *Royal Air Force Ornithol. Soc. J.* 14:1–80.

Johnsgard, P. A. 1993. *Cormorants, Darters, and Pelicans of the World*. Smithsonian Inst. Press, Washington, D.C.

———. 1997. *The Hummingbirds of North America*. 2nd ed. Smithsonian Inst. Press, Washington, D.C.

———. 2000. *Trogons and Quetzals of the World*. Smithsonian Inst. Press, Washington, D.C.

Jones, H. L. 2002. Erroneous and unconfirmed bird records from Belize: setting the record straight. *Bull. B.O.C.* 122(3):201–216.

———. 2000–2003. Central America. In *North American Birds*, vols. 54–57. American Birding Assoc. [Four seasonal reports annually of noteworthy bird observations in Belize and elsewhere in Central America.]

Jones, H. L., and Vallely, A. C. 2001. *Annotated Checklist of the Birds of Belize*. Lynx Edicions, Barcelona.

Jones, H. L., McRae, E., Meadows, M., and Howell, S. N. G. 2000. Status updates for selected bird species in Belize, including several species previously undocumented from the country. *Cotinga* 13:17–31.

Jones, H. L., Balderamos, P., Caulfield, J. and A., Crawford, G., Donegan, T. M., McRae, E., Meadows, M., Muschamp, M., Saqui, P., van der Spek, V., Urbina, J., and Zimmer, B. 2002. Fourteen new species reported for Belize. *Cotinga* 17:33–42.

Juniper, T., and Parr, M. 1998. *Parrots: A Guide to Parrots of the World*. Yale Univ. Press, New Haven, Conn.

Kaufman, K. 1987. The practiced eye: notes on female orioles. *Amer. Birds* 41(1):3–4.

———. 1988a. The practiced eye: female dabbling ducks. *Amer. Birds* 42(5):1203–1205.

———. 1988b. The practiced eye: immature night-herons. *Amer. Birds* 42(2):169–171.

———. 1988c. The practiced eye: notes on female tanagers. *Amer. Birds* 42(1):3–5.

———. 1989. The practiced eye: Blue Grosbeak and Indigo Bunting. *Amer. Birds* 43(3):385–388.

———. 1990. *A Field Guide to Advanced Birding*. Peterson Field Guide Series. Houghton Mifflin, Boston.

———. 1991. The practiced eye: Yellow Warbler and its I.D. contenders. *Amer. Birds* 45(1):167–170.

———. 1992. The practiced eye: Western Kingbird identification. *Amer. Birds* 46(2):323–326.

Kluza, D. A. 1998. First record of Shiny Cowbird *(Molothrus bonariensis)* in Yucatán, Mexico. *Wilson Bull.* 10:429–430.

König, C., Weick, F., and Becking, J.-H. 1999. *Owls: A Guide to the Owls of the World*. Yale Univ. Press, New Haven, Conn.

———. 2002. *Owls: A Guide to Owls of the World*. Yale Univ. Press, New Haven, Conn. Two CDs.

Kricher, J. C., and Davis, W. E., Jr. 1992. Patterns of avian species richness in disturbed and undisturbed habitats in Belize. In *Ecology and Conservation of Neotropical Migrant Landbirds* (J. M. Hagan III and D. W. Johnston, eds.), pp. 240–246. Smithsonian Inst. Press, Washington.

Land, H. C. 1970. *Birds of Guatemala*. Livingston Publishing Co., Wynnewood, Pa.

Land, H. C., and Kiff, L. F. 1965. The Band-tailed Barbthroat, *Threnetes ruckeri* (Trochilidae) in Guatemala. *Auk* 82:286.

Lane, D., and Jaramillo, A. 2000a. Identification of *Hylocichla/Catharus* thrushes, Part 1: molt and aging of spotted thrushes and field I.D. of Wood Thrush and Hermit Thrush. *Birding* 32(2):120–135.

———. 2000b. Field identification of *Hylocichla/Catharus* thrushes, Part 2: Veery and Swainson's thrush. *Birding* 32(3):1242–1254.

———. 2000c. Field identification of *Hylocichla/Catharus* thrushes, Part 3: Gray-cheeked and Bicknell's thrushes. *Birding* 32(4):318–331.

Lanyon, W. E. 1965. Specific limits in the Yucatan Flycatcher *Myiarchus yucatanensis*. *Novitates* 2229.

Lasley, G. W., Miller, B., and Miller, C. 2000. Cassin's Kingbird *Tyrannus vociferans* documented in Belize. *Cotinga* 15:60–61.

Lee, C., and Birch, A. 1998. Field identification of female and immature Bullock's and Baltimore orioles. *Birding* 30(4):282–295.

Lee, D. S., and Clark, C. T. 1988. Point/counterpoint: plumage morphs of Reddish Egrets. *Birding* 20(1):44–45.

Lehman, P. 1983. Point/counterpoint: Laughing/Franklin's gulls. *Birding* 15(6):229.

———. 1988. Orchard and immature Hooded orioles: a field identification nightmare. *Birding* 20(2):98–100.

———. 1994. Photo note: Franklin's vs. Laughing gulls, a "new" perspective. *Birding* 26(2):126–127.

Lethaby, N. 1996. Identification of Tree, Northern Rough-winged, and Bank swallows. *Birding* 28(2):111–116.

Liguori, J. 2000. Identification review: Sharp-shinned and Cooper's hawks, with an emphasis on a challenging wing-on perspective. *Birding* 32(5):428–433.

Lousada, S. 1989. *Amazona auropalliata caribaea*: a new subspecies of parrot from the Bay Islands, northern Honduras. *Bull. B.O.C.* 109:232–235.

Lousada, S. A., and Howell, S. N. G. 1996. Distribution, variation, and conservation of Yellow-headed Parrots in northern Central America. *Cotinga* 5:46–53.

Lowery, G. H., Jr., and Berrett, D. G. 1963. A new Carolina Wren (Aves: Troglodytidae) from southern Mexico. *Occas. Papers Mus. Zool. Louisiana State Univ.* 24.

Madge, S., and Burn, H. 1988. *Waterfowl: An Identification Guide to the Ducks, Geese, and Swans of the World*. Houghton Mifflin, Boston.

———. 1994. *Crows and Jays: A Guide to the Crows, Jays, and Magpies of the World*. Houghton Mifflin, Boston.

Madge, S., and McGowan, P. 2002. *Pheasants, Partridges, and Grouse, including Buttonquails, Sandgrouse and Allies*. Christopher Helm, London.

Mallory, E. P., and Brokaw, V. L. 1997. *Impacts of Silvicultural Trials on Birds and Tree Regeneration in the Chiquibul Forest Reserve, Belize*. Consultancy Report no. 20, Forest Planning and Management Project, Ministry of Natural Resources, Belmopan.

Mason, C. R. 1976. Cape May Warblers in Middle America. *Auk* 93:167–169.

Matola, S. 1990. The Columbia River Forest Reserve Expedition 9–16 December 1990. Unpubl. report.

Means, D. B. 1997. *Natural History of Mountain Pine Ridge, Belize*. N.p.; available at Hidden Valley Inn, Mountain Pine Ridge, Belize.

Meerman, J. C. 1993. Checklist of the birds of the Shipstern Nature Reserve. *Occas. Papers Belize Nat. Hist. Soc.* 2:70–82.

Mennill, D. J. 2001. Song characteristics and singing behavior of the Mangrove Warbler (*Dendroica petechia bryanti*). *J. Field Ornithol.* 72:327–337.

Miller, B. W., and Miller, C. M. 1991. The status of the Black Catbird *Melanoptila glabrirostris* on Caye Caulker, Belize. *Bird Conserv. Int.* 1(3):283–292.

———. 1992. Distributional notes and new species records for birds in Belize. *Occas. Papers Belize Nat. Hist. Soc.* 1:6–25.

———. 1996. New information on the status

and distribution of the Keel-billed Motmot *Electron carinatum* in Belize, Central America. *Cotinga* 6:61–63.

Mills, E. D., and Rogers, D. T., Jr. 1988. First record of the Blue-throated Goldentail *(Hylocharis eliciae)* in Belize. *Wilson Bull.* 100: 510.

———. 1990. Nearctic passerine fall migration in central Belize. *Wilson Bull.* 102(1):146–150.

———. 1992. Ratios of Neotropical migrant and Neotropical resident birds in winter in a citrus plantation in central Belize. *J. Field Ornithol.* 63(2):109–116.

Mlodinow, S. G., and Karlson, K. T. 1999. Anis in the United States and Canada. *N. Amer. Birds* 53(3):237–245.

Monroe, B. L., Jr. 1963. Notes on the avian genus *Arremonops* with description of a new subspecies from Honduras. *Occas. Papers Mus. Zool. Louisiana State Univ.* 28.

———. 1968. *A Distributional Survey of the Birds of Honduras.* American Ornithologists' Union. Allen Press, Lawrence, Kans.

Monroe, B. L., Jr., and Howell, T. R. 1966. Geographic variation in Middle American parrots of the *Amazona ochrocephala* complex. *Occas. Papers Mus. Zool. Louisiana State Univ.* 34.

Moore, J. V. 1992. *A Bird Walk at Chan Chich.* Astral Sounds Recording, San Jose, Calif. Audiocassette.

Moore, R. T. 1945. Sinaloa Martin nesting in western Mexico. *Auk* 62:308–309.

Morgan, J. G., Eubanks, T. L., Jr., Eubanks, V., and White, L. N. 1985. Yucatan Vireo appears in Texas. *Amer. Birds* 39(3):245–246.

Morlan, J. 1991. Identification of female Rose-breasted and Black-headed grosbeaks. *Birding* 23(4):220–223.

National Geographic Society. 1999. *Field Guide to the Birds of North America.* 3rd ed. National Geographic Society, Washington, D.C.

Nelson, J. B. 1978. *The Sulidae: Gannets and Boobies.* Oxford Univ. Press, New York.

Olsen, K. M., and Larsson, H. 1997. *Skuas and Jaegers: A Guide to the Skuas and Jaegers of the World.* Yale Univ. Press, New Haven, Conn.

———. 2002. *Gulls of Europe, Asia, and North America.* Christopher Helm, London.

Orians, G. 1985. *Blackbirds of the Americas.* Univ. of Washington Press, Seattle.

Ornat, A. L., Lynch, J. F., and de Montes, B. M. 1989. New and noteworthy birds from the eastern Yucatan Peninsula. *Wilson Bull.* 101:390–409.

Parker, J. W., Byers, E., and Bonaccorso, F. 1987. Aspects of the population biology of *Fregata magnificens* in Belize. *Amer. Birds* 41(1):11–19.

Parker, T. A., III, Holst, B. K., Emmons, L. H., and Meyer, J. R. 1993. *A Biological Assessment of the Columbia River Forest Reserve, Toledo District, Belize.* Conservation International.

Parkes, K. C. 1974. Variation in the Olive Sparrow in the Yucatan Peninsula. *Wilson Bull.* 86:293–295.

———. 1979. Plumage variation in female Black-throated Blue Warblers. *Cont. Birdlife* 1(6):133–135.

———. 1982. Parallel geographic variation in three *Myiarchus* flycatchers in the Yucatan Peninsula and adjacent areas (Aves: Tyrannidae). *Annals Carnegie Mus.* 51:1–16.

———. 1990a. A critique of the description of *Amazona auropalliata caribaea* Lousada, 1989. *Bull. B.O.C.* 110:175–179.

———. 1990b. A revision of the Mangrove Vireo *(Vireo pallens)* (Aves: Vireonidae). *Annals Carnegie Mus.* 59:49–60.

Patten, M. A. 1993. Notes on immature Double-crested and Neotropic cormorants. *Birding* 25(5):343–345.

Paynter, R. A., Jr. 1957. Rough-winged Swallows of the race *stuarti* in Chiapas and British Honduras. *Condor* 59:212–213.

Pelzl, H. W. 1969. *Birds of the British Honduras Keys.* Publ. by author, St. Louis.

Peterson, R. T., and Chalif, E. L. 1973. *A Field Guide to Mexican Birds.* Houghton Mifflin, Boston.

Petit, D. R., Petit, L. J., and Smith, K. G. 1992. Habitat associations of migratory birds overwintering in Belize, Central America. In *Ecology and Conservation of Neotropical Migrant Landbirds* (J. M. Hagan III and D. W. Johnston, eds.), pp. 247–256. Smithsonian Inst. Press, Washington, D.C.

Phillips, A. R. 1986. *The Known Birds of North and Middle America, Part 1.* A. R. Phillips, Denver, Colo.

———. 1991. *The Known Birds of North and Middle America, Part 2.* A. R. Phillips, Denver, Colo.

Phillips, A. R., and Hardy, J. W. 1965. *Tanagra minuta,* an addition to the Mexican list. *Wilson Bull.* 77:89.

Pierson, J. E. 1986. Notes on the vocalizations of the Yucatan Poorwill *(Nyctiphrynus yucatanicus)* and Tawny-collared Nightjar *(Caprimulgus salvini).* *MBA Bull. Board* 1(86-1):3–4.

Pittaway, R. 1992. Point/counterpoint: dowitcher subspecies. *Birding* 24(5):309–311.

Poole, A., and Gill, F., eds. 1992–2002. *The Birds of North America.* Birds of North America, Inc., Philadelphia. [Series of booklets by various authors; one booklet for each species regularly occurring in North America. Of these accounts, 190 pertain to birds that have been recorded in Belize. Excellent series for detailed information on systematics, distribution, migration, habitats, vocalizations, behavior, and breeding biology, but not field identification.]

Pranty, B. 2000. Possible anywhere: Shiny Cowbird. *Birding* 32(6):514–526.

Pyle, P. 1997. *Identification Guide to North American Birds, Part 1: Columbidae to Ploceidae.* Slate Creek Press, Bolinas, Calif.

Pyle, P., and Henderson, P. 1990. On separating female and immature *Oporornis* warblers in fall. *Birding* 22(5):222–229.

Pyle, P., and Howell, S. N. G. 1996. *Spizella* sparrows: intraspecific variation and identification. *Birding* 28(5):374–388.

Raffaele, H., Wiley, J., Garrido, O., Keith, A., and Raffaele, J. 1998. *A Guide to the Birds of the West Indies.* Princeton Univ. Press, Princeton, N.J.

Ranft, R., and Cleere, N. 1998. *A Sound Guide to Nightjars and Related Nightbirds.* Pica Press, East Sussex, England. Audiocassette.

Rangel, S. J. L., and Vega-R., J. H. 1991. The Great Potoo *(Nyctibius grandis)* as a probable resident in southern Mexico. *Ornithologia Neotropical* 2:38–39.

Reichelt, B. 1995. *A Faunal Survey of Freshwater Creek Forest Reserve.* Occasional Series no. 10. Forest and Management Project, Ministry of Natural Resources, Belmopan.

Ridgely, R. S., and Gwynne, J. A. 1989. *A Guide to the Birds of Panama, with Costa Rica, Nicaragua, and Honduras.* Princeton Univ. Press, Princeton, N.J.

Rising, J. D. 1996. *A Guide to the Identification and Natural History of the Sparrows of the United States and Canada.* Academic Press, New York.

Romagosa, C. M., and McEneaney, T. 1999. Eurasian Collared-Dove in North America and the Caribbean. *N. Amer. Birds* 53(4):348–353.

Roselaar, C. S. 1990. Identification of American and Pacific golden plover in the Netherlands. *Dutch Birding* 12:221–232.

Russell, S. M. 1964. *A Distributional Study of the Birds of British Honduras.* American Ornithologists' Union, Allen Press, Lawrence, Kans.

———. 1966. Status of the Black Rail and Gray-breasted Crake in British Honduras. *Condor* 68:105–107.

Saab, V. A., and Petit, D. R. 1992. Impact of pasture development on winter bird communities in Belize, Central America. *Condor* 94(1):66–71.

Scott, P. E., Andrews, D. D., and de Montes, B. M. 1985. Spotted Rail: first record from the Yucatan Peninsula, Mexico. *Amer. Birds* 39:852–853.

Selander, R. K., and Alvarez del Toro, M. 1953. The breeding distribution of *Chordeiles minor* in Mexico. *Condor* 55:160–161.

Semo, L. S., and Booher, D. 2002. Possible anywhere: White-collared Swift. *Birding* 34(1):16–22.

Sherrard-Smith, D. 1982. Reports from Belize. Big Falls Ranch. *Army Birdwatching Soc. Bull.* 1982(2):F2–F3.

Short, L. L., and Horne, J. 2001. *Toucans, Barbets, and Honeyguides.* Oxford Univ. Press, New York.

Sibley, C. G., and Monroe, B. L., Jr. 1990. *Distribution and Taxonomy of Birds of the World.* Yale Univ. Press, New Haven, Conn.

Sibley, D. A. 2000. *The Sibley Guide to Birds.* Alfred A. Knopf, New York.

———. 2002. *Sibley's Birding Basics.* Alfred A. Knopf, New York.

Skutch, A. F. 1994. The Gray-necked Wood-Rail: habits, food, nesting, and voice. *Auk* 111(1): 200–204.

Smith, P. W. 1987. The Eurasian Collared-Dove arrives in the Americas. *Amer. Birds* 41(5): 1370–1379.

Smith, P. W., and Sprunt, IV, A. 1987. The Shiny Cowbird reaches the United States. *Amer. Birds* 41(3):370–371.

Smith, P. W., Robertson, W. B., and Stevenson, H. M. 1988. West Indian Cave Swallows nesting in Florida, with comments on the taxonomy of *Hirundo fulva. Florida Field Nat.* 16:86–90.

Smithe, F. B. 1960. First records of Cattle Egrets *(Bubulcus ibis)* in Guatemala. *Auk* 77:218.

———. 1966. *The Birds of Tikal.* Natural History Press, New York.

Snow, D. 1982. *The Cotingas.* Cornell Univ. Press, Ithaca, N.Y.

Stattersfield, A. J., and Capper, D. R., eds. 2000. *Threatened Birds of the World.* Lynx Edicions, Barcelona, and BirdLife International, Cambridge, U.K.

Stevenson, H. M., and Anderson, B. H. 1994. *The Birdlife of Florida.* Univ. Press of Florida, Gainesville.

Stiles, F. G., and Skutch, A. F. 1989. *A Guide to the Birds of Costa Rica.* Cornell Univ. Press, Ithaca, N.Y.

Stotz, D. F., Fitzpatrick, J. W., Parker, T. A., III, and Moskovits, D. K. 1996. *Neotropical Ornithology: Ecology and Conservation.* Univ. of Chicago Press.

Taylor, B. 1998. *Rails: A Guide to the Rails, Crakes, Gallinules, and Coots of the World.* Yale Univ. Press, New Haven, Conn.

Terrill, S. B., and Terrill, L. S. 1981. On the field identification of Yellow-green, Red-eyed, Philadelphia, and Warbling vireos. *Cont. Birdlife* 2(5/6):144–149.

Thurber, W. A. 1972. House Sparrows in Guatemala. *Auk* 89:200.

Traylor, M. A. 1979. Two sibling species of *Tyrannus* (Tyrannidae). *Auk* 96:221–233.

Triggs, P. 1987. The Royal Air Force Kinloss Expedition to Belize March 1987. *RAFOS Newsletter* 45:3–7.

Turner, A., and Rose, C. 1989. *Swallows and Martins: An Identification Guide and Handbook.* Houghton Mifflin, Boston.

Udvardy, M. D. F., de Beausset, C. S., and Ruby, M. 1973. New tern records from Caribbean Honduras. *Auk* 90:440–442.

Vallely, A. C., and Aversa, T. 1997. New and noteworthy bird records from Belize including the first record of Chestnut-collared Swift *Cypseloides rutilus. Bull. B.O.C.* 117(4): 272–274.

Vallely, A. C., and Whitman, A. A. 1997. The birds of Hill Bank, northern Belize. *Cotinga* 8:39–49.

Veit, R. R., and Jonsson, L. 1984. Field identification of smaller sandpipers within the genus *Calidris. Amer. Birds* 38(5):853–876 and 41(2):212–236.

Verner, J. 1961. Nesting activities of the Red-footed Booby in British Honduras. *Auk* 78(4):573–594.

Vinicombe, K. E. 1989. Field identification of Gull-billed Tern. *Brit. Birds* 82(1):3–13.

Walters, R. 1993. Some records of birds from Belize, Central America, including three first records. *Bull. B.O.C.* 113(3):145–147.

Warner, D. W., and Harrell, B. E. 1957. The systematics and biology of the Singing Quail, *Dactylortyx thoracicus. Wilson Bull.* 69:123–148.

Weyer, D. 1984. Diurnal birds of prey of Belize. *Hawk Trust Annual Report* 14:22–39.

Wheeler, B. K., and W. S. Clark. 1995. *A Photo-*

graphic Guide to North American Raptors. Academic Press, New York.

Whitney, B. M. 1996. Flight behaviour and other field characteristics of the genera of Neotropical parrots. *Cotinga* 5:32–42.

Whitney, B. M., and Kaufman, K. 1985a. The *Empidonax* challenge, Part 1: Introduction. *Birding* 17(4):151–158.

———. 1985b. The *Empidonax* challenge, Part 2: Least, Hammond's, and Dusky flycatchers. *Birding* 17(6):277–287.

———. 1986a. The *Empidonax* challenge, Part 3: "Traill's" Flycatcher: The Alder/Willow problem. *Birding* 18(3):153–159.

———. 1986b. The *Empidonax* challenge, Part 4: Acadian, Yellow-bellied, and Western flycatchers. *Birding* 18(6):315–327.

Wilds, C. 1982. Separating the Yellowlegs. *Birding* 14(5):172–178.

———. 1993. The identification and aging of Forster's and Common terns. *Birding* 25(2): 94–108.

Wilds, C., and DiCostanzo, J. 2002. *A Guide to the Terns and Skimmers of the World.* Yale Univ. Press, New Haven, Conn.

Wilds, C., and Newlon, M. 1983. The identification of dowitchers. *Birding* 15(4/5):151–165.

Williams, S. O., III. 1983. Distribution and migration of the Black Tern in Mexico. *Condor* 85:376–378.

Williamson, S. L. 2001. *A Field Guide to the Hummingbirds of North America.* Peterson Field Guide Series. Houghton Mifflin, Boston.

Willis, E. O. 1961. A study of nesting anttanagers in British Honduras. *Condor* 63: 479–503.

Winkler, H., Christie, D. A., and Nurney, D. 1995. *Woodpeckers: An Identification Guide to the Woodpeckers of the World.* Houghton Mifflin, Boston.

Wood, D. S., and Adams, R. J. 1985. First Central American recovery of Blue-winged Warbler. *J. Field Ornithol.* 56(4):424–425.

Wood, D. S., and Leberman, R. C. 1987. Results of the Carnegie Museum of Natural History expedition to Belize. 3. Distributional notes on the birds of Belize. *Annals Carnegie Mus.* 56:137–160.

Wood, D. S., and Paulson, D. R. 1988. Status of Couch's Kingbird in Belize. *J. Field Ornithol.* 59(4):405–407.

Wood, D. S., Leberman, R. C., and Weyer, D. 1986. Checklist of the birds of Belize. *Carnegie Mus. Spec. Publ.* no. 12.

RANGE MAPS

Map 1
Thicket Tinamou

Map 2
Slaty-breasted Tinamou

Map 3
Red-footed Booby

Map 4
American White Pelican

Map 5
Double-crested Cormorant

Map 6
*Magnificent Frigatebird
(nesting colonies)*

Map 7
Pinnated Bittern

Map 8
Least Bittern

Map 9
Great Blue Heron (nesting colonies)

Map 10
Great Egret (nesting colonies)

Map 11
Snowy Egret (nesting colony)

Map 12
Tricolored Heron (nesting colonies)

Map 13
Reddish Egret (nesting colonies)

Map 14
Cattle Egret (nesting colony)

Map 15
White Ibis

Map 16
Glossy Ibis

Map 17
Roseate Spoonbill (nesting colonies)

Map 18
Jabiru

Map 19
Wood Stork (nesting colonies)

Map 20
Lesser Yellow-headed Vulture

Map 21
Fulvous Whistling-Duck

Map 22
American Wigeon

Map 23
Northern Pintail

Map 24
Ring-necked Duck

Map 25
Lesser Scaup

Map 26
Hook-billed Kite

Map 27
Swallow-tailed Kite (breeding)

Map 28
Snail Kite

Map 29
Double-toothed Kite

Map 30
Black-collared Hawk

Map 31
White Hawk

Map 32
Solitary Eagle

Map 33
White-tailed Hawk

Map 34
Red-tailed Hawk

Map 35
Crested Eagle

Map 36
Harpy Eagle

Map 37
Black-and-white Hawk-Eagle

Map 38
Ornate Hawk-Eagle

Map 39
Barred Forest-Falcon

Map 40
Aplomado Falcon

Map 41
Orange-breasted Falcon

Map 42
Ocellated Turkey

Map 43
Black-throated Bobwhite

Map 44
Spotted Wood-Quail

Map 45
Singing Quail

Map 46
Gray-breasted Crake

Map 47
Black Rail

Map 48
Clapper Rail

Map 49
Rufous-necked Wood-Rail

Map 50
Uniform Crake

Map 51
Spotted Rail

Map 52
Purple Gallinule

Map 53
Collared Plover

Map 54
Wilson's Plover

Map 55
American Oystercatcher

Map 56
American Avocet

Map 57
Red Knot

Map 58
Sanderling

Map 59
Laughing Gull

Map 60
Gull-billed Tern

Map 61
Caspian Tern

Map 62
Sandwich Tern

Map 63
Roseate Tern (nesting colonies)

Map 64
Least Tern

Map 65
Bridled Tern (breeding range)

Map 66
Sooty Tern (nesting colonies)

Map 67
Brown Noddy

Map 68
Black Skimmer

Map 69
White-crowned Pigeon

Map 70
Red-billed Pigeon

Map 71
White-winged Dove

Map 72
Common Ground-Dove

Map 73
Plain-breasted Ground-Dove

Map 74
White-tipped Dove

Map 75
Gray-fronted Dove

Map 76
Caribbean Dove

Map 77
Gray-chested Dove

Map 78
Scarlet Macaw

Map 79
Brown-hooded Parrot

Map 80
White-fronted Parrot

Map 81
Yellow-lored Parrot

Map 82
Mealy Parrot

Map 83
Yellow-headed Parrot

Map 84
Striped Cuckoo

Map 85
Smooth-billed Ani

Map 86
Crested Owl

Map 87
Spectacled Owl

Map 88
Great Horned Owl

Map 89
Central American Pygmy-Owl

Map 90
Ferruginous Pygmy-Owl

Map 91
Black-and-white Owl

Map 92
Stygian Owl

Map 93
Striped Owl

Map 94
Common Nighthawk

Map 95
Yucatan Poorwill

Map 96
Yucatan Nightjar

Map 97
White-collared Swift

Map 98
Lesser Swallow-tailed Swift

Map 99
Band-tailed Barbthroat

Map 100
Long-billed Hermit

Map 101
Scaly-breasted Hummingbird

Map 102
Wedge-tailed Sabrewing

Map 103
Violet Sabrewing

Map 104
White-necked Jacobin

Map 105
Brown Violet-ear

Map 106
Black-crested Coquette

Map 107
Canivet's Emerald

Map 108
Violet-crowned Woodnymph

Map 109
Azure-crowned Hummingbird

Map 110
Buff-bellied Hummingbird

Map 111
Cinnamon Hummingbird

Map 112
Stripe-tailed Hummingbird

Map 113
Purple-crowned Fairy

Map 114
Collared Trogon

Map 115
Slaty-tailed Trogon

Map 116
Tody Motmot

Map 117
Keel-billed Motmot

Map 118
Amazon Kingfisher

Map 119
White-whiskered Puffbird

Map 120
Rufous-tailed Jacamar

Map 121
Emerald Toucanet

Map 122
Acorn Woodpecker

Map 123
Black-cheeked Woodpecker

Map 124
Red-vented Woodpecker

Map 125
Ladder-backed Woodpecker

Map 126
Scaly-throated Foliage-gleaner

Map 127
Buff-throated Foliage-gleaner

Map 128
Tawny-throated Leaftosser

Map 129
Scaly-throated Leaftosser

Map 130
Wedge-billed Woodcreeper

Map 131
Strong-billed Woodcreeper

Map 132
Spotted Woodcreeper

Map 133
Streak-headed Woodcreeper

Map 134
Great Antshrike

Map 135
Western Slaty-Antshrike

Map 136
Russet Antshrike

Map 137
Plain Antvireo

Map 138
Slaty Antwren

Map 139
Dot-winged Antwren

Map 140
Dusky Antbird

Map 141
Bare-crowned Antbird

Map 142
Yellow-bellied Tyrannulet

Map 143
Northern Beardless-Tyrannulet

Map 144
Caribbean Elaenia

Map 145
Sepia-capped Flycatcher

Map 146
Paltry Tyrannulet

Map 147
Slate-headed Tody-Flycatcher

Map 148
Common Tody-Flycatcher

Map 149
Ruddy-tailed Flycatcher

Map 150
Sulphur-rumped Flycatcher

Map 151
Greater Pewee

Map 152
Black Phoebe

Map 153
Vermilion Flycatcher

Map 154
Rufous Mourner

Map 155
Yucatan Flycatcher

Map 156
Fork-tailed Flycatcher

Map 157
Rufous Piha

Map 158
Speckled Mourner

Map 159
Cinnamon Becard

Map 160
White-winged Becard

Map 161
Lovely Cotinga

Map 162
White-collared Manakin

Map 163
Mangrove Vireo

Map 164
Plumbeous Vireo

Map 165
Yucatan Vireo

Map 166
Green Shrike-Vireo

Map 167
Rufous-browed Peppershrike

Map 168
Yucatan Jay

Map 169
Ridgway's Rough-winged Swallow

Map 170
Band-backed Wren

Map 171
Carolina Wren

Map 172
Plain Wren

Map 173
Sedge Wren

Map 174
White-bellied Wren

Map 175
Nightingale Wren

Map 176
Blue-gray Gnatcatcher

Map 177
Eastern Bluebird

Map 178
Slate-colored Solitaire

Map 179
White-throated Robin

Map 180
Black Catbird

Map 181
Tropical Mockingbird

Map 182
Tropical Parula

Map 183
Mangrove Warbler

Map 184
Grace's Warbler

Map 185
Gray-crowned Yellowthroat

Map 186
Golden-crowned Warbler

Map 187
Rufous-capped Warbler

Map 188
Gray-throated Chat

CABOTI

MEXICANA

Map 189
Bananaquit

Map 190
Common Bush-Tanager

Map 191
Black-throated Shrike-Tanager

Map 192
Red-crowned Ant-Tanager

Map 193
Rose-throated Tanager

Map 194
Hepatic Tanager

Map 195
Flame-colored Tanager

Map 196
White-winged Tanager

Map 197
Crimson-collared Tanager

Map 198
Passerini's Tanager

Map 199
Yellow-winged Tanager

Map 200
Elegant Euphonia

Map 201
Olive-backed Euphonia

Map 202
White-vented Euphonia

Map 203
Golden-hooded Tanager

Map 204
Green Honeycreeper

Map 205
Shining Honeycreeper

Map 206
Slate-colored Seedeater

Map 207
Variable Seedeater

Map 208
Thick-billed Seed-Finch

Map 209
Blue Seedeater

Map 210
Yellow-faced Grassquit

Map 211
Grassland Yellow-Finch

Map 212
Orange-billed Sparrow

Map 213
Olive Sparrow

Map 214
Botteri's Sparrow

Map 215
Rusty Sparrow

Map 216
Chipping Sparrow

Map 217
Grasshopper Sparrow

Map 218
Buff-throated Saltator

Map 219
Black-faced Grosbeak

Map 220
Northern Cardinal

Map 221
Blue-black Grosbeak

Map 222
Blue Bunting

Map 223
Red-winged Blackbird

Map 224
Eastern Meadowlark

Map 225
Giant Cowbird

Map 226
Hooded Oriole

Map 227
Yellow-backed Oriole

Map 228
Orange Oriole

Map 229
Altamira Oriole

Map 230
Chestnut-headed Oropendola

Map 231
Red Crossbill

Map 232
Black-headed Siskin

Map 233
Lesser Goldfinch

Map 234
House Sparrow

INDEX